FURTHER STUDIES IN INTERNATIONAL LAW

Further Studies in International Law

F. A. MANN, C.B.E., F.B.A.
LL.D. (Lond.), Dr. Jur. (Berlin)
Hon. D.C.L. (Oxford), Hon. Dr. Jur. (Kiel and Zürich)

Member of the Institut de Droit International
Honorary Member of the American Society of International Law
Honorary Professor of Law in the University of Bonn
Solicitor of the Supreme Court
London

CLARENDON PRESS · OXFORD
1990

Oxford University Press, Walton Street, Oxford OX2 6DP
Oxford New York Toronto
Delhi Bombay Calcutta Madras Karachi
Petaling Jaya Singapore Hong Kong Tokyo
Nairobi Dar es Salaam Cape Town
Melbourne Auckland
and associated companies in
Berlin Ibadan

Oxford is a trade mark of Oxford University Press

Published in the United States
by Oxford University Press, New York

British Library Cataloguing in Publication Data
Mann, F. A. (Frederick Alexander)
Further studies in international law.
1. International law
I. Title
341
ISBN 0–19–825247–1

Library of Congress Cataloging in Publication Data
Mann, F. A. (Frederick Alexander,) 1907–
Further studies in international law/F. A. Mann.
Continues: Studies in international law. 1973.
Includes index.
1. International law. I. Title.
JX68.M28 1989 341—dc20 89–9450
ISBN 0–19–825247–1

Set by CentraCet, Cambridge

Printed and bound in
Great Britain by Courier International Ltd
Tiptree, Essex

Preface

> Semper enim in his studiis laboribusque viventi non intelligitur quando obrepat senectus.
>
> For he who lives always for his studies and work does not notice when old age creeps up.
>
> *Cicero, De Senectute, xi.38*

When *Studies in International Law* appeared in 1973, it seemed unlikely that there would be enough life, time and material left to publish further studies in international law. In spite or, perhaps one should say, by reason of a mixture of good fortune and adversity and with the help of a benevolent publisher such an undertaking has now become possible.

The new volume is only in two respects a continuation of the earlier one. In 1984 the Hague Academy of International Law generously extended a fourth invitation for a course of lectures and thus rendered it possible to consider again the doctrine of international jurisdiction, a topic to which the 1964 Hague lectures, reprinted in 1973, were devoted and which, incidentally, five years later could again do with fresh investigation. The 1984 series of lectures now opens the present volume. The other work included in it which offends against the principle of *ne bis in idem* is the paper on the International Enforcement of Public Rights. It continues attempts first made in 1955 and published in *Studies* (p. 492) and resumed in Rec. 132 (1971 i) 115, 166. It originally appeared in an American journal whose editors not only 'americanized', but also edited, i.e. rewrote it in many respects. The present version is the original one, but takes care of the remarkable developments which since 1987 occurred both in England and the Commonwealth. This is the only article in the present volume, which has been brought up to date.

A word of explanation is necessary to justify the inclusion of the case notes on Judicial Recognition of an Unrecognised State and on the *Rumasa* litigation. Normally there would have been no place for case notes in this volume. But both topics are so important and show up what is believed to be such unfortunate developments of English law that it seemed appropriate to make an exception in the hope of stimulating discussion and, possibly, promoting reform.

My thanks are due to my grandson Mr. Martin Thomas B.A. who is responsible for the Tables of Cases and the Index.

London, 4 June 1989. F.A.M.

Contents

Table of Statutes

Table of English Cases

Table of Scottish and Commonwealth Cases

Table of Cases decided by Courts of the United States of America

Table of Decisions of International Tribunals

OTHER TRIBUNALS

INTERNATIONAL ARBITRATIONS

1

The Doctrine of International Jurisdiction Revisited After 20 Years

Recueil des Cours, 186 (1984 ii), 9–98.

I. LEGISLATIVE JURISDICTION

I

SINCE a review of the international doctrine of jurisdiction was first attempted 20 years ago[1] its implications in a variety of fields have attracted much attention, mainly on account of American measures and their repercussions. Yet scholarly investigations of the doctrine's history, foundation and scope, of the principles underlying it, their formulation, general character and effect have remained few and far between.[2] To revert to the subject today with a view to exhaustive treatment of the doctrine in the practice of the law would require an enormous apparatus that would exhaust the resources and powers of a single student, for the doctrine has become so pervasive that completeness cannot be achieved; in many instances, such as air law, expert knowledge of the particular field as well as access to unfamiliar sources are the prerequisites of a comprehensive study. Anyone lacking such facilities cannot at present attempt more than a survey of some of the material accumulated over two decades and of the changes of the law that have occurred or the new problems which have arisen or are liable to come to the forefront. Nor is it necessary to pursue all the details, for it is the general principle that matters and that, subject to appropriate adjustments or exceptions, has to be applied in particular cases. And it is the general principle that is at the root of the difficulties. If it is understood and appreciated its application and implementation will follow almost as a matter of course. Emphasis on the fundamentals and the treatment of specific aspects as examples will, it is hoped, render it possible to present a course of lectures which stands on its own feet, that is to say, is independent of the earlier essay which provides the background, but knowledge of which is not required to understand the present discussion.

[1] 'The Doctrine of Jurisdiction in International Law', *RdC* 111 (1964–I), 9, reprinted in *Studies in International Law* [1973], 1.

[2] See, however, Jennings, *RdC* 121 (1967–II), 515; Akehurst, *British Year Book of International Law*, 1972–1973, 145; Bowett, *British Year Book of International Law*, 1982, 1; Higgins, in *Extraterritorial Application of Law and Responses Thereto (1984); Klaus Vogel, der räumliche Anwendungsbereich der Verwaltungsrechtsnorm* (1965); Rudolf, 'Territoriale Grenzen der staatlichen Rechtsetzung', *Berichte der Deutschen Gesellschaft für Völkerrecht*, 1971, 17. There also exists an immense literature on individual subjects. Only some of it can be referred to in the following pages. It proved impossible to aim at completeness. These lectures are not intended not intend to achieve more than a survey of some of the more pressing problems at present troubling theory and practice and of their solution.

II

International jurisdiction is an aspect or an ingredient or a consequence of sovereignty (or of territoriality or of the principle of non-intervention—the difference is merely terminological): laws extend so far as, but no further than, the sovereignty of the State which puts them into force nor does any legislator normally intend to enact laws which apply to or cover persons, facts, events or conduct outside the limits of his State's sovereignty. This is a principle or, perhaps one should say, an observation of universal application. Since every State enjoys the same degree of sovereignty, jurisdiction implies respect for the corresponding rights of other States. To put it differently, jurisdiction involves both the right to exercise it within the limits of the State's sovereignty and the duty to recognize the same right of other States.

Or, to put the same idea in positive and negative form, the State has the right to exercise jurisdiction within the limits of its sovereignty, but is not entitled to encroach upon the sovereignty of other States. In the United States of America, as will appear on more than one occasion, there exists a strong tendency to found international jurisdiction on the existence of interest and a process of balancing of interests. Indeed, a casebook edited by prominent authors[3] suggests in terms that 'under international law the jurisdiction of a State depends on the interest that State, in view of its nature and purposes, may reasonably have in exercising the particular jurisdiction asserted'. There is, however, outside the United States no support for such a theory to be found in any of the traditional sources of international law, and it should be firmly rejected.

Since in the present world sovereignty is undoubtedly territorial in character, in assessing the extent of jurisdiction the starting point must necessarily be its territoriality such as it was developed over the centuries and defined by the Huber–Storyan maxims: as a rule jurisdiction extends (and is limited) to everybody and everything within the sovereign's territory and to his nationals wherever they may be.

It is difficult to believe that these elementary propositions of public international law will be contested. On the contrary, the principle as defined is universal in the sense that prima facie it applies to all legislation and all State intervention derived or sanctioned by the competent authority, i.e., the legislator himself as well as those judicial and executive authorities controlled and empowered by him. Accordingly there is no room for distinguishing between criminal, public and private laws. The suggestion that the doctrine applies to criminal and public law as well as

[3] *International Law, Cases and Materials*, by Henkin, Pugh, Schachter and Smit (1980) 421.

the prerogative rights of the State such as taxation, but 'that there are no rules of international law limiting the legislative jurisdiction of States in questions of what might loosely be described as private law'[4] is untenable: a legislator who were to invalidate all marriages not celebrated in church and declare the children of such marriages illegitimate would act *ultra vires* and could not expect his statute or the judgments of his courts giving effect to it to be internationally recognized. It may well be that 'the cases in which a State violates international law, e.g., by applying its own substantive law to a given situation must be extremely rare'.[5] The point is that if such a rare case were to occur it would constitute an international wrong; the very absence of examples in the legislative, though not the judicial,[6] practice of States is likely to contribute to the proof of the rule. This remains as first stated by Lord Russell of Killowen in 1896[7] and since then frequently reaffirmed in the Anglo–American world:[8] normally no State is allowed to apply its legislation

> to foreigners in respect of acts done by them outside the dominions of the sovereign power enacting. That is a rule based on international law, by which one sovereign power is bound to respect the subjects and the rights of all other sovereign powers outside its own territory.

When this statement of the rule refers to legislation, it contemplates, of course, not only statutes or common law, but also all judicial and executive acts giving effect to the sovereign's will. International law, therefore, employs the term 'legislation' in a very wide sense indicating regulation rather than merely enactment.

III

The general principle which has been suggested is subject to exceptions or refinements required by the character or, more particularly, the limits of the State's sovereignty. These exceptions can best be clarified if one starts from a hypothetical case which to the observer of the international scene in recent years is not as far-fetched as may at first sight appear: Britain enacts a statute according to which 'all persons'[9] are required to sell

[4] Akehurst (above note 2), at p. 187.

[5] Sir Otto Kahn-Freund, *RdC* 143 (1974–III), at p. 176.

[6] The principal examples occur in the field of international criminal law.

[7] *The Queen* v. *Jameson,* [1896] 2 Q.B. 425, 430.

[8] For the United States of America see *Lauritzen* v. *Larsen*, 345 US 571 (1953), at p. 578.

[9] Such phraseology is a popular device of all legislators in all countries of the world. Thus, to give a single example from English practice, under s. 36 (2) of the Restrictive Trade Practices Act 1976 or s. 44 (2) of the Fair Trading Act 1973 or s. 3 (7) of the Competition Act 1980, the Director of Fair Trading may require 'any person' to give information or produce documents. That such wording cannot be interpreted in a literal sense is obvious.

whisky at a certain minimum price. It is not to be doubted that, according to the principle, this statute applies to all persons in the United Kingdom and therefore subject to its sovereignty. But the question arises: who is within the United Kingdom? And who are 'all persons'—all persons in the world or certain persons in the world outside the United Kingdom?

1. The first part of this question comprises the case of the temporary visitor who happens to be in the United Kingdom and, to adapt the language of certain regulations issued by the United States, comes within the terms of 'any person subject to the jurisdiction' of the United Kingdom; the United States regulations also include, *inter alia*, any corporate body controlled by persons 'actually within' the United States.[10] Or so long as the Exchange Control Act 1947 was in force in Britain, i.e., until 1979, when this most unfortunate legislation was for all practical purposes neutralized rather than repealed, Section 5 provided: 'No person shall . . . in the United Kingdom . . . make any payment to . . . a person resident outside' the United Kingdom. On the face of it this meant that no American visitor could in Britian pay $1 or £1 to another American visitor—a totally absurd, but in law probably inescapable conclusion. Taken literally, the hypothetical British statute about the price of whisky seems to catch even the French trader who is on a holiday of two weeks in Britain and whose shop manager, in his absence, sells whisky at less than the prescribed price. It is submitted that this result can be avoided and that so to stretch the conception of territoriality would go too far. The temporary visitor is certainly subject to local legislation which regulates conduct within the territory of the State: the temporary visitor, like all other residents, is not allowed to steal, or to drive on the wrong side of the road, or to gamble, or to drink after licensing hours or perhaps pay foreign currency to another visitor. But his conduct outside the territory in which he merely sojourns is of no concern to the local sovereign. It would, therefore, be unreasonable to allow the local sovereign to regulate the temporary visitor's conduct abroad. The formulations 'subject to the jurisdiction' and 'actually within' the State demand a restrictive interpretation so as to exclude the temporary visitor's activity abroad.

An even more impressive illustration of this aspect of the problem is provided by a long line of cases decided by the courts of the United States of America and relating to foreign ships 'transiently in a United States port'. It has established that notwithstanding the wide words of the statutes, the internal management of foreign ships cannot, even while in the United States, be touched by such legislation as the Merchants

[10] These very wide words occur in many United States statutes, for instance, in s. 385 (2) *(c)* of the Export Administration Regulations referred to in the *Sensor* case, *RabelsZ, 1983, 141 or Int.L.M.1983, 66.*

Seamen's Act or the Jones Act or the National Labor Relations Act, even if the vessel is owned by United States citizens.[11] On the other hand there is the intimidating case of *United States* v. *Field*,[12] a decision of the United States Court of Appeals, Fifth Circuit. Field, a Canadian citizen, was the manager of a banking establishment in the Cayman Islands, British West Indies. Upon the conclusion of a visit to the United States he was in the waiting hall of Miami Airport whence he intended to fly back to his place of residence, the Cayman Islands. At this moment he was served with a subpoena ordering him to appear before a grand jury and to give evidence about the accounts and the business interests of certain of his bank's customers. According to the law of the Cayman Islands, giving evidence about matters protected by banking secrets was a criminal offence. If the question is asked whether the subpoena was validly served, the answer is clearly in the affirmative; for the purpose of service Field's connection with the United States was amply sufficient to render the service legitimate. But could Field be compelled to give evidence about his bank's customers merely because he happened to be a fleeting visitor to the territory of the United States? Was he *for the purpose of giving such evidence* subject to the sovereign control by the United States? The court gave an affirmative answer. To use the familiar language of European systems of law, it relied on *ordre public* in that it invoked the interest of the United States and allowed it to prevail over the competing interest of the Cayman Islands, as United States courts almost invariably do when they purport to embark upon a process of balancing interests. Field had specifically invoked international law by suggesting 'that as a matter of international comity' the subpoena should not be enforced. In balancing the relevant factors or, as we would say, in assessing the force of *ordre public* the court regarded 'the relative interest of the States involved' as the most important factor. The requirements of United States tax legislation, of course, prevailed over Cayman Islands bank secrecy laws. In the last resort this is a political argument.

The question of law was whether a temporary foreign visitor, properly served with a subpoena in the United States, could be compelled in breach of his foreign employer's law to give evidence in the United States about that employer's foreign business. Did jurisdiction over the employee extend to jurisdiction over the employer? The answer should be in the negative. However this may be, the case shows the extreme danger which

[11] The starting point is *Benz* v. *Compania Naviera Hidalgo*, 353 US 138 (1957). There followed *McCulloch* v. *Sociedad Nacional de Honduras*, 372 US 10 (1963); *Incres* v. *International Maritime Workers*, 372 US 24 (1963); *Lopez* v. *S.S. Ocean Daphne*, 337 F.2d 777 (1964) and many other cases, some of which were discussed in 1964.

[12] 532 F.2d 404 (1976); see already *US* v. *Germann*, 370 F.2d 1019 (1964) relating to a Swiss citizen.

a temporary visitor to the United States (if it is not a ship) may run or rather to which an enterprise is exposed if any one of its employees happens to visit the United States of America.

There are many other examples which illustrate the problem. In England and the United States of America it is still the law that a foreigner who is found at London Airport where he changes planes may be effectively served with a writ and thus be subjected to the jurisdiction of the English courts, for he was undeniably served on British soil. But the rule is mitigated by the exception of *forum non conveniens*, which in the United States of America is given wide scope, while in England it is limited by the requirement that there is another forum where justice can be done at less inconvenience and expense and where the plaintiff is not deprived of a substantial advantage.[13]

2. The second special case arises where the State exercises jurisdiction over its nationals abroad. There cannot be any doubt that it can do so in certain respects which avoid collision with the foreign sovereign, for instance, by requiring them to do military service or by entering into treaties renouncing their rights to foreign property[14] or by depriving them of titles of nobility, as happened in the Soviet Union and many other Communist-controlled countries: where the right to a name or title depends upon nationality rather than domicile, as, for instance, in Germany, the law of countries of the Communist bloc is applicable and by virtue of a generally recognized principle of international law this extends to all nationals wherever they may be.[15] It is much more doubtful whether it can tax them, as for about 20 years the United States of America, seemingly alone among Western States, has done.

Does personal allegiance justify that economic allegiance upon which the principle of taxation is founded?[16] Were it not for the fact that the practice of the United States appears to be undisputed and even free from citicism by diplomatic protests one might have been inclined to condemn it, as 20 years ago it seemed possible to do.[17] Can the State of the

[13] On England see Dicey and Morris, p. 182, and on the United States see Scoles and Hay, pp. 263–8, both with many references. And see below, p. 54.

[14] The most authoritative evidence is provided by two decisions of the Federal Supreme Court of Germany, which are founded on much international material: 22 June 1960, RzW 1960, 533; 2 October 1963, RzW 1964, 34. See McNair, *Law of Treaties* (1961), 324.

[15] Curiously enough it was the Bavarian Supreme Court which in numerous cases was called upon so to decide. See, e.g., 13 October 1961, IPRspr. 1960 and 1961, No. 19; 9 March 1971, IPRspr. 1971, No. 18, both with references to numerous other cases. These decisions also exemplify the inter-play of public and private international law and make a substantial contribution to the former. Independently of these cases dealing with special facts it was frequently held in Germany that the right to a name depends on nationality: BGHZ 56, 193; 59, 261. In Switzerland the law of ordinary residence governs: BGE 106 II 103 and 206.

[16] Above note 1, at pp. 110 and 95 respectively.

[17] Above note 1, at pp. 116 and 101 respectively.

nationality go a step further and prescribe the minimum price at which its nationals can sell whisky? Can it take similar action to regulate the commercial conduct of its nationals abroad? It is submitted that to allow this would interfere far too much with the sovereign right of the State of the residence to prescribe or permit trade within its own frontiers. Britain clearly has a commercial interest in maintaining internationally a price level for whisky, which is as high as possible. Britain can prescribe it with effect for its own territory. It can prescribe it for the purpose of export. But once the goods are out of Britain's reach it cannot even for its own nationals legislate about matters which come within the sovereign power of other States, simply because they are so much closer to them than to the distant State of the goods' origin. Goods, once put into circulation, are without nationality. They are subject to the control of the local sovereign, just as traffic or the system of customs duties. It is a matter of closeness of contact, and, therefore, a matter of degree. Lines have to be drawn. It is submitted that the proposed lines flow from a realistic attribution of rights, powers and reason.

Another example is once again provided by exchange control. The attempt by a State to subject the foreign transactions of its non-resident citizens to its exchange control regulations would seem to be improper. In such cases nationality is a wholly inadequate nexus. It is necessary, therefore, to repeat great regret about the House of Lords which in 1950 took the opposite view[18] and thus reached not only a most unjust result in the case before it, but undermined the limitations which, as a matter of principle, should be imposed upon a State in directing the activities of its non-resident citizens.

Finally it is interesting to observe that the nationality of the defendant is now probably an insufficient link to provide the courts of his home State with jurisdiction over him. Numerous dicta in the opposite sense which over a long period have emanated from English judges are now probably discredited[19] and have been rejected by a court of first instance in Eire.[20] Moreover the notorious Article 15 of the French Civil Code is no longer in force where the 1968 Convention on Jurisdiction and the Enforcement of Judgments in Civil and Commercial Matters applies, i.e., within the European Economic Community (or large parts of it). Curial jurisdiction is territorial in character and therefore rejects the old idea according to which allegiance implies submission.

3. The last and most difficult exception concerns the cases which have no territorial or personal link with the legislating State: nationals of

[18] *Boissevain* v. *Weil,* [1950] A.C. 327, on which see above note 1, at pp. 124 and 108 respectively.

[19] See Dicey and Morris, pp. 1055, 1056, with references.

[20] *Rainford* v. *Newell-Roberts, Irish Reports,* 1962, 95 or *Int.L.R.* 30, 105.

Ruritania agree in Ruritania to sell British whisky at less than the minimum price prescribed by Britain. Can Britain prosecute them when they enter British territory? Can Britain obtain an injunction against or recover damages from them, if British courts have jurisdiction? Or, to take a different case, can Britain impose a tax upon the profits which the Ruritanian importer makes by reselling the whisky in Ruritania?[21] The effect of the Ruritanian deviation from the minimum price is that British exporters of whisky find it more difficult, perhaps even impossible to export to Ruritania at a higher price than that prevailing there. Accordingly the British economy is prejudiced. The Ruritanians, however, are in no way subject to British legislative jurisdiction. The purely commercial effect which makes itself felt in Britain should be insufficient to confer upon Britain any international right to prescribe conduct abroad. Mere commercial effect, it is submitted, provides an insufficient link with the legislating State. The persons are outside its territory. The conduct takes place outside its territory. It would accordingly be unreasonable to expect foreign parties to adapt their conduct to the commercial interests of a State with which they have no legally relevant contact.

IV

The question in all the cases discussed in the preceding section is ultimately the same: can we formulate a principle which in an all-embracing manner defines the extent and, more particularly, the limits of a State's jurisdiction? On this point it may be useful to recall the wise observations of one of the great judges of the International Court of Justice, the late Sir Gerald Fitzmaurice:[22]

> It is true that under present conditions international law does not impose hard and fast rules on States delimiting spheres of national jurisdiction in such matters—namely bankruptcy jurisdiction (and there are of course others—for instance in the field of shipping, 'anti-trust' legislation, etc.)—but leaves to States a wide discretion in the matter. It does, however, *(a)* postulate the existence of limits—though in any given case it may be for the tribunal to indicate what these are for the purposes of that case; and *(b)* involve for every State an obligation to exercise moderation and restraint as to the extent of the jurisdiction assumed by the courts in cases having a foreign element, and to avoid undue encroachment on a jurisdiction more properly appertaining to, or more appropriately exercisable by, another State.

[21] As India does (or did): see above note 1, at pp. 117–18 and 102 respectively.

[22] Case concerning *Barcelona Traction, Light and Power Co. Ltd.*, *ICJ Reports*, 1970, at p. 105.

This was said in that disastrous case which failed in the International Court of Justice on the most technical of grounds, namely the case brought by Belgium against Spain arising out of the fact that in 1948 a Canadian company, Barcelona Traction, Light and Power Co. Ltd. without an office or property in Spain, was declared bankrupt by an obscure Spanish court and subsequently deprived of all its assets by the bankruptcy organs' device of printing and selling 'duplicate' certificates of the bearer shares which were held in Canada by a Canadian trustee as security and which represented interests in vast Spanish assets.[23]

The task of the academic lawyer is to attempt to go beyond Sir Gerald's deliberately general statement and to search for a principle. Such an undertaking will be facilitated by the historical approach. For centuries jurists have been concerned with the problem which constitutes the kernel of the doctrine of international jurisdiction, viz., the reach of legislation, its territoriality or its extra-territoriality. It was the problem which dominated the statute theory as it developed in and since the 13th century and as, curiously enough, it was revived in the United States of America in the 20th century when, ignoring the historical background, the 'neo-statutists',[24] i.e., Currie and Ehrenzweig put forward their most unfortunate, but influential theories about governmental interests and the predominance of the *lex fori*.[25] The statute theory was derived from the idea of the sovereignty of States, an idea which about four centuries later under the guidance of Grotius was at the bottom of what became known as public international law. From the point of view of the latter the reach of legislation always was one of the foremost problems to be solved. There thus existed for many centuries a single idea and a single task. It still pervaded the work of Ulricus Huber in the late 17th century, which is often regarded as the first fruit of the modern conflict of laws in that it was marked by a fresh assessment of the statute theory, but was also 'part of the *jus gentium*, a kind of secondary public international law'.[26] The division of the two subjects was initiated only by Joseph Story's *Commentaries on the Conflict of Laws*, the 150th birthday of which we are

[23] On that case see below p. 59, and, generally, Mann, *American Journal of International Law*, 1973, 259 or below p. 217.

[24] They have frequently been so described: see, for instance, Lipstein *RdC* 135 (1972–I), at p. 143; Kahn-Freund, *RdC* 143 (1974–III), 244; Scoles and Hay, *Conflict of Laws* (1982), 16.

[25] Many aspects of their theories can also be explained by a wholly extravagant application of *ordre public*, though once again this conception, its history and scope is largely ignored by the American theorists, while the courts have adopted it under the heading of balancing of interests.

[26] The writer is ashamed to confess that he cannot now identify the author who made this very acute comment noted by him without reference to the source. But see Martin Wolff, *Private International Law* (2nd ed., 1950), 11: when private international law 'was born, it was thought of as a supernational law'.

celebrating this year. Yet even Story largely proceeded from Huber's teachings which combined the flavour of the statute theory with the evolving theory of public international law.

If one realises the history of and the inter-relation between the conflict of laws and public international law in respect of the problem of the reach of legislation, i.e., of international jurisdiction, it becomes plausible, perhaps even obvious that today both continue to give rise to the same fundamental question: does there exist a sufficiently close connection between a given set of facts and, on the one hand, a particular legal system called upon to govern it or, on the other hand, a particular legislator qualified to regulate it? The former question belongs to private, the latter to public international law.

In the conflict of laws it is possible to refine the generality of the formula and to derive from it a number of rules which are or claim to be expressive of the closeness of connection: the law of nationality or domicile governing status, the *lex situs* governing property, the *lex loci delicti* governing torts are familiar examples. In the field of legislative jurisdiction in international law we can, for the time being, only offer general formulae. In 1964 it was suggested that the public international lawyer should ask 'whether the legally relevant facts are such that they 'belong' to this or that jurisdiction'[27] or whether there existed 'a reasonable relation',[28] or

> that a State has legislative jurisdiction if its contact with a given set of facts is so close, so substantial, so direct, so weighty that legislation in respect of them is in harmony with international law and its various aspects (including the practice of States, the principles of non-interference and reciprocity and the demands of inter-dependence). A merely political, economic, commercial or social interest does not in itself constitute a sufficient connection.[29]

A German scholar has called this the theory of the meaningful contact which he adopted for the realm of anti-trust law.[30] In 1981 the Tentative Draft No 2 of the Revised Foreign Relations Law of the United States

[27] Above note 1, p. 45 and p. 35, respectively.

[28] Above note 1, p. 46 and p. 37, respectively.

[29] Above note 1, p. 49 and p. 39, respectively. This sentence has met with the approval of Professor Jennings (as he then was), *RdC* 121 (1967–II), 515, and the Swiss Government (*Annuaire Suisse de droit international 1981*, 247 sqq., at p. 251). On the other hand Professor Jiménez de Aréchaga, *RdC* 159 (1978–I), 182, suggests that international law knows only 'a loose criterion of a purely negative character rather than a positive rule of public international law: a State is not entitled to exercise jurisdiction over matters, persons or things with which it has absolutely no concern'.

[30] Meessen, *Völkerrechtliche Grundsätze des internationalen Kartellrechts* (1975), at p. 101, whom Verdross-Simma, *Universelles Völkerrecht* (1976), 571, follows.

adopted the principle of reasonableness[31]—a suggestion which appears unobjectionable, so long as it is understood that mere political, economic, commercial or social interests are to be disregarded when it comes to the weighing which every test of reasonableness implies. It is reasonableness in international law, a weighing of legally relevant elements, that is decisive. Sometimes it is said that the limits imposed by international law, for instance in the field of nationality, are 'the principles of prohibition of abuse of rights and arbitrary action';[32] this is not essentially different from the test suggested here, for arbitrariness is substantially the same as unreasonableness. Nor will the process of weighing be the same in each field of law. Thus criminal law, civil procedure, taxation, bankruptcy, nationality or restrictive practices each involve and demand the consideration of different aspects. In each case the overriding question is: does there exist a sufficiently close legal connection to justify, or make it reasonable for, a State to exercise legislative jurisdiction?

We know that in certain fields other than the conflict of laws such rules have been developed. Criminal law is perhaps the most prominent example where one speaks of the theory of universality or the objective principle and so forth. Perhaps in the course of time similar rules applicable to other fields will emerge. We must be patient and not expect too much too quickly. We are protected against such a danger if we consider ourselves as a small item in a long and slow historical process.

A particularly significant development has taken place in the field of taxation. In 1964 it was submitted that a State's right to levy taxation depended on some reasonable link between the State and the person, property or transaction it seeks to tax. Almost 20 years later this starting point was strikingly affirmed by Germany's Federal Constitutional Court, when, relying on the suggestions of 1964, it said:[33]

[31] Section 403 and Comments. This was anticipated by a most valuable and thoughtful article on legislative jurisdiction by Professor Willis L. M. Reese, 78 (1978) *Col.L.R.* 1586. He was primarily concerned with constitutional law, but describes it as the fundamental question 'whether it would be reasonable in the context of our federal system of government for the state in question to apply its law in the particular case. The same principle could be made applicable to international situations by substituting "the international system" for "our federal system of government"' (p. 1592). The learned author suggests a twofold test: 'whether application of the law of the particular state to the point at issue would be fair to the parties and also consistent with the needs of the federal (or international) system.' It is for the reasons indicated by Professor Reese that already in 1964 it was attempted to show that international law may find the constitutional law of a federal state a useful guide to decision. Professor Brownlie, *Principles of Public International Law* (3rd ed., 1979), 309, demands 'a substantial and *bona fide* connection'. On extraterritorial jurisdiction in a federal system of constitutional law see O'Connell, 75 (1959) *L.Q.R.* 318, relating to Australia, and Edinger, (1982) 14 *Ottawa L.R.* 57, relating to Canada.

[32] In this sense Germany's Federal Administrative Court, 24 February 1966, BVerwG 23, 274 or (in English) *Int.L.R.* 57, 307.

[33] BVerfGE 63, 343, at p. 369 (22 March 1983).

> The imposition of taxes upon a foreigner living abroad, which is founded upon a set of facts wholly or partly implemented abroad requires sufficiently appropriate points of contact for taxation by the taxing State to prevent interference, contrary to public international law, with the foreign State's claims to sovereignty. These points of contact and their factual closeness must, from the point of view of public international law, satisfy a minimum of reasonableness.
>
> This requirement constitutes an essential legal limitation of the sets of fact which according to the rules of its own legal system a State may lawfully lay hold of, i.e., a restriction of its international legislative jurisdiction. The legal possibility of imposing taxes upon foreigners is subject to clear limits by the necessity of contact, for instance, with nationality, establisment, residence or sojourn, the realization of a set of taxable facts or the achievement of a legally relevant result within the State.

The only remarkable aspect of this summary is the fact that nationality is unhesitatingly included as a permissible point of contact for purposes of taxation. Yet on the whole it still seems to be the prerogative of the United States of America to subject all its citizens wherever resident to United States tax in respect of the whole of their taxable assets. It seems that the community of nations has accepted this, though doubts about the relevance and adequacy of the test of nationality, which were alluded to 20 years ago, remain. Is the State in which the United States citizen resides not liable to be severely prejudiced by American demands for tax in respect of capital, income or transactions which have no connection with the United States at all and which from the point of view of an 'economic allegiance' belong exclusively to the State of residence? The United States makes its citizens pay for the passport they hold, for the right to return to the United States, to exercise civil rights such as voting rights and for such protection as it decides to afford to its citizens. Yet a case can be made for the suggestion that in relation to the State of residence these are facts which do not reasonably justify the withdrawal from its economy of funds that originate from and, in the sense of economics, 'belong' to it. However this may be, taxation offers many examples of the effect, and a few of the disregard, of the principle. On the one hand there is the disappearance of the German provision which purported to tax certain foreign subsidiaries of German parent companies[34] and on the other hand one may mention

[34] This was section 15 (2) of the Steueranpassungsgesetz on which see H. H. Jakobs, *Steuer und Wirtschaft*, 1970, 589 and Peter Müller, *Deutsche Steuerhoheit über ausländische Tochtergesellschaften* (1970). The Federal Finance Court held in an interesting decision that the provision was not contrary to public international law: 18 December 1963, *Juristenzeitung*, 1965, 21. At that time the court denied that in the field of taxation there existed customary, i.e. generally recognized and applied public international law. The court also applied (but did not cite) the *Lotus* formula that there existed no rule of public international law, which *prohibits* the imposition of German tax upon a foreign subsidiary. A few years later section 7 of the German 'Aussensteuergesetz', as well as section 482 of the United States

the English rule according to which in certain cases the sale of shares in a foreign company will subject the non-resident seller to capital gains tax in England.[35]

An interesting phenomenon which has appeared in the United States should be emphasized. Just as in the field of conflict of laws a theory of the analysis of interests has, under the calamitous influence of Currie, gained ground,[36] so in the field of international jurisdiction we hear of a theory of a balance of interests. The parallelism is fascinating to everyone who is conscious of the historical interconnection between private and public international law.[37] But whether one speaks of analysis or of balancing, interests are in law a bad and misleading guide. It is contact that matters, though this may be a 'territorialist turn of phrase that should make interest analysts cringe',[38] particularly if it is used by the Supreme Court of the United States.[39] The so-called balancing of interests is nothing but a political consideration: it is not the subjective or political interest, but the objective test of the closeness of connection, of a sufficiently weighty point of contact between the facts and their legal assessment that is relevant. The lawyer balances contacts rather than interests.

V

Since the test which determines the existence of legislative jurisdiction and the content of a rule of the conflict of laws is the same and since it has, from a historical point of view, the same root, it cannot be surprising that the doctrine of international jurisdiction has considerable bearing upon the formation of private international law. Whatever the universalist theory of earlier days may have attempted,[40] it cannot today be open to doubt that public international law is not normally the source of private international law in the sense that the former does not lay down effective rules, still less a system of the latter. Public international law does not tell

International Revenue Code and section 80 of the English Finance Act 1984 permit, subject to various conditions, the apportionment of the subsidiary's profits among its shareholders and the imposition of tax upon them.

[35] This is achieved by section 38 of the Finance Act 1973 in conjunction with section 12 of the Capital Gains Tax Act 1979 and thus by the fiction that in the case of oil exploitation companies such gains as are mentioned in the text will 'be treated as . . . gains . . . carried on . . . in the United Kingdom through a branch or agency'.

[36] For an excellent and fortunately convincingly critical survey of a most unfortunate, though fashionable doctrine see Juenger, *American Journal of Comparative Law* 32 (1984), 1.

[37] See *RDC* 111 (1964–I), at pp. 24–31, or *Studies in International Law*, 16–20.

[38] Juenger, loc. cit. 25.

[39] In *Allstate Insurance Co.* v. *Hague*, 449 US 302 (1981) the 'aggregation of contacts' is used to justify the 'state interests'.

[40] See, e.g., Kahn-Freund, *RdC* 143 (1974–III), at pp. 166 sqq.

us what law is to be applied in a given case, though there are exceptions; thus as recently as 1982 Lord Denning spoke of 'the rule of international law which says that no country can legislate so as to affect rights of property when that property is situated beyond the limits of its own territory',[41] a rule which of course does not apply to the incidental effects of general assignments such as death or bankruptcy, but does explain a good deal of our law on expropriation. However this may be, by its adoption of the test of closeness of contact public international law limits the reach of legislative jurisdiction and imposes a duty of making a choice. Public international law, therefore, does not prescribe the application of either the law of the nationality or of the law of domicile to questions of personal status. But it would not permit the law of the forum as the solely applicable law.[42] (This, incidentally, is the reason why it is so misleading to say (as many courts have done,[43] particularly in the United States) that foreign law has no extraterritorial effect or is being applied by the forum only by comity. As so often, comity may in truth mean public international law, but if it does not have this meaning the dictum is wrong, for it would involve the conclusion that the forum would be *entitled* to apply its own law to all foreign facts—a conclusion which in truth is wholly devoid of support.) Nor would public international law permit the application of any arbitrarily selected system of law. Rather it requires a choice between two systems each of which may claim to be closely connected with the issue at hand. Public international law, therefore, has a limiting function in its relation to private international law.[44] This function is underlined by those principles which originate from treaties, but are likely to have become part of the customary international law of human rights. An example is provided by the rule prohibiting discrimination on the ground of sex. It has far reaching influence upon the State's freedom of legislative jurisdiction and thus upon the formation of its private international law.

The situation is very similar, when we consider the problem of the competence of courts or of what frequently is called curial jurisdiction. Thus many years ago it was said in Germany that, as under German law a court has jurisdiction if property of the foreign defendant is found within

[41] *Attorney-General of New Zealand* v. *Oritz,* [1982] 3 All E.R. 450, at p. 456. Cf. *Bank voor Handel en Scheepvaart* v. *Slatford,* [1953] 1 Q.B. 248.

[42] That a State which prohibits the application of any legal system other than its own commits an international wrong is, it is to be hoped, generally recognized. Martin Wolff taught this since 1933: *Internationales Privatrecht* (1st ed., 1933), 7.

[43] *Huntington* v. *Attrill,* 146 US 657, at p. 669 (1892), or *J. Zeevi & Sons Ltd.* v. *Grindlays Bank (Uganda) Ltd.*, 37 NY 2d 220 (1975).

[44] Lipstein, *RdC* 135 (1972–I), 171–3, accepts the limiting function of public international law in regard to what he calls public law (p. 173). Private international law does not have a fundamentally different character and it is impossible to see why public international law should not be capable of imposing limits upon State action in this field.

its district, a claim of many millions could be pursued if the foreigner's shoes are found outside his hotel room. Or, as we have seen, it was said in England, since service of the writ upon the defendant in England is a ground of jurisdiction, a foreigner becomes subject to English curial jurisdiction if he sets foot on English soil at London Airport to change planes and during this time is served with a writ.[45] Today it is very doubtful whether in either case the connection with the State of the forum is sufficiently close to permit the exercise of jurisdiction.

The relationship between public and private international law cannot, therefore, be determined by theoretical or verbal disputations or formulations. The problem can be solved only by recognizing the pervading influence of public international law, the continuity and steadiness of its development and the slow emergence of rules which define and limit the jurisdiction of competing States not necessarily in a uniform manner, but with a sufficient degree of reliance upon relevant and reasonable contact.[46]

VI

It may be asked, in conclusion, where this test, common to public and private international law, comes from, how its existence can be proved, what evidence supports it. The answer, it is believed, is that the principle is derived from the totality of the sources upon which, according to Article 38 of the Statute of the International Court of Justice, international law rests. There are treaties, there is a vast and universal State practice in numerous different, yet related fields, there is a substantial body of academic opinion that can be invoked in its favour. It is quite true that there exist deviations. But the broad lines of the conduct of civilized States as expressed by their legislative activity regarded as a whole cannot leave any doubt in the mind of any observer. Decisions by international tribunals are admittedly rare. But it is difficult to believe that an international court, faced with the problem in all its starkness, would deny the pervasive influence of international law and assert an unrestrained liberty of States to act even in the field of private international law. Even the discredited majority opinion in the *Lotus* case recognized some limits of a State's legislative jurisdiction. Since then more than 50 years have expired. During that period international law has not stood still. If its development has not always been progressive, it is the duty of international lawyers to try to contribute positively to a doctrine which they recognize as sensible and

[45] Above p. 8.

[46] The theory of the relationship between public and private international law has been very fully treated by Professor Pierre Mayer, *Rev. Crit.* 1979, 1, 349, 547. In the result he is probably not opposed to the submission in the text, though he sees the primary function of public international law in the field of enforcement jurisdiction.

sound and to which modern methods of comparative law lend their aid. Each such contribution adds a little to the foundation upon which international law rests.

It may be, indeed it has been said that international law cares, not about legislative jurisdiction, but only about enforcement jurisdiction: if Ruritania imposes an unreasonable tax upon a Utopian citizen (or adopts an unreasonable rule of private international law about the law governing the formalities of marriage), this, so it may be suggested, is *brutum fulmen* and does not concern Utopia, because the tax cannot be recovered there. The victim, however, may possess or in the future acquire property in Ruritania or he may, voluntarily or involuntarily, set foot on Ruritanian territory, so that the tax could be enforced against him. It would be a most unattractive system of law which would preclude a State from protecting its citizens against an international wrong before it is implemented or, in other words, compel a State to defer its objection to a time when protection may be too late and ineffective. Hence a doctrine of legislative jurisdiction is a necessary ingredient of an adequately developed system of international law.[47]

II. ENFORCEMENT JURISDICTION

I

Enforcement jurisdiction[48] to which the last few words of the preceding chapter refer concerns not the law prescribed by a State to *regulate, inter alia*, acts outside its own territory, but the lawfulness of the State's own *acts* to give effect to such regulation. Enforcement jurisdiction, therefore, is concerned with the question whether and if so in what circumstances a State may act in the sense of exercising sovereign authority, performing acts *jure imperi*. The case of a State entering into a commercial transaction or being a party to commercial arbitration, acting *jure gestionis*, being involved in '*actus qui a rege sed ut a quovis alio fiant*', is entirely outside the scope of the present discussion.

Three propositions about enforcement jurisdiction may be suggested and ought to meet with little opposition.

[47] Nothing has been said in this chapter about what in Tentative Draft No. 2 of the Revised Foreign Relations of the United States the American Law Institute calls jurisdiction to adjudicate (ss. 401, 441). This conception which did not appear in the original version is really no more than an aspect or an emanation of legislative jurisdiction or what the Americans call jurisdiction to prescribe. It therefore does not deserve to be treated as a distinct category equal to legislative jurisdiction. See above p. 5 and below p. 51.

[48] On enforcement generally see, apart from the literature referred to above, Chapter 1, note 1, Rigaux, *Droit public et droit privé dans les relations internationales* (1977), 311 sqq.

1. No State may exercise enforcement jurisdiction outside its own territory in the absence of its own legislature authorizing it to do so, that is to say, in the absence of legislative jurisdiction. Suppose Britain sends policemen to Holland in order to check whether whisky is being sold there at less than the minimum price prescribed by British law. If Britain is not entitled to regulate the price of whisky in Holland the dispatch of officials to and their activity in Holland would be unlawful, irrespective of whether or not it is lawful under Dutch or international law.

2. The mere existence of legislative jurisdiction is insufficient to justify the State to exercise enforcement jurisdiction in another State's territory. Thus if Britain were permitted to prescribe the price of whisky in Holland the legality of the despatch of investigators to Holland to check Dutch sales of whisky does not by any means follow.

Curiously enough it is far from certain whether Professor Brownlie accepts this rule, for he says that there 'is no essential distinction between the legal bases for and limits upon substantive (or legislative) jurisdiction, on the one hand, and, on the other, enforcement (or personal or prerogative) jurisdiction. The one is the function of the other. If the substantive jurisdiction is beyond lawful limits, then any consequent enforcement jurisdiction is unlawful'.[49] And this view seems to have been accepted by the Swiss Government:[50]

> La distinction . . . entre la compétence législative et la compétence en matière d'enforcement, soit entre la législation extraterritoriale et l'application extraterritoriale de cette législation ne sera pas reprise ici. Avec Brownlie il faut admettre que l'une des deux compétences est fonction de l'autre et que leurs limites coïncident.

Yet this must surely be due to some misunderstanding: the fact that a State has legislative jurisdiction does not authorize its enforcement abroad. There can be no question of the two jurisdictions necessarily coinciding. The international order could be gravely prejudiced if it were otherwise.

3. The mere fact that a State can enforce its legislation within its own territory and in this sense has enforcement jurisdiction, does not mean that it necessarily has legislative jurisdiction, and does not therefore render the enforcement valid in public international law.

It is at this point that it becomes necessary to consider a very interesting, but also very difficult decision of a majority of the House of Lords in a tax

[49] *Principles of Public International Law* (3rd edn., 1979), 309.

[50] *Annuaire Suisse de droit international* 1981, 247 sqq., at p. 248. It seems possible that the confusion arises from the use of the word 'application'. If legislation and its application occur in the same State and if application is meant to be the same as enforcement, the two types of jurisdiction, of course, coincide. But enforcement is something quite different from mere application.

case.[51] Under English law an employer is also a tax collector in that he is bound to deduct tax from the wages paid to his employees and to pay it over to the State which has the power by a variety of means to check the correctness of the payments received by it and to enforce its rights against the employer. A Panama company resident in Antwerp pays wages in dollars outside Britain to an employee who is also resident outside Britain in respect of duties performed in Britain. If the Panama company fails to deduct income tax which is due under the law of Britain from the employee can Britain's Inland Revenue recover it from the non-resident Panama company? Lord Scarman, Lord Wilberforce and Lord Roskill answered in the affirmative, Lord Edmund-Davies and Lord Lowry dissented. It is by no means easy to ascertain the precise *ratio decidendi* which the majority adopted, for it would seem that Lord Scarman and Lord Wilberforce put forward different reasoning and Lord Roskill agreed with both. It seems, however, that it was a very important, perhaps a decisive point that the Panama company had what was called a 'tax presence', i.e., assets, including a business in Britain and also an address for service of documents. In other words the tax liability if any could be enforced in Britain. But was it lawful to render a non-resident foreign company liable to make the payments? The House was fully conscious of the territorial limitation which normally characterizes British legislation in general and tax legislation in particular and reaffirmed the principle which has dominated English law for more than a hundred years. Lord Scarman, it seems, thought that the principle was being observed, because it applied to 'foreigners who by coming to the United Kingdom, whether for a short or a long time, have made themselves subject to British jurisdiction';[52] therefore, though non-resident, the Panama company was present in Britain. The concept of a company's 'tax presence' as opposed to residence is entirely new, but is, it is submitted, without any bearing upon the real question. This was whether the law made the non-resident Panama company liable; it was not whether any liability could be enforced. It is submitted, therefore, that Lord Wilberforce was right to search for such liability or, as we would say, for the legislative jurisdiction. He regarded 'as critical'[53] a provision which rendered the non-resident company liable to British tax in respect of profits arising in Britain. But, surely, this has nothing to do with the imposition upon a non-resident of a liability to deduct tax from the employee's income, i.e., to pay *his* tax. What you have to look for is a section imposing this liability upon a non-resident. As Lord Edmund-Davies said:[54]

[51] *Clark (Inspector of Taxes)* v. *Oceanic Contractors Inc.* [1983] 2 A.C. 130.
[52] P. 139. [53] P. 143. [54] P. 147.

Granted that the activities of Oceanic, with its design office at Wembley, its fabrication yard near Inverness and its Aberdeen branch constitute carrying on a trade in the United Kingdom, through a branch or agency within the meaning of the subsection, I respectfully find it difficult to appreciate the bearing of that conclusion on the application of s. 204 of the 1970 Act to emoluments paid abroad to employees of the North Sea division with headquarters in Brussels and an operational centre in Antwerp.

And as to the concept of 'tax presence' the same learned law lord said that even if it existed[55]

it would still not have served . . . to establish that personal liability to tax has any rational or legal connection with a duty to make deductions in respect of the chargeability of others.

In short the case is a striking example of the rule that the undoubted existence of enforcement jurisdiction does not suffice to establish legislative jurisdiction.

However this may be, the decision of the House of Lords concerns exceptional facts. In practice the real problem of enforcement jurisdiction lies in ascertaining the limits within which a State can act in a foreign State to enforce its own laws. On this point the starting point must now be an important dictum by the highest German court, the Federal Constitutional Court, in a recent tax case to which more detailed reference will have to be made in another connection:[56]

According to general public international law a State is in principle under no duty within the limits of its sovereignty to tolerate the performance or execution of acts of sovereignty by another State . . . or by way of judicial assistance to render facilities; on the other hand public international law does not prohibit such tolerance or co-operation; it makes them available to States. Extreme diffidence is being displayed by States particularly where the execution within their own sphere of sovereignty of foreign criminal judgments or the collection of foreign revenue claims are concerned . . .

Indeed, the fact that a State has legislative jurisdiction in respect of a crime committed abroad does not authorize it to send police officers into a foreign State to arrest the criminal and carry him across the frontier, or to send its judges into the foreign State to sit there as a court and try the case. There can be no question of the two jurisdictions coinciding. That a State which has legislative jurisdiction may apply and enforce it in its own

[55] Ibid.

[56] 22 March 1983, BVerfGE 63, 343, at p. 361. Citations of material have been omitted. See further on the case below p. 29.

territory is undoubted and involves no problem. Enforcement jurisdiction, however, is concerned with putting a State's legislative jurisdiction into effect in another country. As a matter of firm principle this cannot be done without the consent of the State in which the act of enforcement takes place. The rights and privileges of the territorial sovereign prevail. The international order would be gravely prejudiced if it were otherwise.

The real problem, therefore, is to define and delimit the measures of enforcement which one State may be authorized by its internationally valid law to take and those to which another State may object.

II

Twenty years ago five types of enforcement jurisdiction were distinguished. In many respects little has happened that would require renewed discussion. Yet it may be helpful to review a few developments which throw new or additional light on the legal position.

When one considers *the use of physical force* by or on behalf of a State in the territory of another State, it is advisable to disregard events which one may describe as macro-political, such as the invasion of Lebanon by Israel or of Grenada by the United States of America. These are events of a war-like character which, on account of their political implications, in the last resort are still unsuitable for, and exceed the scope of, a strictly legal appreciation, at any rate until the factual background has become much clearer. What the law can more readily cope with are such cases as that of Colonel Argoud[57] who on 25 February 1963 was kidnapped in Germany and abducted to France in all probability by agents of the French Government headed by General de Gaulle. Fortunately no similar case seems to have become known since then, but the details of Argoud's case are to a large extent established.

On 16 November 1963 the German Parliament requested the German Government to secure Argoud's return. Accordingly on 30 December 1963 a Note claiming his return was presented to the Quai d'Orsay. That was the very day on which the Cour de sûreté de l'Etat sentenced the Colonel to imprisonment for life, stating that the Ministry for Foreign Affairs, at the time no doubt truthfully, had informed it that Germany had not demanded his return. (The dates seem to be remarkable and, one suspects, were not accidental and the presentation of the German Note may have been deliberately delayed.) Even now it is not known whether and how France ever replied to the German protest; it is certain that

[57] See, in particular Doehring, *Zeitschrift für ausländisches öffentliches und Völkerrecht* 28 (1965), 209, and Rigaux, *Droit public et droit privé dans les relations internationales* (1977), 315 sqq., both with many further references.

France did not follow the example of Nazi Germany which, it will be remembered, had in 1933 abducted the German citizen Jacob Salomon from Swiss territory, but upon Switzerland's request returned him. On 4 June 1964 the Cour de Cassation dismissed Argoud's appeal on the principal ground that any violation of public international law could be relied upon, not by Argoud, but only by Germany.[58] The decision, arrived at with obvious discomfort,[59] is unsatisfactory, because, as Professor Doehring has pointed out[60] and as is highly important for our purposes, a grave violation of human rights had been alleged and nowhere is the rule of French municipal law identified which prevented the courts from remedying the wrong. Almost 20 years later, when pronouncing upon the legality of M. Mitterrand's measures of nationalization, the Conseil Constitutionnel made it clear that the fundamental rights proclaimed by the Déclaration des Droits de l'Homme et du Citoyen of 1789 were incorporated into the French Constitutions of 1946 and 1956.[61] It is to be expected that today no French, indeed no European Government would feel able to defend the most regrettable events in the case of Colonel Argoud, for it is this type of case which pre-eminently comes within the protective functions of the Strasbourg authorities. Admittedly the case of a person who is unlawfully detained and entitled to immediate release, but convicted before the release is obtained is not expressly dealt with by the European Convention on Human Rights, but a conviction obtained in such circumstances would, it is submitted, itself be unlawful.[62]

III

When one comes to the exercise of sovereign authority in a foreign State *without the use of force*, it is in the first place necessary to refer to the problem of the service of documents by post. Apart from the Hague Convention of 15 November 1965 which has been adopted by a large group of countries two events of great significance stand out. On the one hand in the United States the Court of Appeals, District of Columbia Circuit, decided in 1980 that, at any rate in the face of protest by the

[58] Cass. Crim., 4 June 1964, *Clunet* 1965, 93 or in English *Int.L.R.* 45, 90.

[59] The decision itself speaks of circumstances 'si déplorables qu'elles puissent apparaître'. The Rapporteur, M. le Conseiller Comte, obviously felt most uncomfortable. He did not arrive at a firm conclusion, as he found himself 'en face d'une situation dont certains aspects ne laissaient pas d'apparaître troubles et déconcertants (c'est le moins que j'en veuille dire)'. His speech is printed in *Clunet, loc. cit.* The decision is unconvincing and it is a matter of regret that the court did not display that firmness and independence which characterized its attitude in *l'affaire Dreyfus*.

[60] Above note 57, at p. 221.

[61] *Clunet* 1982, 336.

[62] There does not seem to be any case law on the point raised in the text. In the event of unlawful detention the European Convention on Human Rights provides for satisfaction. It may be suggested that this may involve *restitutio in integrum*, i.e. the release of the detained person even if in the meantime he has been lawfully convicted.

French Government, it was not legitimate for the Federal Trade Commission to serve a subpoena upon a party of French nationality by sending a registered letter to France, for 'the act of service itself constitutes an exercise of American sovereign power within the area of the foreign country's territorial sovereignty';[63] accordingly service was invalid.[64] The decision which, incidentally, makes a clear and well-justified distinction between the service of notice which merely involves the supply of information and compulsory process, is likely to be a landmark and will, it is hoped, be strictly observed by those numerous agencies all over the world that have in the past disregarded what should have been an elementary rule frequently proclaimed, for instance, by the Swiss Federal Tribunal,[65] among other courts.

On the other hand there is a decision of the European Court of Justice in 1972[66] which stands in striking contrast to the United States case, though in strict law it may be distinguishable. The Commission of the European Economic Community served a notice of objections under its anti-trust legislation upon a Swiss company by posting a letter to the Swiss head office. It was argued that this method was contrary to Swiss and to international law. This is how the Court dealt with the point:[67]

> It appears from the file that the authorities of the third State in question do not for the present envisage any practical possibility of service, considered by them to be valid under internal law, on the territory of that State. Therefore international law cannot be invoked in order to deny the Community the power to take the necessary steps to ensure the effectiveness of measures taken with a view to curtailing conduct adversely affecting competition which has arisen in the Common Market, even if the registered office of the undertaking responsible for such conduct is situated in a third country.

Professor Pierre Mayer has described this reasoning as untenable.[68] In fact it makes the reader blush, not only because of the lack of logic (the word 'therefore' expresses a *non sequitur* of unusual obviousness), but also on

[63] *Federal Trade Commission* v. *Compagnie de Saint-Gobain-Pont-à-Mousson,* 636 F.2d 1300 (1980), and *Int.L.R.* 69, 92.

[64] This is one of the points on which the decision of the German Federal Constitutional Court of 22 March 1983, BVerfGE 63, 343, is unconvincing. The court assumes that service of an Austrian tax demand by post in Germany was contrary to public international law. But it holds that this does not create personal rights for an individual and has no bearing upon the effect of any violation within Germany. But if there was a violation there must have been nullity of service and nothing except waiver by the Federal Republic could cure it.

[65] The most recent case probably is the decision of 4 May 1979, BGE 105 Ia 307. But see Müller and Wildhaber, *Praxis des Völkerrechts* (2nd edn., 1982), 282.

[66] *J. R. Geigy* v. *E.E.C. Commission, Reports of European Court of Justice,* 1972, II, 787.

[67] At p. 823.

[68] See the decision of the case referred to in note 63 above at first instance: 493 F. Supp. 286 (1980), at p. 290, note 7.

account of the lack of respect for international law. There is no trace of the universal rule, once again affirmed by the American decision above referred to,[69] according to which 'courts are bound wherever possible to construe . . . statutes conferring subject-matter jurisdiction on domestic agencies to avoid possible conflicts with contrary principles of international law'. One can only hope that the European Court of Justice will never again be guilty of a similar blunder.

If in the absence of treaty arrangements a State cannot lawfully serve compulsory process in the territory of another State at any rate in cases in which the recipient is not a national of the serving State,[70] it will not cause surprise that the performance of other acts of authority comes within the scope of the same rule. Thus a judge even if sitting in his country's embassy does not exercise his country's judicial functions in respect of witnesses who are not its nationals and do not appear voluntarily; he can act only under the authority of an appointment by the territorial sovereign or his courts,[71] for while the premises of the mission are inviolable, the idea that they are extraterritorial in the sense of being part of the sending State's territory has long since been discarded.[72]

Similar problems arise in connection with marriages solemnized by diplomatic or consular officers. The matter is dealt with in numerous multilateral and bilateral treaties,[73] but apart from them the picture is not uniform. Consular officers of the United States of America are not permitted to celebrate marriages of nationals[74] and apparently foreign consular officers cannot do so in the United States.[75] In France, on the other hand, it is regarded as a firm principle of public international law that a consul can perform the marriage ceremony of two of his country's

[69] At p. 1323, and passim.

[70] That United States nationals may be served with a subpoena in a foreign country has for many years been the view of the Unites States: *Blackmer* v. *United States*, 284 US 421 (1932), discussed in the course of the 1964 lectures. Since then the United States enacted Public Law 88–619 of 3 October 1964 (*Int.L.M.* 1964, 1081) which amended section 1783 of title 28 of the United States Code and now provides that a national or resident of the United States who is in a foreign country may be served with a subpoena, apparently by post. On the 1964 Act see Smit, 65 (1964) *Col.L.R.* 1015.

[71] *Rio Tinto Zinc* v. *Westinghouse Electric Corporation,* [1978] A.C. 547, at p. 628.

[72] *Radwan* v. *Radwan,* [1972] 3 All E.R. 967, a case which has not received the attention of public international lawyers that it deserves.

[73] See in particular the Vienna Convention on Consular Relations of 1963 which by Article 5 *(f)* authorizes a consul to act 'as notary or civil registrar . . . provided that there is nothing contrary thereto in the laws and regulations of the receiving State'. On the British bilateral treaties see Clive Parry, *Cambridge Essays in International Law in Honour of Lord McNair* (1965), 122.

[74] For a full discussion see Whiteman, *Digest of International Law*, 7, 606 sqq. (1970), and the article by Clive Parry, 67 (1954) *Harv.L.R.* 1187, who exposes a curious misunderstanding by numerous textbook writers who read 'in the presence of' as meaning 'by' and thus completely misunderstood the effect of a United States statute of 1860.

[75] *Jung* v. *Novaya,* 47 NY Supp. 2d 48 (1944).

nationals, and this applies both to French consuls outside France and to foreign consuls in France.[76] But since it is only by virtue of special legislation that a French consul can perform the ceremony if the bridegroom is French,[77] no similar rule prevails in regard to the powers of consuls in France.[78] It is very likely, therefore, that Cumming-Bruce J. (as he then was) was wrong, when he held that as a matter of French law the Egyptian Consul-General in Paris had authority to marry an Egyptian man and an English woman.[79] A German consul can celebrate a marriage if one of the spouses is German and neither has the nationality of the receiving State, but he is instructed not to act in cases in which the validity of the marriage is not certain to be recognized.[80] The British Foreign Marriage Act 1892 authorizes a British consular officer to perform a marriage ceremony if one of the spouses is British,[81] but instructs him not to do so 'if in his opinion the solemnization thereof would be inconsistent with international law or the comity of nations'; the last few words are interesting, but have never been judicially considered, so that it can only be suggested that they envisage the case in which the receiving State either prohibits consular marriages or regards them as an offensive or discourteous act. In any case the conclusion is that the enforcement of domestic marriage legislation by consuls abroad is greatly limited by international law and practice.

IV

While *investigations* carried out by or on behalf of a State in a foreign country do not appear to have given rise to fresh problems,[82] it is necessary

[76] Battifol and Lagarde, *Droit international privé* (7th ed., 1983), sections 423 and 424; Loussouarn and Bourel (2nd edn., 1980), section 290; Pierre Mayer, sections 539 to 541.

[77] This does not apply in the case in which the bride is French and the bridegroom is foreign. It seems doubtful whether this rule is maintainable in an age of non-discrimination on the ground of sex. See Article 14 of the European Convention on Human Rights.

[78] See the authors referred to in note 76.

[79] *Radwan* v. *Radwan* (No. 2), [1972] 3 All E.R. 1027. See also the following note.

[80] Section 8 of the Consular Act of 11 September 1974 and see the comments, for instance, by Marquordt in Erman, Article 13, note 16, or Schwimann, MünchKom, Article 13, note 114. The German Supreme Court held (3 March 1930, JW 1931, 1335) that a marriage between an Egyptian man and a German woman celebrated by a German consul in Egypt was in German law valid, notwithstanding any invalidity under Egyptian law, because the Egyptian Government had by implication permitted such acts of sovereignty by a German consul.

[81] Sections 1 and 19 of the Foreign Marriage Act 1892. On the opposite case of a consul performing a marriage ceremony in England there is no judicial authority. On the views and practice of the Foreign Office see Clive Parry, *British Digest of International Law* 8, 631–45.

[82] See, however, Rigaux, *Droit public et droit privé dans les relations internationales* (1977), 321, who, surpringly, considers such investigations lawful. It should, however, be clear that enquiries carried out by the police in a foreign country without its consent are illegal, and in a great decision of 15 July 1982 the Swiss Federal Tribunal refused the extradition of a

once again to revert to the question whether a State can *enforce its public law by proceedings in the courts of another State*. The problem was discussed not only in 1964,[83] but also in 1971,[84] when the rational foundation of the doctrine was more elaborately developed:

The State which tries to recover penalties or taxes within the territory of another State purports to exercise extraterritorial enforcement jurisdiction. This is so, whether it sends troops or a bailiff, whether it issues letters of demand or institutes proceedings in the courts of the forum, thus using the latter's system of judicial administration and machinery. Even the last-mentioned method involves the assertion that the claimant State is entitled to recover its penalties and taxes in the territory of the State of the forum. It is the assertion of the right to have its sovereign powers in regard to penalties and taxes respected and enforced that constitutes the infringement of the sovereignty of the State of the forum and therefore is contrary to international law. No judge is able or entitled to allow such a claim to proceed and thus to permit an excess of international jurisdiction. Such permission can only be given by the sovereign authority itself and almost everywhere presupposes a treaty and legislation. A judge who would take it upon himself to forego his sovereign's right of jurisdiction would prejudice him greatly: he would be deprived of the opportunity to secure reciprocity of treatment.

Thus the plaintiff State's assertion to be entitled to enforce its prerogative rights in the forum State without that State's permission is the act which constitutes unlawful enforcement jurisdiction. Such is the true reason for a generally accepted practice which has often been bedevilled by the absence of analysis and explanation.[85]

On the level of treaty practice the continued force of the rule cannot be doubted. It is true that in 1981 the OECD's Committee on Fiscal Affairs presented a draft model convention for mutual administrative assistance in the recovery of tax claims and that a few conventions have provided for it,[86] but there is no sign of any general intention to accept it.

It is much more significant that the Brussels Convention on jurisdiction

---

Belgian who had been induced by stealth of the German police to enter Swiss territory; to give effect to the German request would have made Switzerland a party to the violation of Belgian sovereignty of which Germany was guilty (not yet fully reported, but see Annuaire Suisse de Droit International 1983, 228.

[83] At p. 141. [84] *RdC* 132 (1971–I), at p. 166.

[85] The decision of the House of Lords in *Government of India* v. *Taylor*, [1955] A.C. 491 has been criticized on the ground that it is entirely 'positivistic' and gives no rational explanation of the result reached. It must be admitted that the absence of such reasoning weakened the force of the decision.

[86] See, for instance, the German-Austrian Convention referred to below p. 29, or the American-French Convention of 28 July 1967, in force since 11 July 1968, which imposes an obligation to lend assistance in the collection of taxes due from nationals other than those of the State where enforcement is sought (Article 27).

and the enforcement of judgments (as amended) which is in force between the original six member States of the European Economic Community and which is now in force in the remaining four member States applies only 'in civil and commercial matters' and does not extend 'in particular to revenue, customs or administrative matters'.[87]

As regards judicial practice there is not a single recent case which concerned an attempt to recover penalties. There is, on the other hand, strong evidence to the effect that revenue claims in the strict sense of the term, i.e., claims for taxes or customs duties have been universally rejected. It is true that, using language which is perhaps less than judicial and purports to support a wholly unconvincing majority decision, the Court of Appeals of New York in 1975 described the rule according to which one State does not enforce the revenue laws of another as 'an old chestnut'.[88] In truth even in the United States the rule is a blooming flower, at least in international cases.[89] It was applied when in 1979 the Court of Appeals, 9th Circuit, refused to enforce a British Columbian judgment for arrears of taxes[90] and many recent dicta are to the same effect.[91] So is the decision of the Supreme Court of Canada of 1963 which denied enforcement to a United States judgment for taxes.[92] In England there is equally strong evidence of the continued force of the rule which has been applied to deny claims for income tax, capital gains tax, customs

[87] Article 1, as set forth in the 1st Schedule to the Civil Jurisdiction and Judgments Act 1982.

[88] *Banco Frances e Brasileiro* v. *John Doe,* 36 NY 2d 592 (1975). The case has been discussed by Mann, *The Legal Aspect of Money* (4th ed., 1982), at pp. 429, 430 and 432. It was concerned with exchange control regulations which are not revenue laws. The defendants were alleged to have obtained United States dollars for the proper amount of Brazilian currency in circumstances in which under Brazilian exchange control regulations they were not entitled to them. The plaintiffs clearly did not suffer any damage and the action ought to have been dismissed, though if they had to pay and did pay a penalty they probably were entitled to that extent to be indemnified. The reasoning of the majority refers to the irrelevant fact that revenue claims of a domestic character are enforceable in the States of the Union. It also makes the illogical remark that the I.M.F. Agreement, while not requiring a judgment in favour of the plaintiffs, does not preclude it. It is possible that this argument was the *ratio decidendi.* In short the decision of the majority is based on such faulty reasoning as to render elaborate criticism both impossible and redundant.

[89] That as a result of the provisions of a Constitution in a federal State different rules may apply in interstate cases is obvious. Scoles and Hay, *Conflict of Laws*, Section 24.23, state that 'policy considerations support a broad view in favour of enforcement of both interstate and international claims'. But in regard to the latter claims no policy considerations are mentioned or discernible.

[90] *Her Majesty The Queen in Right of British Columbia* v. *Gilbertson,* 597 F.2d 1161 (1979).

[91] See, e.g., Justice Harlan and Justice Goldberg in their wholly convincing dissent in *United States* v. *First National City Bank*, 379 US 378 (1965), at 395, 396 and note 94 below.

[92] *United States* v. *Harden,* [1963] S.C.R. 366, on which see Lysyk, *Canadian Yearbook of International Law,* 1964, 245.

duty, succession duty, profits tax, rates and national insurance contributions.[93] The Commonwealth takes the same view.[94] So does South Africa.[95] And on the Continent Germany's Federal Constitutional Court stated as recently as 1983 that as a general rule States do not render assistance in the execution within their own sovereign sphere of foreign revenue judgments and consider revenue claims as unenforceable, though public international law does not go so far as to prohibit such assistance and therefore occasionally treaties such as a recent treaty between Germany and Austria may permit it.[96] The Court of Appeal in Hamburg applied the principle in circumstances which were suggested more than 30 years ago, but never before judicially considered: a Dutch bank guaranteed the taxpayer's tax debts and discharged them. It then claimed against the taxpayer by virtue of subrogation (as opposed to contract). The claim failed and was bound to fail, 'for it is an internationally recognized rule of law that public law claims, in particular tax and customs duty claims of the State cannot be pursued in a foreign country', and subrogation does not turn the claim into one of private law.[97] The reason for this impressive body of law is not, as the New York Court of Appeals thought,[98] that 'an analogy is drawn to foreign penal laws'. The reason is to be found in the great principle of international law which has been suggested and which also requires the non-enforcement of claims by or on behalf of States to enforce their export restrictions[99] or their exchange control laws[100] or their securities law[101] or, generally, in the words of the Brussels Convention of

[93] For a list of cases see Halsbury (Hailsham), *Laws of England*, 4th ed., Vol. 8, paragraph 420, note 1, or Dicey and Morris, Rule 3.

[94] *Bath* v. *British & Malayan Trustees* (1969) 2 N.S.W.R. 114; *Re Reid,* 17 *D.L.R.* 3rd 206 (1971), a decision of the British Columbian Court of Appeal. Also South Africa: *Jones* v. *Borland* 1969 (4), South African L.R. 29. These cases deal with the problem which arose in *Re Lord Cable deceased,* [1976] 3 All E.R. 417, and in contrast to this English decision decide it correctly. The reasons were developed by Mann, *The Legal Aspect of Money* (4th edn., 1982), 432, 433.

[95] *Commissioners of Taxes* v. *McFarlane,* 1965 (1) S.A. 470.

[96] BVerfGE 63, 343 (22 March 1983), at pp. 361, 362.

[97] IPRspr. 1958/1959 No. 61 (25 November 1959); in this sense Mann, 40 *Transactions of the Grotius Society* (1955), 25, at p. 36, or *Studies in International Law* (1973), p. 492, at p. 503.

[98] See note 88 above.

[99] *King of Italy* v. *De Medici* (1918) 34 T.L.R. 623.

[100] See the cases discussed by Mann, *The Legal Aspect of Money* (4th ed., 1982), 428–33, in particular the Court of Appeals, Second Circuit, in *Menendez* v. *Saks & Co.*, 485 F.2d 1355, at p. 1366, (1973). Here and elsewhere exchange control laws are described as a 'species of revenue laws'. This is both incorrect and unnecessary. In *Attorney-General of New Zealand* v. *Ortiz*, [1982] 3 All E.R. 450, at p. 459 Lord Denning M. R. suggested that two of the English cases on the subject 'might be [or ought to have been?] solved by adopting the distinction between acts done in the exercise of sovereign authority within its own territory, and those outside it'. This is in line with the submission in the text and in the book referred to at the beginning of this note.

[101] *Schemmer* v. *Property Resources Ltd.*, [1975] Ch. 273, at p. 288, where the Securities and Exchange Act of the United States is quite unnecessarily described as a penal act. This

1968, their administrative laws. In short, the principle applies to all claims which are derived from public laws or, as Turner L.J. put it so well, involve the enforcement of prerogative rights.[102] In the words of Lord Denning M.R.[103]

> by international law every sovereign State has no sovereignty beyond its frontiers. The courts of other countries will not allow it to go beyond the bounds. They will not enforce any of its laws which purport to exercise sovereignty beyond the limits of its authority.

As the Court of Appeal in England summarized the rule in 1980:[104]

> It is a well-established rule that our courts will not enforce a foreign revenue, penal or public law. This means that our courts will not try and either punish or give a remedy for the breach of such a law committed in a foreign country.

Interesting questions arise where the State claims reimbursement for services rendered by it or has discharged liabilities of the defendant; these were discussed in 1971 and do not now have to be reconsidered.

Quite apart from the great principle of international law requiring the non-enforcement of foreign prerogative rights there exists a weighty practical reason supporting the rule. In very many cases the proof of foreign public law such as revenue law would cause enormous practical difficulties of fact and law. The ordinary courts of most countries have succeeded in closing their doors to claims based on domestic public law. They cannot be expected to do for foreign sovereigns what in numerous contexts they refuse to do for their own sovereign.

V

Finally it is necessary to deal in general terms with that long line of American cases[105] which have already been referred to and will have to be

---

is certainly true, but even if it were not so the Act would still be unenforceable outside the United States.

[102] *Emperor of Austria* v. *Day* (1861) 3 De G.F. & J. 217, at p. 251.

[103] At p. 457 of the case referred to in note 100. That great judge's formulation is in line with the submissions in the paper referred to in note 97.

[104] *R.* v. *Governor of Pentonville Prison* [1980] 1 All E.R. 701, at p. 714. The case was not cited in the course of the argument in *Attorney-General of New Zealand* v. *Oritz, ubi supra*. If it had been cited Ackner and O'Connor L.JJ. at pp. 467 and 468 respectively would probably not have rejected 'a third category of foreign laws . . . namely public laws'. Indeed they would not have spoken of categories. There is one single group of which penal laws, revenue laws, etc., are mere illustrations. The terminology should be wholly immaterial. It is to be hoped that in future Lord Denning's searching analysis and conclusion will prevail.

[105] Most of them are mentioned in the decision of Judge Milton Pollack in *Securities and Exchange Commission* v. *Banca della Svizzera Italiana*, 92 F.R.D. 111 (1981).

noticed in many connections and which purport to solve the conflict of enforcement jurisdiction, a conflict that usually arises from American demands for information requested by subpoena, interrogatories, orders for discovery of documents and so forth, and from local prohibitions to suppy it. Section 40 of the Restatement (Second) of the Foreign Relations Law of the United States has become almost a statutory text sanctioning that unfortunate doctrine of the balancing of interests. It reads as follows:

Where two States have jurisdiction to prescribe and enforce rules of law and the rules they may prescribe require inconsistent conduct upon the part of a person, each State is required by international law to consider, in good faith, moderating the exercise of its enforcement jurisdiction, in the light of such facts as
(a) vital national interests of each of the States,
(b) the extent and the nature of the hardship that inconsistent enforcement actions would impose upon the person,
(c) the extent to which the required conduct is to take place in the territory of the other State,
(d) the nationality of the person, and
(e) the extent to which enforcement by action of either State can reasonably be expected to achieve compliance with the rule prescribed by that State.

It is submitted that even if the American courts were less chauvinistic in applying these rules and did not regard the preponderance of American interests as a matter of public policy there is, from the point of view of international law, a fundamental objection to the ideas expressed by or underlying Section 40. This is that, as a matter of international law derived from the practice of States and general principles of law, no State is in general entitled to require the commission of a criminal offence or an illegality within the territory of another State. There exists much material supporting such a rule[106] as well as its exceptions.[107] To collect it would far exceed the scope of the present observations. It must suffice to ask a rhetorical question: can it be doubted that a State which through its executive or judicial organs commands a person to commit a murder or a

[106] *De Wütz* v. *Hendricks,* (1824) 2 Bing. 314; *Ralli Bros.* v. *Compañia Naviera Sota y Aznar* [1920] 2 K.B. 287; *Foster* v. *Driscoll*, [1929] 1 K.B. 470, and many other cases. It is, of course, necessary carefully to analyse the facts. Thus *Kleinwort Sons & Co.* v. *Ungarische Baumwolle Industrie A.G.*, [1939] 2 K.B. 678, may well have involved the defendants in an illegality under Hungarian law. But there was no term in the contract to the effect that the money was to be paid in or from Hungary. In the case of monetary obligations it is, in the absence of express terms, immaterial where and how the debtor procures the money required to discharge his debt.

[107] It is surely illegal to pay someone for assisting a prisoner kept in prison in a foreign country to escape. But this is not so if he is unlawfully kept in a concentration camp. This is the idea underlying the decisions of the Federal Supreme Court of Germany upholding contracts for the payment of a fee for assisting an East German to escape into the West: 29 September 1977, BGHZ 69, 295 and 302.

theft in the territory of a foreign sovereign would be guilty of an international wrong? The attack on the integrity of the foreign territory and its legal order is obvious. It is inconsistent with the demands of peaceful co-existence and cannot be justified by any of the five considerations which section 40 enumerates. In particular the interests of the State giving the order cannot be invoked as a justification, whether they be vital or not. They are needs subordinate to the duty to respect foreign sovereignty. Nor is it necessary to discuss the other headings mentioned in section 40. What is most remarkable about that paragraph is the fact that it makes no reference at all to the essential point, viz. the legality or illegality under the local law of compliance with the demand. The failure even to mention so decisive a matter undermines the authority of the judicial decisions which have accepted the text. It is a great pity that the practice of the United States does not appear to have observed the wise words spoken in 1967 by Judge Ryan:[108]

> I cannot, of course, direct and order anybody to violate the orders of his native court, and I do not do so, and I do not intend the United States Court to be so presumptuous as to attempt to intrude upon the sovereignty of any foreign nation . . .

III. INDIRECT ENFORCEMENT JURISDICTION (ALSO HEAD OFFICE AND BRANCH)

I

The preceding chapter has established that, whatever may be said about legislative jurisdiction, enforcement jurisdiction is strictly territorial: a State having legislative jurisdiction cannot enforce rights, particularly its own prerogative rights, in the territory of another State. It can in principle enforce them in its own territory: taxes which it is lawful for it to impose, judgments which it can properly render, punishment that it may inflict can be enforced by it wherever its sovereignty exists, and international law has no complaint.

There remains, however, another question of an exceptional character: is the State free to enforce rights in its own territory exclusively or primarily for the purpose of bringing about an act or omission in foreign territory, i.e., in order indirectly to enforce its jurisdiction abroad? It must be assumed that the State in fact has legislative jurisdiction to punish or to tax or to make the demand in issue—for if this is not so any enforcement must be illegal. But on the basis of the assumption made for the purpose

[108] *Federal Maritime Commission* v. *DeSmedt*, 268 F. Supp. 972 (1967), at pp. 974, 975.

of the present discussion, can the State enforce its rights within its own territory to achieve its ends in a foreign country?

II

1. The prime example in which this question arose in recent years is the injunction restraining the defendant from doing or ordering him to do something in a foreign country. Such an injunction would be enforced (for instance by contempt of court proceedings) in the State in which it is granted, though its effect would take place abroad.

English courts have dealt with numerous cases in which *proceedings* in a foreign country have been restrained. Indirectly this involves interference with foreign courts and it has therefore been emphasized on many occasions that the jurisdiction is to be exercised with 'extreme caution'.[109] What has been less frequently stated in recent years, but is no less important is the fact that the jurisdiction should and will be exercised only if the defendant is a British subject[110] or a foreign defendant resident in England or otherwise properly before the court.[111] Even so recent decisions of the House of Lords have further restricted judicial discretion: the court to which the application for an injunction to restrain foreign proceedings is made must be the natural forum to hear the case and the injunction must not deprive the defendant of a legitimate advantage which is available to him by proceeding abroad.[112]

These are vague tests[113] which involve a weighing of circumstances and one can well understand that differences of opinion, sometimes expressed in very strong language, have arisen between American and English

[109] In this sense Sir John Donaldson M.R. delivering the judgment of the Court of Appeal in *British Airways Board* v. *Laker Airways Ltd.*, [1983] 3 W.L.R. 544, at p. 576. It is regrettable that the decision of the House of Lords in this case was not rendered by the time these lectures were given.

[110] As in *British Airways Board, ubi supra*, or in *Smith Kline & French Laboratories Ltd.* v. *Bloch*, [1983] 1 W.L.R. 730.

[111] As in *Castanho* v. *Brown & Root (U.K.) Ltd.*, [1981] A.C. 557, a case which is by no means free from doubt and the decision of Lord Denning M.R. in the Court of Appeal in the opposite sense has in the eyes of many much greater persuasive force. An interesting decision of Germany's Federal Supreme Court should be mentioned: 10 March 1978, IPRspr. 1978, No. 40. The owners of German property adjoining the Salzburg Airport claimed an injunction against the Airport authorities to protect them against the noise. Although the Austrian legislature had sanctioned any interference through noise, the German plaintiffs succeeded.

[112] See the case mentioned in the preceding note and the cases there referred to. In most of them a stay of English proceedings was an issue, but the applicable principles are the same in the case of an application to restrain foreign proceedings.

[113] The tests employed by the courts in the United States of America are no less vague: see, e.g., *Piper Aircraft* v. *Reyno*, 453 US 435 [1981].

courts.[114] Notwithstanding much criticism by judges in the United States and their sometimes immoderate language, it is submitted that English courts have not granted injunctions except in circumstances in which the institution or continuation of proceedings in the United States would have done great hardship to the defendant there and conferred an unfair advantage upon the American plaintiff. In truth English practice is in almost complete harmony with that of the United States, where the courts have frequently restrained foreign proceedings and where the power to do so is stated to exist, when they would frustrate the policy of the forum, be vexatious or oppressive, threaten the court's *in rem* jurisdiction or other equitable considerations.[115] On the other hand there is very grave doubt whether the American courts had legislative (as opposed to *in personam*) jurisdiction permitting them to restrain Belgian and Dutch defendants from applying against a British plaintiff to the British courts for injunctive relief.[115a] There is a strong argument, ignored by the American courts, for suggesting that no principle of international law permitted such interference in foreign litigation between foreigners.

It is, however, necessary to stress the implied restrictions upon the court's right to grant injunctive relief. Suppose that a French newspaper published in Paris, but distributed in France as well as in England proposes to publish a statement which involves a disclosure of confidential information entrusted by the plaintiff to the French defendant. Suppose that the disclosure and publication is unlawful in England and in France. Although the English court has curial jurisdiction because an unlawful act is about to be committed in England and although the court may well prohibit distribution in England, it ought not to prohibit publication in France, for it would be an excess of enforcement jurisdiction if the English court were to restrain a French defendant resident in France from acting in France. It is a different matter where damages are claimed: they are payable in England. An English judgment may or may not be enforceable in France—this is a matter for the French courts. The question, however, whether the French defendant should be allowed to act in France and thus to commit a tort in France is outside the scope of England's international jurisdiction.

2. Another important case of indirect enforcement relates to the *production of documents*, where either the head office (whether owned by an individual or a company) or the branch and the required documents are in a foreign country. For reasons which will become apparent it is

[114] For the American counterparts of the English cases see, e.g., *Laker Airways Ltd.* v. *Pan American World Airways.*, 731 F.2d 909 (1984).

[115] *Seattle Totems Hockey Club Inc.* v. *National Hockey League*, 652 F.2d 852 (1981), at p. 855 (Court of Appeals, 9th Cir.); *Cargill Inc.* v. *Harford Accident & Indemnity Co.*, 531 F. Supp. 710 (1982), at p. 715. See Scoles and Hay, *Conflict of Laws*, section 10.5, note 3.

[115a] See *Laker* v. *Sabena*, 731 F.2d 909 (1984).

probably necessary to distinguish between the two types of cases that may arise. It should be made very clear that neither of them relates to the production of documents between the parties to litigation in which the courts have ordered discovery; it should be obvious that if a party starts or defends proceedings in a country which has adopted the process of discovery it accepts the implications of the procedural rules of the forum and has to afford discovery in accordance with them.[116] The production of documents in issue here arises where the State, exercising its prerogative rights, makes the demand for the purpose of investigating, prosecuting or taxing the head office or the foreign branch of the individual or company within its jurisdiction and the documents are abroad.

(*a*) In principle it should be clear that the head office, in particular the company (to which, for the sake of simplicity, it is convenient to refer in future) cannot resist the demands of the State to which it belongs on the ground that the required documents are held outside the country. This is particularly so where they are in the posssession of a foreign branch, for in law the company and its branches are a single unit.[117] The location of the documents, therefore, is not a relevant element.

There are only two exceptions. The first and most important one arises where the documents relate, not to the company's own affairs, but to those of a third party. If the company's State proposes to impose a tax upon its subject and in this connection requires production of documents relating to the property, the profits or gains of the branch, production cannot be refused. If, on the other hand, the tax is to be imposed upon a

[116] It is an odd feature of American practice that in the context of the problems discussed in the text almost invariably reference is made to *Société Internationale* v. *Rogers*, 357 US 197 (1958), although the case was of an entirely different character. The plaintiff, a Swiss company, demanded delivery of the shares of General Aniline and Film Corporation, a United States company, which during the war the Custodian of Enemy Property had seized as belonging to a German national and which the plaintiff alleged were its property. Although the plaintiff had genuinely tried to obtain documents taken into the control of the Swiss authorities, it could disclose 'only' 190,000 of them. For this reason the lower courts dismissed the action. For reasons of constitutional law the Supreme Court held that the lower courts should have decided on the merits of the case and that, when weighing the evidence, they should have given to the absence of the remaining documents, the plaintiff's genuine efforts to obtain them and the alleged failure of these efforts such weight as the circumstances required. In this type of case the rule should be that a party who submits to the jurisdiction of a court is bound to obey its procedural rules. The cases discussed in the text are quite different.

[117] Lord Denning seems to doubt this. In *Power Curber* v. *Bank of Kuwait*, [1981] 3 All E.R. 607, at p. 613, he said: 'Many banks now have branches in many foreign countries. Each branch has to be licensed by the country in which it operates. Each branch is treated in that country as independent of its parent body. The branch is subject to the orders of the courts of the country in which it operates: but not to the orders of the courts where its head office is situate.' Lord Denning referred to *R.* v. *Grossman*, [1981] Crim.L.R. 396, where the Court of Appeal refused to make an order allowing the Inland Revenue to inspect books of the Isle of Man branch of Barclays Bank.

third person such as a customer of the foreign bank branch different considerations apply. Here the first question is whether the demand is made for a purpose which from the point of view of legislative jurisdiction is legitimate: is the State entitled to impose the tax to which the investigation relates? If the answer is in the affirmative, is the State entitled to enforce its legitimate demand upon the third party by measures directed in form against its national, the company, but in substance against the customer of the branch who is subject to the jurisdiction of another State? No question of international law arises between the State and its subject, the company (except in the field of human rights which are unlikely to be threatened in the present context). But if the State imposes steadily increasing fines upon its subject does it, indirectly, bring such pressure to bear upon the foreign branch's customer as to be guilty of the indirect enforcement of its rights against it? This depends on the circumstances, but may well be so and in that event would give the third party's State a just cause of complaint on the ground of misuse of rights.

The second exception occurs where the demand made upon the State's subject exposes it or its foreign branch to the risk of committing an illegality or possibly a mere breach of contract in the foreign country, for no-one can be ordered to do what in fact or in law is impossible.[118] This is the approach which in the past some American courts have adopted, though others have far too frequently found a way of disregarding the foreign law. A representative and probably leading case is *United States* v. *First National City Bank*,[119] where in the course of an investigation of a German company, C. F. Boehringer & Soehne G.m.b.H., for alleged violation of United States anti-trust legislation the Frankfurt branch of the bank was asked to produce documents relating to Boehringer's affairs. The court started from a proposition with which it is necessary fundamentally to disagree:

> It is no longer open to doubt that a federal court has the power to require the production of documents located in foreign countries if the court has *in personam* jurisdiction of the person in possession or control of the material.

Such an approach completely overlooks the fact that legislative jurisdiction is by no means identical with *in personam*, i.e., curial jurisdiction. The court then proceeds with 'a careful balancing of interests'. It admits that a risk of criminal liability or a conflict with public policy would be expressive of Germany's superior interest, but the mere risk of civil liability towards the bank's customer, not in fact asserted on the course of proceedings in Germany, is insufficient. Hence this process of 'balancing' led to a result

[118] See above, p. 31.

[119] 396 F.2d (1968). The case has frequently been followed.

favourable to the United States. It is submitted, however, that the true question is quite different. It is whether as a matter of international law the United States has the right to demand the production of documents belonging to Boehringer. The report does not disclose any facts which have a bearing upon this point. It would seem likely, however, that in most countries the customers of American bank branches can obtain an injunction against them, as Krupp did against the Deutsche Bank in the District Court of Kiel[120] and as Marc Rich AG did against the Chase Manhattan Bank's London branch,[121] and this ought to be recognized by American courts, though, as will appear, even here the result is far from certain.

It is possible, however, that a less rigid attitude will develop as a result of the most recent decision in *United States* v. *First National Bank of Chicago*.[122] In this case the Internal Revenue Service sought to obtain from the defendant's Athens branch documents relating to the alleged tax liability of two Greek residents and citizens. Since Greek law forbids under penalties of imprisonment disclosure of the information, 'a sensitive balancing of the competing interests of States' led to a dismissal of the application. It is suggested that such balancing is a wholly unnecessary detour and that even if the United States had any legislative jurisdiction the Greek law created an impossibility of enforcement.

The result would seem to be that an injunction against the branch by a local court or the risk of the branch manager's punishment by the local courts will cause American courts to refrain from exercising enforcement jurisdiction against the head office in the United States.

(*b*) The problem is even more serious and the practice of the United States deserves even stronger condemnation in the converse case: the Deutsche Bank is a German company which has a branch in New York. One of its customers in Germany is Krupp. The United States is investigating whether Krupp is guilty of activities illegal under the law of the United States. It serves a subpoena upon the bank's New York branch. Even assuming that the United States has legislative jurisdiction in respect of Krupp it should be plain that the existence of the Deutsche Bank's branch in New York, though this may permit service upon the bank, does not give the United States enforcement jurisdiction over the bank's documents situate in Germany and relating to its relations in Germany with a German national. Yet on 10 June 1982 the District Court for the Western District of Michigan ordered the bank to produce the documents,[123] and it did so in the face of an *ex parte* injunction obtained by

[120] Below notes 123, 124.

[121] The case is reported under the names of *X. A.G.* v. *A. Bank*, [1983] 2 All E.R. 465, but it is widely known that the parties' true names were those stated in the text.

[122] 699 F.2d 341 (1983).

[123] *International Legal Materials*, 1983, 742.

Krupp against the bank in Germany and affirmed after an *inter partes* hearing on 30 June 1982.[124] The injunction stated that failure to obey it exposed the bank to a fine of up to DM 500,000 and to imprisonment of up to six months and pointed out that the production of the documents would not only constitute a breach of contract, but also an infringement of constitutional guarantees, so that Germany public policy was at stake. Nor did the court consider it relevant that there existed a treaty between the United States and Germany which may have permitted the issue of letters rogatory—it was 'convinced that the United States' interest in enforcing its criminal laws outweighs any countervailing interests or hardships asserted by the bank'. It is difficult to imagine a clearer case in which American legal chauvinism has led to the disregard of elementary rules of international law. One can only hope that the Deutsche Bank appealed and that on the analogy of the decision in the case of the First National City Bank of Chicago above referred to the appeal will succeed.[124a] In the light of the decision of the 11th Circuit in *United States* v. *Bank of Nova Scotia*[125] this must, however, seem doubtful: the bank, a Canadian corporation with a branch in the United States, upon which the subpoena was served, was ordered to disclose its documents and those of its Bahamas branch relating to bank accounts of a customer, although the bank was exposed to criminal prosecution in Nassau and the court assumed 'that the bank will be subject to criminal sanction in the Bahamas'.[126] The decision, it is submitted, constitutes a clear breach of international law.

3. There is a third type of case in which the courts of the United States are liable to exceed their international jurisdiction. They think it right to make freezing orders in respect of property of foreign nationals held for them by foreign defendants who are subject to *in personam* jurisdiction in the United States. This, it is true, is probably not so in England, where an injunction blocking property outside England would not be granted and where the attachment by a Kuwaiti court of a debt due from a Kuwaiti bank would not be effective so as to preclude payment by the bank's London branch.[127] But in the United States the frightening decision of the majority of the Supreme Court in *United States* v. *First National City Bank*[128] is to the opposite effect: the Internal Revenue Service of the United States claimed to be entitled to a large sum from Omar SA, a Uruguayan company which had an account with the defendant's branch in

[124] District Court Kiel, *International Legal Materials*, 1893, 740 or (in German) *Recht der internationalen Wirtschaft* (RiW), 1983, 206.

[124a] We now know that there was no appeal, because the case was settled.

[125] 691 F.2d 1384 (1982). [126] See note 110.

[127] See the cases mentioned in note 117 and also *Intraco Ltd.* v. *Notis Shipping Corporation*, [1981] 2 Lloyd's L.R. 256.

[128] 379 US 378 (1965). The opinion of the court was delivered by Mr Justice Douglas.

Montevideo. The injunction blocking Omar SA's claims against that branch was held to be permissible, for the branch bank's affairs were

> as much within the reach of the *in personam* order entered by the District Court as are those of the home office. Once personal jurisdiction of a party is obtained the District Court has authority to order it to freeze property under its control, whether the property be within or without the United States.

It is not only the theory, but, as Mr Jutice Harlan and Mr Justice Goldberg in their dissenting judgment point out, the practical effect of this ruling that is unacceptable, for it involves the 'procedural cake-walking' of an officer appointed by the federal court being 'sent to Montevideo to make demand upon the Citibank branch in the name of the United States', and of an action being brought in New York in the (certain) event of a refusal. It is obvious that the activity of the court official in Montevideo would constitute a breach of international law and in any event the demand would be illegal and invalid under the law of Uruguay. The injunction, therefore, is *brutum fulmen* and involves a total disregard of international law. If the Internal Revenue Service cannot directly levy execution into Omar SA's Uruguayan property, it surely cannot do so indirectly by obtaining an injunction against the Montevideo bank's head office in New York. But the decision also exemplifies the dangers of banking with foreign branches of American banks.

III

The preceding observations render it appropriate to review in a few words the general problem of the relations of head office and branch for the purpose of international jurisdiction.

If one assumes the unity of the enterprise (as, in principle, one must, though bank and insurance branches may have to be treated differently), it is fairly clear that the head office is subject to the commands of its sovereign and that they may extend to foreign branches except in so far as international law renders them subject to the local sovereign—and examples of this situation have been given. But the sovereign controlling the branch does not thereby control the head office. It may be possible to bring proceedings against the head office by serving them on the branch, and this may be so not only in respect of disputes arising out of the business of the branch, but also of the head office; this in fact is so in Anglo-American countries, although under Article 5 (5) of the Brussels Convention of 1968 the jurisdiction of the courts of the branch is limited. Curial jurisdiction, however, does not have any bearing upon the question of substantive law whether or not there exists legislative jurisdiction, i.e.

whether the applicable law is intended to, and can, reach the foreign head office. It must again be emphasized that there are few statements more misleading than that frequently to be found in Anglo-American decisions, according to which proper service of a document upon a defendant necessarily makes him in all respects subject to the court's *in personam* jurisdiction.

The law thus summarized came to the forefront in a wholly extreme fashion in the case of Marc Rich SA which in 1982 and 1983 created a sensation in Switzerland and came before the courts not only of New York,[129] but also of England,[130] though in the latter country the names of the parties remained anonymous. Marc Rich SA is a Swiss company which, in the words of Leggatt J. conducts its business wholly outside the United States and has no employees, books or records there. A wholly-owned subsidiary is Marc Rich International SA, also a Swiss company which carries on business in Switzerland, but has a branch in New york. That branch was served with a subpoena in pursuance of which it produced some 75,000 documents to the Department of Justice. In 1982 a subpoena *directed to Marc Rich SA* was served upon the New York branch of the *subsidiary*. This led to many unsuccessful applications in New York, to interventions by the Swiss Government and to an injunction against the London branch of the Chase Manhattan Bank with which, curiously enough, the Swiss parent banked. In England the case was really a simple one: the bank's duty of confidentiality precluded the London branch from disclosing documents in pursuance of the subpoena served upon the New York head office. In Switzerland the case depended on an equally clear point of international jurisdiction: even if the service upon the subsidiary's New York branch was effective in relation to the Swiss head office, it cannot possibly have had any effect upon the Swiss parent. It is a matter of great regret that judiciary and executive of the United States failed to recognize the breach of international law which those authorizing and serving the subpoena committed.

IV. PARENT AND SUBSIDIARY

I

The case of Marc Rich AG mentioned at the end of the preceding chapter was unique in that, without any discussion of the problem clearly governed by Swiss law, the New York courts assumed jurisdiction over the Swiss

[129] *Marc Rich & Co. A.G.* v. *United States*, 707 F.2d 663 (1983) The decision does not make it clear that the subpoena served on the New York branch required the production of documents belonging to the Swiss head office's parent.

[130] Above note 121.

parent company on the ground that its Swiss subsidiary had a branch in New York. This extraordinary case conveniently introduces the problem of jurisdiction arising as between parent and subsidiary, to which it is now necessary to turn.

Since the International Court of Justice has extolled the separate legal existence of corporations[131] there can be no doubt about the starting point in international law:

> Separated from the company by numerous barriers the shareholder cannot be identified with it. The concept and structure of the company are founded on and determined by a firm distinction between the separate entity of the company and of the shareholder, each with a distinct set of rights,[132]

and, so one is tempted to add, of duties. A subsidiary (as Barcelona Traction, Light & Power Company Ltd was) is a separate legal entity and therefore necessarily distinct from its parent. It follows that as a matter of international law parent and subsidiary are each subject to the exclusive jurisdiction of their respective sovereigns. They cannot be identified.

Nowhere was this made clearer than in the decision of the Supreme Court of the United States in *Sumitomo Inc* v. *Avagliano*[133] in 1982. It was there held that a wholly-owned subsidiary incorporated in the United States by a Japanese parent was a United States corporation and therefore subject to the anti-discrimination provisions of the Civil Rights Act 1964 rather than Japanese law.

From these basic propositions a number of consequences follow.

II

1. The State of the parent is without jurisdiction in respect of a foreign subsidiary even if it is wholly owned. Both are distinct entities subject to distinct jurisdictions.

It is unfortunate that the United States of America has rejected this principle. Thus section 418 (2) of the Restatement of the Foreign Relations Law (revised) states in terms that as a general rule

> the United States has jurisdiction to apply its law to corporations (or similar juridical entities) organized under the laws of a foreign State that are substantially owned or controlled by nationals of the United States (including corporations organized under the laws of the Unites States).

[131] Case concerning the *Barcelona Traction, Light and Power Co., Ltd.*, *ICJ Reports*, 1970, 4.

[132] Above note 131, Paragraph 41.

[133] 457 US 176 (1982).

Or section 385 (2)*(c)* of the Export Administration Regulations applies them to 'any person subject to the jurisdiction of the United States' and defines this term as including

(i) any person, wherever located, who is a citizen or resident of the United States,
(ii) any person actually within the United States,
(iii) any corporation organized under the laws of the United States or of any State, territory or district of the United States, or
(iv) any partnership, association, corporation, or other organization, wherever oganized or doing business, that is owned or controlled by persons specified in paragraphs (i), (ii) or (iii) of this section.

Provisions of this type enable the United States to proceed direct against the foreign subsidiaries of United States corporations. This seems to have led to strong protests by other countries. A particularly telling incident occurred, when the United Kingdom took up the case of the 3M United Kingdom Ltd, which together with its parent, the 3M Company of St Paul, Minnesota, was a defendant in proceedings instituted against them by the Department of Commerce under the anti-boycott regulations of the United States. The British subsidiary, like its parent, entered into a consent decree whereby, in effect, it submitted to the American regulations. This caused the British Government on 31 March 1981 to address a Note to the United States Government[134] which, *inter alia*, demanded a release of the British company 'from the obligations purportedly imposed on it under the terms of the Consent Decree' and in the course of which it was said:

It is not acceptable to Her Majesty's Government that 3M UK, being a United Kingdom company as defined in the preceding paragraph of this Note, should be proceeded against by a United States authority for activities outside United States territory which are not illegal in the United Kingdom, nor that it should be subjected to purported requirements to report on such activities to an authority of a foreign State. Such proceedings and requirements are objectionable to Her Majesty's Government both as a matter of infringement of jurisdiction and as being likely to damage the trading interests of the United Kingdom.

The United States replied by a Note of 30 June 1981 in which it relied on the familiar argument that international trade transactions have effect in more than one State and that (apparently) each such State may 'seek to exercise its jurisdiction over such conduct'. The British point of view was further developed with considerable force in a Note of 4 September 1981.

[134] The three Notes mentioned in the text are printed in the *British Year Book of International Law*, 1982, 442–6.

The outcome of this exchange is not known. It is submitted, however, that the British position as set forth in these Notes is sound in law and is likely to be in line with the attitude of the majority of nations.

The principle that a foreign subsidiary is free from control by its parent's sovereign prevails even where under the domestic law of the parent's State a wholly-owned subsidiary is or may be treated as a mere branch of the parent. This is so in certain countries, for instance, for purposes of taxation.[135] But the international standard as expressed in a very large number of Double Taxation Conventions is different. Consequently, although the parent's sovereign cannot proceed against a foreign subsidiary for, say, the production of documents, it may be entitled to do so under its own law, on its own territory, against its own national, the parent, for as between that sovereign and the parent no question of international jurisdiction can arise. Yet even in such a situation international law may have a role to play. In the Tentative Draft No 2 of the Foreign Relations Law of the United States one can read with reference to section 418 above referred to:[136]

> under this section regulations that cannot be applied to a subsidiary directly may not be applied indirectly by mandate to the parent corporation or to its officers on the basis of their United States nationality.

This may be particularly so where such indirect application would lead to a risk of unlawful conduct in the foreign country. International law, so it may be suggested, does not allow pressure to be brought upon a domestic corporation, the parent, in order to compel a foreign corporation, the subsidiary, to act in a foreign country in a manner unlawful under its own law.

No rule of this kind was in the minds of the judges of the Ninth Circuit who decided the almost frightening case of *Vetco Inc* v. *United States*.[137] Vetco Inc was the parent of a wholly-owned Swiss subsidiary. The Internal Revenue Service of the United States required the parent to produce certain documents, not specified in the report, which belonged to and were in the possession of the Swiss subsidiary; as from March 1980 Vetco Inc as well as its co-defendants, Deloitte Haskins & Sells, the accountants, had to pay $500 per day as a penalty for what was held to be contempt of court committed by the failure to produce the documents. The defence was that under the criminal law of Switzerland it was a criminal act for the subsidiary to make business secrets available to a foreign State or its agent.[138] The court rejected the defence. It did not even mention the

[135] In substance this is the effect of section 482 of the United States Internal Revenue Code and of section 7 of the German Aussensteuergesetz.

[136] Comment *a*. [137] 644 F.2d 1324 (1981). [138] Section 273 of the Criminal Code.

separate legal personality of the Swiss subsidiary, although the United States/Swiss Double Taxation Convention expressly treats subsidiaries as independent entities. The court preferred to base its reasoning on the balancing of interests—a process which, as almost always, led to the paramountcy of the interests of the forum. Nothing whatever was said by the court about the action which the defendants were supposed lawfully to take. Should they institute proceedings against the subsidiary (which would have been bound to fail) or remove the Swiss directors and appoint American directors and what could they have lawfully done? Or should the subsidiary have been liquidated? The Court of Appeals seems to assume that the American defendants can just purloin the documents and leave it to Switzerland to try to prosecute them. If this is the law of the United States it would be propagating lawlessness.

2. The principle of the separate personality of parent and subsidiary is subject to qualification in the case in which the parent lawfully exercises its corporate rights to impose upon the subsidiary a course of action consistent with the law of the parent's and the subsidiary's sovereign.

Suppose the American parent company of 3M United Kingdom Ltd. had wished its subsidiary to act in accordance with the anti-boycott regulations of the United States. Suppose that for that purpose it had held a general meeting of the subsidiary and passed a resolution requiring it to act in the desired manner or, alternatively, removing the directors and appointing new directors who could be expected to comply. And suppose that under English company law such resolutions were valid (which in the case of the former resolution is unlikely). It is submitted that in such circumstances no rule of international law would have been infringed, and in view of the assumptions made no rule of English law would have been disregarded, the subsidiary having been wholly-owned, nor would any English legislation have been infringed. This would be so even if the parent company exercised its English corporate rights at the request of the Government of the United States. The parent would not thereby become a mere instrument used by the United States for the purpose of the extraterritorial enforcement of its prerogative rights, though this is a far from easy and wholly provisional conclusion which to some extent may depend on the precise facts.

However one may decide this particular point, it may be urged that the distinction here drawn is artificial: if a State can order its subject, the parent, to cause the foreign subsidiary to adopt a certain conduct which is lawful under the local law, why should such an order not be capable of being given directly? Why, indeed, should the parent's State not be allowed to adopt the control theory and treat the foreign subsidiary as its own national? The answer is that the control theory of nationality lacks such general recognition as to render it an internationally permissible test.[139]

The failure to distinguish between the command of the parent's sovereign and the lawful exercise of the parent's corporate control over the subsidiary explains the much-discussed *Frühauf* case decided by the Paris Court of Appeal in 1965.[140] The United States parent, the Frühauf Corporation in Detroit, held 70 per cent of the capital of the French subsidiary, Frühauf (France) SA; the remaining 30 per cent was held by French interests which also provided three directors out of eight, including the Managing Director. The French company had a contract with another French company for the supply of trucks destined for China, export to which was at the time not allowed by the United States to any person coming within the definition set forth at the beginning of the present Section II. In accordance with express instructions given to it by the United States Treasury the parent required the French subsidiary to cancel the contract. This led not only to diplomatic protests by the French Government which relied on traditional arguments of public international law, but also to an application to the French courts by the three French directors for the appointment of an administrator to carry on the business of the company until completion of the contract with Berliet. The application was granted on grounds which are derived from the elementary and generally recognized principle of company law, according to which cancellation of the contract and the resulting liability to pay heavy damages would have been oppressive to the minority: the judge 'doit s'inspirer des intérêts sociaux par préférence aux intérêts personnels de certains associés, fussent-ils majoritaires'. There is no justification for the suggestion that 'French interests were what decided the case in the French court'.[141]

The problem re-appeared 17 years later, when the United States, again relying on the same wide definition, tried to prevent European companies from exporting to the Soviet Union machinery and equipment which directly or indirectly derived from United States sources and was required in connection with building the Siberian gas pipeline. The export regulations made on 5 January and 22 June 1982 under the Export Administration Act 1979[142] were addressed not only to United States corporations,

[139] See, for instance, the Comments which accompanied the diplomatic Note sent by the Commission of the EEC to the United States on 10 August 1982, paragraph 7, and which are published in *Int.L.M.* 1982, 891, or the British Note of 4 September 1981 (above note 134 at p. 444). And see the case referred to above note 131.

[140] 22 May 1965, *Dalloz & Sirey* 1968, 147; for an English extract see *Int.L.M.* 1966, 476.

[141] In this sense, however, Professor Andreas Lowenfeld, *Rd*C 163 (1979–II), at p. 343. At the relevant time he was Deputy Legal Adviser to the Department of State and, as the preceding pages indicate, much concerned with the diplomatic side of the case which he describes in detail.

[142] These regulations, expressed in incredibly complicated terms, are published at *Int.L.M.*

but also to their foreign subsidiaries.[143] This led to diplomatic protests by many States, including Britain,[144] and also by the Commission of the European Economic Community.[145] The regulations provoked Dresser Industries Inc. and its French subsidiary, Dresser (France) SA, to apply for an injunction against the Secretary of Commerce, but they failed to obtain relief.[146] It is noteworthy that Mr Monroe Leigh, a former Legal Adviser to the Department of State, regarded it as 'apparent that neither of the traditional principles of jurisdiction—territoriality and nationality—justified the extension of United States export regulations to Dresser (France)', a French national.[147] A similar case occurred in Holland, when at the request of a French buyer the President of the District Court at The Hague ordered Sensor Nederland BV, a sub-subsidiary of Geosource Inc, a Texas corporation, to fulfil a contract for the supply of seismographic equipment destined for the Siberian pipeline; the court held the extension of the American export restrictions to the Dutch company to be contrary to public international law.[148] The incident is relevant here, because the question arises what the legal position would have been if the United States parent had by means of lawful corporate measures imposed United States policy upon the subsidiary. It is submitted that from the point of view of international law this would have been unobjectionable, though orders made in Britain under the Protection of Trading Interests Act 1980 or in France under similar French legislation[149] would have nullified any

---

1982, 864. The Export Administration Act 1979 is printed at *Int.L.M.* 1979, 1508. Orders denying export privileges are published at *Int.L.M.* 1982, 1099. The whole problem raised by these regulations on the international scene is discussed by Audit, *Rev Crit.* 1983, 401.

[143] As defined in the usual wide sense.

[144] See the diplomatic Note of 18 October 1982, *British Year Book of International Law*, 1982, 453–5.

[145] The Note of 12 August 1982 does not seem to have been published. It was accompanied by Comments on the legal position, which are referred to above note 139.

[146] 549 F.Supp. 108 (1982). From the point of view of international law the decision is without interest.

[147] *American Journal of International Law*, 1983. 627.

[148] The English text of the decision is at *Int.L.M.* 1983, 66. A German version is published in *RabelsZ*, 1983, 141, with a detailed note by Basedow who has usefully collected much relevant material. The decision finds that the contract between Sensor and the French buyer was governed by Dutch law. This alone would have justified the judgment. The discussion of public international law was unnecessary. How a Dutch contract to be performed by delivery of goods by a Dutch company to a French buyer could be affected by export regulations of the United States cannot readily be appreciated.

[149] In Britain an Order was made: see *British Year Book of International Law*, 1982, 452. On the British legislation see Lowe, *American Journal of International Law*, 1981, 257. On the French legislation which is published in *Rev. Crit.* 1980, 871 see Herzog, *American Journal of International Law*, 1981, 382; Nevot, *Rev. Crit.* 1981, 421; Cohen–Tanugi, *ibid.*, 1983, 213. See also Mann, *International and Comparative Law Quarterly*, 1982, 199. For the Dutch court any French order ought to have been irrelevant, since the contract was governed by Dutch law. See the preceding note.

such step taken by the United States parent, for the subsidiary would have had to obey the commands of its sovereign.

3. The parent can, and may be required to, impose its sovereign's commands upon its subsidiary not only by lawful corporate measures, but also by including appropriate terms in contracts, provided they do not conflict with the law of the country to which the subsidiary belongs and in which the contract is to be performed. Indeed by a contractual term requiring buyers to observe American law in general and export restrictions in particular the American supplier can bind buyers who are complete strangers. This will be obvious to any private international lawyer. There is, however, a somewhat ambiguous passage in the Note which the British Government addressed to the United States on 18 October 1982.[150] It includes the memorable phrase: 'Goods have no national identity which overrides changes of ownership of these goods.' It is there also correctly stated

> that a provision in a contract between two private parties providing that an overseas party will observe the law of the United States in regard to any re-export of items of United States origin is not capable of replacing or overruling the national law of the country concerned.

This, of course, depends on the proper law and if the proper law is that of the United States the statement is wrong, except in cases in which the buyer's sovereign makes specific provision under such legislation as the Protection of Trade Act 1980 which under the law of the United States would presumably create a case of impossibility of performance. But the British Note continues: 'Any attempt by a State to further the use of such clauses in private contracts concluded by its nationals for the purpose of extending the jurisdiction of the State would be objectionable.' The British may dislike contracts governed by the law of a state of the Union or an English contract incorporating a clause which renders American export restrictions applicable. Yet neither method is contrary to law or can properly be described as 'objectionable'. It is in law perfectly legitimate.[151]

[150] See above note 142 at p. 455.

[151] For a different, but wholly unconvincing view see the elaborate discussion by Kreuzer, in *Zum Deutschen und Internationalen Schuldrecht* (1983), 89, particularly pp. 106 sqq. He proposes to exclude legislation such as the Export Administration Act from application both in case of the law of the United States being applicable to the contract as a whole and in case of the Act and the regulations made under it being specifically referred to. Yet he would allow the incorporation of appropriate terms (p. 110), i.e. 'materiellrechtliche Verweisung' in place of reference. That in any case the *ordre public* of the forum may have something to say is obvious. Private international lawyers should beware of what many would regard as mere sophistry.

III

If one now turns to the converse case of the State of the subsidiary trying to exercise jurisdiction over the foreign parent, the legal position is simpler inasmuch as it is self-evident that the subsidiary cannot exercise control over its parent. Consequently both in law and in fact the parent cannot as a rule be subject to the jurisdiction of the subsidiary's sovereign.

Nevertheless some legal systems have discovered ways and means of obtaining jurisdiction over the foreign parent and have in fact gone very far in disregarding its separate legal status. Again it is the United States of America which, particularly in anti-trust, tax and civil jurisdiction cases, has developed very broad theories of the unity or integration of the enterprise, of acting as 'alter ego' or whatever other phrases may have been employed to establish that the foreign parent is in fact present, resident or 'found' in the United States. The number of decisions dealing with this point is vast. Almost always American courts have been able to 'find' the foreign parent in the United States. Merely by way of example three cases should be referred to. One,[152] an anti-trust case, lists nine factors each one of which is apparently sufficient to justify the court in 'finding' the parent in the United States: (1) business activities which the parent would perform if there was no subsidiary; (2) partnership in world-wide business competition; (3) the parent's capacity to influence decisions of the subsidiary; (4) the part played by the subsidiary in the over-all business of the parent; (5) the existence of an integrated sales system; (6) the status of the subsidiary as a marketing arm of the parent; (7) the subsidiary's use of a trademark owned by the parent; (8) the transfer of personnel between the two corporations; (9) the presentation of a common marketing image. In a tax case the court regarded it as decisive that the sixth of these nine factors existed: Toyota Sales USA Inc. was the 'marketing conduit' which made the 'purposeful exploitation of the forum market' possible for the Japanese parent.[153] As regards civil jurisdiction the Supreme Court of the United States has reaffirmed the standard of reasonableness and rejected the test of the foreseeability of a sale in the forum; at the same time it has conceded that if the sale in the forum 'arises from the efforts of the manufacturer or distributor to serve, directly or indirectly, the market for its products in other States, it is not unreasonable to subject it to suit in one of these States'. The exercise of jurisdiction is reasonable if the parent 'delivers its products into the stream of commerce with the expectation that they will be purchased by consumers in the

[152] *Zenith Radio Corporation* v. *Matsushita,* 402 F. Supp. 262, 327 (1975). See, generally, Atwood & Brewster, *Antitrust and American Business Abroad* (2nd edn., 1981), s. 5.10.

[153] *United States* v. *Toyota Motor Corporation,* 561 F. Supp. 354 (1983), discussed by Langbein, *RiW* 1983, 747, among others.

forum State'.[154] The fact is that, whatever verbiage may be employed, the parent will always satisfy one of these conditions and, therefore, a foreign parent will always be 'found' within the United States and thus come within the jurisdiction of the United States.

Similarly in the numerous American states which exercise civil jurisdiction over anyone 'doing business' there the parent will almost always be held to do business through a wholly-owned subsidiary, whether it is incorporated in the United States or elsewhere.[155] As a leading textbook puts it,[156] "conducting economic activities through a subsidiary has little distinction from conducting those activities through the officers and employees of the parent corporation'. Mere ownership of the shares, it is true, is insufficient to subject the foreign parent to the jurisdiction of, say, New York, but almost anything going beyond this is likely to change the result. In 1967 the New York Court of Appeals decided a case against the Royal Bank of Canada as well as the Royal Bank of Canada (France) SA.[157] The former was before the court, because it had a branch in New York and this does not give rise to comment. As to the latter a Special Referee had investigated the facts and on the basis of his findings the court reached the conclusion that the French company was 'nothing more than the name under which the defendant Royal Bank of Canada did business in France', that the French company 'is not merely a subsidiary of the Royal Bank of Canada, but is in fact, if not in name, the Royal Bank of Canada itself'. Common directorships or common design of the letter-head are circumstances which tend to establish identity. Not many years later assessment of a factual situation hardens into firm conclusion.[158] In the case of the Beatles,[159] the New York courts held that the New York subsidiary of their English company was 'the alter ego through which it acts' and that Ringo Starr was doing business in New York on account of 'composing activities which he has exploited in the United States through attorneys and accountants whom he has retained in New York on a continuing basis'.

In the United States the tendency thus displayed is likely in many respects and possibly altogether to substitute a single unit for what is in law a group of separate companies. It is difficult to reconcile this result

[154] *World-Wide Volkswagen Corporation* v. *Woodson,* 444 US 286 (1980), particularly at p. 297.

[155] The identification of a foreign parent and a foreign subsidiary is exemplified by the *Marc Rich* case referred to above, p. 40.

[156] Scoles and Hay, *Conflict of Laws*, s. 9.8.

[157] *Public Adminstration* v. *Royal Bank of Canada,* 19 NY 2d 127, 278 N.Y.S.2d 378 (1967).

[158] See, e.g., *Taca International Airlines S.A.* v. *Rolls Royce*, 15 NY 2d 97, 256 N.Y.S.2d 129 (1965), or *Boryk* v. *de Havilland Aircraft Co.*, 341 F.2d 666 (1965).

[159] *ABKCO Industries Inc.* v. *Lennon,* 384 N.Y.S. 2d 781 (1976).

with customary international law or the conventional international law expressed by the 21 Friendship Navigation and Commerce Treaties concluded by the United States.

It is a matter of some surprise, however, that the European Court of Justice in Luxembourg is taking the same line. In *Imperial Chemical Industries Ltd.* v. *Commission of the EEC*,[160] one of the so-called dyestuffs cases decided in 1972 before Britain joined the Community, the court held that the British parent, like the Swiss parent, of the subsidiary companies in the Common Market countries, was subject to the Community's jurisdiction and could be fined. There existed, so it was held, a 'unity of the group', so that 'the activities of the subsidiaries may, in certain circumstances, be imputed to the parent company'. What are these circumstances? Firstly, ownership of 'the whole or at any rate the majority, of the capital of these subsidiaries', secondly the ability 'to influence in a decisive manner the sale price policy' of the subsidiaries and thirdly the fact that on one occasion[161] the parent 'made use of this power'.[162]

The jurisdiction of the subsidiary's State over the parent is, of course, only an aspect of the very much wider problem of the 'piercing of the corporate veil'.[163] This arises everywhere and in numerous different connections. It cannot be discussed here. But it can be suggested with some confidence that outside the United States and the European Economic Community it will be difficult to find support for piercing the veil where there is no misuse of the corporate structure and where the subsidiary does not act in accordance with directives given by the parent so as to become the latter's mere *negotiorum gestor*.[164]

[160] *Common Market L.R.* 1972, 557, at p. 629, or *European Court Reports*, 1972, 619, at p. 662 discussed by Goldman, *Clunet* 1973, 925 and by Mann, *I.C.L.Q.* 1973, 35. Later cases are to the same effect. See, in particular, *Continental Cann, European Court Reports*, 1973, 215.

[161] This is the most deplorable passage in a wholly unsatisfactory judgment. The court was referring to a telex message of 1964 the text of which is not reproduced, so that it is unknown how the parent decided the subsidiary's sales policy. Moreover the court thought it right to continue that 'in the absence of contrary indications it must be assumed' that in 1965 and 1967 the parent acted in the same way to decide the sales policy of the subsidiaries. In a matter of a criminal character which led to heavy fines this is a most objectionable conclusion. The corresponding German decision of the Federal Supreme Court relates to a slightly different point, but is reasoned in a wholly exemplary fashion: *NJW* 1971, 521.

[162] See also the remarks above, p. 40, about the case of *Marc Rich SA* which is most remarkable, because there the United States exercised jurisdiction over the Swiss head office of the New York branch *and* over the Swiss parent of the Swiss subsidiary (head office). The decision of the Court of Appeals above referred to does not even mention the existence of the Swiss subsidiary which had the New York branch.

[163] The literature is immense and is referred to in the usual textbooks. A good survey of American practice is given by Weltins, *RiW*, 1983, 713. An impressive German study was recently published by Wilhelm, *Rechtsform und Haftung bei der Juristischen Person* (1981).

[164] This very helpful suggestion was recently made by Flume, *Die Juristische Person* (1983), 88 sqq.

IV

At this point many lawyers would probably find it necessary to embark upon a discussion of what has come to be called a multinational company. The subject has produced a considerable literature[165] and no doubt some of it has a bearing upon the problem of international jurisdiction. Yet it is suggested that the so-called multinational company is not a legal conception or at any rate that there are no legal problems peculiar to a company that deserves the name multinational. IBM undoubtedly has numerous shareholders and numerous subsidiaries and sub-subsidiaries in numerous countries. Yet the legal problems would not in any way be different if it had a single shareholder, an individual, and a single subsidiary in a single foreign country. From a legal point of view nothing is gained by characterizing a company as multinational. It is always the problem of parent and foreign subsidiary that requires solution. The problem of the multinational company is one of degree rather than legal nature.

Nor is there anything to be gained from a consideration of the draft guidelines on transnational corporations prepared by the United Nations.[166] It is not surprising to gather from paragraph 50 that there is wide disagreement on the question of jurisdiction.

V. CIVIL JURISDICTION

I

The international jurisdiction to adjudicate is, as has been pointed out,[167] not a separate type of jurisdiction, but merely an emanation of the international jurisdiction to legislate: a State's right of regulation is exercised by legislative jurisdiction which includes adjudication. It follows that both aspects of jurisdiction are co-extensive. Yet the public international law governing civil jurisdiction has remained more firmly rooted in territoriality than most other branches of the law. When in 1977 Lord Diplock referred to 'the general rule that the jurisdiction of the English court over persons is territorial',[168] he stated an undeniable truth about which one cannot be surprised, because it supplies a firm basis in a branch

[165] For a recent discussion of International Law Problems of Multinational Corporations see *Berichte der Deutschen Gesellschaft für Völkerrecht*, Volume 18 (1978), with contributions by Wildhaber, Grossfeld, Sandrock and Birk on public international, tax, civil and labour law respectively. Detailed references to literature on pp. 8 and 9. See also, for instance, C. D. Wallace, *Legal Control of the Multinational Enterprise* (1982).

[166] See the Report by the United Nations Commission on Transnational Corporations, *Int.L.M.* 1983, 177, with draft guidelines on p. 192.

[167] Above, note 47. [168] *The Siskina*, [1979] A.C. 210, at p. 254.

of the law where certainty and foreseeability is perhaps more necessary than in most others. Yet the prevailing firm adherence to territorial sovereignty is surprising or at least interesting, for a tendency towards flexibility could have been caused by two developments of potentially great influence.

In the first place it has been shown that the strictly territorial charcter of the doctrine of international jurisdiction has been much relaxed by the need to treat reasonable closeness of contact as a substitution for or, to put it at its lowest, a supplementary element in, the commanding position of territorial sovereignty. Comparative surveys of civil jurisdiction do not, however, seem to provide any evidence of the flexibility which such an approach would imply. In particular there is no indication anywhere that in the international field the requirements of the plaintiff which occasionally indicate a very intimate connection with the forum have succeeded in superseding the rule which almost 2,000 years ago was expressed by the maxim *actor sequitur forum rei*, the plaintiff has to submit to the defendant's court.[169]

Nor has the international scene so far to any extent been restructured by the almost sensational changes which, relying on the Due Process clause of the Constitution, the Supreme Court of the United States of America achieved in the field of civil jurisdiction since 1945. In that year the strict territoriality of jurisdiction which had prevailed since 1877,[170] or in the words of Professor Arthur von Mehren the power theory of jurisdiction was replaced by what the same learned author calls the fairness theory,[171] for in 1945 Mr. Chief Justice Stone declared on behalf of the court[172] that 'de facto power over the defendant's person' was no longer the test, that

> due process required only that in order to subject a defendant to a judgment *in personam*, if he be not present within the territory of the forum, he have certain minimum contact with it such that the maintenance of the suit does not offend traditional notions of fair play and substantial justice.

Later he added that[173]

[169] On this see, e.g., Jochen Schröder, *Internationale Zuständigkeit* (1971), at p. 239. This is a most learned and valuable book the practical value of which is unfortunately diminished by the fact that it is difficult to find the passages one is looking for. He does not, however, accept that in the field of civil jurisdiction public international law has any substantial contribution to make. See p. 367 about the exclusive jurisdiction where the title to immovables is in issue, and p. 766 sqq. about the so-called exorbitant jurisdictions. The effect of the Convention of 1968 is hardly taken into account.

[170] *Pennoyer* v. *Neff*, 95 US 714 (1877).

[171] See, in particular, *Boston University L.R.* 63 (1983), 279; see already von Mehren & Trautman, *Harv. L.R.* 70 (1966), 1121.

[172] *International Shoe Co.* v. *Washington*, 326 US 310 (1945).

[173] P. 317.

> those demands may be met by such contacts of the corporation with the state of the forum as make it reasonable . . . to require the corporation to defend the particular suit which is brought there. An estimate of the inconvenience which would result to the corporation from a trial away from its home or principal place of business is relevant in this connection.

Reasonableness, fairness, convenience have, therefore, become the catch-words. The tests were developed in a number of later cases of great interest to the constitutional lawyer,[174] but if such tests have been applied in wholly international contexts (which is not entirely certain) they have led the lower courts to results which in many cases are unattractive and, as a matter of international law, unsatisfactory. It is true that these cases, to some of which attention will have to be drawn, have not provoked any diplomatic protests or other action on an international level. But this does not preclude academic lawyers from suggesting how those cases should be evaluated in terms of international law. The general impression which they create in the international lawyer's mind is that due process as understood in modern American law cannot provide firm guidance to the doctrine of international civil jurisdiction. It must be admitted, however, that none of the critical cases has yet come before the Supreme Court.

From the point of view of public international law the outstanding event during the last 20 years has been the conclusion of the Convention on Jurisdiction and the Enforcement of Judgments in Civil and Commercial Matters which the six original member States of the European Economic Community signed in Brussels in 1968 and which will soon be in force in the four new member States. This convention, it is true, has created a dual régime in that it applies as between the member States, but in regard to non-members a different law applies or may apply. Yet, unwelcome though it is in very many respects, the convention has to be recognized as an important step in the evolution of an international law of civil jurisdiction. However sceptical and even hostile one may be to many of the provisions of the convention, its pervading influence must be acknowledged. In other words the international lawyer has to recognize that what the convention accepts is likely to be consistent with the demands of international law and that what it leaves to the individual States for application in their relations with third parties may not necessarily be inconsistent with international law, though rejection by the Ten may be a blemish, an argument for criticism and the starting point for a progressive development of international law.

[174] See, in particular, *McGee* v. *International Life Insurance Co.*, 355 US 220 (1957); *Hanson* v. *Denckla*, 357 US 235 (1958); *Shaffer* v. *Heitner*, 433 US 186 (1977); *World-Wide Volkswagen Corporation* v. *Woodson*, 444 US 286 (1980); *Allstate Insurance Co.* v. *Hague*, 444 US 320 (1980), and many other cases.

II

The basic principle adopted by the convention is that jurisdiction to adjudicate depends on the defendant being ordinarily resident[175] or, if a corporation, having its seat, i.e., being incorporated within the jurisdiction of the court. This is, of course, fully in harmony with the classical rule and the demands of territorial sovereignty. But by proclaiming this principle the convention, either expressly or impliedly, condemns some other bases of jurisdiction, in so far as persons ordinarily resident in a Contracting State are concerned, whatever their nationality.

1. Jurisdiction can no longer be founded upon the title to property within the country. This applies, in particular, to Germany, where the general law, applicable outside the province of the convention, remains to the effect that if I have property, however small, in Germany I can be sued there for unlimited sums. This surely is an exorbitant jurisdiction in the most literal sense of the term and one would hope that if tested international law would disapprove it.

2. The famous Articles 14 and 15 of the French Civil Code do not apply. This means, in particular, that the French nationality of a defendant resident in a convention country does not render him subject to the jurisdiction of French courts. In other words nationality as a point of contact for purposes of jurisdiction has been rejected. International law does not require this, but the provision was unique to France and the countries influenced by French law and its limitation should be welcomed.

3. Mere presence in a country does not render a person subject to its courts. This is directed against Britain where, as in the whole of the common law world, even a person changing planes at London Airport could be served with a writ and thus be brought before an English court in a matter which had no connection of any kind with Britain. Only a few years ago the Maharanee of Baroda served Mr Wildenstein, the well-known art dealer, with a writ, while he was on a visit from Paris to attend the Ascot horse races, and the Court of Appeal refused to set aside the writ, since it regarded the English court as a *forum conveniens*.[176] The law is the same in the United States. There does not seem to be a case which held that jurisdiction over a foreigner obtained in such circumstances was unreasonable, unfair or inconvenient.

4. The fact that a contract is made in the country of the forum does not

[175] The convention uses the term 'domicile'. This is specifically defined by sections 41 sqq. of the Civil Jurisdiction and Judgments Act 1982. The text uses a shorthand term which may be adequate, though not entirely accurate. On the definition see L. Collins, *The Civil Jurisdiction and Judgments Act, 1982* (1983), 37 sqq.

[176] [1972] 2 Q.B. 283.

confer jurisdiction upon its courts. Such a head of jurisdiction exists in England, but is surely exorbitant[177] and, perhaps, contrary to international standards.

5. Another head of jurisdiction rejected by the convention is the purely English practice according to which an English court may assume jurisdiction in respect of a contract which is governed by English law.[178] This results from what undoubtedly are reasons of convenience, but must be admitted to be exorbitant,[179] as is supported (though not conclusively proved) by the fact that an English court would not recognize a foreign judgment which, in the absence of submission by the defendant, is based on a similar ground. Altogether it may be suggested that if one desires to test the international validity of a head of jurisdiction it is helpful to ask whether the court would give effect to a foreign judgment based on a corresponding type of jurisdiction. The legal ideal and, perhaps, the legal rule should be complete congruity between the two problems.

6. The test of doing business, adopted by numerous American states, is not accepted either by the convention or, indeed, by any European country. It is true that a resident of a member State may be sued as regards a dispute arising out of the operations of a branch, agency or other establishment in the courts of the place in which such branch, agency or establishment is situated.[180] But this is a test which in a wholly traditional manner confers jurisdiction on the local court. What the convention rejects is the American conception of doing business (in the absence of an establishment), which has led to results that European observers regard as unacceptable and international lawyers are likely to describe as extravagant and, probably, contrary to every principle of international law, whether it be territorial sovereignty or reasonably close linkage. The material illustrating this most serious practical problem is enormous.[181] It is frequently being discussed in connection with products liability where its unusual character is less evident, for introducing goods into the mainstream of commerce in circumstances in which the planned or foreseeable economic conduct results in foreseeable events in the United States,[182] may well be the foundation of civil jurisdiction in respect of tortious liability. Some may think that this goes very far, but it is not unacceptable, for the traditional search for the *locus delicti* could well lead to the same result. The wholly extreme character of the

[177] O. 11, r. 1, paragraph 1 *(d)* (i). [178] Ibid., paragraph 1 *(d)* (iii).

[179] Lord Diplock in *Amin Rasheed Shipping Corporation* v. *Kuwait Insurance Co.*, [1984] A.C. 50, at p. 65. [180] Article 5 (5).

[181] See, in general, Scoles and Hay, *Conflict of Laws* (1982), s. 8.25 and s. 9.3.

[182] See the *World-Wide Volkswagen* case, above note 174.

interpretation given to 'doing business' is more vividly exposed by a different type of case.

The problem of international law that arises may be made clearer by referring shortly to three recent cases.[183] In one of them the defendant, a Zurich businessman who held an American patent, wrote a letter from Zurich, in which he complained of patent infringement and threatened proceedings. This was held to be doing business in Massachusetts. Although the court added qualifying words to the effect that the defendant also conducted or planned some patent-related business and the plaintiff corporation was pursuing a competing business, the indication is that the letter would have been sufficient on the analogy of a single visit made for the purpose of signing a contract constituting the transaction of business for the purpose of jurisdiction.[184] In a third case it was held that if the representative of an English company has a single luncheon meeting in Chicago, from which eventually business results, this means that the English company is doing business in Illinois: 'A defendant's participation in the state in substantial preliminary negotiations leading to the contract in issue' is a sufficient basis for jurisdiction.[185]

Many similar examples could be given. It is submitted that their legal basis is unacceptable. The root trouble is that American courts and lawyers think in terms of constitutional requirements. The decisions which have been mentioned may be in conformity with the Constitution, because they satisfy the minimal requirements of justice and fairness which prevail since 1945. But whether they come up to the level which international law demands is an entirely different matter never even alluded to by the courts of the United States. There is much to be said for giving a negative answer.

If anyone asks for practical advice in the situation that has been described one can only say this: never hold any discussions or negotiations in the United States and if a contract is concluded sign it outside the United States and provide for the exclusive jurisdiction of a non-American court or include a well-drafted and carefully considered arbitration clause. And if you are a lawyer or accountant or banker keep out of the United States, for you may only too readily be made a party to proceedings against your client.[186]

[183] See also *ABKCO Industries Inc.* v. *Lennon*, 384 N.Y.S. 2d 781 (1976), referred to above note 159.

[184] *Nova Biomedical Corporation* v. *Moller*, 629 F.2d 190 (1980), citing *Carlson Corporation* v. *University of Vermont*, 402 N.E. 2d 483, at p. 485 (1980).

[185] *Neimann* v. *Rudolf Wolff & Co. Ltd.*, 619 F.2d 1189 (1980).

[186] See, e.g., *Leasco Data Processing Equipment Corporation* v. *Maxwell*, 468 F.2d 1320 (1972), where apart from Mr Robert Maxwell the defendants were Robert Fleming & Co. Ltd., and two of its directors, Chalmers Impey & Co., Chartered Accountants in London who were dismissed from the suit, and Mr. Isidore Kerman, a London solicitor.

III

Under the Brussels Convention of 1968 provisional or protective measures such as, in particular, a *saisie d'arrêt*, Arrest, Mareva injunction, sequestration or attachment may be ordered either by the court having jurisdiction in respect of the substantive case or by the court in the country in which the property is situate.[187] This is so notwithstanding the fact that the convention does not permit the exercise of civil jurisdiction based on the ownership of local property such as is known to German law.[188] Nor does the convention require such minimum contact of the defendant with the forum as the Constitution of the United States apparently requires for the attachment or sequestration of property or at any rate a civil suit brought to uphold it.[189]

It is, therefore, safe to suggest that at any rate for the purpose of protective measures international law does not reject the locality of property belonging to the debtor as a permissible head of civil jurisdiction. This is particularly so in light of the fact that in respect of cases falling within the scope of the 1968 Convention England has expressly assumed the power to grant protective measures[190] based on the location of property and in respect of other cases England may act similarly, but has for the time being upheld the rule laid down by the House of Lords in 1979 that an English court can grant interim relief only in cases in which it has jurisdiction in respect of the principal action.[191] This is a most unfortunate situation which, let it be emphasized, is not required by international law. In part Lord Diplock's reasoning was founded on the abolition of the German rule according to which the existence of assets belonging to the defendant within the territorial jurisdiction of the German court justifies it in assuming jurisdiction. From this Lord Diplock drew the conclusion that

> comity [he probably meant and certainly should have said: international law] . . . would seem to be against a Mareva injunction as a procedural device to found jurisdiction in the English courts to adjudicate on the merits of actions against foreign defendants.[192]

But this is an unconvincing point, since the issue related to protective measures (which the convention does not touch) rather than to the main

[187] Article 24. See Collins, loc. cit. p. 98.

[188] Section 23 of the Code of Civil Procedure.

[189] See the difficult case of *Shaffer* v. *Heitner*, 433 US 186 (1977). It would seem that the case relates to jurisdiction in respect of the main action, but does not deal with jurisdiction to attach property only. But this may be a wrong interpretation.

[190] Section 25 of the Civil Jurisdiction and Judgments Act 1982.

[191] *The Siskina*, [1979] A.C. 210. [192] P. 259.

action. 'Comity', therefore, was not opposed to an attachment in the case before the House of Lords. Nor has international law ever any objection against protective measures in the country in which the debtor's property is located, even if neither party has any other connection with it.

IV

When one comes to bankruptcy jurisdiction, it is necessary to begin by eliminating two sources of confusion. In the first place in the common law countries corporations are not made bankrupt, but are wound up. There exist usually procedural differences, though bankruptcy rules may be applicable to winding up. But in most respects relevant for present purposes both the prerequisites and the effects of bankruptcy and winding up are in broad terms similar. Secondly there are numerous countries in which the bankruptcy or winding up procedure is used, not to administer the estate of the foreign individual as a whole or to wind up the foreign corporation as such, but merely as a means of execution in respect of local assets. The same terms, the same legal provisions and the same techniques are used as in the case of the bankruptcy of an individual or the winding up of a domestic corporation. Yet the distinction is striking: the winding up or the bankruptcy order in respect of local property leaves the status of the debtor abroad completely intact. Thus in England the local property of a foreign corporation may be 'wound up' or, perhaps one should say, may be made available for creditors by way of winding up procedure, although in its home country the corporation is flourishing or, alternatively, is dissolved.[193] For the purposes of the Bankruptcy Reform Act 1978 of the United States of America the definition of 'debtor' includes a person 'that . . . has . . . property in the United States'. Such procedures have only local effect.[194] They should be distinguished from the true bankruptcy or winding up with which the following observations are concerned.

Bankruptcy in the true sense of the term and also winding up (which henceforth will not be separately dealt with) occurs exclusively in the country to which the debtor is subject in the territorial sense, because he is domiciled or resident, carries on business or has an establishment,

[193] *Russian and English Bank* v. *Baring Brothers & Co.* (1936) A.C. 405. The odd logical difficulties which so many judges felt in that case would not have arisen if they had realized that the issue related to the winding up of assets. That the existence of an asset is sufficient for purposes of a winding up in the sense explained in the text has been firmly established law in England for many years. For the latest decision the point in depth see *Re Compania Merabello*, [1973] Ch. 75.

[194] The decision to the opposite effect by the German Supreme Court, 11 July 1934, IPRspr. 1934, No. 12, is therefore likely to be wrong.

whether principal or secondary[195] or is similarly connected. It is believed that a comparative survey would bear out this statement, though the formulations differ considerably. There is no treaty or draft treaty which is inconsistent with them;[196] thus the proposed Bankruptcy Convention of the European Economic Community would confer jurisdiction on the country of the debtor's centre of administration or if this is outside the Common Market, on the State of the EEC where the debtor has an establishment.[197] All conventions relating to civil jurisdiction and the recognition of foreign judgments exclude bankruptcy from their ambit[198] and thus make it clear that other bases of jurisdiction than territorial connection do not apply to bankruptcy.

The most important case relating to international bankruptcy jurisdiction is the decision of the International Court of Justice in the case of *Barcelona Traction, Light and Power Company, Ltd.*[199] In a decision of almost incredible narrowness the Court, it is true, discussed only the right of affording diplomatic protection to shareholders of a practically defunct company and thus avoided all problems of substance. But the documents which unfortunately have never been printed, but are available in some of the principal law libraries, as well as the pleadings and oral arguments which are printed contain a vast amount of interesting comparative material. Moreover, as we shall see, one of the judges whose learning and wisdom was such as to entitle him to special respect and authority made some pronouncements on questions of substance, which deserve the attention of scholars.

Barcelona Traction was a holding company incorporated, resident and operating in Canada to such an extent that according to the Court only the Canadian Government was or would have been entitled to afford it diplomatic protection and the application made by Belgium had to be dismissed. The company had no branch, no business, no assets in Spain. Its only assets were the bearer shares in another Canadian company, Ebro, which were held by a Canadian trustee as security for sterling bonds issued by Barcelona Traction on the London market. Ebro had

[195] In France, in particular, 'un établissement secondaire' is sufficient: Batiffol–Lagarde (7th ed., 1983), No. 674, note 8.

[196] Nadelman, N., *University of Pennsylvania L.R.* 93 (1944), 58, reprinted in *Conflict of Laws: International and Inter-state* (1972), 299.

[197] *Bulletin of the European Communities*, Supplement 2/82. The report states on p. 57: 'An examination of the existing laws and conventions on this matter reveals that, in the case of natural persons, jurisdiction is generally exercised by the court of their domicile, i.e. in the case of traders, by the court of their principal commercial establishment; with regard to companies, it is in principle the court of the place where the company's head office is situated which must declare the company bankrupt'.

[198] In particular Article 1 of the Brussels Convention of 1968.

[199] *ICJ Reports* (1970) 4. On this case see also above pp. 10, 41. Contrary to many erroneous statements, the case had nothing whatever to do with expropriation.

not only a branch in Spain, but also owned the shares of a number of Spanish subsidiary companies which had built virtually the whole of the electricity system in Catalonia. Since Franco Spain did not allow Ebro to remit money to Canada, Ebro could not declare dividends, Barcelona Traction was without cash resources and the interest on the sterling bonds was not paid. In this situation a protégé of Franco, one Juan March, caused a few bonds to be bought. Disregarding the terms of the bonds which included a no-action clause vesting the sole right of action in a trustee, the purchasers obtained from a judge at Reus a bankruptcy order, not against Ebro (which had an establishment in Spain, but was not the debtor), but against Barcelona Traction which was the debtor, but had no legally relevant connection with Spain. Belgium attacked Spain, *inter alia*, on the ground that it had no international jurisdiction to make any bankruptcy order against Barcelona Traction. Although Judge Sir Gerald Fitzmaurice agreed with the Court on the question of Belgium's *jus standi*, he gave some attention to the problem of jurisdiction and arrived at the conclusion[200] that if it were necessary to form a view

> it could in my view be only in the sense that the whole bankruptcy proceedings were, for excess of jurisdiction, null and void *ab initio*, and without effect on the international plane.

Barcelona Traction's lack of territorial connection with Spain was not the ground of decision, but this pronouncement constitutes an important contribution to the doctrine of international jurisdiction in bankruptcy. The Court's failure to afford relief against a unique act of piracy and the failure of democratic Spain to undo an injustice of a kind typical of a totalitarian régime will for ever strike international lawyers as a painful experience.

It is, however, impossible to put the *Barcelona Traction* case aside without mentioning one of the defences put up by Spain, which is not reflected at all in the opinions, but must be treated as rejected. This was the theory of the so-called unity of enterprise, *unité de l'entreprise*. The theory apparently was that the whole complex of Barcelona Traction and its subsidiary and sub-subsidiaries represented a single unit which was carrying on business in Spain and was, therefore, subject to Spanish jurisdiction. In law no such conception exists, just as in law the conception of a multinational corporation does not exist.[201] Of course all countries know the group of companies, the *Konzern*. But all countries treat the constituent elements as separate bodies, unless there are special

[200] P. 106. [201] Above p. 51.

circumstances which permit or compel a different conclusion. The point was recently put by a unanimous House of Lords[202] in words of Lord Diplock's which may claim general applicability. In rejecting the argument that, if A Ltd. and B Ltd. belong to the same shareholder they can be identified the learned law lord said:

> The reason why English statutory law, and that of all other trading countries, has long permitted the creation of corporations as artificial persons distinct from their individual shareholders and from that of any other corporation even though the shareholders of both corporations are identical is to enable business to be undertaken with limited financial liability in the event of the business proving to be a failure. The 'corporate veil' in the case of companies incorporated under the Companies Act is drawn by statute and it can be pierced by some other statute if such other statute so provides; but in view of its raison d'être and its consistent recognition by the courts . . . one would expect that any parliamentary intention to pierce the corporate veil would be expressed in unequivocal language.

There is every reason to believe that the International Court of Justice took a similar view and rejected the theory of the unity of the enterprise. If it had been accepted the Belgian majority shareholders of Barcelona Traction would have formed part of that enterprise and Belgium's diplomatic protection would have been effective. Moreover, the Court said very much the same thing as the House of Lords:[203] 'Separated from the company by numerous barriers, the shareholder cannot be identified with it.' And later[204] it continued:

> The law has recognized that the independent existence of the legal entity cannot be treated as an absolute. It is in this context that the process of 'lifting the corporate veil' or 'disregarding the legal entity' has been found justified and equitable in certain circumstances and for certain purposes.

For purposes of bankruptcy *jurisdiction* the doctrine of piercing the corporate veil can hardly ever be invoked as a basis. It is an entirely different matter that once a bankruptcy has properly been pronounced circumstances may permit that doctrine to be invoked for the purpose of *collecting the bankrupt's assets*. In the present context we must adhere to what that great expert, the late Professor Nadelmann, said exactly 40 years ago when discussing bankruptcy treaties:[205]

[202] *Dimbleby & Sons Ltd.* v. *National Union of Journalists,* [1984] 1 W.L.R. 427, at p. 435.

[203] P. 34.

[204] P. 39. The very important statement on page 51 (paragraph 102) is also relevant.

[205] Above note 196, at p. 314 of the reprint.

With almost no exception the court of the domicile of the debtor is the court which is given exclusive bankruptcy jurisdiction or . . . jurisdiction with extraterritorial effect.

VI. THE REGULATION OF TRADE

I

In the course of the preceding chapters numerous references have already been made to attempts by States to regulate business outside their frontiers. In particular it has been shown that export restrictions, trade embargoes, anti-boycott regulations or licensing requirements which States purport to impose on the foreign purchaser of goods, in the absence of contractually imposed terms, plainly constitute an excesss of international jurisidiction.[206] The same applies to attempts to impose such restrictions on foreign subsidiaries otherwise than by lawfully enforced corporate policies. And in the case of foreign branches the local manager's submission to policies adopted by the head office in accordance with the law of its sovereign cannot be complained of, unless they are in conflict with contractual obligations or with the law of the territorial sovereign of the branch. In short no State can directly exercise jurisdiction in foreign countries, but there is no legal rule which precludes it from doing so indirectly by giving directions to its own subjects in their own territory, provided they can be implemented without violation of the corporate or other law of the foreign sovereign or of contractual obligations and provided that no undue pressure is brought upon foreigners to enforce compliance with legal rules to which they are not subject. It follows, for instance, that prima facie the American attempt during the Iranian crisis to block Iranian assets held by subsidiaries or branches of American banks in foreign countries was not supported by principles of international jurisdiction. In particular dollar balances like goods have no nationality and it could not be argued that, since the United States has control over the dollar as a currency, it also had control over all contracts denominated in dollars, wherever they may have been made, wherever they may have to be performed and by whatever law they may be governed.[207]

[206] See above p. 32 and passim. Some of the Export Control Regulations of the United States are published in *Int.L.M.* 1982, 853 sqq.

[207] It does not follow that Iranian actions for payment or delivery up had to succeed. If the contract was governed by the law of a member state of the Union (which in most cases seemed unlikely) the actions would succeed, for the law of the United States could not be rejected by reason of the excess of international jurisdiction or of *ordre public*, since it was enacted as a sanction against a grave violation of international law as established by the International Court of Justice. Indeed, even where the contract was subject to the local law (as it probably was in the majority of cases), the international wrong was of such gravity as

There remain, however, numerous other aspects of the regulation of trade, which are independent of the relationship between parent and subsidiary or head office and branch, which involve less exceptional circumstances and which have caused great difficulties. To them it is now necessary to turn.

II

Corporate rights and duties. A lawyer outside the United States of America who is concerned with a problem involving the relationship between corporation and shareholder or between shareholders as such would turn to the conflict of laws to find a solution and thus avoid all problems of international jurisdiction. In all probability he would apply the *lex societatis*, the law governing the corporation's status, whether this is the law of its incorporation or domicile or the law of its 'seat' or its residence.[208] Thus, to take a few examples, if the allegation is that the corporation has wrongfully repaid capital to shareholders their liability depends on the *lex societatis*. Or if according to the corporation's law membership depends on the proof of certain conditions such as nationality, registration, residence and so forth, the absence of such evidence precludes the creation or the continuation of membership, for, in the words of the French Cour de Cassation, no other law can decide upon 'les conditions dans lesquelles s'acquiert, se conserve et se perd la qualité d'actionnaire'.[209] Similarly the corporation's ability to purchase its own shares is determined by the *lex societatis* and so is the question whether shareholders are liable for the debts of the corporation or, in other words, whether the corporation's veil may be pierced; in the last resort this concerns the status or, more particularly, the existence *pro tanto* of the corporation (its *Rechtsfähigkeit*), and its law must therefore govern, as Austrian, British and German courts have in fact decided.[210] Nor is the applicable law altered by the fact that the corporation's shares are quoted in more than one country: the Deutsche Bank, it is submitted, has not become subject to the corporate

---

to permit the wholly exceptional argument that the American regulations should be given effect by way of *ordre public* in its positive form. In the case of Euro-dollars there existed probably a special argument based on illegality of performance: see Mann, *The Legal Aspect of Money* (4th edn., 1982), 193, 194. Article VIII (2) *(b)* of the IMF Agreement had nothing to do with the problem: Mann, loc. cit. p. 393, note 90.

[208] See, generally, Mann, 'Bemerkungen zum Intenationalen Privatrecht der Aktiengesellschaft und des Konzerns', *Festschrift für Carl Heinz Barz* (1974), or in *Beiträge zum Internationalen Privatrecht* (1976), 70.

[209] *Rev. Crit.* 1973, 520 (Royal Dutch). In the same sense the Swiss Federal Tribunal, 2 February 1954, BGE 80 II 53 (Royal Dutch).

[210] Supreme Court, 17 June 1981. *Juristische Blätter*, 1982, 257; *Bateman* v. *Service*, 6 App. Cas. 386 (1881), at p. 389; BGHZ 76, 316, 334.

law of England and New York (and many other countries) by reason of the fact that its shares are listed not only in Germany, but also in London, New York and elsewhere.

In many contexts the approach by the courts of the United States does not seem to be fundamentally different, especially where the solution is to be found in the common law.[211] A prominent and impressive example is a decision of the Court of Appeals, Second Circuit.[212] The plaintiffs were minority shareholders of a Venezuelan company which had sold American properties to an American corporation. The claim was a derivative one, made in the name of the Venezuelan company against the purchaser with a view to nullifying the transfer of title to him. At the same time a claim for damages against the directors was made. The defence was that the plaintiffs' right to sue in opposition to the directors and the majority shareholders depended on the law of Venezuela which denied it, although the procedural law of New York affirmed it. The primary question therefore was whether the minority's right was governed by the *lex societatis* or the *lex fori*. The court decided in the former sense, for the claim

> concerns the very nature and quality of their substantive rights, powers and privileges as stockholders of a Venezuelan corporation. The Venezuelan law . . . reflects a deliberate policy that such actions ought to be brought not only when the claims may have merit, but when the stockholders as a body are of the opinion that the corporate welfare is best promoted by suing upon them. The issue is not just 'who' may maintain an action or 'how' it will be brought, but 'if' it will be brought.

Yet the remarkable fact is that when the action is brought on the basis of a statute the atmosphere changes, the guidance given by the conflict of laws is abandoned and the court purports to give effect to the statute with the result that very frequently the limits of international jurisdiction are exceeded. No case has illustrated the contrast more clearly than that of the Court of Appeals, Second Circuit, in *Schoenbaum* v. *Firstbrook*.[213] The plaintiff was an American shareholder of a Canadian corporation, Banff Oil Ltd. He brought a derivative action based on the Securities Exchange Act 1934[214] against the company's directors as well as two corporations which were the majority shareholders and to which Banff Oil had sold treasury shares[215] at an alleged undervalue. The shares of Banff

[211] See, generally, Scoles and Hay, *Conflict of Laws*, Ch. 23.

[212] *Hausmann* v. *Buckley,* 299 F.2d 696 (1962).

[213] *Schoenbaum* v. *Firstbrook,* 504 F.2d 200, 215 (1968), also *Int.L.R.* 60, 28.

[214] It was, therefore, the same type of action as in the case mentioned in note 212.

[215] This is the American term for shares of a corporation which the corporation has under its own control, whether as a result of acquisition or otherwise, and of which it can dispose.

Oil were registered with the Securities Exchange Commission and traded upon both the American and the Toronto Stock Exchange. Although the impugned transaction was wholly Canadian in character the court held that the Act was intended to have extra-territorial effect and to be applicable in respect of violations taking place outside the United States 'at least when the transactions involve stock registered and listed on a national securities exchange and are detrimental to the interests of American investors'.[216] It is only fair to add at once that later cases seem to have established that the essential element in *Schoenbaum* was the fact that the plaintiff was an American resident in the United States or, alternatively, that the shares were listed on an American stock exchange.[217] But even so the reach of the Securities Exchange Act, as interpreted by judicial decisions, is excessive. It seems that corporate transactions, governed by the law of the corporation, come within the purview of the American Securities legislation, merely because the injured plaintiff is American. Even if one could understand, though not approve, the listing of the securities on an American exchange as a relevant and sufficient connecting factor, the mere residence (or nationality?) of the plaintiff establishes too weak a connection with the American legislation, as the next section will render apparent.

There exists, however, a second reason why the law of the exchange should not have any influence upon corporate rights and liabilities. This is the principle of the equality of shareholders. If the listing in New York creates special and, indeed, novel rights for the benefit of American shareholders who bought in New York, shareholders in other countries may be gravely prejudiced, or, alternatively, the company must adjust the whole of its corporate law to New York law. This is a consequence which, it is submitted, runs counter to fundamental principles of the conflict of laws and is liable to cause unacceptable clashes with the *lex societatis*. There is nothing unjust in holding the purchaser of foreign shares subject to the corporate law of the foreign company.

III

Dealings with securities. Where a question arises as to the liabiltiy of the seller of securities or of persons involved in their issue and sale, such as promotors, banks, brokers, lawyers and accountants, most countries again would apply conflict principles relating either to contractual or tortious liability. In the United States of America, however, an entirely different

[216] P. 208.

[217] See, e.g., *Leasco Data Processing Equipment Corporation* v. *Maxwell*, 468 F.2d 1326 (1972), at p. 1333, also *Int.L.R.* 60, 51.

problem arises in consequence of the extreme width of section 10 *(b)* of the Securities Act 1934. This renders it

> unlawful for any person, directly or indirectly . . . to use or employ in connection with the purchase or sale of any security . . . any manipulative or deceptive device or contrivance in contravention of such rules and regulations as the Commission may prescribe as necessary or appropriate in the public interest or for the protection of investors.

This text could potentially have world-wide application. It contains the typically wide language which legislators tend to employ and which it is for the courts to restrict in the light of appropriate principles of international law. In a long series of cases the courts of the United States have done this, so that today a fairly clear picture exists. Since 1975[218] it is established that the anti-fraud provisions of the securities legislation

(1) apply to losses from sales to American residents in the United States,
(2) apply to losses from sales of securities to American residents abroad if, but only if, acts of material importance in the United States have significantly contributed thereto,
(3) do not apply to losses from sales of securities to foreigners outside the United States, unless acts within the United States directly caused such losses.

It may be that this formulation which leaves a number of uncertainties, though it comes from the pen of Circuit Judge Friendly, could have been much compressed by stating that it is conduct in the United States that is the essential requirement. In fact a year later another Circuit Court of Appeals put the point succinctly: jurisdiction attaches

> whenever there has been significant conduct with respect to the alleged violations in the United States. And this is true even though the securities are foreign ones that had not been purchased on an American Exchange.[219]

[218] *Bersch* v. *Drexel Firestone Inc.*, 519 F.2d 974 (1975), at p. 993. Most recently in *Fidenas AG* v. *Compagnie Internationale* 606 F.2d (1979), with reference to other cases.

[219] *Travis* v. *Anthes Imperial Ltd.* 473 F.2d 515 (1973), at p. 524. The question how significant the conduct in the United States must be to give the United States courts subject-matter jurisdiction is usually answered in a most liberal manner. In *Continental Grain (Australia)* v. *Pacific Oilseeds*, 592 F.2d 409 (1979) the 8th Circuit Court of Appeals affirmed the applicability of the Act, although the transaction involved the sale of shares in an Australian company in Australia by American sellers to Australian buyers. Letters written and telephone conversations held in the United States were held to constitute significant conduct. Many readers of the decision are likely to consider it minimal.

Such a principle is wholly traditional in character and is in no way different from that which prevails, for instance in England, to establish tortious liability: the court has to answer the question 'where in substance did this cause of action arise'?[220] Where did the material conduct such as the sale, the offer, the misrepresentation and so forth occur?

While, notwithstanding the wealth of material, this seems to be a relatively straightforward point, a much more difficult question relates to the extent to which the Securities Exchange Act provides the Securities Exchange Commission with inquisitorial powers over foreigners merely by reason of the fact that they engaged in dealings on an American exchange. It will be readily accepted that anyone who purchases shares or other property on an exchange subjects himself to the rules and regulations and, indeed, to the law governing the exchange. Does he also become subject to regulatory provisions of the law of the country to which the exchange belongs and which asserts jurisdiction over all aspects and implications of every transaction taking place on it? The problem is one of extreme difficulty, because an affirmative answer jeopardizes the certainty and smooth functioning of international trade and frequently exposes the trader to unexpected and unusual risks. Yet one is reluctanly driven to the conclusion that an affirmative answer is required. The point arose a few years ago in the notorious case of *Securities Exchange Commission* v. *Banca della Svizzera Italiana*[221] where Judge Milton Pollack gave the decisive reason. The Bank, a Swiss corporation, bought 'through a subsidiary corporation'[222] a parcel of shares on the Philadelphia and New York Stock Exchanges in circumstances which, if true, supported a strong suspicion of insider trading. The plaintiff, therefore, required the bank to answer certain interrogatories. To do so involved the bank in a violation of its duty of secrecy. Yet the judge thought[223]

It would be a travesty of justice to permit a foreign company to invade American markets, violate American laws if they were indeed violated, withdraw profits and

[220] *Distillers Co. (Biochemicals) Ltd.* v. *Thompson* (1971) A.C. 458, 468, per Lord Pearson, followed by the Court of Appeal in *Multinational Gas and Petrochemical Co.* v. *Multinational Gas and Petrochemical Services Ltd.*, [1983] 3 W.L.R. 492. The odd point is that United States courts are so fascinated by the problem of the statute's scope that they do not ask whether general principles of the conflict of laws do not apply. Thus in *Grünenthal GmbH* v. *Hotz*, 511 F.Supp. 582 (1981), the action was dismissed for lack of 'subject-matter jurisdiction', but since much conduct took place in California, the question whether a tort was committed in California could have arisen, but was never asked.

[221] 92 F.R.D. 111 (1981).

[222] It is odd, but typical, that the existence of an American subsidiary was completely ignored and obviously thought immaterial.

[223] P. 119. On insider trading and international co-operation see, e.g., Szak, 40 (1983) *Washington and Lee L.R.* 1149 and the material there referred to.

resist accountability for itself and its principals for the illegality by claiming their anonymity under foreign law.

There does not seem to be an answer to the argument that he who invades a foreign market must accept its law. If this is right the Swiss banking secret obviously was no defence and much of Judge Pollack's elaborate discussion is otiose. It was almost exclusively based on the assessment of the balance of interests, with the inevitable result that the interest of the United States prevailed. What should have been a judicious weighing of connecting factors became a discussion of policies and politics.

IV

Merger. The international implications of the merger of companies give rise to much difficulty, because the available academic material of a comparative character is limited,[224] the possible transactions carried out to achieve what may be called a merger are numerous and the statutory techniques are diverse. For the purpose of the following discussion it would seem appropriate to proceed on the basis of a logical, though considerably simplified, classification of the types of merger of companies (including branches, but excluding such other methods as joint ventures, licensing of patents and trademarks, distribution agreements and similar devices).

1. It cannot be doubted that the merger of two (or more) companies being incorporated and doing business in a given State is subject to such State's control. This is so even if one or both of the companies are subsidiaries of foreign enterprises which merge abroad with the result that such foreign merger brings about the merger of the domestic subsidiaries. This has frequently been accepted in the United States, where the matter was rightly regarded as so obvious that it was dealt with by consent,[225] for no State is required to allow foreigners by their action abroad to create a monopoly within its own frontiers.

The point arose in Germany, where the Court of Appeal in Berlin made extremely heavy weather of a simple situation.[226] Philip Morris, the American manufacturer of cigarettes, which had a wholly-owned subsidiary in Germany, bought a parcel of shares of Rothman's Ltd., an English company. The purchase gave it *de facto* control over the company.

[224] One of the best recent surveys is Roth, *RabelsZ*, 1981, 501, who refers to much further material.

[225] See, e.g., *United States* v. *CIBA Corporation*, 1970 Trade Cases 73, 269, among others mentioned by Atwood and Brewster, *Antitrust and American Business Abroad*, s. 12.16, note 71.

[226] See *Der Betrieb*, 1984, 231, discussed, for instance, by Ebenroth, ibid., p. 597.

Rothman controlled, through a subsidiary, a German company, Martin Brinkman AG. The latter company and Philip Morris (Germany) thus came under common control and commanded a joint market share of more than 30 per cent. The Federal Cartel Office was entitled to prohibit the merger of the two German companies. The court so held. The point was not really open to doubt. The argument arose from the unfortunate formulation of the Cartel Office's order; in truth it was unambiguous, so that the whole Berlin case is without any realistic foundation.

It is implied in what has just been said about the domestic effect of a foreign merger that if there are no domestic subsidiaries or branches the domestic administration is likely to be powerless. What it most certainly cannot do is to prohibit the foreign merger. Such a prohibition would not only be useless in fact, but also inadmissible in law, since it would amount to a plain excess of international jurisdiction. This has been recognized in the United States, where the result was derived from difficulties of enforcement and from 'comity consideration' which is merely another word for considerations of international law.[227] On the other hand the foreign merger may seriously prejudice domestic competition and the domestic adminstration will therefore search for means of eliminating such consequences. In all probability these will be very limited. A prohibition of imports would in many cases be possible, but aggravate rather than solve the problem.

2. The other possibility of a merger arises where a domestic company, directly or indirectly, acquires a foreign company (or vice versa). Such an acquisition may have far-reaching consequences in the domestic market, as it did in the American case of *United States* v. *Schlitz*.[228] Schlitz, the American brewers, intended to acquire a Canadian brewery which owned a controlling interest in a regional brewery in the west of the United Sates. This brewery had plans of extending towards the Eastern States. The acquisition was likely to eliminate or reduce such competition and therefore the acquisition was disallowed. No problem of international law arose. Nor would it have been different if the Canadian acquisition had been effected through a Canadian subsidiary company. A decision of the Court of Appeal in Berlin[229] is unlikely to be opposed to this conclusion. The French subsidiary of Bayer, the German chemical group, intended to purchase the French factories of Firestone, a United States corporation. In order to maintain employment the French Government strongly favoured the purchase. The effect on the German market was likely to be minimal. In these circumstances the court raised no objection. In the particular circumstances of the case the court took the view that, though it

[227] See Atwood and Brewster, s. 12.13.

[228] 385 US 37 (1966).

[229] *RiW*, 1981, 406.

had the power to prohibit the merger in France, its exercise would be unreasonable and at the same time amount to unlawful intervention in essentially French affairs. This, it is suggested, is exemplary reasoning. The case raised a question of degree. It is not difficult to imagine circumstances in which the German court would have been perfectly justified in prohibiting the German parent company from allowing its French subsidiary to proceed with the purchase. This would have been so if the transaction entered into or allowed by the German parent would have resulted in a serious distortion of competition on the German market. Again it is the act or omission of the German company in Germany and its effect on the German market that provides the German authorities with jurisdiction.[230] If the unlikely case of a foreign subsidiary acting independently, i.e., without the active concurrence of the parent, should arise, the purely commercial effect upon the domestic market would have to be tolerated.

V

Restrictive practices. In considering the public international law relating to restrictions of competition, whether they be brought about by agreements or monopolies, it is necessary to avoid terminological quibbles which tend to dominate the discussion. They centre around the word 'effect'. The legislation of many countries is intended to apply, whenever acts done abroad have 'effect' within the legislating country. The real question is what may legitimately be meant by this word. As Germany's Federal Supreme Court said:[231]

> In order to prevent the limitless extension of the international field of application of the substantive provisions of the cartel law, which in view of the multitude of repercussions are imaginable . . . it is necessary to delimitate and specify the relevant domestic effects according to the protective purpose of the law in general and of the particular substantive norms from time to time to be considered.

When on numerous occasions[232] the British Government rejected and protested against the theory of effects, it did not intend to deny that there

[230] No question of public international law arises if a German company whose American subsidiary purchases an American enterprise so as to affect competition on the German market has to notify the German authorities: 29 May 1979, BGHZ 74, 322.

[231] 29 May 1979, BGHZ 79, 322 at p. 325.

[232] One of the earliest published statements is the Aide-Mémoire of 20 October 1969 addressed to the Commission of the EEC and published, for instance, by E. Lauterpacht, *British Practice* 1967, 58 or Brownlie, *Principles of Public International Law* (3rd edn., 1979), 310, with accompanying Statement of Principles; see further numerous Notes addressed to the United States of America and published in the *British Year Book of International Law*.

were some effects of foreign anti-competitive action, which international law allowed States to treat as a violation of their own law.

The dispute which divides the world relates to one specific type of effect which 20 years ago was described as follows; suppose Dutch manufacturers enter in Holland into a minimum price agreement in respect of their products. The agreement is lawful under Dutch law. The products are sold by the Dutch manufacturers partly to consumers in Holland, the United States and elsewhere, partly to Dutch distributors for resale. To a varying extent and in varying circumstances the Dutch restraint of trade affects the price level of the Dutch and other competitive goods sold in the United States, among other nations. Is this an effect caught by section 1 of the Sherman Antitrust Act of 1890, which declares 'every contract combination in the form of trust or otherwise, or conspiracy, in restraint of trade or commerce among the several States, or with foreign nations' to be illegal?

The United States statute, as will be seen, does not refer to 'effects'. But since 1945 the United States courts have put a gloss on the statute, not by applying traditional methods of statutory interpretation which would have excluded the extra-territorial reach of the statute, but by applying the statute to every foreign act, event or conduct that is intended to have and does have effect in the United States that is foreseeable and significant. In other words the problem arises from the fact that the term 'effect' is meant to indicate the *purely commercial effect* such as in the above example the Dutch agreement would have in the United States, it being uncertain whether that effect has to be direct, substantial, intended or foreseeable,[233] for, while the Foreign Trade Antitrust Improvement Act 1982[234] renders the Sherman Act inapplicable to domestic trade (other than imports) and to export trade unless there is conduct having 'direct, substantial and reasonably foreseeable effect', the omission from the definition of other types of trade would seem to necessitate the *argumentum e contrario* that the limiting words do not apply to them.

Although during the last two decades an enormous literature dealing with this problem, among many cognate ones, has sprung up everywhere,

[233] In *Dominicus Americana Bohio* v. *Gulf & Western*, 473 F.Supp. 680 (1979), the court said that the *American Banana* case was an 'aberration' and 'obsolete' and that is was 'not necessary for the effect on foreign commerce to be both substantial and direct, so long as it is not *de minimis*' (p. 687). In *National Bank of Canada* v. *Interbank Card Association*, 666 F.2d 6 (1981), the plaintiffs complained about the termination of a licence agreement to operate in Canada Master Charge business through the issue of Master Charge credit cards. The action under the Sherman Act failed, because 'some effect' in the United States was insufficient and that what mattered was 'whether the challenged restraint has or is intended to have anti-competitive effects upon United States commerce'.

[234] It constitutes Title IV of the Export Trading Company Act 1982 (Public Law 97–290), *Int.L.M.* 1983, 363.

particularly in Germany,[235] there has been a remarkable dearth of judicial decisions. Such cases as have occurred in the United States have adopted a method that is far from convincing.

They have described as 'subject-matter jurisdiction' what is here considered as legislative jurisdiction. Having ascertained in a given case that it exists they have asked themselves whether it should be exercised. They have treated this question as one of discretion, the exercise of which was said to be governed by considerations of comity. In truth 'comity' is only another word for international law. In truth, moreover, no question of discretion should arise. If, construed in the light of international law, a statute applies the judge is not entitled to reject it. If the rules of international law preclude its application the judge has no discretionary power to enforce it. Consequently the distinction between the existence and the exercise of jurisdiction and, on the latter point, the reliance on discretion constitute a misleading approach which should not be followed and which is not being followed in other branches of the law.

The case which on its facts is closest to the crucial set of facts is the decision of the Court of Appeals, Seventh Circuit, in *Westinghouse Electric Corporation* v. *Rio Algom Ltd.*[236] The difficulty arises from the fact that, rightly or wrongly, the plaintiffs had alleged (apparently in regard to all defendants) that the conspiracy to fix the price of uranium in the world market had taken place in Illinois, among several other places. This allegation, made, it seems, without any evidence, surprisingly compelled the court to 'accept all properly pleaded allegations as true for purposes of determining jurisdiction'.[237]

This allegation (which may well be adopted by future litigants and, if established by evidence, make the whole legal problem otiose) gave to the case an almost unarguable character, for it cannot be doubted that if part of the actual illegal conduct takes place in the United States it has not only curial, but also legislative jurisdiction on the basis of the classical doctrine of territoriality.

Nor are the other two cases, famous though they have become, directly in point. Both of them, viz. that of the Ninth Circuit in *Timberlane Lumber Co.* v. *Bank of America*[238] and of the Third Circuit in *Mannington Mills Inc.* v. *Congoleum Corporation*,[239] relate to illegalities allegedly

[235] In particular Schwartz, *Deutsches Internationales Kartellrecht* (1962); E. Rehbinder, *Extraterritoriale Wirkungen des deutschen Kartellrechts* (1965); Meessen, *Völkerrechtliche Grenzen für die Anwendung kartellrechtlicher Verbotsnormen* (1975), and much further literature collected by Meng, *Zeitschrift für ausländisches öffentliches Recht und Völkerrecht* 41 (1981), 469.

[236] 617 F.2d 1248 (1980). [237] P. 1254.

[238] 549 F.2d 597 (1976), also printed by Lowe, *Extraterritorial Jurisdiction*, 15. See the second case at 749 F.2d 1378 (1984).

[239] 610 F.2d 1059, also printed by Lowe, loc. cit. p. 31.

committed by United States nationals in Honduras and in a variety of foreign countries respectively with the results that imports to and/or exports from the United States were restricted. It was in this context that for the purpose of determining the extraterritorial reach of the Sherman Act the court in *Timberlane* favoured a jurisdictional rule of reason which involved a balancing of the foreign and American interests involved.[240] The elements to be considered were later enumerated in *Mannington Mills* as follows:[241]

1. Degree of conflict with foreign law or policy.
2. Nationality of the parties.
3. Relative importance of the alleged violation of conduct here compared to that abroad.
4. Availability of a remedy abroad and the pendency of litigation there.
5. Existence of intent to harm or affect American commerce and its foreseeability.
6. Possible effect upon foreign relations if the court exercises jurisdiction and grants relief.
7. If relief is granted, whether a party will be placed in the position of being forced to perform an act illegal in either country or be under conflicting requirements by both countries.
8. Whether the court can make its order effective.
9. Whether an order for relief would be acceptable in this country if made by the foreign nation under similar circumstances.
10. Whether a treaty with the affected nation has addressed the issue.

No case has as yet become known in which this process has in fact been carried out. Although the 10th Circuit obiter approved the *Timberlane* and *Mannington Mills* approach[242] and although the Department of State subscribes to it,[243] the 7th Circuit seems to reject it.[244] It is therefore difficult to form a view of the practical implications of these ten points. It is unlikely that they will all point in the same direction. Nor is it easy to foresee how a court will deal with the conflicting elements which will

[240] The 'effect' had to be supplemented, because it neglected in particular 'the additional question . . . whether the interests of and links to the United States . . . are sufficiently strong, *vis-à-vis* those of other nations, to justify an assertion of extraterritorial authority': p. 613.

[241] At pp. 1297, 1298.

[242] *Montreal Trading Ltd.* v. *Amax Inc.*, 661 F.2d 864 (1981). The facts were only too clear for argument: the plaintiffs claimed damages, because the defendant's Canadian subsidiaries refused to sell to the Canadian plaintiffs Canadian potash for delivery in Canada. The court held that American interests were 'minimal' and that the defendants' action in the United States had only 'a speculative and insubstantial effect'.

[243] Mr Atwood, then Assistant Secretary of State in a letter of 27 September 1979, *American Journal of International Law*, 1980, 179; Mr Robertson, then Legal Adviser to the Department of State, ibid, 1982, 839, 845.

[244] *Westinghouse Electric Corporation* v. *Rio Algom Ltd.*, 617 F.2d 1248 (1980), at p. 1255.

become apparent. If one takes the facts of the *Westinghouse* case it is by no means certain that the court would have found in favour of the foreign defendants, even assuming that none of them acted in Illinois.

The conclusion is that, while the introduction of the ten balancing factors is to be welcomed as likely to reduce cases of excessive jurisdiction, the more objective, more general approach suggested in these lectures is preferable: if one considers the act complained of, i.e., the agreement, and asks with which country it has the closest contact the answer is obvious and entirely independent of any political or legally irrelevant aspect. Nor does it render governmental interventions necessary or desirable, so that such very embarrassing events as occurred in the course of the *Westinghouse* litigation would be avoided.[245] This case not only involved the Governments of Britain, Canada, Australia and South Africa which submitted briefs as *amici curiae*,[246] but also led to one of the few occasions in legal history, when a government (successfully) protested against the terms of a judicial decision. Moreover it resulted in decisions by the highest courts of Britain[247] and Canada,[248] which held that letters rogatory issued by courts in the United States consituted an encroachment upon the sovereignty or were contrary to the public policy of the State. In fact in the *Westinghouse* case Judge Marshall clearly recognized the invidious nature of the balancing process which the *Timberlane* approach required him to undertake. In a lengthy statement he said:[249]

> Aside from the fact that the judiciary has little expertise, or perhaps even authority, to evaluate the economic and social policies of a foreign country such a balancing test is inherently unworkable in this case. The competing interests here display an irreconcilable conflict on precisely the same plane of national policy . . . It is simply impossible to judicially 'balance' these totally contradictory and mutually negating actions.

[245] The intervention of the Governments of Australia, Canada, South Africa and the United Kingdom provoked the 7th Circuit Court of Appeals to say that 'shockingly to us the governments of the defendants have subserviently presented for them their case against the exercise of jurisdiction'. Some or all of the governments immediately protested to the Department of State which wrote to the Associate Attorney-General to draw the attention of the court to the concern it had given to the United States Government: letter of 17 March 1980, *American Journal of International Law*, 1980, 665. Thereupon the Associate Attorney-General wrote to the court pointing out that the foreign governments 'are entitled to appropriate deference and weight in resolving legal questions that turn at least in part on considerations of international comity': letter of 6 May 1980, *American Journal of International Law*, 1980, 928.

[246] The essential parts of the briefs are printed by Lowe, loc. cit., pp. 156 sqq.

[247] *In re Westinghouse Electric Corporation Uranium Contracts Litigation* [1978] A.C. 547.

[248] *Gulf Corporation* v. *Gulf Canada Ltd.*, 111 D.L.R. 3d 74 (1980), a unanimous judgment of the Canadian Supreme Court delivered by Laskin C.J.C.

[249] 480 F.Supp. 1138, at p. 1148 (1979).

This statement which may be said to correspond to common sense and has significance far beyond the field of restrictive practices forcefully points to the weakness of the *Timberlane* reasoning, however well-meant it may be. It is in line with the views of Australia[250] and of the British Government. After the *Westinghouse* case had been settled at enormous expense another American company, Washington Public Power Supply System, brought a fresh action against Rio Tinto Zinc Corporation, in which the British Government again filed an *amicus curiae* brief in October 1982,[251] repeating the arguments it had submitted in the *Westinghouse* litigation.[252] But the British Government also addressed a Note to the Government of the Unites States[253] in the course of which it said:

> If the balancing of interests of two or more sovereign States is a matter properly to be left to the courts of one such State at all (a proposition as to which Her Majesty's Government have serious reservations) it is clear that such an exercise cannot be left to those courts without assistance from the appropriate department of the government concerned. It is clear from the conduct of the court in the *Westinghouse* litigation that leaving such matters to the courts alone cannot always resolve such problems. Indeed, it can lead to additional friction between governments which might otherwise be avoided.

These are indeed serious problems. None of them arises if one follows the approach suggested above. Whether one calls it the territorial theory (which, as a principle, the British Government[254] as well as Canada, Australia, France and South Africa seem to favour) or the theory of the close or reasonable—or 'meaningful'[255]—contact does not matter. It is the object that matters, viz. the object of bringing the problem back to dimensions with which a judge is familiar and with which he can cope. The assessment of objective points of contact complies with such a requirement.

[250] It seems that Australia, speaking through her Attorney-General, rejects the *Timberlane* principle and regards it as 'offensive to Australian sovereignty for a United States court to evaluate Australian interests': see Sutherland, *I.C.L.Q.* 1984, 230, footnote 6.

[251] *British Year Book of International Law*, 1982, 455 and following.

[252] Above note 246.

[253] 23 June 1982, *British Year Book of International Law*, 1982, 430, at p. 431, also Lowe, loc. cit. pp. 175, 176.

[254] For the latest statement see the brief referred to in *British Year Book of International Law*, 1982, 456: 'The longstanding belief of the British Government is that territorial principles of jurisdiction should govern in the field of economic competition'.

[255] Meessen (above, note 235) uses the expression 'sinnvoll' which is intended to be a German version of genuine or reasonable used in the 1964 lectures. The word used in the text is intended to be a retranslation of this German word.

VI

Shipping. The limits of international jurisdiction in the case of restrictive practices are well exemplified and particularly significant where shipping, among other methods of transportation, is concerned. This is a type of business which by its very nature is international in character and of necessity involves contact with numerous countries and their laws. It is easy to imagine the chaos that would occur if, for instance, every country which allows a ship to enter its territorial waters were to arrogate to itself jurisdiction in respect of such of the ship's conduct as originates in other countries, especially in the home port, and is highly likely to have effects everywhere.[256]

Yet the Sherman Act of 1890 creates the very perplexity that is so alien to international transportation. It treats so-called shipping conferences,[257] i.e. agreements between carriers fixing rates of freight and possibly other terms of the transportation of goods, as an illegal restraint of trade within the meaning of section 1, and it does so at the very moment, when in England the House of Lords by a Committee of seven law lords decided that shipowners who agree upon terms of carriage, but have no intention to cause injury other than that resulting from legitimate competition are not guilty of unlawful obstruction, molestation, intimidation, conspiracy or restraint of trade.[258] This is still the law in England, where shipping conferences were invariably exempted from any legislation controlling

[256] But this may be the attitude of the United States. Speaking about dual-rate contracts the then Assistant Secretary of State Mr G. Johnson said (*Int.L.M.* 1964, 1128): 'Carriers in international trade have long been aware that they must comply with the laws of each country involved.'

[257] In 1974 a United Nations Convention laying down a Code of conduct for Liner Conferences was accepted by 72 votes against those of Denmark, Finland, Norway, Sweden, Switzerland, the United Kingdon and the United States, while the Netherlands, Canada, Greece, Italy and New Zealand abstained: *Int.L.M.* 1974, 910. The Convention which is discussed, for instance, by Grewlich, *Zeitschrift für ausländisches öffentliches Recht und Völkerrecht* 35 (1975), 742, entered into force on 6 October 1983 after 24 ratifications had been deposited as provided in Article 49. Neither the United Kindgom nor the United States have ratified. See Council Regulation (EEC) No. 954/79 of 15 May 1979 concerning the ratification of member States of or their accession to the United Nations Convention on a Code of Conduct for Liner Conferences (*Official Journal*, 17 May 1979, No. L121/2)—a Regulation which is probably of little consequence, as no European country is likely to adopt the Convention. The Report of the Rochdale Committee of Inquiry into Shipping (1970) *Cmnd.* 4337, includes an illuminating description of shipping conferences (paragraphs 401 sqq.) which have existed for more than 100 years (paragraph 401) and of which there exist more than 300 throughout the world. The Committee's judgment was (paragraph 476) that 'on balance it would not advance the public interest to prevent shipowners . . . from entering into some arrangements for the regulation of the trade'. But 'a published code of conference practices' was recommended (paragraph 481).

[258] *Mogul Steamship Co.* v. *McGregor Gow & Co.* [1892] A.C. 25.

trade restrictions.[259] It is also the law in many other countries and even the EEC allows shipping between member States to be subject to the provisions of conference agreements.[260] Perhaps it is not surprising that the United States felt compelled to deviate from the severity of the Sherman Act. Section 15 of the Shipping Act 1916 grants antitrust immunity to shipping conferences notified to and approved by the Federal Maritime Commission. Nevertheless there remains a considerable quantity of agreements between carriers which are not covered by such immunity. As recently as 1981 a number of shipping lines, including a German and an English one, were heavily fined in the United States.[261] And in January 1978 the Consultative Shipping Group Governments which include 12 European countries[262] and Japan addressed a Note to the Government of the Unites States, in which they stated that they

> accept neither the right of the United States Government to impose its own views on the regulation of events and activities taking place wholly or largely within the territories of other nations, nor the concept that one government should seek to regulate unilaterally and in its own interest activities of an industry which are international by nature and of equal and vital concern to other governments.[263]

In October 1981 the same 13 Governments spoke of the 'regrettable friction in our relations with the United States' caused by the United States interpreting its law 'as applying outside United States territory and even to dealing between European citizens taking place on European soil'.[264] Nor was the problem solved by Recommendations issued by the Council of the OECD for consultation and conciliation in the event of investigations being undertaken.[265]

Shipping conferences are a pre-eminent example of the working of the 'effects doctrine'. On the one hand the United States and its courts have accepted that its laws do not reach the internal management of foreign

[259] See the Restrictive Trade Practices (Services) Order 1976 (Statutory Instruments 1976 No. 98), s. 3 (1) *(c)*, and paragraph 2 of the Schedule, made under the Fair Trading Act 1973; Anti-Competitive Practices (Exclusion) Order 1980 (Statutory Instrument 1980 No. 979), s. 2, and Schedule 1, made under the Competition Act 1980.

[260] Council Regulation 141 of 26 November 1962 exempting transport from the application of Regulation 17. A draft regulation laying down detailed rules for the application of Articles 85 and 86 of the Treaty of Rome to maritime transport was submitted by the Commission on 16 October 1981 (Official Journal of 5 November 1981, No. C 282/4), but has not yet been adopted.

[261] See *British Year Book of International Law*, 1979, 352; 1981, 459.

[262] Belgium, Denmark, Finland, France, Germany, Greece, Italy, the Netherlands, Norway, Spain, Sweden and United Kingdom.

[263] Note addressed to the United States, extracts printed in *British Year Book International Law*, 1978, 386.

[264] Lowe, loc. cit. p. 220.

[265] They are printed by Lowe, loc. cit., 243–5, 251–4. They relate to trade in general and are not limited to shipping.

ships while they are in American waters. Thus American labour or similar legislation does not apply to them.[266] Nor does the United States object if a single shipowner lays down and applies a tariff for carriage of goods to the United States. But if several shipowners, i.e., a conference, agrees to apply a similar tariff then section 15 of the Shipping Act 1916 or, if it is not complied with, section 1 of the Sherman Act 1980 applies, irrespective of the fact that the agreement is made abroad between a group of foreign shipowners under the protection of foreign law by which it is perfectly legal. The basis of this doctrine was laid as early as 1913 in a case which related to shipping, though not to a conference.[267] Section 19 of United States Immigration Act 1907 prohibited the owner of a vessel from making any charge for the return passage of aliens brought to the United States, but not permitted to land. Return tickets Bremen–New York–Bremen were sold under German law in Germany. In holding that this was an indictable offence the Supreme Court of the United States, while denying the extra-territorial effect of statutes, stated that 'the parties in Germany could make a contract which would be in force in the United States . . . they created a condition which was operative in New York'.[268] Two other Supreme Court cases which are usually cited in support of the 'effects doctrine' in the sphere of shipping conferences are not really in point,[269] so that it is only the application of the *Alcoa* rule that caught them. In fact in 1961 the Federal Maritime Board (as it was then called) obtained an order for discovery of documents against a foreign conference[270] and in 1964 it was expressly stated:[271]

> The vital principle to be applied . . . is whether the performance of contracts or effectuation of those arrangements operated in this country so as to affect our foreign commerce directly and materially.

[266] See *McCulloch* v. *Sociedad Nacional de Marineros de Honduras*, 372 US 10 (1963) and the many later cases founded on it; *Lauritzen* v. *Larsen*, 345 US 571 (1953).

[267] *United States* v. *Nord Deutscher Lloyd,* 223 US 515 (1913).

[268] At p. 518.

[269] *United States* v. *Pacific & Arctic Co.,* 228 US 87 (1913); this was a case in which American and Canadian carriers concluded in the United States an agreement relating to carriages from the United States to Alaska; yet the court said (at p. 106): 'If we may not control foreign citizens or corporations operating in foreign territory, we certainly may control such citizens and corporations operating in our territory, as we undoubtedly may control our own subjects and our own corporations.' *Thomsen* v. *Cayser,* 243 US 66 (1917): this was the case of an agreement concluded between foreign firms abroad, but relating to carriage from New York to South Africa. The court said (at p. 88): 'It is contended that the combination was formed in a foreign country and that, therefore, it was not within the Act of Congress . . . As was said in the Circuit Court of Appeals, the combination affected the foreign commerce of the country and was put into operation here . . . It, therefore, is within the law.' Of course.

[270] *Montship Lines Ltd.* v. *Federal Maritime Board,* 295 F.2d 147 (1961), also *Int.L.R.* 32, 100.

[271] *United States* v. *Anchor Line,* 232 F. Supp. 382 (1964), also *Int.L.R.* 35, 103.

These cases vividly illustrate not only the 'effects doctrine', but also the practical implementation of a theory based on the assessment of a reasonable contact or link. A shipping conference agreed in the United States between American and Canadian carriers is surely subject to the Sherman Act.[272] But a shipping conference agreed between foreign carriers in respect of the carriage of goods from New York to South Africa[273] or in respect of carriage to and from the United States has, it is submitted, insufficient contact with the latter State and, therefore, should not be under the control of the legislation of the United States. The substance of the agreement concerns the way in which foreign carriers transact their business outside the United States. Admittedly there exists contact with the United States which is by no means negligible, but the connection with the United States is very much less close than with the carriers' home countries. One must not forget that it is the agreement that matters, and this was concluded outside the United States; for if each shipowner, separately, individually and independently, had adopted the terms corresponding to the agreement no American prohibition would have existed. That freight is paid in the United States at a rate that reflects the conference agreement made outside the United States is one of the purely commercial repercussions or 'effects' of foreign policies and events which every State must put up with, unless it decides to prescribe rates applicable in its territory. Merely to prohibit the foreign agreement which stipulates such rates, is different in character and beyond the limits of a State's jurisdiction. One may, as the British Government prefers to do,[274] describe this as the territorial principle, but it is perhaps less crude than what one normally means by that approach.

The didactic value of the pre-1984 shipping law remains even after the coming into force of the Shipping Act 1984 in June 1984. On certain conditions, particularly on notification to the Federal Maritime Commission, conference agreements are now exempt from the antitrust legislation. The burden of proof as regards the violation of public interest now rests with the Commission which, in order to obtain an injunction will have to prove that the agreement 'is likely by a reduction in competition to produce an unreasonable increase in transportation cost'. These and other changes are substantial. As a symptom they are encouraging. Whether in practice they will be so applied as to achieve the far-reaching changes which seem to be intended remains to be seen.

[272] See the first of the cases mentioned in note 269.
[273] See the second of the cases mentioned in note 269.
[274] Note of 27 July 1978, *British Year Book of International Law*, 1978, 390.

EPILOGUE

At the end of these lectures a few general remarks may, it is hoped, be appropriate.

In the first place there may be some to whom the preceding submissions appear to include too harsh a criticism of American practices. Such an impression would be entirely unfounded. Criticism of American practice in one particular field is a sign, not of antagonism, but of concern. The United States of America, though greatly admired by most observers on this side of the Atlantic, has gone astray and all who mean well ought to try to expose the error and to eliminate it. There is a simple method of proving the error: where the large majority of nations co-exists harmoniously but there is tension and disagreement between them and a single other State, the presumption is that the latter is wrong in law. This is the position in the field of international jurisdiction.

It may, secondly, be asked how it is possible to refer so frequently to (allegedly prevalent) rules of international law when there is so little firm evidence of their existence, when, in particular, they lack the authority which decisions of international tribunals tend to confer. It is, indeed, regrettable that no State has invoked judicial remedies of an international character to test the validity of the practices which the United States, almost alone among the nations of the world, observes. It is surprising, because in all probability there exist tribunals which would have jurisdiction; the fear that the optional clause which the United States has signed as a result of the Connally Amendment prevents the International Court of Justice from assuming jurisdiction is likely on closer investigation to be open to doubt. And although a prominent American lawyer has thought it right to say that at 'the present the International Court of Justice simply does not enjoy such a level of esteem as to make it a generally acceptable arbiter of jurisdictional disputes',[275] there is no reason to believe that the United States or, indeed, any other civilized State would not accept and implement that Court's verdict. However this may be, the suggestion that rules of international law do exist and are binding is founded on other sources of international law than decisions of international tribunals. It is derived from the practice of States (which includes their municipal practice) and from the authority of academic writers. Each of them has a contribution to the development of an international rule to make. Some of them are entitled to great respect or to greater respect than others—this is a difficult matter of assessment, perhaps only of taste or preference. None of them should be rejected as worthless to the process of the

[275] Professor Detlev F. Vagts, *Wirtschaft und Recht* 35 (1983), 95.

evolution of international law. What are suggestions today, may or may not become legal rules. In the last resort it is their persuasiveness and their acceptance that counts, and the latter is not jeopardized by differences in formulation or terminology.

Next a word should be said about the function and the value of inter-State agreements on problems of international jurisdiction. If they are observed (and, as in the course of a thoughtful paper[276] Professor Frank Vischer has pointed out, the United States of America may well be only too ready to disregard them) they are in many respects of the greatest importance and will, it is hoped, attract much support. This applies, for instance, to double taxation treaties, to treaties relating to civil and criminal jurisdiction, to treaties on mutual assistance in criminal matters such as the United States of America and Switzerland concluded in 1973,[277] or even to such Agreements made under private law as that concluded in 1982 between the Swiss Bankers Association and its members as well as the Securities and Exchange Commission of the United States,[278] or the so-called Basel Concordat concluded by representatives of the central banks of Belgium, Canada, France, Germany, Italy, Japan, Luxembourg, the Netherlands, Sweden, Switzerland, the United Kingdom and the United States and defining the principles for the supervision of foreign banking establishments in regard to solvency, liquidity and foreign exchange operations by the parent and host authorities.[279] In these cases legally enforceable duties are created which are clearly defined and can be readily understood. On the other hand there is room for some scepticism, when one considers an Agreement such as that concluded in 1982 between the United States of America and Australia relating to co-operation in anti-trust matters,[280] which stems from suggestions originally put forward by the Australian Attorney-General.[281] Anti-trust investigations have to be notified (Article 1) and lead to the two nations' duty to consult (Article

[276] *Wirtschaft und Recht* 35 (1983), 98, at pp. 106–8, which points out that the American–Swiss Treaty of 1973 has far-reaching consequences for civil proceedings or rather for what the Americans call civil proceedings.

[277] Treaty of 25 May 1973, *UTS* 27, 2019, and see the Swiss statute of 20 March 1981, *Int.L.M.* 1982, 1339.

[278] Agreement XVI of 2 September 1982: *International Legal Materials*, 1983, 1. It establishes a Commission of the Swiss Bankers Association. If within 25 days prior to a merger or the offer for at least 10% of the shares of a company a customer gives to a Swiss bank an order for purchase of the shares, the United States Government may address an Inquiry to the Commission through the Swiss Government. The Commission may require the bank to disclose the information. If the customer is an 'insider' his name is to be disclosed to the United States and his account may be blocked.

[279] Published in *IMF Survey* 1983, 201 (11 July 1983).

[280] *Int.L.M.* 1982, 702. On this Agreement see Sutherland, *I.C.L.Q.* 1984, 230; Ramsey, *Virginia Journal of International Law* 24 (1983), 127, among many others.

[281] See the speech by Mr Durack, Q.C., printed in A. V. Lowe, *Extra-territorial Jurisdiction* (1983), 90. The Agreement is printed at p. 233.

2), i.e., to 'seek earnestly to avoid a possible conflict between their respective laws, policies and national interests and for that purpose to give due regard to each other's sovereignty and to considerations of comity'.[282] A prohibition to give information or disclose documents shall not be issued automatically, but, so it seems, only if the laws, policies or national interests of the State are adversely affected (Article 5) and in the case of private anti-trust proceedings, the goverment concerned shall upon request 'report to the court on the substance and outcome of the consultations'.[283] This shows the very limited value of such treaties. They impose certain duties on States, but they have no effect upon proceedings between private parties and they may have only a delaying effect upon proceedings instituted by the government and its agencies. It is a little optimistic to suggest (as an American author does)[284] that the diplomatic approach 'will serve the needs of the international system to resolve such conflicts with emphasis on co-ordinating competing interests in a climate of international co-operation, not on unilateral resolutions enabled by coercive local power' and 'will contribute to the development of a community consensus by means of international dialogue on jurisdictional restraints that will further facilitate the flow of transnational commerce'. On the other hand it is noteworthy that the same author recognizes that the balancing of interests as practised in the United States 'leads to the assertion of the primacy of United States interests in the guise of applying an international jurisdictional rule of reason'[285] and that interest balancing belongs to diplomacy rather than to the judicial forum. Such insight can only be welcomed. But it does not solve the problem of international jurisdiction. That problem can only be solved by the law, that is to say, by rules of municipal law which conform to the demands of public international law. It is their development rather than the pursuance of national interests that is the task of the lawyer. Professor Bowett who, incidentally, is by no means entirely adverse to the process of balancing interests,[286] would prefer negotiation and consultation, but rightly fears that it would be 'a somewhat sterile exercise' and concludes that 'the onus lies on the United States to initiate the necessary changes internally'.[287] This, unfortunately, is unlikely to happen. It is to be expected, therefore, that the problem of

[282] In view of this elaboration of what the duty to consult involves it will hardly be possible to turn it into a duty to negotiate, as the Arbitration Tribunal in the *Aminoil* case did: *Int.L.M.* 1982, 976, paragraphs 18 to 24.

[283] Article 6. In view of past experience it does not seem very likely that the court will be much interested in what happened in the course of the consultations.

[284] Maier, *American Journal of Comparative Law*, 1983, 579, at pp. 581, 582.

[285] P. 590. This is, of course, the view expressed in these lectures, but it is rarely heard in the United States.

[286] *British Year Book of International Law*, 1982, 18 sqq.

[287] Loc. cit., p. 26.

international jurisdiction and its limits will remain a source of friction and uncertainty.

Finally, while diplomatic efforts should not be discouraged, the immediate remedy of limited scope lies in the 'blocking statutes' such as Britain's Protection of Trading Interests Act 1980[288] or similar legislation adopted by numerous countries.[289] From the point of view of international law there cannot, in present circumstances, be any objection to, and from a political point of view there cannot be any surprise at, the fact that such legislation was thought necessary. It constitutes an act of self-defence or reprisal or sanction against the international wrong inherent in the assumption of excessive jurisdiction by other States. Its scope varies from country to country and it may well be that Britain has gone further than any other State by enacting that in certain circumstances two-thirds of the damages awarded in the United States, i.e., the punitive part of the award, may be recovered in an English court.[290] The United States specifically protested against this provision,[291] but its legality cannot be in doubt. On the other hand there exists strong reason for regretting the necessity for such retaliation. If, by once again placing individual problems into the wider framework of the general doctrine of international jurisdiction, these lectures should have contributed to a revision and moderation of excessive claims to jurisdiction, if they should at least have stimulated lawyers to reflect again and think afresh, they would have fulfilled their purpose and achieved all that could be expected.

[288] For an excellent review of the circumstances leading to the enactment of this statute see Lord Mackay's speech in the House of Lords, *British Year Book of International Law*, 1980, 444 sqq. For somewhat intemperate criticism of the Act see Lowenfeld, *American Journal of International Law*, 1981, 628. The learned author seems to think that if three American companies cannot join together to fix the price of a product, two British companies are necessarily also precluded from doing so. He forgets that it is open to the three American companies to sell in Britain at prices fixed by them.

[289] See the legislation enacted by Australia, Belgium, Denmark, Finland, France, Germany, Italy, the Netherlands, Phillippines, South Africa, Sweden, Switzerland. Many of these statutes are limited to shipping documents. They are printed by Lowe (above note 281), pp. 79–225. On proposals for similar United States legislation directed against legally unjustifable requirements of the EEC see Vagts, *American Journal of International Law*, 1982, 591. As to Canada see *Canadian Extra-territorial Measures Act* 1985, *Int.L.M.* 1985, 794.

[290] Section 6.

[291] See the Note by the United States of 9 November 1979, printed in Lowe (above note 281), 178–82 or in *British Year Book of International Law*, 1979, 362.

2

The Doctrine of *Jus Cogens* in International Law

I

FUNDAMENTAL laws are not only inalienable, but, by virtue of their authority, character and content, also exist independently of any text which may attempt to formulate them, and bind the community, whether or not it submits to them. The Ten Commandments are fundamental laws: their binding and law-making force is universal and eternal and would be so even if they had not been given formal expression.

The question whether there are fundamental laws which form part of or underlie public international law or, to put it differently, which, while included in public international law, have a higher status and sanction than the ordinary rule of international law—that question does not seem to have arisen before the present century.[1] On the contrary, until very recently it was believed by many that it is open to States by their treaty to derogate from every rule of international law. The impetus for a reconsideration of the problem[2] came, when the codification of the law of treaties and its implications had to be pondered. The international legislator was confronted by a dilemma. If he refrained from saying anything about *ordre public*, this could be understood to mean that every treaty, however obnoxious its terms might be, would be valid, unless there existed one of the well-known types of *vice de consentement* such as error or fraud. On this hypothesis it would be open to a State by treaty to sell one of its racial minorities as slaves to another State, and international law would, by its silence, sanction the validity of such an arrangement. Or the legislator

[1] References to the very limited pre-war literature are supplied, for instance by Verdross, *Völkerrecht* (5th edn., 1964) p. 129; or by Monaco, *Rec.* 125 (1968 iii) p. 203 n.1.

[2] It has been extensively discussed by modern writers, though usually with primary emphasis upon contractual aspects which, as a result of the Vienna Draft Convention on Treaties mentioned below, are now very much less pressing. For references to the literature see, for instance, Brownlie, *Principles of Public International Law* (2nd edn., 1973) p. 499 n.4, or O'Connell, *International Law* (2nd edn., 1970) I, 244 n. 74. Add, among others, Zotiades, *International Jus Cogens* (Thessaloniki, 1968); Barberis, *ZaöRVR* 30 (1970) 19; or Jaenicke, *Berichte der Deutschen Gesellschaft für Völkerrecht* 7 (1965) pp. 80 sqq. who at p. 82 n. 7 gives a very full bibliography and himself suggests (p. 81) the term '*ordre public* of the international community.'

Festschrift für Ulrich Scheuner (Berlin, 1973), 399–418.

would provide for the nullity of treaties contrary to *ordre public international*. He thus had to face the problem of definition and identification. At the same time he would be unlikely to be troubled by the more philosophical problem whether international law recognized the existence of fundamental laws which a priori restricted the States' freedom of action. Applying his mind to the point at any time after the Second World War he would not be burdened by positivist clogs. He would know that, as a result of elementary and eternal laws of nature and morality, a treaty such as that instanced above could not possibly be upheld by any tribunal worthy of its function, that it would and ought to be held null and void and that in truth his task was limited to finding a form of words to describe the inevitable, yet to confine it within acceptable bounds. Thus it happened that Sir Hersch Lauterpacht was compelled to grapple with it, when in 1953 he presented his First Report on the Law of Treaties to the International Law Commission.[3] In a period of rapid movement it is not without interest to quote the central passage of that great scholar's exposition:[4]

> It would thus appear that the test whether the object of the treaty is illegal and whether the treaty is void for that reason is not inconsistency with customary international law pure and simple, but inconsistency with such overriding principles of international law which may be regarded as constituting principles of international public policy (*ordre international public*). These principles need not necessarily have crystallized in a clearly accepted rule of law such as prohibition of piracy or of aggressive war. They may be expressive of rules of international morality so cogent that an international tribunal would consider them as forming part of those principles of law generally recognized by civilized nations which the International Court of Justice is bound to apply by virtue of Art. 38 (3) of its Statute.

Accordingly Lauterpacht suggested that a treaty should be void 'if its performance involves an act which is illegal under international law and if it is declared so to be by the International Court of Justice'. Finally, in 1969 the Vienna Draft Convention on the Law of Treaties[5] adopted Art. 53 in the following terms:

> A treaty is void if, at the time of its conclusion, it conflicts with a peremptory norm of general international law. For the purpose of the present Convention a peremptory norm of general international law is a norm accepted and recognized by the international community of States as a whole as a norm from which no derogation is permitted and which can be modified only by a subsequent norm of general international law having the same character.

[3] *Year Book of the International Law Commission*, 1953 ii 90. [4] Ibid. p. 155.
[5] For the text see, for instance, *American Journal of International Law*, 1969, 875

Since 1969, therefore, it is difficult to deny the existence of a fundamental law of the family of nations, of an international public policy or *jus cogens*. But there remains the grave question of its emanations. Indeed, already in 1965 Germany's Federal Constitutional Tribunal had given a remarkable, though very general answer:[6]

> Only some elementary legal commands will have to be considered as rules of customary international law which do not permit contracting out. The quality of such peremptory norms can be attributed only to those legal rules which are firmly embedded in the legal conscience of the community of States, which are indispensable to the existence of public international law as an international legal system and the observance of which may be demanded by all members of the community of States.

To that question Ulrich Scheuner made a further important contribution[7] which it is useful to analyse and to which, by way of a tribute to a distinguished scholar and a friend, it is proposed to add a postscript; like Scheuner's article and for the same reasons that presumably motivated him, it is written in the English language.

On a strict interpretation Art. 53 employs terms which almost constitute the denial of the very idea it sanctions. In order to be a 'peremptory norm of general international law' a norm must be 'accepted and recognized by the international community as a whole'. The formula clearly demands more than is required for a simple rule of international law. This requires a custom, viz. extensive and virtually uniform State practice expressive of a legal obligation,[8] or a general principle of law recognized by civilized nations.[9] While for the latter purpose a principle must be general, recognized and common to civilized nations,[10] Art. 53 requires it to be universal as well as accepted and recognized. Are there such norms? Scheuner, like many others, answered in the affirmative. He also proposed to distinguish three groups of norms:[11] firstly, rules protecting 'the foundations of law, peace and humanity', such as the prohibition of genocide, slavery or the use of force; secondly, rules of peaceful co-operation

[6] 7 April 1965, *BVerfG* 18, 441, at p. 448, or *Archiv des Völkerrechts* 13 (1966/67) 122, at p. 126. The decision on which see Riesenfeld, *American Journal of International Law*, 1966, 511 affirms Federal Finance Tribunal, 1 March 1963, *BStBl* 1963 iii 300, or *Archiv des Völkerrechts* 11 (1963/64) 246, also *Int.L.R.* 44, 149.

[7] *Zeitschrift für Ausländisches Öffentliches Recht und Völkerrecht* 27 (1976) 520.

[8] North Sea Continental Shelf Cases, *ICJ Reports* 1969, 4 at p. 43.

[9] Art. 38 (1) (c) of the *Statute of the International Court of Justice*.

[10] In the *North Sea Continental Shelf Cases*, ubi supra, pp. 132–5, Judge Ammoun objects to the use of the word 'civilized', which he regards as 'discriminatory' in character. This can hardly be taken as a useful contribution. One may decide to call all nations civilized; this is a question of terminology. But it is a fact of life that some are more civilized than others, and Art. 38 (1) (c) contemplates their law rather than the law of the less civilized ones.

[11] Above n. 7, at p. 526.

protecting fundamental common interests such as the freedom of the seas; and, thirdly, rules protecting humanity in so far as they 'protect human dignity, personal and racial equality, life and personal freedom'. Such classifications are probably as good as any other. It is probably also true that they comprise norms which may fairly be said to come within the terms of Art. 53 and which, in particular, are 'accepted and recognized' by the community of nations. It is, however, also true that they are not being universally practised and observed. Indeed, it would not be difficult to think of numerous norms which, on many occasions, have been shamelessly disregarded by States who, on a purely verbal level, purport most strongly to favour those very norms. Nevertheless it is neither helpful nor appropriate for this reason to approach Art. 53 in a destructive manner. It is beside the point to generalize by describing the doctrine of *jus cogens* as 'perfectly adapted to the idiosyncrasies of a hypocritical age' or as having 'all the trappings of fashionably "progressive", if unrealistic, thinking' or 'as a means of undermining the sanctity of the pledged word'.[12] Nor is it profitable to express the fear that Article 53 might give rise 'à des considérations d'ordre politique ou idéologiques imposées par voie majoritaire et abusivement érigées en règles pseudo-juridiques'.[13] Seen in the light of actual conditions in the present world and, in particular, in the United Nations Organisation, these are wholly justified assessments upon which it will be necessary to expand. Seen against the background of the particular task in hand, viz. the codification of the law of treaties, they are unacceptable. Nor should it be forgotten that there is in law and in fact a great distinction between an agreement to commit an unlawful act and the commission of the act itself. That, for a variety of reasons, the latter cannot always be punished or otherwise condemned does not entitle a judge to uphold and enforce the former.

We must conclude (and we should do so without hesitation) that there exists an international *jus cogens*, that its identification may not always be easy and will certainly be a slow process, but that where it is infringed the treaty, or the provision in question,[14] is null and void, and that within the context of Art. 53 no other solution is conceivable.

The much more serious question, however, is what implications, outside the law of treaties, the existence of *jus cogens* carries into international law as a whole. It is this question to which the following observations are primarily devoted.

[12] Schwarzenberger, 'International Jus Cogens', 43 (1965) *TexasL.R.* 455, reprinted in *The Concept of* Jus Cogens *in International Law* (Papers and Proceedings of the Conference on International Law. Lagonissi, April 1966), pp. 117 sqq., at p. 140; also *Current Legal Problems* 1965, 191.

[13] Rousseau, *Droit International Public*, I (1970)s. 131.

[14] Art. 53 treats the case in which the treaty as a whole offends against a peremptory norm. If only one provision does so, Art. 44 applies.

II

The Vienna Conference on the Law of Treaties had not yet concluded its work, when in February 1969 the International Court of Justice delivered its judgment in the *North Sea Continental Shelf Cases*.[15] In broad terms the Court was called upon to define the rules governing the delimitation of the Continental Shelf adjacent to territories of neighbouring States. The Court held that the Geneva Convention on the Continental Shelf of 1958 was not applicable as between the Parties and that its Article 6 did not express customary international law when, in principle, it adopted the equidistance rule. On this point it had been sought to derive an argument from Article 12 which, in effect, allows acceding States to make reservations to, *inter alia*, Article 6. It is in this way that in some of the Separate or Dissenting Opinions, remarks on the relationship of reservations and *jus cogens* can be found.

Thus Judge Padilla Nervo stated[16] that 'customary rules belonging to the category of *jus cogens* cannot be subjected to unilateral reservations':

> It follows that if the convention by express provision permits reservations to certain Articles this is due to recognition of the fact that such Articles are not the codification or expression of existing mandatory principles or established binding rules of general international law, which as such are opposable not only to the Contracting Parties, but also to third States.

Similarly, Judge Tanaka intimated that a reservation would be null and void if it were 'contrary to an essential principle of the Continental Shelf institution which must be recognized as *jus cogens*'.[17] Finally, Judge *ad hoc* Sorensen said:[18]

> The acceptance of a reservation . . . does not have the effect of depriving the Convention as a whole or the relevant article in particular of its declaratory character. It only has the effect of establishing a special contractual relationship . . . Provided the customary rule does not belong to the category of *jus cogens*, a special contractual relationship of this nature is not invalid as such.

These three Judges, therefore, accepted the view that a reservation expressly permitted by the terms of a Convention cannot be made so as to compromise provisions belonging to the category of *jus cogens* (and, according to Judge Tanaka, an 'essential principle' of an institution such as, in the case of the Continental Shelf, the equidistance principle, excludes the validity of a reservation).

If States cannot enter into a treaty contrary to a peremptory norm, then

[15] *I.C.J. Reports* 1969, 4. [16] Pp. 97, 98. [17] P. 182. [18] P. 248.

it makes good sense that they cannot agree upon a reservation to and, therefore, a departure from a provision embodying a peremptory norm. In the latter case, however, it would be desirable if the Convention was so framed as to identify provisions in respect of which a reservation is impossible. This is particularly so, when it is remembered that the suggestions made by Judges Padilla Nervo, Tanaka and Sorensen constitute a wholly new development which before 1969 is unlikely even to have been considered by any draftsman. Take the European Convention on Human Rights of 1950. According to Article 64 'any State may, when signing this Convention or when depositing its instrument of ratification, make a reservation in respect of any particular provision of the Convention to the extent that any law then in force in its territory is not in conformity with the provision'. Suppose such a reservation is made in respect of a law then in force which permits any Minister to order the detention without trial of any person in a concentration camp for an indefinite period, and which is therefore contrary to Articles 3, 4 and 5 of the Convention—Articles which it will be difficult not to accept as peremptory norms, as *jus cogens*. Is it really the law that such a reservation is null and void? In the case of the example given the idealist, even if he is a lawyer, may be readily inclined to give an affirmative answer. But would this be a result consonant with the intentions of the High Contracting Parties in 1950? It is submitted that much progress has been made since 1950, that as a matter of construction based on the intentions of 1950 the reservation was probably intended to be effective, but that in 1973 *ordre public international* should be so understood as to invalidate it.

Such a conclusion, it is true, goes far beyond the terms, but is in no sense inconsistent with the spirit, of the advice which in 1951, i. e. before the recognition of the idea of *ordre public international*, the International Court of Justice gave in relation to *Reservations of the Convention on the Prevention and Punishment of the Crime of Genocide*.[19] That Convention was silent on the admissibility and scope of reservations. At the same time the prohibition of genocide is certainly a matter *d'ordre public* of the highest degree. The view of the majority was as follows:[20]

> The object and purpose of the Convention thus *limit* both the freedom of making reservations and that of objecting to them. It follows that it is the compatibility of a reservation with the object and purpose of the Convention that must furnish the criterion for the attitude of a State in making the reservation on accession as well as for the appraisal by a State in objecting to a reservation. Such is the rule of conduct which must guide every State in the appraisal which it must make, individually and from its own standpoint, of the admissibility of any reservation.

[19] *I.C.J. Reports* 1951, 15. [20] P. 24.

The Court, therefore, thought it possible that even in the case of the Genocide Convention and in the absence of any provision on reservation it was possible that a State might make reservations. If today that possibility were held to be excluded the law would have moved forward in a manner which could only be welcomed. In fact Art. 19 of the Vienna Draft Convention on Treaties allows reservations only if they are specified by or compatible with the object and purpose of the treaty.

III

Since 1969 the existence and the scope of fundamental laws have received much emphasis and their legal significance has been greatly extended, perhaps even modified, by the judgment of the International Court of Justice in the *Case of Barcelona Traction*.[21] That case, it will be remembered, was concerned with the question whether and in what circumstances it was open to the State of the corporation's shareholders to afford them diplomatic protection *vis-à-vis* a State which was alleged to have committed an international tort against, and caused injury to, the corporation rather than the shareholders. In introducing the discussion the Court set aside a category of absolute and unqualified rights the infringement of which could be pursued by every State and did not come under the heading of diplomatic protection at all:[22]

> In particular, an essential distinction should be drawn between the obligations of a State towards the international community as a whole, and those arising *vis-à-vis* another State in the field of diplomatic protection. By their very nature the former are the concern of all States. In view of the importance of the rights involved, all States can be held to have a legal interest in their protection; they are obligations *erga omnes*. Such obligations derive, for example, in contemporary international law from the outlawing of acts of aggression, and of genocide, as also from the principles and rules concerning the basic rights of the human person, including protection from slavery and racial discrimination. Some of the corresponding rights of protection have entered into the body of general international law ('*Reservations to the Convention on the Prevention and Punishment of the Crime of Genocide*', *ICJ Reports* 1951,23); others are conferred by international instruments of a universal or quasi-universal character. Obligations the performance of which is the subject of diplomatic protection are not of the same category . . .

[21] *I.C.J. Reports* 1970, 4.

[22] Paragraphs 33–5. It is noteworthy that already Wengler, *Völkerrecht* (1964) p. 412 suggests that in the case of certain norms of customary international law all States have the right to demand their observance in a given case. The learned author does not attempt to define those norms. On the same point see also above n. 6. Doubt about the theory referred to in the text is expressed by Charpentier, *Annuaire Français de Droit International*, 1970, 312.

Thus, within a few months of the conclusion of the Vienna Conference on the Law of Treaties, one finds the International Court of Justice adopting the doctrine of 'the obligations of a State towards the international community as a whole', the clear implication being that their enforcement is open to every State and independent of the conditions in which diplomatic protection can be exercised. It would seem once again that this doctrine is unprecedented. It gives rise to at least three comments of varying importance.

Firstly, if obligations existing *erga omnes* 'are the concern of all States' and 'all States can be held to have a legal interest in their protection', it is likely that their infringement will entitle every State to the exercise of remedies. This would mean that the use of force against one State involves the use of force against all States, so that all States can use force in what one presumably must call self-defence. But it would probably also mean that every State has a cause of action and can exercise judicial remedies. If this is the Court's intention the Foreign Offices of the world will be advised to review their acceptances of the optional clause. State A is alleged to practise or permit slavery. It has submitted to the jurisdiction of the International Court of Justice in relation to every State other than Z. Can Z apply to the Court for an injunction? The question cannot be answered *in abstracto*. Its mere existence must give much food for thought.

Secondly, let it be assumed that State Z can apply to the Court and claim not only a declaration and an injunction, but also damages for the benefit of the group of persons held to be in slavery such as all the inmates of a concentration camp. Let it further be assumed that no damage of any kind is suffered by State Z or its nationals, that Z has not even allowed refugees from A to take residence within its territory. Would it not be a wholly novel step if, in the absence of any legally relevant ties between Z and the subjects of A, the former could, in its own right, claim damages when it has not suffered any damage? The question is one of substance rather than procedure. The assertion of the rights is unlikely to offend the sense of justice of anyone who welcomes additional opportunities for the judicial settlement of disputes and the enforcement of international rights. What is difficult to believe is that those States which have failed to sign the optional clause, which are only too ready to deny the jurisdiction of international tribunals, which are wont to invoke the exclusivity of their domestic jurisdiction and in every other respect succeed in remaining outside the network of international legal control, will be prepared to recognize in fact and in law an enforceable legal duty of almost sensational novelty.

Looking at the matter from the historical point of view it may well be that, in principle and subject to far-reaching limitations to which it will be necessary presently to revert, a majority of the International Court of

Justice would be willing to allow State Z to demand at least a declaration against A. This arises from the aftermath of the *South West Africa Cases* of 1966[23] in which, by the President's casting vote,[24] a Court of seven denied the 'legal right or interest' of Ethiopia and Liberia, independently of the League of Nations itself, to ask for a declaration that by its policy of apartheid South Africa acted in violation of its Mandate over South West Africa. In that case which, as is well known, led to somewhat vehement reactions both within and outside the Court the dissenting Judges (one cannot speak of a minority) went very far in advocating the sufficiency of a general interest to permit the Applicant States' *locus standi*—a sufficiency which, as will appear, by their narrow and incredibly doctrinaire reasoning in *Barcelona Traction*,[25] they disclaimed as a general proposition four years later in no uncertain terms and which, therefore, is likely to be confined to the type of 'right' in issue in the *South West Africa Cases*. Thus in 1966 one finds Judge Koretsky stating[26] that in international courts 'the character of relations and rights is of another kind. Here one cannot think in civil law categories. The notion of a "general interest" finds wider scope in international law'. Or Judge Tanaka (who in 1970 in an entirely consistent manner upheld the right of Belgium to protect the shareholders) in 1966 asserted that 'international law has long recognized that States may have legal interests in matters which do not affect their financial, economic or other material or so-called physical or tangible interests', and he treated as outstanding examples 'the recognition of the legal interests of States in general humanitarian causes, the international efforts to suppress the slave trade, the minorities treaties, the Genocide Convention and the Constitution of the International Labour Organization'.[27] He even went so far in 1966 as to admit at some length that in the field of corporation law the possibility of an individual member being able to 'act as an organ of the whole' was 'highly developed'.[28] We find the same point made in the dissenting opinions delivered by Judges Jessup,[29] Padillo Nervo[30] and Forster.[31] Judge Jessup's analysis ends with the statement[32] 'that there is no generally established *actio popularis* in international law. But international law has accepted the established situations in which States are given a right of action without any showing of individual prejudice or individual substantive interest as distinguished from the general interest.' There is a direct line which leads from these

[23] *I.C.J. Reports*, 1966, 4.

[24] O'Connell (above n. 2) at p. 340 wrongly states: 'by a bare majority'.

[25] See Mann, *American Journal of International Law*, 1973, 259 or below p. 217.

[26] Above n. 23, at p. 242. [27] P. 252. [28] P. 254.

[29] Pp. 373 sqq., particularly p. 374.

[30] Above n. 23, pp. 460 sqq., particularly pp. 462, 463.

[31] Pp. 478, 479. [32] Pp. 387, 388.

and similar utterances in 1966 to the *dictum* in 1970 that obligations *erga omnes* can be enforced by all States, because 'all States can be held to have a legal interest in their protection'.

The third and by far the most important point, alluded to in the preceding paragraph, arises from the limitation inherent in the phrase 'the basic rights of the human person', 'les droits fondamentaux de la personne humaine', a phrase which, somewhat ominously, seems to distinguish between human rights which are not basic rights, and basic human rights. Of the latter the Court gives two examples, namely slavery and racial discrimination. It thus poses the problem of drawing a hitherto unknown line between human rights and basic human rights but also of defining the specific mischiefs which the Court intended to bring within the terms 'slavery and racial discrimination'.

As regards the former point, there exists the depressing suspicion that the Court intended to exclude from the scope of basic human rights those which only the old guard of highly civilized Western States practise and which are not accepted by nations practising inhumanity such as concentration camps, killing without trial, stifling of all freedoms, whether of religion, speech, thought, association and so forth. This, it is to be feared, would be in line with the description which one of the greatest men of our time, Alexander Solzhenitsyn,[33] gave of the United Nations Organization, the judicial organ of which is the International Court of Justice. It

> equates those governments which were freely elected, those which were imposed by force, and those which seized power by force of arms. Thanks to the venal prejudice of the majority of its members, the UN jealously guards the liberty of certain nations and neglects the liberty of others. It obsequiously voted against investigating private grievances—the groans, cries and entreaties of simple, humble individuals, insects too tiny for such a large organisation to concern itself with. The best document it put out in all its twenty-five years was the Declaration of Human Rights, yet the UN did not endeavour to make endorsement of it an obligatory condition of membership, and thus it left ordinary people at the mercy of governments not of their choosing.

That the guarantee of a fair judicial hearing or the protection of property are not basic human rights, must, notwithstanding Articles 10 and 17 of the Universal Declaration of Human Rights, be inferred from the decision in the *Case of Barcelona Traction* itself, for Belgium, acting on behalf of Belgian shareholders, was not allowed to pursue claims arising from denials of justice, excess of jurisdiction and *abus de droit* which were alleged to have been committed by Spain against a Canadian corporation.

[33] One Word of Truth . . . (The Nobel Speech, London 1972) 21.

Indeed, as the Court itself put it with complete frankness and at the same time with a surprising lack of consistency,[34]

> With regard more particularly to human rights, to which reference has already been made in paragraph 34 of this Judgment, it should be noted that these also include protection against denial of justice. However, on the universal level, the instruments which embody human rights do not confer on States capacity to protect the victims of infringements of such rights irrespective of their nationality.

When the Court refers to 'the universal level', it presumably is thinking of the Universal Declaration of Human Rights of 1948. Its Article 10 in fact purports to protect against a denial of justice. Its text does not include any provision relating to methods of protection or enforcement. The Court's statement quoted above is, therefore, correct. But it also applies, for instance, to slavery which the Court had proclaimed to be the subject-matter of universal protection. There is nothing in the Universal Declaration which would render slavery 'the concern of all States', which would 'confer on States the capacity to protect the victims of' slavery irrespective of their nationality. Yet it is this very capacity which the Court asserted. In so doing it created its own scale of values. It introduced distinctions which, it must be suggested with deep regret, can only be described as arbitrary. It allowed contradictions to arise that must lead to much uncertainty.[35]

In these circumstances it is not impossible that in asserting the universal *jus standi* the Court intended to limit it to what the present majority of the United Nations regard as the right of self-determination the denial of which implies the acceptance of slavery and racial discrimination. In other words, it is possible that the Court was merely proclaiming the familiar anti-colonialist policy of the United Nations, without wishing to assert the right of self-determination of such countries as Hungary, Czechoslovakia or East Germany, including the German Democratic Republic. One is reminded of the Declaration on the Granting of Independence to Colonial Countries and Peoples pronounced by the General Assembly of the United Nations in 1960:[36]

[34] Paragraph 91.

[35] Judge Gros (p. 274) said very aptly that 'it is paradoxical, to say the least, to invoke the protection of human rights in the name of universality while at the same time excluding from it the protection of property from unlawful acts in the name of a particular way of thinking which contests that right'. On the point made in the text see also Seidl-Hohenveldern, *Österreichische Zeitschrift für öffentliches Recht*, 1971, 255, at pp. 276–9. It should be made clear that the right to the protection of property was not really in issue in *Barcelona Traction*. In view of the outlook of many of the present members of the International Court of Justice that right would probably have even less of a chance of protection than the right to a fair hearing.

[36] Resolution 1514 (XV), adopted 14 December 1960.

The subjection of peoples to alien subjugation, domination and exploitation constitutes a denial of fundamental human rights, is contrary to the Charter of the United Nations, and is an impediment to the promotion of world peace and co-operation.

It is the 'New Higher Law of Anti-Colonialism' of which Professor Rupert Emerson wrote a few years ago[37] and which Judge Ammoun likes to introduce into his judicial pronouncements. Thus in *Barcelona Traction* itself (which by no stretch of the imagination could be said to have had anything to do with the right of self-determination) he made, among numerous similar observations, the following statements:[38]

Against the defenders of the last bastions of traditional law, there thus stand arrayed, once again, with the support of a Western minority, the serried ranks of the jurists, thinkers and men of action of the Latin-American and Afro-Asian countries, as well as of the socialist countries. For all of them self-determination is now definitely part of positive international law. As is known furthermore, a majority of States, through their representatives at the 1969 Vienna Conference on the Law of Treaties, pronounced in favour of a solution to the problem, of *jus cogens* capable of giving definitive sanction to the principles of the Charter, regarded by them as imperative juridical norms.

And in the course of his Separate Opinion in the *Case of Legal Consequences of the Continued Presence of South Africa in South West Africa*[39] in 1971 Judge Ammoun again spoke at length about the 'imperative character of the right of peoples to self-determination'[40] which, he complained, was 'still not recognized as a juridical norm in the practice of a few rare States or the writings of even rarer theoreticians'.[41] It is true that he also asserted[42] the imperative character 'of the human rights whose violation by the South African authorities' the Court denounced: 'To establish instead, and to enforce, distinctions, exclusions, restrictions and limitations exclusively based on grounds of race, colour, descent or national or ethnic origin which constitute a denial of fundamental human rights is a flagrant violation of the purpose and the principles of the Charter'.[43]

With this view few will disagree, yet the conclusion to which the

[37] The New Higher Law of Anti-Colonialism in 'The Relevance of International Law', *Essays in honour of Leo Gross*, (1968), p. 153. See also Emerson, 'Self-determination', in *American Journal of International Law*, 1971, 459. While this article went through the press, there appeared Sir Gerald Fitzmaurice's Special Report on *The Future of Public International Law* for the Rome Meeting of the Institut de Droit International in September 1973. What the learned author says in paragraphs 42–4 about the 'double standard' and the notion of self-determination is very much in line with the submissions in the text.

[38] P. 312.

[39] *I.C.J. Reports*, 1971, 16.

[40] P. 72.

[41] P. 75.

[42] P. 72.

[43] Paragraph 131.

preceding discussion leads is far from encouraging. It is very likely indeed that there now exists, as part of customary international law, an *actio popularis* where a violation of *jus cogens* is alleged.[43a] For the purpose of this rule, however, not all rights normally having the character of *jus cogens* are certain to be so considered. The prohibition of acts of aggression and, indeed, the use of force and of genocide are clearly peremptory norms the enforcement of which is a community interest, although it is more than doubtful whether in these cases the disregard of the prohibition can ever usefully give rise to the judicial process: an *actio popularis* against a war-like operation seems, to put it at its lowest, a little incongruous. Another case of a peremptory norm coming within the rule arises in the event of a violation of 'the basic rights of the human person'. Here the trouble is that it is far from certain whether this means anything else than the right to freedom from colonial domination. Other human rights may be basic in the eyes of 'the defenders of the last bastions of traditional law', but they are not necessarily basic to others some of whom in certain instances may be found to practise double talk and double standards. Nevertheless those traditionalists might be well advised to put the matter to the test and to avail themselves of a suitable opportunity for challenging prevailing tendencies by bringing an *actio popularis* in defence of rights which are basic to them, but leave 'the serried ranks of the jurists, thinkers and men of action of the Latin-American and Afro-Asian countries as well as of the socialist countries' indifferent. The right to personal freedom might be conveniently asserted. The cases in which that right has been violated in some of the Latin-American, Afro-Asian and socialist countries are numerous. If they were to become 'the concern of all States', if the international community had the legal right and interest to proceed against them, if the defence of the exclusivity of domestic jurisdiction were to disappear from the field, then and only then would the Court's interpretation of the doctrine of *jus cogens* be truly progressive and command universal approval. So long as there is a danger of it being used solely as a weapon against colonialism, there is room for suspecting it as a political exploit.[44]

[43a] See, generally, Schwelb, 'The *actio popularis* and International Law', *Israel Yearbook of Human Rights*, II (1972) 47.

[44] It should be noted that there exists a tendency to create not only peremptory norms of liability, but also crimes—provided of course, that they are limited to certain types. Thus in the Advisory Opinion on South West Africa of 1971 (above n. 39) Judge Ammoun said (p. 79) that 'violations of human rights by the practice of apartheid . . . are no less punishable than the crimes against humanity and war crimes upon which the Charter of the Nuremberg Tribunal visited sanctions', though at p. 80 he added that apartheid should be 'punished as any other attempt upon human equality and individual or national liberty would be'. In his *Third Report on State Responsibility* Professor Ago speaks of similar trends, and reports that Soviet doctrine regards 'genocide, aggression and colonial oppression' as international crimes: *Year Book of the International Law Commission*, 1971 or *UN Document A/CN. 4/246*, 5 March 1971, at p. 33.

IV

The fourth emanation of the doctrine of *jus cogens* which has so far made its appearance is to be found in the law of recognition. It is possibly of the greatest practical significance, for we may be witnessing the emergence of a clearly defined customary duty of non-recognition.

The remarkable Advisory Opinion which the International Court of Justice rendered in 1971 on *South West Africa*[45] was concerned with the question of 'the legal consequences for States of the continued presence of South Africa in Namibia,[46] notwithstanding Security Council Resolution 276 (1970)'. By that Resolution the full text of which cannot, *mirabile dictu*, be found anywhere in the 340 pages of judgment and opinions, but an extract of which is included in Judge Onyeama's Separate Opinion,[47] the Security Council 'declares that the continued presence of the South African authorities in Namibia is illegal' and 'calls upon all States . . . to refrain from any dealings with the government of South Africa which are inconsistent' with the preceding declaration. This followed upon the General Assembly's much discussed Resolution 2145 of 27 October 1966 the terms of which, one notes with even greater surprise, can only be found towards the end of Judge Sir Gerald Fitzmaurice's Dissenting Opinion.[48] By that Resolution the General Assembly 'decides' that South Africa's Mandate 'is . . . terminated'. The Court reached the conclusion that by virtue of both or either of these Resolutions the Mandate had been effectively terminated and South Africa's presence in South West Africa was illegal. The Court then proceeded to rule that member States of the United Nations were under a duty of non-recognition which, in general terms, involved the 'obligation to recognize the illegality of South Africa's presence in Namibia and the invalidity of its acts on behalf of or concerning Namibia, and to refrain from any acts and in particular any dealings with the Government of South Africa implying recognition of the legality of, or lending support or assistance to, such presence and administration'.[49]

These aspects of the Advisory Opinion, happily, do not in the present context require any analysis. There is nothing new in the fact that an international organization, acting within its constitutional powers, finds one of its member States guilty of a breach of duty or an illegality and imposes upon member States a duty of non-recognition in the nature of sanctions. In 1932 the League of Nations adopted a Resolution directed against Japan's aggression in Manchuria, according to which 'it is incumbent upon the members of the League of Nations not to recognize any

[45] *I.C.J. Reports*, 1971, 16.

[46] The General Assembly of the United Nations, it appears, gave to South West Africa the name of Namibia. In the course of the present paper it will not be used.

[47] P. 147. [48] P. 305. [49] P. 48.

situation, treaty or agreement which may be brought about by means contrary to the Covenant of the League of Nations or to the Pact of Paris',[50] and in 1933 American States concluded treaties precluding the recognition of territorial acquisitions achieved by aggression.[51] Nor can there be any doubt that, whatever the legal and factual basis in the specific case of South West Africa may have been, in general the United Nations Organization enjoys the power, subject to clearly defined conditions, to impose upon its members a duty of non-recognition as one of the 'measures not involving the use of armed forces' which by Art. 41 of the Charter of the Security Council may require member States to take 'to give effect to its decisions'. Assuming, therefore, that the Mandate was validly terminated, that the presence of South Africa in South West Africa is illegal and that the Security Council acted, and was entitled to act, in accordance with Art. 41,[52] the Advisory Opinion does not up to this point have any direct bearing upon the subject matter of the present essay. It merely provides, and is here without discussion accepted as providing, the background to the grave problem arising from the further legal principles which the Court, in the face of dissents by Judges Sir Gerald Fitzmaurice, Gros, Petren and Onyeama, laid down in regard to non-member States.

The rule applicable to them may probably be formulated as follows: if a member State of an international organization has committed a breach of the treaty constituting the organization and for this reason has been judicially found to be acting illegally, a non-member State cannot disclaim any concern with the treaty to which it is not a party, but is bound, within its own sphere, to implement the duty of non-recognition which the illegality imposes upon member States. The illegality exists *erga omnes*. More particularly the Court stated:[53]

> In the view of the court, the termination of the Mandate and the declaration of the illegality of South Africa's presence in Namibia are opposable to all States in the sense of barring *erga omnes* the legality of a situation which is maintained in violation of international law: in particular, no State which enters into relations with South Africa concerning Namibia may expect the United Nations or its Members to recognize the validity or effects of such relationship or of the consequences thereof. The Mandate having been terminated by decision of the international organisation in which the supervisory authority over its administration was vested, and South Africa's continued presence in Namibia having been

[50] H. Lauterpacht, *Recognition in International Law* (1947), p. 417.

[51] Ibid., p. 419.

[52] The remarkable fact is that the Opinion does not rest upon Art. 41 the conditions of which were lacking. The Court believed to be able to found upon Articles 24 and 25 of the Charter. This is, perhaps, the most astonishing part of the opinion.

[53] Paragraph 126.

declared illegal, it is for non-member States to act in accordance with those decisions.

Accordingly, the Court expressed its opinion[54] 'that it is incumbent upon States which are not Members of the United Nations to give assistance' within the scope of the duties imposed upon Members in the action taken with regard to South West Africa.[55]

What is the legal basis of the Court's rulings in relation to non-member States? No reason of any kind is vouchsafed by the Court itself. No satisfactory explanation is supplied by Art. 2 (6) of the Charter according to which the 'Organisation shall ensure that States which are not Members of the United Nations act in accordance with these Principles so far as may be necessary for the maintenance of international peace and security'. This provision imposes a duty upon the United Nations rather than non-members and at the same time confines it to a case which does not arise in South West Africa, viz. the maintenance of international peace and security. Nor can there be any doubt that even if the Security Council had imposed the duty of non-recognition by way of sanctions under Art. 41, this could not have extended to non-member States, and the opposite has so far not been suggested.[56] Nor is an acceptable explanation furnished by Judge de Castro[57] according to whom the United Nations' right to have the termination of the Mandate respected by non-members is the same 'as that of an owner of property who withdraws the mandate given by him to administer his property'. It is by no means certain that under the law of civilized nations a third party commits a tort and is guilty of an illegality if he has dealings with an administrator of property merely because the latter's mandate has been withdrawn.

It is suggested that the true rationale of the Court's holding ought to be found in the admittedly unexpressed idea that he who assists in the consummation of an illegal act must be treated as a party to it.[58] By giving assistance to or having intercourse with South Africa in relation to South West Africa a non-member State would become an accessory to an international illegality. This may well be said to be a rule of customary international law derived from the general principles of law recognized by

[54] P. 58, paragraph 3.

[55] Perhaps it would have been preferable if the Court had defined the duty of non-members in a negative manner: it is incumbent upon them not to give assistance to anyone in the commission or the continuation of acts flowing from the illegality.

[56] It is clearly not suggested by Brownlie, (above n. 2) pp. 100, 101. That the policy of sanctions against Rhodesia does not bind such countries as Germany or Switzerland would seem to be accepted: von Schenck, *ZaöRVR* 29 (1969) 257, particularly at pp. 269–79; R. L. Bindschedler, ibid. 28 (1968) 1. As to Austria where the position is, of course, different, as she is a member State, see Zemanek, ibid. p. 16.

[57] P. 219.

[58] There must, of course, be a clear case of illegality. In the view of some lawyers it is not certain whether the Advisory Opinion has established such a case.

civilized nations and by no means limited to the sphere of international organizations. Such a rule would seem to constitute an impressive and progressive development of the law and would, in principle, be entitled to support.

Probably, however, it is a novel proposition. The suggestion, it is true, has been made that if the judicial organs of a State give effect to the law of a foreign country, which results from an international illegality, they may assist in the consummation of an international delinquency and thus incur responsibility.[59] But what is believed to be a salutary rule in the hands of tribunals does not necessarily (yet) apply universally. In fact in customary international law there is as yet no clear trace of the assertion of a duty of non-recognition where a violation of *jus cogens*, an illegality, an infringement of *ordre public international* falls to be considered, and it is almost with incredulity that one finds so cautious a lawyer as Judge Dillard speaking without qualification of 'the obligations of States to refuse official recognition to a government illegally in control of a territory'.[60] Sir Hersch Lauterpacht whose exposition of the principle of non-recognition[61] is perhaps not the most succinct of his contributions did not suggest the existence of a duty. Elsewhere recognition and non-recognition are treated as matters of policy or discretion[62] and no distinction is made as to whether or not the situation is brought about by *injuria*. Professor Brownlie has in recent months helpfully indicated a line of inquiry:[63] according to him the specific content of peremptory norms 'involves the irrelevance of protest, recognition and acquiescence: prescription cannot purge this type of illegality. Moreover it is arguable that *jus cogens* curtails various privileges . . .' But the irrelevance of recognition, i.e. the fact that a situation created in disregard of a rule of international *jus cogens* cannot become valid and effective as a result of recognition, is a far cry from the duty of non-recognition such as the Advisory Opinion lays down.

Above all, however, the explanation of that Opinion offered above cannot pray State practice in aid. If non-intervention in matters of domestic jurisdiction is a rule of *jus cogens* the occupation of Czechoslovakia by the Soviet Union in 1968 ought to have required, but did not

[59] See Mann, *Studies in International Law* (1973) p. 380 or 70 (1954) *L.Q.R.* 181, at pp. 193, 194; and see Wortley, *Expropriation in Public International Law* (1959) p. 17: 'Indeed, to recognise a title so acquired might itself be a breach of international law'. Or Kraus, *Festschrift für Laun* (1953) 231: 'the Judge would be compelled to become an instrument in implementing a breach of public international law'. Similarly Dahm, *Festschrift für Kraus* (1964) pp. 79–81.

[60] *I.C.J. Reports*, 1971, 165.

[61] Above n. 50, at pp. 409 sqq.

[62] Sir Hersch Lauterpacht himself (loc. cit. at pp. 1, 61 sqq., 158, 240) admits that this is the predominant view. In the same sense, for instance, Brownlie (above n. 2) p. 94 or Bindschedler, *Berichte der Deutschen Gesellschaft für Völkerrecht* 4 (1961) 20. See, however, Dahm, I, pp. 132 sqq.

[63] Above n. 2, at p. 501.

meet with, non-recognition. If annexation by the use of force is peremptorily prohibited, the conquest of Goa by India in 1961 might have attracted the sanction of non-recognition.[64] If self-determination is *d'ordre public international*, many countries, among them, for instance, West Irian[65] between 1963 and 1969, would have suffered a different fate at the hands of the community of nations. In particular, the right of self-determination, so forcefully put forward as a fundamental law, was most recently and most strikingly disregarded and infringed in the case of the German Democratic Republic. Neither the creation nor the continuation of that State was accompanied by the exercise of the right of self-determination, and it is no more than a sad and cynical case of lip-service, when the 'Fundamental Treaty' between the Federal Republic and the German Democratic Republic provides in Article 2 that both States will be guided by the 'purposes and principles which are laid down in the Charter of the United Nations, particularly . . . the right of self-determination, the protection of human rights and non-discrimination'.[66] Nor did the absence of any right, opportunity or, indeed possibility for the East German people 'to choose for themselves a form of political organization and their relations to other groups'[67] prevent any State at the end of 1972 or early 1973 granting recognition to a State which in other respects as well might be said to disregard the fundamental laws of nations. In short, there is no evidence that the community of States has as yet abandoned the principle that the grant or withdrawal of recognition is a political act which no State is under a duty, but every State is at liberty, to perform and which regulates the relationship between the two states concerned, irrespective of the position in regard to third States[68] and irrespective of the legality of the situation.

It cannot, in fact, be denied that a general duty of non-recognition, arising wherever an international illegality and its consequences are in issue, would involve far too high a standard and would be impracticable. It would go far beyond the Stimson doctrine[69] which expressed a policy rather than a duty, and even so could not be consistently applied. It would strain the powers and resources of international law as at present practised. It would, in short, be wholly unrealistic and, therefore, unsound.

[64] On the incident see Sohn, *Cases on United Nations Law* (1967) 415, 416, with further references.

[65] For an informative survey see von Mangoldt, *ZaöRVR* 31 (1971) 197.

[66] for the text see *Europa-Archiv*, 1973 D 13.

[67] See the definition by Brownlie (above n. 55) p. 575.

[68] The fact that recognition has effect (only) between the recognizing and recognized State or Government and has always such effect is frequently overlooked, but is quite fundamental. It helps to understand the futility of most of the theories which dominate the literature on the subject.

[69] On which see MacNair, *British Year Book of International Law*, 1933, 65.

How, then, did the International Court of Justice come to propound a non-member State's duty of non-recognition?

The only possible, though wholly unattractive, explanation would seem to be that once again the Court created a special legal duty peculiar and confined to anti-colonialism: colonialism is an illegality of such singular character that, in the view of the Court, it requires and permits a wholly unique reaction on the part of all members of the family of nations, whether they are or are not members of the United Nations, viz. assistance in its elimination. Even such a principle is devoid of any legal basis, unless one subscribes to the much wider rule of customary international law which has been suggested. But it would confine the doctrine within reasonably acceptable bounds. It would also make it clear that at the present time much of the doctrine of *jus cogens* is hardly more than an anti-colonialist device. There only remains the hope that in the fullness of time it will acquire broader scope and a firm foundation in law.

V

In conclusion it is apparent that the doctrine of *jus cogens*, outside the sphere of treaties, is still in an early state of development. It is accordingly too soon to pass judgment upon its scope and strength. Yet it is characterized by an unusual feature. Judicial tribunals in general and international tribunals in particular have in the past proved diffident in pronouncing upon new legal theories. This tendency has been treated as the product of that caution and perhaps even conservatism which is both expressive of and peculiar to the judicial mind. *Jus cogens*, on the other hand, derives its momentum from the International Court of Justice which in the short space of about five years extended it from the law of treaties to reservations, diplomatic protection and recognition. What is even more significant is that in a large degree it originates from dicta which were unnecessary to the decision and which convey the impression of having been studiously planted in the text or artificially dragged into the arena.[70] It would be a great pity if a potentially fruitful doctrine of wide and general impact came to be regarded as the outcome of a specific and limited approach, of a narrow-minded and prejudiced attitude or involved a political programme dear to the General Assembly of the United Nations, that is to say, 'value judgments', evaluations of a political rather than a legal character. This is the danger against which lawyers must guard.

[70] Seidl-Hohenveldern (above n. 35) suggests that the dictum in *Barcelona Traction* (above n. 21) was a reaction against the decision in the *South West Africa Case* of 1966 (above n. 25).

3

Britain's Bill of Rights

I

BLACKSTONE did not know the conception of human or fundamental rights. Quoting Montesquieu he spoke, it is true, of England as 'a land, perhaps the only one in the universe, in which political or civil liberty is the very end and scope of the constitution.'[1] This liberty meant 'the power of doing whatever the laws permit; which is only to be effected by a general conformity of all orders and degrees to those equitable rules of action, by which the meanest individual is protected from the insults and oppression of the greatest.'[2] And later in his *Commentaries*[3] he dwells on the personal liberty of individuals which 'the law of England regards, asserts and preserves' and which, with the right of personal security and the right of property, constitutes 'in a peculiar and emphatical manner the rights of the people of England.'[4] All these rights and their incidence to Blackstone were aspects of the law of nature or of natural law which he treats as the source and origin of the common law. But while, of course, he emphasizes the privileges conferred by such specific instruments as the Great Charter, the petition of right, the bill of rights and the act of settlement,[5] the idea that human beings could have enforceable rights against the State which no legislator can destroy, that such rights are capable of being spelled out, defined and enumerated so as to override legislation, that there could be a real Bill of Rights such as first appeared in the Constitutions of the American States in 1776 and as the United States adopted in 1791, that there could be judicial review of the constitutional validity of legislation—that idea was as alien to Blackstone in 1765 as it is to most English lawyers today.

Blackstone, however, at least admitted one qualification: 'acts of parliament that are impossible to be performed are of no validity; and if there arises out of them collaterally any absurd consequences, manifestly contradictory to common reason, they are, with regard to those collateral consequences, void.'[6] He does not tell us what type of case he had in

[1] *Commentaries on the Laws of England*, p. 6. At the time Blackstone wrote the statement was no doubt true.

[2] P. 6. [3] P. 134. [4] P. 129. [5] See, e.g, pp. 127, 128. [6] P. 91.

This is the text of the Third Blackstone Lecture delivered in the University of Oxford under the auspices of Pembroke College on May 27, 1978. *Law Quarterly Review* 94 (1978) 512–33.

mind. Was he thinking of no more than Holt C.J.'s far-fetched example:[7] 'An act of parliament may not make adultery lawful, that is, it cannot make it lawful for A to lie with the wife of B'? Such absurd and unrealistic reasoning makes it apparent that there is little difference between Blackstone in 1765 and Lord Reid in 1974 who summarized the doctrine developed in the nineteenth century under the influence of Bentham and Austin and universally accepted by English lawyers at the present time:[8]

> In earlier times many learned lawyers seem to have believed that an Act of Parliament could be disregarded in so far as it was contrary to the law of God or the law of nature or natural justice, but since the supremacy of Parliament was finally demonstrated by the Revolution of 1688 any such idea has become obsolete.

This seems to sound the death-knell of any residual vestige of fundamental rights in modern English law. Nonetheless, in passing, one feels bound diffidently and most respectfully to put a question. Suppose Parliament enacts a statute depriving Jews of their British nationality, prohibiting marriages between Christians and non-Christians, dissolving marriages between blacks and whites or vesting the property of all red-haired women in the State. Is it really suggested that English judges would have to apply and would in fact apply such a law? Do not evade the issue, do not avoid the legal test by asserting that, as we all hope and believe, no English Parliament would ever pass such a statute. Would the hypothetical question really have to be answered in the affirmative, while a similar German statute was condemned by four Law Lords as constituting 'so grave an infringement of human rights that the courts of this country ought to refuse to recognise it as a law at all'?[9] We certainly cannot forget that Lord Pearson in the House of Lords[10] and Buckley and Orr L.JJ. in the Court of Appeal[11] felt reluctantly constrained to bow to the 'supremacy' of a German 'law-giver' whose régime had ended more than 30 years earlier. Nor can we forget that Dicey taught almost a century ago that 'a modern judge would not listen to a barrister who argued that an Act of Parliament was invalid because it was immoral or because it went beyond the limits of parliamentary authority.'[12] The possibility of the literal application of Lord Reid's statement of the law, therefore, cannot be

[7] *City of London* v. *Wood* (1701) 12 Mod. 669, 688.

[8] *Pickin* v. *British Railways Board* [1974] A.C. 765, 782, and see Lord Simon of Glaisdale at p. 798. In the same sense *Madzimbamuto* v. *Lardner-Burke* [1969] 1 A.C. 645, 723.

[9] *Oppenheimer* v. *Cattermole* [1976] A.C. 249, 278, *per* Lord Cross of Chelsea, and see Lord Salmon at p. 282. Lord Hailsham of St Marylebone and Lord Hodson agreed. On the point of English constitutional law discussed in the text see the extremely cautious remarks in Wade & Phillips, *Constitutional and Administrative Law* (9th edn., 1977, by Bradley), at pp. 64, 65.

[10] At p. 265. [11] [1973] Ch. 264, 273 and 274 respectively.

[12] *Lectures on the Law of the Constitution* (2nd edn., 1886), Lecture II (p. 59).

excluded. Yet the likelihood should be denied. For more than 300 years England has been spared the necessity of facing the question which was raised as a hypothesis. Lord Reid as well as many English lawyers before him failed, so one may confidently suggest, to have it in view. In the extreme and revolutionary circumstances which have been put English judges could no doubt find a legally convincing reason for reverting to the tradition of the fundamental law. The real question would be whether, in the condition which has been assumed, they would have the strength of character to search for it. They might remember that no less a connoisseur of the English tradition than Sir Winston Churchill wrote that Magna Carta raised 'the underlying idea of the sovereignty of law . . . into a doctrine for the national state. And when in subsequent ages the State, swollen with its own authority, has attempted to ride roughshod over the rights or liberties of the subject it is to this doctrine that appeal has again and again been made, and never, as yet, without success.'[13] Sovereignty of the law, however, presupposes judicial review, that hallmark of constitutional government,[14] and is in the last resort irreconcilable with the sovereignty of Parliament.

However this may be, it must be emphasized that at the present time Britain has nothing in the nature of a Bill of Rights which embodies human rights and fundamental laws and is superior to and immune against parliamentary legislation. Such human rights as the law of this country recognizes are almost entirely judge-made and in many instances involve no more than a rebuttable presumption to the effect that Parliament is unlikely to have intended to interfere with or destroy them. Thus judges have allowed the principle of personal freedom to be carried to the absurd length that every British subject can at any time and as often as he pleases change his name and so become untraceable, possibly by means of a passport obtainable with a minimum of formality at every post office. Judges have established the rule that 'everyone charged with a criminal offence shall have the right to be presumed innocent until proved guilty according to the law.'[15] Judges have laid it down that no one is 'to be

[13] *A History of the English-speaking Peoples* (1956), Vol. I, p. 201 (end of Chap. VII).

[14] It is most important to realize that judicial review is an essential feature of a real, genuine, living Constitution. Judicial review is the great contribution of the Framers of the American Constitution, as is rightly emphasized by Professor Bernard Schwartz, *The Great Rights of Mankind* (New York 1977), p. 19. See also pp. 93, 116, 169, as well as p. 168 with a reference to Madison's description of judicial review as an 'impenetrable bulwark against every assumption of power.' The writer would like to pay a most grateful tribute to Professor Schwartz's excellent book as well as to his earlier publications on the American Constitution to which he is deeply indebted. The title of the book repeats Madison's memorable phrase quoted on p. 160.

[15] Art. 14 (2) of the International Covenant on Civil and Political Rights (Cmnd. 6702), and Art. 6 (2) of the European Convention, and as to English Law see the discussion by Glanville Williams, *Criminal Law* (2nd edn., 1961), Section 286.

compelled to testify against himself.'[16] The right of peaceful assembly,[17] the right to freedom of association[18] and the right to a fair hearing (or due process of law)[19] is judge-made. The freedom of the press has been proclaimed by judges.[20] So has the most important rule that an executive act resulting from an abuse of discretion is void[21] or that the exclusion of a legal remedy against such an act presupposes the executive observing the limits of their functions.[22] Judges have developed a presumption against the restrospective effect of legislation.[23] It is the judiciary which is responsible for the important presumption that no crime can be committed without a guilty mind (*mens rea*).[24] The judges have laid down the rule of statutory interpretation according to which legislation is presumed not to intend to violate international law[25] or to take property without compensation.[26] These and many similar rules are ordinary rules of law which cannot fairly be described as forming part of a Constitution in the traditional sense of the term. They can at any time be abolished or reduced by a Parliament which, in contrast to the medieval monarch, is not *legibus tenetur*, which is 'sovereign' and, therefore, can act by a simple majority—and this can conceivably consist of a minority of the Members of Parliament as a whole, may represent a minority of popular votes and may act upon the command of whips who in turn are subject to the orders of the few men forming the Cabinet, yet the process (which Madison described as the greatest danger, viz. 'Prerogative of Majority'[27] and which

[16] Art. 14 (3) (*g*) of the Covenant mentioned in note 15 and as to English law *R.* v. *Boyes* (1861) 1 B. & S. 311 and many later cases.

[17] Art. 21 of the Covenant mentioned in note 15 or Art. 11 of the European Convention on Human Rights, and as to English law *Hubbard* v. *Pitt*, [1976] QB 269, 281 *per* Lord Denning M.R. The right includes peaceful picketing.

[18] Art. 22 of the Covenant mentioned in note 15 or Art. 11 of the European Convention, and as to English law see Halsbury (Hailsham), *Constitutional Law*, Vol. 8, para. 837. Cf. as to Trinidad and Tobago (another country to which by S.I. 1961 No. 1875 the United Kingdom gave a Constitution containing a Bill of Rights) see *Collymore* v. *Attorney-General* [1970] A.C. 582, a decision which is not without interest to the law of the United Kingdom: freedom of association is not affected by restrictions on the freedom to strike or to bargain collectively.

[19] In England referred to as the principles of natural justice.

[20] Art. 19 (2) of the Covenant mentioned in note 15 or Art. 10 of the European Convention, and as to English law see *Bonnard* v. *Perryman*, [1891] 2 Ch. 269, 281.

[21] *Padfield* v. *Minister of Agriculture, Fisheries and Food*, [1968] A.C. 997; *Congreve* v. *Home Office* [1976] Q.B. 629.

[22] *Anisminic Ltd.* v. *Foreign Compensation Commission*, [1969] 2 A.C. 147.

[23] Art. 15 of the Covenant mentioned in note 15 and as to English law see *Phillips* v. *Eyre* (1870) L.R. 6 Q.B. 1; *Ingle* v. *Farrand* [1927] A.C. 417.

[24] *Brend* v. *Wood* (1946) 62 TLR 462, *per* Lord Goddard C.J., as frequently approved in subsequent cases.

[25] Maxwell, *Interpretation of Statutes* (12th ed., 1969), p. 183.

[26] For a recent dictum see *Westminster Bank* v. *Beverley Borough Council*, [1969] 1 Q.B. 499 or *Central Control Board (liquor traffic)* v. *Cannon Brewery Co Ltd.*, [1919] A.C. 744, 752 *per* Lord Atkinson.

[27] Quoted by Schwartz (above note 14), p. 169.

Lord Hailsham called Elective Dictatorship) is said to constitute the democratic ideal and to be the guardian of the rule of law.

At the same time Britain is a party to three and possibly four Conventions guaranteeing human rights and fundamental laws. None of them has been directly incorporated into English law. This creates a paradox in no less than three respects. Firstly Britain has assumed international obligations, but prima facie done nothing to secure their implementation, and even where their terms are at present being observed nothing has been done to prevent future inconsistent legislation coming into force and superseding the present law by virture of the rule *lex posterior derogat priori*. Nor can it be asserted that as a result of a non-legal, non-binding convention Parliament would in fact refrain from interfering with such rules of constitutional significance as the common law has developed. In respect of each of them exceptions are to be found in the statute book; it must suffice merely by way of example to refer to the War Damage Act 1965 setting aside the decision of the House of Lords in *Burmah Oil Co. Ltd.* v. *Lord Advocate*[28] or to section 18 of the Petroleum Submarine Pipelines Act 1975 unilaterally altering the terms granted by earlier licences. It should, secondly, be remembered that, while such is the position in Britain, it was in Britain also that the idea of fundamental laws originated and it was from Britain that it spread all over the world, probably no country other than Britain even in recent years having brought about the independence of so many modern States and secured for them Constitutions which contained (but frequently no longer contain or practise) long chapters on the 'Protection of Fundamental Rights and Freedoms of the Individual.'[29] Thirdly, it is a remarkable fact that in England the very body of intellectual opinion which one would expect to be passionately in favour of fundamental rights and their guarantee by judicial review is hostile to it. Thus the late Professor Harold Laski has stated[30] that

> the tendencies of the modern State run counter to the main principles upon which the common law has been built. The result is an effort on the part of the judiciary to minimise the consequences of those tendencies in a way which consciously hampers the purposes of the administrator. The judges spare no pains in attacking parliamentary decisions it is not their function to criticise. They are occupied in the construction of what is hardly less than a fundamental law which they use to confine the ambit of statutes within the limit of policies they happen to approve . . . They interpret the "rule of law" as though they are themselves the masters of a "higher law" than that of sovereign legislator the consent of which they

[28] [1965] A.C. 75.

[29] See, for instance, Sierra Leone Independence Order 1961, S.I. No. 741; Malawi Independence Order 1964, SI No. 916; Zambia Independence Order 1964, S.I. No. 1652. And see above note 18.

[30] *Parliamentary Government in England* (1945), pp. 367, 368.

themselves determine and the particular relevance of which they themselves decide. It is at least not excessive to say that they bring to the interpretation of the modern State and its processes habits of interpretation which, at least by implication, deny the validity of many of the ends to which its power is devoted.

And the friend and distinguished Blackstone lecturer in 1977[31] followed similar lines of thought, when in the context of labour law he revived the perennial argument that a bill of rights shifts much of the power of policy- and law-making (but also of protection) 'from the democratically elected legislature' to the judiciary. This, indeed, is the reason why in the words of an eminent Italian lawyer[32] judicial review 'remains an enigmatic institution. It is, on the one hand, an aspect of man's never-ending attempt to find something immutable in the continuous change which is his destiny. Laws change, but the Law must remain, and with it the fundamental values; a law which contravenes that Higher Law is not law at all.' On the other hand judicial review claims the right 'to frustrate, in certain situations, the will of the majority. Its decisions are often pre-eminently political, yet they are made by men not themselves responsible to the electorate.' Do not let us overrate the point: in essence, though to a lesser degree, not only judicial review, but the judicial process as a whole is exposed to the dilemma.

Yet there remains a question of paramount significance: seeing that Britain has assumed far-reaching international obligations, what is their status and effect in Britain today?

II

Neither the European Convention for the Protection of Human Rights and Fundamental Freedoms ratified by Mr Attlee's Government on behalf of the United Kingdom on 22 February, 1951, nor the International Covenant on Economic, Social and Cultural Rights nor the International Covenant on Civil and Political Rights, both ratified by Mr Callaghan's Government on behalf of the United Kingdom on 20 May, 1976, and in force since 20 August, 1976, have been incorporated into the law of the United Kingdom. They do not form part of its law and cannot be applied

[31] Sir Otto Kahn-Freund [1976] *Camb.L.J.* 240, 266, 270. The argument goes back at least to the debates preceding the ratification of the Constitution of the United States of America in 1789. See, for instance, the *Brutus* letter and its refutation in *The Federalist*. In fact the argument is perennial. In 1940 Mr. Justice Frankfurter rightly spoke of judicial review being 'a deliberate check upon democracy through an organ of government not subject to popular control' (*Law and Men*, p. 17). This is and always has been the very characteristic, but also the very virtue of judicial review. But, as has frequently been pointed out, an institution democratically created cannot be called undemocratic: see Edgar Bodenheimer, *A Treatise on Justice* (New York, 1967), pp. 136 sqq.

[32] Cappelletti, *Judicial Review in the Contemporary World* (1971), pp. vii and 98.

as law by its courts.[33] Nor can they be indirectly applied, for instance by invoking them as a head of public policy, for if they were applied for the purpose of setting aside a result required by the ordinary law of England they would be put into operation without parliamentary sanction, and this would be contrary to a firmly established principle of British consitutional law.[34]

On the other hand there is no reason why those treaties should not be resorted to for the purpose of interpreting, testing and even developing common law as well as statutory rules. This in fact is what English courts have in the course of the last few years done in application of the European Convention, while the two international Covenants have until now been ignored not only by the courts, but also by the Grunwick Court of Inquiry which was presided over by Lord Scarman and which in its Report of August 1977 referred to the Universal Declaration of Human Rights of 1948 (which undoubtedly never was or was intended to be legally binding) rather than the International Covenants.[35]

Probably the first reference to the European Convention on Human Rights in an English decision occurs in Lord Reid's speech in *Waddington* v. *Miah*[36] in 1974, when the penal provisions of the Immigration Act 1971 fell to be construed. Denying retrospective effect to them Lord Reid referred to Article 7 of the European Convention according to which 'no one shall be held guilty of any criminal offence on account of any act or omission which did not constitute a criminal offence under national or international law at the time when it was committed.' In view of this prohibition it was thought 'hardly credible that any government department would promote or that Parliament would pass retrospective criminal legislation.' This is a perfectly legitimate and, indeed, welcome argument, for it is in line with the presumption that Parliament intends to comply with the country's international obligations.[37]

The relevance of the European Convention became a much more serious issue in three further cases relating to the Immigration Act 1971, for they involved the question whether and in what sense the Executive can allow itself to be guided by the terms of the Convention as interpreted at Strasbourg. The development of the law on this important point started in 1975. In the first case, decided in May of that year,[38] the applicant was an illegal immigrant from India who, while detained pending deportation, requested facilities to marry a woman previously unknown to him. His application for an order of mandamus was based, *inter alia*, on Article 12

[33] The principal authority probably still is *Attorney-General for Canada* v. *Attorney-General for Ontario*, [1937] A.C. 326, but there are numerous more recent authorities.

[34] Mann, *Studies in International Law*, pp. 340 sqq.

[35] Cmnd. 6922, paras. 55 and 56. [36] [1974] 1 W.L.R. 692, 694. [37] See above note 25.

[38] *R.* v. *Secretary of State for the Home Department, ex p. Bhajan Singh*, [1976] Q.B. 198.

of the Convention according to which men and women of marriageable age have the right to marry and found a family. Dismissing the application Lord Denning M.R. with whom Browne and Geoffrey Lane L.JJ. agreed stated 'that the immigration officers and the Secretary of State in exercising their duties ought to bear in mind the principles stated in the Convention. They ought, consciously or unconsciously, to have regard to the principles in it, because, after all, the principles stated in the Convention are only the principles of fair dealing and it is their duty to act fairly.'[39] Later in 1975 the Court of Appeal had to consider the case of two women from India and Bangladesh respectively, to whom the Home Office had denied the opportunity of joining their husbands who were lawfully in this country. Their applications for orders of mandamus succeeded. Neither Lord Denning M.R. nor Lawton L.J. referred to the European Convention, though the latter emphasized that 'fundamental legal rights' were involved. Scarman L.J. (as he then was), however, stated that the hallowed principles enshrined in Magna Carta were now reinforced by the European Convention 'to which it is now the duty of our public authorities in administering the law, including the Immigration Act 1971, and of our courts in interpreting and applying the law, including the act, to have regard,' and he invoked Article 8 which guarantees to everyone the right to respect for his private and family life.[40] Finally one comes to a case in 1976[41] in which another foreign wife, this time unsuccessfully, asked for an order enabling her to join her husband in England and relied on Article 8. Lord Denning M.R. expressly amended the statement made by him a year earlier.[42] He now thought that he had been 'asking too much of the immigration officers. They cannot be expected to know or to apply the Convention. They must go simply by the immigration rules laid down by the Secretary of State and not by the Convention the terms of which give rise to much uncertainty and Article 8 of which is so wide as to be incapable of practical application.'[43] Both Roskill and Geoffrey Lane L.JJ. not only agreed, but expressly dissociated themselves from Lord Scarman's *obiter dictum*. In the most recent case the latter reiterated his view in striking circumstances.[44] The question was whether the Inner London Education Authority had acted 'reasonably' within the meaning of the Trade Union and Labour Relations Act 1974, when they dismissed a devout Muslim teacher, who, while receiving full pay and in breach of his

[39] p. 231. It was held, however, that Art. 12 does not simply give the right to marry, but was subject to Art. 5 (1) (*f*).

[40] *R.* v. *Secretary of State for the Home Department, ex p. Phansopkar*, [1976] Q.B. 606, 626.

[41] *R.* v. *Chief Immigration Officer, Heathrow Airport, ex p. Salamat Bibi*, [1976] 1 WLR 979.

[42] Note 38.

[43] Pp. 847, 848.

[44] *Ahmad* v. *Inner London Education Authority*, [1978] Q.B. 36.

contractual terms, absented himself every Friday afternoon for about three-quarters of an hour from his teaching duties in order to attend prayers at the nearest mosque. The Industrial Tribunal and the Employment Appeal Tribunal held the dismissal to be fair. In the Court of Appeal Lord Denning M.R. and Orr L.J. agreed and their decision commands respectful approval. What matters in the present context is that they saw nothing in Article 9 of the European Convention to protect the plaintiff. This guarantees freedom of thought, conscience and religion and the right of worship, but in the words of Lord Denning 'must be subject to the rights of the education authorities under the contract and to the interests of the children whom he is paid to teach.'[45] Scarman L.J. disagreed. His judgment is very detailed, but its kernel is probably contained in the rejection of the consequence that[46]

> a Muslim who took his religious duty seriously could never accept employment as a full-time teacher, but must be content with the lesser emoluments of part-time service. In modern British society with its elaborate protection of the individual from discrimination arising from race, colour, religion or sex, and against the background of the European Convention, this is unacceptable, inconsistent with the policy of modern statute law, and almost certainly a breach of our international obligations.

In the result the present technical position without doubt is that, since the Convention is not part of the law, it cannot be used otherwise than as a not very strong guide to statutory interpretation.

Yet the question arises whether Lord Denning's original approach, shared by Lord Scarman, does not have much to commend it. No doubt the Convention not being part of English law cannot be applied or resorted to in the face of inconsistent statutory provisions, though it may provide some guidance in solving any ambiguity of the words used by the legislator. Still less can the Convention override statutory provisions, so that legislation plainly contrary to the Convention has to be given full effect by the Judiciary and the Executive. But should it not be taken into account where the exercise of discretion falls to be considered or where general terms such as 'fair', 'reasonable', 'expedient', 'arbitrary', 'abuse' have to be applied to a specific set of facts, where in other words judgment has to be passed in the light of values or standards?[47] The reason why an affirmative answer may not be out of place is that the Convention is not

[45] At p. 41.

[46] At p. 50. It is submitted with great respect that Lord Scarman's judgment goes much too far and that, in particular, the restrictive interpretation which the majority put on Art. 9 is compelling.

[47] In *Ahmad's* case (above note 44) Art. 9 of the European Convention was used in such a context, but was rightly held by the majority to be inapplicable.

altogether on a par with other treaties which have not been incorporated into English law and which, therefore, can and must simply be disregarded in the domestic sphere. On 14 January, 1966, the United Kingdom lodged a declaration in accordance with Article 25 of the Convention. Consequently any person, even a national acting against his own government, who claims to be prejudiced by a violation of the Convention may, after exhaustion of local remedies, apply to the Commission for relief with the result that an Act of Parliament, any executive act, any judicial decision, inlcuding decisions of the House of Lords may become subject to the various remedies which the Convention envisages. In the light of this almost sensational development the United Kingdom has the greatest possible interest in avoiding the violation of the letter and the spirit of the Convention, for it is exposed to remedies by individuals, which are of a wholly unique character. It follows that where the domestic law of the United Kingdom has not erected an effective barrier every reasonable attempt should be made to comply with the Convention as interpreted by the considerable body of case law which has been built up in the course of more than 20 years. Admittedly the terms of the Convention are general and uncertain and, in the words of Lord Denning,[48] 'not the sort of thing which we can easily digest.' But like other countries we simply have to digest them, for we cannot possibly assume that English law and practice are necessarily such as to conform to the standards of the Convention. In fact it is by no means extravagant to suggest that the right of individual petition which the United Kingdom has accepted and, therefore, the submission to the Strasbourg Commission of Human Rights, the Committee of Ministers and the European Court of Human Rights have resulted in a type of judicial review which is more incongruous and uncongenial than the traditional procedures. In the limited field covered by the Convention there now exists, unbeknown to many, an international system of fundamental laws and judicial review which, in years to come, may *pro tanto* lead this country back to the beginning and supersede much of the present domestic system—another paradox in this remarkable story. There is, indeed, an almost mephistophelean twist behind the fact that by virtue of a wholly undemocractic process, namely a stroke of the Executive's pen, the United Kingdom has allowed international tribunals to do what is denied to British tribunals. The peculiarly English doubt whether a Constitution in general or a Bill of Rights in particular is compatible with the sovereignty of Parliament, whether it is logically and legally possible to safeguard it from abolition or amendment or at least so to entrench it as to render change difficult, whether judicial review is a democratic process and a wise and fruitful institution—every such doubt was removed

[48] See note 41.

from debate and, in effect, negatived by the simple device of the Government's declaration entrusting judicial review to the Strasbourg authorities charged with the enforcement of what unquestionably is a Bill of Rights, though it does not by any means cover all the human rights which one would like and is accustomed to see protected.

III

Having considered the status of the Conventions within the United Kingdom one thus comes to examine English law from without, that is to say, the international attitude towards breaches of conventional international law.

The first point is that neither the International Covenant on Economic, Social and Cultural Rights nor the International Covenant on Civil and Political Rights includes an even indirectly effective method of enforcement. The former provides for a system of reporting to and recommendations by the Agencies of the United Nations. The latter provides for a Human Rights Committee (Art. 28) to which reports on the measures taken for the implementation of the Covenant have to be rendered (Art. 40) and which, if a State makes the required Declaration, as the United Kingdom has done, may consider complaints by another State about the alleged failure to fulfil obligations under the Covenant (Art. 41).

This is not to say that in law the Covenants fail to impose effective legal duties upon the contracting States. The duties exist. Their disregard constitutes a breach of treaty. States in general and the United Kingdom in particular would do well to review their legal systems with a view to eradicating or avoiding such breaches. Thus in England it is a matter for serious reflection that the country has undertaken 'to ensure that any person whose rights or freedoms as herein recognised are violated shall have an effective remedy'[49] or 'to have respect for the liberty of parents . . . to choose for their children schools other than those established by the public authorities'[50] or that 'everyone convicted of a crime shall have the right to his conviction and sentence being reviewed by a higher tribunal according to law'[51] or that every one shall have the protection of the law against arbitrary or unlawful interference with his privacy.[52] Or to mention another, very topical and particularly serious discrepancy, both Covenants emphasize the right of association and, in particular, the right to form and

[49] International Covenant on Civil and Political Rights, Art. 2 (3) (*a*).
[50] International Covenant on Economic, Social and Cultural Rights, Art. 13 (3).
[51] International Covenant on Civil and Political Rights, Art. 14 (5).
[52] Ibid., Art. 17.

join trade unions[53]—a right which is also guaranteed by the European Convention[54] and which, as the European Commission of Human Rights decided already in 1970, is what it says, namely a right, not a duty, and therefore necessarily implies the negative freedom or right not to join.[55] In other words the closed shop is contrary to all three Conventions.[56]

If, then, a judicial pronouncement upon any violation of human rights is unlikely to be made by anyone other than the European Commission and the European Court, the legal thinking of these bodies becomes a matter of some significance for English lawyers who will have to become familiar with the sometimes astonishing principles of construction prevailing at Strasbourg. If they are expressive of a method it is so liberal and, indeed, so free and unrestrained that it can fairly be described as lacking in precedent anywhere except possibly in the European Court of Justice. If in the latter tribunal it is pursuit of integration that is the test, in Strabourg it is the activist ideal of the Convention's 'reason and spirit' (to use language taken from American constitutional history)[57] that seems to be decisive. In fact the Commission has argued forcefully that the Convention, 'although in form a treaty,' was not 'a treaty in the traditional sense,' but was something in the nature of a 'constitutional instrument,' the intention being to suggest that established rules of treaty interpretation can and must be disregarded in order to make room for the functional and political freedom which the 'reason and spirit' of a Constitution implies.[58]

[53] Arts. 8 and 22 respectively. [54] Art. 11.

[55] *Yearbook of the European Commission on Human Rights* (1970), Vol. 13, pp. 708, 718.

[56] On Art. 11 see most recently Lucius Wildhaber, *Gedächtnisschrift für Peter Jäggi* (Fribourg, 1977), p. 365, and *German Yearbook of International Law* (1976), Vol. 19, pp. 238, 244.

[57] Apparently the phrase first occurs in the *Brutus* letter of 31 January 1788, here quoted from Professor Julius Goebel Jr.'s work, *History of the Supreme Court of the United States*, Vol. I, p. 310.

[58] These passages are taken from para. 9 of Judge Sir Gerald Fitzmaurice's Separate Opinion in the *National Union of Belgium Police* case decided on October 27, 1975, and reported Series A, Vol. 19. Sir Gerald's Opinions in this case and in the case of *Golder* referred to in the text below contain a most impressive and forceful statement of the principles guiding an international as opposed to a constitutional lawyer or, so one is tempted to say, a lawyer as opposed to a politician. In fact, in para. 10 of the same Opinion Sir Gerald quotes Counsel of the Commission as saying 'that law is always the instrument of policy.' In the case of *Ireland* v. *United Kingdom*, judgment of 18 Jan. 1978, the attitude of the Court is most vividly expressed by the astonishing reasoning that notwithstanding the existence of a public emergency (Art. 15) it felt entitled to investigate violations of Articles 5 and 6—a procedure which is unanswerably criticized in paras. 37 to 45 of Sir Gerald Fitzmaurice's opinion. *Pace* Sir Gerald (para. 6 of his opinion), however, there could be no objection if the Court merely attributed to itself 'a teleological role'; see Art. 31 of the Vienna Draft Convention on Treaties and *Stock* v. *Frank Jones (Tipton) Ltd.* [1978] 1 All E.R. 948, in particular at pp. 952, 953 *per* Lord Simon of Glaisdale. Nor can the Court be reproached for its object 'to elucidate, safeguard and develop the rules instituted by the Convention.' The objection is to the Court's substitution of law-making activism for judicial restraint.

This fundamental approach has not been expressly adopted by the European Court of Human Rights. But it is probably no exaggeration to say that in substance it is to a large extent being followed, so that from without a Bill of Rights is being imposed upon the United Kingdom and developed with a breadth and intensity that has in the past been unknown to the law of England. It is for present purposes impossible and unnecessary to analyse the whole of the rapidly increasing practice of the European Court of Human Rights or even to analyse a single case in all its ramifications. It must suffice to devote a little attention to one case which, as some may think, is of outstanding significance.

According to Article 6 'in the determination of his civil rights and obligations or of any criminal charge against him everyone is entitled to a fair and public hearing within a reasonable time by an independent and impartial tribunal established by law.' While it is arguable, and has in fact been held recently, that the phrase may include administrative proceedings,[58a] it is difficult to imagine how it can be so interpreted as to apply to anything else than the hearing of pending proceedings to the exclusion of the institution of proceedings, of access to the courts. It is true that traditionally the failure to provide reasonable access to the courts has been considered by international law as an aspect of the denial of justice in the narrow sense of the term, and it may indeed be surprising that the Convention does not refer to this case. One would have thought that no amount of sophistry could assert the contrary. Yet this is what, over the forceful dissent of Judge Sir Gerald Fitzmaurice, the European Court of Human Rights did in the almost grotesque case of *Golder* v. *United Kingdom*,[59] and since the judgment was rendered by no less than nine judges against three and in part even unanimously it is entitled to great respect.

In October 1969 Golder, a United Kingdom citizen, was serving in Parkhurst Prison a sentence of 15 years' imprisonment for robbery with violence. A disturbance occurred in an area of the prison where Golder happened to be. Prison officers made various reports and details of possible charges to be made against Golder were entered in his prison record by an officer named Nairn. Later the record was marked: 'Charges not proceeded with.' In March 1970 Golder wrote to the Home Secretary asking for 'permission to consult a solicitor with a view to taking civil action for libel in respect of this statement' (in the prison record). The Home Secretary refused permission. Golder was released in July 1972. No proceedings for libel were brought; whether Golder consulted a solicitor is not known. On these facts the majority of the Court held that the United

[58a] *König* Case, judgment of June 28, 1978.

[59] European Court of Human Rights, Series A, Vol. 18 or *Int.L.R.* 57, 200.

Kingdom had violated Article 6 (1). The effect of the decision can be summarized as follows: everyone, including a convicted prisoner while in prison, has the right at any time to consult a lawyer on any question on which he believes he needs or desires advice, and if he is denied such a right his entitlement 'to a fair and public hearing within a reasonable time by an independent and impartial tribunal established by law' is infringed, even if in fact no case is ever commenced. There must be many to whom the result so stated is likely to appear striking. The Court not only treated words clearly referring to the conduct of a case actually pending before a tribunal as comprising a reference to access to the tribunal, but also included in the latter phrase the right of a convicted prisoner to immediate advice from a lawyer on a complaint which, if pursued, would probably have been struck out as an abuse of the process of the court.

If one looks at the reasoning upon which the Court's conclusion is based its insufficiency becomes apparent. The Court admits in no uncertain terms[60] that 'the right to a fair, public, expeditious judicial procedure can assuredly apply only to proceedings in being.' The Court continues to make the correct, but irrelevant statement that it does not 'necessarily follow that the right to the institution of such proceedings is thereby excluded'—as if the decisive question had not been whether such a right was granted rather than excluded. Where is such grant to be found? The Court refers to the rule of law,[61] to the fact that 'the principle whereby a civil claim must be capable of being submitted to a judge ranks as one of the universally recognised fundamental principles of law,' 'the principle which forbids the denial of justice'—principles in the light of which Article 6 (1) must be read and which render it 'inconceivable' that Article 6 (1) 'should not first protect that which alone makes it in fact possible to benefit from such guarantee, that is, access to a court. The fair, public and expeditious characteristics of judicial proceedings are of no value at all if there are no judicial proceedings'[62]—a statement which either stems from a complete misunderstanding or is an incredible exaggeration. What the Court has overlooked is the fact that since the time of Vattel international law and practice have clearly distinguished between the refusal of an opportunity to assert rights, viz. the denial of justice in the narrow sense, the failure to provide a just procedure and the failure to render a just decision. These distinctions have been maintained by publicists of the highest authority, by international tribunals and by the treaty practice of the leading States.[63] The different torts are different in character, although

[60] Para. 32. [61] Para. 34. [62] Para. 35.

[63] See in particular Jiménez de Aréchaga in Sorensen, *Manual of International Law* (1968), p. 554. Access alone is most frequently guaranteed in treaty practice; see, e.g. Whiteman, Vol. 8, pp. 753 sqq. Wilson [1953] *American Journal of International Law*, 20, 47. Or see as a further example the Anglo-Greek Treaty referred to in the award in the case of *Ambatielos*

they are sometimes given the same name. The commission of the one does not imply the commission of either of the others. You can have a fair hearing of a case but a most unfair result and, conversely, you can have an unfair hearing but a fair decision. Similarly, you can have fair access but an unfair hearing or an unfair, namely delayed or impeded access but a fair hearing. There may be good reasons for the restriction of the guarantee to one set of facts. Just as Article 6 (1) does not guarantee a just decision, so it does not guarantee access to court. To describe this result as 'inconceivable' is neither a sufficient nor a legally acceptable argument. One might just as well say that it is inconceivable that Article 6 (1) guarantees a fair procedure but should not protect that which alone makes it worth while to benefit from such guarantee, that is a fair result.

In fact what international law forbids is the denial of, rather than the difficulty in obtaining, justice. Were it not so, every obstacle, such as the payment of court fees or the requirement of consent to proceedings, would be a denial. Certainly, according to the striking but imprecise adage, justice delayed is justice denied, and in the same sense justice made difficult may be justice denied; the Court, therefore, was not altogether wrong in stating[64] that 'hindering the effective exercise of a right may amount to a breach of that right, even if the hindrance is of a temporary character.' But these are questions of degree and in the circumstances of *Golder's* case the permissible limits which were hardly explored by the Court cannot possibly be said to have been exceeded.

Finally, as a matter of construction, it should be certain that if Article 6 (1) includes a right of access it must be access qualified by the word 'fair.' The Court, perhaps a little surprisingly, accepts the substance of this point by searching for implied limitations[65] and on the facts reaches the conclusion[66] that 'Golder could justifiably wish to consult a solicitor with a view to instituting legal procedings.' Quite apart from many obvious but minor points this sentence and the argument on which it rests so completely disregards the requirements of prison discipline, the practical implications of punishment, prisoners' supervision and the protection of the prison staff that the attitude of the Home Secretary who had to weigh up the interests concerned cannot possibly be described as unfair, particularly if it is remembered that of necessity he must be allowed a measure of discretion or, as the Court has frequently admitted, a 'power of appreciation.' Its abuse was not established in *Golder's* case.

If, therefore, one is bound to disagree with the view of the majority on

---

v. *United Kingdom* (H.M. Stationery Office, 1956), or the Harvard Research Draft on State Responsibility, p. 173. On the other hand the American Draft Foreign Relations Law distinguishes in s. 180 between denial and unfairness of hearing.

[64] Para. 26. [65] Para. 37–40. [66] Para. 40.

Article 6 (1), the unanimity of the Court in finding a violation of Article 8 of the Convention causes bewilderment. This Article reads as follows:

1. Everyone has the right to respect for his private and family life, his home and his correspondence.
2. There shall be no interference by a public authority with the exercise of this right except such as is in accordance with the law and is necessary in a democratic society in the interests of national security, public safety or the economic well-being of the country, for the prevention of disorder or crime, for the protection of health or morals, for the protection of the rights and freedoms of others.

It may be open to doubt whether the Home Secretary failed to show 'respect' for a convicted prisoner's correspondence, for, let it be noted, not even a free and innocent person is entitled to freedom of rather than respect for his correspondence. However this may be, is it not obvious that in the case of a convicted prisoner it is 'the prevention of disorder' and 'the protection of the rights and freedoms of others' that requires the severe limitation of correspondence? The Court was unable[67] to see anything that 'could oblige[68] the Home Secretary to prevent Golder from corresponding with a solicitor with a view to suing Laird for libel,' since he 'was seeking to exculpate himself of a charge.' How an orderly prison administration can be carried on, how a reliable prison staff can be found if every prisoner who has a complaint to make has the immediate right to consult a solicitor and, perhaps, to institute proceedings for libel—such a situation will astonish even those who know little about the vicissitudes of prison discipline and the activities of certain types of prisoner.

In sum one cannot help feeling that, quite apart from purely legal defects, the decision of the Court which, inevitably, provoked a series of prisoners' cases against the United Kingdom, lacks in common sense and that the Court would have been well advised to learn from the experience of prison administrations in the most civilized countries, which Lord Denning had epitomized with his usual precision and insight:[69] 'If the courts were to entertain actions by disgruntled prisoners the governor's life would be made intolerable. The discipline of the prison would be undermined.'

[67] Para. 45.

[68] This, of course, misses the point. The question involved the Home Secretary's *right*.

[69] *Becker* v. *Home Office*, [1972] 2 Q.B. 407, 418—a most illuminating decision. See also *R.* v. *Board of Visitors of Hull Prison, ex p. St. Germain*, [1978] 2 W.L.R. 598. D. J. Harris, [1974–75] *British Year Book of International Law* at p. 395 thinks that in *Golder's* case 'the Court's teleological approach would seem a permissible one in the circumstances.' It is submitted that the Court's approach was legislative rather than teleological.

There remain a few general remarks with which the detailed, but by no means exhaustive discussion of *Golder's* case may be concluded.

In the first place it is highly significant that it was Article 8 which in *Golder's* case was held to have been infringed, but of which Lord Denning, certainly no positivist lawyer adverse to reform or impervious to the 'great rights of mankind,'[70] said that it was 'so wide as to be incapable of practical application.'[71] This, with deference, is likely to be an overstatement in the opposite direction. It may be that English lawyers will have to learn the technique of interpreting and developing constitutional texts. The English lawyers in the England of the seventeenth and in the American colonies of the eighteenth century had no such difficulties. Since the end of the eighteenth century Americans have learned to transform and even to revolutionize such texts to a wholly unexpected extent. That freedom of speech guaranteed by Article I of the First Amendment should invalidate laws against peaceful picketing[72] or that the guarantee of personal liberty and privacy proclaimed by or implicit in the Constitution should invalidate a law prohibiting abortion during the first three months of pregnacy[73] or that freedom of the press should restrict the law of libel[74] or the secrecy of sensitive official documents[75]—these are some examples of what provisions of the Constitution of the United States have produced as a result of the judicial review exercised by the Supreme Court. In due course, when European lawyers become more alive to the immense possibilities the European Convention offers, the practice of the Strasbourg authorities may become similarly daring, although the European Convention wisely includes many qualifications which will impose restraint. Hence English lawyers may have to retrieve the spirit of their forefathers; to remember that a Constitution such as the European Convention with its peculiar method of judicial review is different from an English statute and built upon the idea expressed by Madison in 1789 that it is 'impossible to confine a government to the exercise of express powers, there must necessarily be admitted powers by implication, unless the constitution descended to recount every minutiae',[76] and to take to heart the words of one of the great constitutional lawyers of our time[77] according to which what a constitutional court exercising judicial review must apply 'is a

[70] See above note 14. [71] Above note 42 at p. 848.

[72] For details see Sir Otto Kahn-Freund [1976] *Camb.L.J.* 258, 399.

[73] *Roe* v. *Wade*, 410 U.S. 147 (1973).

[74] *New York Times* v. *Sullivan*, 376 U.S. 284 (1964) and many other cases.

[75] *New York Times* v. *United States*, 403 U.S. 713 (1971).

[76] Quoted by Schwarz (above note 13) at p. 178. The legal doctrine expressed by these words was fully developed in the famous case of *McCulloch* v. *Maryland* (1819) 4 Wheat. 316. Those who criticize the wide terms of the European Convention should study the memorable opinion delivered in that case by Chief Justice Marshall.

[77] Schwarz (above note 14) at p. 215.

broad standard rather than a closely defined precept. But the same thing is done in most important areas of modern law. Indeed, it is in the application of such standards instead of only mechanical rules that a developed legal system differs most from a primitive one.'

Secondly, the English Parliament and English judges will have to be much more conscious of the control and supervision liable to be exercised by those who, though sitting at Strasbourg, effectively are the guardians of great parts of the English constitution. Apart from many illuminating cases against the United Kingdom, including one in which the Court of Appeal and the House of Lords escaped embarrassing criticism by Strasbourg,[78] there is the decision of the House of Lords in *Attorney-General* v. *Times Newspapers Ltd.*[79] which the Strasbourg Commission by a majority of eight to five held to constitute a violation of Article 10 of the Convention guaranteeing freedom of expression and on which the European Court is now called upon to pronounce. The case involved contempt of court in pending proceedings, one of the most exemplary contributions of English law to civilization, the maintenance of personal liberty and the improvement of standards of public life. The offence may be thought to have been glaring and indisputable.

Anyone familiar with conditions on the Continent will be conscious of the great evil which trial by newspaper is doing there. It would surely be perplexing if foreign judges who are unaware of the high-minded purposes and the lofty rationale of the English rule were to condemn an institution which, however uncertain some of its ramifications may be, is far superior to anything known to their own national legal systems. What matters in the present context is that English courts should appreciate the necessity for adapting their reasoning to the Strasbourg terminology and mentality. The House of Lords whose decision, as expressed in particular by Lord Diplock and Lord Simon of Glaisdale, may seem so persuasive as to be almost inevitable, would and ought to have framed their reasoning in slightly different and more elaborate terms if they had been conscious of a possible review in the light of Article 10. Sometimes it is not so much the result as the grounds provided for it that would make all the difference for the foreign observer who knows little about the virtues of a legal tradition grown over the centuries and whose instruction in a strange field presupposes special sympathy, seeing that he is not always representative of the highest judicial or even legal quality in his own country.

Thirdly, the English lawyer will have to ask himself whether it would not be sounder policy to entrust judicial review in the light of a Bill of Rights to a tribunal imbued with the spirit and history of English

[78] *Firestone Tire and Rubber Company* v. *United Kingdom* [1973] *Yearbook of the European Commission on Human Rights* 152.

[79] [1974] A.C. 273.

fundamental law rather than to a tribunal that is predominantly foreign in nationality, training and standards, that includes judges from nineteen countries as diverse as Malta and Iceland, Turkey and Portugal, Cyprus and Luxembourg, and that displays little inclination to seek guidance from comparative material or, in particular, from the wealth of American learning and its English ideological base. To raise such a question[80] at the present moment may seem audacious. But developments may lead to the time when this country will have to choose between Strasbourg, withdrawal from Strasbourg and possibly the creation of its own institution of judicial review. The debate will involve controversy about great moral, political and also legal issues. When that time comes the truly English tradition which manifested itself in the United States during the memorable 15 years from 1776 to 1791 may provide much guidance.

IV

It may be something of an anticlimax, but the preceding survey would be incomplete without a few words about the latest development in the field of Britain's Bill of Rights—a development which comes to Britain by way of the European Communities Act 1972 and which has so far attracted singularly little attention in this country.

On April 5, 1977, Signor E. Colombo on behalf of the European Parliament, Dr David Owen on behalf of the Council and Mr Roy Jenkins on behalf of the Commission signed what is called a Joint Declaration reading as follows:[81]

THE EUROPEAN PARLIAMENT, THE COUNCIL AND THE COMMISSION,

Whereas the Treaties establishing the European Communities are based on the principle of respect for the law;

Whereas, as the Court of Justice has recognized, that law comprises, over and above the rules embodied in the treaties and secondary Community legislation, the general principles of law and in particular the fundamental rights, principles and rights on which the constitutional law of the Member States is based;

Whereas, in particular, all the Member States are Contracting Parties to the European Convention for the Protection of Human Rights and Fundamental Freedoms signed in Rome on 4 November 1950,

HAVE ADOPTED THE FOLLOWING DECLARATION:

1. The European Parliament, the Council and the Commission stress the prime importance they attach to the protection of fundamental rights, as derived in

[80] It was raised by some, in particular by Lord Scarman's Hamlyn Lecture on *English Law—The New Dimension* (1974), pp. 10–20. See already Mann, 'The United Kingdom's Bill of Rights,' *The New Law Journal*, March 30, 1972.

[81] *Official Journal*, 27 April 1977.

particular from the constitutions of the Member States and the European Convention for the Protection of Human Rights and Fundamental Freedoms.

2. In the exercise of their powers and in pursuance of the aims of the European Communities they respect and will continue to respect these rights.

It is submitted that this Joint Declaration, which has no basis in any specific provision of the Treaty, is expressive of the Community's legal policy, but has no legal force. Bearing in mind Article 164 of the Treaty which requires it to observe 'the law' the European Court of Justice has on numerous occasions emphasized that 'fundamental rights form an integral part of the general principles of law the observance of which it ensures' and that in safeguarding them it 'is bound to draw inspiration from constitutional traditions common to the Member States and it cannot therefore uphold measures which are incompatible with the fundamental rights recognised and protected by the Constitutions of those States.' In this connection international treaties binding the member-States 'may supply guidelines which should be followed within the framework of Community law.'[82]

In member States such as the Federal Republic of Germany whose Constitution includes a catalogue of fundamental rights and provides for judicial review and thus for their observance and enforcement the Joint Declaration will be read with satisfaction and understanding and may assist in straightening out some doubt which, very justifiably, a recent decicision of the Federal Constitutional Court provoked.[83] Nor will the Joint Declaration cause much excitement in France, where by virtue of Article 55 of the Constitution, the European Convention on Human Rights is accepted and overrides all inconsistent French law, whether earlier or later,[84] the Cour de Sûreté de l'Etat having recently decided[85] '*que cette Convention est applicable en France et a, en vertu de la Constitution, une force supérieure à toute loi interne qui lui serait contraire*.'

[82] The most important decision is *Nold* v. *Commission* [1974] 2 C.M.L.R. 338. But there were earlier cases: See H.P. Ipsen, *Europäisches Gemeinschaftsrecht* (1972), pp. 716 sqq. with a very full and interesting discussion. For a later case which, however, does not carry the development further, see *Rutili* v. *Minister of the Interior* [1976] 1 C.M.L.R. 140, 155.

[83] BVerfGE 37, 271. It was held that Community law could not necessarily override fundamental rights enshrined in the German Constitution. The decision must be described as wholly convincing and almost self-evident, but it has been widely criticized and also led to some diplomatic representations by the Commission *vis-à-vis* the Government of the Federal Republic. Perhaps the Joint Declaration was intended to reassure the Federal Constitutional Court. In view of its character it is, however, unlikely to achieve this. In particular the protection of property afforded by the German Constitution (Art. 14) is not clearly guaranteed by the Community; cf. Mann, *Beiträge zum Zivil- und Wirtschaftsrecht* (Festschrift für Ballerstedt), p. 421, at p. 432. Other examples could be given.

[84] On the French development see Mann [1976–77] *British Year Book of International Law*, 26, 27.

[85] May 6, 1976, *Rev.Gén. de Droit Int.Public* 1977, 897.

But in this country the Joint Declaration should give rise to some heart-searching. Is English constitutional law based on the general principles of law and on fundamental rights within the meaning of the Joint Declaration? Does English law attach 'prime importance' to the protection of fundamental rights in the sense of securing them against an omnipotent legislature? Certainly English law accepts the indirect and remote control of the Strasbourg authorities. But it lacks that indigenous judicial control which many other European countries practise, which to a certain extent even Canada introduced a few years ago,[86] and which alone prevents a 'Constitution' from being 'a mere rope of sand,' to use the telling phrase coined in 1768 by the then Lieutenant-Governor and Chief Justice of Massachusetts, Thomas Hutchinson.[87] In the result it is less the incorporation of the Convention into English law than domestic as opposed to foreign judicial review that is the kernel of the issue. Does it not deserve a much more learned, intensive and purposeful debate than it has had in the past? Is it not perhaps worthy of some positive action?[88]

[86] On the Canadian development see Wade and Phillips, *Constitutional and Administrative Law* (9th edn., 1977, by Bradley), pp. 541–3. It is certain that the Bill of Rights (the scope of which is very limited) renders earlier inconsistent legislation inapplicable, and it is very likely that the courts will apply it to nullify such legislation subsequently enacted.

[87] Quoted by Schwartz (above note 14) at p. 92. On Hutchinson see Goebel (above note 57) at p. 93.

[88] While this article went through the press, there appeared the Report of the Select Committee on a Bill of Rights (House of Lords) and the author became aware of the Minutes of Evidence taken before the Select Committee. There is much that may have to be said at a later date about both publications, but the argument in the above article is not affected by them.

4

The Consequences of an International Wrong in International and National Law

THE doctrine of the international wrong, that is to say, the violation of a duty imposed by public international law, is both one of the most important and one of the most intricate chapters of public international law. It is, on the one hand, so important because it is that part of public international law with which the practising lawyer most frequently comes (or ought to come) into contact, for wrongs suffered by a physical or legal person at the hands of a foreign State are unfortunately a matter of daily occurrence, although they are not always diagnosed as such, and even if they are, the absence of diplomatic protection or the lack of submission by the wrongdoing State to a tribunal is likely to render a remedy illusory. On the other hand, the intricacy arises from the existence of a relatively large amount of material on State responsibility, from which, however, in many respects a firm rule has not yet been evolved. Thus even such elementary questions as the scope of *abus de droit* as a cause of action[1] or the imputability of acts occurring within its jurisdiction to the State[2] are to some extent controversial and in need of that clarification which only a developed body of judicial decisions can provide.

Moreover, assuming an international tort to have been established, the nature of the rights which it is open to the claimant State to assert is not free from doubt. This, indeed, is the first topic to which in the following observations it is proposed to turn (below, section I). There then arises the question how national legal systems treat, or should treat, a set of facts which in public international law would be considered an international wrong. This is a problem which requires discussion, from the point of view of legal principle, with reference to the effects of violations of customary (below, section II) and conventional (below, section III) international law by the forum and by a foreign country (below, section IV). But no contribution to its solution is likely to be useful without the illustration which practical cases can supply; accordingly a review of three

[1] See, most recently, Taylor, this *Year Book*, 46 (1972–3), p. 323 with further references.
[2] On this subject see the weighty Reports by Professor Ago, *Yearbook of the International Law Commission*, 1971, vol. 2, p. 199; 1972 vol. 2, p. 71.

British Year Book of International Law, 49 (1975–1976), 1–65.

entirely different sets of facts which have arisen in the practice of courts and arbitral tribunals will have to be analysed (below, sections V to VII).

Each aspect of the general problem which has thus been indicated has in the past led to much discussion. On certain points extensive material has been collected by scholars and many different suggestions have been made, sometimes with a measure of emphasis and even special pleading. It is not proposed in the course of the following remarks to review the whole field, to analyse every point or to aim at completeness of citation. Sufficient references will, it is hoped, be given to facilitate the student's further research in a branch of the law which is in a state of continuous and rapid evolution and is, therefore, liable to undergo unexpected changes. Nor will the expert have any difficulty in ascertaining what the author intends to accept or to reject, or any novel point that he may venture to suggest.

I. THE EFFECTS OF INTERNATIONAL WRONGS IN INTERNATIONAL LAW

The rights which, as a result of an international wrong, the claimant State acquires against the wrongdoing State are frequently (and rightly) said to include such remedies as intervention, reprisals, satisfaction or apology. These are somewhat esoteric means of redress which may safely be ignored in order to permit a closer look at the great problems which continue to bedevil the more usual rights States prefer to pursue.

1. It is probably no exaggeration to say that *reparation* is still the primary and most frequently sought form of relief. After almost fifty years the definition of its legal nature remains to be found in the often quoted and characteristically precise statement by the Permanent Court of International Justice in the *Chorzów Factory* case, which does not become less weighty by reason of the fact that to some extent it was *obiter*:[3]

> The essential principle contained in the notion of an illegal act—a principle which seems to be established by international practice and in particular by the decisions of arbitral tribunals—is that reparation must, as far as possible, wipe out all the consequences of the illegal act and re-establish the situation which would, in all probability, have existed if that act had not been committed. Restitution in kind or, if this is not possible, payment of a sum corresponding to the value which a restitution in kind would bear; the award, if need be, of damages for loss sustained which would not be covered by restitution in kind or payment in place of it—such are the principles which should serve to determine the amount of compensation due for an act contrary to international law.

[3] *P.C.I.J.*, Series A, No. 17 (1928), p. 47. Germany had actually claimed damages.

Reparation may thus take two different forms, restitution in kind or the payment of damages, the former being clearly the primary remedy, although, as the Court said elsewhere in the same judgement, monetary compensation 'is even the most usual form of reparation' and was in fact 'selected' by Germany in that case.[4]

Restitution in kind, it is true, is largely unknown to the common law which, in principle and somewhat paradoxically, adheres to the rule of Roman law *omnis condemnatio est pecuniaria* and calls it *restitutio in integrum* (which it is not[5]). Yet it should not be overlooked that even in England, for instance, the plaintiff in an action for detinue is by no means confined to monetary relief, but is entitled to delivery-up of the chattel.[6] This, in fact, is the approach adopted in most continental countries where, broadly, in many cases the victim will obtain *naturalis restitutio* and where the law allows him such relief as in the circumstances is most appropriate. Thus in Switzerland it is the judge who determines 'le mode ainsi que l'étendue de la réparation d'après les circonstances et la gravité de la faute'.[7] In France, if the circumstances permit it, the victim has the choice.[8] In Germany, in cases which do not involve injury to a person or thing, the victim can claim damages only where restitution in kind is impossible or insufficient.[9]

In the first place it seems fairly clear that as a rule public international law has for long recognized restitution in kind as a right, probably as the principal right, against the wrongdoing State. Many writers of authority have not only asserted, but also explained, developed and applied the rule;[10] few have denied it.[11] None has asserted the exclusivity of the claim

[4] Ibid., pp. 27, 28.

[5] In English municipal law the expression 'restitution in *integrum*' is used to indicate the measure of damages to which the victim is entitled: see, e.g., McGregor, *Damages*, 13th edn. (1972), Section 10. It was in this sense that the expression was employed by Sir Hersch Lauterpacht, *Private Law Sources and Analogies* (1929), p. 147.

[6] See the illuminating judgment of Diplock LJ (as he then was) in *General and Finance Facilities Ltd* v. *Cooks Cars (Romford) Ltd.*, [1963] 2 All E.R. 314. See now the Torts (Interference with Goods) Act 1977.

[7] Art. 43 of the Code of Obligations.

[8] See, for instance, Mazeaud, *Lçcons de Droit Civil*, vol.2 (1966), No. 621.

[9] Sections 249 to 251 of the Civil Code. See Federal Constitutional Court, 11 Oct. 1985, *NJW* 1986, 1426: restitution in kind is a general principle of public international law.

[10] Jiménez de Aréchaga in Sørensen, *Manual of Public International Law* (1968), pp. 565, 566, who regards restitution in kind as the normal remedy; Berber, *Lehrbuch des Völkerrechts*, vol. 3 (1977), pp. 25, 26, who says in terms that in law restitution in kind is the primary right; Brownlie, *Principles of Public International Law*, 2nd edn. (1973), p. 448 who regards it as exceptional; Dahm, *Völkerrecht*, vol. 3 (1961), pp. 232, 233; Duckwitz, *Rechtsfolgen bei Verletzung völkerrechtlicher Verträge* (1975), p. 31; Eagleton, *Responsibility of States in International Law* (1928), p. 182; François, *Recueil des cours*, 66 (1938–1), p. 281; Lais, *Rechtsfolgen völkerrechtlicher Delikte* (1932), p. 29; O'Connell, *International Law*, 2nd edn. (1970), p. 1114; Reuter, *Droit international public* (1958), p. 157; Salvioli, *Recueil des cours*, 28 (1929 III), p. 237; Schüle in Strupp-Schlochauer, *Wörterbuch des Völkerrechts*, vol. 1, pp. 337, 338 and vol. 3, p. 843; Schwarzenberger, *International Law*, 3rd edn. (1957),

for damages;[12] such a theory would, indeed, be unacceptable in that it would favour the defaulter and deprive the victim of a useful right. One author of authority has subdivided the wrongdoer's duty into a duty to restore where a situation has been illegally created and a duty to make good (*Nachholepflicht*) where the wrongdoer has wrongfully failed to create a situation.[13] The Harvard Draft Convention, prepared under the auspices of Professors Sohn and Baxter, recognizes the principle by providing in Article 27 that the reparation which a State is required to make for a wrongful act or omission may take the form of 'measures designed to re-establish the situation which would have existed if the wrongful act or omission . . . had not occurred', damages or a combination thereof.[14] A proper sense of responsibility will require full weight to be given to so unanimous a body of scholarly opinion which, as will appear,[15] is in harmony with the practice of numerous States and which was judicially approved already in 1917, when the Central American Court of Justice decided the case of *El Salvador* v. *Republic of Nicaragua*.[16] Nicaragua had entered into the so-called Bryan–Chamorro Treaty with the United States of America, which, so El Salvador alleged, was in violation of treaty and other rights due from Nicaragua. The Court found[17] that 'the Government of Nicaragua is impressed with the obligation to take all possible means sanctioned by international law to re-establish and maintain the legal status that existed between the two countries prior to the conclusion of the Bryan–Chamorro Treaty'. And the actual order made by the Court was framed in similar terms.[18]

Next it appears to depend on the circumstances of the case and on the claimant State's choice whether the wrongdoing State can or should make restitution in kind or pay damages. Thus if a person has been illegally

---

pp. 653 sqq.; Spiropoulos, Niemeyer's *Zeitschrift für internationales Recht*, 35 (1925/6), p. 59; Strupp, *Das völkerrechtliche Delikt* (1920), p. 209; Verdross, *Völkerrecht*, 5th edn., p. 400; Verdross and Simma, *Universelles Völkerrecht* (1976), pp. 630, 631, who state particularly clearly that restitution in kind is the primary right and damages are only subsidiary in the sense that they can only be claimed if restitution in kind is impossible; Verzijl, *Jurisprudence of the World Court*, vol. 1 (1965), p. 172 and *International Law in Historical Perspective*, vol. 6 (1973), pp. 742 sqq.; Weil, *Recueil des cours*, 128 (1969–III), p.225 with references; Wengler, *Völkerrecht* (1964), pp. 503, 510; Dupuy, *Clunet*, 1977, pp. 384–7, as Sole Arbitrator.

[11] The most important, perhaps the only, one of them is Kelsen, 'Unrecht und Unrechtsfolge im Völkerrecht,' *Zeitschrift fur öffentliches Recht*, 12 (1932), p. 481. Against him Verdross, *Völkerrecht*, 5th edn. (1964), p. 398.

[12] For a possible exception see Baade, *American Journal of International Law*, 54 (1960), p. 801.

[13] Wengler, op. cit. (above, n.10), pp. 503, 510.

[14] Sohn and Baxter, *American Journal of International Law*, 55 (1961), p. 545, at p. 580.

[15] See below, n. 22, n. 31, n. 37, where examples of recent cases are given in which States have claimed and sometimes obtained restitution in kind.

[16] *American Journal of International Law*, 11 (1971), p. 674.

[17] Ibid., p. 728.

[18] Ibid., p.730.

abducted from the territory of the claimant State, as happened in the case of Jacob-Salomon who was abducted by Nazi Germany from Swiss territory,[19] it is the return of the person that can, and usually will, be claimed, because it alone will undo the wrong. There is, however, no reason why damages should not be claimed and this would in any event be the only claim if, for instance, the individual in question had been killed. Or take the *Barcelona Traction* case.[20] There the Belgian State claimed[21] that the reparation due to it 'must be complete and must, so far as possible, reflect the damage suffered by its nationals . . . since *restitutio in integrum* is, in the circumstances of the case, practically and legally impossible, the reparation of the damage suffered can only take place in the form of an all-embracing pecuniary indemnity'. Nor did Spain attack the Belgian decision to claim damages rather than restitution in kind. The latter relief would have been inappropriate and impracticable, seeing that some twenty-two years had passed since the date of the alleged wrong and the property in question had entirely changed its character. On the other hand, in the *Interhandel* case[22] Switzerland asked and could ask the Court to 'declare . . . that the government of the United States is under an obligation to restore the assets' of the Swiss company. These few examples make it clear that too much must not be read into the fact that many treaties have provided for the assessment of financial compensation rather than restitution in kind or that some arbitral tribunals have even described such compensation as the normal remedy.[23] It may well be that the cases in which compensation is adequate are more numerous or that States prefer to agree upon the payment of compensation, but this experience does not permit a legal principle to be inferred. At the same time it would be equally unjustifiable to state in categorical terms that damages are the only alternative entitlement available if and when restitution in kind fails, or to discuss what is the rule and what is the exception. The true position, it is submitted, is that the claimant State has an option which it must reasonably exercise:[24] no tribunal will be bound by a choice which is arbitrary or inappropriate in the light of the facts.[25]

[19] On this well-known incident see, among others, Oppenheim (ed. Lauterpacht), *International Law*, vol.1, 8th edn. (1955), p. 295. It should, however, be noted that many of the authors mentioned at n. 10 above, emphasize the primacy of the right to restitution in kind. See, for instance, Schwarzenberger, Spiropoulos, Verzijl, or Eagleton.

[20] *I.C.J. Reports*, 1970, p. 3.

[21] Ibid., p. 23.

[22] *I.C.J. Reports*, 1959, p. 9.

[23] See, e.g., in the *Lusitania* case the United States–German Mixed Claims Commission, *Reports of International Arbitral Awards*, vol.7, pp. 32. Cf. *Affaire des Forêts du Rhodope Central*, ibid., vol. 3, p. 1405, at p. 1432: the question whether restitution in kind or payment should be awarded was left to the arbitrator, who decided in the latter sense.

[24] This is, in substance, what is suggested by Oppenheim (ed. Lauterpacht), *International Law*, vol. 1, 8th edn. (1955), p. 353.

[25] For this qualification see, in particular, Verdross, op. cit. (above n. 10), p. 401, and Berber, op.cit. (above, n. 10), p. 25.

Finally it must be emphasized that, whatever form of reparation the claimant State may be entitled to claim, it may be satisfied with something less or different and that the question of remedies is to be clearly distinguished from that of entitlement. Remedies depend on the jurisdiction and procedure of the tribunal. They may not always coincide with the substantive right. In addition the latter may have to be considered independently of proceedings between the claimant and the defaulting State. Thus it may have a bearing on the interpretation of treaty provisions which give effect to it, as the Peace treaties with Italy and other States did after the Second World War when they imposed a duty to restore the property of United Nations nationals.[26] Or the substantive right may be relevant in proceedings before a municipal court, and in such event the question whether and how it could be enforced in an international court would not be allowed to blur the issue. This may occur, for instance, if an individual is being sued for conspiring by instigating or exploiting the international tort.

2. The second question, much less frequently explored, is whether international law contemplates *nullity* as a possible consequence of an international wrong—and, regardless of the many refinements which dominate the sparse literature on the subject,[27] nullity will be understood as signifying something that is, in a broad sense, null and void rather than voidable and as primarily affecting acts of municipal law which constitute an international illegality.[28]

Obviously the problem arises only where it is a juristic act such as legislation, an executive order or a judicial decision that is alleged to be tortious. In such cases it may happen that nullity, and possibly a judicial declaration of nullity, is the only effective method or at least the necessary concomitant of an effective method for the protection of the victim State. It may in fact be little more than a step in the practical implementation of the idea of restitution in kind. If, as a matter of the restoration of the status quo, the wrongdoing State may be ordered to abrogate or nullify

[26] For a convenient survey see Whiteman, *Digest of International Law*, vol. 8, pp. 1202 sqq.

[27] Verzijl, *Revue de droit international*, 9 (1935), p. 284—a fundamental contribution; Guggenheim, *Recueil des cours*, 74 (1949–I), p. 237 and *Traité de droit international public*, 2nd edn. (1967), p. 67; Jennings, *Cambridge Essays in International Law* (1965), p. 64; Baade, *Indiana Law Journal*, 39 (1964), p. 497 (who does not consider the validity of internal acts which are contrary to international law: p. 512); Paul de Visscher, *Recueil des cours*, 136 (1972–II), p. 90. On the effects of illegal acts of international organizations see E. Lauterpacht, *Cambridge Essays in International Law* (1965), p. 88.

[28] Acts of general international law in connection with which the problem of nullity arises are infrequent. As to treaties see now Articles 42 sqq. of the Vienna Draft Convention. The case of the premature recognition which is sometimes mentioned is a doubtful one, because it is far from obvious *vis-à-vis* whom there is a duty of non-recognition.

one of its acts, it is by no means extravagant to suggest that, at least *vis-à-vis* the claimant State that act is null and void. This is no new suggestion. Thus Professor Guggenheim, among others,[29] has said:[30] 'La nullité joue également un rôle en tant que modalité de la réparation d'un acte illicite.' The association of ideas is also clearly indicated in the award in *l'Affaire Martini*[31] where the Arbitrator decided that on account of the international wrong inherent in a Venezuelan judgment 'le Gouvernement Vénézuélien est tenu de reconnaître, à titre de réparation, l'annulation des obligations de paiement imposées à la Maison Martini & Cie.'. The close connection with the idea of reparation had led one author even to suggest that an international wrong does not create a nullity at all, but that the tortious act 'according to the principles of restoration of the status quo must be reversed by the wrongdoing State';[32] but, as will appear, so extreme a view is opposed to prevailing practice.

If the sanction of nullity fits well into the fundamental principles of public international law, it leads to the continued existence and recognition of the status quo. Indeed, in the words of Sir Hersch Lauterpacht, 'the absence of more direct means of enforcement tends to endow the principle of nullity of illegal acts with particular importance in the international sphere'.[33] This is well exemplified by the effects of non-recognition of States or governments: it implies non-existence in relation to the non-recognizing State. Moreover, nullity of the wrongful act is demanded or at least suggested by the basic principle of public international law, *ex injuria non oritur jus*.[34] Another little-known illustration is provided by a diplomatic incident which occurred in September 1919:[35] Article 61 (2) of the German *Reich's* Weimar Constitution envisaged that Austria would delegate representatives to sit in the German Second Chamber (*Reichsrat*).

[29] See O'Connell, op. cit. (above, n. 10), p. 116, or Baxter, *Syracuse Law Review*, 16 (1965), p. 745 at p. 750, who speaks of the 'sanction of nullity'; Brownlie, op. cit. (above, n. 10), p. 448, who says that 'to achieve the object of reparation tribunals may give "legal restitution" in the form of a declaration' of invalidity. And see Verdross and Simma, op. cit. (below, n. 34).

[30] *Recueil des cours*, 74 (1949–I), p. 237; but see the same author in *Traité de droit international public*, 2nd edn. (1967), vol. 1, p. 67. For the important award of 19 January 1977, see below, p. 197.

[31] *Reports of International Arbitral Awards*, vol. 2, p. 975, at p. 1002.

[32] Wengler, op. cit. (above, n. 10) p. 421.

[33] *Recognition in International Law* (1947), p. 421.

[34] It is referred to in connection with nullity by Guggenheim, Jennings, Lauterpacht, loc. cit. (above, n. 27), and by Verdross and Simma, *Universelles Völkerrecht* (1976), pp. 65, 244. Paul de Visscher, loc. cit. (above, n. 27) rightly stresses that the 'mécanisme de nullité' is necessary to render the international legal order effective. On the principle see also Fitzmaurice, *Recueil des cours*, 92 (1957–II), p. 117 and Singapore Court of Appeal, I.L.R. 23 (1956), pp. 810, 831, 837.

[35] The incident is frequently described by German authors. See, e.g., Lais, op. cit. (above, n. 10), pp. 30, 31.

The Allies regarded this as a violation of the Treaty of Versailles. In response to a demand made by them, Germany confirmed that all provisions of the Constitution which were inconsistent with the Treaty were 'invalid'. It would indeed be odd if a wrongful act were in law to be treated otherwise than as null and void. The analogy of municipal law would lend no support to such a conclusion: an act done in contravention of the law may have a variety of legal effects, but as a rule it cannot be the foundation of a valid legal title.

Thus in the *Eastern Greenland* case,[36], the Permanent Court of International Justice, having held the disputed area not to belong to Norway, proceeded to hold that the Royal Proclamation of 10 July 1931 whereby the Norwegian Government purported to occupy the area 'and any steps taken in this respect by that government constitute a violation of the existing legal situation and are accordinly unlawful and invalid'. In the *Barcelona Traction* case[37] Judge Sir Gerald Fitzmaurice inquired whether the Spanish courts were entitled to render a judgment of bankruptcy against Barcelona Traction, a Canadian company without office, property or business activity in Spain. His conclusion was 'that the whole bankruptcy proceedings were, for excess of jurisdiction, internationally null and void *ab initio* and without effect on the international plane'. It is submitted that this represents sound law and should in no way be confined to cases of excess of jurisdiction. A slightly more troublesome position arose in the *Fisheries Jurisdiction* case[38] where the International Court of Justice held that certain Icelandic legislative acts 'are not opposable to the government of the United Kingdom'. The relative nullity so pronounced was deliberate: the Court did not hold that the Icelandic legislation was, as suggested by the United Kingdom, 'invalid *erga omnes*', and for this reason a number of Judges, in a Joint Separate Opinion, felt it possible to concur.[39] The result is a little surprising, because previously it had been thought that a breach of customary international law or of a treaty was an international tort which produced absolute nullity. Both aspects were in issue, namely the United Kingdom's preferential fishing rights and the breach of a treaty of 1961.[40] The Court refrained from discussing the reasons for preferring the concept of relative nullity. It is not easy to discover a legally acceptable reason. The point which matters for present purposes is that the international wrong committed by Iceland led to some form of nullity of its legislation.

The very opposite type of difficulty is created by the International Court's Advisory Opinion in the *Namibia (South West Africa)* case.[41]

[36] *P.C.I.J.* Series A/B, No. 53 (1933), p. 24.

[37] *I.C.J. Reports*, 1970, p. 106.

[38] *I.C.J. Reports*, 1974, p. 3, at p.34.

[39] Ibid., p.46.

[40] See, in particular, p. 29 (paragraph 67).

[41] *I.C.J. Reports*, 1971, p. 16.

Having held that South Africa's Mandate over South West Africa had been terminated by the United Nations[42] and that *vis-à-vis* Members of the United Nations South Africa's presence in South West Africa was illegal, the Court proceeded to state that such termination and illegality 'are opposable to all States in the sense of barring *erga omnes* the legality of a situation which is maintained in violation of international law'.[43] It may be that in the particular case the view of the Court, especially the duty of non-recognition which it inferred from the absolute illegality, went very far.[44] Yet the general attitude towards the consequences of an international illegality which the Court contemplates is in line with what has been submitted to be the correct approach, and now constitutes the most authoritative and impressive statement of principle.

There are, on the other hand, cases of treaties in which States have found it necessary expressly to exclude nullity as a consequence of an international wrong, but exceptions may be said to prove the rule. Thus the European Convention for the Peaceful Settlement of Disputes[45] provides[46] that if the execution of the international tribunal's decision would conflict with a judgment on another measure put into effect by a party to the dispute and if the municipal law of such party precludes 'the consequences of the judgment or measure in question to be annulled', the international tribunal 'shall, if necessary, grant the injured party equitable satisfaction'. This is very much in line with a number of Treaties for Conciliation, Judicial Settlement and Arbitration concluded by Switzerland,[47] for instance the one with the United Kingdom,[48] which provides that if and in so far as annulment is impermissible, the international tribunal 'shall determine the nature or extent of the reparation to be awarded to the injured party.'[49]

3. Next it is necessary to turn to the distinct problem of the consequences of a *breach of treaty*. That such a breach, at any rate if it is substantial,[50] constitutes an international wrong and cannot simply be likened to a breach of contract is generally recognized[51] and is in line

[42] On this basic point of the Opinion and the compelling doubts surrounding it see, in particular, Kewenig, *Festschrift für Ulrich Scheuner* (1973), p. 259.

[43] *I.C.J. Reports*, 1971, p. 56.

[44] Mann, *Festschrift für Ulrich Scheuner* (1973), p. 399, at pp. 414 sqq. or above p. 97.

[45] *United Kingdom Treaty Series*, No. 10 (1961) (Cmnd. 1298).

[46] Art. 30.

[47] See Guggenheim, loc. cit. (above, n. 27), p. 69 n. 1.

[48] *United Kingdom Treaty Series*, No. 42 (1967) (Cmnd. 3285).

[49] Art. 33.

[50] This qualification would seem to be obvious and hardly worth making.

[51] *Interpretation of Peace Treaties with Bulgaria etc., I.C.J. Reports*, 1950, p. 228: 'It is clear that refusal to fulfil a treaty obligation involves international responsibility'. Or see, among many others, Oppenheim (ed. Lauterpacht), *International Law*, vol. 1, 8th edn. (1955), p. 339; Berber, *Lehrbuch des Völkerrechts*, 2nd edn. (1975), vol. 1, p. 505; Wengler, op. cit. (above, n. 10), pp. 503, 504; Schüle (above, n. 10), vol. 1, p. 330; Mosler, *Recueil des cours*, 140 (1974–IV), p. 172. In view of the decision of the International Court of Justice in the *Fisheries Jurisdiction* case, *I.C.J. Reports*, 1974, p. 3, the question arises whether the rule has not now been jeopardized. See above, p. 131.

with the fact that even in private law a breach of contract is an unlawful act.[52]

In the words of Lord NcNair,[53] 'One point is clear: a breach by one party (including an unlawful denunciation) does not automatically terminate the treaty, for the other party may prefer to maintain it in existence.' Accordingly the breach confers upon the innocent party the *right* to terminate the treaty. It would be shocking if this view, which has frequently been expressed,[54] were not treated as compelling. If by a breach of a treaty a State could effectively put an end to it or force the other party to treat it as ended, one of the basic principles of international law and society and of law as a whole, viz. the principle of *pacta sunt servanda*,[55] would be undermined and destroyed, for one would be making the wholly irresponsible admission that by assuming an undischarged liability to pay damages the defaulting party could, against the wishes of the innocent party, terminate a treaty. No wonder, then, that so paradoxical a view has nowhere been put forward. It may be that the principle of the continuing validity of a treaty rests on a basis of considerable, perhaps even extreme, generality, but this is surely one of the cases in which there is no room for qualifications or distinctions.

If it were necessary to look for support, it could be stated with certainty that the world's municipal systems of law are to the same effect. A material breach of the contract by the defaulting party does not discharge the contract, but provides the injured party with the option of accepting the repudiation (in which event both parties are discharged) or holding the defaulter to the contract and requiring its performance. Damages are payble in both cases, though their nature and extent will depend on how the option is exercised. No legal system has become known which, whatever phraseology or techniques it may employ, does not in substance and in the result correspond to the rule as stated in terms of the common law.[56]

In fact the existence of the rule in public international law which was stated already by Grotius and judicially applied for the first time in 1796

[52] *Rookes* v. *Barnard*, [1964] A.C. 1129.

[53] *Law of Treaties* (1961), p. 553.

[54] *Yearbook of the International Law Commission*, 1963, vol. 2, p. 204; Oppenheim (ed. Lauterpacht), op. cit. (above, n. 19), p. 947; Brownlie, op. cit. (above, n.10), pp. 596, 597; Berber, op. cit. (above, n. 51), p. 493; Clive Parry in Sørensen, *Manual of Public International Law*, p. 239; Verdross and Simma, *Universelles Völkerrecht* (1976), pp. 409, 410; Verzijl, *International Law in Historical Perspective*, vol. 6 (1973), p. 338; Dahm, op. cit. (above, n. 10), vol. 3, p. 137.

[55] Now recognized by Art. 26 of the Vienna Draft Convention.

[56] As to English and Scottish law, in particular, see *White and Carter (Councils) Ltd* v. *McGregor*, [1962] A.C. 413.

by the Supreme Court of the United States[57] and reaffirmed in 1913[58] is now implied in Article 60 of the Vienna Draft Convention on Treaties: 'A material breach of a bilateral treaty by one of the parties *entitles* the other to invoke the breach as a ground for terminating the treaty or suspending its operation in whole or in part.' This implies that the injured State, if it does not exercise its entitlement to terminate the treaty, rightfully holds the wrongdoer to the treaty. To suggest that Article 60 does not do more than authorize and require a formal declaration to the effect that performance by the injured party will come to an end is a proposition inconsistent with the wording of the Article, the clear option it presupposes and the effect of the acceptance of a repudiation, namely the release of both parties from the duty of performance. Nor is it possible to subscribe to the view that the injured party 'must make up his mind within a reasonable time, otherwise he will lose his right to abrogate the treaty'.[59] If there is a single act which once and for all constitutes the breach of a treaty, such as the sinking of a ship, it may well be that even after protest the right to accept the repudiation is lost as a result of estoppel, acquiescence, delay or some similar legal principle. But if the wrong is a continuing one, if, for instance, the wrongdoer captures and holds the ship or occupies territory, there does not appear to be any good reason why the injured State, which, so it is assumed, has expressed its protest should suffer any loss of rights while the illegality lasts.

As a matter of principle, therefore, it is an indubitable rule of law in general and of international law in particular that a treaty fundamentally broken or abrogated by one party continues in force and is to be performed indefinitely by the defaulting party until the innocent party elects to declare it terminated.

4. It is against the background of the substantive law thus far expounded that it becomes possible to consider the *remedies* which international law permits the innocent party to exercise. In this connection it is particularly necessary to guard against unchecked generalizations, for by their *compromis* the parties may agree upon particular forms of remedy. The resulting decision, while often useful as an example, does not lend itself to the formulation of a widely applicable rule; nor does the absence of cases in which a particular remedy was applied for or used prove that in suitable circumstances it would not be available. Much, perhaps everything,

[57] *Ware* v. *Hylton*, 3 U.S. (3 Dall.) 199 (1796).

[58] In *Charlton* v. *Kelly*, 229 US 447 (1913), at p. 473, the Court said in relation to the possible violation of a treaty by Italy that this would justify the United States in denouncing the treaty. The Court continued: 'If the United States elected not to declare its abrogation so as to come to a rupture, *it would remain in force*. It was only voidable, not void; and if the United States should prefer it might waive any breach' (italics supplied).

[59] Lord McNair, *Law of Treaties* (1961), pp. 553, 571; Dahm, op. cit. (above, n. 10), p. 138.

depends on the terms of the claimant State's application, though the decision eventually pronounced by the tribunal will rest on the exercise of its own discretion: the tribunal cannot go beyond the terms of the application, but is not compelled to grant relief in the very terms requested or suggested by the claimant.

The most usual remedy is undoubtedly *declaratory* relief. International decisions ordinarily are 'not imperative in tone'.[60] The reason or at any rate the theory is that declarations are less likely to offend the susceptibilities of States, that no question of enforceability in any event arises on the international level and that it may normally be taken for granted that even in the absence of a direct order States act in accordance with their legal duties once these have been declared by the tribunal to which they have submitted (or have been held to have submitted); the failure of highly civilized States to do so or even to submit argument showing why they should not do so is a very recent phenomenon which has done grave and most regrettable harm to the idea and the ideal of the pacific settlement of disputes, but, it is hoped, will not in the long term render the value of a declaratory judgment less cogent. Already forty years ago Judge Hudson said:[61]

> In international jurisprudence, however, sanctions are of a different nature and they play a different role, with the result that a declaratory judgment will frequently have the same compulsive force as a mandatory judgment; States are disposed to respect the one not less than the other.

Similar views have frequently been expressed.[62] It is, therefore, the almost invariable practice of States to ask for a declaration designed to clarify the legal position and to lay the foundation for such additional claims for relief as may be necessary or expedient in order to work out more specific effects and implications of the declaration. This is what happened, for instance, in a striking fashion in the *Fisheries Jurisdiction* case.[63] While the United Kingdom, using a formula which by now has become traditional,[64] asked the Court to 'adjudge and declare' that as against the United Kingdom Iceland was 'not entitled unilaterally' to assert certain exclusive fisheries rights or to exclude British fishing vessels from certain areas,[65] the Court 'finds' for the United Kingdom and thus declares the parties' respective rights.[66] Nor is the power and the duty of an international tribunal to make a declaration in any way impaired by the extraordinary judgment of the

[60] Hudson, *International Tribunals* (1944), p. 120.

[61] *Diversion of Water from the Meuse* case, *P.C.I.J.*, Series A/B, No. 70, p. 79.

[62] In particular the statement was endorsed by the Joint Dissenting Opinion referred to below, n. 71.

[63] *I.C.J. Reports*, 1974, p. 3.

[64] See the case referred to below, n. 67, at p. 263 (paragraph 30).

[65] *I.C.J. Reports*, 1974, p. 3 at p. 7.

[66] Ibid., at p. 34.

International Court of Justice in the *Nuclear Tests* case,[67] which is the most recent of a series of disquieting decisions and may have done more than any other case to jeopardize the authority of the World Court. By an application dated 9 May 1973 Australia asked the Court 'to adjudge and declare that . . . the carrying out of further atmospheric nuclear weapon tests in the South Pacific Ocean is not consistent with applicable rules of international law.' Australia also asked for an order 'that the French Republic shall not carry out any further such tests'.[68] The oral argument was concluded on 11 July 1974. The Court found that unilateral statements made by French authorities between 25 July and October 1974 (on which Australia was not heard)[69] and indicating an intention to discontinue atmospheric tests after the end of 1974 met the object of Australia's second claim and that Australia's first claim 'cannot be regarded as being a claim for a declaratory judgment', that such a judgment 'would be only a means to an end and not an end in itself' and that, so one reads with amazement, 'the present case is not one in which such a declaratory judgment is *requested*'.[70] That this was factually and legally 'untenable'[71] was convincingly shown by the Joint Dissenting Opinion of Judges Onyeama, Dillard, Jiménez De Aréchaga and Sir Humphrey Waldock and the further Dissenting Opinions of Judges De Castro and Sir Garfield Barwick. The Court gravely prejudiced, *inter alia*,[72] the usefulness of declarations: if a declaration so clearly requested is held not to have been requested on account of its allegedly subsidiary character one of the remedy's most useful functions is likely to suffer. Nor was there any basis for the assumption made by the Court, for in respect of the years 1973 and 1974 Australia did not obtain any measure of satisfaction, clarification or guidance. One can only express the hope that it is not necessary to infer from this remarkable incident that the Court has broken with its long practice[73] and that it will not in future fail to decide disputes between States by way of a declaratory judgment (however embarrassing the circumstances may be) or to attribute to such judgments the primacy which they have for so long enjoyed.

[67] *I.C.J. Reports*, 1974, p. 253.

[68] Ibid., at p. 256.

[69] It may be that this is one of the gravest aspects of the decision. Had it been a municipal case the fact mentioned in the text would have brought the decision within Art. 6 of the European Convention on Human Rights which guarantees the right to a 'fair hearing'.

[70] *I.C.J. Reports*, 1974, p. 253 at p. 263 (italics supplied). The statement that no declaration had been requested is such that it is preferable to suppress any comment.

[71] Ibid., at p. 312 (paragraph 3).

[72] For an excellent and moderate comment upon the decision see Kewenig, in *Recht im Dienst des Friedens* (Festschrift für Menzel, 1975), p. 323.

[73] A declaratory judgment has frequently been described as the 'normal' judgment asked for and given in international proceedings. See, e.g., Wengler, op. cit. (above, n. 10), p. 720.

There is, however, another and more positive lesson which this judgment teaches. It seems to indicate, and even to rest on, the logical assumption that Australia was acting properly in making its second claim and that, accordingly, international law allows a State to claim and in a suitable case to obtain an order in the nature of a *negative injunction*. In fact Judge De Castro in his Dissenting Opinion spoke *obiter*[74] of Australia's right 'to ask the Court to uphold its claim that France should put an end to the deposit of radio-active fall-out on its territory'. Similar claims have frequently been made, apparently without objection, though even such claims are sometimes clothed in the form of a declaration. Thus in the *Case Concerning Right of Passage over Indian Territory*[75] Portugal asked the court to 'adjudge and declare' that India must 'abstain from any act hampering or impeding' the alleged right of passage. Or a significant dictum by Judge Sir Gerald Fitzmaurice in the *Case Concerning the Northern Cameroons*[76] illustrates the close interconnection between declaration and injunction:

> Now it is in no way singular that an allegation that a breach of treaty has occurred should not be accompanied by any claim for compensations or other reparation, where the treaty is still in force and operating, for in that case any finding in favour of the plaintiff State functions as a prohibition on the continuance or repetition of the breach of treaty, and this may be all that is required, and in any event makes the judgment effective.

In the *Fisheries Jurisdiction* case[77] the United Kingdom again did not apply for an order restraining Iceland from excluding British fishing vessels from the area in question, but asked the Court to 'adjudge and declare . . . that Iceland is not entitled unilaterally to exclude British fishing vessels'. The difference in formulation does not involve a difference of substance in the field of international law where no judgment, howsoever it may be expressed, is capable of being compulsorily executed except possibly within the scope of Chapter VII of the Charter of the United Nations.

Nor is there, finally, any reason why an international tribunal should not render a *mandatory order*. Thus an order for payment—a very frequent type of order—was made against Germany,[78] an order that it 'must withdraw its customs line' was made against France,[79] Thailand was

[74] *I.C.J. Reports*, 1974, p. 253 at p. 389. The value of the award in the *Trail Smelter* arbitration is, however, reduced as a result of Art. III of the Special Agreement between the United States of America and Canada, which conferred express powers upon the tribunal.

[75] *I.C.J. Reports*, 1960, p. 10.

[76] *I.C.J. Reports*, 1963, p. 98.

[77] *I.C.J. Reports*, 1974, p. 7.

[78] *The Wimbledon, P.C.I.J.*, Series A, No. 1 (1923).

[79] *Case of the Free Zones of Upper Savoy and the District of Gex, P.C.I.J.*, Series A/B, No. 46 (1932), p. 172

held to be 'under an obligation to restore to Cambodia' certain chattels.[80] Apart from the *Interhandel* case already referred to,[81] one can mention Liechtenstein which claimed that it be adjudged and declared that Guatemala 'should restore to Mr Nottebohm all his property which they have seized and retained'.[82] There is also academic authority for the proposition that an international tribunal may order the doing of an act such as the evacuation of territory.[83]

Where the claimant State desires to enforce its treaty rights (and only in such a case), the question arises whether the mandatory order may take the form of an order for *specific performance*.[84] No actual example of such an order has been found, but there is no reason in logic or justice why such an order should not be made. That it cannot be enforced is no obstacle, for no order by an international tribunal can ever be enforced. Nor is it material that in the common law countries specific performance is not invariably granted by the courts. The refusal usually occurs where enforcement would be impracticable or difficult, but, as has just been pointed out, in the context of international law this is not a relevant point. Even in the common law countries the courts have become much less reluctant to grant specific performance; even the obligation to pay may now be ordered to be specifically performed.[85] In any case, ever since the fusion of law and equity in 1873 it was incorrect to suggest that in the common law the structure of the contractual obligation was such as to imply no more than a duty to pay damages in case of breach; a somewhat dogmatic statement by Mr Justice Oliver Wendell Holmes[86] has led to much misunderstanding on the Continent.[87] There is certainly nothing in

[80] *Case concerning the Temple of Preah Vihear, I.C.J. Reports*, 1962, p. 37.

[81] Above, n. 22.

[82] *Nottebohm case, I.C.J. Reports*, 1955, p. 7. A curiously vague order was applied for by the United Kingdom in the *Anglo-Iranian Oil Co case, I.C.J. Reports*, 1952, p. 93, at p. 96, when it asked the Court 'to adjudge that the Imperial government of Iran should give full satisfaction and indemnity for all acts . . . which are contrary to international law or the aforesaid Convention, and to determine the manner of such satisfaction and indemnity'.

[83] Dahm, *Völkerrecht*, vol. 2 (1961), p. 540.

[84] It is very important to emphasize this. Much confusion has been caused as a result of use by some international lawyers of the phrase 'specific performance', when they mean restitution in kind. The two conceptions are entirely different. Specific performance is limited to the enforcement of contractual obligations. The confusion may be due to the fact that in order to describe the measure of damages the victim has frequently been said to be entitled to such sum as would afford him *restitutio in integrum*. See above, n. 5. Mosler, Hastings International & Comparative LR 4 (1981) p.441, also on declarations.

[85] *Beswick* v. *Beswick*, [1968] AC 58.

[86] *The Common Law* (1882), p. 301; *Collected Papers*, p. 175.

[87] An early work by Rheinstein, *Die Struktur des verträglichen Schuldverhältnisses im anglo-amerikanischen Recht* (1932), has much contributed to the false impressions on the Continent. For a good survey see Zweigert and Kötz, *Einführung in die Rechtsvergleichung*, vol. 2 (1969), pp. 162 sqq., and on the common law, pp. 177 sqq. Modern practice is illustrated, e.g. by *Evans Marshall & Co Ltd* v. *Bertola*, [1973] 1 W.L.R. 349, where a

the common law system that would compel an analogy to the effect that international tribunals cannot grant a mandatory order in the form of an order for specific performance.

5. Lastly it should be clear that the existence of an international wrong is to be distinguished from and is entirely independent of any procedural question to which the enforcement of the liability may give rise. Neither the absence of a tribunal having jurisdiction over the matter nor the claimant State's failure to proceed nor its decision not to exercise any remedies open to it nor its failure to afford diplomatic protection can affect the substance of the obligation and its breach. In particular, in the course of discussions about the exercise of the *jus standi* formulations may be found which suggest that the wrongdoing State's responsibility rests on the State of the victim's taking up the claim. But such formulations must be read in their context which usually did not require any emphasis upon the distinction which is here made and which is unlikely to meet with much opposition. It can in any event pray in aid a very clear and persuasive statement by Judge Sir Gerald Fitzmaurice, who said[88] that if a State acts illicitly

> it stands in breach of international law irrespective of whether any other State is qualified to take the matter up. For instance, if an individual were concerned, he might be stateless. If in the present case there have been contraventions of international law, they are in no way legitimized nor do they become any the less illicit, because Canada has not (or even possibly could not) pursue the matter, and because Belgium is held to possess no *locus standi in judicio* for doing so.

This, it is believed, is sound law, for a wrong committed by the standards of objective law does not become a right by virtue of the impossibility of pursuit or unwillingness to pursue it.

II. THE EFFECTS OF BREACHES OF CUSTOMARY INTERNATIONAL LAW BY THE FORUM STATE

1. As a matter of public international law it is free from doubt that, except in very special circumstances,[89] the rights accruing from an international wrong are vested in the victim State and lie against the wrongdoing State.

---

unanimous Court of Appeal granted an interlocutory injunction, although it was uncertain whether a permanent one would be granted, and specific performance would certainly have been denied.

[88] *Barcelona Traction Co* case, *I.C.J. Reports*, 1970, at p. 66.

[89] The European Convention on Human Rights, with its remedy of individual petition, provides the principal exception.

Nor can such rights be asserted otherwise than on the level of public international law, that is to say, in an international court or before an international arbitration tribunal. Does it follow that in municipal law an international tort is to be treated as nonexistent and that a municipal court or arbitrator cannot take cognizance of it? No unqualified answer is possible. A number of distinct aspects demand consideration.

The starting-point must be the lawyer's inclination and, indeed, his determination and duty to contribute to the pervasive influence of public international law and to secure its effectiveness. In pursuing this object municipal law, as history has proved, has an important role to play, for even if one disregards the academic, though morally attractive, monistic theory it would be most unfortunate if there arose a wide discrepancy between public international and municipal law. A cleavage cannot at the present stage of development be avoided altogether. Yet it can, and ought to be, reduced to the greatest possible extent by using domestic legal systems as an instrument in extending the scope and cementing the effectiveness of public international law. Admittedly such a tendency, demanded by the highest interests of the law and its supremacy, has in recent years been exposed to considerable strain. In far too many cases public international law has been flagrantly violated or proved powerless; international legal institutions, in particular the International Court of Justice, have frequently, for the sake of expediency, failed to live up to their responsibilities; academic lawyers, in the name of realism, have decried the creative tradition of the practice of municipal courts;[90] domestic lawyers have become sceptical of the effectiveness, the precision, the guiding force and even the value of public international law; for a period of more than a dozen years, now perhaps approaching its end, one of the most authoritative and enlightened tribunals in the world, the Supreme Court of the United States, had caused that high-mindedness and idealism which is necessary for the implementation of public interational law by municipal courts to be paralysed and undermined.[91] Yet the scholar

[90] The most unfortunate and at the same time the work which in the United States of America has proved most influential is Falk, *The Role of Domestic Courts in the International Legal Order* (1964) on which see Mann, this *Year Book*, 40 (1964), p. 399.

[91] This is the result of *Banco Nacional de Cuba* v. *Sabbatino*, 376 U.S. 398 (1964), on which see Mann, *Virginia Law Review*, 51 (1965), p. 604 or *Studies in International Law* (1973), p. 466. A change has been brought about by the Hickenlooper Amendment, s. 620(e) (1) of the Foreign Assistance Act 1961, by the decision in *Alfred Dunhill of London Inc.* v. *Republic of Cuba*, 425 U.S. 682 (1976), and, most strongly, by the letter from the Legal Adviser to the Department of State of 26 November 1975 (*International Legal Materials*, 15 (1976), pp. 164–6 or *Digest of U.S. Practice in International Law*, 1975, pp. 372–5) which concludes as follows: 'In general this Department's experience provides little support for a presumption that adjudication of acts of foreign States in accordance with relevant principles of international law would embarrass the conduct of foreign policy. Thus, it is our view that if the Court should decide to overrule the holding in *Sabbatino* so that acts of State would

as well as the practitioner, particularly the municipal judge, must not at any time allow his temporary disillusionment to overshadow the ultimate unity of the law. To put it differently, he must always remember and put into effect the aim of establishing the greatest possible harmony between public international and municipal law. To compel the municipal judge to commit or sanction an international wrong, or conversely, to force the international judge to reach a decision inconsistent with an established body of municipal law—these would be consequences which every inspired lawyer will strive to avoid as much as possible.

By the nature of things the (relative) harmony between the international and the municipal legal order can, in the sphere of State responsibility, be achieved only in so far as the nullity of the internationally wrongful act is concerned. Monetary compensation lies outside the reach of a municipal court. So does restitution in kind in the strict sense. But nullity, as has been shown, acknowledges the continued existence of the status quo and is, therefore, a type of *restitutio in integrum*. It exists *erga omnes*. Hence it should, in principle, be fully cognizable by municipal courts, though the circumstances in which such recognition is appropriate need definition. At the same time it must again be emphasized that it is only a legal act as opposed to a set of facts that is capable of being struck down by nullity. Hence the international lawyer cannot complain of the universal practice of municipal courts[92] to proceed against an offender who had been illegally seized in a foreign territory; the seizure is a fact against which the foreign State may have a just cause of complaint or which it may waive,[93] but which cannot be a nullity so as to deprive the forum of jurisdiction over a person in its actual control. Similarly the seizure of a ship in neutral waters is a fact so that the captor's prize court has jurisdiction over it, though the neutral State whose territorial sovereignty was infringed has a right to restitution in kind; on this point, therefore, the Anglo-American practice[94]

---

thereafter be subject to adjudication in American courts under international law, we would not anticipate embarrassment to the conduct of the foreign policy of the United States.' Such a statement, supported as it is by common sense and sound law, would seem entirely to remove the 'underpinnings' of the Act of State doctrine. And see below, n. 211.

[92] For a comprehensive review see the decision of 29 May 1962 by the Supreme Court of Israel in *Eichmann's* case, I.L.R., 36, pp. 57 sqq., where all the law up to 1962 is disucssed; on this case see the literature referred to by O'Connell, *International Law*, 2nd edn. (1970), p. 833 n. 3. Since then, in the same sense, *Argoud's* case decided by Cass. Crim., 4 June 1964, *Clunet*, 1965, pp. 93, on which see Doehring, *Zeitschrift für ausländisches öffentliches Recht und Völkerrecht*, 25 (1965), p. 209; see also pp. 295–300 where the attitude of the German Government is set forth.

[93] As Argentina eventually did in Eichmann's case, though Germany might have had a claim to restitution: see Mann, *Studies in International Law*, pp. 113, 114.

[94] As to the United Kingdom see, e.g., *The Düsseldorf*, [1920] A.C. 1034, or *The Pellworm*, [1922] 1 A.C. 292. As to the United States see, e.g., *The Sir William Peel*, 5 Wall. 517 (1867).

would seem to be unobjectionable, while the continental practice,[95] based on the alleged 'nullity' of the capture, rests on faulty legal analysis.[96] International law is in these respects in harmony with municipal practice: thus if a party to proceedings has illegally obtained a document, this is a fact which does not render the document inadmissible in evidence.[97]

The definition of the boundaries of nullity, then, is the task to which it is necessary to turn and which cannot be discharged without making a fundamental distinction between the consequences of an international wrong committed by the State of the forum and that committed by a State foreign to the forum. The former depend on the force which the constitutional law of the forum allows public international law to exercise over its own law. Accordingly it becomes necessary to distinguish between the status of customary and the status of conventional international law within the municipal system—in each case exclusively for the purpose, not of forming, developing or adapting a rule of municipal law, but of examining whether and to what extent both branches of international law or either of them can prevail over and nullify emanations of municipal law violative of it.

2. As regards customary international law there is no doubt that it was England that gave impetus to the idea of the municipal application of international law, and English law might have taken such a course as to confer supremacy upon the latter. The eighteenth century produced a number of cases[98] which in 1765 Blackstone summarized by the famous statement:[99]

> The law of nations (whenever any question arises which is properly the object of its jurisdiction) is here adopted in its full extent by the common law of the land.

This could have meant that public international law was not only directly applicable, but also conclusive in England except that even at that time it probably could not invalidate an Act of Parliament. During the following two hundred years many lofty pronouncements were made which pointed

[95] On it see O'Connell, *International Law*, 2nd edn. (1970), p. 836 or Morgenstern, this *Year Book*, 29 (1952), p. 265, at p. 274, whose observations on this aspect of the law merit close study.

[96] It is necessary to invoke first principles: possession is a fact. Its acquisition cannot be either valid or invalid. Even the thief has possession. On all this see, for instance, M. Wolff-Raiser, *Sachenrecht*, 10th edn. (1957), pp. 40, 59.

[97] *Karuma* v. *The Queen*, [1955] AC 197; *Lord Ashburton* v. *Pape*, [1913] 2 Ch. 469; and see Phipson on *Evidence*, 11th edn. (1970), section 584. The question whether there are countries in which the rule is different cannot be pursued in the present context.

[98] *Barbuit's* case (1737), Cas. temp. Talbot 281; *Triquet* v. *Bath* (1764), 3 Burr. 1478—a case decided by Lord Mansfield and argued by Blackstone; *Heathfield* v. *Chilton* (1767), 4 Burr. 2015.

[99] *Commentaries*, vol. 4, chapter 5.

in the same direction, and some high-minded scholars[100] attempted to assert and preserve the supremacy of international law; in fact to this day many continental observers are prone to represent English law as if the spirit of 1765 were still alive.[101] The truth is that the development was quite different and, as some may think, retrograde. It was succinctly summarized in a sentence for which Wynn-Parry J. bore responsibility and which deserves being saved from falling into oblivion:[102] 'The weight of modern authority regards those customary rules as part of English law only in so far as they have been adopted and made part of the law of England by legislation, judicial decision or established usage.' To put it differently, there does not appear to be any evidence at all in support of the suggestion that a British legislative, executive or judicial act, valid under British law, could ever be null and void on the ground of being contrary to customary international law or that a British court could refuse to apply it. And today this is by no means a peculiar characteristic of British law, for the position is the same in many other countries,[103] particularly the United States of America[104] and France, in regard to which a recent survey proved that the French judge, 'serviteur de la loi, il ne se reconnaît en aucune hypothèse le pouvoir de faire prévaloir le droit international . . . sur une règle ayant une valeur législative'.[105]

Notwithstanding its very liberal beginnings, the law of the United Kingdom thus ended up by accepting the principle which in 1919 the German *Reich's* Weimar Constitution formulated in its Article 4 and according to which the 'generally recognized' rules of public international

[100] Notably Sir Hersch Lauterpacht, *Transactions of the Grotius Society*, 25 (1939), p. 51 or *Collected papers*, vol. 1 (1970), p. 154.

[101] See, e.g., Guggenheim, *Traité de droit international public*, 2nd edn. (1967), p. 70: 'L'application immédiate du droit international coutumier est assurée [*sic!*] surtout dans les ordres juridiques anglo-saxons.'

[102] Halsbury (ed. Simonds), *Laws of England*, 3rd edn., title: 'Conflict of Laws', p. 4. The passage does not appear in the current, fourth, edition. The most recent example of a judicial statement of the law is *R.* v. *Secretary of State for the Home Department, ex parte Thakrar*, [1974] Q.B. 684, at p. 701 *per* Lord Denning, p. 709 *per* Lawton, L.J. But see now Lord Denning in *Trendtex Trading Corporation Ltd* v. *Central Bank of Nigeria*, [1977] 1 All E.R. 881,at p. 889.

[103] See, for example, High Court of Australia in *Polites* v. *Commonwealth*, (1945) 70 C.L.R. 6 or *Annual Digest*, 12 (1943–5), p. 208, or Supreme Court of Israel, 19 July 1951,in *Steinberg* v. *Attorney-General*, I.L.R. 18 (1951), p. 10.

[104] The principle that international law forms part of the law of the United States is stated with particular clarity in *The Paquete Habana*, 175 U.S. 677 (1900), at p. 700, where Mr Justice Gray also states the exception when he inserted the words: 'where there is no treaty and no controlling executive or legislative act or judicial decision'. See also *The Over The Top*, 5 F. 2d. 838 (1925).

[105] Dubois, p. 77 in *L'Application du droit international par le juge français* (Paris, 1972). The only decision by a supreme tribunal which is directly relevant is Cass. Crim., 4 June 1964, *Clunet*, 1965, 93 (*Re Argoud*), where the Cour de Cassation approved the lower court's decision that an indictment could not be null and void on the ground of a violation of German sovereignty committed by the abduction of the accused.

law were binding in Germany. This expression, which still governs in the German Democratic Republic[106] and which found its way, though probably with a different connotation, into the Constitutions of Austria[107] and Italy,[108] was understood to mean that nothing could be generally recognized that was not recognized by the *Reich*, and that therefore the *Reich* decided upon the controlling influence of international law. Thirty years later, in 1949, Article 25 of the Basic Law of the Federal Republic of Germany opened the door wide, and perhaps more widely than elsewhere, to public international law by providing: 'The general rules of public international law shall be an integral part of federal law. They shall take precedence over the laws and shall directly create rights and duties for the inhabitants of the federal territory.' Two points require emphasis. First, the general rules of public international law are automatically incorporated into German law, irrespective of recognition by the Federal Republic. Secondly, they take precedence over pre-existing German law (with the exception of constitutional law)[109] and a statute expressly abrogating or inconsistent with them or any one of them would in substance be invalid.[110] No case seems to have occurred in which German law was found to be contrary to customary public international law and for this reason excluded from application. But many judicial *dicta* disclose that German courts are very conscious of the effect of Article 25. On the other hand the federal

[106] Berber, *Lehrbuch des Völkerrechts*, 2nd edn., vol. 1 (1975), p. 100.

[107] According to Article 9 of the Austrian Constitution 'the generally recognized rules of international law are held to be integral parts of the federal law'. According to the Constitutional Court, 24 June 1954, I.L.R. 21 (1954), p. 212, the generally recognized rules of international law are incorporated into Austrian law as ordinary federal law. They do not have the quality of constitutional law. Therefore a statute inconsistent with international law cannot be held to be unconstitutional and, therefore, invalid.

[108] Article 10 (1) of the Constitution of 1948 reads as follows: 'The Italian legal system conforms to the generally recognized principles of international law'. For a survey of Italian law see O'Connell, *International Law*, 2nd edn. (1970), p. 68 or Oellers-Frahm, *Zeitschrift für ausländisches öffentliches Recht und Völkerrecht*, 34 (1974), p. 330. It seems to be accepted that the words 'generally recognized' do not require universality (ibid., p. 334), but those principles seem to have the standing of a constitutional provision (ibid., p. 341). A number of the decisions of the Italian Supreme Court holding the Hague Regulations to be part of customary international law and, therefore, of Italian law are to be found in I.L.R. 17 (1950), p. 419; 18 (1951), pp. 621, 681, 690.

[109] That the general rules of international law have only the status or quality of general law as opposed to constitutional law seems to be the better opinion: see, e.g. *BVerfGE*, 6, 309, 363; 37, 271, 279; *Bonner Kommentar*, Art. 25 note 3; Hamann, *Grundgesetz*, 3rd edn. (1970), Art. 25, note 3; Maunz-Dürig, Art. 25, note 25.

[110] The Federal Constitutional Court avoids the word 'invalidity', but prefers to speak of the general rules of international law breaking or superseding inconsistent municipal law: *BVerfGE*. 6, 309, 363; 23, 288, 316; 36, 342, 365. But it is unlikely that more than a terminological question is involved. A recent decision of the Federal Supreme Court explains wholly accurately that in the event of an inconsistency between international law and German municipal law the latter 'withdraws', but does not become contrary to Art. 25 or unconstitutional: 20 October 1976, *Juristenzeitung*, 1977, p. 67, at p. 68. However it is put, inconsistent German law is inapplicable.

Constitutional Court decided four years before the Vienna Draft Convention on the Law of Treaties[111] that, except in so far as peremptory norms were concerned,[112] customary international law was *jus dispositivum* in the sense that it could be displaced by a treaty to which the Federal Republic is a party.[113] The question whether a treaty concluded by other States can deprive a rule of public international law of the generality of its character has not been decided and is probably a matter of degree, the reference of the Basic Law being to general rather than universal rules.

The conclusion is that, though to a greater or lesser extent the rules of public international law are almost everywhere directly applicable,[114] it is not in many countries that a measure, lawful under the law of the forum, is liable to be held ineffective in the forum on the ground of its inconsistency with customary international law.

III. THE EFFECTS OF BREACHES OF TREATY OBLIGATIONS BY THE FORUM STATE

When one comes to deal with the municipal effects of the violation of treaty obligations assumed by the forum, one cannot help noticing a livelier, speedier and sometimes almost sensational development of constitutional (not international) law which owes much to the impact of the Treaty establishing the European Economic Community.[115]

Three principal sets of facts have to be distinguished.

1. There is, first, the case of the treaty which is binding in public international law upon the State of the forum, but which has not been

[111] See its Art. 53. The text is to be found, e.g., in *American Journal of International Law*, 63 (1969), p. 875.

[112] The Court defined them as follows: 'Only some elementary legal commands will have to be considered as rules of customary international law which do not permit contracting out. The quality of such peremptory norms can be attributed only to those legal rules which are firmly embedded in the legal conscience of the community of States, which are indispensable to the existence of public international law as an international legal system and the observance of which may be demanded by all members of the community of States.'

[113] 7 April 1965, *BVerfGE* 18, 441, at p. 448, or *Archiv des Völkerrechts*, 13 (1966/7), p. 122, at p. 126. The decision, on which see Riesenfeld, *American Journal of International Law*,60 (1966), p. 511, affirms Federal Finance Tribunal, 1 March 1963, *BStBl.* 1963, 3, p. 300 or *Archiv des Völkerrechts*, 11 (1963/4), p. 246, also I.L.R. 44, p. 149.

[114] As to Switzerland see Guggenheim, *Traité de droit international public*, 2nd edn. (1967), p. 73 with reference to cases in n. 4. In Austria public international law has the status of federal law and can therefore be overridden by inconsistent legislation: Constitutional Court, 24 June 1954, I.L.R. 21 (1954), p. 212.

[115] On the law discussed in this section see the discussion and the collection of material by Kaye Holloway, *Modern Trends in Treaty Law* (1967), pp. 151 sqq. and Michel Waelbroeck, *Traités internationaux et juridictions internes* (1969), an excellent work, though unfortunately to some extent already superseded by events; O'Connell, op. cit. (above, n. 10), pp. 56 sqq.; Berber, op. cit. (above, n. 10), pp. 96 sqq.

incorporated into its municipal legal system. The failure to transform the treaty into municipal law will invariably constitute a serious international illegality. But, although in accordance with their general practice municipal courts will usually try so to interpret their municipal law as to avoid a conflict, and there is a presumption in favour of the legislature's intention to observe international law,[116] they are bound to apply the municipal law as they find it, and if this does not include the treaty they can do nothing about it.

It must unfortunately be stated that conflicts of this kind have arisen in the United Kingdom with an alarming frequency. Perhaps the most prominent example is the European Convention on Human Rights which has never been made part of English law. The omission seems to be due to the wholly untenable belief that incorporation was unnecessary because English law was in conformity with the Convention;[117] if that illusion was not shattered earlier, it surely must have been exploded by the decision of the European court of Human Rights in *Golder's* case,[118] which, notwithstanding its obvious fallacy,[119] must have created much embarrassment for the United Kingdom (as well as many other countries). While the failure to transform into English law the Agreement on German External Debts made in London in February 1953[120] did not in England lead to any litigation of a possibly unworthy character, the same cannot be said of the case of *Administrator of German Property* v. *Knoop*,[121] where the judge had to apply English law knowing it to be contrary to a treaty, or of the circumstances which led to the probably even more invidious decision in *Republic of Italy* v. *Hambros Bank*,[122] where the Republic of Italy unsuccessfully tried to prevent an attempt of the Crown, by its agent, the Custodian of Enemy Property, to break a treaty made by it. To this day neither an explanation nor an excuse seems to have been proffered. The

[116] Maxwell, *Interpretation of Statutes*, 12th edn. (1969), pp. 183 sqq. As to the United States, the law goes back to Chief Justice Marshall in *Murray* v. *Schooner Charming Betsy*, 2 Cranch (6 U.S.) 64 (1804), at p. 118. For a more recent case see, e.g., *MacLeod* v. *U.S.*, 229 US 416 (1913), at p. 434 *per* Mr Justice Day. As to Germany see Maunz-Dürig, Art. 25 note 30, and Verdross and Simma, *Universelles Völkerrecht* (1976), p. 437.

[117] Sir Francis Vallat, *International Law and the Practitioner* (1966), p. 12.

[118] I.L.R. 57, 200.

[119] It was held that if a prisoner in an English prison believes he has been libelled in October 1969 and is due for release in July 1972, and if in April 1970 he is not given an opportunity to consult a solicitor about possible proceedings for damages for libel (which he could, but does not, institute on release), he has 'in the determination of his civil rights' been deprived of his entitlement 'to a fair and public hearing within a reasonable time' in the sense of Article 6 of the Convention. Quite apart from the extraordinary construction placed on Article 6, the elevation of the 'right' of a prisoner to consult a lawyer at will to a human right can only be noted with astonishment.

[120] *United Kingdom Treaty Series*, No. 7 (1959) (Cmnd. 626).

[121] [1933] Ch. 439.

[122] [1950] Ch. 314. On this case and on the case mentioned in the preceding note see Mann, *Studies in International Law*, pp. 351, 354, 356.

most serious, because the most authoritative, judicial breach of a treaty committed as a result of the omission of incorporation occurred through the decision of the House of Lords in *Black-Clawson International Ltd.* v. *Papierwerke Waldhof-Aschaffenburg A.G.*,[123] a decision which has so far failed to attract the close attention of public international lawyers which it merits. In 1960 the United Kingdom and the Federal Republic of Germany entered into a Convention for the Reciprocal Recognition and Enforcement of Judgments in Civil and Commercial matters.[124] It provided, *inter alia*, that a judgment entitled to recognition 'shall be treated as conclusive as to the matter thereby adjudicated upon in any further action between the parties . . . and as to such matter shall constitute a defence in any further action between them in respect of the same cause of action'.[125] Further, recognition 'shall not be refused merely on the ground that the original court has applied, in the choice of the system of law applicable to the case, rules of private international law different from those observed by the court or authority applied to'.[126] An action was dismissed by the District Court of Munich. The reason was that the claim was statute-barred under German law which, in the view of the court, was applicable. The majority of the House of Lords (Viscount Dilhorne, Lord Wilberforce and Lord Simon of Glaisdale)[127] held that, since the German judgment was based upon what English law regarded as a procedural matter it was not 'conclusive' and therefore not entitled to recognition under Section 8 of the Foreign Judgments (Reciprocal Enforcement) Act 1933. The Convention, not having been made part of English law, was not applied. In the course of a powerful dissenting opinion Lord Diplock wisely invoked the text of the Convention (which had been settled long before 1960 and, indeed, before 1933) as well as the material preceding it, for[128]

> where an Act of Parliament is passed to enable or to require United Kingdom courts to give effect to international obligations assumed by Her Majesty's Government under a treaty, it is a well-established rule of construction that any ambiguity in the words of the Act should be resolved in favour of ascribing to them a meaning which would result in the performance of those international obligations—not in their breach.

[123] [1975] A.C. 591. The comments on this case by Edler, *Rabels Zeitschrift für ausländisches und internationales Privatrecht*, 40 (1976), p. 43 do not deal with the point made in the text.

[124] See S.I. 1961, No. 1199. [125] Article III (4). [126] Article III (3).

[127] Lord Reid was of the opinion that the Act of 1933 did not apply at all in regard to foreign judgments in favour of a defendant. It may be expected that this will remain an isolated view, though unfortunately it was not expressly rejected by the majority.

[128] Pp. 640, 641. And see Lord Denning M.R. in *R.* v. *Chief Immigration Officer, exparte Bibi*, [1976] 1 W.L.R. 979, at p. 984, and see above, n. 115.

He found that the words 'question adjudicated upon' in the Convention threw light on the word 'conclusive' in the Act and referred to the actual decision, i.e., the operative part of the judgment, as opposed to the grounds or reasons supporting it. There can be no doubt that this interpretation corresponds to the German text of the Convention[129] and has in fact never given rise to any problem in Germany, where the Convention was adopted as part of the law, and the dismissal of the action in fact meant that the plaintiffs could not recover.[130] By looking at the reasons for the result reached by the German court and interpreting them in the English rather than the German sense, i.e., by treating them as procedural rather than substantive, the House of Lords, in the words of Lord Diplock, sanctioned a breach of the Convention, which, whether it could have been avoided by the judiciary or not, would almost certainly not have happened had the Convention been made part of English law. It remains a matter for regret, though perhaps not a matter of international responsibility, that the majority of the House of Lords did not avail itself of the opportunity of remedying a grave, albeit unintended, violation of international law by the United Kingdom.

In these circumstances it must be described as comforting that absence of transformation into domestic law occurs also abroad and is, therefore, not by any means a defect peculiar to the United Kingdom. Thus publication of treaties is the necessary and at the same time sufficient condition of their judicial application in France.[131] It appears that there are a number of cases in which treaties were not or were improperly published and for this reason excluded from application.[132] That States are liable to observe less than the strictest care in these matters is a surprising fact and calls for radical remedies.

2. A treaty, duly incorporated into the domestic legal system by legislative action, clearly prevails over pre-existing municipal law[133] even where the constitutional law of the forum does not include a clause such as Article VI clause 2 of the Constitution of the United States of America according to which treaties are the supreme law of the land, or Article 55 of the French Constitution of 1958 which provides that 'les traités ou

[129] The German text has for the English word 'matter' the word '*Anspruch*' and is, therefore, much clearer.

[130] Curiously enough Viscount Dilhorne, using these very words, said that that was 'all that the German court decided': p. 626. What else could or should the German court have decided? If an action is dismissed, the plaintiff cannot recover. If he cannot recover, it is conclusively established that he does not have a cause of action.

[131] Article 55 of the Constitution of 1958.

[132] See on the subject Batiffol and Lagarde, *Droit international privé*, 6th edn. (1974), vol. 1, no. 36, in particular n. 53, with references.

[133] The question whether it also prevails over constitutional law is a distinct one and has not met with a uniform answer. It cannot be pursued in the present context.

accords régulièrement ratifiés ou approuvés ont, dès leur publication, une autorité supérieure à celle des lois'. Such treaties, expressly or by necessary implication, repeal the earlier municipal law which is inconsistent with them. The reason lies in the rule *lex posterior derogat priori*. It is not public international law as such that has the effect of setting aside the earlier inconsistent law. The question which the judiciary faces is purely one of construction. It is governed by the general rules of statutory interpretation, though in the United States of America it has been held that the earlier law will be treated as repealed only if the incompatibility is clear and not merely implied.[134]

3. A much more difficult problem arises in the converse case of the incompatibility between a duly incorporated treaty and a subsequent inconsistent statute. Everywhere the courts have gone far to adopt a process of construction which will avoid such a clash,[135] and in the United States of America it has even been held that for a later statute to prevail over an earlier treaty the legislator's intention must be clearly expressed and in the absence of such expression the presumption against implied repeals of treaty law controls.[136] The position is similar in France where the leading formulation of the principle is to be found in the submissions of the celebrated Procureur Général Matter in 1931, who said that there exists 'en quelque sorte une présomption que la loi n'a pas voulu empiéter sur le traité et cette présomption ne peut être détruite que par une déclaration formelle de la loi'.[137] Thus, even before and independently of Article 55, above referred to, the supreme tribunals of France adopted a firm practice[138] which, more particularly, led to the rule that, where the earlier treaty conferred a benefit upon a foreigner, the later statute 'réserve *nécessairement* le cas où l'étranger peut invoquer une convention internationale'[139]—a rule which very recently was affirmed by the Conseil

[134] *Johnson* v. *Browne*, 205 US 309, 321 (1907). On Italy, see now Constitutional Court, 14 July 1976, *Europarecht*, 1977, p. 171.

[135] As to Germany see the references by Klaus Vogel, *Der räumliche Anwendungsbereich der Verwaltungsrechtsnormen* (1965), pp. 398, 399, and see below, n. 139. As to Austria see the references by Binder, *Zeitschriftfür ausländisches öffentliches Recht und Völkerrecht*, 35 (1975), p. 299 n. 75, and, generally, see above, n. 110.

[136] This goes back to Marshall C.J. in *The Charming Betsy*, 6 U.S. (2 Cranch) 64 (1804), and has frequently been reaffirmed. See *Chew Heong* v. *U.S.*, 112 U.S. 536 (1884); *US* v. *Payne*, 264 US 446 (1924); *Cook* v. *U.S.*, 288 U.S. 102 (1933); *Moser* v. *U.S.*, 341 U.S. 41, 45 (1951).

[137] Cass. Civ., 22 December 1931, *Clunet*, 1932, p. 687 with the submissions of M. Matter, also S. 1932, 1. 257. The principle is generally accepted.

[138] See the cases collected, e.g., by Batiffol-Lagarde, op. cit. (above, n. 132), no. 39, n. 69.

[139] Cass. Civ., 4 February 1936, S. 1936, 1. 257. On one occasion a German Court, the Supreme Finance Court, *RFH* 3, 10 (14), in effect took a similar course by treating a treaty as *lex specialis* in relation to a subsequent statute, so that, in the words of Vogel, op. cit. (above, n. 135), *lex generalis posterior non derogat legi priori speciali*.

d'État in spectacular circumstances:[140] even where the statute specifies the categories of foreigners entitled to the benefits which it grants, such a provision 'ne saurait être compris comme ayant eu pour effet d'en exclure les étrangers, même non visés par le décret du 4 septembre 1962, qui sont à même de se prévaloir d'une convention internationale'. Nothing less than an express exclusion by the new law of those covered by the earlier treaty is sufficient.

It is with regret that one notices the different and somewhat cavalier manner in which in recent years English courts have approached the problem. Although the starting-point is a rule which is similar to, though much less strongly formulated than, the French counterpart, the practice displays a striking cleavage. In *Collco Dealings Ltd.* v. *Inland Revenue Commissioners*[141] an Anglo-Irish Agreement of 1926, duly adopted by English legislation, provided for the exemption from certain British taxation of residents of Eire. In 1955 an English statute imposed tax on 'a person entitled under any enactment to an exemption from income tax'. The plaintiff, a company resident in Eire, was assessed to tax under the last-mentioned provision, but claimed that on its true construction it ought not to be applied to persons who were entitled under an enactment which incorporated a treaty benefiting foreign residents into English law. The claim failed. The argument that a wide construction of the relevant phrase would be contrary to 'the comity of nations and the established rules of international law' involved to the mind of Viscount Simonds no more than 'high-sounding phrases', and to invoke the Agreement with Eire '(which the appellant company, to add weight to the argument, prefers to call a treaty)' for the purpose of disregarding 'the plain words of the statute' was 'an extravagance'.[142] Although the other members of the House (Lord Morton of Henryton, Lord Reid, Lord Radcliffe and Lord Guest) gave the plaintiff company's case equally short shrift, the decision is far from convincing. Generality of expression should be insufficient to impute to Parliament the intention to involve the United Kingdom in a plain breach of obligations arising from a treaty, for notwithstanding Lord Simonds's disdain no less than a treaty was in issue.[143] However general, however 'clear' the words of a statute may appear to be, there always is room for the question whether they are intended to apply to a case to which, as a matter of international law, they ought not to and, therefore, may not apply. If we are serious in our desire and object to avoid a breach of international law by the United Kingdom it is *nihil ad rem* simply to point

[140] 25 July 1975, *Revue critique de droit international privé*, 1976, p. 60, with note by Valticos.

[141] [1962] A.C. 1. [141] [1962] A.C. 1, pp. 18, 19.

[143] This was the legal position, irrespective of any designation used by the High Contracting Parties.

to words which are sufficiently general and wide to comprise the uninviting result. Britain should not fail to adopt and give effect to the presumption which, for the discharge of their international duties, other countries have introduced into their law. It is very necessary to make this suggestion with respect yet with firmness, for in the House of Lords there were also remarks made to the effect that a breach of the treaty was a matter for the governments concerned, the implication being that the courts were at liberty to decide what they thought right.[144] Such a thought, it is submitted, indicates a dangerous road leading to the courts being relieved of all restraint which international law and the danger of its violation may impose. It also disregards the rationale of the presumption or the rule which earlier generations accepted. This is to protect the nation against complaints by a foreign State. The restraint which international law expects the courts to observe is imposed, not in the interest of a litigant, but in the interest of the State of the forum. Scrutton L. J.,[145] it will be remembered, went so far as to state that to hold foreign legislation to be contrary to essential principles of justice and morality would be 'a serious breach of international comity' and possibly a *casus belli*. We now know that this surely was an exaggeration, wrong in law and rejected by many later cases. But the approach was soundly based in that the observance of international law, where its rules apply,[146] is required of judges no less than of other organs of the State in the interest of their sovereign who is bound by it.

Although courts should and usually will strive by a process of construction to avoid a conflict between a treaty and a later statute, there are likely to be cases in which a clash is inescapable. If this happens the attitude of the courts will again be determined by constitutional rather than international law. It depends on constitutional law whether precedence is accorded to the earlier treaty or the later inconsistent statute. Until a short time ago an answer in the latter sense was supported by almost universal practice in most countries, but the EEC Treaty gave new impetus to the problem and its solution is undergoing remarkable changes. It is proposed to consider their effect on the general law and at the same time to ask whether the EEC Treaty itself is to be dealt with differently.

In Germany and Italy it is widely accepted that, since the incorporated treaty has the rank of an ordinary statute, it can be modified or repealed

[144] This appears particularly clearly from the opinion of Lord Reid, p. 22: 'Although the infringement of a treaty may cause loss to individuals, the only person properly entitled to complain of such infringement is the other party to the treaty.' Yet Lord Reid also said: 'there is a presumption that Parliament did not intend to act contrary to the comity of nations'.

[145] *Luther* v. *Sagor*, [1921] 3 K.B. 532, 558, 559.

[146] They did not apply in the case before Scrutton L.J., nor was there any rule of international law which could have precluded an English court from having resort to *ordre public*.

by subsequent legislation, even though this is likely to involve an infringement of the earlier treaty;[147] in particular it is difficult to see how in either country a different rule should apply in relation to the EEC Treaty, and in fact no court of final jurisdiction has as yet attributed any privileged status to it.[148] The only argument which could be put in both countries[149] and which is not by any means peculiar to the EEC Treaty is to the effect that the rules of customary international law have overriding force and that, therefore, the question arises whether these rules could invalidate legislation inconsistent with an earlier treaty of any kind. This might be so if the rule *pacta sunt servanda* could be treated as a general rule of international law within the meaning of the constitutional provisions,[150] particularly if it were to be supplemented by another general rule, curiously enough invariably overlooked by those participating in the discussion, according to which 'a State cannot adduce as against another State its own Constitution with a view to evading obligations incumbent upon it under international law or treaties in force'.[151] Such an argument is usually rejected, though the arguments are not always convincing. Thus when it is said that the rule cannot turn conventional into customary international law[152] this misses the point, for it is the breach of the treaty which international law does not permit and which the constitutional rule precludes from prevailing. Or it is suggested that the rule is intended to

[147] Apart from the literature referred to above, n. 115 see as to Germany, for instance, Maunz-Düring, Art. 25 note 29 and as to Italy Oellers-Frahm, *Zeitschrift für ausländisches öffentliches Recht und Völkerrecht*, 34 (1974), p. 337.

[148] In both countries the Constitutional Court held that EEC legislation is directly applicable, but that the fundamental rights guaranteed by the Constitution cannot be overridden by EEC law—a most welcome decision which unfortunately has met with much criticism (see, e.g., Scheuner, *Archiv des öffentlichen Rechts*, 100 (1975), p. 30). In both countries the question whether subsequent national legislation can set EEC law aside is unsettled. See Italian Constitutional Court, 27 December 1973, [1974] C.M.L.R. 372 and 30 October 1975, *Europarecht*, 1976, p. 246, and German Federal Constitutional Court, 29 May 1974, *BVerfGE* 37, 272.

[149] In Germany one of the chief exponents of the idea that EEC law prevails even over subsequent German legislation is Ipsen, *Europäisches Gemeinschaftsrecht* (1972), pp. 277–308.

[150] As mentioned above, Italian law speaks of generally recognized rules of international law, but this is not regarded as a form of qualification: Oellers-Frahm, loc. cit. (above, n. 141), p. 334.

[151] As to this principle see, generally, Brownlie, op. cit. (above, n. 10), p. 37 or, for instance, Permanent Court of International Justice in *Exchange of Greek and Turkish Populations*, Series B, No. 10 (1925), p. 20; *Jurisdiction of the Courts of Danzig*, Series B, No. 15 (1928), pp. 26, 27; *Free Zones of Upper Savoy and the District of Gex*, Series A, No. 24 (1929), p. 12; *Greco-Bulgarian Communities*, Series B, No. 17 (1930), p. 32. The two first-mentioned cases related to the failure to incorporate treaties into the municipal system of law.

[152] German Federal Constitutional Court, 9 June 1971, *BVerfGE* 31, 145, at p. 178. On the problem see W. K. Geck, *Bundesverfassungsgericht und Grundgesetz* (Festgabe für das Bundesverfassungsgericht, 1976), p. 135.

secure the international commitment, not the domestic law of the State and applies, therefore, only among States.[153] The international rule, however, requires observance of the treaty. It may leave it to the State to decide how the international rule is to be implemented. But it undoubtedly does require the fact of observance and if constitutional law renders international law obligatory in domestic courts it comprises all such international law as is self-executing, irrespective of the fact that originally international law is addressed to States and their instrumentalities, including their courts. In sum, one cannot help being impressed by those German and Italian scholars[154] who submit that the constitutional requirement of the paramountcy of customary international law precludes the recognition of a statute which is contrary to an earlier treaty.

This is the result which recently was arrived at in the Netherlands, France, Belgium and, apparently, Luxembourg. In the two first-mentioned countries there was probably little cause for surprise, for in the Netherlands Article 66 of the Constitution of 1966 expressly provides that treaties duly adopted and published have precedence over domestic law, whether they be concluded before or after the latter came into force, and in France Article 55 of the Constitution of 1958 attributes 'une autorité supérieure à celle des lois' to treaties which have been duly ratified and published. It is true that, notwithstanding the width of the formulation, it was until a short time ago almost generally believed that a later statute had to be applied even if it was inconsistent with an earlier treaty.[155] As recently as 1972 Monsieur Ange Blondeau, then Advocate General, ventured to predict that 'aussi bien les Chambres civiles que les Chambres criminelles appliqueraient la loi', not the treaty, the reason being that a French court cannot examine the constitutional validity of a statute and, therefore, lacks 'le moyen de faire triompher le traité sur la loi postérieure manifestement contraire'.[156] Yet on 24 May 1975[157] the highly authoritative Chambre Mixte of the Cour de Cassation, following the submission of the Procureur général Touffait, confounded all expectations and in relation to the EEC

[153] Berber, op. cit. (above, n. 10), pp. 100, 101, with references to those holding opposite views, including a decision of the German Federal Supreme Court.

[154] In Italy in particular Quadri and his school. See Quadri, *Recueil des cours*, 113 (1964–III), pp. 304–7.

[155] Batiffol-Lagarde, op. cit. (above, n. 132), no. 40.

[156] Reuter and others, *L'Application du droit international par le juge français*, p. 61.

[157] *Clunet*, 1975, p. 801, with note by Professor Ruzié who rightly emphasizes that the decision is not limited to EEC law, but as a result of the express reference to Art. 55 of the Constitution 'implique, de la part de la Cour de Cassation, sa volonté de faire prévaloir n'importe quel traité ou accord, regulièrement ratifié ou approuvé, sur toute loi postérieure'. The decision is also reported in *Revue critique de droit international privé*, 1976, p. 347 with Note by Jacques Foyer and D. Holleaux and in [1975] C.M.L.R. 336, at p. 367 in English, at p. 377 in French. The submissions by Monsieur Touffait had expressly requested the court (pp. 363, 364) not to invoke Art. 55, but to base the decision on the peculiarity of Community law. This the court refused to do.

Treaty deduced from Article 55 of the constitution the wholly general rule that a treaty 'a une autorité supérieure à celle des lois' and that consequently a provision of the treaty 'devrait être appliqué en l'espèce, à l'exclusion de l'article 265 du Code des Douanes, bien que ce dernier texte fut postérieur'.

If many French lawyers must have regarded this decision as startling, the development in Belgium was even more remarkable. Article 68 of the Belgian Constitution of 1831 provides no more than that treaties which bind individuals 'n'ont d'effet qu'après avoir reçu l'assentiment des Chambres'. Nevertheless, in a case involving the EEC Treaty, but on entirely general grounds, the Belgian Cour de Cassation, in accordance with the submissions of its Procureur Géneral, held[158]

> que la règle, d'après laquelle une loi abroge la loi antérieure dans la mesure où elle la contredit, est sans application au cas où le conflit oppose un traité et une loi; attendu que, lorsque le conflit existe entre une norme de droit interne et une norme de droit international qui a des effets directs dans l'ordre juridique interne, la règle établie par le traité doit prévaloir; que la prééminence de celle-ci résulte de la nature même du droit international conventionnel.

In view of the restricted scope of the constitutional provisions, the paucity of such reasoning as the Court advances is palpable rather than surprising and it remains to be seen how Belgian law will develop in years to come.

However this may be, it is hardly open to doubt that in other countries such as, in particular, the United States of America,[159] Switzerland[160] and the United Kingdom the later statute, in spite of its inconsistency with an

[158] Cass. 21 May 1972, [1972] C.M.L.R. 330, at p. 375.

[159] See, generally with reference to numerous cases, Hyde, *International Law*, vol. 2 (1947), pp. 1463–5. See, in particular, the *Head Money* cases, 112 U.S. 580 (1884); *Whitney* v. *Robertson*, 124 U.S. 190 (1888); *U.S.* v. *Lee Yen Tai*, 185 U.S. 213 (1902).

[160] In view of the British practice to which reference has been made, Swiss law is particularly instructive. The leading case is the decision of the Federal Tribunal of 22 November 1968, *BGE* 94 I 669. The question was whether a nineteenth-century treaty guaranteeing freedom of navigation on the Rhine to 'everyone' was made subject to the then existing Swiss postal monopoly or, alternatively, was repealed by a statute of 1924. Both questions were answered in the negative. As to the latter point it was stated as a principle of law (p. 678) 'that the federal legislator intends validly concluded treaties to remain effective, unless he expressly accepts that municipal law inconsistent with international law should come into existence. In case of doubt municipal law must be construed in conformity with international law'. It was found as a fact that the legislator of 1924 did not intend to create a state of affairs violating the treaty. In a decision of 2 March 1973, *BGE* 99 Ib 39 (in Italian); *Annuaire suisse de droit international*, 1974, p. 110 (in French); *Praxis des Bundesgerichts*, 1973, no. 106, p. 291 (in German) the Tribunal affirmed the principle and added: 'En règle générale et en cas de conflit ouvert le principe en question reconnaît la primauté du droit international, que celui-ci soit antérieur ou postérieur à la règle de droit interne.' In view of the *travaux préparatoires*, however, the Tribunal found that in the case before it Parliament had in fact intended to override the treaty obligation. On this case see Wildhaber, *Annuaire suisse de droit international*, 1974, p. 195.

earlier treaty, albeit the EEC Treaty, will prevail. As regards the United Kingdom[161] there is simply no legal basis which would enable any British court to disregard the will of Parliament as expressed in the subsequent statute. Nor has any, or any serious, argument to the contrary effect ever been put forward. It would run counter to a fundamental principle of constitutional law of the United Kingdom.

The conclusion to which the preceding survey leads is that in most municipal systems of law treaties have a much greater force than customary international law. Moreover in a growing number of countries treaties have a greater degree of legal force than subsequent but inconsistent municipal law. It must be hoped that these tendencies will become more pronounced so as eventually to establish and fortify the supremacy of international law. But however fervently international lawyers will be tempted to share this hope, they should be fully aware of the great dangers which legislation by treaty may involve if it is not entrusted to strict and continuous parliamentary control. There are many students of international and constitutional law who regard the substitution of bureaucratic for parliamentary control as one of the principal dangers to which international organizations such as the European Economic Community are exposed. One cannot but hope that a radical reform will be required in order to avoid the risk of national legislatures passing statues which violate treaty obligations.

IV. THE EFFECTS IN THE FORUM STATE OF FOREIGN VIOLATIONS OF INTERNATIONAL LAW (THE GENERAL RELATIONSHIP BETWEEN *ORDRE PUBLIC* AND INTERNATIONAL LAW)

When one comes to consider the effects which the forum State can or should attribute to international wrongs committed by a foreign State, the judge is rid of the fetters his own constitutional law may impose upon him. Both in law and from the point of view of sentiment or psychology he is free to render the requirements of public international law effective. Non-recognition or nullity in relation to a foreign State's international tort presupposes a judicial attitude that must appear to many as attractive or at least as natural. It is not difficult to make this clear by reverting to the

[161] See, among numerous other cases, *Madzimbamuto* v. *Lardner-Burke*, [1969] 1 A.C. 645, at p. 723 *per* Lord Reid. On the status of EEC law, in particular, see Lawrence Collins, *European Community Law in the United Kingdom*(1975), pp. 17 sqq., who argues convincingly that there is no room for departing in the case of EEC law from the traditional English law. (The opposite view expressed by Winterton, *Law Quarterly Review*, 92 (1976), p. 615 is wholly unconvincing; his suggestion that the subsequent statute 'was not, in fact, an Act of Parliament' can only be described as untenable.) The position in Eire is the same: *Re Lawless*, I.L.R. 24 (1957), p. 420

case which has already been mentioned[162] and in which English courts believed themselves to be able and compelled to disregard a treaty with the Federal Republic of Germany which had not been incorporated into English law. Suppose in that case the English court, rejecting the defence of the statute of limitations, had given judgment for the plaintiffs whose prior action in Germany had been held to be barred and therefore was dismissed. Suppose the plaintiff had taken the English judgment to Switzerland in order to enforce it there. Would the Swiss court enforce the English judgment, although it was in conflict with the earlier German judgment which, as a result of Britain's breach of international law, had been disregarded there?

The problem in all its sharpness arises only where a foreign country's internal law is applicable in the forum but said to be contrary to public international law. No real difficulty arises in cases in which the foreign State's acts can necessarily be tested only by the tenets of public international law, as occurs in particular in the case of external acts. Thus public international law must decide whether the waters in which a collision happened are the territorial waters of a foreign State or whether the jurisdiction purported to be exercised in, say, criminal or taxation matters is legitimate or excessive or whether the denial of personal immunity to a diplomat is lawful. In order not to extend the scope of the discussion too much, this type of case will have to be excluded, however capriciously the line may appear to be drawn.

It is obvious that in cases of the type intended to be explored the national judge has two different legal tools available in order to avoid, if he so wishes, the duty of giving effect to an international delinquency, viz. *ordre public* or public international law *per se*, and prima facie it does not matter which of these tools the judge may decide to employ, provided he reaches the correct result. Yet differences are liable to arise in a very limited category of facts. Hence on a previous occasion in 1954 it was attempted to show that for many reasons reliance on the objective and absolute standards of public international law was much to be preferred.[163] *Ordre public* is frequently designed to protect or assert the interests or values of the judge's nation, while public international law provides a more neutral and at the same time a uniform standard which has the additional attraction of assisting in rendering public international law more effective—a significant element in the case of a legal system that all *homines bonae voluntatis* wish to develop and strengthen, but the effectiveness of which is limited yet in need of expansion.[164] To suggest public

[162] Above, p. 147.

[163] 'International Delinquencies before Municipal Courts', *Law Quarterly Review*, 70 (1954), p. 181 or *Studies in International Law* (1973), p. 366.

[164] This point is made, for instance, in the thoughtful contribution by Professor Jänicke on

international law as a directly applicable test implies its obligatory character so as to deprive the judge of any discretion.[165] Yet there is no need to shrink from such a conclusion:[166] it has the advantage of being progressive; of facilitating both the reasoning and the decision of the judge and of protecting him against participating in the consummation of an international wrong.

Both the arguments previously put forward and the results then adumbrated are fully maintained; indeed, hardly any criticism of a fundamental nature has become known. Nor is it intended to repeat anything then said. Rather is it proper to review certain recent developments which are likely to lend emphasis to the suggestion that in appropriate cases the national judge should allow himself to be guided by public international law as opposed to his own public policy and that for him the violation of international law by a foreign State should be sufficient and even compelling to reject the application of its law.

For this purpose two aspects of particular significance will be selected for closer investigation. On the one hand something will have to be said about judicial attitudes which disclose a tendency to apply or to purport to apply public international law, though nominally it is public policy that is being prayed in aid. On the other hand it will be shown that public policy is an unsafe rule of decision in that it may enable the national court to reach and justify decisions which are alien to an enlightened system of law and the demands of justice.

Before turning to these two headings one must make it clear that it is

---

'International *Ordre Public*', *Berichte der Deutschen Gesellschaft für Völkerrecht*, 7 (1967), p. 77, particularly p. 84. The learned author is probably to a large extent in agreement with the submissions made in the text, but it is odd that he advocates, not the overriding effect of public international law as such, but only of the 'international *ordre public*' which in his terminology seems to be limited to what is known as the *jus cogens* of public international law. It is difficult to understand the justification or the necessity for such a limitation. In a recent paper of great value ('Le droit international privé face au droit international', *Revue critique de droit international privé*, 1976, p. 261) Professor Rigaux has reminded us (p. 284) that Niboyet in 1928 and since then many others have spoken in favour of giving effect to 'un véritable ordre public international'.

[165] This is really the essential distinction: resort to *ordre public* is in the last resort discretionary, the application of public international law is or ought to be mandatory. For a general discussion of the relationship between public international law and *ordre public* see Lipstein, *Recueil des cours*, 135 (1972–I), pp. 189–92.

[166] Jänicke, loc. cit. (above, n. 164), p. 119, is right in pointing out that it is not at present possible to prove a rule of customary international law imposing a duty not to recognize foreign law which is internationally illegal. But every author who adds an argument in favour of such a duty contributes to its creation, and Jänicke himself suggests with much persuasiveness that 'where a norm is in issue the observance of which decisively interests not only the injured State, but the international community as a whole and which therefore forms part of the international *ordre public* all States should regard it as their duty to refuse recognition to a foreign State's acts of sovereignty which infringe such a norm'.

not proposed to allow room to the doctrine of the sacrosanctity of the foreign act of State, a doctrine which, if it existed, would preclude any investigation into a foreign legal system's reconcilabililty with public international law or, possibly, with public policy. The doctrine with all its implications is peculiar to the law of the United States of America where it is now established to rest on constitutional 'underpinnings',[167] that is to say, it is designed to preserve the sole control of the Executive over foreign affairs. However, not only the legislator,[168] but also the very branch of government in charge of foreign affairs, viz. the Department of State,[169] have to a large extent disowned it, so that even in the United States its disappearance or at least its severe restriction is on the cards. In Europe there exists in a limited type of case some evidence of a kind of immunity *ratione materiae*,[170] but there has never been any trace of a general principle that would undermine the relevance and importance of the questions to be discussed. There is certainly no evidence whatever that in Europe the principle of the separation of powers is so understood or, perhaps one should say, so misunderstood as to compel a court, in deference to the actual or possible views of the executive, to apply a foreign law which is clearly opposed to public international law—and this is the sole point on issue here.[171]

[167] *Banco Nacional de Cuba* v. *Sabbatino*, 376 U.S. 398 (1964), at p. 423 *per* Mr Justice Harlan. The decision and its numerous implications cannot be discussed here in any detail. See, however, *Virginia Law Review*, 51 (1965), p.604 or *Studies in International Law* (1973), p. 466.

[168] See the so-called Hickenlooper Amendment of 1964. The text can be found, e.g., in *International Legal Materials*, 11 (1972), pp. 41, 42. See further the Foreign Sovereign Immunities Act 1976 (*International Legal Materials*, 15 (1976), p. 1388) which provides in s. 1605 (a) (3) that a foreign State shall not be immune in any case 'in which rights in property taken in violation of international law are in issue and that property or any property exchanged for such property is present in the United States in connection with a commercial activity carried on in the United States by the foreign State'. The same applies if the property 'is owned or operated by an agency or instrumentality of the foreign State' which is engaged in a commercial activity in the United States. For a recent review of the Act of State doctrine see Leigh and Sandler, *Virginia Journal of International Law*, 16 (1976), p. 685. Lower courts unfortunately continue to attribute its full strength to the doctrine: see, e.g., *United Bank Ltd* v. *Cosmic International Inc*, 542 F. 2d 868 (1976) or *D'Angelo* v. *Petroleos Mexicanos*, 422 F. Supp. 1280 (1976).

[169] Above, n. 90.

[170] It is possible that the idea is inherent in the decision of the Court of Appeal in *Buttes Gas & Oil Co* v. *Hammer*, [1975] 1 Q.B. 557, and also in such cases as *M. Isaacs & Sons* v. *Cook*, [1925] 2 K.B. 391, where it was held that a communication by the High Commissioner of Australia in his official capacity to the Prime Minister of Australia in execution of his duties is absolutely privileged as an act of State. See also *Szalatnay-Stacho* v. *Fink*,[1947] KB 1, where, perhaps surprisingly, the defence of act of State was disclaimed by Counsel (p. 6); on this case as decided at first instance see Mann, *Modern Law Review*, 9 (1946), p. 179. And see the French decision, Cour de Paris, 26 February 1880, D.P. 1886, 1. 393 and the material referred to by Mann, *Studies in International Law*, p. 430, n. 1. The French practice according to which 'les actes se rattachant aux relations internationales de la France ne sont pas de nature à être déférées à la juridiction administrative' (Conseil d'État, 11 July 1975, *Clunet*, 1976, 126) may also be expressive of the same idea.

[171] It is, however, not without interest to remember the practice of the civil divisions of

1. In the first place one cannot help noticing symptoms of *ordre public* acquiring a more international rather than a national or even nationalistic character, so that direct reliance on international law becomes a more familiar and safer guide.

Unfortunately we cannot, it is true, attach too much importance to a dictum by Sir Hersch Lauterpacht according to which *ordre public* 'must be regarded as a general principle of law in the field of private international law', so that 'it may not improperly be considered to be a general principle of law in the sense of Article 38 of the Statute of the Court' and that 'its content must be determined in the same way as that of any other general principle of law in the sense of Article 38 of the Statute, namely by reference to the practice and experience of the municipal law of civilized nations in that field.'[172] If this were true, the distinction between *ordre public* and a rule of international law would not survive for long. Moreover, Professor Lipstein, in a very moderate, but highly persuasive contribution,[173] has shown that the opinions delivered in the case before the International Court of Justice in which the quoted words occur are open to very considerable doubt. It is, therefore, more prudent to treat them as an interesting thought which is not reflected in actual State practice. Yet it is this practice that has in fact shown a measure of universalism, at any rate outside France where, notwithstanding an earlier lead given by Niboyet,[174] authors of high authority continue to assert that 'en réalité les tribunaux n'apprécient pas la régularité au regard de la loi étrangère, ou même du droit international, de l'acte en cause; ils lui refusent seulement effet en France au nom de conceptions françaises réputées indispensables à sauvegarder'.[175]

One of the strongest cases (in which, however, the foreign law did not constitute an international wrong) comes from Germany, where the Federal Supreme Court held[176] that an insurance policy covering the

---

the French Cour de Cassation according to which the interpretation of treaties is a matter for the government in so far as they 'mettent en jeu des questions de droit public international'. On the other hand the criminal division as well as the Conseil d'État take the view that the interpretation of treaties invaribly belongs to the Executive. The reason lies in the idea of the separation of power. In this sense the French courts, on whose practice see Batiffol-Lagarde, op. cit. (above, n. 132), nos. 37 and 40, give to that principle a wider, though different, meaning than the United States of America. All these matters would be worthy of a fresh, broadly based comparative study.

172 *Case Concerning the Application of the Convention of 1902 Governing the Guardianship of Infants* (Netherlands *v.* Sweden), *I.C.J. Reports*, 1958, p. 55, at p. 92.

173 *International and Comparative Law Quarterly*, 8 (1959), p. 506; cf. Batiffol-Lagarde, op. cit. (above, n. 132), no. 303.

174 See above, n. 164.

175 Batiffol-Lagarde, op. cit. (above, n. 132), no. 357. The approach is similar in Germany.

176 *BGHZ* 59, 82 (22 June 1972). See the detailed analysis of the decision by Bleckmann, *Zeitschrift für ausländisches öffentliches Recht und Völkerrecht*, 34 (1974), p. 112. Another case of considerable interest is the decision of the Court of Appeal in Brussels, 20 January

transport of works of art from Nigeria to Hamburg could not be enforced by the assured who was exporting the works of art in breach of Nigerian law. The rationale was that as a result of a Convention sponsored by UNESCO, but not then adopted by Germany, the exportation of cultural possessions was considered to be contrary to public order and impeding the understanding between nations. 'Within the community of nations there exist definite and fundamental convictions about every country's right to protect its cultural heritage and about the condemnation of practices which jeopardize it and should be suppressed. Therefore, in the interest of the preservation of decency in international intercourse, the exportation of cultural possessions prohibited by the country of origin is unworthy of legal protection.' This is a significant case, because it clearly shows international law as the standard whereby the legality of a transaction is being measured. It is the more remarkable in that in Germany it is by no means certain that there exists a firm and general principle to the effect that the deliberate violation of a foreign prohibition is necessarily contrary to *ordre public*.[177]

Such a principle does exist in England, where at the same time its dangers have become apparent. In England a contract is illegal 'if its performance will involve the doing of an act in a foreign and friendly State which violates the law of that State'.[178] However strongly one may wish to support the condemnation of a contract which by its terms *necessitates the parties or one of them*[179] committing an illegality in a foreign country, so broad, vague and inexact a term as 'involve' creates great dangers,[180] as can be demonstrated by the case in which it occurs and the principle was most authoritatively stated. Under a contract governed by English law the Swiss plaintiff bought from the English defendants a quantity of Indian

---

1965, *Pasicrisie belge*, 1966, vol. 2, p. 19 (in Flemish), or in an abbreviated French version, *Revue belge de droit international*, 1967, p. 566: In 1954 the Governor of Goa caused a letter of credit to be opened. The bank paid, but after the annexation of Goa by India in 1960 a Governor in exile in Portugal claimed repayment. The Court of Appeal dismissed his action, but held that he had *locus standi*: Goa 'a été envahi et occupé à main armée par l'État de l'Inde; qu'aucune conséquence juridique ne peut être reconnue à cet acte de violence, en attendant un traité international; . . . que la reconnaissance de cette violence serait complètement contraire à l'engagement qui a été pris par les États membres des Nations Unies (dont l'Inde et le Portugal), lors de la signature de la Charte'.

[177] See the note by Mann, *Neue Juristische Wochenschrift*, 1972, p. 2179, on the case referred to in the preceding note.

[178] *Regazzoni* v. *Sethia*, [1958] A.C. 301, at p. 317 *per* Viscount Simonds. For the French law on the point see Batiffol-Lagarde, op. cit. (above, n. 132), no. 598.

[179] This probably was the *ratio decidendi* in *Foster* v. *Driscoll*, [1929] 1 KB 470 which related to smuggling of alcohol into the United States during prohibition.

[180] See Mann, *Modern Law Review*, 21 (1958), p. 130. A fresh view of *Regazzoni's* case confirms the impression that it was an unfortunate decision, because the facts did not support it. It is perhaps one of those cases which would have decided differently if the argument had been put less high.

twills c.i.f. Genoa. Both parties knew that the goods were to be resold to South Africa, that the law of India prohibited the export of goods directly or indirectly destined for South Africa and that the sellers intended to find an Indian supplier who would not ask inconvenient questions about the ultimate destination of the goods. In these circumstances, so the House of Lords held, 'deference to international comity'[181] required the contract to be illegal in English eyes, although no acts actually done or to be done in India were proved. 'Comity' may refer to 'rules of politeness, convenience and goodwill'.[182] In this sense the term is an unsafe guide and should be without legal relevance, for it is capable of justifying whatever result judicial discretion may prefer. Or 'comity' is, or is intended to be, synonymous with international law. This would be a welcome guide and it was in fact adopted by Best C. J. more than 150 years ago, when he held that the raising of a loan to support rebels in their revolutionary activities against a friendly State was contrary to 'the law of nations',[183] and similarly, though perhaps a little surprisingly, by the Court of Appeal in Paris when it held in 1966 that a contract made in Geneva between two Liechtenstein corporations for the purchase and sale of war materials was 'contraire à l'ordre public international.'[184] But in 1958 in *Regazzoni's* case the House of Lords implied that even if the legislation of India, a member of the British Commonwealth, had constituted a breach of international law, an English court had no alternative but to disallow an attempt to infringe or evade it, for it is just this consequence which is implied in Lord Reid's remarkable, though imprecise and legally dubious, statement according to which[185]

> it is impossible for a court in this country to set itself up as a judge of the rights and wrongs of a controversy between two friendly countries, we cannot judge the motives or the justifications of governments of other countries in these matters and, if we tried to do so, the consequences might seriously prejudice international relations. By recognizing this Indian law so that an agreement which involves a breach of that law within Indian territory is unenforceable we express no opinion whatever, either favourable or adverse, as to the policy which caused its enactment.

However strongly one may wish to support the condemnation of a contract which by its terms compels the parties or one of them to commit

[181] *Regazzoni* v. *Sethia*, [1958] A.C. 301, at p. 319 *per* Viscount Simonds. See also Lord Keith at p. 327.

[182] Oppenheim (ed. Lauterpacht), *International Law*, vol. 1, 8th edn. (1955), p. 34 n. 1.

[183] *De Wütz* v. *Hendricks* (1824), 2 Bing. 314, 315-16.

[184] 9 February 1966, *Revue critique de droit international privé*, 1966, p. 264 with note by Louis-Lucas.

[185] [1958] A.C. 301, at p. 326. Lord Keith at p. 327 said that the English courts could not 'adjudicate upon political issues between India and South Africa'. This is undoubtedly correct, but not in point.

an illegality in a foreign country, and however warmly one should advocate the existence of a rule of international law to that effect, the far-reaching principle formulated by the House of Lords is in many respects open to considerable doubts. In fact it is peculiarly apt to indicate the wide and disquieting gulf between public policy defined by the idiosyncrasies of the national judge and public international law as a guide. It is not possible within the confines of the present observations to explore in depth the question whether the Indian prohibition of exports to South Africa was contrary to public international law, but there is undeniably material which required consideration of the problem. It is by no means fanciful to suggest that in modern international law economic constraint is illegal; suffice it to recall the United Nations' Declaration on the Inadmissability of Intervention in the Domestic Affairs of States of 1965,[186] according to which 'no State may use . . . economic, political or any other type of measures to coerce another state in order to obtain from it the subordination of the exercise of its sovereign rights or to secure from it advantages of any kind'. It may be that this Declaration is typical of the United Nations' 'double-talk'.[187] It is even more likely that the Declaration is without legal force. Yet it is indicative of a possible legal principle which may find support elsewhere. A second line of investigation arises from the participation of both India and South Africa in the General Agreement on Tariffs and Trade (GATT). According to its Article XIII, 'no prohibition or restriction shall be applied by any Contracting Party . . . on the exportation of any product destined for the territory of any other Contracting Party, unless . . . the exportation of the like product to all third countries is similarly prohibited or restricted'. If for both or either of these reasons the Indian prohibition had been internationally illegal (a hypothesis which, let it be repeated, is for present purposes simply assumed, but in no way accepted), then the House of Lords' somewhat facile reliance on 'comity' or on the irrelevance of 'motives' would have been misplaced. The real question would or ought to have been: does public international law require or even permit the application of national public policy upholding the binding force of Indian legislation or, on the contrary, its condemnation as an international wrong? Is it permissible to treat the violation of a foreign law as contrary to public policy if such law itself is contrary to public international law? The House seemed, perhaps a little faintly, to admit exceptions from the English rule in case of the foreign legislation's being a measure of persecution.[188] Should it not also admit an exception in case of

[186] General Assembly Resolution 2131 (xx), paragraph 2, in *International Legal Materials*, 5 (1966), p. 374.

[187] The majority surely did not intend it to operate in favour of South Africa.

[188] Lord Reid, [1958] A.C. 301, at p. 325, Lord Somervell at p. 330; see also Viscount Simonds at p. 319.

the measure's being discriminatory or for other reasons internationally illegal? It does not matter whether the point is being dealt with by way of rule and exception. What does matter is that a national court should not give assistance to the commission of an international illegality by a foreign State whose laws are applicable. If Indian legislation had constituted an international wrong it should be refused recognition and its violation ought not to be condemned by national judges. There is no reason to regret some lines written in the summer of 1956:[189]

> anyone who thinks of Nazi or Communist laws, of their far-reaching international repercussions and their claims to international enforcement will be bound to read *Regazzoni's* case with a feeling of bewilderment. One also wonders how the decision will work out in the following, not wholly imaginary case: X, a Jewish merchant in Manchester, needs Egyptian cotton. By Egyptian law the direct or indirect supply of Egyptian goods to Jews is prohibited. Y, a merchant in London whom Egyptian law defines as 'Aryan' can obtain Egyptian cotton. He agrees to do so and sell it to X. Will X's action be dismissed on the grounds that . . . the courts of one country should not help to break the laws of another?

2. If one turns, secondly, to consider whether, apart from international law, *ordre public* is sufficient to achieve results which meet the crucial cases of international wrongs committed by the State of the *lex causae* a negative answer is entirely within the realm of possibility. The main reason is that, as a matter of principle, many countries understand *ordre public*, not as the 'essential principle of justice and morality',[190] that is to say, as a rule of a fundamental and general character, but as the specific legal and moral order of the forum; to put it differently, a violation of *ordre public* is liable to be found, not in 'something contrary to the morality of civilized nations as we understand it',[191] but in something contrary to the laws, institutions and conceptions peculiar to the forum. This is known as the relativity of *ordre public* and means that in order to justify resort to it the forum must be affected, there must be a *Binnenbeziehung*, an appropriate relationship or link with a domestic situation. *Ordre public* conceived in so limited and so national, perhaps even chauvinistic, a sense will clearly be determined by standards other than those of public international law and may, therefore, recognize and enforce foreign laws or transactions which international law would condemn—not necessarily because such laws and transactions meet with approval, but because they are not of a sufficiently close concern. The point is made very clear in a recent decision of the

[189] Mann, *Modern Law Review*, 19 (1956), p. 524.

[190] The phrase is used by Buckley L.J. (as he then was) in *Saxby* v. *Fulton*, [1900] 2KB 208, 228.

[191] Ibid., *per* Kennedy L.J. at p. 232.

German Federal Supreme Court.[192] The question was whether the property of the infant son of an Iranian father and mother of both German and Iranian nationality whose marriage had been dissolved and who were both resident in West Berlin was, in accordance with Iranian law, subject to his father's control to the exclusion of the mother. The lower court had invoked *ordre public* to give effect to the German doctrine of equal parental rights. The Federal Supreme Court defined the requirements by stating that what mattered was 'the relationship with domestic law in the individual case. If all interested parties are aliens of the same nationality German *ordre public* does not as a rule demand the non-application of parental rights granted by the *lex patriae*. The opposite would lead to the unnecessary imposition of foreign law. If only certain parties are aliens, the particular circumstances of the given legal situation must be examined . . . If only one spouse is a German national the ordinary residence of the family on German territory does not necessarily involve the right to the recognition of equality between husband and wife. In such a case adaptation is required . . .'

It must, however, be emphasized that this requirement of an intensive link with domestic law which is characteristic mainly of Swiss[193] and German law but is also known in England[194] and France[195] is in practice frequently less formidable than at first sight appears and the textbooks suggest. In a large number of cases it is in fact fulfilled, though this is not always appreciated. The starting-point lies in the indubitable fact that if one of the parties is a national of the forum State the necessary link with its law exists. In a case of great significance (which, however, is hardly ever referred to by commentators) the German Federal Supreme Court held[196] that if a treaty between the forum State and one of the parties' national State confers upon the nationals of one country the right to national treatment in the other country, viz. the right to be treated upon terms no less favourable than the terms accorded in like situations to nationals, then the alien may rightfully and necessarily invoke *ordre public* as if he were a national. Such treaty rights exist in innumerable cases, for they are not only expressly conferred upon nationals of the Contracting State, but also originate from a far-flung net of most-favoured-nation

[192] 20 December 1972, *BGHZ* 60, 68, at p. 79; cf. Kegel, *Internationales Privatrecht*, 4th edn. (1977), p. 239, among many other writers.

[193] See, e.g., Vischer, *Internationales Privatrecht*, p. 535.

[194] Lloyd, *Public Policy*, p. 84; Cheshire and North, *Private International Law*, 9th edn. (1974), p. 150; Kahn-Freund, *Transactions of the Grotius Society*, 39 (1954), pp. 39 sqq. and *Recueil des cours*, 143 (1974–III), pp. 428, 429 and probably many other writers.

[195] This is not very clear, but can possibly be inferred from Batiffol-Lagarde, op. cit. (above, n. 132), no. 367, who discuss what they describe as the 'effet atténué' of *ordre public*.

[196] 8 March 1963, *BGHZ* 39, 220, at p. 232 with reference to Art. 2 of the Paris Union relating to Industrial Property of 1883, as amended.

clauses. If it is remembered that between the end of the Second World War and 1971 the United States of America alone entered into twenty-one Treaties of Friendship, Commerce and Navigation with, *inter alia*, Belgium, Denmark, France, Germany, Greece, Eire, Italy, Luxembourg, Netherlands (to mention only European countries)[197] and that these treaties, as most of their kind, include both the national treatment and the most-favoured-nation clauses, it is easy to imagine the great reduction which the scope of the 'link theory' would suffer if practitioners were aware of these treaties and undertook the often heavy burden of tracing them. Moreover, in so far as the Parties to the European Convention on Human Rights are concerned, it may well be that the denial of a legal right to the national of a member State on the ground of his foreign nationality would be contrary to Article 6 in conjunction with article 14 which in the view of the majority of the European Court of Human Rights 'is complementary to the other normative provisions of the Convention and Protocols: it safeguards individuals, or groups of individuals, placed in comparable situations, from all discrimination in the enjoyment of the rights and freedoms set forth in those provisions'.[198] And in so far as the Parties to the International Covenant on Civil and Political Rights are concerned (which was adopted by the General Assembly of the United Nations on 16 December 1966 and came into force for the United Kingdom on 20 August 1976)[199] it would seem that the equal protection of the law guaranteed by Articles 2, 14 and 16 prohibits any discrimination on the ground of nationality. It is submitted that even where such treaties are not incorporated into the national law (as is frequently the case in Britain), they can and must be taken into account by the court when assessing the scope or intensity of *ordre public*.

Yet, however wholesome the influence of the 'link theory' undoubtedly is in many contexts, within the limited field of the subject-matter of the present discussion it may impede decisions which public international law requires. How do we judge the validity of a marriage between a man and a woman of different race or religion who by the law of their home country are incapable to intermarry? There can be no doubt that public international law condemns such legislation and renders it illegal and void.[200] If

[197] For a list see Mann, *The Legal Aspect of Money*, 3rd edn. (1971), p. 547 n. 2. It is odd that even the United States does not render it easy to ascertain a complete list as it exists from time to time. Whiteman's *Digest* does not seem to contain any list.

[198] *Belgian Linguistics* case, 23 July 1968, paragraph 9 (I.L.R. 45 (1972), p. 114 at p. 164); *National Union of Belgian Police* case, 27 October 1975, paragraph 44, with a strong and logically unassailable Dissent by Judge Sir Gerald Fitzmaurice.

[199] *United Kingdom Treaty Series*, No. 6 (1977) (Cmnd. 6702).

[200] See Art. 16 of the Universal Declaration of Human Rights; Articles 12 and 14 of the European Convention on Human Rights. See also Articles 2 and 23 of the International Covenant on Civil and Political Rights of 16 December 1966 (previous note). When in the

the municipal judge were to have resort to public international law he would not in any circumstances recognize or give effect to such incapacities, and it is submitted that this is how it should be. But if he proceeds by way of *ordre public* no such absolute and general conclusion will be reached. As regards incapacity based on differences in race, it appears that, while it is almost invariably condemned, there are hardly any decisions and some writers make its rejection dependent upon the parties' residence within the forum.[201] There is in fact strong support for such a distinction where the incapacity is derived from differences in religion. The material on this question is enormous.[202] It must suffice to exemplify it by referring to Germany where the point has arisen in an almost dramatic form. In 1931 the German Supreme Court recognized an Austrian provision prohibiting a marriage between a Christian and a non-Christian as compatible with German public policy;[203] the actual case involved a Protestant husband of Austrian nationality and a Jewish wife of Russian nationality. The Austrian law was changed and the German decision of 1931 is today without any substantial support.[204] It is ironical and at the same time very sad that at present particular international importance and interest attaches to the law of Israel which prohibits and invalidates the marriage between Jews and non-Jews.[205] Forty years later, in 1971, the German Federal Supreme Court held that, notwithstanding this state of affairs, a German Registrar of Marriages was permitted to perform a ceremony of marriage between an Israeli national of Jewish faith resident in Israel and a Christian woman of German

---

Case Concerning the Barcelona Traction Light and Power Co (Belgium *v.* Spain) the International Court of Justice spoke of those obligations which exist *erga omnes* and include 'the principles and rules concerning the basic rights of the human person, including protection from slavery and racial discrimination' (*I.C.J. Reports*, 1970, p. 32), it certainly did not wish to have the rights discussed in the text eliminated. See, generally, Brownlie, *Principles of Public International Law*, 2nd edn. (1973), p. 578 with many references, or any other textbook on public international law.

[201] For a summary of the present state of the law see Staudinger-Gamillscheg, Art. 13 n. 452.

[202] For an excellent survey see Staudinger-Gamillscheg, Art. 13 nn. 436 to 451 with a massive collection of material. In England there has never been any doubt about either of the cases mentioned in the text: see, e.g. Dicey and Morris, *Conflict of Laws*, 9th edn. (1973), pp. 73, 231, though there is no decision directly in point. Mann, *Transactions of the Grotius Society*, 44 (1958–9), p. 29 or *Studies in International Law* (1973), pp. 346, 347, expressly relied on the European Convention.

[203] 16 May 1931, *RGZ* 132, 416.

[204] See, however, District Court of Bremen, 12 July 1966, *IPRspr* 1966/7 No. 60: the petition for nullity by a Jewish husband against his Greek-Orthodox wife succeeds on the ground of the Greek law against marriages between a Christian and a non-Christian (Art. 1353 of the Greek Civil Code).

[205] See in particular Gamillscheg (above, n. 201), Art. 13 n. 437. Whether the law of Israel has been correctly interpreted by the German courts is a question which cannot be pursued in the present context.

nationality and residence.[206] One would not wish to quarrel with the decision or anything said in it. But it is in terms confined by its rationale, viz. the statement that it would be 'intolerable if a *German national* were prevented from marrying in the Federal Republic of Germany merely because the parties have different religions'.[207] It is submitted that there ought to be no room for a qualification of this kind and that a judge who applies public international law (as a German judge should do more readily than any other)[208] will treat such legislation as an absolute wrong, as a plain violation of human rights and fundamental freedoms, as discriminatory, however tenuous the factual connection with his own law or country may be. Perhaps the German court would have done so if it had paid attention to the teachings and requirements of public international law.[209]

The conclusions to which these observations lead may be summarized as follows:

1. If in principle a violation of international law should not be sanctioned by the courts of the forum, public policy does not require and perhaps should not allow a court to treat as illegal the violation of a foreign law which constitutes an international wrong.

2. The effect in the forum State of a foreign law which constitutes an international wrong should be assessed by public international law rather than public policy.

V. THE IMPOSITION AND DEPRIVATION OF NATIONALITY

At this point it becomes possible to look a little more closely at some of the groups of cases which are apt to illustrate the largely general propositions developed in the preceding sections and for this purpose to turn in the first place to the law of nationality. This branch of the law has for long been a rich source of cases in which municipal courts have applied (and often misapplied) public international law and, more particularly, refused to recognize the effects of international illegalities. Although many other

[206] 12 May 1971, *BGHZ* 56, 180. [207] Ibid., p. 192. [208] Above, p. 144.

[209] The Federal Supreme Court referred to Art. 16 of the Universal Declaration (p. 190), but failed to discuss or even to mention any other international source. It is particularly remarkable that the European Convention on Human Rights was ignored, although it is formally incorporated into and forms part of German law and although so distinguished an author as Professor K. J. Partsch, *Die Rechte und Freiheiten der Europäischen Menschenrechtskonvention* (1966), p. 214, expressly mentions the inadmissibility of prohibitions based on race or religion. This is not the first time that the Federal Supreme Court has examined the applicability of *ordre public* without considering relevant rules of international law: see 25 March 1970, *BGHZ* 53, 357 where the court failed to have regard to Art. 6 of European Convention on Human Rights.

examples could be adduced and although a vast amount of material, both judicial and academic, is available in England as well as abroad,[210] it is proposed to limit the review to certain aspects of the law of nationality resulting from the delinquencies of Nazi Germany before and during the Second World War. They confronted the world with problems which are highly instructive to the student of law and which may, therefore, be conveniently scrutinized within the context of the present contribution. They will be discussed in the light of the leading decisions only, so that intermediate decisions of lower courts will be no less ignored than certain German statutes which at a relatively late date[211] created a firmer and more specific basis.

1. Beginning with the occupation of Austria in March 1938, Nazi Germany decided upon the *imposition* of her nationality in the territories she purported to annex. The first case which after the war reached the Federal Constitutional Court of Germany[212] arose from the occupation of Czechoslovakia in March 1939. German nationality was immediately imposed upon all Czechs (other than Jews[213]). The restored Republic of Czechoslovakia, on 2 August 1945, enacted a decree whereby persons of Czechoslovakian nationality but German race 'who according to the laws of a foreign occupation authority' had become Germans were deemed on the date of such acquisition to have lost Czechoslovakian nationality.[214] Was a Czech who lived in Czechoslovakia in 1939 a German or a Czech national or stateless? The Federal Constitutional Court accepted that the annexation of Czechoslovakia was contrary to international law, but held that neither Article 4 of the Weimar Constitution nor Article 25 of the

[210] See Brownlie, this *Year Book*, 39 (1963), p. 284 and *Principles of Public International Law*, 2nd edn. (1973), pp. 367, 638, who lists most of the earlier material. As to State succession and nationality generally see Brownlie's article, pp. 319 sqq.; Whiteman's *Digest*, vol. 2, p. 923 and vol. 8, p. 104; O'Connell, op. cit. (above, n. 10), p.391; Batiffol-Lagarde, op. cit. (above, n. 132), no. 74; Mann, *Modern Law Review*, 5 (1942), p. 218 or *Studies in International Law*, p. 515; Gräupner, *Transactions of the Grotius Society*, 32 (1946), p. 87. On the much-discussed question whether in the event of State succession nationality is determined by international or municipal law see Federal Supreme Court, 23 October 1963, *RzW* 1964, 130 or *IPRspr* 1962/3 No. 243 on the position in Israel between 1948 and 1952. Some of the German problems and cases referred to in the following pages were discussed by Mann, 'Zwangseinbürgerungen und das Völkerrecht', *Friedenswarte*, 53 (1956), p. 101 and *Beiträge zum internationalen Privatrecht* (1976), p. 39.

[211] Statutes of 22 February 1955 and 17 May 1956.

[212] 28 February 1952, *BVerfGE* 1, 322 or *IPRspr* 1952/3 No. 316a.

[213] This exception was recognized by the Court of Appeal in Munich, 10 October 1969, *RzW* 1970, 172 or *IPRspr* 1968/9 No. 288—perhaps for benevolent reasons.

[214] This was changed in 1953 in regard to persons who had continued to live in Czechoslovakia, but this very change was held to be contrary to Art. 25 of the German Constitution, because it was held to be a generally recognized principle of law that nationality could not be compulsorily imposed: Court of Appeal in Cologne, 18 May 1960, *IPRspr* 1960/1 No. 239, partly in I.L.R. 32, p. 166—again perhaps for benevolent reasons.

Constitution of 1949[215] nor the general principles of international law required the acquisition of German nationality in 1939 to be held null and void, for a State's nationality was a matter exclusively for its municipal law and its invalidity in international law could be ignored. The decision was, it is submitted, wholly unsatisfactory. Germany had no semblance of right to impose her nationality upon the inhabitants of a foreign country unlawfully invaded. Even if the occupation of the territory had not been illegal, there was much to be said for the conclusion that the compulsory imposition of nationality without the grant of any option would have been an illegal excess of jurisdiction.[216] In any event the decision was self-contradictory: it stated that, on the one hand, the admitted invalidity of the annexations after 1 January 1938 did not support the view 'that all compulsory impositions of German nationality resulting from the annexations are to be considered as null and void'; on the other hand one reads that 'all compulsory naturalizations connected with annexations (after 31 December 1937) are in so far invalid as the persons in question are being claimed as their nationals by the States whose territory was annexed'. Since *ex hypothesi* Czechoslovakia never ceased to exist in law and undoubtedly 'claimed' its nationals at all times up to August 1945, it is difficult to see how in the face of such 'claim' they could ever become German. From a human point of view the decision will be readily understood: there was no point in treating persons as Czechoslovakians (or as stateless) whom Czechoslovakia had in August 1945 deprived of its nationality. Such opportunism, even if it takes the form of humane kindness, may sway the legislator, but should not allow a judge to legalize the effects of an admitted wrong.[217]

The principle so established by the Federal Constitutional Court was followed in regard to Austria: Austrians were held to have become Germans in 1938, and the same applied to the inhabitants of the Sudeten territory.[218]

[215] On these provisions see above, p. 144.

[216] There is much evidence of the existence in customary international law of an option or a 'right to elect'. See, e.g., *Murray* v. *Parkes*, [1942] 2 K.B. 123, at p. 136 *per* Singleton J. And the United States cases mentioned below, n. 224, which require 'their own consent and election'; J. Mervyn Jones, *British Nationality Law and Practice* (1947), p. 40; Brownlie, *Principles of Public Intenational Law*, 2nd edn. (1973), p. 540; Sir Gerald Fitzmaurice, *Recueil des cours*, 73 (1948–II), p. 255, at p. 284; Batiffol-Lagarde, op. cit. (above, n. 132), no. 74. Against an option: Oda in Sørensen's *Manual of Public International Law*, p. 479; O'Connell, op. cit. (above, n. 10), p. 393; Dahm, op. cit. (above, n. 10), vol. 1, pp. 478, 479; Verdross, op. cit. (above, n. 10), p. 290.

[217] See on this point, generally, below, p. 174.

[218] As to Austrians: Federal Constitutional Court, 12 December 1952, *BVerfGE* 1, 322 or *IPRspr* 1952/3 No. 316b; 9 November 1955, *BVerfGE* 4, 322 or *IPRspr* 1954/5 No. 230. As to Sudeten: Bavarian Supreme Court, 21 March 1969, *NJW* 1960, p. 997 or *IPRspr* 1968/9 No. 286. The nationality of the 'Sudeten Germans' depended or ought to have depended on the question whether the Munich Agreement of 29 September 1938 was null and void *ab*

In view of the admitted international illegalities committed by Germany one would have expected the post-war courts to disregard all annexations, to treat annexed States as continuing to exist and to have been merely occupied, with the result that none of the nationals ever lost his original nationality. In other words the courts should have adopted what in Austria was described as the 'occupation theory'. In so far as the courts relied upon the *de facto* recognition which, allegedly, certain Western powers had granted to the territorial changes of 1938 this was in law equally doubtful. The acts of recognition, even if they were initially lawful, were revoked with retrospective effect. Moreover, recognition is of a relative character and therefore has effect only between the recognizing and the recognized States. What the United Kingdom and others did by way of recognition could not bind the States of Austria and Czechoslovakia[219] which *ex hypothesi* continued to exist.

The correct attitude required by international law led to the result that the acquisition of German nationality was properly denied in the case of Poles,[220] just as non-German courts denied it in all relevant cases. That after the war the Belgian Cour de Cassation held the imposition of German nationality upon the inhabitants of Eupen and Malmedy to be

---

initio (as Czechoslovakia always maintained) or subsequently became inexistent (as the Federal Republic of Germany believes). The point was pragmatically and elegantly settled by the Treaty of Prague of 11 December 1973. For an illuminating review of the problem see Kimminich, *Jahrbuch für internationales Recht*, 18 (1975), pp. 62, 77 sqq. with references to the very extensive earlier literature which includes Akehurst, *International Relations* (1974), p. 472.

[219] As to the continuity of Austria, in particular, see Verdross, *Völkerrecht*, 5th edn., p. 251, the fundamental work by Verosta there referred to and the illuminating and richly documented discussion by Krystyna Marek, *Identity and Continuity of States in Public International Law* (1968), pp. 338 sqq., who convincingly proves that as a matter of international law Austria never ceased to exist. In the same sense Reut-Nicolussi, *Transactions of the Grotius Society*, 39 (1954), p. 119, at pp. 125 sqq. with references. (The article by Brandweiner in the opposite sense, which is there cited, appeared in English in *Law and Politics in the World Community* (ed. by G. A. Lipsky, 1953), pp. 221, 230 sqq.) The 'occupation theory' which is the official Austrian version and was on innumerable occasions affirmed by Austrian courts (Seidl-Hohenveldern, *Zeitschrift für ausländisches öffentliches Recht und Völkerrecht*, 14 (1951–2), pp. 219 sqq. and also Supreme Court, 15 October 1947, *Annual Digest*, 14 (1947), No. 15) was generally accepted, particularly by the Nürnberg International Military Tribunal and by the Swiss Federal Tribunal, 23 September 1949, *BGE* 75 I 289 or *Annual Digest*, 16 (1949), p. 184. As to the continuity of Czechoslovakia see the material referred to by Seidl-Hohenveldern, 'Das Münchener Abkommen im Lichte des Prager Vertrages von 1973' in *Recht im Dienst des Friedens* (Festschrift für Eberhard Menzel, 1975), p. 451, and the Dutch decisions referred to at n. 223 below. The treaty which the Federal Republic concluded with Czechoslovakia in December 1973 leaves the general question open (see Frowein, *International and Comparative Law Quarterly*, 23 (1974), pp. 113, 114), though it settles the problem of nationality.

[220] Federal Supreme Court, 18 March 1959, *RzW* 1959, 254 or *IPRspr* 1958/9 No. 228; 12 July 1963, *RzW* 1964, 76 or *IPRspr* 1962/3 No. 241.

invalid[221] or the Netherlands courts disregarded imposition of German nationality upon the people of Danzig[222] and Czechoslovakia[223] is perhaps less remarkable than the practice of courts of the United States of America during the war, when they were called upon to consider the question whether an Austrian who since October 1936 had been living in the United States had in March 1938 become German. This they refused to accept.[224] They started from the principle that they 'must consider not only the municipal law of the foreign nation, but also the accepted rules and practices under international law'. And by these very principles 'Germany could impose citizenship by annexation (collective naturalization) only on those who were inhabitants of Austria in 1938'. While the positive aspect of this conclusion was based on the assumption (as opposed to a finding) that the annexation of Austria had been *de facto* recognized by the United States, in regard to the negative aspect the Court of Appeals, Second Circuit, could rely on much earlier and highly impressive material.

2. When Austria was restored in April 1945 and an Austrian law of 10 July 1945 proceeded on the footing of all those who were Austrians in 1938 being restored to Austrian nationality,[225] the question arose of what effect should be given to such *re-imposition upon those living outside Austria*. The German courts did not doubt that those living in Germany (in addition, of course, to those living in Austria) had also ceased to be Germans.[226] This, so it was said, was necessarily involved in the intention to undo the *Anschluß*. Restoration meant that 'the State of Austria, re-created within its former frontiers, may not be deprived of its former population'. This argument one can well understand. It is concerned with

[221] 19 July 1957, I.L.R. 24 (1957), p. 439. See, generally, Rigaux, *Droit public et droit privé dans les relations internationales* (Paris, 1977), p. 72.

[222] Judicial Division of the Council for the Restoration of Legal Rights, 19 July 1956, I.L.R. 24 (1957), p. 434.

[223] Judicial Division of the Council for the Restoration of Legal Rights, 4 July 1955, I.L.R. 24 (1957), p. 432 (where it is also said that the failure to grant an option was contrary to Dutch public policy); 29 June 1956, I.L.R. 24 (1957), p. 536; District Court of The Hague, 11 December 1956, I.L.R. 24 (1957), p. 435; in the same sense the Court of Appeal in Brussels, 17 March 1959, I.L.R. 47, p. 31, at p. 33.

[224] *United States ex rel. Schwarzkopf* v. *Uhl*, 137 F. 2d 998 (1943) or *Annual Digest*, 12 (1943–5), p. 188. In the same sense *United States ex rel. D'Esquiva* v. *Uhl*, 137 F. 2d 903 or *Annual digest*, 12 (1943–5), p. 23; *United States ex rel. Zeller* v. *Watkins*, 167 F. 2d 279 (1948) or *Annual digest*, 15 (1948), p. 206. On the English cases of *Matter of Application for Patents by AB* (1944) 61 RPC 89 and *Matter of Mangold's Patent* (1951) 68 RPC 1, see Abel, *International Law Quarterly*, 4 (1951), p. 373 and Mann, *Modern Law Review*, 15 (1952), p. 100.

[225] This followed from the 'occupation theory': above, p. 170.

[226] Federal Constitutional Court,9 November 1955, *BVerfGE* 4, 322 or *IPRspr* 1954/5 No. 230 or I.L.R. 22 (1955), p. 430. In so far as the inhabitants of Austria were concerned this was never in doubt: Federal Supreme Court, 18 January 1956, *BGHStr* 9, 53, 175 or *IPRspr* 1956/7 No. 221a and 221b or I.L.R. 23 (1956), pp. 364 and 367; Federal Administrative Court, 28 September 1965, or *IPRspr* 1964/5 No. 306; 30 October 1954, *IPRspr* 1954/5 No. 228 or I.L.R. 21 (1954), p. 175.

the loss of German nationality assumed to have been acquired in 1938 and does not therefore touch upon international law.

It was, however, an entirely different matter whether former Austrians who in 1945 were living outside Austria and had perhaps acquired a nationality other than German had Austrian nationality re-imposed upon them. The United States decision to which reference has just been made[227] ought to have shown the way to the right principle and the correct result. However, the German Federal Supreme Court decided in favour of such re-imposition even in cases in which the persons concerned were living in and had become subjects of the United Kingdom, the United States of America or Israel.[228] It was said that Austrian law applied, because allegedly there were no general principles of public international law relating to nationality in the event of State succession or the restoration of a State. Or it was said that 'as a matter of constitutional and international law the *Anschluß* had been a wrong', but its legality or illegality was irrelevant, for the 'factual change of sovereignty' was alone decisive both as regards the acquisition of German nationality in 1938 and the re-imposition of Austrian nationality in 1945. It is submitted that, on the footing of the German view that such persons had ceased to be Austrians in 1938,[229] these conclusions do not merit approval, and it is satisfactory to observe that they were in fact rejected by the Court of Appeal of West Berlin.[230] The jurisdiction of a State is confined to its nationals and its territory. It has no jurisdiction over persons of foreign or no nationality resident outside its territory. The fact that such persons were at one time its nationals does not provide it with jurisdiction over them, for there exists no continuing or no sufficiently effective link. One is tempted to describe these arguments as elementary,[231] but the regrettable fact remains that in giving effect to only part of Austrian law, viz.

[227] Above, n. 224.

[228] Federal Supreme Court, 21 October 1959, *RzW* 1960, 35 or *IPRspr* 1958/9 No. 230; 27 September 1961, *RzW* 1962, 37 or *IPRspr* 1960/1 No.238; 3 July 1963, *RzW* 1963, 560 or *IPRspr* 1962/3 No. 238. Against these decisions notes by Mann, *RzW* 1960, 182; 1964, 129. In a decision of the Federal Supreme Court, 29 December 1953, *NJW* 1954, 510 at p. 512 one finds the *dictum*: 'As a matter of public international law an imposed nationality will not as a rule be recognized, because in the absence of a lawful connection with its own legal system the granting State interferes with the sovereignty of another State'.

[229] The point would be entirely different if the German courts had followed the Austrian 'occupation theory' and held that no Austrian ever ceased to be Austrian.

[230] 21 December 1965, *RzW* 1966, 167 or *IPRspr* 1964/5 No. 310 or I.L.R. 43, p. 191.

[231] In the same sense Oppenheim (ed. Lauterpacht), *International Law*, vol. 1, 8th edn. (1955), section 219 (p. 553 n. 2), section 240; Lauterpacht at p. 171 of the paper referred to below, n. 245; Brownlie, *Principles of Public International Law*, 2nd edn. (1973), p. 392; Dahm, op. cit. (above, n. 10), vol. 1, p. 470; Verdross, op. cit. (above, n. 10), p. 309; German-Yugoslav Mixed Arbitral Tribunal in *Peinitsch* v. *Germany, Annual Digest*, 2 (1923/4), No. 121 and almost all the material referred to above, n. 210. See Briggs, *The Law of Nations*, 2nd edn. (1952), pp. 503, 504.

the legislation of 1945, but rejecting the full implications of the 'occupation theory', the Federal Supreme Court on its part misapplied the law and exceeded Germany's international jurisdiction.

3. There remains the question whether, if the *compulsory expatriation* of foreign nationals by their national State constitutes an international wrong, other States are entitled and in law bound to refuse recognition to the loss of nationality and to treat the foreigners concerned as having retained their nationality rather than as stateless.

An affirmative answer is inherent in the trail-blazing decision of Germany's Federal Constitutional Court holding that the notorious Nazi decree of 23 November 1941, which deprived all Jews of German nationality who were outside Germany of their nationality and confiscated their property, 'violated fundamental principles. It is to so intolerable a degree irreconcilable with justice that it must be considered to have been null and void *ab initio*', to have been '*Unrecht*', non-law, an act of arbitrary power, with the result that in principle all persons affected by the decree had at all times been and remained Germans.[232] A grave infringement of human rights thus having been established by the highest German tribunal itself, one might have expected every English and, indeed, every court to treat the decree as null and void. The curious fact is that, while expressing their strong condemnation of the decree, the supreme tribunals of Switzerland,[233] France,[234] and Israel[235] as well as the Court of Appeals, Second Circuit, in the United States,[236] admittedly before the great German decision of 1968, and the Court of Appeal in England after 1968,[237] gave effect to the decree and held its victims to be stateless. It was the majority of the House of Lords in 1975[238] which took a different and consistent line by deciding in conformity with the German decision that an English resident had not in 1941 become stateless. According to Lord Hodson, to give effect to the German decree would have been contrary to 'the relevant international law'.[239] In the words of Lord Cross of Chelsea, 'it is

[232] 14 February 1968, *BVerfGE* 23, 98 or *IPRspr* 1968/9 No. 281. On this case and the decision of the Court of Appeal presently to be mentioned in the text see Mann, 'The present validity of Nazi Nationality Laws', *Law Quarterly Review*, 89 (1973), p. 194.

[233] 3 October 1948, *BGE* 74 I 346 or *Annual Digest*, 15 (1948), No. 73, overruling *BGE* 72 I 407 or *Annual Digest*, 13 (1946), No. 58.

[234] Cass. Civ. (Assemblé plénière), 20 December 1950, *Clunet*, 1951, 176 or *Annual Digest*, 16 (1949), No. 176.

[235] 28 October 1954, I.L.R. 21 (1954), p. 197.

[236] Above, n. 224.

[237] *Oppenheimer* v. *Cattermole*, [1973] Ch. 264, reversing Goulding J., [1972] Ch. 585.

[238] [1976] A.C. 249. Lord Pearson at p. 265 differed from the reasoning of the majority in that he agreed with the positivist approach by Buckley and Orr L.JJ. in the Court of Appeal, according to which, if a legislative or executive act of a recognized foreign government, 'however unjust or discriminatory and unfair, has changed the status of an individual by depriving him of his nationality of that country, he does in my opinion effectively cease to be a national of that country'.

[239] Ibid., p. 265.

part of the public policy of this country that our courts should give effect to clearly established rules of international law', and the decree of 1941 'constitutes so grave an infringement of human rights that the courts of this country ought to refuse to recognize it as a law at all'.[240] Lord Salmon, similarly, had 'no doubt that on the grounds of public policy' English courts should refuse to apply the decree,[241] but later he, too, stated that it 'was so great an offence against human rights that they would have nothing to do with it'.[242]

Here, then, the highest tribunal in Britain has given us an exemplary lead in two respects of vital and general importance. Foreign legislation which constitutes an international illegality will in the eyes of an English court be null and void—and it matters not whether the result is reached by the direct application of international law or by way of public policy. It will certainly be necessary to examine each individual case to ascertain whether it does amount to an international wrong in the true sense, but this is a different question and does not affect the principle so clearly enunciated by the House of Lords. Moreover, that principle applies irrespective of whether the result is advantageous or prejudicial to the victim.[243] It is the character of the legislation that precludes the truly judicial mind from having anything to do with it: a judge cannot and ought not to implement a wrong even if it is for the purpose of doing good or of reaching a result that appears to him meritorious. This jurisprudential lesson merits strong emphasis. It has often been ignored. It was ignored by many German courts which, in the words of Lord Hailsham of St Marylebone,[244] saw 'small value in adding hardship to injustice in order to emphasize the cruel nature of the injustice'.[245] It was invariably for the

[240] Ibid., p. 278. [241] Ibid., p. 282.

[242] Ibid., p. 283. It remains, however, a matter for regret that both Lord Cross of Chelsea and Lord Salmon seemed to accept Scrutton L. J.'s notorious *dictum* in *Luther* v. *Sagor & Co*, [1921] 3 K.B. 532, 558, 559, about the alleged limits and risks of applying public policy: pp. 277, 282, 283. In particular Lord Cross of Chelsea went out of his way to stress that refusal to recognize a foreign law 'may be embarrassing to the branch of the executive which is concerned to maintain friendly relations between this country and the foreign country in question': pp. 277, 278. And see Lord Salmon at p. 282 E to F. Such a *dictum* which, fortunately, was immediately followed by the unqualified statement 'that our courts should give effect to clearly established rules of international law', smacks of the American version of the Act of State doctrine (above p. 158). It is opposed to another strand of the British tradition which does not find 'the fear of the embarrassment of the executive a very attractive basis upon which to build a rule of English law': *Kawasaki Kisen Kabushiki Kaisha of Kobe* v. *Bantham Steamship Co Ltd*, [1939] 2 K.B. 544, 552 *per* Sir Wilfred Green MR; *Bank voor Handel en Scheepvaart* v. *Slatford*, [1953] 1 Q.B. 248, 266 *per* Devlin J. (as he then was); and see *Studies in International Law*, pp. 408–12.

[243] This—jurisprudential—point was one of the principal reasons for the article mentioned at n. 232, above, which seems to have resulted in the unusual procedural history of the decision in *Oppenheimer* v.*Cattermole, ubi supra*.

[244] [1976] A.C. 249, at p. 263 C–D.

[245] It has been pointed out that the same thought may have influenced German courts on more than one occasion: above, nn. 213, 214, and 217.

advantage of the victim, his successors-in-title or his wife that other courts proceeded from the statelessness created by the decree of 1941. It was for humanitarian reasons that Sir Hersch Lauterpacht[246] argued forcefully that effect had to be given to the decree, however odious, in order not to impose a nationalilty upon persons who were most anxious not to possess it. Yet one can only conclude with Lord Cross of Chelsea[247] that 'it surely cannot be right for the question whether the decree should be recognized or not to depend on the circumstances of the particular case'.[248]

VI. CONFISCATIONS CONTRARY TO INTERNATIONAL LAW

I

While there is no doubt that a State lacks international jurisdiction to take property situate outside its territory and such takings are, therefore, necessarily ineffective,[249] the international effects of the confiscation of property within the confiscating State's territory are in many respects unclear. At the same time they are of great practical importance; it may well be that they are the most important ones within the scope of the

[246] 'The Nationality of Denationalized Persons' in *Jewish Yearbook of International Law*, 1948, p. 164.

[247] [1976] A.C. 249, at p. 278 D–E.

[248] The question of German law decided by the House of Lords lies outside the purview of the present observations. Perhaps it is permissible to say very shortly that it is still believed that the result ought to have been based upon s. 25 of the Nationality Act of 1913 (although the House obviously disliked this reasoning). S. 25 operates automatically and, in particular, independently of the former national's state of mind or knowledge. Moreover, that the Constitution of 1949 should have deprived a German of his nationality is more than the 'oddity' of which Lord Cross of Chelsea speaks (p. 271 G–H). It may be that the House attached too much importance to the decision of the Federal Constitutional Court, 10 July 1958, *BVerfGE* 8, 81 or *IPRspr* 1958/9 No. 215. This was a case in which an emigrant, having been naturalized in the United States, returned to Germany and, therefore, by virtue of Art. 116 sub-section 2, sentence 2 of the Constitution was deemed not to have been expatriated. The Court held that, the deeming provision having come into force only in 1949, the individual could not at the time of his earlier naturalization in the United States rely upon or retain his German nationality, which was apparently assumed to have been lost as a result of the expatriation. The case of Mr Oppenheimer was different, because it is the very basis of the decision of 1968 that he had never lost his German nationality. It was not new legislation which in 1949 retrospectively made him a German. The distinction between the retrospective effect of legislation which is constitutive and the 'retrospective' effect of a judicial decision which is declaratory is well known. German comment on the point does not seem to be available. The result defended in this note seems to be approved by Drobnig, *American-German Private International Law* (1972), pp. 72, 73. But see Federal Administrative Court, 8 March 1977, *RzW* 1977, 194 and Mann, Festschrift Coing, p. 324.

[249] This rule is so obvious and so well established that it would be futile to refer to the enormous amount of supporting material. The only question is whether expropriation against compensation should have extra-territorial effect. The answer is in the negative. Not even a benevolent taking can have such effect: *Bank voor Handel en Scheepvaart* v. *Slatford*, [1953] 1 QB 248.

present survey, for confiscations are unfortunately frequent and the fate of what the Americans call 'hot products',[250] i.e. products confiscated in and by a foreign State and subsequently exported to and found in the forum State, is likely to come up often for judicial consideration.

Two questions stand out: What are the circumstances in which a taking of a foreigner's property is contrary to public international law? What are the international implications of an illegality thus established? The former question is outside the confines of the present discussion. This must assume the commission of an international wrong. Such an assumption is not unreasonable, for however obscure many details may be, certain principles may be taken to be firmly based. Thus an international wrong undeniably occurs where an alien's property is taken in breach of a treaty,[251] or where the taking is arbitrary, abusive or discriminatory and therefore has the character of punishment,[252] or where it is unaccompanied by the payment of or at least the clearly defined and readily enforceable right to compensation, whether it be reasonable, equitable, just, adequate or appropriate.[253] No lawyer familiar with, or willing to ascertain, the sources of international law[254] will find it difficult to prove the existence of

[250] The expression occurs in the statement of 8 May 1974 by the Department of State concerning its policy with regard to such products: *Digest of United States Practice*, 1974, 275.

[251] This was the basis of the decision of the Permanent Court of International Justice in the *Chorzów Factory* case (Germany *v*. Poland), above, n. 3. In the Indonesian cases far too little attention was paid to the Round Table Conference Agreements between the Netherlands and Indonesia, 27 December 1949, *United Nations Treaty Series*, vol. 69, pp. 3, 230–58. These Agreements deprived the Indonesian measures of any semblance of justification.

[252] See, for instance, Brownlie, *Principles of Public International Law*, 2nd edn. (1973), pp. 523, 524, 527, or O'Connell, *International Law*, 2nd edn. (1970), pp. 776–80, with further references. This merely constitutes, in the realm of international law, the application of principles developed in municipal law as a result of a long historical process: see Mann, 'Outlines of a history of expropriation', *Law Quarterly Review*, 75 (1959), p. 188.

[253] The importance of the various formulations should not be overrated. In the large majority of cases they do not matter, because in fact the property is simply taken and no compensation of any kind is effectively paid, with the result that in the end the victim or the State to which it belongs accepts a fraction of what is due even on the footing of the least generous formula.

[254] It may be helpful to indicate the sources which are relevant and the neglect of which constitutes the gravest criticism to which the *dicta* in the majority opinion of the Supreme Court of the United States of America in *Banco Nacional de Cuba* v. *Sabbatino*, 376 U.S. 398 (1974), at pp. 428–30 *per* Mr Justice Harlan, are exposed. Those sources include: (1) *Treaties*: It must suffice to mention the innumerable Treaties of Commerce concluded in the course of the current century and represented by the twenty-one Treaties of Friendship, Commerce and Navigation made between 1946 and 1971 by the United States of America and followed by numerous similar treaties such as treaties between the United Kingdom and Japan or Iran or between Germany and Italy, Portugal, Greece or Spain. All of them contain elaborate provisions against confiscation. In addition, between 1945 and May 1976 no less than 141 Treaties for the Protection of Capital Investments were concluded (see *Bilateral Treaties for International Investment* published in January 1977 by the International Chamber of Commerce). As a result of the most-favoured-nation clause the network created by these treaties is greatly extended. In the course of his recent discussion of the protection of private

these principles, but for present purposes it must suffice to profess adherence to them.

II

Where the foreign State has taken property in circumstances which, for one or the other reason, are contrary to international law, the forum should treat the taking as null and void. In its courts the original owner should continue to enjoy title.

---

property by public international law Rigaux, *Droit public et droit privé dans les relations internationales* (Paris, 1977), p. 255, suggests that a minimum standard 'n'a jamais été reconnu comme tel ni par les États socialistes ni par les pays sous-développés ayant accédé à l'indépendance depuis 1945. Dans un ordre international essentiellement fondé sur l'adhésion tacite ou expresse des États, ce phénomène ne saurait être ignoré.' The treaties referred to establish the opposite and prove that the States contemplated by Rigaux and many of their supporters or defenders have a habit of being double-tongued; their standard is not the law, but their interest. (2) *Diplomatic Notes*: For a few recent examples see the Dutch Note, *American Journal of International Law*, 54 (1960), p. 484, or the American Notes, Digest of United States Practice in International Law 1975, 489, 490 or the British Note of 23 December 1971 (*Int.L.R.*, 53, 317), where the classical principles are clearly stated and where it is expressly asserted 'that the measures in question amount to a breach of international law *and are invalid*'. And see the Department of State's declaration of 30 December 1975, *Digest of United States Practice in International Law*, 1975, pp. 488, 489. (3) *National legislation*: Reference should be made to numerous constitutional provisions (see the fourteen volumes of Blaustein and Flanz, *Constitutions of the World*) and to the equally numerous Investment Codes enacted in many countries (see the six volumes of *Investment Laws of the World* published by Oceana Publications Inc). (4) *Judicial decisions*: Up to 1959 they were collected by Lord McNair, *Nederlands Tijdschrift voor Internationaal Recht*, 6 (1959), p. 218. Since then numerous decisions of municipal courts have become known which reaffirm the principle and to some of which reference will be made. Special weight should be attached to the *dictum* by Judge Gros in the *Case Concerning the Barcelona Traction, Light & Power Co* (Belgium *v*. Spain), *I.C.J. Reports*, 1970, p. 275, who spoke of 'la règle de droit international prohibant les confiscations sans indemnité'. A clear statement of the rule is provided by the Austrian Constitutional Court, 15 October 1968, *Entscheidungen*, 1968, No. 5382 or I.L.R. 47, p. 40, where it was said that the seizure of a foreigner's private property 'is only permissible under international law against full and immediate compensation and that the taking of property has to be regarded as confiscation contrary to international law if full and immediate compensation is not forthcoming'. See the same Court, 24 June 1954, I.L.R. 21 (1954), p. 212. (5) *Academic opinion*: There is hardly any writer of standing who has failed to support the rule. It would be impossible to give a list which could claim any degree of completeness. (6) *State practice*: This is perhaps the most significant and the most interesting piece of evidence. The confiscators continue to recognize the rule by providing in their confiscatory legislation for compensation, though often in so circuitous, indefinite or vague a form as to make the pretence obvious. Numerous examples up to 1960 are collected by Mann, *Virginia Law Review*, 51 (1965), p. 604 or *Studies in International Law* (1973), p. 466, at pp. 479–83. Since then the same technique was followed by Bolivia in 1969 (*International Legal Materials*, 10 (1971), pp. 173, 182, 1113, 1201), Algeria, Libya and Chile in 1971 (ibid., 10 (1971), p. 847; 11 (1972), p. 380; 10 (1971), p. 1067) or Iraq in 1972 (ibid., 11 (1972), p. 380). The intended violation of a legal rule implies the recognition of its existence. If the confiscators think it right and necessary to provide for compensation they thereby prove the rule with which they pretend to comply and which in fact they disregard. They should be held to the appearance they create.

Such a result should cause no difficulty in countries in which public international law or its general or generally recognized rules are directly applicable. Certain it is that in international law the rights and remedies against international wrongs are vested in the State whose nationality the victim possesses. Certain it is also that these comprise reparation in the sense of restitution in kind (which in the case of confiscation means return of the property[255]) or damages at the State's option, but, as we know, they do extend to the nullity of the wrongful act. When we come to the effect of the international rule in a municipal system of law, we must look to the latter for the appropriate solution, for international law expects, and indeed, requires municipal systems of law to observe and enforce it,[256] but prescribes no method of doing so. International law leaves it to municipal law to decide how obedience is to be achieved.[257] Hence municipal law is the source which indicates to the municipal judge the transformation of the international rule. The decisive question is not (as it has been wholly unjustifiably put in Germany[258]) whether there exists a generally accepted principle whereby *public international law* imposes upon the municipal *judge* the *duty* to treat an internationally illegal foreign act as void *ab initio*. That question was rightly answered in the negative, but misses the point altogether, for *ex hypothesi* public international law which, as a rule, addresses the State provides no answer.

Where, as is the almost universal practice, transformation of customary international law occurs, the judge will implement it in pursuance of the principle of effectiveness, i.e. so that within the national system of law the international rule can most effectively be worked out and the court can reach results most closely conforming to the international rule. Thus in Germany it is Article 25, in Italy Article 10, of the Constitution, in the Anglo-Saxon countries it is the common law which in regard to the foreign illegal confiscation permits and requires the recognition of the nullity contemplated by international law.[259] The victim's home State, it is true, may at any time dispose of the international claim and thus deprive the victim of any rights in national courts by a waiver of the wrong, by demanding financial compensation and thereby foregoing the nullity or by

[255] This example is expressly mentioned by Berber, op. cit. (above, n.10), at p. 25.

[256] See, generally, Brownlie, op. cit. (above, n. 10), pp. 36–8 with numerous references, among them the cases mentioned above, n. 150.

[257] This is stated expressly by Berber, *Lehrbuch des Völkerrechts*, 2nd edn. (1975), p. 107 or Dahm, *Völkerrecht*, vol. 1, p. 55, or Verdross and Simma, *Universelles Völkerrecht* (1976), pp. 56, 430, 431. See also Guggenheim, *Traité de droit international public*,2nd edn. (1967), vol. 1, p. 70: 'En vertu d'une délégation du droit des gens, le droit étatique est chargé d'exécuter les règles de droit international public qui se rapportent à son domaine territorial.'

[258] Particularly in the decision of the Court of Appeal at Bremen, 21 August 1959, *IPRspr* 1958 and 1959, 746, also I.L.R. 28, pp. 16, 24 sqq., and following it the District Court at Hamburg, 22 January 1973, *AWD* 1973, 163 or *International Legal Materials*, 12 (1973), p. 251.

[259] See above, pp. 129 sqq.

otherwise disposing of its subject's rights.[260] But so long as this has not happened, nullity means invalidity or ineffectiveness on all levels, for and against all, independently of proceedings in international tribunals, and constitutes the remedy, indeed the only remedy, which by virtue of municipal law is available to the municipal judge in order to give shape to the international facts and legal requirements.

This thesis[261] is, it is believed, in line with the most fundamental demands of justice, for notwithstanding a very odd *dictum* by an American court, fortunately in an entirely different context,[262] the Eighth Commandment 'Thou shalt not steal' surely is part of the law of nations, simply because, as the court admitted, 'every civilized nation doubtless has this as a part of its legal system.'[263] This is so even if modern positivists, particularly those who invoke positivism to oust or fetter the law, attempt to discredit the thesis as a product of natural law[264]—a description which, though intended to be derogatory, in fact carries the hallmark of commendation and dignity. Thus the Federal Supreme Court of Germany has impressively stated[265] that 'statute meets its limits where it is contrary to the generally recognized rules of public international law or to natural law', that in the event of such inconsistency municipal courts must start from the unlawfulness of the measure and that public international law 'as the inalienable kernel of law has precedence over all municipal law'. The fundamental approach which it is at this juncture intended to indicate has, as will appear, in the result much judicial and other support, but it may also claim specific endorsement by such authorities as, among many others, Sir Hersch Lauterpacht,[266] and

[260] As a matter of international law there can be no doubt about these rights of the State; they were expressly recognized by the Federal Supreme Court of Germany: 22 June 1960, *IPRspr* 1960 and 1961 No. 61; 2 October 1963, *Archiv für Völkerrecht*, 1965, 331, 335. In the same sense *The Blonde*, [1922] 1 A.C. 313, at p. 335. The effect of such arrangements in municipal law is another matter.

[261] See already Mann, 'International Delinquencies before Municipal Courts', *Law Quarterly Review*, 70 (1954), p.181 or *Studies in International Law* (1973), p. 366, and the German article 'Völkerrechtswidrige Enteignungen vor nationalen Gerichten', *Neue Juristische Wochenschrift*, 1961, p. 705 and Festschrift Duden (1977), 287.

[262] *IIT* v. *Vencap Ltd*, 519 F. 2d 1001 (1975), at p. 1015 *per* Judge Friendly.

[263] Cf. Art. 38 (1) (c) of the Statute of the International Court of Justice of which the American court may have been unaware.

[264] One of the most recent of such attempts is made by Behrens, *Rabels Zeitschrift für ausländisches und internationales Privatrecht*, 37 (1973), p. 394, particularly pp. 404, 418. The extent of this author's positivist efforts in the interest of the immunity of confiscatory measures is astonishing. The requirements of public international law are described as relative and optional, the question of the public interest involved in a taking as well as the question of the discriminatory character of a taking are said to be non-justiciable.

[265] *BGHZ* 3, 94 (107); *BGHStr* 1, 391 (399); also Federal Administrative Court, *NJW* 1961, 2225.

[266] Sir Hersch Lauterpacht in Oppenheim, *International Law*, vol 1, 8th edn. (1955), pp. 269, 270; *Cambridge Law Journal*, 12 (1954), p. 20.

Professors Verzijl,[267] Dahm[268] and Jennings[269] some of whose observations merit quotation, though the scholar may do well to ponder the whole of his thoughtful exposition:

> If, then, the claim to compensation and the claim to reparation are quite different claims in law, with different parties, and if the latter arises when there is already not only a failure to satisfy the former but even an impossibility of satisfying the former, it follows that it is not at all logical or even permissible to explain the situation in terms of a mere outstanding obligation to pay compensation. And it would seem to follow from this that it is both logical and proper for a municipal court to refuse to recognize, i.e., to treat as a nullity for all purposes of the forum, a foreign expropriation decree that fails to satisfy any international rule requiring the payment of prompt compensation.

III

The strength of the thesis which has just been developed is frequently obscured by an invidious and arid problem of methodology which has already been discussed,[270] but must in the present context be resumed on account of the special significance given to it. It is said that, while any violation of international law as such, committed as a result of the foreign confiscation, is legally immaterial in the forum, it is or at least may be contrary to its *ordre public* and on this ground incapable of recognition. Public policy is, of course, a conception which has much wider scope than international law; thus it may well invalidate in the forum a foreign measure which by international law is not open to criticism, for instance because the victim is a national of the confiscating State and no violation of human rights, such as discrimination on grounds of religion or race, arises.[271] But where a violation of international law is in issue it should

[267] 'The Relevance of Public and Private International Law for the Solution of Problems arising from Nationalization', *Festschrift für Makarov, Zeitschrift für ausländisches öffentliches Recht und Völkerrecht*, 19 (1958), p. 531.

[268] *Völkerrecht*, vol. 1 (1958), pp. 264, 270.

[269] 'Nullity and Effectiveness in International Law', *Cambridge Essays in International Law* (1965), p. 80. The list could be considerably extended. It must be sufficient to mention a few others: Martin Wolff, *Das internationale Privatrecht Deutschlands*, 3rd edn. (1953), p. 12; Kraus, *Festschrift für Laun* (1953), p. 234; Niederer, *Festschrift für Lewald* (1953), pp. 547, 554; Wortley, *Expropriation in Public International Law* (1959), pp. 17, 18, 155; Verdross and Simma, *Universelles Völkerrecht* (1976), p. 589.

[270] Above, pp. 159 sqq.

[271] In the Chilean copper case, which was recently decided by the District Court at Hamburg (above, n. 258) and which has led to a disproportionally large literature in Germany, the victim of the confiscation was a Chilean corporation in which the Chilean State held 51 per cent and an American corporation held 49 per cent of the share capital. It is difficult to see how any question of international law could arise in this case. The plaintiff was held to be a 'split corporation' represented by a Hamburg lawyer as a curator and said to be of German nationality: District Court Hamburg, 13 March 1974, *AWD* 1974, 410 or

make no difference whether non-recognition is based on the international rule or on *ordre public*, for the difference should be little more than a verbal and, therefore, unattractive one. This is particularly so if one remembers that where courts invoke *ordre public*, they in substance affirm the general rules of international law or contribute to their formation, for what is material to the creation and to the evolution of a general principle of public international law is often the result reached rather than the precise legal reasoning on which it rests. How irrelevant the problem of method is can readily be shown by the decision of the House of Lords in the case of *Oppenheimer* v. *Cattermole*[272] to which reference was made in another connection. It was held that a foreign 'breach of international law' and a violation of human rights could not be recognized in England, because 'it is part of the public policy of this country that our courts should give effect to clearly established rules of international law', and similar evidence of international law being treated as a head of public policy can be found elsewhere.[273] Whether one considers a foreign violation of international law as a nullity on account of its character *per se*, or on account of its inconsistency with the domestic public policy, is not a matter worthy of prolonged discussion and one will, therefore, be inclined to shrug one's shoulders at German attempts to construct a difference without a distinction, that is to say, to deny the relevance of a violation of international law, yet to condemn the same violation by means of public policy.[274] It is, indeed, paradoxical for a public international lawyer so to proceed and to end by developing on many pages the view that in relation to foreign illegal confiscations a generous resort to public policy is required and that, therefore, 'the courts of the forum should refuse recognition to all acts of foreign States which in the eyes of the court are contrary to international law'.[275] This is precisely what, particularly in Germany, can be done by giving effect to the nullity provided for by international law and transformed into German law by the Constitution.

The difference, however, becomes material and, moreover, dangerous if it is utilized for the purpose of condemning the foreign delict, yet neutralizing its effect by asserting the absence of a sufficiently intensive

---

International Legal Materials, 13 (1974), p. 1115. These are processes of artificiality which outside Germany should be considered wholly inadmissible, although in unexplained circumstances a similar course was taken in *Banco Nacional de Cuba* v. *Sabbatino*, above, n. 254, see on this point Mann, *Studies in International Law*, p. 466 n. 2.

[272] *Oppenheimer* v. *Cattermole*, [1976] A.C. 249, 278 *per* Lord Cross of Chelsea.

[273] See, e.g., the approach by Lipstein, *Recueil des cours*, 135 (1972–I), pp. 190, 191 or Jennings, loc. cit. (above, n. 269), p. 81.

[274] Both the decisions mentioned at n. 258, above, proceed in this fashion, though in the end they reject *ordre public* for the reason presently to be mentioned in the text.

[275] In this sense Seidl-Hohenveldern, 'Völkerrechtswidrige Akte Fremder Staaten vor innerstaatlichen Gerichten', in *Recht im Wandel*, p. 591, 618.

link between the facts of the case and the forum (*Binnenbeziehung*). The requirement of such a link is a universal feature of the doctrine of *ordre public* and also exists in English law, although legal terminology ignores a technical term for it.[276] The reach of the doctrine within the context of foreign illegal confiscations is probably limited to a single type of case (which renders the methodological point referred to even more trivial). On the one hand continental courts which so far have alone had occasion to consider the point have held the necessary link to exist whenever the plaintiff is a national of the forum State[277] or a foreigner, but the subject of a State whose nationals are entitled by virtue of a treaty to what is known as national treatment, i.e., to the same treatment as nationals;[278] in view of the far-flung network of most-favoured-nation clauses this is, as must again be emphasized, a most significant extension to which effect should be given even in countries such as Britain[279] in which treaties of commerce or similar instruments are not usually incorporated into the domestic legal system. Moreover, if the defendant is a national of the forum State and claims to be interested in the property the link is said to exist; this is so both where he claims to have acquired title and where he acts merely as a sales agent earning commission.[280] On the other hand the link is allegedly missing where the defendant is merely in possession of the property which he holds for another.[281] The result is unconvincing, for it is

[276] See above, p. 163.

[277] In this sense the Federal Supreme Court of Germany, *BGHZ* 28, 385; Kegel, *Internationales Privatrecht*, p. 239 or Soergel-Kegel, Art. 30 n. 17. The same thought underlies the very important decision *BGHZ* 39, 220 (232). It is, however, doubtful whether the nationality of the plaintiff should really be allowed to matter where a violation of the law is concerned. Cf. the strange study by Sperduti, *Mélanges Charles Rousseau* (1974), p. 249: he first tries to prove that, notwithstanding such provisions as Art. 10 of the Italian Constitution, 'il manque dans l'ordre juridique du for une norme d'adaptation au droit international qui qualifie d'illicite une expropriation étrangère'. He then says that *ordre public* does not help, because it 'tend à sauvegarder des principes fondamentaux de l'ordre juridique du for et non point des principes étrangers'—as if the maintenance of international law was not a major interest of the forum. But he concludes that 'l'ordre public . . . réagit vis-à-vis de la violation du droit international perpétrée au préjudice d'un citoyen, en privant l'acte étranger illicite de la possibilité de produire, dans le for, tout effet juridique utile quelconque.'

[278] This is a significant point upon which the decision of the Federal Supreme Court, *BGHZ* 39, 220 (232) rests.

[279] A treaty, not incorporated into English law, cannot normally provide a head of public policy so as to require observance in defiance of the general law: see the discussion by Mann, *Studies in International Law*, pp. 340–4. The point mentioned in the text is, however, different. What the judge has to do is to assess the scope of public policy. If, in doing so, he has regard to the nationality of the plaintiff he should not exclude from the benefits granted to a British subject such foreigners as can invoke treaty rights.

[280] This was so decided by the Court of Appeal at Bremen, above, n. 258.

[281] In this sense the District Court at Hamburg, above, n. 258, but there is much academic opinion against this view. See, in particular, Stoll (Staudinger), n. 219 after Art. 12 and Seidl-Hohenveldern, *AWD* 1974, 427, among others.

also generally admitted that the graver the violation of (international) law is the looser the link may be to justify the intervention of *ordre public*. A flagrant international wrong should invariably be deemed to be so grave a matter as to be contrary to the public policy of the forum. It is an absolute wrong and leaves no room for a doctrine of relativity.

While, therefore, there should be no disadvantage in relying upon *ordre public* rather than international law, one can perhaps discern a slight advantage in doing so. Public policy is determined by the conceptions of law, justice and morality prevailing in the forum. Public policy is independent of the attitude adopted in foreign States. The latter is not necessarily or universally exemplary. If, as some believe, it were necessary to take account of the views of all countries in order to ascertain the general principles of law recognized by civilized nations or, in other words, of international law it would, in the present world, be almost impossible and certainly difficult to discover the common standard. Fortunately international law does not require universality of practice, but considers only the practice of civilized nations. In the result, therefore, there should be no practical difference between the standards of international law and the demands of public policy, though it must be admitted that in most civilized countries the latter can more readily be met.

IV

Whichever route judicial practice has followed, the legally relevant reasoning has largely been in harmony with the preceding suggestions, even though the actual result of the decisions may, on factual grounds or on account of the specific appreciation of the character of foreign events, have differed from what could be expected. Those decisions have not always been analysed with the precision they merited. A short comparative survey cannot, therefore, be dispensed with.

The strongest lead was given by the *French* Cour de Cassation which for half a century has consistently refused to recognize confiscations carried out in the Soviet Union, Spain or Algeria.[282] In recent years it employed the often repeated formula

> Aucun effet de droit ne peut être reconnu en France à une dépossession opérée par un État étranger sans qu'aucune indemnité équitable soit préalablement fixée.

[282] Cass. Req., 5 March 1928, *Clunet*, 1928, 674; Cass. Civ., 11 March 1939, *Clunet*, 1939, 615; Cass. Civ., 23 April 1969, *Clunet*, 1969, 914 and numerous other decisions published only in the *Bulletin*, but collected *Revue critiquede droit international privé*, 1970, p. 751; 1971, p. 796; 1973, p. 775. See in particular the decision Cass. Civ., 17 November 1969, *Bulletin civil*, 1969 I no. 343. The frequently repeated formula was also applied in the Chilean copper case decided by the President of the 1st Chamber of the Tribunal de grande instance in Paris, 19 November 1972, *Clunet*, 1973, 227. See, generally, Batiffol-Lagarde, *Droit international privé*, vol. 2 (1976), no. 523.

To the French Cour de Cassation we also owe one of the clearest rejections of the relevance of the merely verbal, unperformed and frequently disingenuous promise of compensation:[283]

> que semblables dispositions de pur principe, qui, après dépossession immédiate, laissent le soin à l'Administration de fixer, dans un délai indéterminé et discrétionnairement, une indemnité en indiquant seulement le montant qu'elle ne pourrait pas dépasser, sont contraires à l'ordre public français.

This point was strongly made in *Switzerland*[284] and *Austria*[285] also, but it misled *Japanese* courts[286] and lower *Italian* courts:[287] while they decided clearly that a title acquired by a foreign State in violation of international law would not be recognized, they considered the vaguest of promises to pay compensation sufficient to legitimate the foreign takings. No such error occurred in the *United States of America* where, after many vicissitudes, Cuban confiscations were treated as ineffective to transfer title on the ground that they were so discriminatory as to be contrary to international law;[288] this meant that, in accordance with the more recent and, one is tempted to say, the more enlightened attitude of both the legislative[289] and executive[290] branch of the Government of the United states the Act of State doctrine no longer applies to illegal confiscations.

[283] Cass. Civ., 23 April 1969 (above, n. 281).

[284] Federal Tribunal, 25 September 1956, *BGE* 81 I 196, 199 or I.L.R. 23 (1956), pp. 24, 26.

[285] Supreme Court, 3 February 1954, *Revue critique de droit international privé*, 1956, p.259. Constitutional Court, 15 October 1968, *Entscheidungen*, 1968 No. 5382 or I.L.R. 47, p. 412, at p. 416. In the same sense as to Czechoslovakia the United States Foreign Claims Settlement Commission re *Wyman's* claim, 14 September 1962, I.L.R. 40, p. 97.

[286] Court of Appeal at Tokyo, I.L.R. 20 (1953), p. 305.

[287] Court of first instance in Venice, 11 March 1953, *Foro Italiano*, 1953, vol. 2, p. 719 or I.L.R. 22 (1955), p. 19; Court of first instance in Rome, 13 September 1954, *Revue critique de droit international privé*, 1958, p.519 or I.L.R. 22 (1955), p. 23. For a more realistic and wholly satisfactory appreciation see, however, Court of Appeal, 28 April 1956, *Rivista di diritto internazionale*, 40 (1957), p.264 which is likely to supersede the decisions mentioned in the preceding sentence. Cf. the decision of the Italian Supreme Court, 19 April 1960, I.L.R. 40, p. 17. But see also the *dicta* in the decision of the Corte di Cassazione, 14 November 1972, *Italian Yearbook of International Law*, 1975, p. 238, at p. 251.

[288] *Banco Nacional de Cuba* v. *Farr Whitlock & Co*, 383 F. 2d 166 (1967), cert. den. 390 US 956 (1968), which followed the earlier decision of the same court in *Banco Nacional de Cuba* v. *Sabbatino*, 307 F. 2d 845 (1962) and thus brought the *Sabbatino* litigation to an end.

[289] Above, n. 168.

[290] Its recent attitude appears from the statements referred to above, n. 91; n. 254. If one compares these recent statements with views expressed by the same Department of State in the course of and after the *Sabbatino* litigation (*A.J.* (1978), 398, also *International Legal materials*, 2 (1963), pp. 1012, 1019, and 3 (1964), p. 1077), the radical change of attitude becomes obvious. It is, indeed, most welcome. On the general problem see Henkin, 'Is there a "Political Question" doctrine?', *Yale Law Journal*, 85 (1976), p. 597 and, in particular, Henkin, *Foreign Affairs and the Constitution* (1972), where the problem is dealt with on pp. 210–16—unfortunately a little shortly.

Accordingly the law of the United States is now in harmony with that of *Holland*[291] and, in particular, *Britain*,[292] where foreign confiscations which are discriminatory are incapable of transferring title. What is still an open question in these countries is whether the non-payment of compensation for the property of an alien is accepted as a violation of international law recognizable by municipal courts.[293] The Federal Supreme Court of *Germany*, like the *Swiss* Federal Tribunal, has not yet had an opportunity of dealing with the fate of 'hot products', but the general tendency of both courts' decisions seems to justify the expectation that they will allow the true owner to recover them.[294] Nevertheless it must be noted with regret that lower German courts have not yet established a firm practice: takings in the Soviet zone of occupation[295] as well as takings of Indonesian tobacco to the detriment of Dutch owners[296] and of Chilean copper[297] have been recognized, but takings by Czechoslovakia of the property of Sudeten Germans[298] were held to be illegal and invalid.

[291] This was clearly decided by the Supreme Court, 17 October 1969, *International Legal Materials*, 9 (1970), p. 758—a decision which in other respects is difficult to follow and probably unconvincing. As to Indonesian measures which were held to be contrary to *ordre public*, see Supreme Court, 17 April 1969, I.L.R. 40, p. 7 and Court of Appeal Amsterdam, 4 June 1959, I.L.R. 30, p. 28.

[292] On this point the decision of Upjohn J. (as he then was) in *Re Helbert Wagg & Co Ltd*, [1956] Ch. 323, 344 sqq., is quite clear: the learned Judge did not challenge the decision in *The Rose Mary*, [1953]1 W.L.R. 246 on the ground that the confiscation by Iran there in issue was discriminatory in character. It would have been absurd if in the latter case a British court had not found a way of retaliating against a hostile act specifically directed against Britain or British interests.

[293] On this point Upjohn J. (see preceding note) thought that *Luther* v. *Sagor*, [1921] 3 KB 532 and *Princess Paley Olga* v. *Weisz*, [1929] 1 K.B. 718 included *dicta* of such general nature and impact that the principles there laid down also extended to cases in which the property of persons was involved who are subjects of a State other than the confiscating State. The *dicta* in those cases have frequently been analysed and criticized. They have had a most unfortunate influence, though no one doubts the correctness of the actual decisions in these cases. It can only be hoped that Upjohn J.'s interpretation will one day be reviewed by a higher court in the light of the learning to which those decisions have given rise and much of which should carry considerable weight. This applies, in particular, to Professor Lipstein's contributions.

[294] As to Germany see the general approach of the cases mentioned above, n. 265, and the tendency of such cases as LM No. 2 on s. 96 EVO (decision of 28 February 1956); *BGHZ* 31, 168; 39, 220 to which Arndt in Erman (6th edn.), Art. 30 n. 9 rightly attaches great importance. As to Switzerland see the decisions collected by Frank Vischer, *International Privatrecht* (1973), pp. 659, 660, who believes 'hot products' should be recoverable if the defendant knew of the confiscation or if this was discriminatory.

[295] Court of Appeal Hamburg, *IzRspr* 1945–53 No.7a; Court of Appeal, Oldenburg, ibid., p.22; District Court Mannheim, ibid., No. 7; in the same sense Raiser, *Süddeutsche Juristenzeitung*, 1950, p. 279. For the opposite view see Court of Appeal Nuremburg, *IzRspr* 1945–53 No. 5; District Court Berlin, ibid., No. 3 and No. 5.

[296] Court of Appeal Bremen, above, n. 258.

[297] District Court Hamburg, above, n. 258.

[298] Court of Appeal Munich, *IPRspr* 1950–1 No. 5 or *Clunet*, 1954, 1012; Court of Appeal Nuremburg, ibid., No. 13; Court of Appeal Hamburg, *IPRspr* 1952–3 No. 36; District Court Kassel, *IPRspr* 1945–9 No. 3. In the same sense the majority of authors, in particular

In the result there appears to be a substantial body of judicial practice which in a very wide variety of factual circumstances allows the dispossessed owner to recover his property. The survey which could be undertaken for present purposes is far from complete. It also fails to analyse the prevailing practice in depth. A more comprehensive and more detailed investigation could easily assume excessive proportions, but would be unlikely to achieve more than to fill in rather than revise the picture that has emerged.

V

There remains the task of defining a little more closely the consequences which the nullity flowing from the illegality of the confiscation entails.

1. The chattel confiscated in a manner considered to be internationally illegal should be treated as having been stolen. The original owner, therefore, has retained his title except where a subsequent purchaser in accordance with the general law of the *lex situs* has acquired it. Where title to stolen property can be acquired at all, the purchaser will usually have to act without actual or constructive notice. If the person in possession of 'hot products' knows their origin he may also become liable in damages to the true owner, not only for such a tort as conversion, but also for conspiracy committed by co-operating with others to deprive the true owner of his rights.

2. The nullity extends not only to the transfer of title to chattels or movable property generally, but also to immovables. The latter effect will usually be without international relevance, but special circumstances may occur. Thus it may happen that timber cut in confiscated forests can be found and identified in the forum. It is submitted that the true owner should be allowed to recover it.[299] The broad principle from which nullity is derived requires the court to look at the substance of the matter rather than legal technicalities. The fact that at the moment of confiscation the timber formed part of the land and that the latter, by its very nature, is not and cannot be a 'hot product' found in the forum should not make any difference. Similar considerations apply to coal or oil which at the moment of confiscation is in the ground and by virtue of the *lex situs* belongs to the owner of the land.

3. Does this also apply if the coal or oil in the ground belongs to the

---

Beitzke, *Rabels Zeitschrift für ausländisches und internationales Privatrecht*, 15 (1949), p. 145.

[299] Such a case came before the Austrian Supreme Court. Its decision in the opposite sense is criticized by Schwind, *Handbuch des österreichischen internationalen Privatrechts* (1975), p. 274.

confiscating State and according to the *lex situs* becomes the property of the owner of the mining rights only at the time of extraction by him? In other words, does the nullity of the taking comprise such chattels as at the moment of confiscation were the property of the plaintiff as well as chattels title to which the plaintiff would have acquired if there had been no confiscation? It is submitted that the answer to these questions should be in the affirmative and that, in particular, the local law relating to the acquisition of title should not be allowed any relevance at all.[300] As the Federal Supreme Court of Germany has said, if the substance of the property has not changed hands, the fruits of property cannot have a different fate.[301] If an international illegality has occurred, the acquisition by the confiscator of the fruits of the property is as illegal and, therefore, as void as the acquisition of the thing itself. In the words of the Permanent Court of International Justice[302] the latter is to be wiped out, so consistency no less than justice requires the former to be wiped out as well. A broad brush is necessary, for the law relating to the acquisition of title by the owner of mining rights who is not the owner of the land is very technical and varies from country to country. International law, when it assesses the consequences of an international delinquency, does not take account of legal technicalities or refinements, nor can the wrongdoing State expect it to do so. Any different view would impose upon the plaintiff a burden of proof which as a rule he cannot discharge and which in any event would be so elusive as to render the plaintiff's rights illusory or, to look at the other side of the coin, to allow the wrongdoing State to enjoy the benefit of its tortious act. This the law ought not to allow.

4. A much more difficult question arises where a process of manufacture is interposed by the confiscator. Suppose a car-manufacturing business has been illegally confiscated. Suppose that at the moment of confiscation there were in the factory finished cars as well as raw materials from which after the date of the confiscation cars were produced. Can the dispossessed owner recover both types of cars? If the preceding submissions are correct he can certainly recover the former. But the same should apply to the latter. The line will, however, have to be drawn if the confiscator buys raw materials and then uses them to manufacture cars. Even if all the raw materials were bought with money found in the confiscated business the right of recovery probably cannot extend to the cars produced from them. They constitute a new departure and their connection with the confiscation is too remote.

5. A question of some practical importance relates to the validity of an

[300] Court of first instance of Syracuse, 15 February 1972, *International Legal Materials*, 13 (1974), p. 114 is, therefore, wrong.

[301] *BGHZ* 39, 220, at p. 230. [302] Above, n. 3.

insurance contract made by or on behalf of the confiscator in regard to 'hot products'. If they are in the same category as stolen goods then by the law of most countries the insurance contract would not be concluded for the purpose of protecting a lawful interest of the assured in the goods. Goods obtained in pursuance of an international wrong are to be considered as stolen. No valid insurance contract can, it is submitted, be made in respect of them.[303]

6. The effects described in the preceding paragraphs should occur wherever the victim is the subject of a State other than the confiscator. It does not matter whether the victim is a national of the forum State or of a third State. Such a distinction could possibly be material within the sphere of *ordre public*, but even there no country ought to adopt so parochial an attitude as to grant rights to its subjects which it refuses to grant to foreigners. If international law is applied to reject the consequences of the foreign illegality there would in any event be no room for the distinction. On the other hand, where the victim is a national of the confiscating State no international responsibility falls to be considered except where the foreign State's act amounts to a violation of human rights. This may happen in the event of arbitrary discrimination on some such ground as political views, religion or race, and where it occurs the law of civilized nations should not hesitate to interfere.

VII. BREACH OF CONTRACT AND INTERNATIONAL WRONG

I

If one asks in what circumstances an international wrong committed by a foreign State may involve a breach of a contract made by the same State with an alien, the field, properly analysed, is very limited, for the question makes sense only where three conditions coincide.

In the first place the contract must be governed by the law of the State which is a party to the contract and has committed the wrong. If the contract is governed by any other legal system, the breach is most unlikely to be in any sense legally relevant. Thus a contract of concession granted, but wrongfully repudiated or modified, by a given State in law necessarily continues to exist unaffected if it is governed by the law of another State or by international law (assuming the latter alternative to be possible[304]).

[303] The 'purchaser' does not have a right in or against the property, as required by *Stockdale* v. *Dunlop*, (1840) 6 M. and W. 224. As to Germany see Federal Supreme Court, 24 May 1962, *NJW* 1962, 1436; 22 June 1972, *BGHZ* 59, 82.

[304] It was first developed in 1944: Mann, this *Year Book*, 21 (1944), p. 11 or *Studies in International Law* (1973), p. 179; see further this *Year Book*, 35 (1959), p. 34 or *Studies in International Law*, p. 211 or (in German) *Jus et Lex* (Festschrift für Max Gutzwiller, 1959),

Discharge or variation of a contract is subject to its proper law. This will not recognize interference by another legal system except as a fact creating impossibility of performance. Even so, it is hard to imagine any legal system which would allow a party to a contract to rely on self-induced impossibility to get rid of its legal obligations or to bring a contract to an end against the will of the other party to it.

Secondly, in the present context the contracting State's intervention must be not merely a simple breach of contract, but so grave and so specific a breach as to constitute an international wrong. If the contract provides, for instance, for the building of a harbour and the contracting State does not pay the sums due from it or does not accept delivery or, while the work proceeds, evinces an intention not to perform some obligation and thus repudiates the contract, and such repudiation is (or is not) accepted by the contractor, a simple breach of contract occurs with which the law is familiar and upon which, for present purposes, it is unnecessary to enlarge. But if the State passes legislation purporting to discharge or vary the contract, then it becomes a matter of significance to ascertain whether the legislation is general and irreproachable in character, scope and purpose or has the specific quality of an international wrong[305]

---

p. 465, and more recently *Revue belge de droit international*, 1975, p. 562, below p. 264 (the author is not responsible for the numerous printing errors in this publication). Since 1944 the subject has produced an enormous amount of academic discussion. The contributions by Professors Prosper Weil, *Recueil des cours*, 128 (1969–III), p. 101, Böckstiegel, *Der Staat als Vertragspartner ausländischer Privatunternehmen* (1971) and Sacerdoti, *I Contratti tra Stati e Stranieri nel Diritto Internazionale* (Milan, 1972) deserve special mention. See also O'Connell, op. cit. (above, n. 10), pp. 978 sqq. As to concessions in particular see Peter Fischer, *Die internationale Konzession* (1974), on whom see Mann, *Rabels Zeitschrift für ausländisches und internationales Privatrecht*, 41 (1977), p. 185. See also Roland Brown, *Modern Law Review*, 39 (1976), p. 625.

[305] For the legal basis of the distinction drawn in the text see Mann, 'State Contracts and State Responsibility', *American Journal of International Law*, 54 (1960), p. 572 or *Studies in International Law* (1973), p. 302. If the contract as a whole is subject to the law of the legislating State neither logic nor justice nor authority can support the suggestion that, in its effect upon the State's contracts, general legislation of a wholly unobjectionable type should be treated as a breach of contract. The submission of a contract to the proper law implies the submission to the law of the country as it is from time to time (for references see Mann, *The Legal Aspect of Money*, 3rd edn. (1973), pp. 304, 305 and add Upjohn J. (as he then was) in *Re Helbert Wagg & Co Ltd*, [1950] Ch.323, at pp. 341, 342, 353, 354). There is no exception in cases in which the legislating State is a party to the contract (see, e.g., the Supreme Court of Norway, 2 May 1962, mentioned by Mann, *The Legal Aspect of Money*, p. 126 n. 7). No rule of international law has become known which would render it an international tort for a State on the level of municipal law to rely on its own legislation. To invoke *pacta sunt servanda* does not help in a case in which by its very nature and the law supporting it the *pactum* is liable to become subject to new legislation. Nor is it possible to suggest a proprietary right in the continued existence of legislation rendering the contract immune: *French* v. *Banco Nacional de Cuba*, 23 N.Y. 2d. 46 (1968), at p.55 *per* Chief Judge Fuld, approving Mann, *The Legal Aspects of Money*, p. 495. The discussion by Delaume, *Transnational Contracts*, vol. 1. (1975), pp. 20 sqq. does not meet these points and lacks

and whether, for this reason, in a foreign tribunal it is deprived of the effect which legislation enacted by the proper law usually has. The building contract may include a clause allowing the contractor to employ foreign labour. A general law prohibiting or restricting the employment of foreign labour will hardly ever be internationally wrongful. It would be different if it applied to the particular contractor only, because in such event it would in all probability be discriminatory or arbitrary, or if there was a denial of justice. It may be suggested with some force that the question whether this type of legislation is an international wrong is otiose, for it would in any event be contrary to the *ordre public* of most States. The distinction is, or at least ought to be, in most municipal tribunals without practical import, unless, of course, any such tribunal takes the narrow and unsatisfactory view that *ordre public* cannot be resorted to in the absence of a link based on the nationality of one of the parties or some similar national interest.[306] Since such a view is reflected in judicial practice and implies a sharp distinction between non-recognition on the ground of *ordre public* and non-recognition on the basis of international law and since, moreover, the question of an international delict may have to be decided in a truly international court, it will be assumed that the legislation in issue does amount to what may fairly be described as a breach of international law.[307]

Thirdly, the issue before the court must be a contractual rather than a proprietary one. It must concern, for instance, the continued existence of the contract. Where, possibly as a result of or in connection with the

---

persuasiveness. Although in parts Jennings, this *Year Book*, 37 (1961), p. 156 gives a different impression, he does not in substance differ from these submissions (see his conclusions 2, 3 and 5 on pp. 181, 182). They are also supported by Sir Gerald Fitzmaurice, this *Year Book*, 37 (1961), p. 64, to a large extent by Weil, *Recueil des cours*, 128 (1969–III), pp. 226–9 and Brownlie, op. cit. (above, n. 10), p. 530 or O'Connell, op. cit. (above, n. 10), pp. 986 sqq. with numerous references. That a State cannot avoid its responsibilities arising under public international law by invoking its municipal law is *nihil ad rem*. It is, of course, possible that expressly or impliedly contracting parties submit only part of the contractual relationship to the law of the contracting State; this is a special case which does not lend itself to analysis in general terms.

[306] See above, p. 163.

[307] It has frequently been suggested that such a breach occurs in any event in those numerous cases in which the contract includes a clause submitting it to the law of the contracting State as existing at the time of the contract, or a clause precluding the State from passing or relying upon subsequent legislation. But whether a breach occurs depends in the first place on the proper law. If such clauses are overridden by new legislation of a general and unobjectionable nature, which is sanctioned by the proper law, no breach of contract nor any international illegality can be established. None of the relevant headings applies, because anyone contracting with a State on the footing of such State's law must be taken to have assumed the risk of new and inconsistent legislation. As was shown in the paper mentioned at n. 305, above, in so far as the American Constitution creates an exception, it cannot be generalized. For a particularly valuable discussion see Weil, *Mélanges Charles Rousseau* (1974), p. 301.

dissolution of the contract, property is taken, the rules discussed in the preceding chapter apply.

If, and only if, these three conditions are fulfilled there arises the question of what effect, if any, such internationally wrongful legislation enacted under the auspices of the proper law will be accorded by a tribunal outside the legislating State.

II

It is submitted that legislation which involves an international wrong leaves the contractual relationship unaffected, for it will be disregarded as unworthy of recognition and, consequently, the rights and liabilities of the parties remain in full force and effect, just as they would do in the more familiar case of *ordre public* precluding the application of some foreign statute. Of course, the legislation, so we assume, involves repudiation of the contract, to use English terminology to describe an event that all legal system are conversant with. Repudiation which is wrongful and not accepted by the innocent party is everywhere incapable of discharging the contract. It must be so,[308] for otherwise the wrongdoer could at will terminate his contractual duties and leave it to the innocent party to pursue a claim for such damages as he can prove. No legal system has become known in which so perverse a result prevails. It would be tedious to refer to the innumerable legal systems in which the opposite rule is established. One is confronted with one of those elementary rules of which one can only say: let those who assert the absurd come forward and prove it.

This, therefore, is not a situation to which the idea of reparation would be germane. Where the contractual tie exists or is deemed to exist (because in law the wrongful act cannot be allowed any effect, however different the factual position created in defiance of the law may appear), it is performance which is due from both parties, though in some legal systems the innocent party may be entitled to withhold performance, while the other party is in default.

To take an example, assume the oil concession which Libya granted to British Petroleum Ltd in 1957 had been subject to Libyan law.[309] The

[308] See above, p. 133.

[309] In fact it was not so subject. The clause read: 'This concession shall be governed by and interpreted in accordance with the principles of law of Libya common to the principles of international law and in the absence of such common principles then by and in accordance with the general principles of law, including such of those principles as may have been applied by international tribunals.' See Delaume, *Transnational Contracts*, vol. 1 (1975), p. 46 who discusses this clause and correctly concludes that 'the general principles constitute the test whereby Libyan law retains a vocation to govern the relationship, since in the event of a contradiction the general principles would prevail'. (For a similar clause see Art. XXI of

Libyan Nationalization Act of 7 December 1971[310] purported to cancel it. Suppose the concession had included an arbitration clause and an arbitration tribunal sitting in, for example, Geneva found the Libyan legislation and the repudiation of the concession inherent in it clearly contrary to public international law in that it was enacted for purely extraneous political reasons and was arbitrary and discriminatory in character. Suppose further the arbitrators had to decide the question whether in law the concession continued to exist, not merely for the purpose of their own jurisdiction,[311] British Petroleum having refused to accept the repudiation and the British Government not having waived the international tort. If, as mentioned, the Act of 1971 was rejected as an international illegality or, in the language of the British and American Diplomatic Notes on the subject,[312] was 'invalid', the answer can only be in the affirmative. The opposite would be tantamount to denying the fundamental and universal principle of the binding force of contractual obligations.[313] Accordingly it has been impossible to find any legal provision, any decision or any author of repute asserting the almost paradoxical theory that, as a matter of law, an illegal breach committed by one party brings the contract to an end against the will of the other party. To revert to the example given, no reasonable person would deny that in Libya the concession came to an end in fact and perhaps in law. But the assumption is that a tribunal

---

the Concession Agreement between Egypt and Esso of 1974 in *International Legal Materials*, 14 (1975), p. 915.) In fact the clause renders international law paramount and primarily applicable. Under the first part of the clause, Libyan law and international law must coincide; in other words if, and in so far as Libyan law does not conform to international law it is inapplicable and one has to turn to the second part of the clause which renders general principles of law applicable. But this is merely another description for international law. The general principles of law are nothing else than one of the sources of international law (see Art. 38 (1) (c) of the Statute of the International Court of Justice). They are not a legal system which alone can give life and legal force to a contract. Nor can it be assumed that parties intend to submit their contract to rules which do not constitute a law, a legal system, but merely one of its sources. The distinction is by no means a purely verbal one. There is no general principle of law which would preclude a State from enacting legislation which interferes with or even abrogates contracts governed by its law and covers contracts made by itself; such legislation occurs everywhere and extremely frequently without objection. But where international law applies, a State is precluded from relying on its own legislation to limit the scope of its international obligations (see above, p. 152.). On this point, in particular, see the article of 1975 mentioned at n. 304, above, at p. 567.

[310] *International Legal Materials*, 22 (1972), p. 380.

[311] That an arbitration clause survives the discharge of a contract by an accepted repudiation was decided in England by the House of Lords in *Heymann* v. *Darwins Ltd*, [1942] A.C. 356, and is likely to be the law in most countries. It would also seem to be international law: *Council of I.C.A.O.* case, *I.C.J. Reports*, 1972, p. 54; *Fisheries Jurisdiction* case, *I.C.J. Reports*, 1973, p. 3; see, in particular, Judge Sir Gerald Fitzmaurice's Separate Opinion, at p. 31.

[312] For references see above, n. 252.

[313] It would be wrong to accumulate quotations in support of an elementary principle. See, however, above, p. 133.

outside Libya has held the Libyan legislation to be inapplicable in law. Hence, in the eyes of such a tribunal, it cannot be allowed any effect. This is the inexorable consequence of the violation of public international law or, if one prefers it, of *ordre public*.

To avoid misunderstanding two further thoughts should be added.

The innocent party may decide at a time exclusively to be determined by itself[314] to accept the repudiation and thus to terminate the contract as from the date of such acceptance. The consequence would be that that party's rights would then become limited to damages of such an amount as to afford it as far as possible *restitutio in integrum*. Moreover, in most legal systems the innocent party will be entitled to damages even while, in the absence of acceptance, the contract is in existence. But the type and amount of such damages is quite different from those due for the loss of the contract as a whole.

Further, by the law of some countries certain types of contract concluded by the State are subject to termination by it either at discretion or *sub modo*, either conditionally or unconditionally, the condition usually being the payment of compensation or the absence of a contractual renunciation of the right by the State. Where this is the law, the termination of the contract in accordance with it would not be a breach. Discharge of a contract in a manner authorized by the proper law and conforming to the *lex fori's* notions of public international law or *ordre public* will inevitably meet with recognition and raises no problem requiring academic discussion. The assumption on which the present discussion proceeds is, however, quite different.

III

It is against the background of the effect of an internationally wrongful breach of contract by a State under the substantive rules of the proper law as applied and recognizable by the forum that it is now possible to turn to the distinct question of the remedies available to the innocent party in such forum.

Difficulty arises only where the innocent party has not accepted the repudiation brought about by the breach of contract which *ex hypothesi* is treated by the forum as flowing from the legislation enacted by the State party. If the repudiation has been accepted the idea of reparation and of damages enters the picture. Whether such damages are to be paid in money or whether and in what circumstances the innocent party is entitled to restitution in kind (as, for instance, it would frequently be under the

[314] Municipal legal systems do not seem to prescribe any time limits. As to international law see above, p. 134 sqq.

German Civil Code) is a question for the *lex fori*, for it relates to the remedy and raises procedural matters. It would be pointless and, moreover, wrong to allow a tribunal, usually an arbitration tribunal, to make an order for restitution in kind if according to the *lex fori* such an order was not permitted or could not be enforced. The question, therefore, is in substance the same as that which arises when the repudiation is not accepted and the innocent party asks for an order for specific performance rather than a declaration of the continuing existence of the contract.

This, again, is a matter for the *lex fori*[315] which in the only material case of arbitration is the same as the procedural law of the country where the arbitration tribunal has its seat, or the *lex arbitri* as it was called in 1967[316] and is now widely described; different views, it is true, have from time to time been put forward,[317] but experience shows that the *lex arbitri* is almost universally followed by arbitrators, including arbitrators on State contracts,[318] and has to be followed if they wish to avoid the risk of rendering an award which is null and void or liable to be set aside or to be held unenforceble. Specific performance may be subject to general limitations, as in the Anglo-American countries. Or the respondent State may, under its own law, be exempt from an order for specific performance (as the Crown is in the United Kingdom), and the same may apply to the State of the forum. Or it is possible that under the proper law of the contract specific performance is excluded in clearly defined types of contract to which the contract in issue belongs; such contracts may therefore at the outset suffer from certain congenital infirmities which a foreign tribunal may not be able to disregard. In short, it is difficult to generalize, as Professor Schwebel felt able to do in one of the few studies devoted to the subject, viz. an article[319] which, significantly, is entitled

[315] Dicey and Morris, *Conflict of Laws*, 9th edn. (1973), pp. 1101, 1119.

[316] 'Lex facit arbitrum', in *International Arbitration (Liber amicorum for Martin Domke)*, p. 160.

[317] Notably by Gentinetta, *Die lex fori internationaler Handelsschiedssprüche* (1973), on whom see Mann, *Rabels Zeitschrift für ausländisches und internationales Privatrecht*, 38 (1974), p. 763. The view expressed in the text does not rest on doctrine, but on hard facts, that is to say, on the legal texts to be found in most countries and often giving the courts power to a larger or smaller extent to supervise or interfere with arbitration proceedings pending within their jurisdiction. See, e.g., ss. 1025 sqq. of the German Code of Civil Procedure; Art. 1019 of the French Code de procédure civile: 'les arbitres et tiers arbitres décideront d'après les règles du droit, à moins que le compromis ne leur donne pouvoir de prononcer comme amiables compositeurs'; the English Arbitration Act 1950; and most significantly the Swiss Concordat which applies to every arbitration (Art. 1) which has its seat within the meaning of Art. 2 in one of the participating Cantons, and according to which the procedure is subject to Federal law, unless the parties or failing them the arbitrators have within the limits permitted by Art. 25 adopted a different procedure (Art. 24).

[318] See Mann, 'State Contracts and International Arbitration', this *Year Book*, 42 (1967), p. 1 or *Studies in International Law*, p. 256.

[319] *Rights and Duties of Private Investors Abroad* (1965), p. 201.

'Speculations on Specific Performance of a Contract between a State and a Foreign National'. He starts from the assertion[320] that 'the question of the remedies which the law affords for violation of a contract depends on what law governs the contract and upon the terms of the contract itself'. With respect to the learned author, this is hardly accurate. If the proper law of the contract does not allow the innocent party the right to insist upon the performance of the contract, the question whether the *lex fori* would allow it does not arise. If, on the other hand, the proper law (which, we know, may be international law) does, or is deemed to, allow such a right, then it is for the *lex fori* to say whether under its procedural law it will enforce that right by granting the remedy of specific performance. A detailed investigation of the relevant legal systems, including their special rules relating to State contracts, will be required; Professor Schwebel seems to conclude[321]

> that the case for according specific performance may be more compelling as respects a contract between a State and a foreign national than as respects one between a State and its citizen. Admittedly, the distinctions between the cases are not conclusive. And, whatever their force, the fact that specific performance normally is not afforded against a State in the national sphere suggests that it normally will not be accorded in the international sphere. An international lawyer would not counsel his international client prudently were he to advise that specific performance is a remedy to be expected.

With this comment one could readily agree if it referred to claims made in national tribunals; but it appears under the heading of 'Specific Performance in International Law',[322] and in that sphere it would, as has been submitted,[323] be unfounded: there is no reason at all why an international tribunal (with which the present chapter is not concerned) should not be able and entitled to make a decree of specific performance for the benefit of the plaintiff State which grants diplomatic protection to enforce 'a contract between a State and a foreign national'. On the other hand, when speaking about arbitrations on contracts between States and aliens[324] (which necessarily proceed on a national level and are subject to the *lex arbitri*) Professor Schwebel probably goes too far in the opposite direction when he suggests[325] that 'specific performance may well be the remedy which is more than a cure—the remedy which can give new life to the living law of a contractual relationship'. In practice it will not often be possible in law or useful in fact for a tribunal in the forum State to order a foreign State specifically to perform a contract made by it. Within the

[320] Ibid., p. 202. [321] *Rights and Duties of Private Investors Abroad* (1965), p. 210.
[322] Ibid., p. 206. [323] Above, p. 138.
[324] Loc. cit. (above, n. 321), p. 210. [325] Ibid., p. 212.

territory of the respondent State such an order will in any case be unenforceable, because even if it will recognize the tribunal at all it will not recognize the holding that the legislation terminating the contract is refused application—and such a holding must be the foundation of any award made against the respondent State. Outside its territory the rules relating to immunity of execution, among other obstacles, will make enforceability of an order for specific performance even more speculative and futile than the enforceability of a money judgment against a foreign State, which in turn is hardly anywhere enforceable. If, in addition, by the *lex arbitri* the arbitrators are not assured of jurisdiction to make an order for specific performance against a foreign State or at all, their award as a whole may be vulnerable. The result, therefore, is that, except on the level of truly international proceedings, specific performance is a very dubious remedy against a foreign State and that a prudent claimant should not claim and a national court or arbitrator should not grant it except after the most careful and comprehensive investigation of the legal position in the relevant legal systems.

This, then, leaves the declaratory judgment or award as the only other remedy to establish (but only to establish) the rights of the party to a State contract, which has failed to accept the State's repudiation of the contract. Such a remedy is readily and almost always and everywhere available to the innocent party, and it may in particular include a forthright declaration to the effect that the contract continues to be in force. Practically all legal systems permit declaratory relief,[326] and even where judicial discretion comes into the picture they are most willing to grant it just in cases in which no other effective remedy is available so as to clarify the legal rights and duties of the parties. In England, where at the time no order for the reinstatement of a wrongfully dismissed employee, i.e., no order for specific performance of the contract of service, could be made, it was even held that the court could declare the wrongful dismissal to be invalid; the purpose of the declaration was 'to make it clear to all the world what was the plaintiff's position in the eyes of the law'.[327] Accordingly, he who asks for a declaration as to his rights does not ask either for *restitutio in integrum* (reparation) or specific performance. The three remedies are entirely distinct. Nor is the distinction subtle. It is an elementary one, and an extraordinary confusion of thought would be required to suggest that where the claimant is not entitled to reparation in the sense of restitution in kind or to specific performance he is also excluded from declaratory relief. It may well be that by virtue of its moral force, though by no means

[326] See the impressive survey in Edwin Borchard, *Declaratory Judgments*, 2nd edn. (1941).

[327] *Vine* v. *National Dock Labour Board*, [1957] A.C. 488, at p. 504 *per* Lord Morton of Henryton.

as a matter of law, a declaratory judgment may in exceptional circumstances be similar in effect, though not in character, to an order for specific performance. Where the respondent State is told by the declaratory order what its obligations are and decides to implement them, it in fact acts as if an order for specific performance had been made against it. Such an attitude would be rare, but welcome and a tribute to the authority of the law. But in the strictly legal sense it is voluntarily adopted. There were, indeed, times when claimant States thought that, when making a claim in an international court, they should confine themselves to claiming a declaration, because if granted it could reasonably be expected to be implemented by the respondent State.[328] No reasonable person could or would wish to describe this as a subtle device and to refuse a declaration on the ground that in reality an order for specific performance is requested, but would have to be refused. Such reasoning could only be described as perverse, for it would test the actual and plainly permissible order requested by the plaintiff by an order which is not requested and which, if it were requested, would be entirely different in legal character.

The conclusion, therefore, is that the innocent party who has not accepted the repudiation by illegal legislation of a contract by the State party to it is entitled to have the continued existence of the contract and the legal rights and liabilities flowing therefrom clarified and established by a declaratory judgment or award. Indeed, so long as the repudiation has not been accepted (and in law it does not ever need to be accepted and acceptance certainly cannot be imposed by the defaulting State), a declaration may be the only remedy of relative effectiveness which is available to the innocent party and which no judge or arbitrator can reasonably withhold. While an order for the payment of money or specific performance would almost invariably be unenforceable against the wrongdoing State and, therefore, useless, a declaration would not only vindicate the innocent party in the eyes of the world, but might also serve as a defence or as *res judicata* in other proceedings and thus have some value for the victim.

While this paper went through the press, part of an Award rendered by Professor Dupuy on 19 January 1977 in a dispute between two American companies and Libya was published.[329] It arose from oil concessions which had been granted apparently in 1971 and which Libya was alleged to have

[328] Above, p. 135.

[329] *Clunet*, 1977, p. 350. On this decision (also in *Int.L.R.* 53, 422) Rigaux, *Rev. Crit.* 1978, 4350. It does not appear where the seat of the arbitration was. Some observations of Mr J.-F. Lalive, however, indicate that the Arbitrator held the arbitration to be subject to public international law (p. 324). For the reasons developed in the paper referred to above, n. 318, this was an indefensible conclusion. It was perhaps also a dangerous one: Klein, in *International Law and Economic Order (Essays in honour of F. A. Mann)*, p. 617.

broken by nationalizing the companies' Libyan property in 1973 and 1974. The claims were for a declaration[330] that the concessions 'ont un caractère obligatoire' (which one would have thought to be obvious), that as a result of the nationalization Libya 'a manqué aux obligations découlant par elle des contrats' and that Libya was 'tenue d'exécuter les contrats et de leur donner plein effet'. In substance the Sole Arbitrator, in the absence of the respondent State, so held except that he seems to have intended to make an order for *restitutio in integrum*[331] rather than for a declaration. The discussion is elaborate, though the question of the nullity of the nationalization was not in terms referred to. Professor Dupuy in effect decided in favour of nullity, though the odd terms of the application[332] compelled him to talk in terms of restoration.[333] With the possible exception of the third remedy granted, the result is in conformity with the preceding submissions, and the same applies to much of the reasoning.

[330] *Clunet*, 1977, p. 350.
[331] Ibid., pp. 387, 388.
[332] Ibid., p. 350.
[333] Ibid., pp. 380–8.

5

State Corporations in International Relations

I

Not long ago it was said by the Supreme Court of the United States of America:

> Increasingly during this century, governments throughout the world have established separately constituted legal entitities to perform a variety of tasks. The organisation and control of these entitites vary considerably, but many possess a number of common features. A typical government instrumentality, if one can be said to exist, is created by an enabling statute that prescribes the powers and duties of the instrumentality and specifies that it is to be managed by a board selected by the government in a manner consistent with the enabling law. The instrumentality is typically established as a separate juridical entity, with the powers to hold and sell property and to sue and be sued. Except for appropriations to provide capital or to cover losses, the instrumentality is primarily responsible for its own finances. The instrumentality is run as a distinct economic enterprise; often it is not subject to the same budgetary and personnel requirements with which government agencies must comply.[1]

This description certainly fits conditions in the United Kingdom, where there exist such diverse corporations as the British Steel Corporation, the National Coal Board, the Independent Broadcasting Authority,[2] the Secretary of State for Defence (who is a corporation sole[3]), or the regional health authorities, the area health authorities, the Special Health Authority, and the Family Practitioners Committee, each of which is a body corporate.[4] The list could be considerably extended, but one of the cardinal questions always is whether, and in what respects, the corporation

[1] *First National City Bank* v. *Banco Para El Comercio Exterior de Cuba*, 462 US 611, 624 (1983).

[2] It is a body corporate: s. 1(1) of the Broadcasting Act 1981; but by para. 4(2) of Schedule 1 of the same Act it is, for purposes of privilege, not to be treated as a body exercising functions on behalf of the Crown.

[3] Defence (Transfer of Functions) Act 1964, s. 2.

[4] National Health Service Act 1977, Schedule 5, para. 8. On public corporations see, in particular, the illuminating survey by Sir William Wade, *Administrative Law*, 5th edn. (1982), 139–56.

Liber Amicorum for Lord Wilberforce (Oxford, 1987), 131–48.

can be identified with, or is to be considered, a department or organ of government, or, on the contrary, is independent of, and distinct from, the Crown, or, as one should perhaps say more accurately,[5] the State. The problem of the immunity of the Crown and its emanations from proceedings in the United Kingdom is today of little or no importance,[6] but subjection to legislation or privilege in respect of discovery may be a matter of difficulty; thus the Secretary of State for Social Services is clearly entitled to privilege, although he is a corporation sole,[7] but the health authorities have by statute been deprived of it[8] although they exercise their functions on behalf of the Crown. The Custodian of Enemy Property is,[9] but the British Transport Commission is not,[10] a servant or agent of the Crown or a government department, yet if the latter body cannot pay the loss falls on the Consolidated Fund.[11] The Independent Broadcasting Authority is a body corporate exercising functions on behalf of the Crown, but for purposes of privilege is excluded from privilege.[12] As regards the status of British State corporations in international relations, there does not seem to be any material except one rather curious incident.[13] In connection with American anti-trust proceedings, Mr Geoffrey Lloyd, then Minister of Fuel and Power, in October 1952 ordered the Anglo-Iranian Oil Company 'not to produce any documents which were not in the United States of America and which do not relate to business in the United States without in either case the authority of Her Majesty's Government'. In November 1952 Sir Anthony Eden, then Foreign Secretary, certified to the United States court that Mr Lloyd's letter was signed

> in his capacity as Minister of Fuel and Power in Her Majesty's Government in the United Kingdom and was issued with the official approval and under the full authority of Her Majesty's Government in the United Kingdom. This letter from the Minister of Fuel and Power embraced a claim of sovereignty in that it was addressed to British subjects and organisations by Her Majesty's Government in the exercise of their Governmental authority and in the British public interest including the economic, strategic and political interests of Her Majesty's Government.

[5] In *Town Investments Ltd.* v. *Department of the Environment*, [1978] AC 359 Lord Diplock suggested (381) that it would be appropriate 'if instead of speaking of "the Crown" we were to speak of "the goverment"'. But it is submitted with great respect that the Government is the agent of the Crown which is synonymous with the State—i.e. the United Kingdom of Great Britain and Northern Ireland.

[6] This is due to the Crown Proceedings Act 1947.

[7] Halsbury, *Laws of England*, viii, para. 1239.

[8] National Health Act 1977, Schedule 5, para. 15(2).

[9] *Bank voor Handel en Scheepvaart* v. *Administrator of Hungarian Property* [1954] AC 584.

[10] *Tamlin* v. *Hannaford* [1950] 1 KB 18.

[11] Ibid. 23, per Denning L.J. (as he then was), on behalf of the Court.

[12] Broadcasting Act 1981, s. 1(1) and Schedule 1, para. 4(2).

[13] See, generally, Mann, *Foreign Affairs in English Courts* (1986), 6, 7.

In the light of this correspondence and of the fact that the British Government owned 35 per cent of the capital and the majority of the voting rights in the Anglo-Iranian Oil Company, the American court held that 'the corporation Anglo-Iranian Oil Company is indistinguishable from the Government of Great Britain'.[14]

It would be wrong to draw any general conclusion from this isolated case, which may well have involved an excess of power on the part of Mr Lloyd.

The problems arising in international relations are much more richly illustrated by cases relating to the State corporations which in the Communist world (and this expression is intended to include Cuba) have been established to carry on foreign trade. As Professor Knapp of the University of Prague has described the position in some detail,[15] in pursuance of complete control of each country's entire economy, the Communist States have created foreign trade corporations which are legal persons, and which 'are as a rule exclusively, i.e. by virtue of a monopoly, entitled to export and import certain kinds of merchandise that are strictly defined or to carry on another foreign trade activity'. In order to prevent misunderstanding it should be added that State corporations having the monopoly of trading in certain goods also occur in some other than Communist countries; an important example coming from Franco Spain will have to be considered later.

In discussing the international problems of State corporations, it is important to give due weight to two characteristic aspects. On the one hand, it should never be overlooked that, whatever the formal position may be, it is always the State which owns the entity. Though, for instance, the Secretary of State for Social Services in the United Kingdom is a corporation sole in whom hospitals and other property are vested,[16] he holds them on behalf of the Crown,[17] just as he exercises his functions on behalf of the Crown.[18] In the United States of America sovereign immunity is enjoyed by an instrumentality of a foreign State which is a separate legal person and a majority of whose 'ownership interest' is owned by the State.[19] Yet an American judge of first instance arrived at the surprising

[14] *In re Investigation of World Arrangements relating to Petroleum*, 13 FRD 280, 291 (1952), in part also in Int. LR 19 (1952), 197.

[15] *Sources of the Law of International Trade*, ed. Schmitthoff (1964), 61.

[16] The original vesting occurred by virtue of s. 6 of the National Health Service Act 1946.

[17] This follows from the case mentioned in n. 5.

[18] In *Nottingham Area No. 1 Hospital Management Committee* v. *Owen* [1957] 3 All ER 358 it was held that since 1946 hospitals have been Crown property occupied for the public service of the Crown; and in *Pfizer* v. *Ministry of Health* [1965] AC 512 it was held that National Health Service authorities exercise their functions on behalf of the Crown.

[19] S. 1603(b) of the Foreign Sovereign Immunities Act 1976, the text of which is conveniently printed in *Int. LR* 63, 655.

conclusion that this condition was not fulfilled by a Yugoslav workers' organization founded for the purpose of constructing and operating nuclear power stations, for it was mere 'political theory' that in a Socialist state all property ultimately belongs to the State.[20] On the other hand, there are many State corporations which are limited companies of the familiar type; this applies to the German Salzgitter A.G.[21] and the Portuguese shipbuilding company known as Setenave.[22] For international purposes it would be desirable if it made no or little difference which formal structure the state has chosen to attribute to its corporations.[23]

However this may be, one legal conclusion is common to all forms of State corporations and, it seems, to all countries. The status assigned to the entity, in particular its corporate character, is universally recognized. To quote once again the Supreme Court of the United States:

> Due respect for the actions taken by foreign sovereigns and for principles of comity between nations . . . leads us to conclude—as the courts of Great Britain have concluded in other circumstances—that government instrumentalities established as juridical entities distinct and independent from their sovereign should normally be treated as such.[24]

The same attitude has been adopted, for instance, by courts and authoritative writers of the Federal Republic of Germany,[25] where, in particular, it was emphasized that there was no room for denying the legal personality of State enterprises on the ground of *ordre public*.[26]

II

The principal problem created by the international activities of State corporations[27] used to arise from claims to sovereign immunity, though such a claim was rarely made by a State corporation in a Communist country, because the character as a legal entity was believed to exclude the 'danger that the foreign trade corporations would claim for themselves the immunities and prerogatives which belong to the state and its property'.[28] That problem, however, has for all practical purposes disappeared.

[20] *Eldow International Co.* v. *Nuklearna Elektrarna Krsko*, 441 F. Supp, 827 (1977); also *Int. LR* 63, 100.

[21] The whole of this commercial company's share capital belongs to the Federal Republic.

[22] It is the principal debtor referred to in *Settebello Ltd* v. *Banco Totta* [1985] 1 WLR 1050.

[23] This point is emphasized by Böckstiegel, *Der Staat als Vertragspartner ausländischer Privatunternehmen (1971) 49, 73.*

[24] See above, n. 1, 626–7.

[25] Ebenroth, in *Münchener Kommentar*, n. 440 after Article 10, with ref.

[26] Grossfeld, *Internationales Gesellschaftsrecht (1981),* in Staudinger, n. *133, 153.*

[27] A most useful survey is provided by Fischer and von Hoffman, 'Staatsunternehmen in Völkerrecht und im internationalen Privatrecht,' *Berichte der Deutschen Gesellschaft für Völkerrecht* 25 (1984).

[28] Knapp (above, n. 15), 63.

Since the State itself, its government or its organs, such as, for instance, an officer comparable to Britain's Secretary of State for Defence, cannot invoke immunity in relation to 'a commercial transaction' or, indeed, to any contract of any kind wholly or partly performable in Britain,[29] no separate entity, however closely connected with the State it may be, can make such a claim; nevertheless the legislator has made it clear that no entity which is distinct from the executive organs of the State and capable of suing or being sued is entitled to immunity, except in rare cases which presuppose, *inter alia*, that the entity has exercised sovereign authority.[30] For all practical purposes, therefore, foreign State corporations will in future not be entitled to claim immunity, and the cases in the past in which such immunity was allowed will in future have to be decided differently.[31] This applies, in particular, to *Krajina* v. *The Tass Agency*,[32] the case which led to the setting-up of the unproductive Inter-Departmental Committee in 1949.[33] Yet it must be noted with some surprise that in the United States the Tass Agency, as well as the Novosti Press Agency, were not only identified with the Soviet State,[34] but were also held not to carry on a commercial activity.[35]

[29] See s. 3 of the State Immunity Act 1978.

[30] See s. 14 of the State Immunity Act 1978. Before the Act there was room for the unfortunate impression that it was not the nature of the transaction at issue, but the nature of the act constituting the breach which was decisive for the question of whether immunity was to be granted; if the latter event was a sovereign act, there was a tendency to deny immunity. See *I Congreso* [1983] 1 AC 244, particularly *per* Lord Wilberforce, and the discussion by Mann, 31 [1982] ICLQ, 573. See also the decision by Donaldson J. (as he then was) in *Uganda Co. (Holdings) Ltd.* v. *The Government of Uganda* [1979] 1 *Ll. LR* 481, where the learned Judge reached the conclusion that a guarantee given by a Ugandan company could not be enforced, because the company had been confiscated by the State of Uganda, which by decree succeeded to the liabilities of the guarantors. The question of enforcement was a purely procedural matter, which in an English court ought not to have arisen. But the Judge said (488) that 'the litigation would involve the Court in expressing an opinion upon the meaning and effect—and perhaps the propriety—of Ugandan legislation in a suit to which the government of that State would not be a party. I do not think that even the most enthusiastic supporter of the restrictive doctrine of sovereign immunity would hold that it extends thus far.' The learned Judge's thought was wrong. To consider the meaning, effect, and perhaps the propriety of foreign legislation in the absence of the foreign legislator is a matter of daily occurrence and necessity. The case was similar to, and as unfortunate as, the decision of the Swiss Federal Tribunal, BGE 102 la 574 (5 May 1976), on which see Pierre Lalive, *Zeitschrift für Schweizerisches Recht* 97 (1978), 529; Delaume, *American Journal of International Law* (1981), 789; and Mann, *Festschrift für Zweigert* (1981), 280. The Swiss decision is universally regarded as wrong, but it had the advantage, at any rate, that immunity was never even considered as a possible defence. The same confusion between the cause of action (which is the exclusively relevant test) and the history of the defendant State's acquisition of title marks the decision of the Italian Corte di Cassazione, 17 Oct. 1956, *Rivista di diritto internazionale*, 40 (1957): 248, also *Int. LR* 24, 211.

[31] This also applies to *Mellenger* v. *New Brunswick Development Corporation* [1971] 1 WLR 604, a corporate body which was held to be a department of the Province of New Brunswick. For the reasons see Mann, BYBIL, 1979, 49 or below p. 309.

[32] [1949] 2 All ER 274.

[33] See Mann (n. 31) 45 and 53 or below p. 305.

[34] *Yessenin-Volpin* v. *Novosti Press Agency*, 443. Supp. 849 (1978) also *Int. LR* 63, 127.

[35] The decision will not, it is hoped, be followed in this country.

In most other countries too, the fact of the State corporation having a distinct legal personality and carrying on business will exclude any claim to immunity. This is so, for instance, in Germany,[36] Holland,[37] and, in particular, France, where the law was clarified by a very recent decision of the Cour de Cassation.[38] The Algerian Société Nationale de Transport et de Commercialisation des Hydrocarbures, better known as Sonatrach, had a claim against the French organization Gaz de France. One of its creditors obtained a garnishee order in respect of that claim. The Cour de Cassation upheld its validity:

à la différence des biens de l'Etat étranger, qui sont en principe insaisissables, sauf exceptions, . . . les biens des organismes publics, personnalisés ou non, distincts de l'Etat étranger, lorsqu' ils font partie d'un patrimoine que celui-ci a affecté à une activité principale relevant du droit privé, peuvent être saisis par tous les créanciers, quels qu'ils soient, de cet organisme . . . la Sonatrach ayant pour objet principal le transport et la commercialisation des hydrocarbures, activité relevant par sa nature du droit privé. . . .

Two points should be noted. The court speaks of a public organization which need not be a corporation, but which has its own property and which is distinct from the State. The idea that incorporation is not required to deprive the organization of immunity seems to be very sensible, since this is a purely superficial and fortuitous feature. Furthermore it is sufficient that the organization's principal activity relates by its nature to private law. It need not necessarily be a commercial activity. Nor is the degree of government control of any relevance.

On the other hand, if the State corporation is made liable for sovereign acts of the State owning it, the immunities to which the State is entitled enure to its benefit. This follows from a decision of the French Cour de Cassation[39] which, if read together with the decision of the *judex a quo*, the Cour d'Appel d'Aix-en-Provence,[40] may safely be described as so

[36] Federal Supreme Court, 7 June 1955, *BGHZ* 18, 1 (9,10); Federal Constitutional Court BverfGE 64, 1, also *Int. LR* 65. 215.

[37] *Cabolent* v. *National Iranian Oil Co.*, 28 Nov. 1968, *Int. LR* 47, 138.

[38] Cass. Civ., 1 Oct. 1985, *Semaine Juridique*, 1980 No. 20566 with note Synvet, (or *Clunet*, 1986, 170, with note Oppetit; or *Rev. Crit.* 1986, 527, with note Audit). See also Cass. Civ., 19 May, 1976; *Rev. Crit.* 1977, 359, and *Int. LR* 65, 63: in so far as the privately owned Bank of Japan exercises functions of an exchange control authority—i.e. sovereign functions—it is entitled to immunity.

[39] Cass. Civ., 4 Feb. 1986, *Rev. Crit.* 1986, 718 with note Pierre Mayer.

[40] 20 Nov. 1984, *Rev. Crit.* 1985, 358, note Remond-Gouilloud. The underlying facts are not repeated in the text, because they seem to be irrelevant in law, but they are politically of great interest. *The Astor*, a vessel belonging to Marseille Fret and chartered by Ras et Hilal, carried 10 Russian tanks and ammunition destined for Idi Amin in Uganda. There was no bill of lading, and the cargo was seized at Durban. The Libyan courts held Marseille Fret responsible for the absence of a bill of lading.

extremely astringent that it is almost impossible to unravel the facts and to understand the law.

A French shipping company, Marseille Fret, obtained from a Marseille court the attachment of *The Ghat*, a vessel which, according to the Court of Appeal, belonged to General National Maritime Transport Company (GNMT), a Libyan corporation described by the Court of Appeal, as 'une émanation de l'Etat libyen et comme telle appelée à répondre sur son patrimoine de la créance invoquée contre celui-ci'. The object was to secure a sum of $7,300,000 allegedly due to Marseille Fret on account of the arbitrary retention of its vessel *The Rove*, which, on the application of the Libyan company Ras et Hilal, had been authorized by a Libyan court. Ras et Hilal was, according to the Court of Appeal, a 'simple intermédiaire' acting as a screen ('paravent') for the Republic of Libya and making its claim in the Libyan courts for the benefit of the latter. According to the Cour de Cassation the attachment had to be lifted, because 'les conditions nécessaires pour le jeu de l'immunité existant au profit d'un Etat étranger *ou d'un organisme agissant sur son ordre ou pour son compte* se trouvent remplies.' The reason was that the French shipowner's claim existed 'à l'encontre de l'Etat libyen', since it resulted 'du préjudice occasionné par un acte de puissance publique émanant de cet Etat'. What is not clear is whether the 'acte de puissance publique' was the judgment of the Libyan court or the detention by Ras et Hilal, and why the damage caused by the latter could not be recovered from GNMT since both corporations seem to have been emanations of the Republic of Libya.

III

It is a much more serious question whether and in what circumstances a State corporation and the State owning or controlling it can be identified for the purpose of liability or, in other words, for the purpose of piercing the corporate veil. The rule, accepted by learned writers,[41] undoubtedly is that the very fact of incorporation isolates the corporation from the State. It is by no means only the law of the Socialist countries that justifies the general conclusion[42] that 'the state is not liable for the obligations of foreign trade corporations or for those of other enterprises and that the enterprises are not liable for the obligations of other enterprises or organizations or for those of the State.'

Thus, as long ago as 1934, the Soviet Arbitration Commission decided

[41] Riad, *Rec. Des Cours* 108 (1963–i), 646, an early and excellent contribution; Seidl-Hohenveldern, *Recht in Ost und West* (1966), 1; Wolfgang Friedmann, 'Government (Public) Enterprises', in *Encyclopedia of Comparative Law*, xiii. 43 ff.; von Hoffman (*supra*, n. 27), 66 ff.

[42] Knapp (above n. 15), 63.

the much-discussed case of the British ship *King Edgar*.[43] The ship's cargo was lost in territorial waters of the Soviet Union. When a Soviet State enterprise made a claim for salvage charges, the British ship replied that the loss was due to the salvor—namely, the Soviet Union—which was responsible for the failure of signals and thus for the accident. The Arbitration Commission in Moscow held that Sovtorgfott, the salvor, was a separate corporate entity to which any negligence of another Soviet legal entity could not be attributed. A closely reasoned judgment of the Swiss Federal Tribunal[44] is to the same effect. A Swiss creditor of the Polish State attached the debt due by a Swiss bank to the Polish National Bank on the theory that the bank was identical with the State. It was held that, according to Polish law, the National Bank was distinct from the State and could not be held responsible for the latter's liabilities.

The question however, arises, here no less than in the case of a private limited company of the familiar type, whether there are exceptions to the rule.

The most radical solution, amounting almost to a rule rather than an exception, has been adopted by the French courts, at least for the case of confiscation. In a decision of 1978 the Cour de Cassation was confronted with the following set of facts: Sapvin, a French company at Marseille, had a subsidiary in Algiers which obtained credits from Crédit Populaire d'Algerie, a state-owned bank. The parent company guaranteed them. In 1971 Algiers confiscated all the assets of the subsidiary, so that Crédit Populaire could not obtain payment from its debtor. It therefore sued the guarantor in France. In its defence the guarantor invoked Article 2037 of the Code Civil according to which the guarantor is discharged if the subrogation 'ne peut plus, par le fait de ce créancier, s'opérer en faveur de la caution'. The Cour de Cassation accepted the Court of Appeal's holding that the Crédit Populaire 'était une émanation de telle sorte que les actes de puissance publique accomplis par ledit Etat, et non par le Crédit Populaire algérien lui-même, étaient opposables à ce dernier'. Without denying the separate legal personality of the Crédit Populaire, the French courts deduced from the circumstances, typical of State corporations in Socialist countries, which are summarized in the appeal and, in short, involved the complete ownership, control, and supervision by the Algerian State, that the bank was to such an extent identified with the State that the facts created by the latter and rendering the subrogation inoperative were to be attributed ('étaient opposables') to the former.[45]

[43] *Rec. des décisions de la Commission d'arbitrage maritime* (1934), 13.

[44] BGE 76 III 60.

[45] Cass. Civ., 14 Feb, *Rev. Crit.* 1980. 708, note Pierre Mayer. The result of this decision is highly satisfactory, but in countries which do not have a provision similar to Article 2037 it may not be easily achievable. It is to be feared that in England, in particular, the courts are

This goes far, but the result is attractive and persuasive. The solution was perhaps even more radical in an earlier case decided by the Cour de Cassation.[46] The respondent, the Banque Populaire et Industrielle in Algiers, claimed from the appellant various sums of money advanced to him. The latter's property in Algiers had been confiscated, and the respondent had become an Algerian State bank, 'une émanation de l'Etat algérien'. This fact was considered capable of operating as a discharge of the appellant. The reasons are far from clear. Was he entitled to claim a violation of *ordre public* or to rely on *force majeure*? Or did he have a counter-claim against the State for compensation which he could puruse *vis-à-vis* the respondent? Professor Pierre Mayer thinks so: 'la mise en jeu de la responsabilité de l'Etat algérien . . . peut seule expliquer, par le biais d'une compensation, que l'on ait envisagé de libérer le rapatrié de sa dette envers l'émanation de l'Etat.'[47] It will have to be submitted below that this explanation, though it may be the only possible one, is in law untenable.

This brings us to the remarkable decision of the Supreme Court of the United States in *First National City Bank* v. *Banco para el Commercio Exterior de Cuba*,[48] the only American decision on the subject, which, in view of the great eminence of its authors, requires careful analysis. On 15 September 1960 the Cuban branches of the First National City Bank were nationalized by the Cuban Government. On 20 September 1960 Citibank credited the amount due under a letter of credit to the account of Banco Nacional de Cuba as assignee for collection of a letter of credit due to Banco para el Comercio Exterior de Cuba (Bancec), and 'applied the balance in Banco Nacional's account as a set-off against the value of its Cuban branches'—that is, the compensation claimed by it from the Cuban confiscator. Bancec had been established by law in April 1960 as the Cuban Government's exclusive agent in foreign trade. The Government owned all the shares, received all the profits, and nominated the governing board. On 23 February 1961 Bancec was dissolved. Its banking business was vested in Banco Nacional, and its trading business was transferred to another State corporation, Empress, which was subrogated in the rights and obligations of Bancec as regards commercial export business. In

likely to be governed by the fixed rules which have governed this subject for so long. The case of *Bank Saderat Iran* v. *S. H. Farshneshani*, which was decided by Nourse J. on 30 Mar. 1982 and is reported in [1982] *Com. LR* 111, does not inspire much hope. The plaintiff bank had made sterling loans to the defendant. They were secured by the deposit of 370 shares in the bank. Later the bank was nationalized in Iran, apparently by the confiscation of its shares. The bank was allowed to recover, although the shares (the certificates of which it was prepared to return) had become valueless as a result of the confiscation. The result may strike some as grossly inequitable.

[46] Cass. Civ., 9 Mar. 1971, *Bull. I*, No. 75.

[47] *Rev. Crit.* 1980, 714, 715 and *Clunet*, 1986, 15, 16.

[48] Above, n. 1.

December 1961 Empress was dissolved, and its sugar business was transferred to Cubazucar, also a State trading corporation. In 1980 the District Court gave judgment for Citibank; the Court of Appeals, Second Circuit, reversed, but the Supreme Court restored the District Court's judgment. In the course of its reasoning three questions were (or ought to have been) discussed.

In the first place the court had to decide 'which body of law determines the effect to be given to Bancec's separate judicial status'.[49] The Supreme Court rejected the view that the law of the State of incorporation determines not only issues relating to the internal affairs of a corporation but also the rights of third parties external to it. It is much more difficult to say which legal system was affirmatively held to be applicable. Without deciding the general question, the Supreme Court, in a somewhat puzzling passage, seems to have held[50] 'that the principles governing this case are common to both international law and federal common law which in these circumstances is necessarily informed both by international law principles and by articulated congressional policies'. It is difficult to interpret these words, for neither international law nor any branch of law of the United States can define the extent of a Cuban corporation's corporate existence. It would seem that the Court invoked American public policy as derived from 'international law principles and . . . articulated congressional *policies*'. No other solution of the conflict of laws problem can be inferred from the Court's phraseology. In fact, it may be that no other solution was available, for the only real and strongly supported contender,[51] the law of the corporation whose veil was to be pierced, was Cuban law, which in no circumstances would have permitted the disregard of one of its State corporation's corporate status.

The impression that the Court relied upon *ordre public* to solve the conflict problem is strengthened by the manner in which the Court dealt with the substantive problem of whether Bancec could be held liable for the compensation due from the Cuban Government so as to create the identity of parties, which was the pre-condition of a set-off. On this point the Court started from a clear and definite recognition of the corporate status of State corporations and concluded 'that government instrumentalities established as juridical entities distinct and independent from their sovereign should normally be treated as such'.[52] Here, however, 'equitable

[49] Ibid. 621. [50] Ibid. 623.

[51] In private international law it is the general view that the question whether the shareholder is personally liable for the company's debts is governed by the law governing the company's status, the *lex societatis: Bateman* v. *Service,* 6 App. Cas. (1881) 386, at 389 *per* Sir Richard Couch; Austrian Supreme Court, 12 June 1981, *Juristische Blätter*, 1982, 257; German Federal Supreme Court, 5 Nov. 1980, *BGHZ* 78, 318, at 334.

[52] Above, n. 1, 627. On this point the Court cited with approval *I Congreso* [1983] AC 244, 258 *per* Lord Wilberforce; *Trendtex Trading Corporation* v. *Central Bank of Nigeria*

principles' (which governed the problem of the corporate veil in American municipal law) had to be applied. Since 'the Cuban Government could not bring suit in a United States Court without also subjecting itself to its adversary's counterclaim', and since 'the Cuban Government and Banco Nacional . . . would be the only beneficiaries of any recovery', the Court declined 'to adhere blindly to the corporate form where doing so would cause such an injustice'[53]—namely the injustice 'that would result from permitting a foreign state to reap the benefits of our courts while avoiding the obligations of international law'.[54] In the result, therefore, the Court held Bancec (or Banco Nacional) to be identical with the Cuban Government. However, it confined this judgment to the very specific case in which a State corporation had succeeded in the American courts, but the State had failed to perform its obligations under international law. Even so, the result is surprising. It is difficult to see why obligations under international law, if repudiated by the foreign State, should have a different force from any other obligations. Is it not equally inequitable that a State corporation should recover its debts in the United States, while the States creating it or a sister State corporation are in default in respect of their commercial debts? And if this question is answered in the affirmative (as logic would seem to demand and equity, in the eyes of many, may permit), what then remains of the Court's wish to avoid a decision which 'would result in substantial uncertainty over whether an instrumentality's assets would be diverted to satisfy a claim against the sovereign and might thereby cause third parties to hesitate before extending credit to a governmental instrumentality without the government's guarantee'?[55] From a legal point of view the Court's reasoning is by no means compelling.

There remains however, a third point which the Court did not discuss at all (perhaps because it was not put forward by Cuba[56]), and which causes the greatest difficulty and surprise. It may safely be assumed, and is undoubtedly correct in law, that in respect of the confiscation of American property, Cuba is liable to pay compensation and has failed to do so. But was such a claim for compensation available to Citibank for set-off? On this point one does not think of the provisions which are frequently to be found and may exist in the United States and in Cuba limiting a set-off

---

[1977] QB 529, 559, and *Czarnikow Ltd.* v. *Rolimpex* [1979] AC 351, 364 *per* Lord Wilberforce.

[53] Above, n. 1, 632 [54] Ibid. 634. [55] Ibid. 626.

[56] See *Banco Nacional de Cuba* v. *Chase Manhattan Bank*, 505 F. Supp. 412 (1980), at 429. In *First National City Bank* (above, n.1). 26, the Supreme Court refers to 478 F 2d 191 (1973) where the decisions holding the Cuban confiscations inconsistent with international law are mentioned (194). But in none of them did the question arise; nor was it considered by the court in whom the claim for compensation was vested. This is very odd.

against State claims.[57] The real problem is that the claim to compensation arises under public international law and is vested in the State of the victim, in this case the United States of America, rather than the victim itself. Is it possible in law that an individual can set off a claim arising under international law against a debt resulting from a credit to a bank account? And is it possible for that individual to set off a claim which under international law only the national State can prosecute and dispose of? Perhaps the two questions merge into one. In any case it is more than likely that they require a negative answer.[58]

This is not to say that a debt due to a State corporation can never be subject to a set-off, with a claim against the State creating it. It should be possible where (to use the language of section 14 of the State Immunity Act 1978) the entity is part of the executive organs of the government. In England 'the mere fact of incorporation which is only for administrative convenience does not make a Secretary of State or a minister or a ministry an entity separate from the Crown',[59] so it seems possible that outside England a claim made by the Secretary of State for Social Security or even a regional health authority may be subject to a set-off with a claim against the Secretary of State for Defence. They are all the Crown (and, probably, for the purpose of Part 2 of the State Immunity Act 1978, the United Kingdom). There may be foreign countries in which the legal position is

[57] In England, Order 77, Rule 6, of the Rules of Supreme Court excludes a counter-claim or set-off where the claim or counter-claim is based on taxes, duties, or penalties and can be made with the leave of the court only where claim and counter-claim are made by or directed against different Government departments. This is probably a procedural rule, which before a foreign court or arbitrator would not be effective. In Germany s. 395 of the Civil Code permits set-off against a claim by the Republic, a *Land*, or a municipality if payment has to be made to the office which is liable to pay. This is a rule of substantive law, but in England it may possibly be classified as procedural.

[58] The most recent authority is embedded in the decisions of the European Court of Human Rights in the cases of *Lithgow* v. *United Kingdom* and *James* v. *United Kingdom*, where the reference in Article 1 of the First Protocol to the general principles of international law was explained by the legislator's wish to eliminate the rule according to which non-nationals 'would have to seek recourse to diplomatic channels or to other available means of dispute settlement' (para. 115 and/or para 62).

[59] *Town Investments Ltd.* v. *Department of Environment* [1978] AC 359, at 399 *per* Lord Simon of Glaisdale; and see Parker L. J. (as he then was) in *Baccus S.R.L.* v. *Servicio Nacional del Trigo* [1957] 1 QB 438, at 472: 'Many Ministers are constituted corporations sole. Some, as in the case of the Minister of Transport, for all purposes; some, as in the case of the Minister of Health, for limited purposes; and I do not think anybody could say that under English law the Minister of Transport or the Minister of Health was not the Crown'. See also *Commissioners of Works* v. *Page* [1960] 2 QB 274, at 290 *per* Devlin L. J. (as he then was): 'It has been admitted that the Crown is one and indivisible and acted as much through the Commissioners of Works as through the Commissioners of Crown Lands'. The former were created by the Minister under the Minister of Works and Planning Act 1942; the latter were a body corporate constituted under the Crown Lands Acts 1829–1943 and were reconstituted by the Crown Estates Act 1956. The case of *Baccus* is an excellent example of a situation (in this case in Spain) in which a trading corporation is an organ or part of the executive, and is therefore under the common law entitled to immunity.

similar. In such cases the constitutional law of foreign countries may require very careful investigation.

It may well be that in the case decided by the Supreme Court of the United States, Bancec could have been considered an organ of the Cuban State. If so, a set-off with a trade debt properly vested in Citibank might well have been possible. No such point arose. But if one looks at the status of Servicio Nacional del Trigo, Spain's National Wheat Corporation, the example may be instructive. It had the monopoly of buying and selling wheat as a department of the Ministry of Agriculture.[60] It formed part of the governmental organization. That it was a corporation did not necessarily mean that it could not be part of the Spanish State organization, as the Court of Appeal in fact held by granting it State immunity. On this basis it was the State of Spain which was the party to the proceedings. No question of piercing the corporate veil arose. The single State was represented by its various organs, of which the Servicio Nacional del Trigo was one.

IV

The final and most serious difficulty in the law relating to State corporations involves the question whether, and in what circumstances, contracts concluded by State corporations may be discharged by legislation of the State which created and controls them. In searching for an answer it is necessary to make a familiar distinction.

1. If the contract is governed by the law of the corporation's country, this will have to be given effect and, accordingly, impossibility of performance created by such country's legislation will normally have to be recognized. In particular, this seems to be the law in the Socialist countries. Thus the Polish Chamber of Foreign Trade has held since 1958 that a State enterprise of the German Democratic Republic was without remedy, when as a result of a change in the export plan of the Polish Council of Ministers the quantity of coal to which it was contractually entitled was reduced by one-sixth.[61] In Bulgaria, it appears, the law was the same between 1956 and 1961, on the basis of the theory that the identification of State and State corporation had to be rejected, and that, therefore, new governmental directives could create impossibility of performance. But the law seems to have changed in 1964, since when it has been held that, *vis-à-vis* foreign parties, changes in the economic plan could not relieve the Bulgarian State

[60] See the case of *Baccus* (above, n. 59), 441.

[61] Award of 11 Feb. 1958; see *Yearbook of Commercial Arbitration*, 5 (1981) 147.

corporation of its contractual duties.[62] The law of the Soviet Union seems to have been settled by the much discussed decisions of the Foreign Trade Arbitration Commission in Moscow in the matter of the Israel-Soviet Oil Arbitration.[63] Sojuzneftexport, a Soviet oil export corporation, agreed to sell quantities of oil to two Israeli companies. On account of the Suez Canal hostilities of 1956, the Soviet Ministry for Foreign Trade refused the export licences which the seller had to procure. The buyer's claim was dismissed on the ground that the legal prohibition rendered performance impossible, the underlying theory being that the State and the State corporation were different entities.[64]

Where the law of a Socialist State applies, foreign courts cannot avoid this practice, unless public policy may be invoked. This may be possible in either of two situations. In the first, it may be possible to identify the seller with the Socialist State, a point to which it will be necessary to revert. Secondly the supervening legislation may be designed to cover one particular contract or to apply to one particular State corporation, so that it may be discriminatory in character and offend against accepted standards of State conduct; though even then there may be countervailing circumstances, such as an emergency or economic necessity, which justify a State in taking special and unusual measures to protect the national interest, a condition which in the case of the Soviet–Israeli deal may have been fulfilled. Such measures, it is true, may amount to expropriation entitling the victim or its national State to compensation, but this is by no means a universally available remedy.

As far as can be seen there is only one award by an arbitration tribunal sitting in Holland and consisting of Professor Brunner, Mr R. A. MacCrindle, QC and Professor Frank Vischer, which held that emergency legislation of a Western State encroaching upon the terms of a contract was contrary to *ordre public*, on the ground that the legislation in question was enacted for the sole purpose of striking at one particular contract. It is however, very necessary to observe the utmost caution in resorting to public policy in the present context, for it is plain that no country can, or can be expected to, forgo the right of legislation in the general interest and that such legislation may apply to the State's own contracts. As the

[62] Kozucharov in D. Pfaff, *Die Aussenhandelsschiedsgerichtsbarkeit der sozialistischen Länder* (1973), 650–2. See, generally, Kemper–Strohbach–Wagner, Die AL Bedingungen des RWG 1968 in *der Spruchpraxis sozialistischer Aussenhandelsschiedsgerichte* (East Berlin, 1957), 273–7.

[63] *American Journal of International Law*, (1959), 800, or *Int. LR* 27, 631. See the discussion by Domke, ibid., 787; Berman, *RabelsZ*, 1959, 449; Riad (above, n. 41) 651; Böckstiegel (above, n. 23) 72

[64] The decision has been widely criticized, but on the basis mentioned in the text it is difficult to find fault with it. See Mann, 9 [1960 ICLQ, 691.

Supreme Court of the United States has said,[65] 'the United States when sued as a contractor cannot be held liable for an obstruction in the performance of the particular contract resulting from its public and general acts as a sovereign.'[66] And the same applies to England[67] and (probably) Germany.[68]

2. If the contract is governed by the law of a country other than that to which the State corporation belongs, foreign legislation is material only if it creates an impossibility within the meaning of the proper law, or if a *force majeure* clause is included in the contract. Such a case fell to be considered by arbitrators sitting in Switzerland. A contract was made with a Polish State corporation for the installation of a plant for the production of heating gas in January 1980. In December 1981 Poland's Council of Ministers prohibited the importation of this plant, as well as twenty-three others. An award of unusual diffuseness rejected the defence of *force majeure*, probably because the State corporation and Poland were held to be identical.

In a similar case Kerr J. (as he then was), the Court of Appeal (Lord Denning, M. R. and Lane and Cumming-Bruce L.JJ.)[69] and the House of Lords (Lords Wilberforce, Dilhorne, Salmon, Fraser of Tullybelton, and Keith of Kinkel)[70] rejected such a conclusion. This unanimous decision by nine English judges, with which, it seems, the Supreme Court of the United States agrees,[71] is undoubtedly at present the leading authority. Yet is has been subjected to much criticism by Western traders and their associations. The truth of the matter is that the decision is founded upon the arbitrators' findings of fact as the nine judges understood them,[72] while the legal principle was never in doubt. Lord Wilberforce, the eminent judge and jurist and friend to whom these pages are dedicated, stated it very clearly: 'Rolimpex cannot on the evidence be regarded as an organ of the Polish State'.[73] This means, on the one hand, that the question whether or not Rolimpex was an organ of State was decisive, and on the other,

[65] *Horowitz* v. *United States*, 267 US 458, at 460 (1925), and other cases referred to by Mann, *American Journal of International Law*, 1960, 584, 585.

[66] See, generally, Mann, *Studies in International Law*, 316 ff.

[67] *Commissioners of Crown Lands* v. *Page* [1960] 2 QB 274, at 292 *per* Devlin L. J. (as he then was): any promise made by the Crown 'must by neccesary implication be read to exclude those measures affecting the nation as a whole which the Crown takes for the public good'.

[68] *RGZ* 25, 354; on the problem see J. A. Frowein, *Festschrift für Werner Flume* (1978), i, 301.

[69] 2 [1977] *Ll. Lr*, 201.

[70] [1979] AC 351.

[71] Above, n. 1.

[72] These included the fact that the contract was for *Polish* sugar f.o.b. *Polish* port. A purchase on the world market was therefore ruled out. Furthermore, the *force majeure* clause was invoked solely on account of the governmental decree, not on account of the failure of the crop, which was the motive for it. If the sellers had alleged impossibility on the ground that only a fraction of the expected quantity was available for export, entirely different questions would have arisen.

[73] Above, n. 70, 364.

that, had the evidence shown Rolimpex to be an organ of State, the plea of *force majeure* would have failed. From the point of view of the law in general these are very important conclusions, with which one can only respectfully agree and which should guide the approach to cases which may arise in the future.

The problem in the *Rolimpex* case, therefore, is one of fact: did the arbitrators make adequate findings of fact, and did the courts correctly understand such findings as were made? An outsider cannot, of course, form a view on these questions, but Mr Lasok suggests some gaps.[74] It may indeed be doubtful whether the finding in paragraph 52 (c)[75] that 'Rolimpex is an organisation of the Polish state' really meant 'no more than that it was set up by the Polish state and controlled by the Polish state', as Lord Wilberforce stated;[76] for Mr Lasok also draws attention to the much neglected paragraph 22 of the arbitrators' findings, according to which Rolimpex 'is in Polish law a unit or organisation of the socialist economy',[77] a conclusion which, so he suggests,[78] 'betrays its status as a sub-division of the State apparatus'. In view of Mr Lasok's explanations and of what is generally known about the State and the economy in Communist countries, it is indeed difficult to believe that Polish State corporations can be put on the same level as, say, the National Coal Board in England. When the arbitrators described Rolimpex as 'a unit or organisation of the socialist economy', did they not perhaps intend to attribute to it the character of an organ of State?

The attitude of the English courts towards a problem of this kind is even more vividly illustrated by the decision of the Court of Appeal in *The Playa Langa*,[79] which concerned our old friend the Cuban state corporation Cubazucar. On 27 September 1973 Cuba enacted legislation freezing all Chilean property. Consequently Cubazucar was precluded from performing a contract for the sale of sugar concluded with a Chilean corporation. The buyers contended that Cubazucar was the agent or servant of the Cuban State and could therefore not rely upon the impossibility brought about by its principal or master. It was accepted

that Cubazucar was not a department of the Cuban State. Its senior management was appointed by the Minister of Foreign Trade and it derived its working capital in the form of interest-free finance from the National Bank of Cuba, Cuba's central bank. Any profits returned, in one form or another, to the Cuban State. At all material times Cubazucar acted as the instrumentality through which the State of Cuba conducted its export trade in Cuban sugar. It purchased its sugar from provincial sugar manufacturers, state trading enterprises operating under the aegis of the Minister of Sugar. Each year a national plan for the use, allocation and sale

[74] 44 [1981] *MLR*, 249 [75] Above, n. 69, 204. [76] Above, n. 70, 364.
[77] Above, n. 69, 203. [78] Ibid. 255. [79] [1983] *Ll. LR* 171.

of Cuban sugar is drawn up through the National Planning Board and enacted into law. This plan determines how much sugar is to be allocated for home consumption and how much for export.[80]

In these circumstances it is perhaps not fanciful to suggest that if and in so far as, in the realm of public law, such conceptions as agent or servant are appropriate at all,[81] Cubazucar was an instrumentality and, therefore, an agent of the State. However, the Court of Appeal tells us that the Chileans did 'not contend that Cubazucar were the agents or servants of the Cuban government'.[82] What they did argue is not stated. The Court of Appeal simply relied on its impression that they could not see 'any crucial differences between Rolimpex and Cubazucar'. Perhaps it is sufficient to suggest that in *Rolimpex* the agency point does not seem to have been taken.

However this may be, it is submitted with respect that in construing a *force majeure* clause,[83] arbitrators and courts should take a much more realistic view of the character and function of State corporations in Socialist countries. They may enjoy a measure of independence. They may not come within the strict definition of an agent. But they admittedly are 'the instrumentality through which the State' conducts its trade. To use the language of Lord Simon of Glaisdale, in England they would be 'aspects of the Crown'.[84] Or to use the language of Professor Riad of Cairo University, in the eyes of the law of many Continental countries they constitute 'un service de l'Etat'.[85] Are they not in England to be seen as organs of the Communist State?

V

At this point we reach the crucial general problem which touches on many subjects not discussed in the preceding pages, a problem which the judiciary of the Western world will have to solve and to which French scholars, stimulated by their rich judicial practice, have devoted much attention.[86] Should we decide to identify the State corporations of Socialist States with the State itself? In practice it would not make much difference

[80] Ibid. 174.

[81] We know from the case of *Town Investments Ltd.* (above, n. 59) that in England they would be inappropriate; and it is most likely that the same applies to the law of the Communist countries.

[82] Above, n. 79, 192.

[83] A detailed discussion of a *force majeure* clause is outside the scope of this paper. A helpful German paper on the subject discussed in the text here is Khadjavi–Gontord and Hausmann, *RIW*, 1980, 533, with much further material, particularly relating to Iran.

[84] Above, n. 81, 400.

[85] Above, n. 41, 651, 652.

[86] See, in particular Paul Lagarde, *Études Colliard* (1982), 539; Pierre Mayer, *Clunet*, 1986, 5 at 15, 16, with further references.

if we asked the question suggested by a well-known writer[87] whether there should be a readily rebuttable presumption in favour of identification. An affirmative answer would have far-reaching consequences, but may be required by a realistic assessment of the specific policy of the Socialist State. There is no validity in suggesting that if in the capitalist State parent and subsidiary companies are not normally so identified, the same should apply to State and State corporations in Socialist States. In the usual capitalist case the subsidiary company carries on an independent activity, and is by law expected to do so; the parent exercises its rights as a shareholder, and it if exceeds the limits so drawn, it runs the risk of being identified with the subsidiary. In the Socialist State the structure is totally different. The degree and manner of control in a given case will, of course, have to be proved, but no court should close its eyes to what is general knowledge: it is more than likely that in a totalitarian State (and a Socialist State is totalitarian—who would deny it?) the control of the State is all-pervasive. We should not hesitate to draw the appropriate conclusions. We should not pretend that a State corporation, whether we call it an 'emanation' or an instrumentality or an *alter ego*, has any degree of independence, except, possibly, in matters of mere routine, or that the State has no other function or influence than as a majority shareholder.

Nor should English courts and arbitrators be more diffident than their French colleagues; if one compares the facts found by the Cour d'appel at Aix-en-Provence[88] and those found by the arbitrators in *Rolimpex*, they are so similar that it is odd that the former led to affirmation and the latter to denial of the corporation being an 'emanation' of the State.

The idea that the State corporation of the Socialist State will, as a result of identification, be liable for the debts of the State itself may come as a surprise, and perhaps as a disappointment, to some of the corporation's creditors. But there will be others who will welcome the State's liability for the debts of its corporations. Such arguments cut both ways and are, therefore, not decisive. We should search for the principle, a principle founded on reality rather than make-believe.[89]

[87] Böckstiegel, (above, n. 23), 55–75.

[88] They appear from the 'moyen unique de cassation' printed with the report of Cass. Civ., 14 Feb. 1978, *Rev. Crit.* 1980, 707.

[89] There may be some arbitrators who will prefer to solve the problems discussed in the text by substituting discretion for law, and describe their decision so arrived at being based on transnational law or *lex mercatoria* or general principles of law such as *pacta sunt servada* or good faith. The courts should firmly disapprove such methods which, in substance, lead to decisions *ex aequo et bono*. They are rarely authorized by the parties.

6

The Protection of Shareholders' Interests in the Light of the *Barcelona Traction* Case

I

PROFESSOR Briggs' summary[1] of the decision of the International Court of Justice in the *Case Concerning the Barcelona Traction, Light and Power Company Limited*[2] fairly recapitulates the principal reasons which led the Court to deny 'the existence of any general rule of international law or of any special circumstances or considerations of equity which confer a right of diplomatic protection of national shareholders in a foreign company where the acts complained of were directed by authorities of a third state against the company rather than against any legal rights of the shareholders as such.'

If the rule is formulated in these terms one is, however, liable to perpetuate the impression which the judgment of the Court creates: it is to the effect that the case was concerned with no more than the taking by Spain of an item of property, or the withdrawal of a concession of Barcelona Traction, giving rise to a complaint by its shareholders. That something of this kind was in issue would be a misconception. Its origin lies in the truly astonishing fact that the unique and outstanding event that was at the root of the whole case, namely the bankruptcy of Barcelona Traction, a Canadian holding company, pronounced in Spain on February 12, 1948, is not once referred to in paragraphs 26 to 103 of the judgment, which contain the Court's reasoning. To put it differently, no part of the Court's discussion was at any point directed to the fundamental event that gave to the case its specific character and rendered it entirely different from such type of facts as the reasoning of the Court seems to contemplate.

In 1964, when joining the third preliminary objection to the merits, the Court had stated:[3]

> It can be asked whether international law recognizes for the shareholders in a company a separate and independent right or interest in respect of damage done

[1] 65 *JIL*327 (1971) [2] [1970] *ICJ Rep*. 3. [3] [1964] *ICJ Rep*. 6, at 42.

American Journal of International Law 67 (1973), 259–74.

to the company by a foreign goverment; and if so to what extent and in what circumstances and, in particular, whether these circumstances (if they exist) would include those of the present case.

Later the Court referred to the third preliminary objection involving 'a number of closely interwoven strands of mixed law, fact and status,'[4] and to the objection and the merits being 'too intimately related and too closely interconnected'[5] to permit a separate decision of the objection. In 1970 the Court upheld the third preliminary objection on grounds which, without exception, were available and could have been used in 1964 and which were wholly independent of the facts of the case.[6] In the judgment of the Court in 1970 there was not a single express reference to or express finding upon the merits. In 1970 the special circumstances, arguments, and problems arising from the bankruptcy were to such an extent ignored that readers of the judgment seem to be unaware of them. Thus it is not without significance that in the course of the discussion during the Annual Meeting of the American Society of International Law[7] in 1971 none of the participants even mentioned the bankruptcy and its peculiarities or implications. Yet if it desired to grasp the full impact of the judgment, Professor Briggs' formulation as repeated above will have to be amplified by reference to some of the conclusions which will be summarized below and which, at this juncture, may be stated as follows: 'this applies even if the respondent state claims to have such control over the foreign company as to be entitled to exercise bankruptcy jurisdiction over it and in fact exercises such jurisdiction by declaring the foreign company bankrupt on the ground of insolvency and by selling the whole of its property even insofar as it is situate within the state to which the foreign company belongs'.

The failure to define the full content and scope of the decision cannot be allowed to continue. This is so for at least two reasons. Firstly, it cannot be assumed that the Court did not take cognizance of the material submitted to it. On the contrary, the Court must have taken the view that, for some reason, that material could in law be disregarded. It follows that those who are looking for legal or rational explanations of the decision ought to

[4] Ibid. 46. [5] Id.

[6] It is possible that the criticism of Secretary of State William P. Rogers to which Professor Briggs refers (above note 1, at 331, 332) and which he describes as 'ill-considered' was directed to the remarkable fact stated in the text rather than to the alleged delay for which the Court bore no responsbility.

[7] Proc. Amer. Soc. of Int. Law 65 *AJIL* (No. 4) 340–58 (1971) Significantly, Professor Lowenfeld (66 *AJIL* 803 (1972) referring to *Barcelona Traction*, speaks of the 'refusal of the International Court of Justice to get drawn into the issue' which, in the context, can only be intended to mean the act of state doctrine or confiscation. Is it possible that the learned author failed to realize that *Barcelona Traction* had nothing to do with either issue but was a case of bankruptcy and its effects?

learn what argument it is that the Court impliedly rejected. Secondly, there is the problem of what one may call the 'philosophy' of the Court. Is its approach positivistic, doctrinaire, traditional, strict, perhaps even narrow? Or is it the Court's policy to take a broad view, to rely on a detailed review of the facts of the case before it, to decide according to the standards of a still formative equity? Is the Court, in Sir Hersch Lauterpacht's words, pursuing a policy of judicial caution or judicial legislation? How far is it prepared to go in either direction?

In order to answer these questions the student ought to have access to the pleadings, the supporting documents, the speeches of Counsel. It will take many years until these will be printed and thus become publicly available. In the circumstances it may be helpful (and permissible for one who was privileged to be one of Belgium's Counsel) to collect some of the material submitted to the Court and to state the issues raised by it (see below section II) and, thereafter, to indicate the type of reasoning which, largely by implication, the Court must have found unacceptable.

II

The status of Barcelona Traction in Canada was (and is) free from any doubt. At all material times the legal existence of the company in Canada and under Canadian law was plainly and universally agreed. The effectiveness of the company's Board of Directors and, later, of the Receiver appointed in Canada stood unimpaired; there was, in particular, no question at all of the company having been in Canada and under Canadian law 'reduced to a position of impotence such that it could not have approached its national State, Canada, to ask for its diplomatic protection', and the Court so finds (paragraph 100). Indeed, the bankruptcy pronounced in Spain was expressly denied recognition by the Supreme Court of Ontario.[8] Moreover, under Canadian law the company's property, namely the bearer shares of Spanish and the registered shares of Canadian subsidiaries, all of which was (and is) situate in Canada belonged to it (or rather to the National Trust as trustee for bondholders), free from any control or influence of the Spanish bankruptcy authorities or courts. As Judge Sir Gerald Fitzmaurice stated in terms,[9] in Canada '(and everywhere outside Spain) the original scrip remained and remains perfectly valid', and notwithstanding the purported transfer to Spain of one of the Canadian subsidiaries, its share register, its registered office, and its seat in Toronto 'remained where they were, and are still there today, not only in actuality but in law'.

[8] *National Trust Co.* v. *Ebro*, 30 D.L.R. 326 (1954), quoted without disapproval by Dicey & Morris, *Conflict of Laws*, 481, 485, 496 (8th ed. 1967).

[9] Separate Opinion, para. 71. See also Judge Ammoun at 320.

In Spain and under Spanish law, on the other hand, Barcelona Traction was bankrupt. The legal effect under Spanish law was fully explained in the course of the proceedings and merits analysis. To a large extent it turns on Article 878 of the Spanish Commercial Code which reads as follows:[10]

> Once bankruptcy has been declared the bankrupt shall be incapacitated from administering his property. All his acts of disposal and administration subsequent to the time to which the effects of the bankruptcy are retroactive shall be null and void.

The meaning of this provision is discussed, for instance, in Annex 77 to the Spanish Government's Rejoinder. The reader will find it interesting to see this set forth in some detail:[11]

> Spanish law does indeed prescribe a real lack of capacity in the case of the bankrupt, not only by prohibiting him from administering his property, but also by declaring absolutely null and void all his acts of possession and administration. The nullity of the acts of the bankrupt of his estate is based not only on the need for safeguarding the intangibility of the total estate of the bankruptcy . . ., but also on a personal disability of the bankrupt, which, in the non-controversial spirit of our legal doctrine and our court decisions, amounts to the lack of capacity. On the material plane the bankrupt thus lacks capacity to carry on trade and to administer his estate or to dispose of it. On the procedural plane he lacks capacity to be a party to proceedings. In other words, he cannot sue in the courts or defend his rights as defendant.

A later section dealing with the special case of corporation is even more telling:[12]

> When a corporation is adjudged bankrupt, the adjudication affects its various representatives in different ways. The directors of the company continue to discharge the duties of their office, in the absence of any provision to the contrary in the articles of association. Nevertheless, the disability (inhabilitacion) affects the directors in the sense than any act of disposal or administration performed by them in respect of the estate of the bankrupt corporation is null and void *ipso jure*. The function of the said directors is consequently limited to representing the

[10] The translation is taken from the speech of Professor Uria, *Case Concerning Barcelona Traction*, Pleadings, Oral Arguments, Documents New Application 1962), Vol. IX p. 275. The following references are to this text. Where it is in French, the translations were taken from the official transcripts which are available in many libraries. The author made his copies available to the library of the British Institute of International and Comparative Law. Unfortunately no academic lawyer has ever fully exploited the rich material there buried.

[11] At 144 of the English or 614 of the French version of Vol. II of the Annexes to the Rejoinder.

[12] At 146 of the English and 616 of the French version. Italics supplied.

bankrupt corporation *solely in the bankruptcy proceedings* for the purpose of asserting the rights and discharging the duties which the law grants to or imposes upon the bankrupt. The exercise of the rights and the conduct of actions of the bankrupt corporation in any proceedings other than the bankruptcy proceedings become, on the contrary, the responsibility of the organs of the corporation.[13] The fact that the board of directors of bankrupt corporations continues to exist with these limitations is provided for in Article 929 of the Commercial Code.

This is not by any means a document which remained hidden among thousands of others. Professor Uria, one of Spain's Counsel, referred to it, when he discussed Article 878 and its effects and stated (*inter alia*):[14]

In the Spanish system, as in certain others inspired by a very ancient historical tradition, the effects of the divesting of the bankrupt are much more extensive and rigorous and always entail not only his incapacity but also the automatic placing of bankruptcy authorities in possession of all his property.

A week later we find Professor Jiménez de Aréchaga (as he then was) addressing the Court as follows:[15]

As to the activities in 1949 by a so-called Canadian Board of Ebro, I must point out at the outset one fact carefully passed over by Belgian Counsel: this Canadian board was elected by a general meeting of shareholders held in Toronto in 1949, in which the main participant was the bankrupt company itself, although by Spanish law it is deprived of legal capacity from the day of the adjudication in Bankruptcy and, therefore, could not appear as a shareholder. It is obvious, then, that the power of attorney issued by a board so elected could not be recognized as valid by any Spanish tribunal. Such powers of attorney were therefore ignored . . .

Accordingly, even in Toronto, Barcelona Traction, a Canadian company, could not under Spanish law elect a Board of Directors in the general meeting of Ebro (another Canadian company) so as to be valid and effective in Spain.

Again, Spain's Agent, Professor Castro-Rial, in the course of a formal statement made in reply to a question from Judge Jessup, himself informed the Court that even acts carried out by the Receiver who had been appointed in Canada in respect of Barcelona Traction's property 'would have to be deemed to be void in Spain', but in any event this would apply to all acts of disposition on the part of the bankrupt company, 'whatever their legal weight in Canada'.[16] In the same sense the Counter-Memorial

[13] This is an obvious misprint for 'organs of the bankruptcy'. The French version makes this clear.

[14] Above, n. 10, at p. 275.

[15] Above, n. 10, at p. 478.

[16] Above, n. 10, at pp. 554, 556.

had already stated categorically that 'a bankruptcy adjudication in one State extends its effects to all the assets and documents of the bankrupt wherever situated'[17] and that 'under Spanish law a bankrupt undergoes a sort of *capitis diminutio* or reduction of his capacity, which necessarily entails nullity of any act of transfer or management which he may perform'.[18] The Rejoinder once more picks up the same themes.[19]

Finally, the Belgian Government did not, in general, deny the consequences of the bankruptcy in Spanish law. On the contrary, it invoked them for a variety of purposes. Perhaps it is sufficient to quote here from the speech of Mr E. Lauterpacht who, *inter alia*, attempted 'to specify the injury for which the Government of Belgium now claims reparation'. Having discussed the various measures taken by Spain, he continued:[20]

> Thus for all practical purposes the Board of Barcelona Traction was replaced by the bankruptcy organs in the management of the whole business of the company. I need not remind the Court of the far-reaching consequences that this replacement entailed by reason of the extraordinary use that the bankruptcy organs made of their *de facto* powers of management. The subsequent sale of the assets of the subsidiaries made total and irreversible what might otherwise have been a possibly passing or transient infringement of the shareholders' rights. The injury was made graver by the fact that the assets were sold for an arbitrarily and artificially reduced consideration, hardly sufficient in fact to discharge Barcelona Traction's debts. Not only was the company thus completely destroyed, but nothing was left of the considerable excess of its assets over its liabilities, an excess which precisely and exactly represented the economic content of the share capital. If the shares of Barcelona Traction were thus emptied of all their valuable content, how is it possible to conceive that this was not a damage to the shareholders? The Court thus finds itself confronted with a situation in which the shareholders have been deprived of all three of the traditional elements in a shareholder's right: the right to administration; the right to a share in the profits; and the right to participate in the distribution of assets.

The conclusions on the effects in Spain of the Spanish law of bankruptcy may be summarized as follows. In Spain Barcelona Traction was incapacitated, that is to say its Board's powers of management and administration

[17] Part II, Chapter IV, para. 67, at 36 of the English text, 490 of the French text.

[18] Ibid. 81 of the English or 527 of the French text.

[19] Thus para. 27 (at 292 of the English or 274 of the French version) is headed: 'According to Spanish Law, the Effects of the Adjudication in Bankruptcy of Barcelona Traction Extended to the Bankrupt Company and to its Assets, Wherever Those Assets Were.' A little later para. 29 states: 'As far as Spanish courts are concerned, a bankrupt remains incapable wherever he may be and his acts of management and administration are null and void wherever they may have been carried out, and the dispossession of his property, which is the consequence of such an incapacity, also takes place wherever this property may be located.'

[20] Above, n. 10, Vol. VIII, p. 459. And see the statement at 18, one among many made by numerous Counsel: 'The bankruptcy order left Barcelona Traction without a cent outside Spain.'

were suspended (except for the purpose of the bankruptcy proceedings), it was dispossessed of its property wherever situate, all acts of disposition by any person other than the bankruptcy organs were null and void, wherever they were performed and wherever the property was situate, and this was so to such an extent that, for instance, even a power of attorney granted by the Toronto Board to enable the attorney to vote in Toronto at a meeting of another Canadian company such as Ebro was null and void.

How was the material on the effect of the Spanish bankruptcy law dealt with by the Court? We know that it was not referred to, but the inferences to be drawn from such silence remain to be ascertained.

It will be remembered how the reasoning of the Court proceeded. The starting point was the firmly established rule 'that the company alone, through its directors and management acting in its name,[21] can take action in respect of matters that are of a corporate character' and that the shareholders have mere interests in the company's assets, injury to which does not affect shareholders' rights; hence only the company has rights which its state can diplomatically protect.[22] There may be four exceptions to this rule: the first may arise where the company has ceased to exist or has lost its capacity.[23] Secondly, it is possible that the company's national state lacks capacity to act on its behalf.[24] Thirdly, one of the Applicant Government's own legal rights may have been infringed.[25] Fourthly, there is the question whether 'considerations of equity' do not require the shareholders' state to enjoy a right of protection.[26] The manner in which the Court disposed of these possible exceptions or special circumstances without reference to the Spanish developments or even the bankruptcy requires explanation.

III

In discussing the first exception the Court considered it possible (but did not so decide) that the shareholders' national state may be entitled to afford them diplomatic protection in 'the case of the company having ceased to exist'.[27] It then stated that, while the parties had put forward conflicting interpretations of the present situation of Barcelona Traction,[28] it was clear that Barcelona Traction had 'lost all its assets in Spain' and

[21] Already at this point the Court might have asked whether *vis-à-vis* Spain this situation could fairly be said to subsist after February 12, 1948.

[22] Paras. 42–54. [23] Paras. 65–68. [24] Paras. 69–84.

[25] Paras. 85–91. [26] Paras. 92–102. [27] Para. 64.

[28] The Court does not specify the conflicting interpretations and it is indeed difficult to identify them. There may have been differences in regard to immaterial details, but, broadly and in essence, there was no, nor could there be any, conflict since the facts were beyond dispute.

was 'from the economic viewpoint . . . entirely paralysed'.[29] But did it exist? In paragraph 66 the Court answers as follows:

> It cannot however be contended that the corporate entity of the company has ceased to exist, or that it has lost its capacity to take corporate action. It was free to exercise such capacity in the Spanish courts and did in fact do so. It has not become incapable in law of defending its own rights and the interests of the shareholders. In particular, a precarious financial situation cannot be equated with the demise of the corporate entity, which is the hypothesis under consideration: the company's status in law is alone relevant, and not its economic condition, nor even the possibility of its being 'practically defunct'—a description on which argument has been based but which lacks all legal precision. Only in the event of the legal demise of the company are the shareholders deprived of the possibility of a remedy available through the company; it is only if they became deprived of all such possibility that an independent right of action for them and their government could arise.

This is a vital passage. It gives rise to many questions and comments, particularly if one submits it to close verbal analysis. It must suffice to emphasize a few of the outstanding points.

Thus it should be noted that the court does not indicate the legal system upon which its conclusions are based. Is it Canadian or Spanish law? Or is it international law, particularly that branch of it which relates to diplomatic protection?

A second aspect arises from the simultaneous and intermingled discussion of two different things, viz. existence and capacity. What is said in regard to the latter is somewhat puzzling. We know that in Spain, by virtue of Article 878 of the Spanish Commercial Code (not mentioned by the Court), the company had lost its capacity except within the framework of the bankruptcy proceedings. From the point of view of Spanish law, therefore, it is simply incorrect to state that the company 'has not become incapable in law of defending its own rights and the interests of the shareholders'. The Court failed to explain in what manner and in what circumstances outside the bankruptcy proceedings the company 'was free to exercise such capacity in the Spanish courts and did in fact do so'. Was it possible in law, for instance, for an action to be brought against the purchaser of the duplicated share certificate, Fecsa,[30] for the return of the property acquired by means of those pieces of paper? Would such an action have been successful? If Canada had afforded diplomatic protection to Barcelona Traction could or would it have been met with the reply that those instructing it had no power to do so, as the company had lost its

[29] Para. 65.

[30] See para. 17 of the judgment

capacity and was now under the management and control of the bankruptcy authorities? The Court does not consider such and similar questions. It is not easy to suggest a compelling answer.

Perhaps the most troublesome sentence in paragraph 66 is the last one quoted above in the course of which the Court refers twice to the condition which may give birth to the shareholders' direct right and, consequently, to their state's right of diplomatic protection. That condition is that 'the shareholders [are] deprived of the possibility of a remedy available through the company'. What the Court assumes here is that such a possibility continues so long as the company has not suffered a 'legal demise'. What the Court has refrained from doing is investigating the accuracy in law or in fact of that assumption. In all systems of law, an essential feature of a corporation with limited liability is that shareholders are not bound to make any contributions to the corporate funds beyond the amount of the share capital. If a company has lost all its property, how does it obtain the resources required to buy the ink or to do whatever else may be necessary to exercise 'a remedy available through the company'? It cannot force shareholders to make payments. It is, accordingly, a little difficult to say that the company retains 'the possibility of a remedy'. On the other hand it is obvious that anyone, whether he be a shareholder or not, is at liberty at any time to make gratuitous payments or gifts to the company. What the last sentence of the paragraph under discussion seems to contemplate is that 'the shareholders' (as opposed to the company) are the relevant persons to consider and that so long as it is open to them to make gifts to the company and cause the company to apply such gifts to the exercise of a remedy they have no direct rights. Has the Court ascertained whether this is so in the law of Ontario or in any legal system? And has the Court thought of the fate that would befall money paid to the company by way of gift? One might have expected a comment on whether this question is governed by Canadian or Spanish law. If Spanish law applies, it may well be that monies voluntarily paid to the company would be liable to be taken immediately by the bankruptcy organs as being subject to the process of divestment which Article 878 appears to prescribe. Nor can it be suggested that the Court did not have the underlying facts in mind. It recorded it as 'common ground that from the economic viewpoint the company has been entirely paralyzed. It has been deprived of all its Spanish sources of income, and the Belgian Government has asserted that the company could no longer find the funds for its legal defence, so that these had to be supplied by the shareholders' (paragraph 65); similarly, as regards capital, the judgment refers to the Spanish trustees procuring 'decisions that new shares of the subsidiary companies should be created, cancelling the shares located outside Spain (December 1949), and that the head offices of Ebro and Catalonian Land should henceforth be at Barcelona and not Toronto' (paragraph 17).

There is, however, little point in pursuing the doubts and misgivings which the Court's somewhat cursory method of reasoning creates in the reader's mind. It is of much greater importance—it is, indeed, a matter of fundamental significance—to point out that in the light of paragraph 66 it must be taken to be the view of the International Court of Justice that a corporate shell which has lost all of its property, the activity of which depends on gifts from shareholders and others, which may even be exposed to the risk of having the funds so contributed attacked by the bankruptcy authorities, and which, in any event, has within the respondent state become incapable (except in proceedings relating to the bankruptcy), is yet in a meaningful sense a legally existing entity. It is possible that at this point one reaches the core of the judgment's jurisprudential teachings. In order to reveal it to full appreciation it is necessary to revert shortly to the Belgian argument which, once again on less than express grounds, the Court rejects.

The precise legal and economic position of Barcelona Traction was, for obvious reasons, described on many occasions by almost all Belgian Counsel, particularly by Professor Virally who presented the argument on the *jus standi*. Among many passages in his two addresses which one could quote[31] (in addition to the written pleadings) one is particularly specific and, in the light of the judgment's laconism, striking:[32]

From a strictly formal point of view, and also in terms of municipal law, the company has not been wound up. But, as I already tried to show during the first round of oral argument, it has been, as it were shot down in full flight and annihilated; its corporate objects, its very *raison d'être* have been destroyed and it has been deprived of its estate and of all its means of action. It is not more than a wreck which no force can now set in motion again; indeed, it is less than a wreck, for the latter at least retains its scrap value.

Assuredly the nature and gravity of such damage are no negligible things. The loss which the shareholders have suffered is total and it is final. How can it be denied in the circumstances, that those shareholders have distinct and independent rights and interests to assert, and that their national State, consequently, has the right to obtain compensation, for the loss inflicted on its nationals?

In expressing myself thus, Mr President, I am not putting forward any new idea, not any idea invented by Belgium. Reference to a 'practically defunct' company is already to be found, as the Court knows, in the *Delagoa Bay Railway* case, decided in 1900, and already then the consequences of the shareholders being in the position I have just described were drawn. The expression was again adopted in the *El Triunfo* case, and is further to be found constantly used in legal literature,

[31] See, for instance, above, n. 10, Vol. VIII, pp. 514, sqq.
[32] Above, n. 10, Vol. X, p. 248.

diplomatic correspondence and arbitral awards concerning the protection of shareholders, even in Notes from the British Government rejecting such protection, as in the *Romano-Americana* case (Hackworth V,743) and, still more remarkably, in the preliminary objections of the Spanish Government in the present case.

I was, consequently, astonished that my learned friend, Professor Ago, made no reference to this argument upon which I had myself laid stress in his long address to the Court. I can only conclude from this that the Spanish Government is very wisely sticking to those positions it adopted in the previous stage of the proceedings, when it recognized that the *de facto* destruction of the company entailed direct harm to the detriment of the shareholders.

In the present case that destruction was carried out under such conditions and was so complete that not only were the shareholders' interests injured, but the very rights which they derived from their shares, those famous rights of which so much was said in the Spanish pleadings . . . were directly harmed thereby.

Next day Professor Virally picked up the same theme. It is sufficient to quote two sentences from a long exposition:[33]

The blow delivered literally shattered the corporate shell and the shareholders found themselves directly and personally exposed to the blows directed against the company. The rights which were theirs and were attached to their shares no longer have more than the semblance of existence; they no longer connect with anything, no longer bring anything to the shareholders; they are void of all substance.

The issue was thus clearly put before the Court. It was not that the company was in 'a precarious financial situation'. It was not even the fact 'of its being "practically defunct".' The Court speaks of a possibility 'which lacks all legal precision'[34] rather than a fact, but the fact was not seriously disputed, and indeed could not be, and in any event ought not to have been left open. The issue was whether the Court was to attach weight to the undenied existence of a 'corporate shell' without life or substance and to formal (municipal) law, or to look to facts—to treat the company's '*de facto* destruction' as decisive—and to do so, not generally and for all purposes, but within the limited context of the *international* law of diplomatic protection. The Court's decision went in the former sense: the only event that could have encroached upon the corporation's rights and brought those of the shareholders to life was the strictly 'legal demise' of the company in municipal law. Factual conditions, however grave and far reaching, could not lead to such decapitation as legal precision or, as some might say, legal conceptualism demands.

Those who have read up to this point are likely now to realize the true character and impact of the judgment in *Barcelona Traction*. It has carried

[33] Above, n. 10, Vol. X, p. 286. [34] Para. 66.

a new note into international law. The idea and the ideals of international law have in the past not been circumscribed by legalism. The practice of international tribunals has, on the whole, been characterized by careful analysis of the facts against the background of broad principles of law. Does the judgment in *Barcelona Traction* inaugurate a new trend? Or should it be treated as a special and isolated case to be explained by phenomena, attitudes, or politics peculiar to it?

IV

The next exception which the Court envisages and which was referred to above is that the state of the shareholders' nationality may have a right of protection in the event 'of the lack of capacity of the company's national State to act on its behalf'.[35] What the Court had in mind was, of course, not Canada's general capacity as a state, but rather the question whether Barcelona Traction could be said, for the purpose of the law of diplomatic protection, to have a sufficient connection with Canada. Just as Nottebohm, admittedly a Liechtenstein citizen, was held not to possess the genuine link with Liechtenstein to permit that state to protect him, so it was doubtful whether Barcelona Traction stood in such a relationship with Canada as to entitle Canada to afford it protection. The Court's holding that the company had 'a close and permanent connection' with Canada[36] and that Canada's right of protection 'remains unaffected'[37] stems from an assessment of the facts:[38]

> Not only did the founders of the company seek its incorporation under Canadian law but it has remained under that law for a period of over 50 years. It has maintained in Canada its registered office, its accounts and its share registers. Board meetings were held there for many years; it has been listed in the records of the Canadian tax authorities.

The lesson to be learned from this part of the Court's judgment is that, while reaffirming the need for 'a genuine connection,'[39] the Court finds it in relatively few, easily established facts, does not embark upon a process

[35] Para. 69. [36] Para. 71. [37] Para. 83.

[38] Para. 71; for some further relevant facts see Judge Jessup at 191 *passim*.

[39] It is submitted that this test was in fact reaffirmed by the Court. In para. 70, it is true, the Court expresses the somewhat obscurely formulated opinion 'that there can be no analogy with the issues raised or the decision given' in Nottebohm's case. The intention must have been to state that the facts in Barcelona Traction were such that the Nottebohm test was satisfied or, in other words, there was no room for raising the issues or reaching a decision similar to that in the earlier case. Had this not been the intention then there would have been no logical basis for para. 71 which lists the facts establishing 'a close and permanent connection' with Canada, or for paras. 72–6 which prove that 'the Canadian nationality of the Company had received general recognition'.

of weighing them against other facts pointing in other directions, and therefore does not try to find the state which may claim the most genuine connection of the company with it. If a state has such connection with the company as the Court defines, this is sufficient to confer capacity upon it to protect the company and to exclude a similar right of the shareholders' state even if the latter's connection with the company is in fact closer.

It is, however, important to emphasize the interconnection between Canada's capacity and Belgium's incapacity, which Judge Lachs thought it right to stress. He held that Canada's right 'is an essential premise of the Court's reasoning and that its importance is emphasized by the seriousness of the claim and the particular nature of the unlawful acts with which it charges certain authorities of the respondent State'.[40] Does this mean that if, for one reason or another (which it is difficult to visualize), Canada had never had or had lost or renounced rather than discontinued the right of protection, Belgium would automatically have acquired it? It would probably be too hazardous to read an affirmative answer into the judgment or even Judge Lachs' declaration. But it is possible that such was the intention. In that event one would again be confronted with the Court's determination to allow law to prevail over fact: the non-exercise in fact by Canada of the right of protection since 1952[41] could not outweigh the legal right, continuing to exist in 1970, to afford protection. But Judge Lachs' declaration and perhaps even the Court's observations permit one general conclusion. The cessation in fact of Canada's protection in 1952 and its discontinuation for eighteen years would not have been sufficient to oppose Canada with a plea of delay or prescription. International lawyers will remember other occasions when such delay might have been held to be fatal.[42]

V

A further exception considered by the Court involves the proposition that Belgium would have had a *jus standi* or perhaps more accurately, would have been entitled to pursue its own claim if 'one of its rights had been infringed'[43] by the Spanish measures. Could it be said that foreign investments by a state's nationals 'are part of a State's national economic resources' and that, therefore, 'any prejudice to them directly involves the economic interest of the State?' The Court's conclusion is that, in the absence of treaty arrangements, 'no generally accepted rules in the matter have crystallized on the international plane'.[44]

[40] Judgment at 53, 54. [41] See Judge Jessup at 177.

[42] For references, see Oppenheim (–Lauterpacht) 349 (8th edn. 1955); O'Connell, 2 *International Law* 1066 (2nd edn. 1970); or Dahm, *3 Völkerrecht* 169 sqq. (1961).

[43] Para. 86. [44] Para. 89.

As some of the Separate Opinions and Judge Riphagen's Dissenting Opinion show, this was a problem of some complexity. While it is difficult to say that the Court was wrong, it certainly displayed a very high degree of caution and, in particular, a surprising brevity of reasoning. It is also interesting to note the Court's statement that 'here as elsewhere, a body of rules could only have developed with the consent of those concerned'.[45] If this is intended to suggest that no rule of customary law can ever evolve without the specific consent of those concerned, the area in which customary international law would operate would be greatly reduced.

At this juncture it may be appropriate to mention two additional facts which are not reflected in the judgment.

The first arises from the Belgian attack upon some of the administrative measures which were taken in Spain and were alleged to have been abusive or discriminatory.[46] It was alleged that, in taking those measures, the Spanish authorities not only knew of the Belgian nationality of those controlling Barcelona Traction, but also intended to injure them rather than Barcelona Traction.

Secondly, there was material before the Court to show that not only Barcelona Traction itself, but also certain natural and legal persons of Belgian nationality brought some of the proceedings in the Spanish courts which resulted in a total of 3,267 judgments and orders[47] and which without any exception were decided against the plaintiff or applicant. Allegations of a denial of justice extended to such proceedings as were instituted by Belgian nationals. In this respect the Belgian *jus standi* could not be open to doubt. But the Court did not proceed to deal with the merits at all. In particular it did not think that for the purposes of the judgment it was necessary 'to go into' those orders and judgments.

VI

Finally an important line of inquiry arose in connection with the Court's fourth exception. The Court seemed to think it likely 'that the State of the shareholders has a right of diplomatic protection when the State whose responsibility is invoked is the national State of the company'. The Court summarily disposed of this theory by stating that 'it is certainly not applicable to the present case, since Spain is not the national State of Barcelona Traction'.[48] It is impossible to quarrel with this statement. But is it exhaustive? As a result of the Spanish bankruptcy and the measures of enforcement taken in Spain to bring Barcelona Traction's property

[45] Ibid. [46] See section 1 of the Belgian Submissions, judgment at 17.

[47] This figure appears from para. 18 of the judgment. The Belgian allegations appear from the Submissions at 22, 24, 25, 26, 29 of the judgment. [48] Para. 92.

under the control of the bankruptcy authorities, there arose in Spain an estate, a conglomerate of property, an organism or what the Germans call a 'Zweckvermögen' which was under the exclusive administration of the bankruptcy authorities. The property was held for the benefit of creditors. The directors and shareholders of Barcelona Traction were excluded from control or protection. Under Spanish law, as we know, this state of affairs had extra-territorial effect. The sale of the Spanish asset, in particular, was carried out by the bankruptcy authorities without regard to Barcelona Traction, its directors, and shareholders. Is it so far-fetched to see in the body or organism existing in Spain something distinct and separate from the Toronto Corporation, something entirely Spanish in character? From the point of view of formal law, it is true, no legal entity called Barcelona Traction was created in Spain by the bankruptcy. But this does not touch the true question: were the facts such that for the purposes of the international law of diplomatic protection there existed in Spain a body which was Spanish in character and in respect of which the state of the old Barcelona Traction's shareholders should in equity be allowed to exercise diplomatic protection as if that body were a Spanish body corporate?

Perhaps it is possible to put the same point slightly differently. Rightly or wrongly the Spanish courts held Barcelona Traction to be so closely connected with Spain as to be subject to Spanish bankruptcy jurisdiction.[49] This in itself would seem to allow room for the question whether such a non-Spanish company should not, for the purpose of the law of diplomatic protection, in equity be treated as a Spanish national *pro tanto*. No such question would admittedly arise in the case of a physical person, but the nationality of corporations is a problem which is necessarily so artificial and has in the practice of states met with so many and divers answers that the point might have been worthy of consideration. It must be remembered that a corporation, like a human being, may have two nationalities. The fact that a company has Canadian nationality because it is incorporated in Canada and has its seat there does not exclude the possibility of it having also another nationality, however specific or limited the ambit of the secondary nationality may be. There is much academic support for a system of 'functional nationalities'.[50] Its implications in the field of diplomatic protection are not to be underrated.

Since all the facts were before the Court, it must, however, be assumed that its silence implies the rejection of the reasoning which has been suggested. Belgium, it is true, did not submit that Barcelona Traction was

[49] For a few of the reasons why that holding was illegal, see Judge Sir Gerald Fitzmaurice's Separate Opinion, paras. 67–72.

[50] See in particular, H. F. Van Panhuys, *The Role of Nationality in International Law* 33, 165 sqq. (1959). See also Makarov, *Allgemeine Lehren des Staatsangehörigkeitsrechts* 12, 13, 17 (2nd edn. 1962).

a quasi-Spanish national. But the Belgiam Submissions as a whole were not couched in terms of rule and exceptions employed by the Court, whose duty of clarification could not in any event be confined by the parties' arguments.

VII

It was not the function of the preceding remarks to summarize or explain every aspect of the Court's judgment, still less the Separate or Dissenting Opinions. The intention was to discover the judicial attitudes inherent in the Court's judgment and also to ascertain what, in the light of the factual background, was actually decided by the Court, whether in express terms or by necessary implication.

As regards specific results, the decision seems to establish the following principal rules:

1. In general no state can exercise diplomatic protection, unless one of its nationals is injured in his rights (as opposed to his interests).

2. Where the injury is directed against the rights of a corporation, diplomatic protection cannot, in general, be exercised by the state of the shareholders who possess mere interests in the property of the corporation.

3. The rule stated in the preceding paragraph is, or may be, subject to exceptions.

4. *a* Such an exception may arise if the corporation has suffered 'legal demise', i.e. has in law ceased to exist or has lost its legal capacity to act.

b The question whether this has occurred is governed, not by international law nor by the law of the Respondent state, but by the law of the state of the company's nationality.

c Accordingly, if by such law the company exists even as a mere shell, without any assets and so as to be dependent upon gifts made to it by shareholders and others, it has yet legal existence and the exception does not apply.

d Moreover, the fact that in the Respondent state the company is declared bankrupt, is dispossessed of its property, is incapacitated, and is subject to the management and control of the bankruptcy authorities who claim extra-territorial power is equally inapt to bring the exception into operation.

5. *a* A second exception may arise where the company's national state lacks capacity to act on its behalf, i.e. fails to have some 'genuine connection' with it.

b For this purpose it is not necessary that the company's national state has the closest or a closer connection than any other state with the company. A connection that is real and genuine is sufficient.

c The failure of the company's national state to afford protection for eighteen years does not create a lack of capacity on the part of such state.

d It is an open question whether some legal step in the nature of a formal renunciation would be necessary to create such incapacity of the company's national state as would confer a right of diplomatic protection upon the shareholders' national state.

6. No rule of customary international law has as yet come into existence which would confer a right of diplomatic protection on a state merely by reason of the fact that the value of its nationals' shareholdings and thus its own economic resources suffer damage.

7. *a* It is likely that the shareholders' state has a right of diplomatic protection if the company is a national of the Respondent state.

b Such nationality does not, for the purpose of the international law of diplomatic protection, arise from the fact that the Respondent state claims and has exercised bankruptcy jurisdiction over the company and the legality of these very measures is being challenged.

These conclusions were reached by the Court by way of reasoning which is not only derived from the law of the company's nationality alone, rather than international law, but is also strictly legal, almost abstract in character. It is as if the Court had proclaimed the doctrine that the legal structure of the formal (national) law must prevail, however much the company as a living entity may have been distorted or undermined by realities or by factual disorganization. Even international law is without authority to give relevance to facts created by a law other than the national law.

No other message can be deduced from the Court's disinclination to attend to the facts of the case. It must have thought them wholly irrelevant: the facts created under Spanish law could not touch the strictly legal position under Canadian law and were therefore to be disregarded for the purpose of the international law of diplomatic protection.

The purpose of the present observations has been to dissect the real issues, to prevent them from falling into oblivion, to clarify what, in substance, the Court did decide and what it impliedly rejected as immaterial. The broad result of that inquiry is that the Court subordinated facts to formal law. Legal conceptualism prevailed over realism.

There remains the problem why the Court adopted the course which this article has attempted to outline, and refused to be more explicit, more distinct, more specific. This is unlikely to be an aspect of the decision which raises questions of international law or even international legal policy. It is rather a matter of jurisprudence. Its elucidation must be left to others.

7

British Treaties for the Promotion and Protection of Investments

TREATIES for the promotion and protection of investments[1] have for more than twenty years been a feature of international practice. Since 1959 the Federal Republic of Germany has concluded more than fifty such Agreements.[2] Switzerland started in 1961 and has concluded about thirty.[3] Between 1972 and 1978 France concluded sixteen such treaties.[4] In 1977 the International Chamber of Commerce counted altogether 124[5] and since then the number has increased.

Britain's first Agreement now in force was concluded in 1975 with Egypt,[6] the latest with Paraguay;[7] in addition there are Agreements with Singapore,[8] Korea,[9] Romania,[10] Indonesia,[11] Thailand,[12] Jordan,[13] Sri Lanka,[14] Senegal,[15] Bangladesh,[16] the Philippines,[17] Lesotho,[18] Papua New Guinea,[19] and Malaysia.[20]

In essence all the treaties are very similar in nature, content and structure. This is not surprising, as they are derived from drafts prepared in 1959 by a private group and connected with the names of Abs/Shawcross[21] and in 1967 by the Organization for Economic Co-operation

[1] When this article was written, the United Kingdom had concluded the Treaties mentioned in the following text. Since then numerous similar treaties have been concluded: Sierra Leone, Cmnd. 8501, 9044; Papua New Guinea, Cmnd. 8506; Belize, Cmnd. 8631, extended to Cayman Islands by Cmnd. 9812; Cameroon, Cmnd. 8670; Costa Rica, Cmnd. 8767; Saint Lucia, Cmnd. 8872, 9606; Yemen Arab Republic, Cmnd. 9096; Panama, Cmnd. 9144; Haiti, Cmnd. 9731; China, Cmnd. 9821; Mauritius, Cmnd. 9822, Cm. 65; Malta, Cm. 20; Jamaica, Cm. 99; Antigua and Barbuda, Cm. 197; Dominica, Cm. 252; Hungary, Cm. 281; Poland, Cm. 365; Benin, Cm. 369; Grenada, Cm. 381.

[2] Alenfeld, *Die Investitionsförderungsverträge der Bundesrepublik Deutschland* (1971), lists thirty-eight, but since then many more have been concluded.

[3] Caflisch, *Annuaire Suisse de droit international,* 1980, p. 175 n. 55.

[4] Juillard, *Clunet*, 106 (1979), p. 274.

[5] See the leaflet *Bilateral Treaties for International Investment (1977).*

[6] Cmnd. 6141, 6638. See also Cmnd. 6140. An early Agreement of 1963 with Cameroon (Cmnd. 2133) entered into force on signature but, is no longer in force.

[7] Cmnd. 8329. [8] Cmnd. 6300, 7183. [9] Cmnd. 6510; 9894

[10] Cmnd. 6500, 6722. [11] Cmnd. 6858. [12] Cmnd. 7732.

[13] Cmnd. 7945. [14] Cmnd. 7984, 8186, 8563. [15] Cmnd. 8079 and 9292.

[16] Cmnd. 8013. [17] Cmnd. 8148. [18] Cmnd. 8246.

[19] Cmnd. 8307, 8506. [20] Cmnd. 8269; Cm. 707.

[21] See on this, for instance, Schwarzenberger, *Foreign Investment and International Law* (1969), p.109.

British Year Book of International Law (Oxford, 1981), 241–540.

and Development.[22] Nevertheless, in the course of time a number of improvements and revisions have been introduced into the texts. Although these treaties do not seem to have given rise to much difficulty or contention in practice, it may be helpful, not to write a commentary upon or to embark upon an exhaustive analysis of the thirty-four British treaties, but to discuss some specific points which have occurred to one reader.

In order to facilitate the understanding of what follows, the text of the latest Agreement which at the moment of writing is publicly available, i.e. the Agreement with the Philippines, will be found in the Annexe to this paper and taken as a basis for the following discussion.

It will be seen that these Agreements proceed from the principle of reciprocity: they apply to investments by the United Kingdom in the Philippines no less than to investments by the Philippines in the United Kingdom. In practice, of course, the latter type will be extremely rare and it is probably no exaggeration to suggest that reciprocity is to a large extent a matter of prestige rather than reality. What is primarily intended is the promotion and protection of British investments in the Philippines. It should also be pointed out that the structure and even the wording of these Agreements is almost identical. The first two Articles are concerned with definitions. The following Articles III to VIII contain the substantive obligations. Article IX provides for consultation, but this is hardly more than a nominal duty. Articles X and XI deal with the settlement of disputes between the investor and the host country and between the Contracting Parties respectively. Finally, Article XII regulates the coming into force and the duration of the Agreement. It is noteworthy that the texts in both languages are equally authentic; in the circumstances this may be described as a remarkable concession to the principle of reciprocity. In practice it is likely to be of minor importance, for if the English text provides the standard the language would seem to be simple and reasonably clear, so that disputes about interpretation will probably be infrequent. On the other hand the Agreements include many terms which involve a measure of evaluation and of judgement and may give rise to disputes about degree rather than terminology. This applies, for instance, to the overriding obligation of 'fair and equitable treatment' or to limitations in Article VII which entitle a Party 'equitably and in good faith' to impose protective measures or to transfer 'large amounts' by way of 'reasonable instalments'. These are terms which by no means are withdrawn from, or incapable of, judicial appreciation, but they undoubtedly leave to the State a considerable, albeit controlled, freedom of assessment.

[22] See Schwarzenberger, op. cit. (previous note), p. 153.

I. DEFINITIONS

1. It may be stated at the outset that one of the principal changes that has taken place relates to the definitions. That the early Agreements defined 'returns' rather than 'earnings', occurring in the Agreement with the Philippines, is probably of minor significance. The definition of a United Kingdom company is much more remarkable. Originally it meant a corporation, firm or association incorporated or constituted under the law in force in any part of the United Kingdom or in any territory to which this Agreement is extended.[23] The Agreement with the Philippines speaks of 'a corporation, partnership or other association, incorporated or constituted and actually doing business under the laws in force in any part of the territory of that Contracting Party wherein a place of effective management is situated'.[24] This means that the United Kingdom subsidiary of an American company comes within the definition only if it actually does business in the United Kingdom and has there a place where it is effectively managed. The American parent should not find it too difficult to bring its British subsidiary within these conditions before the latter makes an investment in the Philippines.

Two types of company are not in any case covered by the definition. A Philippine company cannot claim the protection of the Agreement even if all the shares are owned by a British national. Nor can a holding company incorporated, say, in Luxembourg do so. In both cases such treatment as Barcelona Traction suffered in Spain and as Belgium attempted to attack would prima facie remain immune. Where the investment is made by an international consortium, it will have to be carefully considered in which country the head company should be constituted.

2. The definition of the term 'investment' seeems to have remained the same. It includes, in particular, property and property rights, shares, claims under a contract, intellectual property and goodwill as well as concessions. Where it is intended to purchase a factory building in Manila, it may be preferable to do so in the name of a British rather than a Philippine company, for in the former case the company is probably protected against unfair taxation of property, while in the latter case it is by no means certain whether the reduced value of the shares would give rise to any remedy under the Agreement. On the other hand, the protection would seem to extend to activities which are not necessarily envisaged by the term 'investment'. If a British bank or a British firm of management consultants opens a branch in Manila this would perhaps not

[23] Art. I of the Agreement with Egypt.

[24] Art. I.

generally be described as an investment, yet the branch and its assets clearly come within the definition.

More difficult questions arise in the case of lending. A loan of money is no less protected than a loan of cranes for the purpose of building a skyscraper. But can lending a picture for exhibition or lending an aeroplane for temporary use fairly be described as an 'investment'? It is submitted that in such cases it is necessary to look to the permanency of the purpose of the transaction; its temporary character would seem to require a negative answer.

Similar difficulties may arise in the event of the sale of goods. If the goods are destined for consumption, such as oil or wheat, no 'investment' occurs. But where a very expensive machine or ship is supplied, this may well constitute an 'investment'.

In many cases the problem will be solved by the fact that the treaty applies only to investments 'which are qualified for registration and are duly registered by the appropriate government agency of the receiving Contracting Party, if so required by its laws'. Where, however, there are no laws requiring registration, it may become necessary to find an answer to the problems referred to.

II. SUBSTANTIVE LAW

3. The overriding obligation is that investments 'shall at all times be accorded fair and equitable treatment and shall enjoy full protection and security'.[25] This is underlined by the further provision that investors shall not be subjected to 'unreasonable measures'.[26] Although these are very familiar terms, they have hardly ever been judicially considered. Thus, while it may be suggested that arbitrary, discriminatory or abusive treatment is contrary to customary international law, unfair and inequitable treatment is a much wider conception which may readily include such administrative measures in the field of taxation, licences and so forth, as are not plainly illegal in the accepted sense of international law. In particular it is submitted that the right to fair and equitable treatment goes much further than the right to most-favoured-nation and to national treatment, even if in the latter case the foreigner's rights are greatly extended and underlined by the duty not to subject the foreigner to 'unreasonable measures'.[27] Thus if a British national erects a factory to produce cement in the Philippines and the government introduces a maximum price order, a tribunal may be able and compelled to investigate

[25] Art. III of the Agreement with the Philippines. [26] Art IV (2).
[27] Art. IV.

whether the prices so fixed are fair, equitable or reasonable. So general a provision is likely to be almost sufficient to cover all conceivable cases, and it may well be that other provisions of the Agreements affording substantive protection are no more than examples or specific instances of this overriding duty.

It has been suggested that the term 'fair and equitable' is expressive of, or adopts what has for many years been known as, the minimum standard. Thus in 1979 the Swiss Foreign Office stated:[28]

> On se réfère ainsi au principe classique du droit des gens selon lequel les États doivent mettre les étrangers se trouvant sur leur territoire et leurs biens au bénéfice du 'standard minimum' international c'est-à-dire leur accorder un minimum de droits personnels, procéduraux et économiques.

It is submitted that nothing is gained by introducing the conception of a minimum standard and, more than this, it is positively misleading to introduce it. The terms 'fair and equitable treatment' envisage conduct which goes far beyond the minimum standard and afford protection to a greater extent and according to a much more objective standard than any previously employed form of words. A tribunal would not be concerned with a minimum, maximum or average standard. It will have to decide whether in all the circumstances the conduct in issue is fair and equitable or unfair and inequitable. No standard defined by other words is likely to be material. The terms are to be understood and applied independently and autonomously.

In any event it seems clear that the provisions of the Agreement would compel a tribunal to condemn such action as occurred in the *Barcelona Traction* case.[29] If one adapts the facts of that case to the situation under the Agreement with the Philippines, the position is as follows: a United Kingdom company owns all the shares of a Philippine company and deposits such shares with a London trustee as security for bonds issued by it. The Philippine company erects electricity works in the country. It is very prosperous, but does not obtain permission to remit the dividends to its British parent company, so that the latter's bonds cannot be serviced. A Philippine financier, without proper or indeed any notice to the debtor, obtains an order from an obscure court in the Philippines declaring the English parent company bankrupt. Trustees in bankruptcy are appointed and have 'duplicate' share certificates of the Philippine subsidiary printed.

[28] *Annuaire Suisse de droit international*, 1980, p. 178, with references to literature. It may be that it was the intention of the OECD to adopt the so-called minimum standard. The express terms, however, must govern and go far beyond it.

[29] *I.C.J. Reports,* 1970, p.3, on which see Mann, *American Journal of International Law,* 67 (1973), p. 259 or above p. 217.

They then sell these duplicated certificates and thus the whole of the English company's investment. Whether or no such treatment would be lawful under the law of the Philippines, it should not be open to doubt that it is neither fair nor equitable nor reasonable and would, therefore attract the liability of the Philippines.[30]

4. As has just been mentioned, the Agreements include a most-favoured-nation as well as an extended national treatment clause. These are familiar clauses which in the present context do not need any comment, except that the former has been so defined as not to include any existing or future customs union, common market, free-trade area or regional economic organization or anything relating to taxation. In view of the very wide terms considered in the preceding paragraphs it is unlikely that the two well-known standards thus guaranteed will add anything substantial. An example will perhaps help: there are certain countries in which the State accepts liability for wrongful acts of its servants only in cases in which the victim is a national of the State. There are also countries in which certain fundamental rights guaranteed by the constitution can be asserted only by nationals. If a foreigner is entitled to national treatment he must in both cases have the same rights as nationals. But suppose he were entitled merely to fair and equitable or reasonable treatment. Would the result not be the same? Would it not be unfair, inequitable or unreasonable to deny to him the rights which a national enjoys? Nobody will object to most-favoured-nation and national treatment rights being expressly assured. But the cases in which these rights will have independent significance are probably rare.

5. In the normal course of events an investor expects to be able to repatriate his capital and his profits, if any. The treaties invariably guarantee this right.[31] They usually speak of 'the free transfer' of capital and profits. This probably means: free from restrictions such as exchange control restrictions, taxes on transfer or charges for the grant of permissions. No doubt it is intended to emphasize this freedom by the further provision that the rate of exchange applicable to the transfer shall be that 'prevailing at the time of remittance'. This means that the investor, as he should do, incurs the risk of the host country's currency depreciating between the date of investment and the date of repatriation. Yet there remains a point of considerable obscurity in that in many countries

[30] After more than ten years it appears even more remarkable than earlier that the facts summarized in the text were defended by eminent Spanish lawyers instructed by the Franco regime as lawful under Spanish and international law, that no independent tribunal has ever pronounced upon them and that post-Franco Spain, which purports to adhere to democracy, participates in the Council of Europe and its human rights institutions and intends to join the EEC, has done nothing to undo a grave injustice.

[31] Art. VII of the Agreement with the Philippines.

multiple rates of exchange are in force. The differences of commercial value are frequently considerable. The treaties do not provide for the use of the 'official' or any other rate of exchange. The point may lead to difficulties and disputes and it is therefore desirable to regulate it, if possible, in the specific agreements which the investor concludes with the host country. But where the investor introduces money at the official rate it would seem fair and equitable that he should be able to retransfer at the same rate, and here again the duty which has been described as overriding may play a role.

In many treaties the right to 'the free transfer' is expressed to be subject to the host country's power 'to impose equitably and in good faith such measures as may be necessary to safeguard the integrity and independence of its currency, its external financial position and balance of payments'. This is a provision in connection with which the obligation to act fairly, equitably and reasonably may become specially significant. It may lead to the right to free transfer being recognized notwithstanding the absence of bad faith. In other words, it is submitted that good faith is presumed here as elsewhere, and that bad faith need not be proved by the investor if he can establish a breach of the overriding objective duty of acting fairly, equitably and reasonably. If the authorities of the host country are found to be acting unfairly, inequitably or unreasonably they are in bad faith. The latter phrase at first sight carries a subjective connotation, and there may be occasions in the law when this is the correct interpretation. But on account of the primary duties imposed on the host country this, it is submitted, is not one of them.

6. The treaties usually contain a further provision guaranteeing the success of the investment: each party 'shall observe any obligation arising from a particular commitment it may have entered into with regard to a specific investment'.[32]

This is a provision of particular importance in that it protects the investor against any interference with his contractural rights, whether it results from a mere breach of contract or a legislative or administrative act, and independently of the question whether or no such interference amounts to expropriation. The variation of the terms of a contract or licence by legislative measures, the termination of the contract or the failure to perform any of its terms, for instance, by non-payment, the dissolution of the local company with which the investor may have contracted and the transfer of its assets (with or without the liabilities)—these and similar acts the treaties render wrongful.

The provision, it is submitted, does not amount to an unqualified guarantee, but only applies where a party fails to 'observe any obligation'.

[32] Art. III (3) of the Agreement with the Philippines.

Where it is not such failure, but an extraneous event, in particular *force majeure*, that is put forward, the provision does not apply.

Furthermore (and this is a very serious limitation) the provision only covers an obligation arising from a particular commitment either of the Contracting Parties may have entered into. If the investor contracts with a local company, the provision does not apply to its obligations. What is assumed is that the State has entered into a particular commitment which imposes obligations. Such obligations may arise from contract with the State or from the terms of the licence granted by it. It may be express or implied, it may be in writing or oral. But it must be clearly ascertainable as an obligation of the State itself arising from its own commitments. No difficulty occurs where the contract is made with the State itself—and the term may fairly be said to comprise its instrumentalities, even if they are separate legal entities, as well as companies of which it is the sole shareholder. But where the contract is made with a private person, then the provision only applies if and in so far as an obligation of the State arising from its own particular commitment (as opposed to existing general legislation) may be discerned. Thus if the law of the land provides that the State is liable for the torts of its servants this is not an 'obligation arising from a particular commitment' the State may have entered into and may be changed, though in certain circumstances this may become subject to the provisions about expropriation.

7. These last-mentioned provisions are in all treaties contained in what may be called a standard clause of a most comprehensive character.[33] Investments 'shall not be subject to expropriation or nationalization or any measure equivalent thereto, except for public use, in the public interest or in the interest of national defence and upon payment of just compensation'.

The first question is whether this provision invalidates expropriation altogether or permits it on the terms defined by the treaty or at least invalidates it in the event of the terms not being observed. It is submitted that the last-mentioned interpretation is the correct one. It accords with customary international law in general, for the taking of property for private use without the payment of compensation is illegal. Moreover, the breach of an express treaty obligation itself constitutes an illegal act, i.e. an act without legal validity.[34]

It is noteworthy that the conception of expropriation comprises 'nationalizations'. In the past it has often been suggested that far-reaching social changes such as nationalizations usually intend to achieve are on a different level and should not give rise to any right to compensation at all or should

[33] Art. V of the Agreement with the Philippines.

[34] This was submitted in this *Year Book*, 48 (1976-7), at p. 47.

lead to compensation on a lower scale defined as 'reasonable', 'sufficient' or in some similar fashion; the numerous treaties concluded after the Second World War with Eastern countries and providing for compensation at about 10 per cent have sometimes been put forward as models. The treaties now under discussion give the lie to any such theory: they require the payment of 'just compensation' for both expropriations and nationalizations and thus recognize a standard which is entirely in accordance with traditional thought. Moreover the rules applicable to expropriation and nationalization extend to 'any measure equivalent' thereto, i.e. any act depriving the investor of his property or proprietary rights and enriching the State, even if no property is transferred to it. Municipal law supplies innumerable examples of acts which may be said to be an expropriation or at least a measure equivalent to it, the latter expression being so comprehensive as to involve anything that prejudices the investor and benefits the State, whether directly or indirectly.[35]

In view of the difficulties which have arisen in the past, the treaties expressly define the 'just compensation' which they contemplate: it shall amount to the market value or, in its absence, the investor's actual loss, it shall be paid 'without undue delay', shall be effectively realizable and freely transferable in the manner indicated in paragraph 5 above and subject to prompt judicial or independent review. It is clear, therefore, that the mere insertion of recognition of a right to compensation in the expropriating legislation is insufficient to render the expropriation lawful. Such 'paper recognition' has occurred in practically all expropriations which have happened in the last thirty years or so but, as the French Cour de Cassation has so rightly said,[36]

> semblables dispositions de pur principe, qui, après dépossession immédiate, laissent le soin à l'Administration de fixer, dans un délai indéterminé et discrétionnairement, une indemnité en indiquant seulement le montant qu'elle ne pourra pas dépasser, sont contraires à l'ordre public français.

'Market value', it is true, will usually have to be assessed in terms of the host country's currency and this may impose upon the investor the risk of a depreciation of that country's currency. But this is not necessarily so. Thus dollars are the currency of the international oil industry and in

[35] The expression occurs several times in the Treaty of Rome creating the European Economic Community and has been given a very wide interpretation by the European Court of Justice. In certain circumstances the practice of that court may prove useful as a guide in construing the Agreements under discussion.

[36] 23 April 1969, *Clunet*, 96 (1969), p. 914.

certain cases the market value will therefore have to be assessed in dollars, though in fact the market is situate in the host country.[37]

Another point which has caused much difficulty in practice is also expressly clarified: if the investment takes the form of shares in a local corporation, partnership or other body the assets of which are expropriated, the host State shall ensure the payment of the compensation to the foreign investors 'to the extent of their interest in the assets expropriated'. It would seem that in such a case the foreign shareholder will be entitled to obtain judicial review and is not limited by any action taken (or not taken) by the corporation itself; this conclusion is based on the wording ('shall apply the provisions of paragraph 1 of this Article so as to ensure . . .') and from the purpose of the clause, which could easily be defeated if the foreign investor were not given independent rights.

8. A final provision of a substantive character is due to the fact that practically all investments made by Western countries in pursuance of these treaties carry the benefit of an insurance or guarantee agreement,[38] in England by the Export Credits Guarantee Department of the Department of Industry. If the investor suffers any insured loss the Department becomes entitled to his rights by way of subrogation. The treaties expressly, though perhaps unnecessarily, provide for the recognition of the assignment. They also state that the assignee State does not acquire any greater rights than were vested in the assignor; although, strictly, this may again not be a necessary provision it is a useful one, for it makes it clear that the usual rule[39] according to which inter-State monetary obligations are not subject to exchange control regulations does not apply to private law debts assigned to the State. The assignee State or its instrumentality may therefore become the owner of blocked accounts which the assignor could not utilize; the treaties helpfully provide that such accounts shall be 'freely available' to the assignee State 'for the purpose of meeting its official expenditure in the territory'.

III. REMEDIES

9. Among the remedies available to an investor there is in the first place any local remedy which the law of the host country may provide. In the event of expropriation, as has been pointed out in paragraph 7 above,

[37] *B.P. Exploration Co. (Libya) Ltd* v. *Hunt*, (1979) I W.L.R. 783, *per* Robert Goff J., affirmed by the Court of Appeal at (1981) 1 W.L.R. 233. In this case the courts were concerned with the assessment of a 'just sum' and on this aspect their observations may be helpful in construing and applying similar terms occurring in a treaty.

[38] See Meron, *Investment Insurance in International Law* (1976).

[39] Mann, *The Legal Aspect of Money* (4th edn., 1982), p. 559.

there exists the specifically guaranteed right to have both the legality of the expropriation and the valuation of the investments reviewed by a judicial or other independent body though this is without prejudice to the additional remedies presently to be mentioned.

10. Among these there is in the first place the investor's (though not the host country's) right[40] to have any dispute decided by a tribunal set up under the World Bank's Convention on the Settlement of Investment Disputes between States and Nationals of Other States of 18 March 1965.[41] This affords the best legal protection which, probably, in present circumstances is available, though the Convention of 1965 and, in particular, the panel of arbitrators set up by the World Bank cannot by any means be viewed with unqualified enthusiasm.

The right of access to the Convention and the tribunal contemplated by it is considerably strengthened by the express provision according to which a company incorporated in the host country may itself be a claimant if the foreign investor owns the majority of the shares in it; this probably includes an investor who owned the shares prior to expropriation.

On the other hand, the protection afforded to the investor is considerably prejudiced if he fails to obtain a direct undertaking to him to apply the Convention and submit to the jurisdiction of the tribunal. The Investment Protection Agreement is a treaty between the High Contracting Parties, from which the private investor is unlikely to be able to derive any benefit unless he ensures the inclusion of a corresponding clause in the document to which he is a party. In the absence of such a clause, he would depend upon the readiness of his government to apply under Article XI, for according to Articles 25 of the Convention on the Settlement of Investment Disputes it is a condition of the Centre's jurisdiction that 'the parties to the dispute consent in writing to submit to the Centre'.[42]

11. Independently of the remedies available to the investor, any 'dispute between the Contracting Parties as to the interpretation or application of the present Agreement' may be submitted to arbitration 'in accordance with the provisions of this Agreement and the applicable principles of international law'.[43]

This, it is submitted, is not a case of a State affording diplomatic protection to one of its nationals: any legitimate interest of the State in the dispute which concerns the interpretation and application of the Agreement is sufficient to give it *jus standi*. This may be important, for instance, if the disputes involve a company incorporated in the host country if all or most of the shares in its capital are owned by the

[40] Art. X of the Agreement with the Philippines.

[41] On which see, e.g., Schwarzenberger, op. cit. above (n. 21), p. 135.

[42] For other pitfalls see Lalive, this *Year Book* 51 (1980), p. 123.

[43] Art. XI.

protecting State's nationals. This particular result, however, is probably in line with the general rules relating to diplomatic protection; the point is one on which, it will be remembered, important dicta are to be found in the International Court of Justice's judgement in the *Barcelona Traction* case,[44] but which has never been finally decided and is not dealt with in the treaties under discussion. It is, however, possible that even in this procedural connection the overriding entitlement to fair and equitable treatment may have a significant function.

IV. APPRAISAL

12. The importance of the British treaties as well as the numerous foreign treaties for the promotion and protection of investments and, incidentally, the twenty-one Friendship, Navigation and Commerce Treaties concluded, principally, by the United States of America since the end of the Second World War lies in the contribution they make to the development of customary international law, in their being a source of law. In general, as the decision of the International Court of Justice in the *North Sea Continental Shelf* cases has proved,[45] it is very difficult to deduce a rule of public international law from a single treaty. But this decision should not be overrated. It dealt with a very specific case in which specific arguments militated against finding the existence of a customary rule. In the case of the treaties, the subject-matter of this discussion, many other elements combine to facilitate such a finding. There is, in the first place, the very large number of treaties the scope of which is increased by the operation of the most-favoured-nation clause. There is, secondly, the fact that many States which have purported to reject the traditional conceptions and standards included in these treaties have accepted them, when (if the colloquial phrase be permitted) it came to the crunch. There is, thirdly, the most important fact that these treaties establish and accept and thus enlarge the force of traditional conceptions. Is it possible for a State to reject the rule according to which alien property may be expropriated only on certain terms long believed to be required by customary international law, yet to accept it for the purpose of these treaties? The paramount duty of States imposed by international law is to observe and act in accordance with the requirements of good faith. From this point of view it follows that, where these treaties express a duty which customary international law imposes or is widely believed to impose, they give very strong support to the existence of such a duty and preclude the Contracting States from denying its existence.

[44] See p. 238 n. 29 above.

[45] *I.C.J. Reports*, 1969, p. 4.

These remarks apply, in particular, to the overriding effect of the standard of fair and equitable treatment, to the duty not to expropriate except on certain terms and to the duty to 'observe any obligation arising from a particular commitment it may have entered into with regard to a specific investment'. The cold print of these treaties is a more reliable source of law than rhetorics in the United Nations.

ANNEXE

AGREEMENT BETWEEN THE GOVERNMENT OF THE UNITED KINGDOM OF GREAT BRITAIN AND NORTHERN IRELAND AND THE REPUBLIC OF THE PHILIPPINES FOR THE PROMOTION AND PROTECTION OF INVESTMENTS

The Government of the United Kingdom of Great Britain and Northern Ireland and the Government of the Republic of the Philippines, hereinafter referred to as the Contracting Parties;

Taking note of their existing friendly relations;

Desiring to create favourable conditions for greater investment by nationals and companies of one Contracting Party in the territory of the other Contracting Party, and to increase prosperity in their respective territories;

Recognising that agreement on the promotion and protection of such investment will contribute to the furtherance of such purposes;

Have agreed as follows:

Article I

For the purposes of this Agreement

1. (*a*) The term 'Republic of the Philippines' shall refer to the entity as constituted at present, whose territory is that defined in this Article.
   (*b*) The term 'United Kingdom of Great Britain and Northern Ireland' shall refer to the entity as constituted at present, whose territory is that defined in this Article.
2. The term 'territory' means:
   (*a*) In respect of the Republic of the Philippines, the territory defined in Article 1 of its Constitution.
   (*b*) In respect of the United Kingdom of Great Britain and Northern Ireland, the territory of Great Britain and Northern Ireland and those territories for whose international relations the Government of the United Kingdom are responsible and with respect to which the Contracting Parties agree to extend the provisions of this Agreement by an exchange of notes.
3. The term 'nationals' shall mean:
   (*a*) In respect of the Republic of the Philippines, its citizens within the meaning of Article III of its Constitution.
   (*b*) In respect of the United Kingdom of Great Britain and Northern Ireland, any citizen of the United Kingdom and Colonies, and any British subject

not possessing that citizenship or the citizenship of any other Commonwealth country or territory, provided that in every case he has the right of abode in the United Kingdom.

4. The term 'company' of a Contracting Party shall mean a corporation, partnership or other association, incorporated or constituted and actually doing business under the laws in force in any part of the territory of that Contracting Party wherein a place of effective management is situated.

Provided that any particular company may be excluded from the foregoing definition by mutual agreement between the Contracting Parties on the grounds of the need to maintain public order, to protect essential security interests or to fulfil commitments relating to international peace and security.

5. The term 'investments' shall mean every kind of asset and in particular, though not exclusively, includes:
   (i) movable and immovable property and any other property rights such as mortgages, liens and pledges;
   (ii) shares, stocks and debentures of companies or interests in the property of such companies;
   (iii) claims to money or to any performance under contract having a financial value;
   (iv) intellectual property rights and goodwill;
   (v) business concessions conferred by law or under contract.

6. The term 'earnings' shall mean amounts yielded by an investment, particularly, though not exclusively, profits, interest, capital gains, dividends, royalties or fees.

Article II

1. This Agreement shall apply only to investments brought into, derived from or directly connected with investments brought into the territory of one Contracting Party by nationals or companies of the other Contract Party which are qualified for registration and are duly registered by the appropriate government agency of the receiving Contracting Party, if so required by its laws.

2. This Agreement shall not affect the rights and obligations of the Contracting Parties with respect to investments which under the provisions of paragraph 1 are not within the scope of the Agreement.

Article III

1. Each Contracting Party shall encourage and create favourable conditions for investments, consistent with its national objectives, by companies or nationals of the other Contracting Party, subject to the laws and regulations of the Party in whose territory the investment is made, including rules on registration and valuation of such investments, if any.

2. Investments of nationals or companies of either Contracting Party shall at all times be accorded fair and equitable treatment and shall enjoy full protection and security in the territory of the other Contracting Party.

3. Each Contracting Party shall observe any obligation arising from a particular commitment it may have entered into with regard to a specific investment of nationals or companies of the other Contracting Party.

Article IV

1. Each Contracting Party shall extend to investments in its territory of companies or nationals of the other Contracting Party treatment no less favourable than that granted to nationals and companies of any third state.

2. Each Contracting Party shall not subject nationals or companies of the other Contracting Party in its territory, as regards their management, use, enjoyment, or disposal of their investments, to unreasonable measures or treatment less favourable than that which it accords to nationals or companies of any third state.

3. The provisions of this Agreement relative to the grant of treatment not less favourable than that accorded to the nationals or companies of any third state shall not be construed as to oblige one Contracting Party to extend to the nationals or companies of the other the benefit of any treatment, preference or privilege resulting from:

(*a*) any existing or future customs union, common market, free trade area, or regional economic organisation of which either Contracting Party is or may become a member, or

(*b*) any international agreement or arrangement relating wholly or mainly to taxation.

Article V

1. Investments of nationals or companies of either Contracting Party shall not be subject to expropriation or nationalisation or any measure equivalent thereto (in this article referred to as 'expropriation'), except for public use, in the public interest, or in the interest of national defence and upon payment of just compensation. Such compensation shall amount to the market value of the investments expropriated, or, in the absence of a determinable market value, the actual loss sustained, on or immediately before the date of expropriation. The compensation shall be made without undue delay, shall be effectively realisable and, subject to the provisions of paragraph 3 of Article VII, shall be freely transferable. The national or company affected shall have a right, under the law of the Contracting Party making the expropriation, to prompt review by a judicial body, or, if such exists, by other independent authority of that Party of his or its case and of the valuation of his or its investment in accordance with the principles set out in this paragraph.

2. Where a Contracting Party expropriates the assets of a company which is incorporated or constituted under the law in force in any part of its territory, and in which nationals or companies of the other Contracting Party own shares, it shall apply the provisions of paragraph 1 of this Article so as to ensure the compensation provided for in that paragraph to such nationals or companies to the extent of their interest in the assets expropriated.

Article VI

If a Contracting Party makes restitution, indemnification, compensation or other settlement for losses suffered owing to war or other armed conflicts, revolution, a state of national emergency, revolt, insurrection or riot in the territory of such

Contracting Party, it shall accord to the nationals or companies of the other Contracting Party whose investments in the territory of the Contracting Party have suffered such losses, treatment no less favourable than that which the Contracting Party shall accord to companies or to nationals of any third state.

Article VII

1. Each Contracting Party shall in respect of investments permit nationals or companies of the other Contracting Party the free transfer of their capital and of the earnings from it, subject to the right of the former Contracting Party to impose equitably and in good faith such measures as may be necessary to safeguard the integrity and independence of its currency, its external financial position and balance of payments, consistent with its rights and obligations as a member of the International Monetary Fund.

2. The exchange rate applicable to such transfer shall be the rate of exchange prevailing at the time of remittance.

3. In cases where large amounts of compensation have been paid in pursuance of Article V the Contracting Party concerned may require the transfer thereof to be effected in reasonable instalments.

Article VIII

1. If either Contracting Party makes payment under an insurance or guarantee agreement with its own nationals or companies in respect of an investment or any part thereof in the territory of the other Contracting Party, the latter Contracting Party shall recognise the assignment of any right or claim arising from the indemnity paid, by the party indemnified to the former Contracting Party, and that the former Contracting Party is entitled by virtue of subrogation to exercise the rights and assert the claims of such nationals or companies. This does not necessarily imply, however, a recognition on the part of the latter Contracting Party of the merits of any case or the amount of any claim arising therefrom.

2. If the former Contracting Party acquires amounts in the lawful currency of the other Contracting Party or credits thereof by assignment under the terms of an indemnity, the former Contracting Party shall be accorded in respect thereof treatment not less favourable than that accorded to the funds of a private investor deriving from activities and transactions similar to those in which the party indemnified was engaged but subject to those limitations or conditions, if any, that are applicable to the party indemnified. Such amounts and credits shall be freely available to the former Contracting Party concerned for the purpose of meeting its official expenditure in the territory of the other Contracting Party.

Article IX

The Contracting Parties agree to consult each other at the request of either Party on any matter relating to investments between the two countries, or otherwise affecting the implementation of this Agreement.

Article X

1. The Contracting Party in the territory of which a national or company of the other Contracting Party makes or intends to make an investment shall assent to

any request on the part of such national or company to submit, for conciliation or arbitration, to the Centre established by the Convention on the Settlement of Investment Disputes between States and Nationals of Other States opened for signature at Washington on 18 March 1965 any dispute that may arise in connection with the investment.

2. A company which is incorporated or constituted under the law in force in the territory of one Contracting Party and in which before such a dispute arises the majority of shares are owned by nationals or companies of the other Contracting Party shall in accordance with Article 25(2) (*b*) of the Convention be treated for the purposes of the Convention as a company of the other Contracting Party.

Article XI

1. Any dispute between the Contracting Parties as to the interpretation or application of the present Agreement, not satisfactorily resolved through diplomatic channels or other amicable means, shall be submitted, at the request of either Party to a panel of arbitrators for decision in accordance with the provisions of this Agreement and the applicable principles in international law.

2. The panel shall be composed of three members, one selected by each Party within one month of receipt of the request for arbitration, and the third to be chosen by the members thus selected by the Parties within two months from the designation of the second member.

3. If within the periods specified in paragraph 2 of this Article the necessary appointments have not been made, either Contracting Party may, in the absence of any other agreement, invite the Secretary-General of the United Nations to make any necessary appointments. If the Secretary-General is a national of either Contracting Party or if he is otherwise prevented from discharging the said function, the President of the International Court of Justice shall be invited to make the necessary appointments. If the President is a national of either Contracting Party or if he too is prevented from discharging the said function, the Vice-President or the member of the International Court of Justice next in seniority who is not a national of either Contracting Party shall be invited to make the necessary appointments.

4. The panel of arbitrators shall reach its decision by a majority of votes. Such decision shall be binding on both Contracting Parties. The panel shall determine its own procedure.

5. Each Contracting Party shall bear the cost of its own member of the panel and of its representation in the arbitral proceedings; the cost of the Chairman and the remaining costs shall be borne in equal parts by the Contracting Parties.

Article XII

1. This Agreement shall enter into force on the 30th day following its signature.

2. This Agreement shall remain in force for a period of ten years from its entry into force and shall thereafter continue in force unless terminated by either Contracting Party by not less than six months' written notice through diplomatic channels; provided that in respect of investments made whilst the Agreement is in force, its provisions shall continue in effect with respect to such investments for a

period of ten years after the date of termination and without prejudice to the application thereafter of the rules of general international law.

In witness whereof the undersigned, duly authorised thereto by their respective Governments, have signed this Agreement.

Done at London this 3rd day of December 1980 in two original copies, each in the English and Philippino languages, each text being equally authentic.

For the Government of the United Kingdom of Great Britain and Northern Ireland:

P. A. R. BLAKER

For the Government of the Republic of the Philippines:

CESAR VIRATA

8

The *Aminoil* Arbitration

SHORTLY before his death the late Sir Gerald Fitzmaurice wrote to the present writer that he had just finished an arbitration which led to a 'remarkable' award, and that he hoped at an early date to have a discussion about it. Unfortunately, his untimely death rendered such a discussion impossible. In the absence of the advice or at least the comments of a dear and greatly respected friend the present writer must try to unravel the intricacies of this clearly 'remarkable', but also difficult and far from compellingly reasoned award in the case of the *State of Kuwait v. The American Independent Oil Company* (Aminoil).[1] It was rendered by Professor Paul Reuter as President, Professor Hamed Sultan appointed by Kuwait and Sir Gerald appointed by Aminoil. It consists of 70 paragraphs summarizing the facts and 179 paragraphs of reasons together with what Sir Gerald described as a separate opinion of 30 paragraphs, which as to the grounds of decision, though not as to the result, is in effect a dissenting opinion of considerable persuasive force; in memory of a great lawyer characterized by his intellectual integrity as well as his judicial qualities it is permissible to quote in full the last paragraph of his opinion which is likely also to be the last words ever written by him:

> In consequence, and while I naturally hesitate to differ from a view so skilfully constructed and persuasive as that contained in the Award, good faith and my professional conscience compel me to conclude that although the nationalisation of Aminoil's undertaking may otherwise have been perfectly lawful, considered simply in its aspect of an act of the State, it was nevertheless irreconcilable with the stabilisation clauses of a Concession that was still in force at the moment of the take-over.

That in these circumstances the arbitrators agreed on the result is indeed remarkable when the figures are considered: Kuwait claimed some \$225m., Aminoil claimed \$2.5 billion, alternatively \$185m., plus in either case some \$450m. Both parties claimed interest. The arbitrators awarded to the Government \$123m., to Aminoil \$206m., i.e. a net sum of \$83m.

[1] *International Legal Materials*, 21 (1982), p. 976.

British Year Book of International Law (Oxford, 1983), 213

which with interest and an inflation factor came to a total sum of about $179m.

The principal reason why the award merits analysis lies in these figures, for it is one of the relatively few modern documents which deals with the liability for and the quantum of compensation payable in the event of expropriation. In view of the fact that there exist innumerable treaties and contracts which provide for or may lead to a liability to pay compensation for expropriation, the reasoning adopted by a tribunal such as the arbitrators in the *Aminoil* case is entitled to close attention, though it may be open to doubt whether it is also entitled to be treated as a precedent or is rather a very special case. The general impression conveyed by the award is that, as so often in arbitrations, strictly legal considerations may have been allowed to be pushed aside for the sake of achieving unanimity among the arbitrators and giving something to both parties.

I. THE FACTS

On 28 June 1948 the Ruler of Kuwait granted to Aminoil for a period of sixty years a concession for the extraction of petroleum and natural gas. The Ruler was to be paid certain sums of US dollars (with the benefit of a gold clause). At the end of the concession in 2008 all Aminoil's property in Kuwait was to vest in the Ruler. Article 17 was a 'stabilization clause':

> The Shaikh shall not by general or special legislation or by administrative measures or by any other act whatever annul this Agreement except as provided in Article II. No alteration shall be made in the terms of this Agreement by either the Shaikh or the Company except in the event of the Shaikh and the Company jointly agreeing that it is desirable in the interest of both parties to make certain alterations, deletions or additions to this Agreement.

Article 18 was an arbitration clause. After Kuwait had become fully independent a supplemental agreement of 1961 affirmed the concession of 1948 subject to certain amendments; these included an Article 9 according to which

> If, as a result of changes in the terms of concessions now in existence or as a result of the terms of concessions granted hereafter, an increase in benefits to Governments in the Middle East should come generally to be received by them, the Company shall consult with the Ruler whether in the light of all relevant circumstances, including the conditions in which operations are carried out, and taking into account all payments made, any alterations in the terms of the agreements between the Ruler and the Company would be equitable to the parties.

A further draft agreement was prepared in 1973. It abolished the gold clause, included a new arbitration clause, provided for the enactment of a tax law, suggested that in future 'the Company should not be denied a reasonable opportunity of earning a reasonable rate of return (having regard to the risks involved) on the total capital employed in its business attributable to Kuwait', and included the following provision about the applicable law:[2]

> The parties base their relations with regard to the agreements between them on the principle of goodwill and good faith. Taking account of the different nationalities of the parties, the agreements between them shall be given effect, and must be interpreted and applied, in conformity with principles common to the laws of Kuwait and of the State of New York, U.S.A., and in the absence of such common principles, then in conformity with the principles of law normally recognized by civilized states in general, including those which have been applied by international tribunals.

The Company, as the arbitrators held, accepted this draft agreement in December 1973. During the following years many further changes took place either as a result of negotiation or by the Government's unilateral action. Still further changes were under discussion, when on 19 September 1977 Kuwait issued decree No. 124 whereby the concession of 1948 was terminated, all the Company's property in Kuwait was to 'revert' to the State and a compensation committee was to be established to assess the compensation due to the Company and its outstanding obligations to the State.

In light of this only too familiar action by Kuwait the Company started arbitration proceedings in London as envisaged by the arbitration clauses in the contracts between the parties. But these proceedings were discontinued after the parties had concluded in July 1979 a special arbitration agreement which provided for arbitration in Paris; the reasons for this change do not appear from the award.

II. THE LAW OF THE ARBITRATION

The special agreement which the parties concluded in 1979 provided for 'transnational arbitration' and thus introduced into the case a most unfortunate, confusing and misleading conception. Nobody has as yet been able to explain what 'transnational' means, with the result that the term is used when parties or their advisors do not know or do not wish or

[2] One learns with some surprise from para. 6 of the award that the parties made no reference to this clause. On this point see below under the heading 'The Proper Law'.

care to know what they want; one can only agree with Sir John Donaldson M.R. who recently said that he found 'the concept of a supernational or transnational body of law difficult to accept. It seems to me that all private law has a nationality, although I fully accept that laws of different nationalities may be identical, whether by design, by common social pressures leading to common solutions or by common origin.'[3] In the present case, however, the term 'transnational' was continuously being used, although its legal connotation remained unexplained.

The arbitration agreement includes many provisions of a very special character. That the President was to be appointed by the President of the International Court of Justice is by no means unusual and is in law without any significance. On the other hand, the agreement also provided that unless otherwise agreed by the parties and subject to any mandatory provisions of the law of the place in which the arbitration is held, i.e. France, 'the Tribunal shall prescribe the procedure applicable to the arbitration on the basis of natural justice and of such principles of transnational arbitration procedure as it may be applicable'. This obsession with 'transnational' principles enabled the Tribunal to hold that in principle 'the Parties have chosen the French legal system' in regard to any mandatory provisions of the procedural law—an obvious conclusion, for in the absence of a truly international arbitration (which would presuppose the consent of France) it is impossible to imagine an arbitration held in Paris which would proceed according to non-French procedural law except to the extent permitted by French law. The arbitrators in fact settled appropriate Rules of Procedure which contain nothing that a French court could object to. Nevertheless the arbitrators felt unable to part from this aspect of the case without again emphasizing that 'having regard to the way in which the Tribunal has been constituted its international or rather transnational character is apparent' (paragraph 5). The point of this remark which seems to state the obvious is not readily discernible.

III. THE PROPER LAW

If the law governing the relations between the parties had exclusively been that defined by the above Article in the 1973 agreement its identity ought not to have caused much difficulty. If one analyses this verbose and imprecise Article it is plain that the first sentence can be ignored and that the first and the second part of the second sentence is comprised in the third part, for the instruction to give effect to the agreement between the

[3] *Amin Rasheed Shipping Corporation* v. *Kuwait Insurance Co.*, (1983) I W.L.R. 229, at p. 237.

parties and to apply principles common to Kuwait and New York must mean that both are included in the 'principles of law normally recognized by civilized states in general'. In other words, there cannot be principles common to Kuwait and New York which do not form part of generally recognized principles of law. If one then asks which is the *legal system* to which such verbiage refers, it can only be public international law of which the generally recognized principles of law are a constituent part. That contracts between a State and a private person can be submitted to public international law and that a reference to the generally recognized principles is tantamount to a reference to public international law was by 1973 well known[4] to both theory and practice. This is what, on a true construction of the clause, the parties must have meant. The arbitrators seem to agree, for they state in terms (paragraph 7): 'Clearly, it must have been the general principles of law that were chiefly present to the minds of the Government of Kuwait and its associates.' It must only be added that those general principles are not, but are a source of, a legal system.

Curiously enough, hoewever, one learns from the award (paragraph 6) that 'the Parties did not, in the course of the present arbitration proceedings, make any reference to' the text of 1973. The reason no doubt was that the arbitration agreement of 1979 instructed the arbitrators to 'decide according to law' and defined that law as follows (Article III):

> The law governing the substantive issues between the Parties shall be determined by the Tribunal, having regard to the quality of the Parties, the transnational character of their relations and the principles of law and practice prevailing in the modern world.

The meaning of this clause, as the arbitrators seem to have recognized (in paragraph 8), is ambiguous. Does it mean that the Tribunal was to determine the proper law? Or does it mean that the Tribunal was to interpret the proper law as fixed by the parties by taking certain matters, including (once again) 'the transnational character of their relations', into account? The Tribunal did not in clear terms decide this conflict or express its views on the proper law to be applied by it; it used some elegant phrases to gloss over the issue (paragraphs 6 to 10), so that it is impossible

[4] The power to 'internationalize' State contracts was first suggested in the *British Year Book of International Law*, 21 (1944), p. 11 at p. 19, and further developed in the *British Year Book of International Law*, 35 (1959), p. 34, where at p. 51 it was also suggested that a reference to the application of general principles implies a reference to public international law as the proper law. Since then the literature on the subject has grown enormously. The latest publication (including a bibliography) is by Jutta Stoll, *Vereinbarungen zwischen Staat und ausländischem Investor* (1982). The papers of 1944 and 1959 are reprinted in *Studies of International Law (1973)*, pp. 179 and 211 respectively.

to say with precision what rules it applied. There is only one fact that stands out: the Tribunal does not anywhere refer to academic material, but such decisions as are cited are all decisions of international tribunals, particularly the International Court of Justice, and there are also references to Article 38 of the Statute of the International Court (paragraph 6) and to the Vienna Convention on the Law of Treaties (paragraph 32). Does this mean that the Tribunal in fact applied public international law as, it is submitted, the agreement of 1973 required it to do?

IV. THE ISSUES

The issues in the arbitration were defined by Article III of the arbitration agreement. The parties recognized 'that the restoration of the Parties to their respective positions prior to 20 September 1977 and/or the resumption of operations under the 28 June 1948 Agreement (as amended) would be impracticable in any event, and the Company will therefore seek monetary damages instead'. The Tribunal was thus given the task of deciding 'the amount of compensation, if any, payable by the Government to the Company in respect of the assets acquired by the Government under Article 2 of the Decree Law No. 124'; the amount of damages, if any, in respect of the termination of the 1948 agreement by Decree No. 124; the amount payable by or to the government in respect of royalties, taxes or other obligations; and interest.

It appears, therefore, that the principle of liability was in no way admitted, and the Tribunal was under a duty in the first place to establish whether and on what basis either party was liable to make any payment.

On the first two issues Sir Gerald Fitzmaurice's argument is simple. In his view the stabilization clauses, one of which is quoted above, rendered the nationalization or expropriation wrongful. The reasons given in paragraphs 19-30 of his opinion are, it is submitted, convincing and, indeed, irresistible—a characterization which, unfortunately, does not fit the majority's reasoning. Its conclusion was (paragraph 102) that 'the take-over of Aminoil's enterprise was not in 1977 inconsistent with the contract of concession, provided always that the nationalisation did not possess any confiscatory character'. The inconsistency was lacking on account of the fact that 'no doubt contractual limitations on the State's right to nationalise are juridically possible, but what that would involve would be a particularly serious undertaking which would have to be *expressly* stipulated for . . . In the present case, however, the existence of such a stipulation would have to be presumed as being covered by the general language of the stabilisation clauses.' At the same time 'these provisions are far from having lost all their value and efficacity on that account, since, by *impliedly* requiring that nationalization shall not have any confiscatory character,they reinforce the necessity for a proper indemnification as a condition of it' (paragraphs 95 and 96). The prohibition of 1948 and 1961 'not by general or special legislation or administrative measures or by any other act whatever' to annul the concession has little or no meaning except that it implies something nowhere mentioned, viz. the duty to pay proper compensation for that which most readers would hold to be specifically prohibited.

We have long known, of course, that there is nothing for which lawyers cannot find words, but there can be few instances of a more blatant distortion of plain language. One can understand, though one is bound to reject, the argument that the stabilization clauses do not specifically prohibit nationalization, expropriation or confiscation. Yet in an international document it would have been difficult to employ more suitable words to comprise such 'acts' than those in fact used; if, as the Tribunal held, notwithstanding their terms, the stabilization clauses rendered a nationalization lawful, one cannot easily answer the question what affirmative meaning and effect may be attributed to these clauses. But there are no rules of interpretation in any system of law, certainly not in international law (cf. Article 31 of the Vienna Convention) which would permit or require the implication of a duty to pay appropriate compensation into the terms of the stabilization clauses.

There are very many points which arise from the majority's discussion of the question of liability. In truth, however, they relate to quantum, though in view of the odd scheme adopted by the majority for the structure of its award, they are presented as problems of liability. One[5] of them concerns the meaning and effect of Article 9 of the 1961 agreement, which calls for a few words of comment.

Article 9 imposes a duty to consult in the event of a change of certain circumstances. The Tribunal treats this as a duty to negotiate (paragraphs 18 and 20). The latter, as we know, has in the course of the last fifteen years or so in public international law become a legally enforceable or at any rate material and effective duty. That similar principles apply to a duty to consult has, it is believed, nowhere been laid down. Yet we now learn that the duty to consult contemplates 'agreement by mutual consent' (paragraph 24). The interesting and important question which frequently arises in arbitration proceedings concerned with long-term contracts clearly embedded in a municipal system of law is whether an arbitrator has the power to impose the agreement which the parties were unable to

[5] Another interesting but elementary discussion rejects Aminoil's argument that its consent to the 1973 agreement was vitiated by duress (paras. 40 to 46). The argument was indeed untenable and does not require discussion in the present context.

reach. (An arbitration tribunal consisting of Mr Mark Littman QC as Chairman, the Hon Mr Ogilvie Thompson, the former Chief Justice of South Africa, and the present writer, which a few years ago sat in Paris and had to apply South African and/or English law, answered the question in the negative, the present writer dissenting.)[6] The arbitrators in *Aminoil* had 'no doubt that, speaking generally, a tribunal cannot substitute itself for the parties in order to make good a missing segment of their contractural relations—or to modify a contract—unless that right is conferred upon it by law or by the express consent of the Parties' (paragraph 74). Since this is a point of great and general practical importance, the *ratio decidendi* should be quoted in full:

> It is not open to doubt that an arbitral tribunal—constituted on the basis of a 'compromissory' clause contained in relevant agreements between the parties to the case, and seized in the matter unilaterally by one of the parties only—could not, by way of modifying or completing a contract, prescribe how a provision such as the Abu Dhabi formula must be applied. For that, the consent of both parties would be necessary.

The argument on the one hand is that, of course, no tribunal can rewrite a contract: this would far exceed the judicial function. On the other hand, where it is merely a question of, say, adjusting a price according to objective standards of reasonableness, there is, it is submitted, no reason why judges or arbitrators should not be empowered or able to do so. A limited function in this sense is inherent in the arbitration clause: it authorizes arbitrators to decide disputes which come within the scope of the judicial function. The point thus becomes a matter of degree. It ought not to be disposed of by urging some generalities about rewriting contracts. The real question is whether in a given case the specific task which the

[6] The so-called fairness clause read as follows: 'If for any reason or reasons beyond the control of either . . . or . . . (be it by reason of legislation or other unforeseeable events and circumstances including but not limited to a change in parity of currencies other than the U.S. Dollar) the basic premises of this contract or the economic circumstances change in such a way that the execution of this contract or any particular term or terms thereof would cause undue hardship to one of the partners or unduly favour one party to the detriment of the other, the parties shall consult together with the aim of finding a mutually acceptable solution for the removal of such hardship.' The award is dated 17 May 1976 and bears the reference no. 2756 of the International Chamber of Commerce. Both parties were agreed that South African courts would have regard to English law. Hence English law was freely referred to, in particular *Sykes* v. *Fine Fare Ltd.*, (1967) 1 Ll.L.R. 53. It is not to be doubted that normally a judge or arbitrator cannot make or modify a contract for the parties. The question in such cases is whether on its true construction the clause, *combined with the arbitration clause*, exceptionally confers such powers. This can only be so where an objective standard such as reasonableness is set and it is a specific and narrow point such as a price which on the basis of evidence can be judicially decided. See the text.

arbitrators are required to perform falls within the judicial function which they are authorized to exercise.

It may be that, notwithstanding its initial doubts about its own jurisdiction, the *Aminoil* Tribunal is not wholly opposed to the approach which has just been outlined, for the Tribunal concluded (paragraph 79) that within the framework of a general settlement it had jurisdiction to determine the amount due, including some amount owing by Aminoil to the Government under Article 9 and the Abu Dhabi[7] formula. The reason given for this conclusion was (paragraph 75) that the Tribunal was 'not expected to devise new provisions that will govern the contractual relations of the Parties for the future, but to liquidate the various consequences of their past conduct and of the contractual clauses that once bound them but are now at an end'. One need only add that if it is within the jurisdiction of arbitrators to ascertain amounts due in the past, there is no reason why their judicial function should preclude them from assessing the amounts payable in future.

V. COMPENSATION

The crucial section of the award dealing with the quantum of compensation payable by Kuwait for taking a business with a life limited to thirty years and producing so volatile a commodity as oil (paragraphs 137 to 178) makes it clear that the Tribunal was supplied with much evidence by accountants and other experts on the various methods of valuation and calculation, on the facts to be taken into account, and on a variety of figures relating to numerous aspects. The award deals with the whole of this material in a somewhat cursory fashion, so that its significance as a precedent for the process of actual valuation is limited. On the other hand, much was said on the principles which in law should guide that process.

The Tribunal took as its starting-point 'the most general formulation of the rules applicable for a lawful nationalisation', viz. the United Nations General Assembly Resolution 1803 (XVII) of 1962, according to which in the event of nationalization 'the owner shall be paid appropriate compensation, in accordance with the rules in force in the State taking such measures in the exercise of its sovereignty and in accordance with international law'[8] (paragraph 143). This means 'that in the case of the

[7] This formula, developed by the Gulf States in the heyday of their economic power in November 1974, meant the imposition of a royalty rate of 20 per cent of posted prices and a tax rate of 85 per cent in respect of oil income. See para. 53 of the award.

[8] The reference to the rules applicable in the expropriating State is of course the most unfortunate feature of this Resolution. In the present case the point was not material because the Tribunal held that the law of Kuwait had adopted and included the rules of international law: para. 6.

present dispute there is no room for rules of compensation that would make nonsense of foreign investment' (paragraph 146). Accordingly compensation 'must be calculated on a basis such as to warrant the upkeep of a flow of investment in the future' (paragraph 147). The legitimate expectations of the parties refer to the contractural equilibrium and 'cannot be neglected,—neither when it is a question of proceeding to necessary adaptations during the course of the contract nor when it is a question of awarding compensation' (paragraphs 148 to 149). There are several methods of valuation, but the conception which 'must guide the Tribunal' is that adopted by the parties 'in the course of their relations and negotiations,—namely that of the reasonable rate of return' (paragraph 154). Kuwait's contention based on 'precedents resulting from a series of transnational negotiations and agreements about compensation' in the oil industry and allowing 'only the net book value of the redeemable assets' could not be accepted (paragraphs 155 and 156). In particular as a matter of law there was no *opinio juris* such as required by the *North Sea Continental Shelf* cases[9] in support of such a contention; where States or companies had accepted net book value, 'economic pressures . . . lay at the root of' such precedents that 'had nothing to do with law, and do not enable them to be regarded as components of the formation of a general legal rule' (paragraph 157). On the other hand, while 'attitudes taken up by a party over the long course of a negotiation that eventually breaks down cannot be made the basis of an arbitral or judicial decision', the fact is 'that over the years Aminoil had come to accept the principle of a moderate estimate of profits and that it was this that constituted its legitimate expectation' (paragraph 161).

In assessing compensation inflation must be taken into account. Hence 'in calculating the value of depreciating assets it would be unfair to settle it on the basis of a superannuated cost consisting of the original purchase price, when that price has no relation to the actual present cost' (paragraph 166). Indeed 'if it were thought necessary to arrive at the total figure of the capital invested by Aminoil in its undertaking it would be appropriate to do so without holding the dollars of 1977[10] to be equivalent to those of 1948' (paragraph 169).

When, finally, the Tribunal comes to deal with actual figures, it states in a single, almost hidden, sentence in paragraph 176 that 'a balanced

[9] I.C.J. *Reports*, 1969, p. 45, para. 77.

[10] The reference to 1977, the year of the taking, is surprising. Precedent would appear to point in the direction of taking the date of assessment as a basis: see Mann, *The Legal Aspect of Money* (4th edn., 1982), pp. 131–3. The Tribunal could have avoided much of the discussion about the element of inflation if it had based itself on the values in 1982. It is submitted that this should have been done, particularly if the taking had been held to be wrongful so as to entitle Aminoil to damages. In accordance with principle future inflation had to be disregarded.

appraisal of the circumstances leads the Tribunal to fix $10 million as a reasonable rate of return for Aminoil'.[11] How this figure was arrived at is in no way explained except that the Tribunal refers to the fact 'that the important works which were to have been carried out by the Company in the near future, and financed, at least partly out of the profit of the undertaking, ceased to be a charge on it'. Whether the $10m. is high or low and how it is related to relevant circumstances such as value of assets, price of oil, costs of production and so forth or what proportion of a total sum it represents, all this is not vouchsafed. The lack of guidance is a matter for regret. The Tribunal then proceeds to assess the values both of the various components of the undertaking separately considered and of the undertaking itself. As regards the different concrete components a joint report of accountants 'furnishes acceptable indications concerning the assets other than fixed assets'. However, no figure is mentioned. As regards the fixed assets 'it is a depreciated replacement value that seems appropriate'. Again no figure is mentioned. Instead the Tribunal states 'the conclusion that, at the date of 19 September 1977 a sum estimated at $206,041,000 represented the reasonably appraised value of what constituted the object of the takeover' (paragraph 178). Deducting liabilites and allowing for inflation the Tribunal arrived at the final figures mentioned above.

In other words, unless the writer is guilty of a grave misunderstanding, the Tribunal allowed nothing for loss of profit during the remaining thirty years of the concession. If this conclusion is correct it would have been welcome to have it expressed and to read about such support as it has in international (or if the Tribunal should prefer it: transnational) practice, in academic literature and in comparative material, i.e. in the sources which Article 38 of the Statute of the International Court of Justice enumerates.

VI. CONCLUSION

A French author who extended an enthusiastic welcome to the decision describes it as its great merit that 'les éléments les plus juridiques *du nouvel ordre international* ont reçu en quelque sorte leur reconnaissance'.[12] He mentions in the first place 'l'interprétation hardie des clauses de stabilisation qui rappelle . . . que l'on ne peut assimiler complètement un Etat contractant à un contractant privé'. If, as seems likely, the Tribunal applied public international law, then on the very point mentioned by

[11] This was an annual figure which was increased by an inflation factor of 10 per cent.
[12] Philippe Kahn, *Clunet*, 1982, p. 844 at p. 868. Italics supplied.

Professor Kahn it left a gap by its failure to refer to the principle underlying Article 26 of the Vienna Convention on the Law of Treaties[13] according to which treaties and, indeed, all agreements governed by international law are binding upon the parties and must be performed by them in good faith. From this point of view the stabilization clauses, as Sir Gerald Fitzmaurice emphasized, cannot be ignored or distorted in the manner adopted by the majority and it was not possible to speak of a lawful nationalization. Rather the taking became illegal. This is the central problem raised by the award, but it is by no means the only one. Looking at the award[14] as a whole one should hesitate long before attributing persuasive force to it. In fact this award once again raises well-known doubts about the wisdom and, sometimes, the legality of publishing awards which are rendered in arbitrations between parties other than States and, therefore, are not strictly international in character.

[13] Cmnd. 7964.

[14] It includes many points which were not discussed in the present Note. They appeared to be of minor importance, but it could be well understood if on this aspect opinions differed.

9

The Theoretical Approach Towards the Law Governing Contracts between States and Private Foreign Persons

IN discussing[1] the theoretical foundations of the law governing State contracts, that is to say, contracts between States (or other international persons) and private persons it is necessary to start from a hypothesis which is both fundamental and elementary. Every contract is necessarily governed by a specific legal order. Or, to put it negatively, an understanding which is not governed by a specific legal system is not a contract. Or, again, it is the law, the legal order or system which confers the quality of a legally binding contract upon the understanding between parties. They may, it is true, agree that their understanding shall be no more than a gentleman's agreement, but, as we all know, this is unenforceable in law and, therefore, no contract at all. To this day the *vinculum juris*, the obligatory character of the understanding is the essential prerequisite of a contract. This starting point, like many a proposition of law, may in the last resort be a matter of belief, observation and experience incapable of mathematical proof. Lawyers, however, know too much about their subject to assert that any legal relationship can exist outside the law, without being created and sustained by the law. We are not here concerned with that entirely different philosophical question of the origin or basis of law as such, and accordingly can ignore all those well known discussions about natural law, positivism and so forth. We are concerned with a much narrower and simpler point, viz. that it is only the law which by its precepts and sanctions creates legally binding and effective ties.

Moreover, it is the law that establishes the conditions subject to, and the scope within, which the parties are at liberty to create contractual rights and duties. Freedom of contract is conferred, defined and limited by law—an almost self-evident proposition which is far too often ignored. In particular, it is right to emphasise the words 'limited by law'. For nothing is gained by treating freedom of contract as if it meant unlimited

[1] This paper contains nothing that is not already included in the two articles reproduced in *Studies in International Law*, pp. 179 and 211. But on the Continent the present, wholly inadequate article is frequently referred to and is, therefore, included in the collection.

Revue Belge de Droit International (1975), 562–7.

freedom. What we know as *jus dispositivum* in a particular legal order is obviously capable of being adopted, rejected or modified by the parties. No problem arises and, therefore, the general statement that freedom of contract is a generally accepted principle is either platitudinous or inaccurate. Freedom of contract has limits—limits fixed by the mandatory rules which exist in every system and in almost every sphere of law. They lead to difficulties familiar to lawyers, especially if they are introduced during the life of the contract and therefore interfere with the expected manner of its performance. It is on them that attention should be concentrated.

If these propositions are accepted it follows that every contract by whomsoever made must be subject either to a national system of law or to public international law, for these are the only legal orders known to us. Which of them applies in a given case is the question to which it is now possible to turn.

For the purpose of ascertaining the legal system applicable to a State contract we do not, as a matter of principle, follow routes which are different from those prevailing in the case of contracts between private persons. We search for the legal system which the parties expressly or impliedly selected, or, in Dicey's immortal phrase, for the proper law. We need not in the present context discuss its refinements or the relatively few uncertainties surrounding the doctrine or its various implications, its precise definition, foundation or consequences—matters the importance of which is sometimes liable to be exaggerated, seeing that, in essence, as a broad rule, the doctrine of the proper law prevails almost everywhere. It is much more relevant to suggest that the peculiarities which apply to a State contract within a given legal system should be disregarded for the purpose of deciding the logically anterior question which legal system is applicable to the State contract at hand. Take the great conception of the *contrat administratif* in French law. Since classification as well as jurisdictional aspects are usually subject to the *lex fori*, a judge or arbitrator sitting in France may well have to apply the law relating to the *contrat administratif* even if the contract is not governed by French law. But a judge or arbitrator sitting outside France does not apply the French law of the *contrat administratif*, unless he has previously found the French legal system to be the proper law of the contract. For similar reasons nothing is gained by what is no more than a terminological feature. One often sees references to investment contracts or economic development contracts or some such terms. Such contracts may be subject to a special legal regime in certain countries. But where the law of such a country does not apply the description does not matter. From the international point of view a concession, in particular, is simply a contract. Whether it is a contract of a special type can only become material after the legal system applicable to it has been identified. A concession, it is true, may not be a contract at all.

It is conceivably conferred by and contained in a legislative instrument. If and insofar as in such cases a question of classification arises the *lex fori* will answer it. If and insofar as the proper law is to be defined the answer depends on the terms of the instrument or, possibly, on presumptions which judicial practice has developed. The rule that in looking for the proper law of transactions with States very great, though by no means overriding, weight has to be given to the character of the State party is universal, supported by common sense and applicable to legislative instruments with particular force.

If, then, in the case of a State contract the search for the proper law is carried out in the same manner as in other cases (except that the status of the State party is a circumstance of great impact), one will normally end up by applying a specific national system, perhaps that of the contracting State, perhaps that to which the private person belongs, perhaps a third one. Whatever national legal system is found to be applicable, it applies as a whole, for better or worse. Perhaps it is permitted to add that this is so even where the law of the contracting State is applicable: its law has to be observed and the mere change of its law does not constitute an international tort attracting the rules of State responsibility, unless the change by its nature is such as to constitute an international wrong—but this is a remark which probably touches upon a point alien to the present discussion.

Although normally the law of a given State will govern the State contract, precisely 30 years ago another possible solution was suggested. It was said that a contract between a State and an alien private person could be 'internationalized' in the sense of being subjected to the only other legal order known to us, namely public international law. This does not mean or was ever intended to mean that the State contract should be considered to be a treaty or should be governed by public international law in the same way as transactions between States. It simply means that by exercising their right to choose the applicable legal system the parties may make public international law the object of their choice. Certainly French law is designed normally to apply to French people or French transactions. Certainly public international law is designed to apply as a rule to States and the transactions between them. But nothing prevents a contract between the German State and a Dutch firm to be submitted to French law. Similarly the fact that one party is not a State should not prevent the contract from being submitted to public international law. It would thus become subject to the mandatory rules of public international law. No mandatory law of any national system as such could touch it. If the parties desire this, why should we put any obstacle in their way? Just as by their will they can choose a given State order as their proper law, so it is their will, their choice, founded upon and permitted by the private international law of the forum, that may submit a contract to the law of States, to public international law. Of course, we must guard against abuse. For this reason the teachings of private international law in general are to the effect that the choice of the legal system adopted by the parties must be reasonable, free from capriciousness, supported by rational, legitimate grounds. These conditions will be fulfilled if one party to the contract is a State or, one may add, a State corporation, though for reasons of social policy private persons contracting among themselves should be precluded from choosing a legal system other than a national one. The public international law thus applicable within a limited field would normally be found in the general principles accepted by civilized nations. Their ascertainment in the special sphere of State contracts should not cause greater difficulties than in the sphere of treaty relationships. The public international law applicable to the contract would include mandatory rules recognised by general international law, by the great codifications such as the Vienna Convention (when in force), by Conventions or Declarations of Human Rights. The legal certainty and security which the parties would enjoy would be considerable, because public international law is unlikely to undergo sudden or radical changes during the life of a contract.

If in some quarters the idea of the internationalization of State contracts has caused difficulties and hesitations this is largely due to the inability of public and private international lawyers to understand each other, their respective apparatus and thought-processes. Public international lawyers are inclined to overlook that under the rules of private international law a contract containing a foreign element is governed by the legal system determined by the *lex fori* and that it is this which renders the proper law applicable. The internationalization of State contracts is thus founded upon a rule of *private* international law. To put it differently, public international law contains no rule which would render it applicable to a contract between an international and a private person. On the other hand private international lawyers are accustomed to think of a reference to a national system of law. There is, however, no a priori reason why parties should be compelled to choose a national law, why they should not be able to choose public international law. Its pervasiveness, its potentialities and riches, well known to public international lawyers but frequently ignored by others, are such that, within the limited field of application, a wholly adequate body is available to support and explain State contracts—certainly a much more developed body of law than that offered by many a national system of law. Moreover, a reference to foreign law leads almost everywhere to the application of the foreign law referred to, whether or not it wishes to be applied, as is proved by the fact that in the field of contracts most countries deny any place to the doctrine of *renvoi*; hence the fact that public international law normally applies only to international persons does not militate against its application by reference. It is therefore a purely dogmatic or conceptualist objection to found upon the obvious and undoubted fact that 'la nature des sujets auxquels s'adressent les normes internationales est bien différente de celle des sujets des ordres juridiques étatiques'. Such arguments should not stand in the way of a progressive and practically useful manipulation of the instruments provided by private international law and of the body of substantive law developed by public international law.

These submissions which in the present context do not need elaboration involve certain (negative) conclusions which require discussion.

In the first place it is submitted that not even in regard to State contracts is there room for a contract without law, a *contrat sans loi* or a *contrat anational*. The origin of any such general doctrine is as obscure as the precise meaning or its effect. It is plainly untenable, as becomes apparent as soon as one thinks of the various rules of interpretation which prevail in different jurisdictions or of mandatory rules such as those relating to 'vices de consentement'. The legal significance of such 'vices' cannot be assessed without resort to a specific legal order. In the vivid phrase of M. Batiffol, 'par là s'écroulera la construction d'un contrat échappant à toute loi positive'. For State contracts the doctrine emanates from and has on many occasions been developed by Verdross. Originally he seemed to confine his teachings to the suggestion that State contracts should for purposes of interpretation be independent of any legal system and be subject to autonomous interpretation, to what he called the *lex contractus*. This left the crucial question unanswered and accordingly in 1964 Verdross propounded the further thesis that 'such contracts are subject to all general principles of law relating to the conclusion and validity of contracts', though as to interpretation they probably were intended to remain autonomous. This still left the problem of the performance of State contracts and here Verdross relied on that self-evident yet far too general and therefore misleading maxim 'pacta sunt servanda', a maxim of which it has been well said: 'What is *pactum* and when and how and if it is *servandum* are questions which must be answered by a system of law capable of reacting in a sophisticated manner to these problems'. On the whole, however, it seems that there is very little that distinguishes the State *contrat sans loi* from the second method of approach which it is proposed to discuss.

This is to the effect that State contracts may be subject to the general principles of law recognized by civilized nations. Such a doctrine makes sense only if it is intended to be distinct from the other theory already discussed according to which a State contract may be submitted by the parties to public international law. If the two views mean the same thing, if there is only a terminological point involved, if a choice of general principles constitutes in truth a choice of public international law no new problem arises into which it would at this stage be necessary to enquire; on the other hand a reference to public international law obviously includes a reference to general principles which, we know, are one of its sources. What, then, is the distinctive feature of the application of general principles as opposed to public international law? It can only be this, that the general principles do not include certain rules of a mandatory character which public international law affirms and includes. There may be many such rules which are by no means expressive of a general principle. The most important example is the rule which precludes a State from relying on its own legislation to limit the scope of its international obligations. This is a firmly rooted principle of public international law. But it is not a general principle of law. We know from numerous cases that if a contract with a State is governed by the law of such State it may, as a result of supervening legislation, be modified and even destroyed. It would, therefore, be impossible to suggest as a general principle that a State, in entering into a contract, foregoes the right to change its terms. The right and the power to do so depend on the proper law. If the proper law is public international law that power and that right are necessarily excluded.

This short review of the theory of State contracts thus seems to lead to the conclusion that one is left with only two alternatives. Depending on the express or implied choice of the parties, a State contract is governed either by the chosen municipal system of law or by public international law.

10
Uniform Statutes in English Law

UNIFORM statutes are provisions enacted or authorized by Parliament and derived from treaties or similar arrangements which a group of nations agree to incorporate into their respective legal systems with a view to unifying legal rules in a particular field. Even though, as a matter of form, the legislative act itself is, in constitutional law, usually the direct and, indeed, the only source of municipal enforceability, the fact that uniform statutes are the ultimate product of a treaty constitutes their special characteristic. That fact has numerous consequences which it is proposed to examine: Is the interpretation of uniform statutes subject to peculiar rules? In particular, is it possible and perhaps even necessary by some process of interpretation to fill gaps in the uniform text? Do uniform statutes really succeed in unifying the law? If not or not entirely, how are divergences to be overcome or, in other words, what is the relationship between uniform laws and the conflict of laws? Is the idea and object of unification of law a head of public policy and, if so, does it eliminate conflict rules and does it perhaps even have a bearing upon rules of jurisdiction?

When some of these questions were examined on a previous occasion,[1] attention was drawn to, and to some extent a distinction was made between, the various methods practised in England with a view to giving effect in English law to the terms of the treaty. The following observations will deal only with the fourth of these methods, viz. a statute the schedule to which sets forth the text of the treaty and has the force of law. This may now be described as the most usual method and may well be on a different footing from the others, particularly from the second method which involves an Act of Parliament making 'such provision as is contained in this Act' and, perhaps, adding the treaty *informationis causa* only. It is necessary to make the scope of the following suggestions very clear, for some confusion may have been introduced into the subject by a remark of

[1] 'The Interpretation of Uniform Statutes' (1946) 62 *L.Q.R.* 278, also to be found in *Studies in International Law* (1973), p. 614. Since then the literature has grown considerably. See, in particular, Sinclair (1963) 12 *I.C.L.Q.* 508; Brownlie, *Principles of Public International Law* (3rd edn., 1979), p. 50 with further references. For a comparative survey see Schreuer, *British Year Book of International Law* 1971, p. 255. As to Germany see Bayer (1955) 20 *RabelsZ* 603. As to Italy see Giardina (1973) *Rivista di Diritto Internazionale 701.*

Law Quarterly Review, 99 (1983), 376–406.

Lord Wilberforce who said of the decision of the House of Lords in *Ellerman Line Ltd.* v. *Murray*[2] that it was 'atypical and in my opinion should no longer be followed'.[3] That decision related to the interpretation of a statute of the second type as defined, for it translated 'the international language of the Convention into the phraseology of the Merchant Shipping Acts' and directed 'that the Act is to become part of and construed as one with the other acts of that code'.[4] Such a method may now be atypical, although the Arbitration Act 1975 in substance adopts it by the description in the Preamble referring to an 'Act to give effect to the New York Convention on the Recognition and Enforcement of Foreign Arbitral Awards'. But whether or no the method is atypical it is entirely different from the situation with which Lord Wilberforce was concerned and which these pages envisage, namely the case in which Parliament 'is, broadly speaking, merely machinery rather than the source of law' or, in other words, 'is not the real law-giver, but merely the law-transformer',[5] the treaty itself being the (indirect) source of law. *Murray*'s case has therefore lost none if its authority in the field contemplated by it.

THE INTERPRETATION OF UNIFORM STATUTES

The ultimate object in interpreting uniform statutes is not open to doubt. It is to find answers conforming to the wording, purpose and idea of the treaty and acceptable to all or most of those countries which have ratified it. As Scott L. J. put it,[6] 'the maintenance of uniformity in the interpretation of a rule after its international adoption is just as important as the initial removal of divergence . . .'. The real question is how this can be achieved.

It has become fashionable to take as a guide Lord Macmillan's instruction[7] that the language 'should be construed on broad principles of general acceptation'.[8] Today it may be submitted with greater confidence

[2] [1931] A.C. 126.

[3] *James Buchanan & Co. Ltd.* v. *Babco Forwarding and Shipping (UK) Ltd.* [1978] AC 141, 153. In support of the suggestion in the text it is possible to refer to dictum by Lord Denning M.R. in *Corocraft* v. *Pan American Airways* [1969] 1 Q.B. 616, 653, to the effect that in *Murray*'s case 'the English statute was clearly given priority over the Convention'.

[4] *Barras* v. *Aberdeen Steam Trawling & Fishing Co.* [1933] A.C. 402, 431, *per* Lord Blanesburgh, at p. 441, *per* Lord Russell of Killowen. See, already, the former's remarks in [1931] A.C. 126, 133.

[5] See the present author's paper referred to above, note 1, at pp. 268, 290, 630.

[6] *The Eurymedon* [1938] P. 41, 61. Many similar statements are to be found in later cases.

[7] *Stag Line Ltd.* v. *Foscolo Mango & Co. Ltd.* [1939] A.C. 328, 350.

[8] See *James Buchanan & Co. Ltd.* v. *Babco Forwarding and Shipping (UK) Ltd.* [1978] AC 141, 154, *per* Lord Wilberforce, at p. 161 *per* Lord Salmon; *Fothergill* v. *Monarch Airlines* [1981] A.C. 251, 285, *per* Lord Fraser, at p. 293, *per* Lord Scarman; *The Hollandia* [1983] A.C. 565, 571 *per* Lord Diplock.

than ever before[9] that such principles are those prevailing in and developed by public international law. For both Lord Diplock and Lord Scarman have recently stated[10] with the fullest possible justification that the interpretation of uniform statutes is governed by the Vienna Convention on the Law of Treaties and has thus become one of the principal points at which public international and private law meet. The relevant provisions of the Vienna Convention read as follows[11]:

Article 31
General rule of interpretation.

1. A treaty shall be interpreted in good faith in accordance with the ordinary meaning to be given to the terms of the treaty in their context and in the light of its object and purpose.

2. The context for the purpose of the interpretation of a treaty shall comprise, in addition to the text, including its preamble and annexes:
   (a) any agreement relating to the treaty which was made between all the parties in connexion with the conclusion of the treaty;
   (b) any instrument which was made by one or more parties in connexion with the conclusion of the treaty and accepted by the other parties as an instrument related to the treaty.

3. There shall be taken into account, together with the context:
   (a) any subsequent agreement between the parties regarding the interpretation of the treaty or the application of its provisions;
   (b) any subsequent practice in the application of the treaty which establishes the agreement of the parties regarding its interpretation;
   (c) any relevant rules of international law applicable in the relations between the parties.

4. A special meaning shall be given to a term if it is established that the parties so intended.

Article 32
Supplementary means of interpretation.

Recourse may be had to supplementary means of interpretation, including the preparatory work of the treaty and the circumstances of its conclusion, in order to confirm the meaning resulting from the application of Article 31, or to determine the meaning when the interpretation according to Article 31:
(a) leaves the meaning ambiguous or obscure; or
(b) leads to a result which is manifestly absurd or unreasonable.

Admittedly these Articles were designed primarily with a view to texts which are not only concluded under the control of public international

[9] The point of the present author's article referred to above, note 1, was to suggest that uniform statutes should be interpreted according to the principles of public international law. It took 35 years for such a suggestion to be accepted.

[10] *Fothergill* v. *Monarch Airlines* [1981] A.C. 251, 282, 290 respectively.

[11] Cmnd. 7964.

law, but also regulate relations between States. But in law there is no difference between such treaties and those contemplating relations between private persons: Articles 31 and 32 apply to both types. Moreover, it does not matter that, technically, the Vienna Convention applies only to treaties concluded after January 27, 1980, when it came into effect, for, as again Lord Diplock made clear,[12] it 'does no more than codify already existing public international law'.

If, then, Articles 31 and 32 are taken as a starting point for the interpretation of uniform statutes enacted by Parliament, certain consequences follow.

1. The first and foremost guide to construction should be the ordinary meaning of the words used in the uniform statute. This is entirely in accordance with English law, for already half a century ago Lord Atkin said[13]:

> For the sake of uniformity it is, therefore, important that the courts should apply themselves to the consideration only of the words used without any predilection for the former law, always preserving the right to say that words used in the English language which have already in its particular context received judicial interpretations may be presumed to be used in the sense already judicially imputed to them.

The paramount importance of the literal interpretation has in recent years sometimes been neglected.[14] Thus in *Fothergill* v. *Monarch Airlines* Lord Wilberforce stated in terms[15]: 'I *start* by considering the purpose of Article 26 and I do not think that in doing so I am infringing any golden rule'. Lord Diplock, with the concurrence of Lord Keith of Kinkel, Lord Roskill, Lord Brandon or Oakbrook and Lord Brightman, went even further: words forming part of an international Convention 'should be given a purposive rather than a narrow literalistic construction'[16] and the latter,

[12] *Fothergill* v. *Monarch Airlines* [1981] A.C. 251, 282. Contrary to the opinion expressed by Lord Fraser at p. 289 it does not, therefore, matter, when the treaty came into effect.

[13] *Stag Line Ltd.* v. *Foscolo Mango & Co. Ltd.* [1939] A.C. 328, 343.

[14] This is so even outside the field of uniform statutes. See the worrying comment by Lord Diplock upon the construction by Lord Simonds of the Finance Act 1933 in *Fothergill* v. *Monarch Airlines* [1981] A.C. 251, 280.

[15] Ibid. at p. 272. Italics supplied.

[16] *The Hollandia* [1938] A.C. 565, 572, relating to the Carriage of Goods by Sea Act 1971 and the Hague-Visby Rules scheduled thereto. The argument rejected by the House of Lords was that Art. III (8) of the Hague-Visby Rules literally corresponding with Art. III (8) of the Hague Rules renders null and void and of no effect 'any clause, covenant or agreement relieving the carrier from liability . . . or lessening such liability'. A clause providing for the jurisdiction of the Dutch courts and submitting the bill of lading to Dutch law was held to be void, because it 'would have the *effect* of lessening the carrier's liability' as compared with English law (ibid, at p. 574F). In substance, therefore, the House of Lords did not look to the words or to the 'clause, covenant or agreement', but to their effect. The difficulty is

somewhat contemptuous phrase was emphasized by being repeated a little later. The result was the neglect and even the distortion of the statutory words in a manner which in the course of almost 50 years had apparently not ever or anywhere been put forward. It is submitted with great respect that as a matter of construction it is difficult to defend this approach. In general it is the observance of Article 31 of the Vienna Convention rather than the golden rule known to English law or what Lord Diplock called 'a narrow literalistic interpretation' that matters, for the very aim of ensuring uniformity of interpretation is best served by starting from and adhering to the ordinary meaning of the actual words used by the framers of the treaty. Contrary to what is sometimes thought of as continental methods of construction, the predominance of the text has repeatedly been emphasized, for instance, by the Federal Supreme Court of Germany which in a fundamental decision said[17] that a uniform law had to be interpreted 'in good faith in accordance with the ordinary meaning which attaches to its provisions in their context and in the light of its object and purpose'. A later decision is more diffuse, but it should be quoted in full, because it will have to be referred to in several connections:[18]

> German courts are unrestrictedly entitled to construe international Conventions where according to their content they are destined to create uniform private law in the member-States and, after transformation into the municipal legal systems, to be applied directly to the legal relations between private parties . . . In their case the object of uniformity of the law merits special attention. The unification of the substantive law is intended to render it unnecessary to examine the question of the conflict of laws to which the legal system is to be applied and as far as possible to protect the parties from the application of 'foreign' law. It conforms to the object of unification to interpret and if necessary to amplify such Conventions autonomously . . . In this connection generally recognised principles of interpretation of private law are to be applied. Therefore an interpretation is required which starts from the wording, but which, particularly where *travaux préparatoires* do not help, gives effect to the logical-systematic context of the individual provisions and to

---

aggravated, when it is realized that Art. III (8) speaks of a clause being 'null and void and of no effect', while Lord Diplock is compelled to rewrite these words and to hold that a forum and choice-of-law clause is valid at its inception, remains valid in many respects and, if and when a case of invalidity arises, is 'of no effect' only '*pro tanto*' (ibid. at p. 575F)—implications which are plainly irreconcilable with the text. Lord Diplock's interpretation now constitutes English law, but it is to be hoped that the method employed by the House of Lords will be confined to the Carriage of Goods by Sea Act 1971 and will not be followed abroad. It is a method which renders it almost impossible so to draft an international Convention that it does not produce unforeseen and unforeseeable consequences. See further, below p. 299.

[17] BGHZ 52, 220 (June 25, 1969). The statement of principle is almost identical with the text of Art. 31 of the simultaneous Vienna Convention.

[18] NJW 1976, 1583 (March 19, 1976). Citations have been omitted.

their meaning and purpose. Conceptions of municipal law may not be accepted unhesitatingly, because otherwise the purpose of unification of law may be endangered. Rather the interpretation is to be accomplished in the sense of the uniform statute itself with the object of a hopefully uniform application in all member-States.

It is, however, very clear that notwithstanding its primacy the literal or textual interpretation is liable to be inconclusive. The recent decision of the House of Lords[19] on the words 'other charges incurred in respect of the carriage of goods' is significant. These words occur in Article 23 (4) of the Convention on the Contract for the International Carriage of Goods by Road, the so-called CMR, which is scheduled to the Carriage of Goods by Road Act 1965. Was excise duty in respect of stolen whisky paid by the plaintiffs included in those words and therefore recoverable by the plaintiffs from the defendant carriers? All courts gave an affirmative answer, although the majority in the House of Lords was three to two only. The result is noteworthy, since in ordinary language the word 'charges' may not readily include excise duties.

2. It is now established that for the purpose of ascertaining the ordinary meaning of a uniform statute it is legitimate to refer to a foreign text irrespective of whether it is the only authentic one upon which the English text is based or whether its authenticity is equal with that of the English text.[20] Very frequently, however, this is again a fruitless effort, as it was in the two recent English cases. In particular the French phrase 'frais encourus à l'occasion du transport' gives rise to the same problem as its English counterpart: neither 'charges' nor 'frais' would normally signify excise duty.

What is not yet clear is whether an English court is permitted to look at texts translated into other languages. Thus it would hardly be open to doubt that the German counterpart of the English phrase 'charges incurred in respect of the carriage of goods,' viz. the words 'sonstige aus Anlass der Beförderung des Gutes entstandene Kosten' cannot reasonably be understood as including excise duties;[21] the same would probably apply to the Dutch word 'vervoerskosten' which Lord Wilberforce referred to as part of a decision of the Amstersdam court rejecting the carrier's liability for excise duty.[22] It is submitted that a translated text is a permissible and frequently a useful guide to decision, for it is likely to indicate how one of the High Contracting Parties understood the authentic text.

[19] *James Buchanan & Co. Ltd.* v. *Babco Forwarding and Shipping (U.K.) Ltd.* [1978] A.C. 141.

[20] Ibid. See also *Fothergill* v. *Monarch Airlines* [1981] A.C. 251.

[21] Quite apart from the use of the word 'Kosten' the German text speaks of charges payable by reason of the carriage (as opposed to 'in consequence of the carriage').

[22] *James Buchanan & Co. Ltd.* v. *Babco Forwarding and Shipping (U.K.) Ltd.* [1978] A.C. 141. 153–4.

From the point of view of literal interpretation the Dutch court held that excise duty was more of a 'subsequent levy or administrative fine than an item of charges in respect of carriage'. This seems to be plainly right and is not refuted by Lord Wilberforce's observation that it 'seems to overlook the distinction between 'carriage charges' and 'other charges' in Article 23 (4)'. In both cases the text requires 'charges', in the first case charges for the carriage, in the second case charges connected with the carriage such as expenses for packing, unpacking, repacking, customs declarations and examinations, perhaps insurance and similar services of the carrier arising from and connected with the carriage.

The general impression which the decision of the House of Lords on the meaning of 'carriage charges' in Article 23 of CMR leaves on the reader's mind is that the ordinary meaning of the word may not at present receive the primary weight which one might expect, and this is certainly not displaced by a similar approach of the House of Lords in a later, though much clearer, case in which the word 'damage' or 'avarie' was held to include (partial) loss.[23]

3. The terms of the treaty cannot, however, be read in isolation. Rather they should be construed 'in their context'. This is nothing new. Already in 1961, when construing the words 'due diligence to make the ship seaworthy' in Article III, rule 1 of the Hague Rules scheduled to the Carriage of Goods by Sea Act 1924, the House of Lords held it 'necessary to pay particular regard to their history, origin and context'.[24] Accordingly, the meaning of those words was held to be that which since a decision of 1895[25] had been attributed to them in England and was in conformity with that prevailing in Canada, New Zealand and the United States of America.[26] Certainly, as Lord Atkin said,[27] the courts should not display any 'predilection' for the local law preceding the Convention, but where the words have been considered and used by courts highly experienced in the subject it is a reasonable inference that the Convention, when using the same word or phrase in connection with the same subject-matter, in all probability does not intend to reject its established meaning; the term may in such circumstances be said to have a special meaning in the sense of Article 31 (4) of the Vienna Convention. This has nothing to do with the

[23] *Fothergill* v. *Monarch Airlines* [1981] A.C. 251.

[24] *Riverstone Meat Co. Pty.* v. *Lancashire Shipping Co. Ltd* [1961] A.C. 807, 836, *per* Viscount Simonds who, incidentally, relied on dicta in *Barras* v. *Aberdeen Steam Trawling & Fishing Co.* [1933] A.C. 402. It must again be emphasized that, although the dicta were in point, the case, like *Ellerman Line Ltd.* v. *Murray* [1931] A.C. 126, was different from that involved in *Riverstone Meat*.

[25] *G. E. Dobell & Co.* v. *Steamship Rossmore Co. Ltd.* [1895] 2 Q.B. 408.

[26] See, e.g. *Riverstone Meat Co. Pty.* v. *Lancashire Shipping Co. Ltd.* [1961] A.C. 807, *per* Lord Hodson at p. 874.

[27] *Stag Line Ltd.* v. *Foscolo Mango & Co. Ltd.* [1939] A.C. 328, 343.

specifically English rule, first stated in 1870 by James L. J.,[28] according to which, where a word of doubtful meaning has received a clear judicial interpretation, the subsequent statute which incorporates the same word or the same phrase in a similar context must be construed so that the word or phrase is interpreted according to the meaning that has previously been assigned to it.[29] It is simply common sense that if the Convention adopts a phrase which appears to have been taken from one legal system or from some, where it is used in a specific sense, the international legislators are likely to have had that sense in mind and to intend its introduction into the Convention. History, origin and context, therefore, are peculiarly apt to throw light on the literal meaning. These are elements which are capable of proof. They do not involve guesswork. They are free from the hazards which often bedevil the assessment of a rule's rationale or purpose. Thus when the CMR Convention speaks of 'charges', 'Kosten', it is unlikely that in the field of road transport a definite meaning had previously been assigned to any of these terms. Or when the Treaty of Versailles created a 'charge' on enemy property, it could not reasonably be a measure subject to English equitable interests.[30] But when a Convention relating to shipping law speaks of 'due diligence to make the ship seaworthy' and when, since 1895, the English-speaking world had understood these words in a certain sense, one can well sympathize with Lord Simonds who 'emphatically' subscribed to statements by Lord Hailsham and Lord Sumner who said that, when the Convention employs but forbears to define a widely used phrase it shows a clear intention to continue and enforce the old clause as it was previously understood and regularly construed by the courts.[31]

4. The next step in the progress of interpretation is to look at the treaty 'in the light of its object and purpose'—words which in every language seem to be tautological and the distinction between which has never been explained and, apparently, has not even been discussed. Perhaps the Vienna Convention intends to express two different aspects of interpretation, namely in the first place the object or purpose of unification, which the treaty as a whole undoubtedly pursues, and secondly the object and purpose of the particular provision the terms of which fall to be construed. Irrespective of whether or no such was the intention of the Vienna

[28] *Ex parte Campbell* (1870) L.R. 5 Ch. 703, 706.

[29] See *Webb* v. *Outrim* [1907] A.C. 81, 89; *Gosse, Millard Ltd.* v. *Canadian Government Merchant Marine Ltd.* [1929] A.C. 223, 230 *per* Lord Hailsham, at p. 237 *per* Lord Sumner; *Barras* v. *Aberdeen Steam Trawling & Fishing Co.* [1933] A.C. 402, 411, *per* Lord Buckmaster, at p. 430 *per* Lord Warrington, at p. 442, *per* Lord Russell of Killowen, at p. 446 *per* Lord Macmillan; *Riverstone Meat Co. Pty.* v. *Lancashire Shipping Co. Ltd.* [1961] A.C. 807, 837, *per* Viscount Simonds.

[30] *Josef Inwald A.G.* v. *Pfeiffer* (1928) 44 T.L.R. 352 (HL).

[31] For references see above, note 29.

Convention and whether or no the words used by it are apt to express the two aspects, it should not be open to doubt that for the purpose of interpretation both of them are material and significant. Their effect requires deeper consideration than it has so far received.

(a) As regards the first point, that is, the object or purpose of applying the Convention so that it implements and promotes the unification of the law, this means in practice that the courts should adopt that interpretation which has been or is most likely to be applied by the greatest number of countries. To be even more specific, this means that a judge in England should follow the practice of influential foreign courts even if he himself would not have reached the same result. This is 'subsequent practice in the application of the treaty', which Article 31 (3) (b) of the Vienna Convention makes an aid to construction, although in a purely English context subsequent practice may be excluded from consideration.[32] What is necessary, therefore, is a comparative approach and a capacity to assess the weight and the probable impact of foreign decisions and, possibly, of academic work.

It is a remarkable and, probably, regrettable fact that the House of Lords seems to be disinclined to permit such a course. Lord Salmon, it is true, took a step towards it, when he said,[33] 'If a corpus of law had grown up overseas which laid down the meaning of Article 23, our courts would no doubt follow it for the sake of uniformity which it is the object of the Convention to establish. But no such corpus exists.' This would seem to mean that if there exists a uniform practice abroad, the English courts would follow it—nothing else can be meant by the reference to a 'corpus of law'. A practice which is divergent provides little guidance and the English courts have shown themselves markedly and surprisingly reluctant even to have regard to it. Thus both Lord Wilberforce and Lord Diplock[34] have explained in some detail why in interpreting the Warsaw Convention of 1929 on international carriage by air they preferred to ignore foreign decisions; they were not always decisions of the highest courts; they were not binding; the process of law reporting varies; the facts are not always clearly discernible. At the same time considerable weight was given to academic writings—a fact which is not free from perversity if one remembers the reluctance of English courts even to consider the writings of English academic lawyers as well as the reasons for it or, to put it differently, if one is aware of the great circumspection with which

[32] As to contracts see *F. L. Schuler A.G.* v. *Wickman Machine Tools Sales Ltd.* [1974] A.C. 235.

[33] *James Buchanan & Co. Ltd.* v. *Babco Forwarding and Shipping (U.K.) Ltd.* [1978] A.C. 141, 161.

[34] *Fothergill* v. *Monarch Airlines* [1981] A.C. 251, 276, 284.

continental writings must be treated and of the necessity for weighing the standing, reputation and expertise of the author.

It is certainly true that, to take a probably extreme case pointed out by Megaw L. J.,[35] in six member-States 12 different interpretations of the same words may be produced. But if there are few foreign decisions and if one of them is clearly and persuasively reasoned, as happened in a case decided by the House of Lords,[36] the English courts, it is suggested, should follow that case and thus intensify and probably secure a uniform interpretation, albeit that in the absence of the foreign decision they would have reached the opposite result. In particular, where, as in fact happened, two Law Lords adopted the foreign decision and its reasoning,[37] the majority of three Law Lords would have better served the object and purpose of the Convention, viz. the uniformity and harmonization of the law, if they had refrained from going their own way. As so often, Lord Denning M.R. led the way, when he said in *Corocraft* v. *Pan American Airways*[38] that even if he disagreed with certain American decisions he 'would follow them in a matter which is of international concern. The courts of all the countries should interpret the Convention in the same way.' If foreign decisions have been rendered by supreme tribunals and all of them clearly point in one direction only, English courts which go in a different way (as 'indefensibly'[39] happened in connection with Article VIII (2) (b) of the Bretton Woods Agreement) badly neglect what may be described as a plain duty.[40] Academic opinion, on the other hand, is never binding, never completely available and rarely expressed with a view to the particular facts in issue. While it should certainly be considered, it should not necessarily be preferred to judicial practice.

(b) Although the (general) object and purpose of creating a uniform practice does not seem to have been in the forefront of English judges' minds, the (specific) object and purpose of the text requiring interpretation

[35] *Ulster-Swift Ltd.* v. *Taunton Meat Haulage Ltd.* [1977] 1 WLR 625, 646; see also *Michael Galley Footwear Ltd.* v. *Laboni* [1982] 2 All ER. 200.

[36] See the Dutch case mentioned by Lord Wilberforce in *James Buchanan & Co. Ltd.* v. *Babco Forwarding and Shipping (UK) Ltd.* [1978] A.C., 141, 153–4.

[37] Lord Edmund-Davies and Lord Fraser of Tullybelton in the case mentioned in the preceding note.

[38] [1969] 1 QB. 616, 655.

[39] The phrase is Sir Joseph Gold's: Staff Papers of the International Monetary Fund 28 (1981), p. 747.

[40] *Wilson Smithett & Cope Ltd.* v. *Terruzzi* [1976] QB. 683, approved by the House of Lords in *United City Merchants (Investments) Ltd.* v. *Royal Bank of Canada* [1983] A. C. 168, 188. On these cases and the relevant foreign material see Mann, *The Legal Aspect of Money* (4th ed., 1982), p. 384, 599. pp. 397–8 and (1982) 98 LQR 526. These decisions are irreconcilable with the intention, proclaimed in *James Buchanan & Co. Ltd.* v. *Babco Forwarding and Shipping (U.K.) Ltd.* [1978] A.C. 141 and *Fothergill* v. *Monarch Airlines* [1981] A.C. 251, so to construe an international Convention as to promote uniformity. For this reason alone the decisions on Art. VIII (2) (b) are bound to cause misgivings.

in casu has attracted predominant attention—so much so that in England a text is now rarely interpreted 'in accordance with the ordinary meaning . . . in the light of its object and purpose', but 'purposive interpretation' has become the almost paramount guide. The trouble is that the purpose of a provision may not always be obvious. Of course, where 'damage' has to be notified to an airline within a certain time limit, this is required for the protection of the airline which will wish to check the passengers' statements, to make inquiries and to assess the extent of the damage; in such circumstances it is not difficult to hold that 'damage' includes (total or partial) loss.[41] But other cases will be less easy to decide. It is to be noted that in holding that excise duty was covered by the phrase 'charges incurred in respect of the carriage' the majority of the House of Lords did not attempt to found its decision on an investigation of the purpose of the provision. In many cases the danger in fact will be that the object and purpose of a particular provision is speculative or even obscure or equivocal. Thus in reference to the words 'charges incurred in respect of the carriage' Lord Denning M.R. said:[42]

> I ask myself: what was the intention—the design or purpose—behind it all? It seems to me that it was intended that the sender should not be limited to the value of the goods as defined in Article 23 (1) . . . but that he should also be compensated for any additional expense that he incurred directly by reason of the loss.

With great respect, it is impossible to infer this from the Convention. There is much to be said in favour of a conclusion in the opposite sense. It is satisfactory to note that, as mentioned above, not even the majority of the House of Lords (which in the result agreed with Lord Denning) based its decision on purposive interpretation. Nor did Lord Edmund-Davies and Lord Fraser in their dissenting speeches. These did not thereby become less persuasive.[43]

5. As Article 32 of the Vienna Convention makes clear, a supplementary and, one may add, very much subsidiary means of interpretation is recourse to *travaux préparatoires*. For the purpose of construing an international Convention this is now accepted by English law.[44] In the

[41] This was decided in *Fothergill* v. *Monarch Airlines* [1981] A.C. 251

[42] *James Buchanan & Co. Ltd.* v. *Babco Forwarding and Shipping (U.K.) Ltd.* [1977] QB. 208, 214.

[43] It should be made very clear that at any rate in relation to treaties purposive construction is nothing new to English law. Already in *Imperial Japanese Government* v. *P. & O. Steam Navigation Co.* [1895] A.C. 644, 657 Lord Herschell said: 'The treaties must be interpreted according to their manifest spirit and intent. In construing such instruments a too slavish adherence to the letter would be out of place, although, of course, violence must not be done to the language used.'

[44] *Fothergill* v. *Monarch Airlines* [1981] A.C. 251.

light of Article 32 this must be described as a foregone conclusion: indeed, Lord Diplock[45] was probably right in suggesting that in the case of treaties concluded after January 27, 1980, the applicability of Article 32 is obligatory, and in such cases it is by no means free from doubt whether Lord Wilberforce[46] would be entitled to impose two conditions upon the use of *travaux préparatoires*, viz. 'that the material involved is public and accessible, and, secondly, that the *travaux préparatoires* clearly and indisputably point to a definite legislative intention'. These are conditions which go to weight (with which Article 32 is not concerned) rather than admissibility.

The real problem, therefore, is what are relevant *travaux préparatoires* and what weight should in a given case be given to them. These are questions of great general scope, which far exceed the field of treaties, which cannot be comprehensively discussed in the present context and to which it may be necessary to revert. Suffice it to emphasize that the cases in which *travaux préparatoires* can profitably be used must be 'rare',[47] indeed exceptional. That the minutes of September 27, 1955, which the House of Lords considered[48] and which reproduce a discussion on the meaning of 'damage' were inconclusive is so obvious that no detailed reference is required. But by way of example both Lord Diplock and Lord Fraser[49] referred to another minute of September 20, 1955, where, in relation to a vote taken on a certain amendment, it is stated 'The President stated that, in the event of a negative vote on the proposal, the Conference would be understood as having stated that the word 'unreasonable' was not necessary, because it was already implied in Article 19 as at present drafted'. Both Lord Diplock and Lord Fraser seem to have taken the view that a minute of this type could be material and perhaps even helpful. Respectful doubt cannot be suppressed. Suppose the majority or some of the delegates disagreed with the President, but remained silent, not necessarily on account of Machiavellianism which according to Lord Diplock 'is not extinct at international conferences',[50] but, for instance, because they were anxious to avoid a long discussion with a foolish President. Is the opinion expressed by the President relevant material? It would be a different matter if the President had not stated his own view, but had purported to summarize the delegates' intentions or had summarized the result of an informal test. But it is submitted that even in the absence of recorded contradiction the President's statement does not carry any weight. It is no more than a personal opinion. It does not imply any legislative intent or authority.

[45] Ibid. at p. 283. [46] Ibid. at p. 278. [47] Ibid. at p. 278
[48] Ibid. at p. 283, *per* Lord Diplock. [49] Ibid. at pp. 282 and 289 respectively.
[50] Ibid. at p. 283.

FILLING GAPS

Not long ago Lord Denning M.R. carried the technique of 'purposive interpretation' to considerable lengths by suggesting that it would or should enable the court to fill gaps.[51] The House of Lords rejected that suggestion, not only because it denied the existence of a gap as opposed to a question of construction, but also because for the courts to fill it would encroach on the province of Parliament and involve the courts in legislation.[52]

It is likely that, contrary to Lord Denning's assumption, this attitude is in line with continental judicial practice. Thus it is true that in 1976 Germany's Federal Supreme Court stated that it was open to the courts to 'amplify' a uniform statute in order to give effect to its objects and purposes,[53] and it is not difficult to find academic support for such treatment. It would appear, however, that, if one disregards the jurisprudence of the European Court of Justice which stands on its own and is characterized by a unique mixture of literalism and passion for 'integration', actual practice frowns upon the judicial filling of gaps. By way of example it may be useful to consider the Federal Supreme Court's practice on the question of the air carrier's liability for luggage which the passenger takes with him on board the aeroplane. Article 18 of the Warsaw Convention renders the carrier liable for damage sustained in the event of the destruction or loss of or damage to any registered luggage or goods. What is sometimes known as 'cabin luggage' is not dealt with. This is a gap. The German Federal Supreme Court held that it was to be filled by reference to domestic German law, for 'the provisions of German air law are superseded by the Warsaw Convention only to the extent to which they are inconsistent with its rules'.[54] Or Article 21, CMR deals with consignments providing for 'cash on delivery', without defining the meaning of 'cash'. Does it mean payment *in specie* or is payment by cheque or similar methods permitted? There is a gap in the Convention. The German Federal Supreme Court filled it by applying the proper law of the contract, found it to be German and held that under German law payment by cheque is not permitted.[55]

It would no doubt be possible to find other examples pointing in the

[51] *James Buchanan & Co. Ltd.* v. *Babco Forwarding and Shipping (U.K.) Ltd.* [1977] QB 208, 213.

[52] *James Buchanan & Co. Ltd.* v. *Babco Forwarding and Shipping (U.K.) Ltd.* [1978] A.C.. 141. An international tribunal cannot fill gaps; see O'Connell, *International Law* (2nd edn., 1970), p. 256.

[53] See the citation above, note 17.

[54] BGHZ 52, 213, 72, 389 (November 29, 1978).

[55] BGHZ 83, 96, 101 (February 10, 1982). See also B&H NJW 83, 1266.

same direction. Always with the exception of the European Court of Justice, which pursues a practice of its own creation, no court faced with a genuine gap, as opposed to a problem of construction, will wish to become a legislator or adopt a solution other than the German one.

FAILURE OF UNIFICATION BY DIVERGENT INTERPRETATIONS

The preceding observations render it apparent that divergent interpretations of uniform statutes are almost bound to occur, however diligently judges may strive to prevent them. The result is diversity where uniformity ought to prevail. The longer uniform statutes are in force the greater is the extent of differences in interpretation. In 1970 the late Dr O. C. Giles published an illuminating book on the treatment of international Conventions in national courts.[56] After a comparative survey of uniform laws relating to bills of lading, air transport, bills of exchange and miscellaneous other subjects he arrived at the cautious conclusion that it was not possible to proclaim either success or failure, but 'that, as in other fields of human endeavour, the perfect solution has eluded the grasp of those creating uniform law, although important progress has been made'.[57] Thirteen years later the instances of diversity have probably become more numerous and the observer's scepticism in regard to unification as a matter of practical politics has become more pronounced.[58] No complete survey such as that offered by Dr Giles in regard to commerical law can be attempted here, but in order to provide some evidence in support of the subsequent remarks a few particularly significant examples deserve to be mentioned.

In the first place it is necessary to remember that it is not only the judicial interpretation, but also the text of the so-called uniform statute which may differ from country to country. The Hague Rules of 1924 were adopted in many forms: The Protocol to the Hague Rules of 1924 and Article 16 of the Hague-Visby Rules of 1968 permit acceptance by the introduction of their provision in a form adapted to the respective national law. Brandon J. (as he then was) spoke of their Romanian, Greek and English versions.[59] There are States which have failed to accept them in any form, others such as Australia have modified them, some adopted the

[56] *Uniform Commercial Law* (A. W. Sijthoff: Leyden). [57] Ibid. at p. 193

[58] A particularly grave misfortune would happen if the United Kingdom allowed itself to be persuaded to adopt the Convention on the Law Applicable to Contractual Obligations (Cmnd. 8489) which the Commissions of the European Economic Community felt called upon to promote. It is about the worst example of misguided enthusiasm for 'harmonization'.

[59] *The Elefteria* [1970] P. 94, 101–102.

Hague Rules of 1968.[60] Some applied them to outward shipments, others to both outward and inward shipments. Striking differences have occurred in connection with the conversion of monetary limits into local currency. It will be remembered that Article IV (5) of the Hague Rules scheduled to the Carriage of Goods by Sea Act 1924 fixed the limit of liability at £100 (taken at gold value) per 'package'. It appears that in the member-States this sum was translated into local currency at values which varied between US $62.50 and US $1.55.[61] A decision of the Cour d'Appel in Paris[62] throws interesting light on the resulting situation: bills of lading relating to the shipment of goods from New York to Le Havre were issued in New York and submitted to New York law, including the Carriage of Goods by Sea Act 1936. The liability for damage was limited in New York to $500 per unit, in France to £100 gold value; for reasons which are difficult to follow the latter amount in terms of French francs was much less than the former. The court gave judgment for an amount of francs corresponding to £100. Most Conventions which fix maximum amounts of liability permit conversion into local currency; the Warsaw Convention on air transport, for instance, expressly so provides in Article 22 (4). It is obvious that the value of such local sums may frequently and quickly change, so that it differs both from the maximum amount fixed in other countries and from the current value of the amount stated in the Convention itself. A judge in a third country who is called upon to award a sum of money to a plaintiff in country A against a carrier in country B will have to remember that the carrier's costs and, therefore, the amount charged by him to the passenger or shipper were no doubt calculated by reference to a maximum amount of liability contemplated by a particular legal system. To hold him liable for an amount prevailing in another legal system would run counter to his and probably the plaintiff's legitimate expectations.

Differences of judicial interpretation are less easily ascertainable, yet equally telling. Take by way of example Article III (6) of the Hague Rules, according to which liability ceases, 'unless suit is brought within one year', 'à moins qu'une action ne soit intentée', 'wenn der Anspruch nicht innerhalb eines Jahres geltend gemacht wird'. Is the commencement of arbitration proceedings covered by this phrase? In Germany the wording is such that an affirmative answer is required.[63] The same view is held in France, although the wording by no means supports it,[64] and a

[60] According to Chaveau, *Droit Maritime Français* (1978), p. 3 the 1968 version applied only in Denmark, Ecuador, France, Lebanon, Norway, Singapore, Sweden, Switzerland, Syria and the United Kingdom.

[61] Braekhus, *Rec*, 164 (1979 iii), p. 322.

[62] October 24, 1966, *Droit Maritime Français* (1967), p. 23.

[63] Schaps-Abraham, *Seerecht* (4th ed., 1978), s. 612, n. 6.

[64] Rodière, *Traité Général de Droit Maritime*, ii (1968), No. 782.

fundamental decision of the Court of Appeal has in England arrived at the same result.[65] But in the United States of America the Court of Appeals, Second Circuit, rendered the astonishing decision that arbitration proceedings are not covered by the word 'suit' and that therefore an arbitration clause has the effect of excluding any time limit.[66] Another example of great significance is the interpretation put in England upon Article III (1) of the Hague Rules, according to which the shipowner is liable for lack of seaworthiness caused by the negligence of an independent contractor.[67] This conclusion is not universally shared; the Scandinavian countries in particular hold a diffferent view.[68] Or take the famous question whether for the purposes of the Hague Rules the container or each of the cartons contained in it is a package. A decision of the Federal Supreme Court of Germany[69] deals with a situation in which the container had a value of DM 1,250 and the 627 cartons in it had a value of DM 14,000 odd. The court awarded the former amount, but it seems that the American practice takes the opposite view.[70] Again it must be emphasized that the German carrier who contracts under German law and who assesses his freight on the basis of German judicial practice should not suddenly be confronted by an English, American or Swiss judge or arbitrator with a liability according to United States law. The converse conclusion is equally true: the American carrier who expects to be liable for DM 14,000 or takes out an insurance policy accordingly should not suddenly be allowed to invoke German law and make a profit equal to about nine-tenths of his expected liability.

One of the most notorious examples of disharmony surrounds the interpretation of Article VIII (2) (b) of the International Monetary Fund Agreement. In France and Germany, where there exists a rich judicial practice, an exchange contract within the meaning of that provision is a contract which in any way affects a country's exchange resources so as to be liable to reduce them.[71] This was originally accepted by the Court of Appeal in England in 1967.[72] In 1976 the Court of Appeal abandoned this view and defined an exchange contract as a contract to exchange the currency of one country for that of another as well as contracts which are a monetary transaction in disguise and in 1982 the House of Lords, without

[65] *The Merak* [1965] P. 223.

[66] *Son Shipping Co. Inc.* v. *De Fosse & Tanghe, Solel Bond Ltd.*, 199 F. 2d 687 (1925).

[67] *Riverstone Meat Co. Pty. Ltd.* v. *Lancaster Shipping Co. Ltd.* [1961] A.C. 807.

[68] Braekhus, *Rec.* 164 (1979 iii), 329, who wisely adds that a situation such as this renders the conflict rules 'necessary even for cases lying within the area of the application of Conventions adopted by all the States to which the case has connections'.

[69] BGHZ 78, 121 (September 22, 1980).

[70] *The Aegis Spirit* [1977] 1 Lloyd's Rep. 93.

[71] For details see Mann, *The Legal Aspect of Money* (4th edn., 1982), p. 384, 599.

[72] *Sharif* v. *Azad* [1967] Q.B. 605.

a word of independent reasoning, adopted this definition.[73] In this way a far-reaching cleavage has arisen; in creating it the courts were oblivious of their plain duty to construe uniform statutes as far as possible so as to promote uniformity.[74] At the same time the House of Lords allowed a second cleavage to arise:[75] ignoring decisions of the New York Court of Appeals[76] it held that an autonomous English documentary credit was in part an unenforceable exchange contract—a result fraught with danger to the international financial community.[77]

The most vivid picture of what he calls the 'judicial diversification' of the Warsaw Convention on air transport was drawn more than 10 years ago by that great expert, Professor Mankiewicz.[78] From the many examples which he gives it is useful to select the problem raised by the conception of 'place of business' in Article 28 of the original Warsaw Convention which deals with jurisdiction at the option of the plaintiff.[79] The question whether that expression, being a translation of the French 'etablissement', comprises another airline or a mere travel agency which issues the ticket, provoked numerous decisions, particularly in England, France and the United States of America. No uniform practice developed. The results were in 1976 carefully compiled by the Federal Supreme Court of Germany[80] which felt able to avoid a decision. Yet it arrived at the surprising result that a ticket of the Bulgarian airline which had been issued by the Deutsche Lufthansa in Germany where the Bulgarian airline had a 'station' enabled the plaintiff to bring his action in Germany. Since the 'station' of the Bulgarian airline had no contact with the plaintiff or, indeed, the public and seems to have carried out purely internal operations, the decision may go much further than most others.

The list of instances which illustrate differences in the terms or the interpretation of uniform statutes could be continued for many pages and with reference to many uniform statutes. An enumeration of such examples would add nothing to the clarification of the real problem: What is their effect in international legal practice? How are they to be dealt with by a judge? What is the principle guiding towards a reasonably satisfactory solution? To this problem it is now necessary to turn.

[73] *United City Merchants (Investments) Ltd.* v. *Royal Bank of Canada* [1983] 1 A.C. 168.

[74] See above, pp. 271, 279, text to notes 6 and 38.

[75] See the detailed Note in (1982) 98 *L.Q.R.* 526.

[76] See above, note 71 for references.

[77] On 'recklessly' see *Goldman* v. *Thai Airways*, (1983) 1 W.L.R., 1180.

[78] (1972) 21 *ICLQ* 718.

[79] Ibid. at pp. 745–7.

[80] NJW 1976, 1587 (March 23, 1976) or IPRspr. 1976 No. 123c. See the more recent decision of June 16, 1982, BGHZ 84, 339.

UNIFORM STATUTES AND THE CONFLICT OF LAWS

1. In general the solution of the conflict should be achieved by the classical process of applying the *lex causae*, in particular, the proper law of the contract.[81] Irrespective of whether the *lex causae* has adopted or failed to adopt the uniform law or has accepted it subject to variations or has interpreted it in a specific sense, in principle its law should be followed in the forum. This will not by any means render it necessary in every case to investigate the content of the foreign law; where neither party alleges a divergence, the court or arbitrator is entitled and, indeed, required to take the *lex fori* as a guide.

The proposed rule is in harmony with the demands of justice as well as the requirements of established law. To disregard the content of the proper law would in many, perhaps in most, cases lead to the exclusive control of the *lex fori* and therefore to unsatisfactory results, for it would necessarily set aside the expectations of the parties. Take a bill of lading issued in Rio de Janeiro under Brazilian law for a shipment from Rio to Hamburg and providing for the jurisdiction of the English courts or for arbitration in London. The carrier has no doubt calculated freight on the basis of his potential liability under Brazilian law. He has covered himself by insurance to the same extent. The conflict of laws was developed for the very purpose of protecting what used to be called vested rights, i.e. the contractual or other rights and obligations as created by the proper law. To override them cannot be readily supported.

Moreover, it is elementary that whenever a set of facts involves a foreign element we are instructed to ascertain the legal system that applies, the proper law or the *lex causae*.[82] There is no reason of principle, logic or justice why, as a rule and where the circumstances so require, the same process should not be gone through in the case of uniform statutes in particular or statutes in general—for the primary and paramount impact of the conflict of laws is entirely independent of the nature of the substantive law, i.e. of the question whether this is statutory or common law. There cannot be any rational distinction between the two sources of English law. If this were not so all law on the Continent would be

[81] On this see Jaffey, 100 (1984) *L.Q.R.* 1980 and Mann, ibid. p. 369.

[82] That this is the function of the conflict of laws is, more or less clearly, stated in the first paragraph of every single book dealing with the subject. One of the clearest formulations is to be found in Martin Wolff, *Private International Law* (2nd edn., 1950), s. 1, who says that, 'if in the facts of the case there is some foreign element . . . then its legal repercussions can only be examined when the preliminary question as to the applicable law has been answered'. But Cheshire & North, *Private International Law* (10th edn., 1981), p. 3 also say in the first sentence of the book: 'That part of English law known as Private International Law comes into operation whenever the court is seised of a suit that contains a foreign element'.

applicable irrespective of any conflict rule, for there all law is statutory. No such suggestion has ever been made.

The foregoing submissions are by no means devoid of judicial and academic support. Admittedly it has often been suggested on the Continent[83] that uniform laws render the conflict of laws unnecessary, but the case of a contradiction between the statutory texts and the judicial interpretations in various countries has hardly ever been squarely faced. Nor has the general problem been much discussed in this country; in fact it is possible that there are only two statements which clearly propound an accurate assessment.[84] On the judicial level the Warsaw Convention fell to be considered by the Court of Appeal in a case in which the plaintiffs were the owners of two boxes of platinum which were flown by South African Airways from South Africa to London and there transferred to the defendants who were to fly them to the United States of America. Only one box arrived. The other one was held to have been stolen in London by a loader employed by the defendants. The Court of Appeal held that the defendant's servants acting within the scope of their employment had been guilty of wilful misconduct and that therefore the defendants were liable for the full value of the stolen box as provided for by Article 25 of the Warsaw Convention.[85] Eveleigh L. J. said:

> In my opinion the Warsaw Convention should be construed in accordance with the law which governs the contract of carriage, for the Convention is incorporated into that contract. In the present case it is agreed between the parties that the law applicable to the contract of carriage is South African law. No special evidence was called, however, as to the effect of South African law . . . and that being so,

[83] See, for instance, the Federal Supreme Court of Germany, above note 17, but see also note 55.

[84] Martin Wolff, *Private International Law* (2nd edn., 1950), s. 6, says that 'where such unified internal laws have been created, all problems of private international law disappear—unless the agreed rule is variously interpreted in the countries concerned'. And Sir Otto Kahn-Freund, *Hague Rec.* 143 (1974 iii), p. 193 says: 'Not as if such substantive unification obviated a recourse to the rules of private international law . . . Yet this unification of substantial portions of commercial law, whilst far from making conflict rules redundant, reduces the urgency of their unification in practice.'

[85] *Rustenberg Platinum Mines Ltd.* v. *Pan American Airways* [1979] 1 Lloyd's Rep. 19, commented upon by Mann (1979) 95 *LQR* 346. It is a pity that Dicey and Morris ignore this case and the compelling statement by Eveleigh L.J. at p. 24. The decision of Bingham J. in *Bofors-Uva* v. *Scandia Transport* [1982] 1 Lloyd's Rep. 410 is not very clear on the point which does not appear to have been argued. Goods were shipped from Sweden to England under a waybill to which the C.M.R. Convention applied and which was held to be subject to Swedish law and to provide for arbitration in Sweden. In interpreting the C.M.R. provisions the learned judge said that he was 'not, of course, applying Swedish law as the appropriate governing law for interpreting the Schedule to an English Act'. It is submitted that the thought underlying this sentence is incorrect. On the other hand there was no evidence that Swedish law on the point was different from English law. That point involved the question whether the reference to Swedish law (which has accepted the C.M.R. Convention) was a sufficient 'provision' within the meaning of Art. 33.

the court has to proceed on the basis that South African law is the same as English law. Thus we arrive at the position where the court has to decide whether, according to the rules of English law, this servant was acting with wilful misconduct within the scope of his employment.

On the question of principle one should perhaps also mention the important decision of the court in *Monterosso Shipping Co. Ltd.* v. *International Transport Workers Federation*,[86] which clearly proves that the applicability of an English statute depends on the proper law of the contract being English, and that, subject to statutory prohibition, illegality or public policy, a reasonable choice of law bona fide made overrides the mandatory rules of any other law and is the very essence of the doctrine of the proper law.

2. An exception to the proposed rules arises where the uniform law or the statute incorporating it lays down its own conflict rule which eliminates or restricts the parties's choice. Thus a special rule is included in the Australian Carriage of Goods by Sea Act which provides that the Hague Rules shall apply to every bill of lading issued in Australia without regard to any submission to a different system of law (section 9). A special conflict rule, though a limited one, is also supplied by Article 41 of the CMR Convention according to which 'any stipulation which would directly or indirectly derogate from the provisions of this Convention shall be null and void'. If, therefore, the parties agree that a contract for the carriage of goods by road which would normally be subject to the CMR Convention should be governed by the law of a country which has failed to adopt it, then such a choice of laws is null and void.[87] In such circumstances it is legitimate to speak of a choice of law being prohibited. The fact that provisions of a type well known to international practice have not been included in a particular uniform law should make it very difficult to read them into such a Convention (e.g. The Hague-Visby Rules).[88]

It should, however, be clearly appreciated that provisions which define and delimit the scope of the Convention or the statute adopting it do not come within the category now under discussion or involve the prohibition of a choice of law. Provisions which make application dependent upon the nationality of the parties, the type of carriage, cargo or shipment, the countries between which goods are carried or similar enactments are not conflict rules, but have a substantive character in that they indicate the scope of the Convention. They are not conflict rules, because they do not

[86] [1982] 3 All E.R. 841. For an earlier case see, e.g., *Sayers* v. *International Drilling Co.* [1971] 1 W.L.R. 1178.

[87] The principal English provision of the same type is s. 27 of the Unfair Contract Terms Act 1977 on which see Mann (1978) 27 *I.C.L.Q.* 661.

[88] But see below section 3 on the decision of the House of Lords in *The Hollandia* [1983] A.C. 565.

prescribe the application of a particular legal system or rule, but deal with the field of application of a Convention or statute known to be applicable.[89]

One of the most famous examples which has to be considered in the present context is Article X of the Hague Rules or, in an amended form, of the Hague-Visby Rules. The text of both versions leaves no doubt but that it does not constitute a conflict rule, as in fact academic writers have frequently pointed out.[90] Nor is there for present purposes any real difference between the two versions. According to the earlier version the Rules applied if the bill of lading was issued in a contracting State. The more recent version repeats this provision and adds the case of a carriage from a port in a contracting State. But since the bill of lading is almost invariably issued in the port of shipment, this addition cannot have much significance or, in particular, alter the character of the provisions in Article X. Nor should it make any difference that the Carriage of Goods by Sea Act 1924 did not incorporate Article X of the Hague Rules into English law, but that section 1 of the English statute rendered the Hague Rules applicable to shipments from any British port, while the Carriage of Goods by Sea Act 1971 merely refers to the Hague-Visby Rules, including Article X, to which it gives the force of law. *Pace* Dr Morris[91] the mere fact of transposition does not change the character of the provision. The incorporation of Article X as such means that the Hague-Visby Rules have a wider scope in that they cover a shipment, not merely from Britain, but from any contracting State. It ought not to mean that the widened scope dispenses with the precondition of the bill of lading being governed by English law. Dr Morris, it is true, suggests that the move of the self-limiting provision from the legislation implementing the Rules into the Rules themselves means 'that an English court would now hold the Rules to be applicable, e.g. to a shipment between two foreign contracting States'. If this means anything it is that Article X has become a conflict rule with the following unacceptable result: let us assume that both Brazil and Germany apply the Hague-Visby Rules, but Korea does not. A shipment from Rio de Janeiro to Hamburg on a Korean vessel under a bill of lading governed by Korean law, but providing for arbitration in London would be subject to the Rules, although neither German nor Brazilian nor

[89] On this type of self-limiting substantive provisions see Mann, *British Year Book of International Law* 1972–3, p. 117 at p. 121.

[90] See, for instance, Sir Otto Kahn-Freund, *Hague Rec.* 143 (1974 iii), p. 240; Stödter, *Liber Amicorum Algot Bagge* (Stockholm 1956), p. 220, 599; Schaps-Abraham, *Seerecht* (4th ed., 1978), s. 662, n. 8; Röper in Reithmann, *Internationales Vertragsrecht* (3rd edn., 1980), p. 395. That the Hague Rules apply only if the proper law of the contract so directs is well established in Germany and Holland. See Court of Appeal Hamburg, November 30, 1978, IPRspr. 1978 No. 36A and, on the other hand, Hoge Raad, May 13, 1966, *Rev. Crit.* 1967, 522 (shipment from Antwerp to Rio de Janeiro on Dutch vessel; choice of Dutch law valid).

[91] (1979) 95 *L.Q.R.* 59 599, especially at p. 64.

Korean law so permits. Or Dr Morris would have to hold that, although neither Germany nor Brazil nor Korea accept a construction of Article III (1) of the Rules, according to which a shipowner is liable for lack of seaworthiness resulting from an independent contractor's negligence, the English court or arbitrator would ignore the conflict rule and apply the English interpretation in the opposite sense.[92] No international or national legislator can have intended this. On the contrary, he was well aware of the Protocol of Signature to the Brussels Convention of 1924 and Article 16 of the Convention of 1968 both of which allow contracting States to include the Rules in their own legislation 'in a form appropriate to' it (and thus to perpetuate diversity).

3. No exception to the general rule should, however, be derived from the fact that when the English legislator adopts a Convention he gives it 'the force of law'. Such a phrase does not confer upon a uniform law a different or higher status than is enjoyed by any other rule of English common or statutory law and, in particular, does not exempt it from the operation of the conflict of laws or bring about the unacceptable consequence of making the *lex fori* paramount. Yet Dr Morris asserts it as 'the truth . . . that when an international Convention on the law of transport is given the force of law in the United Kingdom, its provisions apply to all disputes within its scope, regardless of the proper law of the contract'.[93]

For the reasons given this submission lacks persuasiveness, but in regard to the Carriage of Goods by Sea Act 1971 it seems, for the time being, to have been accepted as the *ratio decidendi* by the House of Lords in the case of *The Hollandia*.[94] Goods were shipped from Britain to a Dutch port on a Dutch vessel. The bill of lading provided for Dutch jurisdiction and the application of Dutch law. Both clauses were held to be null and void, for, as Holland has not adopted the Hague-Visby Rules, the shipowner's maximum liability was less than in England, so that the two clauses had the effect of lessening the shipowner's liability defined by the English Act of 1971. If in the present context one disregards the question of construction which arose and is referred to above,[95] one asks oneself how the House of Lords arrived at a result which, once again, is embodied in a single opinion

[92] On this see above, note 67. The discussion in the text is subject to the effect of the decision in *The Hollandia* [1983] A.C. 565, referred to in the following s. 3.

[93] Op. cit. above, note 91 at p. 66. It is difficult to understand why the statement is confined to Conventions on the law of transport. On p. 64 Dr Morris imputes to the present writer the view that if both Britain and Norway have adopted the Hague–Visby Rules and the bill of lading in respect of the shipment from Britain to Norway is subject to Norwegian law, it 'can escape the Rules'. Nothing of the kind was suggested. The only suggestion was that the choice of law prevails. If Norway has adopted the Hague–Visby Rules they apply, and they do so in their Norwegian incarnation or interpretation.

[94] [1983] A.C. 565. [95] See above note 16.

by Lord Diplock and which the House seems to have had singularly little difficulty in reaching, though the implications may be far-reaching.[96]

The difficulty lies in ascertaining how Lord Diplock came to apply English law, i.e. to ignore the conflict rule which by virtue of an unquestionably valid choice pointed to Dutch law. Although one is reminded of public policy, when Lord Diplock[97] rejects what nobody has ever suggested, viz. that it could be 'open to *any* shipowner to evade the provisions of Article II (8) by the simple device of inserting' *any* forum or choice of law clause,[98] the *ratio decidendi* cannot have been English public policy, which is not mentioned in the speech at all. It can only have been based on the existence of a statute which was interpreted as invalidating or prohibiting (*pro tanto*) any clause having the effect of lessening the shipowner's liability. The statutory character of the English rule was sufficient to displace the proper law of the contract. Such a conclusion would give rise to enormous problems—should the Sale of Goods Act 1979 prevail over a valid choice of law? Or did Lord Diplock regard Article X of the Hague-Visby Rules as a conflict rule or as a prohibition of a choice of law? An affirmative answer may have been intended, for in the last paragraph of the speech emphasis is put on 'the express inclusion in the Hague-Visby Rules of Article X (absent from the Hague Rules) expressly applying the Hague-Visby rules to every bill of lading falling within the description contained in the Article'.[99] Such an interpretation

[96] It is understood that at the beginning of the argument their Lordships announced that they had read the papers. The appellant's argument was allowed to take about three hours. The respondent's counsel was not called on.

[97] [1983] A.C. 565, 574. Italics supplied. The case in point was one where the genuineness, legality and customary character of the clause could not be doubted. See also below p. 294. The 'familiar "floodgates" argument' used by Lord Diplock has been rejected by Lord Fraser of Tullybelton and Lord Roskill in *Junior Books Ltd.* v. *Veitchi Co. Ltd* [1983] A.C. 520, 532, 539. In these circumstances there exists perhaps additional reason for surprise at Lord Roskill's concurrence with Lord Diplock's speech 'in all respects'.

[98] In so far as the conflict of laws is concerned Lord Diplock's speech in *The Hollandia* includes some remarkable dicta. (1) It is submitted that the possibility of a reference to Dutch law 'including its private international law' (p. 573) cannot in truth be envisaged. (2) If goods are shipped on a Dutch vessel to a Dutch port from a Scots port it is by no means certain that 'the proper law would prima facie at any rate be Scots law' (p. 573). (3) On p. 576 Lord Diplock seems to support the proposition that the validity of a choice of law depends on 'the law of the place where the contract was made' or on 'what, in the absence of such express clause, would be the proper law of the contract'. Such views are likely to be in conflict with accepted teachings. (4) In the last sentence of the speech, doubt is thrown on the meaning of 'wide-ranging dicta' in one of the greatest cases in English law decided by one of the strongest Judicial Committees ever formed, viz. the *Vita Food Products* case [1939] A.C. 277. The alleged obscurities were not specified.

[99] [1983] A.C. 565, 577. It should perhaps be made clear that in so far as 'the force of law' is concerned there is no difference between the Act of 1924 and that of 1971. The former employs the phrase in the Preamble and when in s. 1 it uses the words 'shall have effect' it does not mean anything different: *Vita Food Products* case [1939] A.C. 277, 287, *per* Lord Wright.

would attract the doubts expressed above about Dr Morris's views and provokes the further comment that in so far as shipments from Britain are concerned the Rules applied since 1924, it being irrelevant whether they applied by virtue of the statute or by virtue of the Convention having statutory force, but they had to be part of the proper law. Any 'distinction between the 1924 Act and the 1971 Act' or any 'contrast between the legislative techniques adopted in the two Acts' cannot, therefore, be in point. Or why did Lord Diplock emphasize that the '1971 Act deliberately abandoned what may conveniently be called the "clause paramount" technique employed in section 3 of the 1924 Act'?[100] This is a difference without a distinction, for the essential Article III (8) is identical in both Acts. Once more one can only conclude by regretting the absence of additional speeches.

PUBLIC POLICY

Irrespective of the proper law chosen by the parties the Hague-Visby Rules or, indeed, any uniform statute would be applicable in an English court in its English interpretation if public policy so required. This would be an instance of public policy in its positive form and occurs, in the words of Savigny,[101] where 'laws of a strictly positive, imperative nature' are involved.[102] One may admit that statutes may be expressive of public policy, but it is difficult to see why uniform statutes in general or statutes relating to international transport in particular[103] should be a matter of public policy.

The late Sir Otto Kahn-Freund, it is true, for many years described 'the policy of unification as a paramount international *ordre public*' and in somewhat general terms advocated resorting to it, when uniform statutes fall to be considered.[104] Similarly, in *The Hollandia*[105] Lord Denning M.R. in the Court of Appeal referred to 'the public policy which demands that in international trade all goods carried by sea should be subject to uniform rules'. But English courts have traditionally been most diffident in applying public policy, unless fundamental standards of morality, justice or welfare or, as has been very felicitously suggested, human rights were at stake.[106]

[100] [1983] A.C. at p. 577.

[101] *A Treatise on the Conflict of Laws* (translated by W. Guthrie), s. 349.

[102] Dicey and Morris at p. 22 speak of overriding statutes. The expression is unobjectionable except that it creates a special category of statutes only.

[103] They are being put into a separate class by Dicey and Morris at p. 842.

[104] See (1953) 39 *Transactions of the Grotius Society* 65, also to be found in *Selected Writings* at p. 256; *The Growth of Internationalism in English Private International Law* (Jerusalem, 1960), pp. 43–46.

[105] [1982] Q.B. 872 at p. 884.

[106] In this connection the European Convention on Human Rights may have to be considered.

The unification of law or of transport law in particular is a matter of 'political expediency' in the sense of Parke B.'s phrase.[107] Even in so far as it is a matter of legal policy it cannot be a matter of public policy in the eyes of anyone who remembers how inadequate, illusory and elusive unification is in the real world. In other words unification is an abstract ideal. In the concrete case what is or purports to be done in its name may often contribute to the intensification of diversity.

On the other hand it may be said that it is the specific provision in a uniform statute that should be treated as being expressive of public policy and therefore, requiring application in all situations. From this point of view it must be asked: can it really be a matter of English public policy that, for instance, a shipowner should be liable for each kilo of gross weight rather than for each package or unit lost or damaged? A question of this type (and many similar ones can be formulated), can, it is submitted, only be answered in the negative.

It is possible that an entirely different aspect of public policy was in Lord Diplock's mind, when, as mentioned above, he emphasized that it was not 'open to *any* shipowner to evade the provisions of Article III, rule 8 by the simple device of inserting in his bills of lading issued in, or for carriage from a port in, *any* contracting State'[108] a clause excluding the law of the port of shipment. The point is of such importance that it must be repeated that nobody has ever asserted the contrary. It cannot have been part of the appellant's case in *The Hollandia* to do so. A bill of lading governed by the law of the country to which the carrying vessel belongs and to which the goods are intended to be carried, is not to be condemned on the ground that it is an evasion or a device. It is a perfectly normal and legitimate clause universally used in international trade, embodied in numerous standard forms and supported by weighty reasons of commerical requirements and expectations. The point relates, not to public policy, but to the limits of the parties' freedom of choice. No theory, no form of words has ever been put forward with a view to restricting that freedom in the circumstances underlying the decision in issue. How the limits are to be defined does not need discussion in the present context.[109]

JURISDICTION CLAUSES

Many uniform statutes define the courts in which actions arising from their terms may be brought. Article 31 of the CMR Convention is an example:

[107] *Egerton* v. *Brownlow* (1953) 5 H.L. Cas. 1. 123.

[108] See above, note 97.

[109] On this problem see Mann (1950) *International Law Quarterly* 60, 597; Morris, ibid. at p. 297. It should be emphasized that the problem of evasion is entirely outside the scope of this article.

actions may be brought in the court of a contracting country designated by agreement between the parties, in the place of the defendant's ordinary residence or place of business or the place where the goods were taken over by the carrier or where delivery is to take place. Similarly, Article 28 of the Warsaw Convention on transport by air allows actions to be brought in four jurisdictions. Such rules are of a procedural character and will always have to be applied by a court in a contracting State even in the absence of a provision such as Article 41 of the CMR Convention or Article 32 of the Warsaw Convention which prohibit deviations. Where the uniform statutes do not include provisions of this type, they ought not to be implied on the ground that the statute is mandatory and its implementation could be impeded or evaded by a forum clause. The very fact that, against the background of so many uniform statutes regulating jurisdiction, a particular uniform statute does not include a forum clause precludes, it is submitted, any interpretation limiting freedom of contract.

The problem is by no means confined to uniform statutes, but is a general one.[110] Its correct solution has been most impressively demonstrated by the Supreme Court of the United States in the great case of *The Bremen*:[111] a German company undertook with an American corporation to tow a drilling rig from Louisiana to Italy. The contract which included certain exemption clauses contrary to the public policy of the United States and invalid there provided for the decision of disputes by the High Court of Justice in London. The Supreme Court, in an opinion delivered by Chief Justice Burger, held that the forum clause was valid, 'unless enforcement is shown by the resisting party to be unreasonable'. Such a refusal could not be based on the fact that the English court would give effect to the exemption clauses; the effectiveness of the forum clause was excluded only in the event of enforcement contravening 'a strong public policy of the forum in which suit is brought, whether declared by statute or by judicial decision'. Another telling example of international practice is a decision of the Federal Supreme Court of Germany.[112] A German, resident and working in Germany, was the commercial agent of a Dutch industrial enterprise. His contract was terminated and under mandatory provisions of German law he became entitled to compensation. When he brought proceedings in Germany, the defendant Dutch company relied on a clause in the contract according to which the Dutch courts had jurisdiction and Dutch law (denying compensation) applied. The action failed. The court assumed that in the absence of special terms German courts

[110] The literature is considerable. It must suffice to refer to Sir Otto Kahn-Freund (1977) 26 *I.C.L.Q.* 825, who mentions many earlier writers.

[111] 407 US 1 (1972), particularly at pp. 15, 16 and see the English counterpart, *Unterweser Reederei G.m.b.H.* v. *Zapata Off-Shore Co.* [1968] 2 Lloyd's Rep. 158, both noted at (1972) 88 *L.Q.R.* 472.

[112] NJW 1961, 1061 (30 January 1961).

would have had jurisdiction, German law would have applied and the defendant had intended to eliminate the German provisions about compensation. It also assumed that there could be circumstances in which the clause would have been unreasonable. Yet the connection with Holland was close and constituted 'grounds which justified the defendant in wishing to submit the contract with the plaintiff to Dutch law and jurisdiction'. It is believed that the reasoning of both the American and the German decision is exemplary.

In the case of uniform statutes the same reasoning should prevail, but the picture is much more blurred. The controversy primarily relates to the Hague and Hague-Visby Rules of 1924 and of 1968 respectively. Neither of them deals with jurisdiction. It is apparently only the Australian Act according to section 9 of which any term 'purporting to oust or lessen the jurisdiction of the courts of the Commonwealth or of a State in respect of the bill of lading or document shall be illegal, null and void, and of no effect'. Notwithstanding this model the American Carriage of Goods Act 1936 does not contain a similar term. For this very reason an excellent decision by three judges of the Court of Appeals, Second Circuit, in 1955 held that forum clauses were not inconsistent with the Act or the Hague Rules.[113] In 1967, however, nine judges of the Court of Appeals, Second Circuit, imputed to the legislator the intention to invalidate forum clauses in a bill of lading if they excluded an available jurisdiction of an American court.[114] Belgian courts, particularly the commercial tribunal in Antwerp, have taken a similar line.[115] On the other hand the French Cour de Cassation[116] as well as numerous Courts of Appeal[117] and the supreme

[113] *W. H. Muller & Co. Inc.* v. *Swedish American Line Ltd.*, 224 F. 2d 806 (1955).

[114] *Indussa Corporation* v. *The Ramborg*, 377 F. 2d 200 (1967). It is not impossible that the court felt that in the circumstances of the case the forum clause was 'unreasonable', but the decision is being applied generally and without regard to the implications of the decision in *The Bremen* 407 U.S. 1 (1972). See, e.g., *Northern Assurance Co.* v. *Caspian Career* [1971] *American Maritime Cases* 421; *Misui Co. Ltd.* v. *The Glory River* 464 F. Supp. 1004 (1978); *Pacific Lumber & Shipping Co.* v. *The Star Shipping*, ibid. at p. 1314, where a clause for arbitration in London was set aside.

[115] Cass., 9 June 1932, Pas. 1932 I 183 (goods shipped from Antwerp to Turkey on German vessel; bill of lading providing for German law and jurisdiction; Belgian law held to be *d'ordre public*); Cass., 19 December 1946, Pas. 1946 I 480 (goods shipped from Belgium to Hamburg; bill of lading subject to Belgian law, but jurisdiction of Hamburg courts; held valid, because no reason to think that Hamburg courts would not apply Belgian law); Trib. Brussels, 7 December 1972; Jur. Anv. 1973, 103; Com, Antwerp, 29 May 1973, Jur, Anv. 1974, 250; 4 September 1973, ibid., 1973, 360, 365; Trib. Brussels, 31 October 1974, Droit Europ. Transp. 1975, 50; Com. Antwerp, 8 April 1975, Jur. Anv. 1974, 380; 15 April 1975, ibid. 1975–76, 84; 16 September 1976, ibid., 1976, 453, and many other cases.

[116] Cass. Com., 7 July 1969, *Droit Maritime Français* (1969), p. 671: shipment from Portugal to France on Portuguese vessel; bill of lading providing for exclusive jurisdiction of Lisbon court, held valid.

[117] Court of Appeal Rouen, 14 November 1978, D.M.F. 1979, 274: shipment on Moroccan vessel from Rouen to Casablanca. Bill of lading provides for exclusive jurisdiction of

tribunals of Holland[118] and Germany[119] have decided in the opposite sense and allowed forum clauses, sometimes in circumstances which were quite remarkable. Thus in Germany the forum clause was enforced even if the judgment of the agreed court was not enforceable in Germany, one of the reasons being that 'the internationally usual clauses about jurisdiction in regard to bills of lading regularly determine the court at the carrier's principal seat of business as having jurisdiction' and in the interest of international practices this had to be respected.[120]

Until recently there was strong reason to believe that English law was to the same effect. The binding character of jurisdiction clauses has often been emphasized[121] and in relation to the Hague Rules of 1924 a decision of the Court of Appeal of 1927[122] was widely understood to express the same principle. Goods were shipped from England to Bombay; the bill of lading contained the usual clause conferring jurisdiction on the courts of the place of destination. The action brought by the consignees in England was dismissed, Scrutton L.J. saying: 'The only difference is a question of procedure—where shall the law be enforced?—and I do not read any clause as to procedure as lessening liability'. The point did not arise again

Moroccan courts in the form of the Conlinebill (Baltic and International Maritime Conference). Held valid, because Hague Rules do not forbid forum clauses. In the same sense Court of Appeal, Paris, 11 March 1963, D.M.F. 1964, 375; Rouen, 1 December 1977, ibid. 1978, 590; 15 May 1979, ibid., 1980, 469; 28 August 1979, ibid., 1979, 604 (goods shipped on Belgian vessel from Beira to Le Havre; bill of lading providing for jurisdiction of Belgian courts; held valid and excluding French jurisdiction); Court of Appeal, Paris, 27 June 1980, DMF 1981, 85 (goods shipped from Marseilles to Mauretania on Spanish vessel; bill of lading providing for Spanish law and jurisdiction; held 'que le Convention de Bruxelles ne comporte, en ce qui concerne la comptence, aucune clause dérogatoire au droit commun francais ainsi qu'il resulte des terms de l'article 14 de cette Convention'); 6 December 1980, ibid. 1981, 85.

[118] Hoge Raad, 13 May 1966, *Rev. Crit.* 1967, 522.

[119] 8 December 1968, IPRspr. 1968/9 No. 198 (shipment from USA to Hamburg, so that Hague Rules as understood in Germany applied; Dutch carrier issued bill of lading; 'all questions . . . shall be settled in and in accordance with laws of the country of carrying company.'); 12 February 1970, ibid. No. 112; 21 December 1970, NJW 1971, 325; 8 February 1971, NJW 1971, 985; 9 December 1973, IPRspr. 1973, No. 128b (shipment from Bangkok to Hamburg, so that Hague Rules as applied in Germany prevailed; proper law German, but exclusive jurisdiction Bangkok); Court of Appeal Hamburg, 12 February 1970, IPRspr. 1970, No. 112a, affirmed on other grounds by the decision of 21 December 1970. In one case, however, the Supreme Court treated it as relevant whether the foreign court would apply the Hague Rules: 'In view of the purpose of the law the protection of the mandatory provisions of the Hague Rules must be guaranteed for the German consignee. In this sense the forum clause cannot be held valid irrespective of the foreign court's decision'. 3 December 1973, IPRspr. 1973, No. 128b.

[120] See the decision of 21 December 1970 mentioned in the preceding note.

[121] See Dicey and Morris at p. 255 with references.

[122] *Maharani Woollen Mills Co.* v. *Anchor Line* (1927) 29 Ll.L.R. 169, followed by Scarman J. (as he then was) and by the Court of Appeal in *The Merak* [1965] p. 223. Both cases were referred to by the Court of Appeal, but disregarded in Lord Diplock's speech.

until *The Hollandia*[123] was decided in 1982 under the Carriage of Goods by Sea Act 1971 (which in this respect is in no way different from the Act of 1924). It will be remembered that the House of Lords was concerned with a clause in a bill of lading which in relation to a shipment from Scotland to a Dutch port on a Dutch vessel provided for Dutch jurisdiction and law.[124] Both parts of the clause were considered 'colourable devices'[125] designed to lessen the carrier's liability. As regards the forum clause in particular, the choice of the carrier's and the place of destination's forum was described as 'a court of convenience, viz. one situated in a country which did not apply the Hague–Visby Rules or, for that matter, a country whose law recognised an unfettered right of a shipowner by the terms of the bill of lading to relieve himself from all liability'.[126] In a further passage, Lord Diplock said that if the dispute was about duties referred to in Article III (8) and if the foreign country would award a lower sum than envisaged by Article IV (5) of the Hague–Visby Rules 'then an English court is in my view commanded by the 1971 Act to treat the choice of forum clause as of no effect'.[127] It is most important to realize that there is no difference between the Hague and the Hague–Visby Rules on the point of principle; the latter certainly calculate the compensation differently, but even under the Hague Rules which continue to apply in all but about a dozen countries in the world other differences on numerous points could have arisen. Yet a wide range of countries has given effect to the clause employed by *The Hollandia* and described by the Federal Supreme Court of Germany as the 'internationally usual' one, though in the eyes of the House of Lords it was a 'colourable device'. One cannot help coming back to the same point which in England more than elsewhere one would have expected to be a compelling one: in the case of a uniform statute more than in any other it is impermissible to imply clauses which could have been, but are not included in it, or to allow the ultimate or indirect 'effect' of a contractual provision to override the text of the statute or to treat as a colourable device a clause which has much practical advantage to commend it. But the most unfortunate consequence is that a kind of legal chauvinism ensures the reign of English law and courts whereas international tolerance used to be the hallmark of English commercial law.

[123] [1983] A.C. 565.

[124] The clause also reproduced a provision of Dutch law limiting liability in accordance with the Hague Rules. This did not add anything to the reference to Dutch law as the proper law.

[125] [1983] A.C. 565, 573. It is very difficult to understand how commercial lawyers of great experience could come to accept this characterization. Numerous forms of bills of lading that are in general use and numerous judicial decisions have accepted a reference to the law and the courts of the ship's nationality (and of the place of destination) as the most appropriate choice of law. This is so for strong practical reasons.

[126] Ibid. at p. 574G.

[127] Ibid. at p. 575D.

It should, however, be remembered that, when section 2 of the Civil Jurisdiction and Judgments Act 1982 is put into effect, Article 17 of the 1968 Convention is likely, as between the member States of the EEC, to supersede the law laid down by the House of Lords; Article 57 will not apply, because the Hague–Visby Rules are not a Convention which governs jurisdiction. Moreover, not even the House of Lords asserted the invalidity of the prorogation agreement as such or for all purposes.

ARBITRATION CLAUSES

Arbitration clauses are also a subject which many uniform statutes specifically deal with. Thus reference may once more be made to the CMR Convention which allows an arbitration clause to be included in a contract of carriage on condition that it provides that the tribunal shall apply the Convention. Apart from such express terms arbitration clauses should, in general, have the same fate as forum clauses. Since, however, most countries in the world are members of the New York Convention on arbitration, section 1 (1) of the Arbitration Act 1975 will, in regard to bills of lading, cause a serious problem in England, for where there is an international arbitration agreement, the court is required to stay proceedings. Is it the consequence of *The Hollandia* that where a bill of lading issued in Scotland in respect of a shipment from Britain to the Netherlands on a Dutch vessel provides for arbitration in Amsterdam proceedings brought in England are to be stayed, while in the event of an agreement on the jurisdiction of Dutch courts the English action can proceed? It would be an odd inconsistency and it is not certain whether Lord Diplock gave a convincing answer to it. He seemed to assume that there would also be a choice-of-law clause and continued:[128]

> But if the particular choice of substantive law made by the express clause is such as to make the clause null and void under the law of the place where the contract was made, or under what, in the absence of such express clause, would be the proper law of the contract, I am very far from accepting that it would be open to the arbitrator to treat the clause as being otherwise than null and void or to give any effect to it.

This would seem to mean that in the assumed circumstances the English court would refuse to stay the proceedings on the ground that the arbitration clause was null and void under English law. Since *ex hypothesi* English law would not be the proper law (for the arbitration clause is

[128] Ibid. at p. 576D.

presumed to import a reference to Dutch law)[129] and since validity is governed by the proper law,[130] invalidity could only be based on the clause being contrary to English public policy or being prohibited by statute. For the reasons given, the former argument would constitute a radical departure from tradition, while the latter one cannot be supported by the Hague-Visby (or the Hague) Rules as formulated by the international legislator, but is likely to prevail in the English courts in the curious *pro tanto* fashion discovered by Lord Diplock. The argument seems to imply that whenever a choice of law clause, a forum clause or an arbitration clause would have *the effect* of a departure from the law on bills of lading as laid down in the Carriage of Goods by Sea Act 1971 and as understood and applied in England it is *to that extent* null and void. It is submitted that this would be an extravagant and at the same time a parochial conclusion,[131] which affects international trade with unusual intensity and the implications of which will have to be worked out over many years.[132]

If, following Belgian and rejecting Dutch, French and German practice, the House of Lords had founded its decision (which rests on arguments equally applicable to the Hague Rules)[133] on public policy and clearly defined the circumstance and scope of its application, one could have become reconciled with the result, however regrettable the introduction

[129] Dicey and Morris at p. 1127, notes 28 and 29.

[130] Ibid. at p. 1127, note 27.

[131] The idea of partial nullity which Lord Diplock applied in *The Hollandia* [1983] A.C. 565, and which he had already developed in the *United City Merchants (Investment) Ltd.* case [1983] A.C. 168 is novel, not supported by the text of any statutory rule, difficult to apply in practice and almost arbitrary in character. A search for any precedent has been unsuccessful. The idea of severability is something quite different: nullity of a clause leaves the rest of the contract intact. Here partial nullity means that although the statute prescribes the total invalidity of a certain clause or contract an entirely different clause or contract is held to be invalid only if, when and in so far as it may lead to the result of the proscribed clause or contract being upheld. It is submitted that the fundamental reason for so surprising a theory lies in the neglect of the principles of statutory interpretation which do not permit the radical deviation from the text or the disregard of general rules of the conflict of laws. The comparable case of *The Bremen*, 407 U.S. 1 (1972) is inspired by much more traditional ideas.

[132] The final question which apparently has not ever or anywhere been discussed is whether the nullity of 'any clause, covenant or agreement in a contract of carriage' attracts the nullity of the whole contract evidenced by the bill of lading so as to subject the contract to the general law applicable where no bill of lading is issued, or whether the contract evidenced by the bill of lading less the offending clause remains in force. Nor is there any material on the problem of ascertaining the legal system which provides the answer to that question. It is submitted that the proper law should apply, and that if this is English the nullity of one clause is likely to involve the nullity of the written contract as a whole so as to hold the parties to their common law rights and duties.

[133] For this reason the points made in the last paragraph of Lord Diplock's speech do not, it is respectfully submitted, constitute a convincing answer. The change in legislative technique or the amendment of Article X were not the *ratio decidendi* of the decision of the House of Lords. This is to be found exclusively in Art. III, r. 8 which exists since 1924.

into English law of what are believed to be repugnant ideas would have been. The gravamen of the grievance is that the interpretative approach as well as the basis and reach of the decision are lacking principled explanation and analysis.[134,135]

[134] The unacceptable implications of *The Hollandia* are vividly illustrated by Sheen J.'s decision in *The Benarty*, (1983) 2, Ll.L.R. 50. Goods were shipped at Hamburg, Bremerhaven, Antwerp, Cherbourg and London for carriage to Indonesia on a British ship chartered by Indonesians. At each port the Indonesian charterers issued bills of lading providing for the exclusive jurisdiction of Indonesian courts and the application of Indonesian law. Neither the Hague nor the Hague–Visby Rules apply in Indonesia. The Hague Rules apply in Germany, the Hague–Visby Rules apply in Belgium, France and Britain. The learned Judge applied the Carriage of Goods by Sea Act 1971 and disregarded the express choice of forum and law. It is difficult to think of a more extreme case. To impose British legislation upon German, Belgian and French shippers and Indonesian carriers may be a misapplication of *The Hollandia*, but proves the unprincipled character of the latter decision.

[135] See now (1987) 103 *L.Q.R.* 526.

11
The State Immunity Act 1978

ON 22 November 1978[1] the State Immunity Act 1978 came into force. Its purpose, according to its long title, is 'to make new provision with respect to proceedings in the United Kingdom by or against other States; to provide for the effect of judgments given against the United Kingdom in the courts of States parties to the European Convention on State Immunity; to make new provision with respect to the immunities and privileges of heads of State; and for connected purposes'.

As the Act makes 'new provision', it is a remedial statute.[2] It initiates a new era in the field of sovereign immunity in English law, an era which will throw up problems of a new and different kind that have to be solved by way of statutory interpretation. The Act thus constitutes a break with the past. While the past may, but is unlikely to, have relevance for such purposes as, for instance, the identification of the mischief the Act intends to eliminate, and while the old law will retain its significance in connection with the immunity of international organizations to which the Act does not apply, in principle the new legislation must stand on its own feet. Certainly it will not always be easy to say where the Act intends to preserve and where it intends to break with the past. It will, therefore, be much easier to read it without regard to the history preceding it.[3] On the other hand this supplies the material, the experience, the factual situations which are liable to arise and against which the new Act has to be tested.

In this particular case, however, earlier precedents may have another function of a more academic character. The present article can only mention, but cannot explore them. During the hundred years or so before 1978 or, to be more precise, before 1976, when the Judicial Committee of the Privy Council, and before 1977, when the Court of Appeal with a most remarkable judgment of Lord Denning M.R. (which will for ever remain a landmark of a quite unique kind) brought about a strong change of direction, the development of the law relating to sovereign immunity

[1] SI 1978, No. 1572. By SI 1979, No. 458, operative since 2 May 1979, the Act was extended to overseas territories, particularly Hong Kong.

[2] See Craies, *Statute Law* (7th edn., 1971), p. 60.

[3] See, generally, *Bank of England* v. *Vagliano*, [1891] A.C. 107, at p. 145 *per* Lord Herschell.

British Year Book of International Law (Oxford, 1979), 43–62.

showed the common law or rather the principle of precedent at its worst. Its alleged flexibility had, in the field of sovereign immunity, given place to a most regrettable and, it is believed, avoidable ossification and positivism. The principle of precedent had become something in the nature of a cage of words. It precluded a consideration of modern conditions and of the realities of structural changes in world trade. It allegedly compelled the courts to heed a formula rather than the requirements of justice or sometimes even of logic. It did so unnecessarily, because international law is, or ought to be, treated as being different from municipal law and could have been so treated if the courts had had the strength of mind which comes from reflection rather than adherence to verbiage. An observer who for forty years has on many occasions tried to draw attention to the wrong turns taken by, and, indeed, the isolation of, English law and who has lived to see a brighter path to the future, may be forgiven if he emphasizes the great jurisprudential lesson which can be learned from a study of the case law relating to sovereign immunity before 1978. It covers a relatively small, self-contained field which invites analysis of the reasoning put forward by the courts, its strength, its unspoken motivation, its respect for the rule, its underlying idea, its true scope as opposed to the adherence to textual narrowness. The outcome of such an investigation, it must be feared, would by no means be a tribute to or evidence of the progressiveness and the imaginative foresight of the English judiciary of the twentieth century.

If, then, the earlier law is highly significant from the point of view of jurisprudence, but almost immaterial to the interpretation of the Act, it will suffice very shortly to survey the road leading up to it. The main effect can be directed to the explanation of the principle established by the Act and the ten exceptions to it; the latter are of varying importance in practice and frequently will not justify more than a few words. The final parts will have to devote some attention to a number of procedural matters, though care will have to be taken not to present too detailed and, therefore, somewhat uninviting a commentary upon the statute.

BACKGROUND

For almost a hundred years the law of sovereign immunity was dominated by the decision of the Court of Appeal in *The Parlement Belge*.[4] The action was one *in rem* against a mail packet running between Ostend and Dover, belonging to and being in the possession and control of the King of the Belgians and officered by officers of the Royal Belgian navy. Not

[4] (1880) 5 P.D. 197.

surprisingly, in a judgment delivered by Brett L. J., the Court of Appeal held[5] that it lacked jurisdiction 'over the person of any sovereign . . . of any other State, or over the public property of any State which is destined to its public use' and that in an action *in rem* the owner of the ship was 'indirectly impleaded' in that 'the liability to compensation must be fixed not merely on the property but also on the owner through the property'. This was and has remained sound law. Nothing in the formulation of the decision went beyond the four corners of the case before the court or was required or permitted to be understood as a text of inflexible strictness comprehending many different sets of facts.

It was, however, in this sense that it was understood when forty years later the Court of Appeal, consisting of Bankes, Warrington and Scrutton L.JJ., had to decide *The Porto Alexandre*,[6] another Admiralty action *in rem*. The ship, either the property of or requisitioned by the Government of Portugal, carried a cargo of cork shavings to Liverpool under a bill of lading from which it appeared that the cargo was shipped by and consigned to a private company. The argument that the ship was engaged in 'an ordinary commercial undertaking as an ordinary trading vessel carrying goods for a private individual' was held not to be capable of displacing what was believed to be the rule laid down in *The Parlement Belge*. Such was the case which established the English rule of absolute immunity: the State as trader was no different from the State as sovereign.

Six years later, on 10 April 1926, there was signed in Brussels, by the United Kingdom among many other States, the International Convention for the Unification of Certain Rules concerning the Immunity of State-owned Ships; it was supplemented in 1934.[7] Its principal effect was to overturn the rule of absolute immunity as established by *The Porto Alexandre*.[8] But the United Kingdom failed to ratify it. The reasons have remained obscure and are not made clearer by the Interim Report on State immunities which an Inter-Departmental Committee headed by Sir Donald Somervell, then a Lord Justice, rendered in July 1951. It has not been published, but through the courtesy of the Lord Chancellor's Department this writer was allowed to see and use it. The Committee made the surprising statement[9] that the 'Convention has not been ratified by His Majesty's Government, not, as we understand, because its principles were objected to but because difficulties arose with regard to the necessary legislation in Northern Ireland'. What these difficulties were and why they had to prevent ratification has not been explained. It was only on 3 July 1979 that the United Kingdom ratified the Convention, which entered into force six months later (Cmnd. 7800).

[5] Pp. 214, 215, 217, 218. [6] [1920] P. 30. [7] Cmd. 5672 and 5673.
[8] Above, n. 6. [9] Paragraph 13.

The doctrine of unrestricted immunity, introduced and applied without regard to developments abroad, continued to prevail in the United Kingdom with inexorable rigidity: *vide*, for instance, *The Cristina*,[10] a case in which the Spanish Government of General Franco had, by force, used in implementing the decree of requisition, taken possession of a ship lying in Cardiff harbour. A high-water mark was reached by *Krajina v. The Tass Agency*.[11] The plaintiff claimed damages for a libel contained in *The Soviet Monitor* which the defendants had published through their London office, this having been registered in the Register of Business Names set up under the Registration of Business Names Act 1916. Yet the Tass Agency was treated as a department of the Soviet Union and the plea of immunity was upheld. The decision led to some public disquiet and on 23 November 1949 a debate took place in the House of Lords[12] in the course of which the Lord Chancellor, Earl Jowitt, acknowledged the existence of the grave problem 'whether the law of this country affords to organs of foreign States a wider immunity than is desirable or strictly required by the principles of international law observed in the countries of the world'. He announced the setting-up of an Inter-Departmental Committee to consider and report on the question. In due course Sir Donald Somervell was appointed Chairman and among the nine members were Sir Hersch Lauterpacht, Professor Hamson, Sir Eric Beckett, Sir Denis Dodson, Sir Kenneth Roberts-Wray and Sir Robert Speed. The Committee reported on 13 July 1951. It was only on 13 February 1953 that Mr Nutting, then Under-Secretary of State for Foreign Affairs, announced in the House of Commons[13] that the Committee had found 'such great divergencies in state practice as to make it difficult to establish the exact position under international law'. He continued as follows:

> In view of the differing opinions among the members of the Committee as to what principles it would be best to follow the Committee was unable to reach any final conclusions or make any final recommendations. Since it is clear that further study would not achieve any different result, it has been decided not to call upon the Committee for any further or final report and the Committee must now therefore be regarded as *functus officio*.

In fact it appears that all members reached 'the conclusion that the present law of the United Kingdom grants a greater immunity than is in fact granted by a large number of other States'.[14] But 'on the question as to

[10] [1938] A.C. 485.
[11] [1949] 2 All E.R. 274, noted *Modern Law Review*, 12 (1949), p. 494.
[12] *Hansard*, H.L. Debs., vol. 165, col. 940.
[13] *Hansard*, H.C. Debs., vol. 511, col. 81
[14] Paragraph 21.

what is required by international law we differ'.[15] In particular the Committee did not find 'the *jure gestionis* principle capable of formulation'[16] or, as they said in another place and as in the light of later developments is worthy of quotation in full,[17]

> Although the principle of *jure gestionis* undoubtedly suggests the approach to the problem if there is to be a limitation, we are all agreed that regarded as a principle it presents great difficulties. It is not a principle which, even if justified by international law (and on this point, on our present information, we differ), could be incorporated into our law as a principle. Some countries have sought to apply such a principle in their municipal law and have encountered great difficulties. The raising of State loans, the purchase of arms, the purchase of the raw materials for arms or of other goods for the public services, of food necessary for the civilian population, all these might be regarded as acts done in the exercise of sovereign powers. If a change is to be made in the law as applied in this country it would not in our view be practicable simply to leave the courts to work out this principle.

The only positive suggestion which the Committee felt able to make was that there should be discussions with Commonwealth countries, with the United States of America and perhaps one or two other countries.[18]

After this singular failure of eminent men to reach anything approaching a measure of agreement or a constructive solution it took more than twenty years to find a stepping-stone leading to reform. While the courts of the United Kingdom, in one case in the face of a memorable dissent by Lord Denning,[19] adhered to their rules of absolute immunity with remarkable inflexibility and fervent faith in the rigidity of a formula,[20] the Council of Europe took up the subject and in 1972, after innumerable meetings in Strasbourg, produced its Convention on State Immunity which the United Kingdom signed.[21] Almost simultaneously the United States of America produced a Draft Bill,[22] which on 21 October 1976 became the Foreign Sovereign Immunities Act 1976 and entered into force on 19 January 1977.[23] Also in 1976 the Judicial Committee of the Privy Council, in an

[15] Paragraph 22. [16] Paragraph 26. [17] Paragraph 5.

[18] Paragraph 7.

[19] *Rahimtoola* v. *Nizam of Hyderabad*, [1958] A.C. 379, noted *Modern Law Review*, 21 (1958), p. 165. Much later Lord Denning said about his opinion in that case: 'I took more pains about it than any other case in which I have taken part'. See the case mentioned in the following note at p. 1492.

[20] The last case before the break was *Thai-Europe Tapioca Service Ltd* v. *Government of Pakistan*, [1975] 1 W.L.R. 1485.

[21] Cmnd. 5081. The United Kingdom has not yet ratified the Convention, but it is understood that it will do so. Its substance, however, has been enacted in the State Immunity Act 1978. Absence of ratification would reduce the value of the Convention as a guide to construction. Yet, since it is referred to in the long title, it would in any case seem to be an admissible guide.

[22] *International Legal Materials*, 15 (1976), p. 88. [23] Ibid., p. 1388.

Admiralty action *in rem*,[24] changed the laws both of Hong Kong and of this country[25] by denying immunity to a trading vessel of a foreign sovereign—a sensational development in light of the fact that on the one hand in an action *in rem* in which the defendant has appeared 'the claim is against him personally'[26] and on the other hand 'it may fairly be said to be at the least unlikely'[27] that the House of Lords would eliminate the 'illogical result' produced by distinguishing between actions *in rem* and actions *in personam*. The final point of judicial development occurred early in 1977, when Lord Denning M.R. and Shaw L.J., Stephenson L. J., dissenting, decided that even if the defendant Central Bank of Nigeria was a department of State it was not entitled to immunity in respect of a commercial transaction such as a letter of credit;[28] an appeal to the House of Lords was compromised shortly before the date fixed for the hearing.

This, in summary, was the state of the law when the State Immunity Act 1978 passed through Parliament and became law on 20 July 1978. Most of its provisions do not have retrospective effect,[29] yet it will only be on rare occasions that the old law will again have to be considered in the United Kingdom.

PERSONAL IMMUNITY

The principle established by the Act is the classical one: it is the foreign[30] State that is immune from the jurisdiction of the courts.[31] The Act does not speak of a sovereign State. On the existence of a State (and of many other international facts) the Secretary of State's certificate is conclusive evidence;[32] the question whether an unrecognized State is entitled to immunity will, therefore, not come up for judicial decision and it is quite possible that in a given case the Secretary of State's certificate may, in effect, be able to answer that question in the affirmative and thus, contrary to traditional learning, withdraw a point of law from judicial decision—an unfortunate and, possibly, objectionable[33] result. The beneficiaries of immunity, however, comprise a number of defendants other than a State. Their definition invites a few comments.

[24] *The Philippine Admiral*, [1977] A.C. 373, noted *Law Quarterly Review*, 92 (1976), p. 166.

[25] In this sense Robert Goff J. in *Congreso del Partido* [1978] 1 All E.R. 1169, at pp. 1184, 1185.

[26] *The Cristina*, [1938] A.C. 485, at p. 492 *per* Lord Atkin, noted *Modern Law Review*, 2 (1938), p. 57.

[27] See above, n. 25.

[28] *Trendtex Trading Corporation Ltd.* v. *Central Bank of Nigeria*, [1977] Q.B. 529.

[29] S. 23 (3).

[30] This includes a Commonwealth State: s. 14.

[31] S. 1.

[32] S. 21.

[33] If and in so far as the Foreign and Commonwealth Office purports to decide a question of law there may be a violation of Art. 6 of the European Convention on Human Rights.

1. The reference to a State includes, of course, its sovereign 'in his public capacity'[34] (who and whose family shall enjoy the benefit of the Diplomatic Privileges Act 1964[35]) as well as the government and its departments. No serious difficulties are likely to arise in respect of these defendants.

2. Immunity is also enjoyed by an *entity*, i.e. a body capable of suing and being sued, which is not distinct from, that is to say, is part of, the executive organs of the government.[36] This is to be distinguished from a *separate entity*, i.e. a body capable of suing and being sued and distinct from the executive organs of the government; such an entity is immune only in certain circumstances to be considered later.

The Act, therefore, does not attach significance to the question whether under its own law the entity is a body corporate, a legal person, or not. It is possible that the entity meets the test of the prescribed procedural status, although it is not a body corporate in the English sense. The Act accepts the decision of a majority of the Court of Appeal[37] according to which a legal entity is entitled to immunity if in substance it is a department of State. The frequently difficult question of whether or not a body is a corporate one has become irrelevant.

Whether the entity which is capable of suing and being sued is 'distinct from the executive organs of the government' is a question of fact and depends on foreign law, viz. the status which the foreign law confers upon the entity rather than the factual situation. If the entity is intended by the legislator to be distinct, then the fact that it acts in accordance with the directions of the government does not matter. Conversely, if the entity is not intended by the law to be distinct, its actual independence of government organs cannot deprive it of immunity.

It is distinctness from executive organs that matters. Accountability to Parliament or parliamentary organs such as a Public Accounts Committee is immaterial. And the distinctness, it is believed, must be of an organizational character in the sense that the test is provided by the existence of the right of executive organs to give directions about the conduct of the entity's daily business. Political independence is a different and irrelevant point: the entity may have to observe the general lines of the government's policy, yet be distinct from its executive organs. In practice it will probably be helpful to ask whether in substance the entity is a department of government or carries on its business independently, albeit in line with general government policy.

3. *Constituent territories of a federal State* have been dealt with somewhat oddly. As a rule they are treated as if they were a separate entity

[34] S. 14 (1) (a). [35] S. 20. [36] S. 14 (1).

[37] *Baccus SA* v. *Nacional del Trigo* [1957] 1 QB. 438 (Jenkins and Parker L.JJ. Singleton L.J. dissenting), noted *Modern Law Review*, 20 (1957), p. 273.

except that section 12 relating to service of process and judgments in default of appearance applies to them in any case. An Order in Council, however, may provide for other provisions to apply as they apply to a State.[38] This creates uncertainty and exposes a legal question to political influence and pressure, but in view of an unsatisfactory provision of the European Convention[39] the British legislator probably had to adopt some such solution.

A corporation which is 'part and parcel' of a department or an arm of the government of a constituent territory, such as the New Brunswick Development Corporation was found to be in relation to the Province of New Brunswick,[40] is not specifically mentioned in the Act and would appear to be disentitled to immunity. *Ex hypothesi* it is not and cannot be an entity which is part of the central government and therefore covered by section 14 (1). And section 14 (5) and (6) as summarized above only refers to the immunity of the constituent territory itself (for instance, 'as if *it* were a separate entity'), but does not touch a separate entity or a corporation created by the constituent territory. Nor can such an entity be treated as if it were a department of the constituent territory's government. The wording is so clear that a body corporate which is separate and distinct cannot be put on the same level as its creator. Different reasoning was possible and was in fact adopted under the common law, but is not supported by the accepted canons of statutory interpretation. Nor is there any cause for regretting that such a body as the New Brunswick Development Corporation no longer enjoys immunity in this country. International law did not at any time confer such a privilege upon it.

EXCEPTIONS TO IMMUNITY

The Act includes ten provisions which create exceptions to the rule of immunity established by the first section. Many of them and certainly those which in practice are the most important ones are founded upon the existence of a 'commercial transaction' or of 'commercial purposes'. They adopt the distinction between acts *jure imperii* and acts *jure gestionis*, which in 1951 the Inter-Departmental Committee had rejected as unacceptable. What is more, to a large extent they refrain from a definition, but leave it to the courts to work out the distinction. In fact 'commercial purposes' is defined in section 17 (I) in somewhat circular terms, namely

[38] S. 14 (5).

[39] Article 28. See SI 1979, No. 457 relating to Austria's constituent territories.

[40] *Mellenger* v. *New Brunswick Development Corporation*, [1971] 1 W.L.R., 604; cf. *Swiss–Israel Trade Bank* v. *Government of Malta*, [1972] 1 Lloyd's Rep. 497. On both cases see comment, *Modern Law Review*, 38 (1973), p. 18.

by reference to the definition of 'commercial transaction', in section 3. It is a field which has yielded a large harvest in foreign jurisdictions. Both the Brussels and the European Conventions as well as the recent legislation adopted by the United States of America[41] have accepted exceptions based upon the commercial character of the activity. There can be no question of foreign legal developments being a source of law governing the interpretation of an English statute. Yet where the English statute intends to codify the law in a manner consistent with international law, comparative material will have persuasive authority of varying strength in construing terms that are now accepted to be common to most countries and expressive of the present state of public international law.

Another general point which requires emphasis is that it would be unjustifiable to subject sections 2 to 11 of the Act to a narrow construction of the ground that they contain exceptions to the principle laid down in section 1. The European Convention precluded any such argument by enumerating in Articles 1 to 14 the circumstances in which a State is not entitled to immunity and by providing in Article 15 for immunity 'if the proceedings do not fall within' the former group. In England it has frequently been a technique of statutory interpretation to say that an exception does not derogate from the principle to a greater extent that the words used strictly require, that, in other words, in case of doubt the principle rather than the exception should be held to apply.[42] But this is not invariably so and should certainly not be so in the present case. What the legislator described as exceptions represents a very broad sector of State activity. Its limits should be so drawn as to fit the legislative purpose behind each provision rather than the drafting technique that the legislator followed. The so-called exceptions are a far-reaching group of provisions which are not subordinate, but equal, to on the same level as the so-called principle. Hence the rule usually applicable to the construction of exceptions does not fit.

The ten exceptions and their principal implications are as follows.

1. The State which 'has *submitted* to the jurisdiction of the courts of the United Kingdom' is disentitled to immunity. Submission may come about in four different ways.[43]

First, by a prior written agreement—an important change in the law of the United Kingdom. Whether there is an agreement and how it is to be construed will be a matter for the proper law of the contract.[44] The Act

[41] See above n. 22.

[42] Such suggestions have frequently been made. See, e.g., Cockburn, C. J. in *Sowerby* v. *Smith*, (1874) L.R. 9 C.P. 524, at p. 532, where he said that a certain provision 'being in derogation of the freehold given by the Act . . . must, I think, be construed most strictly'.

[43] S. 2.

[44] This is the effect of the decision of the House of Lords in *Nova (Jersey) Knit Ltd.* v. *Kammgarnspinnerei*, [1977] 1 W.L.R. 713, where the agreement required by s. 1 (1) of the Arbitration Act 1975 was considered to be subject to German law.

states that submission of an agreement to English law is not tantamount to submission to English jurisdiction. On the other hand, if English law applies, a clause such as that authorizing an English solicitor to accept service or process ought to be treated as a submission. Whether the agreement is in writing is likely to be a matter for English law, which would have no difficulty in holding that the exchange of telex or cable messages or a written reference to an unsigned document such as the identifiable printed form of a contract constitutes sufficient writing. Whether a State which repudiates the agreement to submit remains subject to jurisdiction is likely to come up for judicial decision. It is submitted that the question should be answered in the affirmative.[45]

Secondly, submission may occur 'after the dispute giving rise to the proceedings has arisen'. Here no formality would seem to be required. Once there is a dispute (and it may not always be easy to define its beginning) even an oral statement accepting jurisdiction will be sufficient; a submission in proceedings actually pending does not seem to be required.

If the State 'has intervened or taken any step in the proceedings' then it is 'deemed to have submitted'; this is the third method. If one accepts the law relating to the Arbitration Act 1950, an unconditional appearance will not be regarded as a step in the proceedings,[46] nor will the claim to immunity be so regarded, as the Act expressly states.

The fourth case is the obvious one in which the State itself has instituted the proceedings. In such event the State is exposed to a counter-claim which 'arises out of the same legal relationship or facts as the claim'. It is not necessary that a court in the United Kingdom has (local) jurisdiction in respect of the cross-claim made by the defendant. It is possible, therefore, that the defendant may pursue a claim which he could not pursue by a writ.

2. The second exception will in practice be the most important one. According to section 3 the State does not enjoy immunity 'as respects proceedings relating to (a) *a commercial transaction* entered into by the State, or (b) an obligation of the State which by virtue of a contract (whether a commercial transaction or not) falls to be performed wholly or partly in the United Kingdom', provided that the latter rule does not apply 'if the contract (not being a commerical transaction) was made in the territory of the State concerned and the obligation in question is governed by its administrative law'.

The rule laid down by sub-paragraph (b) will be readily understood. It is likely to cover many cases. The legal problem which primarily causes

[45] The analogy of such cases as *Heyman* v. *Darwins*, [1942] A.C. 356 and of the established practice of the International Court of Justice (see, e.g., *Fisheries Jurisdiction* case (*United Kingdom* v. *Iceland*) *I.C.J. Reports*, 1973, p. 3) may prove helpful.

[46] S. 4.

difficulty is whether the requirement of total or partial performance in the United Kingdom is to be determined by English law or by the proper law of the contract which, so it must be assumed, is intended by the legislator to govern the existence as well as the construction of the contract, though not its commercial character. The difficulty thus alluded to has arisen in many contexts and is a famous one in the conflict of laws;[47] it led only recently to a decision of the European Court of Justice.[48] It is suggested, though with much hesitation, that it would be so artificial to subject the construction of the contract and the determination of the place of performance to different legal systems that there will be no alternative but to allow the proper law to prevail in both respects.

Nor will sub-paragraph (a) cause much difficulty in the majority of cases, for the Act defines 'commercial transaction' in the widest terms so as to comprise all contracts (except contracts of employment) and any other transaction into which a State enters 'otherwise than in the exercise of sovereign authority'.

In effect, therefore, not only concession agreements but practically every other type of contract will be within the exception, including those contracts which have given trouble to tribunals as well as scholars. The legislator has decided in favour of the objective test of the nature of the transaction and completely disagreed with the Inter-Departmental Committee which in 1951 thought[49] that the principle of *jure gestionis* (now adopted as an exception) was not one 'which, even if justified by international law . . . could be incorporated into our law as a principle'. The Act of 1978 has provided a definition and made it quite clear that all the contracts which in 1951 were apparently thought to be acts done *jure imperii* are commercial transactions. Government loans, shoes for the army, warships, guns, aeroplanes—all these are the subject-matter of commercial transactions in respect of which immunity cannot be claimed. As mentioned above, even a mining concession agreement, though not a contract within the category of contracts mentioned in (b), would be a commercial transaction, because it would be 'any other transaction' . . . into which a State enters', unless 'the parties to the dispute are States or have otherwise agreed in writing'. A substantial limitation, however, is due to the fact that before immunity or its absence falls to be considered an English court must have (territorial) jurisdiction, and this will frequently be a serious hurdle for the plaintiff. A very important point must be emphasized: the denial of immunity is independent of the nature of the act from which the claim arises. If the transaction or activity into which a

[47] Cf. Mann, *The Legal Aspect of Money* (3rd edn., 1971), pp. 206–8.
[48] *Établissements A. De Bloos* v. *Établissements Bouyer SA.*, [1977] 1 C.M.L.R. 60.
[49] Paragraph 5.

State enters or in which it engages is a commercial one, the State is disentitled to immunity even in cases in which, for instance, the breach of contract arises from an act done in the exercise of sovereign authority. All that matters is the character of the transaction or activity carried on by the State as opposed to the facts on which the claim or the defence is founded.[50] These facts may even constitute an act of State. As the law stands, its validity probably may not be questioned for reasons which have nothing to do with the Act of 1978, but if the court is concerned only with its effects upon what is a commercial transaction it is not precluded from considering them either by the rule of immunity or by the alleged sacrosanctity of the act of State.[51]

The puzzling feature of section 3 lies in the fact that, according to the definition, the term 'commercial transaction' includes 'any . . . activity . . . in which [the State] engages otherwise than in the exercise of sovereign authority'. The State is not immune 'as respects proceedings relating to' such an activity. It is submitted that the definition is such as to render it possible to sue a foreign State in respect of a tort other than those mentioned in sections 5 to 7 which has been committed in England, such a tort providing the court with (territorial) jurisdiction according to Order 11 rule 1 (h) of the Rules of Supreme Court. In this somewhat unexpected manner torts do come within the scope of the Act in such a case as *Krajina v. The Tass Agency*,[52] but also in other cases involving, for instance, claims for damages for fraud or conspiracy. The same applies to cases in which confidential information has been imparted to a foreign State, but misused by it or its agent—a by no means inconceivable situation. The only activity which cannot in any circumstances be a commercial transaction is one exercised by virtue of sovereign authority—a phrase which, it is submitted, only qualifies the word 'activity', not the words 'any other transaction'. The term will have to be construed according to English law.[53] In other words the classification of facts alleged to satisfy a conception used by the English legislator must be provided by English law, however alien to English notions they may be. Even if by Soviet law the publication of *The Soviet Monitor* is an act of sovereign authority, this is unlikely to be so

[50] The decision of Robert Goff J. in *I Congreso del Partido* (above, n. 25) on this point (see pp. 1183, 1184) could not even under the old law easily be supported. It is certainly contrary to the construction which the Act requires.

[51] Cf. The decision of the Court of Appeal in *Buttes Gas & Oil Co.* v. *Hammer*, [1975] Q.B. 557.

[52] Above, n. 11.

[53] The Head of New Scotland Yard who upon request sends a report on the Church of Scientology of California to the Federal Republic of Germany's Federal Criminal Office acts in exercise of sovereign authority and is immune in Germany: German Federal Supreme Court, 26 September 1978, *Neue Juristische Wochenschrift*, 1970, p. 1101.

under English law.[54] According to the Report of the Inter-Departmental Committee, in 1951 an Italian court decided that the publication in Italy by a Brazilian state of a magazine strictly for the purpose of encouraging immigration to Brazil was not an act done *jure imperii* in respect of which Brazil was entitled to immunity.[55] An English court ought to hold similarly that the publication of such a paper is not an act done in the exercise of sovereign authority. It would be different, for instance, if a foreign State were to send a diplomatic note to the Foreign and Commonwealth Office; a libel contained in it could not be pursued by proceedings here if the defendant State raised the plea of immunity. The argument here put forward and based on the words 'proceedings relating to . . . any . . . activity . . . in which [the State] engages otherwise than in the exercise of sovereign authority' cannot be met by a reference to sections 5 to 7, which deal with certain torts committed in England. Section 3 comprises torts wherever committed, provided the English court has (territorial) jurisdiction in respect of the claim or counter-claim. A tort committed abroad may yet have been committed in England if the damage has occurred here. Furthermore, the fact that certain torts are specifically mentioned does not necessitate the conclusion that other torts are not caught by the wide terms of section 3.

It must be made clear, however, that an activity may be in the exercise of sovereign authority even if it is unlawful. Property taken by force may be taken by way of sovereign authority.

The width of the exception allowed by section 3 is likely to be fully recognized only in years to come in the light of experience which practice will bring forth and which at this stage it is hard to perceive and foresee.

3. The third exception relates to a *contract of employment* between the foreign State and an individual who is (only) a national of the United Kingdom or habitually resident there, provided that either the contract was made or the work is to be wholly or partly performed here (section 4). It is open to the parties to agree otherwise in writing, and if the employment is for work in an office, agency or establishment, maintained in the United Kingdom, the State cannot claim immunity except if, at the time when the contract was made, the individual was habitually resident in that State.

Once again the question whether a contract was made and what its terms are must be decided by the proper law. But whether it constitutes a

[54] In *Yessenin-Volpin* v. *Novosti Press Agency, Tass Agency and the Daily World*, 443. F. Sup. 849 (1978), also *International Legal Materials* 17 (1978), p. 720, a United States District Court decided that, although by publishing newspapers the defendants engaged in commercial activity, a libel published in the newspaper was not 'in connection with a commercial activity', for the newspapers were committing 'acts of inter-governmental co-operation'. The decision should not be followed for this reason, among others, that it classifies the terms of a U.S. statute according to Soviet law and practice.

[55] Paragraph 18.

contract of employment, i.e. a contract of service rather than a contract for services, whether it was made in the United Kingdom or where the individual's habitual residence was—these are questions governed by English law. The question where a contract is made is, as one knows only too well, a particularly difficult one and it is at first sight not easy to understand why existence or absence of immunity should be dependent upon the place where the letter of acceptance is posted. Immunity and acceptance of an offer are so different in character that to make the former subject to the latter is a little incongruous.

The section is a narrow one and may support results which will not necessarily appear justifiable. If Nigeria makes in London a contract which is governed by English law and by which a citizen and resident of the United States of America agrees to serve on an oil rig on the high seas it would appear that the employer is entitled to immunity in an English court the (territorial) jurisdiction of which may follow from Order 11.

4. The next exception applies to the case in which the foreign State causes in the United Kingdom *injury to a person or to property*: section 5. The provision and its application are fairly obvious and will only in the most exceptional cases give rise to any problem of construction. One such problem is due to the fact that the section requires the damage to or loss of property to have been caused by an act or omission in the United Kingdom, but does not require the property to be situate there. Suppose a London merchant deposits goods in a warehouse in State X on the understanding that they will be released to him or his order upon production of an authority signed by the merchant and countersigned by the Trade Delegation of X in London. The Trade Delegation is contractually bound, but refuses to countersign. The loss of the goods is said to be caused by the failure of the Trade Delegation to act in London. It would seem that in such circumstances State X is not entitled to immunity in an action for damages.

5. The fifth exception, established by section 6, is in certain respects particularly interesting. Sub-sections 1 to 3 deprive the foreign State of immunity in regard to *immovable property* in the United Kingdom, any interest of the State in property of whatever kind and wherever situate if it arises by way of succession, gift or *bona vacantia*, or any interest in an *estate* of deceased persons, insolvent persons and others and in a trust. In the vast majority of cases the property or the estate will be in the United Kingdom. In such a case the exception is plainly justified and necessary and largely supported by earlier law. In some cases the exception would also seem to apply if the property or estate or trust is situate abroad, but they cannot often occur in an English court.

While the cases thus alluded to may seem fairly clear and even familiar, there is buried among them one particular set of facts which, one may be sure, the legislator did not contemplate but which, it is submitted, may be covered by them. It unfortunately happens quite frequently that States cause the dissolution of corporations and take over their assets and liabilities, sometimes for purposes of a confiscatory character, and that such measures are believed to protect the corporation and its property from the jurisdiction of foreign courts or arbitrators. These are instances of a universal succession and should in future come within the ambit of section 6 (2), so that the State can be made personally liable in respect of the 'deceased' corporation's contracts. Such proceedings would appear to relate 'to any interest of the State in movable or immovable property, being an interest arising by way of succession . . .'. These are words which do not need to be limited to proprietary interests, but may be said to comprise liabilities for the discharge of which the property is, in a loose sense, a security.[56] Even where the State takes only the assets of the dissolved corporation and purports to leave its liabilities unprovided for, *ordre public* would require it to be held liable and for the reasons given it should not be entitled to immunity.[57]

Sub-section 4 reads as follows:

> A court may entertain proceedings against a person other than a State notwithstanding that the proceedings relate to property
> (a) which is in the possession or control of a State; or
> (b) in which a State claims an interest,
> if the State would not have been immune had the proceedings been brought against it, or in a case within paragraph (b) above, if the claim is neither admitted nor supported by prima facie evidence.

If one ignores ships,which are separately dealt with in the Act this is the case of the Bank of England with which the State has deposited gold[58] or of Sotheby's who hold a painting sent to them by the State for sale. If proceedings are brought against the Bank of England or Sotheby's by a plaintiff who claims to be the owner or entitled to immediate possession, no Continental court, so it appears, would ever have thought of immunity

[56] Cf. The French principle of the *patrimoine* of which Carbonnier, *Droit Civil*, vol. 3 section 2, has said: 'c'est la caractéristique de la succession au patrimoine (in universum jus) . . . que d'être, tout à la fois et indivisiblement, succession à l'actif et au passif', and he quotes the maxim: *bona non sunt nisi deducto aere alieno*.

It is believed that, for the reasons given in the text, *Thai-Europe Tapioca Service Ltd.* v. *Government of Pakistan*, [1975] 1 W.L.R. 1485, should today be decided differently. On universal succession generally see *Metliss* v. *National Bank of Greece*, [1958] A.C. 509, and *Adams* v. *National Bank of Greece*, [1961] A.C. 255.

[57] On *ordre public* in case of universal succession see *Metliss*' case, in the Court of Appeal, [1957] 2 QB, 33, at p. 48 *per* Romer L. J.; and *Adams*' case, *ubi supra*, at p. 289 *per* Lord Denning.

[58] *United States of America* v. *Dollfus Mieg & Cie.*, [1952] A.C. 582.

coming into play, because this is conceived as a personal privilege of the defendent who, if he holds property for a State and cannot bring it before the court by interpleader proceedings, must make his own arrangements with it, but cannot confront the plaintiff with the immunity of the third party. In this country, however, the unfortunate idea grew up and was repeatedly sanctioned by the House of Lords[59] that indirect possession or control by a State involved its 'indirect impleading' and entitled the defendant actually in possession to immunity. This, one notices with satisfaction, has been abolished in the sense that the defendant can only claim it if the State in an action against it directly could do so. One is thus directed to look again at section 3 and finds that the outcome depends on whether the proceedings relate to any transaction or activity into which the State has entered or in which it has engaged otherwise than in the exercise of sovereign authority. It would seem, therefore, that in the circumstances of the *Dollfus Mieg & Cie.* case the plaintiff could not today succeed, because the State which had deposited the gold with the Bank of England had done so and, indeed, had obtained the gold in the exercise of sovereign authority, so that an action against the States which were the bailors would be stayed. If, on the other hand, the plaintiff has purchased identifiable gold bars from the State which has deposited them with the Bank of England but refuses to release them he is entitled to succeed in regard to any plea of immunity. Property which has been confiscated without compensation or, indeed, which has been taken without colour of legality cannot be recovered from the State. Accordingly it cannot be recovered from the defendant in England who is in possession of it. *Rahimtoola* v. *Nizam of Hyderabad*[60] is now a more doubtful case. Lord Denning, whose approach is much to be preferred to that of his colleagues, put forward the attractive and, indeed, convincing thought that the facts pointed to 'an international transaction' or, as Upjohn J. had said in the court of first instance, an 'intergovernmental transaction' between the Finance Minister of Hyderabad and the Foreign Secretary of Pakistan, a 'transaction more in the nature of a treaty than a contract or trust'.[61] On this basis the court had to deal with a transaction entered into in the exercise of sovereign authority, with the result that Pakistan or its agent, the defendant, could claim immunity and so could the Westminster Bank if the debt due from it could be said to be property in the possession or control of Pakistan or in which Pakistan claimed an interest. This condition, probably, was under the old law and would now be fulfilled, though, as Lord Denning pointed out, it remains very difficult to understand (and none of the other Law Lords satisfactorily explained) why in

[59] For the first time in *The Cristina*, above n. 26.

[60] Above, p. 19. [61] Pp. 422, 423.

the *Dollfus Mieg* case the claim for damages in respect of the converted thirteen gold bars was allowed to proceed, while the debt due from Westminster Bank to the Nizam of Hyderabad as beneficial owner could not be pursued. The conclusion is not entirely fortunate: two of the most regrettable decisions of the House of Lords in the field of sovereign immunity would appear to have been sanctioned by the legislator who at the same time has done nothing to eliminate the logical inconsistency between them.

The sub-section, it will be noted, makes a curious distinction between property which is in the possession or control of a State and property in which a State claims an interest. In the former case the State will have to prove that it is in possession or control, but in the latter case the claim to immunity, unless admitted, will succeed if it is supported 'by prima facie evidence'. Two things have to be said about this provision. The claim to an interest in property as a basis for immunity seems to originate with Lord Wright who used the phrase in *The Cristina*,[62] when he spoke of interests 'lesser than a proprietary interest or even than a possessory interest'. But he probably treated them merely as an illustration of control,[63] while the section under discussion draws a sharp distinction. It is a serious question whether in a statutory text an imprecise phrase used in a judicial opinion should not be given a strict meaning. If so, 'an interest' could only denote an equitable interest as understood by the general law of England. However this may be, the effect is that from the State's point of view it may be more advantageous to allege 'an interest' rather than 'possession or control'. Moreover, the idea that prima facie evidence is sufficient and strict proof is not required, though it comes from an Admiralty case,[64] used to have universal validity. It is now clearly confined to the single case of a claim to 'an interest' in property other than ships.

6. Exception 6 relates to industrial property rights in the United Kingdom. No immunity exists where the proceedings relate to any such right belonging to the foreign State and protected in the United Kingdom or to the infringement by the State of any such right belonging to someone else or to passing-off in the United Kingdom: section 7.

These provisions, the statutory definition of which is much more detailed and precise, are unlikely to prove troublesome and do not require comment at this stage.

7. Similar remarks apply to the seventh exception. A State which is a

[62] Above, n. 26, at p. 507.

[63] This is how he was understood by Earl Jowitt in the *Dollfus Mieg & Cie*. case (above n. 58), at p. 604.

[64] *Juan Ysmael & Co. Inc.* v. *Indonesian Government*, [1955] A.C. 72, noted *Modern Law Review*, 18 (1955), p. 184

member of a corporate or unincorporated body and involved in proceedings brought by such body or its other members cannot claim immunity: section 8. The only point which deserves emphasis is that the section applies not only to bodies created in the United Kingdom, but also to such body as 'is controlled from or has its principal place of business in the United Kingdom'. In some very special circumstances it may be possible to bring an action here against a foreign State as a member of a corporation which is formed under such State's own law, but controlled from the United Kingdom.

8. The eighth exception is designed to overturn a most unfortunate and at the same time wholly avoidable decision of the House of Lords.[65] Where a State has agreed to arbitration, it is without immunity 'as respects proceedings in the courts of the United Kingdom which relate to the arbitration': section 9. It will be noted that the section is not limited to arbitration in the United Kingdom. English awards made against a foreign State can be turned into judgments of an English court (though this should rarely be necessary or useful) and a foreign award can be made enforceable here, though not enforced except as mentioned below. The section also gives jurisdiction to the court to make interlocutory orders for the security of costs, discovery, etc., such as are provided for in the Arbitration Act 1950.

9. Exception 9 is of great practical importance in that it excludes immunity in respect of *ships* used or intended to be used for 'commercial purposes': section 10. The principle as expressed in sub-section 2 extends to cargo and other property belonging to or in the possession or control of the State or in which it claims an interest (sub-sections 4 and 5). But the whole section is applicable only in Admiralty proceedings or in proceedings on a claim which could be brought in Admiralty (sub-section 1); in such proceedings sections 3 to 5, that is to say, exceptions two, three and four discussed above, do not apply if the defendant State is a party to the Brussels Convention, for the Act does not intend to interfere with the latter as a self-contained code.

The main point to be made in connection with section 10 arises from the term 'commercial purposes' which occurs in many sections and which in the present context has very special significance. It is to be contrasted with 'commercial transaction' in section 3 which is determined by its objective nature rather than its possibly subjective purpose, in the same way as the American Foreign Sovereign Immunities Act 1976 which takes 'commercial activity' as a test and defines it 'by reference to the nature of the

[65] *Duff Development Co.* v. *Kelantan*, [1924] A.C. 797, on which see Cohn, this *Year Book*, 34 (1958), p. 260, and Mann, this *Year Book*, 42 (1967), p. 17, also *Studies in International Law* (1973), p. 276.

course of conduct or particular transaction or act rather than by reference to its purpose'.

The starting point would seem to be clear: the meaning of 'commercial purposes' should be construed according to English notions. The plaintiff has to prove the facts, but it is for English law to say whether they establish 'commercial purposes' in the English sense.

In answering this question it will be necessary to distinguish clearly between ship and cargo.

As regards a ship the State is disentitled to immunity if the ship belongs to it (in the wide sense referred to above) and is used or intended to be used for commercial purposes. Cargo does not enjoy immunity if the cargo belongs (again in the extended sense mentioned above) to the State and both the cargo and the ship are used or intended to be used for commercial purposes. The last-mentioned two words, therefore, are crucial. A warship which happens to be used for carrying motor cars for civilian use cannot be immune, but if a trading ship carries ammunition for military purposes both the ship and the cargo are immune, at least if there is no commercial cargo on board. Cement carried in a trading ship may be immune: the result depends on the purpose for which it will be used. If the consignee intends to sell the cement to the military administration, but is not contractually bound to do so, the non-commercial purpose does not in a legally relevant sense exist. If the consignee has sold an identifiable quantity being part of the cargo of cement for the building of military barracks, immunity extends to such quantity and it would probably be no counter-argument that one must not look beyond the consignee; what matter are the ultimate purposes in so far as they can be proven. Shoes for the army (to revert to an often-discussed example) are cargo for a non-commercial purpose, but if they are consigned to a private merchant who only hopes to sell them to the army, the purpose remains commercial. If the consignee is the State itself and intends to use the cargo for the business of a State monopoly such as a tobacco or alcohol monopoly, this is a commercial purpose, though the consignee may regard it as a public purpose. Conversely, if there exists in England a monopoly for the production and sale of certain goods (as at present is not the case) this would not prove that similar goods carried in a foreign ship are not intended for commercial purposes: a State monopoly as such is not by any means a non-commercial venture.

10. The last exception (section 11) does not require more than mention, for it is unlikely to fall often for consideration. No immunity can be claimed by a defendant State in proceedings brought to recover value added tax, customs duty or any agricultural levy or rates in respect of premises occupied for commercial purposes.

THE SCOPE OF IMMUNITY

Immunity does not only mean the exemption of a foreign State from British jurisdiction, but also entails other procedural privileges.

Thus by section 12 service of proceedings and time limits for appearance are subject to special rules, but these do not apply if the State has agreed to service in another manner. From a practical point of view it is, therefore, very important to ensure that a foreign State which submits to the jurisdiction of English courts or to arbitration in England also agrees to service upon an agent in this country, who is irrevocably authorized to accept service and to enter an appearance.

Further consequences of immunity relate to discovery (section 13, sub-section 1). The failure of a State to afford discovery shall not attract any penalty by way of committal or fine. This, clearly, is a necessary provision, but it is also a harmless one, for it does not in any way preclude the court from drawing the appropriate conclusions from the State's failure to comply with rules of procedure to which, *ex hypothesis*, it has submitted. A robust judge should not feel diffident in such a case, particularly if he remembers that the failure of a State to afford discovery may have to be treated as involving State responsibility.[66]

Next, except with the consent of the State (which it is difficult to imagine will ever be given) the English court is precluded from granting an injunction or making an order for specific performance or for the recovery of property against it: section 13, sub-section 2 (a). This is a most serious and, indeed, worrying aspect, for like the rest of section 13 it seems to apply even in cases in which the State is not entitled to immunity and in which, therefore, proceedings of all kinds and with all types of relief should be available against it. In recent years the *Mareva* type of injunction[67] has become an important feature of commercial practice in England. To deny it against a State which is subject to English jurisdiction will frequently render proceedings nugatory and deprive a successful plaintiff of the fruits of his victory. One only has to look at *Trendtex Trading Corporation Ltd. v. Central Bank of Nigeria.*[68] There Mocatta J.

[66] Cf. the Award in the Arbitration between the United Kingdon and Greece in the *Ambatielos* claim (1956).

[67] *Mareva Compania Naviera S.A.* v. *International Bulkcarriers S.A.* [1975] 2 Lloyd's Reports 509.

[68] Above, n. 28. The new English law should be contrasted with the law of Switzerland as declared by a recent decision of the Federal Tribunal (15 November 1978, BGE 104 1a 367): The Zurich branch of Lloyds Bank International granted a 'time deposit' to a Turkish commercial bank in such a manner as to 'interpose' the Turkish Central Bank in its capacity as guardian of Turkish Exchange Control. When the commercial bank failed to repay, the lender's assignee obtained an attachment of the Central Bank's Swiss assets. The appeal

had granted an injunction blocking some $14 million which stood to the credit of the defendant, the Central Bank of Nigeria, in the books of the Midland Bank. The Court of Appeal, on this point unanimously, held that the injunction was to be continued, for 'if the Central Bank of Nigeria is entitled to immunity from being sued, so also can the funds be immune from being seized. Otherwise not'.[69] This sound law has been changed, with the result that in most cases proceedings in England against a foreign State may prove pointless even if the defendant is not entitled to immunity and the action succeeds.

This is to be contrasted with the further provision in section 13, sub-section 2 (b) according to which the property of a State shall not be subject to any process for the enforcement of a judgement or arbitration award or for the arrest, detention or sale of a ship or other property, unless the exception in sub-section 4 applies, i.e. the property is for the time being in use or intended for use for commercial purposes. The latter exception is in line with a remarkable decision of the Federal Constitutional Court of Germany which in an elaborately and closely reasoned judgment held that a foreign State's German property was available for the enforcement of a judgment if it had a commercial character.[70] In these circumstances the total denial of injunctive relief becomes even more mysterious and regrettable.

The scope of immunity is subject to some additional provisions of a very special kind, which apply to *separate entities and central banks*, and need some analysis.

1. By virtue of section 14, sub-section 2 a separate entity (which, it will be remembered, is an entity capable of suing and being sued, but distinct from the executive organs of government) is immune only if 'the proceedings relate to anything done by it in the exercise of sovereign authority' and the circumstances are such that the State would have been immune. The difficulty arises from the former requirement. When can it be said that a separate entity does something in the exercise of sovereign authority? It is an essential element of the definition that the entity is

---

failed, for the Federal Tribunal held that the nature of the legal relationship with the borrower was commercial in character and that 'mere payment regulations' requiring the interposition of the Central Bank could not affect it. Accordingly the Central Bank, if liable at all, was not entitled to immunity. The question of liability was left to be decided in the main proceedings. It is possible that this decision is contrary to two decisions of the highest French court on the immunity of a Central Bank in matters of exchange control: Cass. Civ., 3 November 1952, *Revue critique de droit international privé*, 1952, p. 425, with note by Freyria, or *Clunet*, 1953, p. 654, with note by Goldman; 19 May 1976, *Revue critique de droit international privé*, 1977, p. 359, with note by Batiffol.

[69] At p. 561.

[70] Federal Constitutional Court, 13 December 1977, *Neue Juristische Wochenschrift*, 1978, p. 485.

distinct from the executive organs of government. Hence 'the exercise of sovereign authority' cannot be the same thing as governmental authority. In fact it is difficult to think of, or to find in the judicial practice of the past the example of a body distinct from the executive organs of government, yet exercising sovereign, i.e. supreme, authority. An Immigration Board or the Civil Aviation Authority may qualify, but are unlikely to be sued in a foreign country. A body such as the National Coal Board in Britain does not exercise sovereign authority in respect of coal. Or the British National Oil Corporation as at present constituted certainly exercises far-reaching authority over oil. But can it be suggested that its authority is sovereign? Even if something in the nature of governmental authority were sufficient, this is vested in the Minister of Energy. It would seem, therefore, that it can only be in rare circumstances that a separate entity will be entitled to immunity. This is particularly so in light of the fact that the phrase 'in the exercise of sovereign authority' should be construed according to English law and foreign constitutional law should be immaterial, though, of course, the foreign facts will have to be ascertained in order to answer the question whether they involve the exercise of sovereign authority in the English sense.

2. If a separate entity other than a central bank is entitled to immunity, but submits to the jurisdiction then, according to section 14 (3), the provisions of section 13, sub-sections 1 to 4 shall apply; in particular, no injunction can be granted nor can any judgment be enforced against the separate entity. When does, in the present context, a submission to jurisdiction occur? Is such submission limited to the entry of an unconditional appearance? Or is the term to be understood in the wide sense of section 2 so as to extend to an agreement to submit or to the institution of proceedings by the separate entity? It is suggested that section 2 should apply on the ground that within the field covered by the Act submission is intended to have a special meaning which is wider than and different from the usual one.

3. Where the separate entity is a central bank section 14 (4) introduces special provisions. It renders section 13, sub-sections (1) to (3) applicable, so that no penalty for defective discovery can be imposed, no order for an injunction or for specific performance can be made and a judgment cannot be enforced. And, irrespective of whether or not the central bank is a separate entity, the last-mentioned consequence is fortified by the express provision that even the bank's property used or intended to be used for commercial purposes is unavailable for execution.

The legislator has thus set aside one of the most important results of the judgment of the Court of Appeal in the *Trendtex* case and rendered proceedings against a central bank almost wholly illusory, notwithstanding the fact that by virtue of section 14 (2) a central bank which is a separate entity will be subject to jurisdiction as such in cases in which the proceedings relate to matters of a commercial character and the State itself would not be immune. The mercenary attitude towards central banks, although shared by the United States (see section 1611 of its Act of 1976), remains a matter for great regret. It is no doubt due to the wish to attract foreign funds to the City of London by assuring their owners that they have nothing to fear from their creditors. Is it in the true interest of Britain and the City of London to assist foreign States or their central banks in avoiding the discharge of their commercial debts? If in the *Trendtex* case the action and, in particular, the application for an injunction had failed this country would have bought popularity in Nigeria with a loss of reputation in the rest of the civilized world which does not confer similar privileges on central banks. Would so cynical an attitude commend itself? Does principle and financial and commercial probity no longer count? The legislator's policy towards central banks merits and requires urgent review.

CONCLUSION

In conclusion it can be stated that the Act of 1978 is better drafted than many other recent enactments. It creates some uncertainties. It also allows much greater scope to the principle of immunity than the state of the law in the world at large necessitates, but in this respect gives expression to a specific legislative policy which is designed to protect this country's alleged financial interests. Two problems, in particular, pervade the whole of the Act. The first involves the question of classification. This, it has been suggested, should almost everywhere be solved in the light of English conceptions, the foreign law being relevant only in so far as the explanation of the factual background is concerned. The second relates to the proof of the relevant facts. It is submitted that, throughout, the State claiming immunity has to prove the facts on which it relies. There is only one exception, in section 6 (4), where it is expressly provided that in the event of the State claiming an interest in property the subject-matter of proceedings against a third party it is sufficient for the claim to immunity to be 'supported by prima facie evidence'. The very fact that the legislator thought it right to express this single exception makes it clear that in all other cases the facts have to be fully proved by appropriate evidence. The burden of proof, it would seem, is throughout on the State claiming immunity, though in many cases this may mean proving a negative, viz. the non-existence of one of the exceptions introduced by the Act. Although the marginal note to section 1 speaks of the 'general immunity from jurisdiction' and this paper, therefore, speaks of a 'principle' and 'exceptions', the preceding review proves that it is only a residual immunity which a foreign State can claim in relatively few cases. The denial of immunity is so far-reaching that it is more appropriate to treat the 'exceptions' as distinct categories. Accordingly it is submitted that what may be described as the usual rules about proving exceptions should not be applicable.

12

'Inviolability' and Other Problems of the Vienna Convention on Diplomatic Relations

I

THE Vienna Convention on Diplomatic Relations of 1961 scheduled to the Diplomatic Privileges Act 1964 (and some similar Conventions) makes much use of the term 'inviolability'. The premises of the missions are 'inviolable' (Art. 22). The archives and documents of the mission, wherever they may be, are 'inviolable' (Art. 24). The official correspondence of the mission is 'inviolable' (Art. 27, paragraph 2). The person of the diplomat is 'inviolable' (Art. 29), the same applies to his private residence, his papers, his correspondence and, in principle, his property (Art. 30).

The definition of the term has in the past provoked little discussion. Such definitions as there are almost invariably express the same meaning—a meaning which is suitable in every case in which the term appears, for it is obvious that throughout the Convention it is likely to have been used in the same sense. This is best expressed by the *Oxford English Dictionary* according to which violence means 'the exercise of physical force so as to inflict injury or damage to a person or property', so that inviolability means the opposite, namely conduct which is free from and protected against such treatment. Inviolability therefore intends to protect freedom from disturbance.

In so far as definitions have become known they are in line with this literal meaning. It must suffice to mention a few which may be described as representative. In *England* the late Professor Clive Parry, writing in the *British Digest*[1] did not consider the term 'particularly precise', but believed that it no doubt implied immunity from all interference,

> whether under colour of law or right or otherwise and connotes a special duty of protection, whether from such interferences or from mere insult, on the part of the receiving State.

[1] Vol. 7, p. 700; Denza, *Diplomatic Law* (1976), p. 110 also rightly speaks of the prohibitions of 'interference'.

K. Hailbronner, G. Ress, and T. Stein. (eds.), *Festschrift für Karl Coehring* Berlin, 1989), 553.

And referring to Art. 30 (2) of the Convention whereby the papers, correspondence and property of a diplomat 'likewise enjoy inviolability', Mrs Denza rightly says that 'these words are generally interpreted as according the same degree of protection as is given under Art. 22 of property on mission premises . . . namely immunity from search, requisition, attachment or execution'.[2] In the *United States of America* the Foreign Service Regulations have prescribed since at least 1941[3]

> Premises which are occupied by a diplomatic representative and members of his staff, either as offices or residences, the goods contained therein, and the records and archives of the mission are inviolable. They cannot be entered, searched or detained by the local authorities even under process of law.

This definition was reaffirmed by the Foreign Relations Law of 1965[4] and is no doubt still valid. In *France* the authoritative *Dictionnaire de la Terminologie du Droit International* published in 1960 defines inviolabilité as

> Immunité . . . en vertu de laquelle les personnes qui en jouissent . . . et les choses qui en sont revêtues (hôtel diplomatique, archives diplomatiques and consulaires, siège de l'ONU, etc.) échappent à tout acte de contrainte de la part des authorités du pays où ils se trouvent . . .

In *Italy* Professor Giuliano wrote, after referring to the principle *omnis coactio abesse a legato debet*, that the object of inviolability was 'd'exempter le représentant diplomatique étranger et ses biens de toute mesure de contrainte de la part des authorités locales'.[5] In *Germany* Verdross-Simma[6] state: 'The inviolability of the mission excludes all types of acts of authority by the receiving State, including service of documents.' Some of these statements to which many similar ones could be added were made before 1961, but the Preamble of the Convention of that year (which, curiously enough, is not reprinted in the Schedule to the Diplomatic Privileges Act 1964) states that the existing customary public international law shall remain in force in respect of all questions which are not expressly regulated by the treaty. Moreover, we know that the treaty's authors intended on the whole to codify the existing customary law.

The conclusion is that inviolability means freedom from any act of constraint, in particular search, requisition, attachment or execution, i.e. the measures specifically enumerated in Art. 22 (3).

[2] Diplomatic Agents and Missions in *Encyclopedia of Public International Law* 9, 97.

[3] Printed by Hackworth, *Digest* IV, 562. [4] s. 77.

[5] *Rec.* 100 (1960 ii), 111. [6] *Universelles Völkerrecht* (3rd edn. 1984), s. 895.

II

It is against this background that it is necessary to analyse the decision which is probably the most important one dealing with the effects of the Vienna Convention that has so far been rendered anywhere. This is the decision of the House of Lords in *Shearson Lehman Brothers Inc.* v. *Maclaine Watson & Co. Ltd., International Tin Council Intervening*.[7] An action arising from the insolvency of the ITC in October 1985 was proceeding between the plaintiffs and the defendants, when the ITC obtained leave to intervene for the purpose of satisfying the court that it was an international organization entitled under English law to the privileges and immunities in substance corresponding to those defined by the Vienna Convention of 1961 and that in respect of a large number of documents in the possession of the parties to the action it was entitled to an order 'that no reliance be made in these proceedings upon ITC documents as described . . . or to the information derived therefrom'.[8] The documents objected to were documents or copy documents supplied to third parties with or without the consent of the ITC by a member of its staff or by one of the Member States, its delegates or advisers, also documents made available to and published by the House of Commons Select Committee or released by the United States authorities under the Freedom of Information Act, or documents prepared by a third party containing information derived from an ITC document and so forth. All such documents and others included in altogether thirteen categories were said to be part of the ITC's 'archives' or documents within the meaning of Art. 24 of the Vienna Convention and corresponding provisions.

This summary will be sufficient to show up the extravagance of the case put forward by an international organization of which in another case an English judge said[9] that it had 'behaved more like a disreputable private debtor concerned only to hinder and delay his creditors than the responsible international organization that it claims to be' and, so one may add, that would have spent its allegedly non-existent resources on satisfying some of its debts rather than on litigation likely to strike some as absurd.

Although Lord Bridge of Harwich who delivered the opinion with which Lord Brandon of Oakbrook, Lord Griffiths, Lord Oliver of Aylmerton and Lord Goff of Chieveley merely agreed,[10] dealt with each of the

[7] [1988] 1 W.L.R. 16.

[8] This was a most curious claim formulated with little regard to grammatical correctness. It was probably tantamount to a declaration to the effect that the documents were inadmissible in evidence.

[9] *Maclaine Watson & Co. Ltd.* v. *International Tin Council (No. 2)*, [1987] 1 W.L.R. 1711, at p. 1713.

[10] It is most regrettable that none of their Lordships added a separate opinion. This was a case of great importance on a subject which rarely falls to be considered by the courts and

thirteen categories and subject-matter of the ITC's application, in substance he rejected it on the ground that documents which reached third parties with the actual or ostensible authority of the ITC could no longer be said to be part of its 'archives' or 'documents of the mission'. This would seem to be an obvious conclusion and the reader can only admire the patience which Lord Bridge devoted to its establishment. But in the course of his observations the learned Law Lord made some observations which provoke comment, though not all of them strictly come under the heading 'inviolability' with which this paper is concerned.

1. The first of them relates to the fact that the House treated the ITC's application as relating to the admissibility of documents emanating from, but no longer in the possession of the ITC.[11] It is submitted that this is an unjustifiable approach. Documents which are in the possession of third parties, but still form part of the 'archives', for instance, stolen documents, are, it is submitted, admissible as evidence in proceedings between A and B. The only right of the ITC or the diplomat, as the case may be, is to recover them, for they continue to be 'documents of the mission'. But if the diplomat does nothing neither the parties to the proceedings nor the court has any duties.

For this reason the decision of the Quebec Court of King's Bench, Appeal Division, in *Rose* v. *The King*,[12] followed and approved by the Quebec Interior Court of Appeal in *R.* v. *Lunan*[13] and in *R.* v. *Gurson*[14] is still good law, though Mrs Denza asserts the contrary.[15] In *Rose* v. *The King* original documents had been stolen by a defector from the Soviet Embassy and were used in criminal proceedings in Canada. Barclay J. said:[16]

> It is not for this court to decide whether or not the Government has violated international law. The documents are legally before this court and should be so dealt with.

Bissionette J. said:[17]

---

which gave rise to numerous different aspects. Some additional words of explanataion would have been very welcome. It was pre-eminently a case in which, in the words of Lord Goff (*Proceedings of the British Academy* 1983, 175) it would have been 'better to have a feast of contrasting courses, festering with ideas, than a single hygienic package wrapped in polythene, insulated not merely from dissent, but from differences in analysis and on points of detail which may later prove to be important'.

[11] See pp. 22, 26 and passim. [12] (1947) 3 D.L.R. 618.

[13] (1947) 3 D.L.R. 710, at p. 715. [14] (1948) 3 D.L.R. 280, at p. 282.

[15] The point is not made in *Diplomatic Law* (1976), p. 109, but appears for the first time in *Encyclopedia of Public International Law* 9, 96 which was published in 1986.

[16] P. 628. [17] P. 647.

The moment the State decided to keep them they became seized in the legal sense of international law and they automatically ceased to enjoy the privilege of immunity.

A State which without the use of force or without exercising executive authority has obtained possession of the diplomat's documents and uses them without his objection cannot be said to 'violate' them within the meaning of Art. 24. And it can certainly not be said that they are inadmissible within the meaning of any rule of evidence. It would be different if the State was responsible for the removal of the documents from the mission, but this is a different case.[18]

2. A second point which arises from Lord Bridge's opinion is that he seems to accept that the protection of confidentiality is not the purpose of Art. 24 which, accordingly, does not apply at all if the duty of confidentiality imposed by the diplomat upon the recipient of one of his documents is broken.[19]

This is a most welcome clarification. The claim of the ITC apparently involved the proposition that if the ITC makes an official, but confidential communication to the representative of a member State and, in breach of confidence, he passes the document on to a party to an action, the ITC can prevent its use on the ground of its confidentiality. With remarkable and undeserved politeness Lord Bridge rejected the proposition. But his rejection also means this: if a visitor to the mission wrongfully copies a document which he happens to see there, its use can be restrained only on the ground of breach of copyright or some similar legal rule, but the idea of 'inviolability' enshrined in the Convention does not apply. The mission's document was not subject to that interference or constraint which the Convention envisages.

3. The third point arises from a passage in Lord Bridge's opinion which must be quoted in full:[19]

Mr Kentridge presented a forceful argument for the defendants based on the proposition that the only protection which the status of inviolability . . . affords is against executive or judicial action by the host State. Hence, it is submitted, even if a document was stolen, or otherwise obtained by improper means, from a diplomatic mission, inviolability could not be relied on to prevent the thief or other violator from putting it in evidence, but the mission would be driven to invoke some other ground of objection to its admissibility. I need not examine this argument at length. I reject it substantially for the reason given by the Court of Appeal. The underlying purpose of the inviolability conferred is to protect the privacy of diplomatic communications. If that privacy is violated by a citizen, it

[18] In such a case there would not only have been an infringement of the Convention, but also a violation of customary international law.

[19] P. 27.

would be wholly inimical to the underlying purpose that the judicial authorities of the host state should countenance the violation by permitting the violator, or any one who receives the document from the violator, to make use of the document in judicial proceedings.

In the Court of Appeal to which Lord Bridge referred Dillon L.J. rejected the submission that the 'inviolability' is only an immunity against action by the British Government. In his judgment[20]

the official archives of the diplomatic mission, or of the international organisation such as the ITC are to be kept inviolate, not only as against the British Government, but against all other interests, public or private.

It would seem fair to suggest that these words do not add much to the reasons for the rejection of an argument which in substance and effect is in accord with the submissions made in section I above—submissions which could not be maintained if Lord Bridge's *obiter dictum* (and, fortunately, it is not more than that) would have to be accepted.

Lord Bridge regards it as the purpose of the inviolability rule to protect the 'privacy', i.e. the private or secret character of the mission's documents. It has been suggested more than once that the true purpose is to protect the mission's unimpaired possession of its documents, their freedom from any act of constraint or interference such as only a government can initiate. This is the meaning in Art. 22 (entry into the mission's premises), Art. 29 (the person of the diplomat), and Art. 30 (the diplomat's residence). There is no reason why the term should have an entirely different meaning in Articles 24 and 27. Nor is it reasonable to attribute to Art. 24 a meaning which would impose a burden on the receiving State that it cannot be expected to carry. It cannot reasonably be expected to protect the diplomat or its mission against violations of privacy. They may take many forms, some obvious, some extremely difficult to discover or prove. It is and should be the general law that provides the remedy against them.

It is noticeable that in a later passage[21] Lord Bridge again referred to the word 'inviolability' and said

An infringement of the protection must amount to a violation of the protected documents. It would surely be a misuse of language to say that a protected document had been violated because an officer of the ITC supplied it to a third party without authority, unless the recipient was or ought to have been aware of the absense or authority.

[20] The judgment of the Court has so far not been reported.

[21] P. 29.

This is entirely in harmony with the argument put forward in these pages. A violation requires an act of interference or constraint such as only a government or its agents can perform. The individual who copies a document or steals it no less fails to violate it than the individual who receives it without the owner's authority.

The conclusion, therefore, is that, while Lord Bridge's actual decision deserves unqualified support, one dictum which is inconsistent with established learning in international law as well as with the true construction of the Vienna Convention as a whole should not be followed. International and, it is hoped, English practice should treat it as remarks without binding authority, which were provoked and are explained by the oddities of the case put forward by the ITC. Mr Kentridge's argument was well founded and neither Lord Bridge nor Dillon L.J. have given any reason for its rejection. It expressed in different words the submissions made in this paper.

For the same reason it should be obvious that if a court makes an order against a State or a diplomatic agent and if, in order to comply with the order, some reference to the archives or the documents of a mission is necessary this does not in any way infringe their inviolability. In *Maclaine Watson & Co. Ltd.* v. *International Tin Council (No. 2)*[22] the defendant was ordered to disclose its assets. Its advisers thought it right to suggest that a proviso should be attached to the order to the effect that 'nothing in it should require the International Tin Council or any of its officers to disclose any information which could only be derived from any document which is inviolable'. The Court of Appeal rightly refused so to qualify its order. The application was misconceived. No question of inviolability can arise merely as a result of the fact that a member of the diplomatic mission has to look at some document. Such inspection does not in any sense involve any constraint or, indeed, anything in the nature of a violation of the integrity or archives or documents.

III

If the preceding submissions on the meaning of inviolability in Art. 24 are correct, there will be no difficulty in concluding that the same meaning applies to Art. 22 dealing with the inviolability of the premises of a mission. In fact it is almost superfluous to look for a definition, for Art. 22 (1), second sentence and Art. 22 (3) provide it by precluding the receiving State's agents from entering, searching, requisitioning, attaching or levying execution in respect of the premises, i.e. from such measures as official

[22] (1988) 3 W.L.R., 1169 at p. 1203, on the other hand an Embassy document is inviolable for purposes of discovery: *Fayed* v. *Al-Tajir*, [1988] B.712.

interference could perform. In other words, if in regard to the inviolability of archives and documents the meaning could perhaps give rise to a difference of opinion, nothing like it is possible, when one comes to consider the inviolability of premises. Germany's Federal Constitutional Court was therefore fully justified in holding in 1962 that the sending State was subject to a judicial order deleting its title to the mission's premises from the Land Registry and requiring their surrender, for 'according to general practice and doctrine the inviolability and immunity of embassy premises implies that the organs of the receiving State cannot enter the premises without the consent of the chief of the mission. Searches and measures of execution within the premises are prohibited';[23] the Vienna Convention does not permit any different construction. Here the problem is not one of definition, but of exceptions to the rule.

This is well exemplified by an incident about which Mrs Denza writes.[24] After referring to the *travaux préparatoires* to which little, if any, weight should be attached,[25] she mentions the case of the Embassy of Iraq in Pakistan, where in 1973 'huge consignments of arms were found to be stored in crates', when armed policemen raided the embassy after the Ambassador had refused to allow a search. Since then there occurred in 1984 the notorious incident outside the Libyan embassy in London, called the People's Bureau. An orderly demonstration by opponents of the present Libyan Government's regime took place, and when shots fired from windows of the Bureau were responsible for the death of a woman police constable ten days later, the Bureau was evacuated. When searched by the British police, arms were found. The incident led to a report by the Foreign Affairs Committee of the House of Commons (which includes the Minutes of Evidence)[26] and to a

[23] BVerfGE 15, 25 or *Int. L.R.* 38. 162.

[24] *Diplomatic Law* (1976), p. 84.

[25] See, e.g., the summary by Mrs Denza, loc. cit., pp. 83, 84, or Herdegen (below n. 26) p. 739 or Hardy, *Modern Diplomatic Law*, p. 44. The upshot was that the difficulties of defining exceptions were such as to make definitions impossible. Amendments proposed to deal with exceptional circumstances were withdrawn, because for one reason or another the majority was against such an exception. It is submitted that such a course of events simply meant that the point was left open. It is unjustifiable to say, as Mrs Denza loc. cit. does, that the Convention 'leaves absolute the inviolability of the premises of the mission'. The history has often been summarized and discussed and certainly shows that a majority of those concerned with the preparation of the Vienna Convention thought that there should be no exceptions to the principle of inviolability. But the *travaux préparatoires* are in no sense binding. They are only a subsidiary means of interpretation, where interpretation is required and permitted. If one looks at the issues in depth, it must be obvious, as not all the delegates to the Vienna Conference seem to have appreciated, that no State can be prepared to give up elementary and indispensable rights of self-preservation. In the course of his excellent article referred to in n. 26 Herdegen, after a full discussion of all revelant aspects, rightly concludes that the duties imposed by the Vienna Convention must give way, 'when diplomatic agents of a foreign State prepetrate or cover acts threatening the security of the receiving State, human life or assets situated within its territorial jurisdiction' (p. 752).

[26] *The Abuse of Diplomatic Immunities and Privileges* (1984), published by H. M.

White Paper issued by the British Government.[27] In the context of the inviolability of the mission's premises under Art. 22 both documents are relevant only in so far as they deal with the effects of an emergency and of abuse of the premises.

The problem was on the whole seen in terms of the application of the doctrine of self-defence. The present writer had done the same in a letter to the editor of *The Times*[28] with which Lord Denning, speaking in a non-judicial capacity in the House of Lords, concurred.[29] Before the Committee Sir John Freeland, then the Legal Adviser of the Foreign and Commonwealth Office, stated:[30]

> It is, of course, the case that the doctrine of self-defence in international law is a very restrictive one. The classic formulation . . . is that self-defence is justified where there is 'a necessity of self-defence instant, overwhelming, leaving no choice of means and no moment for deliberation'. In more modern parlance, we would take the view that the right to resort to self-defence arises where there is a serious threat or actual danger, where there is no other means of averting it or bringing it to an end, and that the action taken in self-defence must be limited to what is necessary and what is proportionate.

Later Sir John was asked whether in the event of someone being killed through the window of an embassy the police had the right to go in immediately in self-defence and seize persons and articles. His reply was:[31]

> I certainly would not exclude the possibility of its being justifiable in a case where, for example, there is continued [*sic*!] firing of weapons from the premises of an embassy, where every other method has been tried and has failed to stop that . . .

Sir Francis Vallat, a former Legal Adviser to the Foreign and Commonwealth Office, when asked a similar question said:[32]

> Suppose the embassy were being used as a kind of fortress for a running battle with people in the street, it [self-defence] might then become justifiable, but I find it difficult to imagine that before an international tribunal of repute one would be held to be justified to run into an embassy because there had been one or two shots fired, even if that happened to cause an injury or death.

This seems to mean that the authorities have to wait for the death of a third person before they can intervene—a proposition which must be

---

Stationery Office. See Herdegen, *Zeitschrift für ausländisches öffentliches Recht und Völkerrecht* 46 (1986), 734; Higgins, *American Journal of International Law*, 1985, 641.

[27] Cmnd. 9497, discussed by Higgins, *American Journal of International Law*, 1986, 135.

[28] 1 May 1984. [29] 16 May 1984, Hansard (House of Lords), col. 1454.

[30] Minutes of Evidence, p. 28. [31] Loc. cit. [32] Loc. cit., p. 34.

described as wholly unacceptable and unrealistic, but to which the Committee seems to have listened with a remarkable lack of concern. On the other hand, in a memorandum submitted to the Committee Professor G. I. A. D. Draper went further:[33]

> It is probably a valid contention in law that an immediate and forcible entry into diplomatic premises of Libya, after the firing incident, was a measure designed to prevent the offender repeating the offence, and the overpowering of him within the embassy precincts would have been a legitimate exercise of the inherent right of self-defence enjoyed by the United Kingdom.

Neither the Committee nor the Government's White Paper (perhaps wisely) makes any definite finding on the problem of the receiving State's reaction to abuse of diplomatic immunities, but Professor Rosalyn Higgins who was specialist adviser to the Committee 'remains sceptical as to the applicability at all of the international concept of self-defence to violent acts by the representatives of one state within the territory of another, directed against the latter's citizens'.[34] She also described Ambassador Arthur Goldberg's suggestion that inviolability was lost by the perpetration from the mission's premises of unlawful acts as a 'popular and ill-informed' view.[35]

In the course of the whole of this discussion no attention was paid to an admittedly *obiter*, yet important *dictum* in a decision of the Court of Appeals of the District of Columbia:[36]

> Only if the criminal act being committed by the diplomat is such as to endanger the public may the police disregard the inviolability of an embassy and enter to seize the offender.

In assessing the limits of the inviolability of a mission's premises it is essential to avoid conceptualism and to preserve a modicum of common sense. Thus, on the one hand, there is a question whether we should speak of self-defence or of self-help[37] or self-preservation[38] and, in relation to self-defence, whether we should be bound by a definition which was

[33] Loc. cit. p. 72

[34] See above n. 26, at p. 647. This is probably not the general view. In favour of the application of self-defence or self-help, see, e.g., Dahm, *Völkerrecht*, I, 351, or Berber, *Völkerrecht* I, 288.

[35] See above n. 26, at p. 646.

[36] *Fatemi* v. *United States* 192 A.2d 525 (1963), also *Int. L. R.* 34, 148.

[37] On self-help see Bryde, *Encyclopedia of Public International Law*, 4, 215 (1982) with references to literature. The term is apparently 'reserved to reactions against violations of a State's rights that do not occur in the form of an armed attack'.

[38] See Hall, *International Law*, (8th edn., 1924), 322 sqq, or Oppenheim (-Lauterpacht) I, 297, sqq., or more recently Partsch, *Encyclopedia of Public International Law* 4, 217.

formulated by Webster as long ago as 1838,[39] i.e. long before the emergence of a multitude of States some of which are characterized by lawlessness. In modern circumstances even the conception of self-defence has acquired a much broader connotation, as recent State practice and academic opinion[40] tends to establish. Danger of an armed attack has frequently been invoked as justifying defensive measures. On the other hand, let us imagine that a large quantity of explosives is stored in the premises of an embassy and constitutes a danger of the utmost gravity to a large, inhabited section of a town. Is there anyone who would suggest that the receiving State is precluded from entering the embassy and removing the explosives or, in other words, that it must wait until the explosion has occurred and enormous damage to persons and property has ensued? Surely there is only one answer. If this is so, the whole problem becomes one of degree. From this point of view it is suggested that, once shots have been fired from an embassy and an undertaking to prevent similar acts has been declined by the diplomat in charge, the receiving State should be entitled to enter the embassy, search it and remove such weapons as may be found. In short the inviolability of premises is conditioned by the lawfulness of their use. Of course the receiving State runs the risk of the evidence of abuse being insufficient. It also runs the risk of reprisals in the foreign country, whether they are in law justifiable or not. These are not legal considerations. They involve a balancing of risks. As a rule it should not be too difficult to decide where the greater risk lies. One thing should be certain: the fate of the British mission or even of British civilians in a lawless foreign country must be subordinate to the fate of civilians in Britain.

In conclusion it is suggested that the inviolability of a mission's premises is by no means absolute, but must give way if the mission has allowed such dangers to arise in its premises as to provoke the receiving State and take measures reasonably necessary to protect the security of the life and property of the inhabitants.

It is therefore impossible to agree with the conclusions of the House of Commons Committee, accepted in paragraph 83 of the Government White Paper, that

[39] On Webster's definition put forward in the context of the *Caroline* incident see Oppenheim (-Lauterpacht) I, 300 or Meng, *Encyclopedia of Public International Law* 3, 81.

[40] Professor Bowett's *Self-Defence in International Law* (1958) is probably still the leading text. He rightly suggests (p. 270) that the function of self-defence is 'to justify action otherwise illegal, which is necessary to protect certain essential rights of the state against violation by other states'. The doctrine of necessity was propounded, probably for the first time, by Grotius and is one of those fundamental ideas which no text and no delegate to a Conference can eliminate. For further material see the well-documented article by Herdegen.

whatever answer is given to the question whether self-defence is a concept applicable to the circumstances of St James's Square, it could not have acted as a lawful basis for the forcible entry of the Bureau premises.

On the contrary, the submission here made is that, once the shots had been fired from the premises of the Bureau and the Police Constable had been killed, it was the British Government's right and, indeed, its duty, after rejection of a prompt request for permission, to enter the premises, to search for and to remove any weapons held there. The conclusions of the White Paper should be reconsidered to ensure that none of the 5000 or so foreign diplomats stationed in London misunderstands his duties and the consequences of their breach.

IV

It remains to add a few words about the inviolability of the correspondence of the mission which is limited to its 'official' correspondence (Art. 27 paragraph 2), and of a diplomatic agent, which is not so limited (Art. 30 paragraph 2).

As regards the former it has been suggested[41] that inviolability prevents it from being used as evidence in the courts of the receiving State. As regards the latter the same learned writer believes that in proceedings properly instituted by or against the diplomat discovery could not be obtained.[42] It is submitted that neither suggestion merits support.

'Inviolability', let it be stated once more, simply means freedom from official interference. Official correspondence of the mission over the removal of which the receiving State has had no control can, as has been submitted above, be freely used in judicial proceedings. And if the diplomat has instituted proceedings or if he is a defendant whose immunity has been waived or otherwise lost or is not recognized by law, he is subject to the rules of the court like any other litigant and cannot invoke privileges. At the Vienna Conference the delegate of the United States proposed to limit the inviolability of a diplomat's papers and correspondence in the same way as his property, i.e. by reference to Art. 31 paragraph 1 which denies immunity from civil or administrative jurisdiction in certain cases, particularly in the case of an action relating to any professional or

[41] Denza, loc. cit., p. 124.

[42] Ibid., p. 145; but in the *Encyclopedia of Public International Law* 9, 97 she says that the words in Art. 30 paragraph 2 'are generally interpreted as according the same degree of protection as is given under Art. 22 to property on mission premises . . . mainly immunity from search, requisition, attachment or execution'. With the latter statement one can readily agree.

commercial activity exercised by the diplomatic agent in the receiving State outside his official functions. That proposal was rejected. According to Mrs Denza[43] this

> means that even where, for example, an action may be instituted against a diplomatic agent in regard to a commercial activity which he has been exercising, it will not be possible to obtain discovery or documents against him in regard to papers in his possession which may be crucial to the case . . . It is difficult to defend this residual immunity either on grounds of logic or as necessary to enable the diplomat to perform his functions.

The last sentence shows that the first sentence cannot be defended. Where the immunity from judicial proceedings does not apply, the diplomat is in the same position as any other litigant. He is in no way procedurally privileged. The amendment proposed by the United States was unnecessary. The fact that it was rejected cannot displace a well-established principle. But the whole incident proves how useless, even dangerous and misleading the resort to *travaux préparatoires* often is and how delegates to international conferences who may not be lawyers may, perhaps for the sake of (unnecessary) clarification, lay the foundation for what can only be described as errors of law. Nor does one know why the proposal was rejected: the majority may have thought that the amendment was inappropriate. *Travaux préparatoires* may be looked at only where there is ambiguity, where there arises a problem of interpretation which cannot otherwise be solved. No such situation exists in the present case.

As the law stands, Art. 30 applies outside proceedings and has in no way precedence over them. Proceedings and their effect are dealt with by Art. 31 and well-established law governs their conduct.

The inviolability of correspondence, however, proves how impossible it is to attribute to the term a wider meaning than it has been given in these pages. A State can be expected not to open letters or letter boxes or not to interfere with the messenger who collects mail from the post office or takes it there. But to ensure the 'privacy' of correspondence, to protect correspondence against acts other than those of the State itself is a practical impossibility and cannot have been within the contemplation of any legislator.

[43] Denza, loc. cit., p. 145.

13

Reflections on the Prosecution of Persons Abducted in Breach of International Law

I

A STATE which authorizes the abduction of a person from the territory of another sovereign State is guilty of violation of public international law. This principle is supported by considerable State practice, numerous decisions of municipal courts and a large body of doctrinal opinion.[1] Its basis is the incontrovertible rule that exercise of physical force by one State in the territory of another State without the latter's consent constitutes an excess of international jurisdiction[2] or a violation of the 'principle of respect for State sovereignty', which is guaranteed not only by Article 2 of the Charter of the United Nations and other texts, for these 'merely respond to firmly established and longstanding tenets of customary international law'.[3]

Notwithstanding the almost elementary character of the rule, some of its implications require comment.

1. The rule presupposes that the abduction is carried out by agents instructed or authorized by the State or by private volunteers whose acts have been adopted or ratified by the State.

[1] The material which appeared before 1960 in English-speaking countries is collected by Paul O'Higgins, 'Unlawful seizure and irregular extradition,' *The British Year Book of International Law* (1960), 278–320, at 279, n.1. Since then, see, in particular Vincent Coussirat-Coustère and Pierre Michel Eisenmann, 'L'enlèvement de personnes privées et le droit international', *Revue général de droit international public* (1972) (76), 346–400; Note in 72 *Michigan Law Review* (1974), 1087 and 1103; M. Cherif Bassiouni, 'Unlawful seizures and irregular rendition devices as alternatives to extradition', *Vanderbilt Journal of Transnational Law* (1973) (7), 25–70; A. Abramovsky & Eagle, 57 *Oregon Law Review* 1978, 51; Martin Feinrider, 14 *Akron Law Review 1880–81*, p. 27, and W. Bauer, *Die Völkerrechtswidrige Entführung* (1968). See also Michael H. Cardozo, 'When extradition fails is abduction the solution?' 55 *The American Journal of International Law* (January 1961), 127–135, who asks the pertinent question: would we be outraged if a war criminal were abducted from his home in California and spirited to Yugoslavia?

[2] The proposition is elementary; perhaps it is sufficient to refer to 1 Oppenheim-Lauterpacht, 295; D. Carreau, *Droit international* (1986), paras. 843 et seq., or almost any other textbook. See also Mann, *Rec.* 111 (1964 i), 129 or *Studies in International Law* (1973), 113, and above p. 22.

[3] *Nicaragua* v. *United States of America*, [1986] *ICJ Reports* 110, para 212.

Dinstein, Y. (ed.), *Essays in Honour of Shabtai Rosenne* (Dordrecht, 1989), 407.

A police officer whose acts are not repudiated by his government always acts as an agent of the State. It is, therefore, impossible to agree with a decision of the Appellate Division of the Supreme Court of South Africa,[4] which related to the following facts. The appellants were apprehended on territory of the Kingdom of Swaziland by individuals whose precise status is not made clear, but whom the Court described as unauthorized officials, i.e. police officers of South Africa, who acted in the seizure without any authority from South Africa. The court said, 'that is not an international delinquency since State B [i.e. South Africa] itself does not perform or purport to perform any act of sovereignty in State A'[5] [i.e. Swaziland]. This in untenable. In the first place, the 'unauthorized official' brought the appellant across the Swaziland frontier to Colonel Dreyer of the South African police who was stationed at a spot some fifteen kilometres from the border and arrested the appellant, who in due course was prosecuted in the South African courts. South Africa, therefore, adopted the international wrong. Moreover, a State can only act through agents. Even if their activity is not authorized *ab initio*, it is the State that acts as soon as it fails to return the abducted person, but arrests and prosecutes him and this ratifies the originally unauthorized acts. The South African Court's *ratio decidendi*, namely 'the narrow factual premises mentioned above, i.e. that the seizure of the appellants in Swaziland was not authorized by the Republic',[6] wholly ignores the realities of the case.

Even if the person acting in the foreign territory is not a police officer, but a private one, subsequent adoption by the State entails its responsibility. For this reason the suggestion that the infamous Eichmann was abducted by private volunteers[7] is irrelevant in law, for even if it had been factually correct (which it does not seem to have been[8]), the essential fact is that Eichmann was imprisoned, prosecuted, and convicted and executed by the State of Israel which thus endorsed the acts of any private person involved. If a State wishes to avoid a finding of ratification, it has the option of returning the abducted person to the State from which he was removed.

It is submitted that a violation of international law occurs also where the State or its agent does not abduct the victim by force, but induces him by fraud or other illegal means to leave the country of refuge and proceed to some other country where he is apprehended. In such circumstances to

[4] *Nduli* v. *Minister of Justice*, [1978] (1) *S.A.* 893; also 69 Int. L.R. 145, see also *Ndhlovu* v. *Minister of Justice*, [1976] (4) *S.A.* 250 also 68 Int. L.R. 7.

[5] *Nduli*, ibid., 909. [6] Ibid., 912.

[7] Helen Silving, '*In Re* Eichmann: a dilemma of law and morality', 55 *The American Journal of International Law*, 1961, 307–58, at 312.

[8] See the statement by Prime Minister Ben-Gurion of 27 May 1960, printed by O'Higgins, above note 1, at 296 where reference is made to 'the extraordinary resource and skill of the staff of the Security Services'.

which further consideration will be given below,[9] the wrong is committed in the foreign State, because the illegal means are used or have their effect there. A State, being sovereign, is not expected to tolerate acts that involve generally recognized illegality, though they are not performed by force. It is not necessarily the use of force, but the illegality, that constitutes the wrong done to the sovereignty of the State.

2. A breach of international law occurs only in the absence of consent by the State whose sovereignty the abduction affects.

Consent may be and frequently is declared subsequently. The real question is the factual one: in what circumstances may consent be said to be given or, alternatively, when may a State be said to have waived the tort? It is submitted that if the State does or says nothing, the illegality remains. It is impossible to infer consent from silence or inactivity. Even if the State declares that it does not require the return of the abducted person, it is at least arguable that it waives the remedy rather than the wrong. This is a matter of construction. In *Eichmann's* case, Israel and Argentina issued a joint communiqué to the effect that they 'have resolved to regard as closed the incident that arose out of action taken by citizens of Israel, which infringed the fundamental rights of the State of Argentina.'[10] According to the Supreme Court of Israel,[11] this 'means that Argentina has condoned the violation of her sovereignty and has waived her claims, including that for the return of Eichmann'. This conclusion would seem to be incontrovertible, though one may have some doubt about another part of the judgment of the District Court approved by the Supreme Court, according to which 'such waiver may be explicit or by acquiescence'.[12] It is generally accepted[13] that a waiver must be shown by conclusive evidence and cannot be presumed. Acquiescence can only rarely have the character of conclusive evidence of waiver, but may exceptionally be inferred from prolonged and deliberate silence.

In these circumstances, it is impossible to agree with a decision of the Court of Appeals, Second Circuit in the case of *United States, ex. Rel. Lujan* v. *Gengler.*[14] The opinion of the Court was delivered by Chief Judge Kaufman and is likely to count amount the least ingenuous judicial

[9] Below, text at 18.

[10] See the judgment of the Supreme Court, Vol. 36 Int. L.R. 306 (para. 13).

[11] Ibid. [12] Ibid., 305; see also p. 64.

[13] See Anne M. Trebilcock, 7 *Encyclopedia of Public International Law* (1984) 533, *sub verbo* waiver, and Jörg-Paul Müller & Thomas Cottier, ibid. 5. On acquiescence, see the fundamental article by I. C. MacGibbon, 'The scope of acquiescence in international law', *The British Year Book of International Law* (1956), p. 143–86 (1954, p. 31). See also, Eugène Borel as Arbitrator in *The Kronprins Gustaf Adolf, The American Journal of International Law*, 1932, 834: 'A renunciation to a right or claim is not to be presumed. It must be shown by conclusive evidence.'

[14] 510, F.2d, 62 (1975); also 61 Int. L.R., 206.

pronouncements ever made. The case, which will have to be considered further in another connection,[15] concerned an Argentinian citizen, Lujan, who was hired by fraudulent representations made by an American agent in Argentina to fly to Bolivia where on arrival Bolivian police officers acting without their superiors' authority, but as paid agents of the United States, took him into custody and after a few days' delay placed him on a plane bound for New York. There he was arrested and arraigned. One of the points taken by the court was that neither Argentina nor Bolivia had 'in any way protested or even objected to his abduction' and that the failure of Argentina and Bolivia to object did 'preclude any violation of international law which might otherwise have occurred'. There is also room for the impression that the Court relied on 'the general principle that consent or acquiescence by the offended State waives any right it possessed and heals any violation of international law.'[16] Or, as it was put in another case, 'absent protest or objection by the offended sovereign Reed has no standing to raise violation of international law as an issue'.[17] It is submitted that every step in this argument is open to criticism. There was no evidence that Argentina and Bolivia even knew of the illegalities which had been committed by and on behalf of the United States within their respective territories. Nor could the accused know whether they lodged a protest in Washington; surely it was for the Government of the United States to disclose whether or not a protest had been received. Nor can consent or acquiescence be inferred from the known facts. And even if Argentina and Bolivia had deliberately and in knowledge of all relevant facts decided to ignore the incident, this would not have abolished the breach of customary or conventional international law. If I wrongfully deprive my enemy of his liberty and if, after his release, he decides not to sue me or to report me to the police, my behaviour retains its character of a wrongful act, a tort and a crime. To suggest that my enemy's failure to take proceedings 'heals any violation' of the law or operates as consent is an untenable proposition.

The fact that somehow consent to the abduction has been given or, in particular, that the State in question has failed to object or has waived its rights is peculiarly within the knowledge of the authorities of the prosecuting State. Consequently it should be called upon to prove consent, express or implied. A strictly legal analysis leads to the same result. The accused has to prove that agents of the prosecuting State abducted him and thus prima facie committed an international wrong. If the prosecuting

[15] Below text at notes 56 ff. [16] Ibid., 67.
[17] *United States* v. *Reed*, 639 F.2d, 986 (1981).

State wishes to establish the elimination of the wrong by consent, it plainly carries the burden of proof.

By way of postscript, it should be noted that a decision of the Federal Supreme Court of Germany[18] was guilty of a comparable error. The accused had been abducted from Holland. The Dutch Embassy addressed a Note to the German Government describing the incident 'as a grave violation of Dutch sovereignty' and asked for the immediate communication of the Foreign Office's views. A request for a return of the accused was not made. The Court, therefore, saw no objection to the continuation of the criminal proceedings. The Dutch request about the outcome of which nothing is known was not much less than a protest, but certainly could not be the basis for an inference of consent. In the United States of America there is even a case in which Mexico whence the prisoner was abducted intervened in *habeas corpus* proceedings brought by him. Yet the application was dismissed, and Mexico was referred to the Department of State.[19]

3. The normal and generally accepted remedy in the event of a wrongful abduction is the return of the victim, i.e. restitution in kind. There are numerous cases in which the injured State has demanded, and the wrongdoing State has agreed to, the return of the victim.[20]

It is important to stress the unanimity of practice and doctrine on this point, for it has often been doubted whether international law recognizes the remedy of restitution in kind: some scholars have asserted the rule that international law knows no remedy other than damages.[21] This view is clearly without foundation, and it is satisfactory to notice that a Committee[22] of the Federal Constitutional Court of the Federal Republic of Germany rendered an important decision[23] on the point, which quite clearly assumes that if France—whence the accused person was removed by fraud—had demanded it, the Federal Republic would have been duty-bound to return him.

[18] 30 May 1985, [1985] NStZ 464. See now below, p. 353.

[19] *In re Lopez*, 6. F. Supp. 342 (1934).

[20] No less than four Swiss cases are collected by Müller & Wildhaber, *Praxis des Völkerrechts*, 273–6 (1982). On the general character of the right to restitution in integrum, see Mann, 'The Consequences of an international wrong', in *British Year Book of International Law* (1975–6), 2–8 above or pp. 126–9.

[21] The principal promoter of this unacceptable view is Mr Lagergren in his, for many reasons, unfortunate award in the case of *British Petroleum v. Libya*, 53 Int. L.R. 297, particularly of 347. See, generally, Gray, *British Year Book of International Law* 25 (1985) who is unnecessarily diffident, and above, p. 126.

[22] In the Federal Constitutional Court there is a Committee that submits each appeal to a preliminary examination and admits only those which are not held to be manifestly unfounded. The decision referred to in the text was a decision of the Committee attached to the Second Chamber and consisting of three judges of the Court.

[23] 17 July 1985 [1986] NJW 1427, on which see Mann, op. cit., p. 2167.

On the other hand if, as has already been pointed out, the return of the abducted person does not eliminate the initial wrong (as is shown by the fact that a claim for damages may be pursued by the injured State even after the return), the failure to comply with a request for the return of the abducted person is a separate wrong which is quite independent of the original one. There is, therefore, no justification for the suggestion which has sometimes been intimated, particularly in Germany[24] and the United States of America,[25] that it is relevant to the question of the court's jurisdiction whether a demand for the return has been made. Nor is it relevant to ask whether 'there exists a general principle of public international law according to which, if the injured State demands the immediate return or a comparable remedy, criminal proceedings against a person brought within the jurisdiction in a manner inconsistent with public international law may not be carried through'.[26] It may be that this question may require an affirmative answer. But it has no bearing upon the antecedent illegality, i.e. the wrongful abduction. This is a separate wrong which the injured State does not waive by its decision not to claim the return of the abducted person and which the wrongdoer's State does not undo by allowing a return.

II

It is against the background of the legal position in public international law as sketched in the preceding section that the question must be answered what rights, if any, the abducted person may derive from the international wrong committed by or on behalf of the State in which he finds himself and is being prosecuted for what may or may not be an offence under the local law, for it must not be assumed that a conviction of the accused is certain.

During the greater part of the last 150 years or so, this problem has been seen as one of jurisdiction: does the State have criminal jurisdiction in respect of the abducted person? It would be idle to deny that such jurisdiction exists, and it exists however abhorrent the circumstances of the abduction may be. *Mala captus bene detentus*, as the old adage teaches. The matter was exhaustively considered by the Israeli courts, when in 1961 and 1962 they had to decide *Eichmann's* case.[27] It would be almost disrespectful to the most learned judgment by eight Israeli Judges sitting

[24] Federal Supreme Court, 2 August 1984, [1984] NStZ 563.

[25] This follows from *United States* v. *Toscanino*, 500 F.2d 267 (1974) and all the subsequent cases discussed below, even from *United States ex rel. Lujan* v. *Gengler*, above note 14.

[26] This is the question which the Commission referred to in note 22 above seems to have thought relevant.

[27] 36 Int. L.R. p. 5 (District Court) and p. 277 (Supreme Court).

in the District Court of Jerusalem and the Supreme Court of Israel if an attempt were made to review once again the ample material from many countries that led them to the conclusion that the abduction of Eichmann from Argentina did not in any way prejudice Israel's jurisdiction over him. English and American decisions of the highest authority, such as *R.* v. *Officer Commanding Depot Battalion Colchester, ex parte Elliott*[28] and *Ker* v. *Illinois*,[29] followed by *Frisbie* v. *Collins*,[30] and many other sources of international law left no doubts, though the Israeli courts did not fail to notice the few voices which 25 years ago were critical of the judicial practice in the world.

Since then at least two supreme tribunals have affirmed the established rule that, irrespective of the circumstances in which the accused has been brought within the country, a court has jurisdiction to try him for any offence he may have committed: the accused stands before the court and this fact alone confers jurisdiction *ratione personae* upon it. Thus it came about that in the case of *Argoud*, decided by the French Cour de Cassation,[31] the principle was not contested. Colonel Argoud was abducted from Munich in February 1963 by French agents in circumstances which can only be described as aggravating. On 16 November 1963, the German Federal Parliament requested the Federal Government to demand Argoud's return. On 28 December 1963 the Court held

> que l'assurance formelle a été donnée, ce jour, par le Ministère public que M. le Ministre des Affaires étrangères n'a reçu aucune note du Gouvernement de la République fédérale d'Allemagne demandant la remise aux autorités allemandes de l'ex-colonel Argoud, alors cependant que celui-ci est détenu en France depuis plus de dix mois.

Although the German note was handed over on 30 December 1963 and the defence so informed the Court, on that day the Colonel was convicted. It is merely of political interest to ask whether it was an accident that the delivery of the Note, which does not seem to have been published, was delayed so as to permit the Court to render its decision of 28 December. It is much more important to mention that the appeal to the Cour de Cassation was dismissed on the footing of a report of M. le Conseiller Comte who, in the course of his concluding words, said: 'Rarement—peut-être jamais—ne s'était posé à la conscience des juges problème plus difficile, plus complexe, plus troublant'.[32]

[28] [1949] 1 All E.R. 373. [29] 119 US 436 (1888).

[30] 342 US 519 (1952); in *United States* v. *Crews* 445 U.S. 463 (1980) it was said: 'An illegal arrest, without more, has never been viewed as a bar to subsequent proceedings'.

[31] 4 June 1964, 93 *Clunet* (1965); also 45 Int. L.R. 90. See, in particular Doehring, 28 *ZaORVR 209* (1965).

[32] Above note 31.

The Federal Supreme Court of Germany also affirmed jurisdiction in cases in which the accused had been abducted by force or by stealth from a foreign country.[33] Both decisions rendered in 1984 and 1985 were considered with astonishing speed by Commissions of the Federal Constitutional Court,[34] which held it to be free from doubt that jurisdiction could not be challenged. The earlier Commission relied on a substantial amount of comparative material, though it refrained from a complete investigation. However this may be, it is regrettable that the Commission failed adequately to explore the broader issues to which the problem gives rise.

Finally, in England and the Commonwealth, there is no doubt about the jurisdiction of their courts in respect of an abducted person, though there as well as in the United States of America, as will appear later, much uncertainty surrounds the real problem. None of the English cases related to a person who, in violation of international law, had been abducted. Usually the accused had been deported from the foreign country at the instigation of the English police, frequently in disregard of extradition treaties which provided for an elaborate procedure. Sometimes it was by stealth that he was induced to return. A New Zealand decision of 1978[35] and following it an English decision of 1985,[36] the latest case on the subject, related to facts of this type.

With rare unanimity and undeniable justification the courts of the world have held that the manner in which an accused has been brought before the court does not and, indeed, cannot deprive it of its jurisdiction, of its right to hear the case against the person standing before it.

III

In so deciding the courts of the world have, however, failed to face the decisive question. This is not whether jurisdiction exists, but whether jurisdiction should be exercised.

In order to answer this question one should not think of a case such as *Eichmann*. This was so extreme, so unique, so horrendous a case that a court which had jurisdiction because the man stood before it could not

[33] 2 August 1984, [1984] NStZ 563; 30 May 1985, [1985] NStZ 464.

[34] Above note 23; 3 June 1986, [1986] NJW 3021.

[35] *R.* v. *Hartley* [1978] 2 NZLR 199.

[36] *R.* v. *Plymouth Magistrates, ex parte Driver*, [1985] 2 All E.R. 681. It completely fails to deal in depth with the problem of the existence of jurisdiction, but simply asserts that 'the court has no power to inquire into the circumstances in which a person is found in the jurisdiction for the purpose of refusing to try him'. The Court deals with all the cases affirming the existence of jurisdiction and then turns to what it describes as 'discretion'. Its conclusion is that there is no discretion. The Court completely fails to deal with the relevant point, namely, that there may be a misuse of power within the meaning of *Connelly* v. *Director of Public Prosecutions*, [1964] A.C. 1254, a decision rendered long after the majority of cases relied upon as precedents in *Driver*'s case.

possibly be expected not to exercise it or even to ask whether it should be exercised. The singular character of the crime was such as to render the exercise of jurisdiction in practice, though perhaps not logically, a duty, but at the same time should not in any sense be allowed to supply the standard applicable in other, different cases.

Where they arise, jurisdiction, it is submitted, cannot lawfully be exercised by virtue of that great and general principle which overshadows the more specific rules to which reference will be made: *ex injuria jus non oritur* and its counterpart in American constitutional law where the Supreme Court developed the so-called exclusionary rule, according to which 'a poisonous tree' must not be allowed to bear fruit, so that as a result of its own lawlessness the government is barred from realizing its fruit by bringing the accused to trial.[37] Similarly, the Dutch Hoge Raad denied any probative value to a Dutch police report about an incident in the course of which a patrol vessel of the Netherlands State police stopped a Dutch boat in German territorial waters.[38] The Swiss Federal Tribunal was very conscious of this principle. It refused the extradition of a Belgian subject to the Federal Republic of Germany. He had been induced by agents of Germany to travel from Belgium, where his extradition could not be obtained, to Switzerland where he was immediately taken into custody to enable Germany to request his extradition. But in a decision the full text of which has unfortunately not been published, the Federal Tribunal held that Switzerland would have become an accessory to a violation of public international law if it had complied with the German request.[39]. This is a decision expressive of an examplary sense of international morality and respect for international law.

The more positivist basis is Article 5 of the European Convention for the Protection of Human Rights and Fundamental Freedoms. According to its opening words, 'everyone has the right to liberty and security of persons'; moreover, everyone arrested or detained shall be brought promptly before a judge and shall also be entitled to take proceedings by which the lawfulness of his detention shall be decided speedily by a court. Very similar provisions are to be found in Article 9 of the International Convenant on Civil and Political Rights which has been signed and ratified by a large number of States, among them the Federal Republic of Germany and the United Kingdom, and in many other international texts.[40] But the ideas expressed in these international documents are also included in many constitutions where they are described by such principles

[37] A representative case is *Wong Sun* v. *United States*, 371 U.S. 417 (1963). A long list of cases is to be found in *Toscanino's* case (below note 47), at 272.

[38] 30 October 1962, 11 *Nederlands Tijdschrift voor International Recht* 373 (1964).

[39] *Annuaire Suisse de Droit International* 228 (1983), and see Hans Schultz, ibid. 93 (1984).

[40] See the literature in note 1 above.

as the dignity of the person, the rule of law, due process of law and many similar headings. These universally recognized principles of municipal law constitute important evidence of State practice and, therefore, supplement the international texts to which reference has been made. One cannot possibly agree, therefore, with an astonishing dictum in a German decision:

> In several States, it is true, there have been decisions which seem to be founded upon the view that the illegality created by the abduction could justify an obstacle to judicial proceedings. This practice, however, is neither sufficiently broad to qualify as a firm practice restricting jurisdiction nor does it sufficiently clearly express the conviction that it is public international law which requires the discontinuance of criminal proceedings against a person abducted in a manner inconsistent with public international law; in some decisions there is in fact an express statement that principles of municipal law (rule of law, due process of law) were preventing the proceedings.[41]

This discloses a curious view of the sources of public international law:[42] they most certainly include State practice, in particular judicial practice of municipal courts and principles of constitutional law.

When, therefore, an English Court held that the prosecution of a person illegally abducted from Zimbabwe was an abuse of process[43] and the proceedings had to be stayed, this throws much light on the international rule.[44] The same applies to the earlier decision of the New Zealand Court of Appeal, which in the exercise of its discretion refused to allow a prosecution to proceed in a case in which, in disregard of an existing extradition treaty, the accused had been illegally abducted from Australia. Woodhouse J. said that 'this must never become an area where it will be sufficient to consider that the end has justified the means. The issues are basic to the whole concept of freedom in society'.[45] Later the learned Judge added that the means which were adopted to make a trial possible were 'so much in conflict with one of the most important principles of the rule of law' that the discharge of the prisoner was unavoidable.[46]. This

[41] Above note 23. The dictum is particularly remarkable because the decision itself invokes State practice as represented by judicial decisions in order to justify its conclusion that 'the courts refuse the prosecution of a wrongfully abducted person only if the State injured by the abduction protests against the wrong and requests the return of the abducted person'.

[42] Cf. Art. 38 of the Statute of the International Court of Justice.

[43] That abuse may result in the prosecution being stayed follows from the decisions of the House of Lords in *Connelly* v. *Director of Public Prosecutions*, [1964] A.C. 1254 and *Director of Public Prosecutions* v. *Humphreys*, 2, All E.R. 497, among other cases. In Germany this is apparently an unsolved problem: Federal Supreme Court, 23 May 1984 [1985] NStZ. 131.

[44] *R.* v. *Bow Street Magistrates, ex parte Mackeson* 72 Cr. App. R. 24 (1981).

[45] Above note 35; see note 68 below.

[46] Cf. Lord Devlin at p. 1354 of *Connelly*'s case (above note 43): 'The courts cannot contemplate for a moment the transference to the Executive of the responsibility for seeing that the process of law is not abused.'

leads to a most interesting modern development in the United States of America, which is worthy of detailed analysis.

The leading modern case is *United States* v. *Toscanino*.[47] The defendant, an Italian citizen, alleged that agents of the United States had kidnapped him in Uruguay, taken him to Brazil where he had been tortured, and finally brought him under sedation to the United States. In a memorable judgment of Judge Mansfield the Court of Appeals, Second Circuit, held that in many cases there was no reason why the rule initiated by the often quoted decision of the United States Supreme Court in *Ker* v. *Illinois*[48] should not be followed and why, accordingly, it should not be held that the right of prosecution is not impaired by the illegality of the method by which the prosecution acquires control over the accused. But in a large number of cases beginning in 1961, the general rule was laid down according to which the government could not realize directly 'the fruits of its own deliberate and unnecessary lawlessness in bringing the accused to trial'. Consequently courts should 'decline to exercise jurisdiction over a defendant whose presence has been secured by force or fraud'. It is interesting to observe that in laying down the new rule, the Court invoked not only 'the underlying principle that the government should be denied the right to exploit its own illegal conduct',[49] but also international law as represented by Article 2 (4) of the United Nations Charter and Article 17 of the Charter of the Organization of American States according to which the territory of a State 'is inviolable' and 'may not be the object . . . of . . . measures of force taken by another State, directly or indirectly, on any ground whatever'.[50]

It is clear, therefore, that the decision rests on two distinct foundations, each of which suffices to support it: firstly, the view that the due process clause of the Fourteenth Amendment requires 'a court to divest itself of jurisdiction where it has been acquired as the result of the government's deliberate, unnecessary and unreasonable invasion of the accused's constitutional rights';[51] secondly, the 1888 rule of *Ker* v. *Illinois*,[52] according to which the circumstances creating jurisdiction are irrelevant, 'does not apply where a defendant has been brought into the district court's jurisdiction by forcible abduction in violation of a treaty'[53] or, probably, of international law[54].

[47] 500 F.2d 267 (1974); re-hearing denied, 501 F.2d, 1380 (1974). Also 61 Int. L.R. 190.

[48] Above note 29.

[49] Above note 47, at 275, quoting *Wong Sun* v. *United States*, 371 U.S. 471, 488 (1963).

[50] Above note 47, at 277. It is odd that the Court did not primarily rely on the rule of customary international law which is undoubted.

[51] Ibid. 275. [52] Above note 29. [53] Above note 47, at 278.

[54] This follows from ibid. p. 279, where in discussing *United States* v. *Cotton*, 471 F.2d 744 (1973), the Court made the statement mentioned in the text. It would have been odd if the Court had intended to deny or to forget a firm and obvious principle of customary international law.

The subsequent history of this judgment[55] is remarkable. Within eight months from the date of its delivery and within three months from the denial (by a majority) of a re-hearing, the same court, differently constituted, decided *United States, ex rel. Lujan* v. *Gengler*,[56] Chief Judge Kaufman delivering the opinion. The facts were held not to constitute 'that complex of shocking governmental conduct sufficient to convert an abduction which is simply illegal into one which sinks to a violation of due process'.[57] Lujan did not allege such 'torture, brutality and similar outrageous conduct'[58], or, as another decision put it,[59] such 'egregious incidents . . . which shock the conscience' as Toscanino had put forward, and suffered 'no deprivation greater than that which he would have endured through lawful extradition' which had not been requested by the United States. The rule in *Ker* v. *Illinois*,[60] which had been 'recognized'[61] by the earlier decision (though some readers may remember it as having been 'eroded') was displaced only 'by the use of torture, brutality and similar outrageous conduct' as opposed to 'any irregularity'.[62] And any violation of foreign territorial sovereignty was irrelevant in the absence of any protest or objection by the foreign State.[63]

It may be doubted whether the reader of the decision in *Toscanino* is persuaded by the distinction so drawn or feels impressed by the crass use of words for the purpose of giving *Toscanino* a flavour that simple-minded lawyers would not suspect. However this may be, it must be admitted that in those Circuits in which any exception advocated by *Toscanino* is admitted at all,[64] it is strictly limited to 'cruel, inhumane and outrageous conduct'[65] and, as Justice Mansfield himself accepted,[66] presupposes 'a finding that the gross mistreatment leading to the forcible abduction of the defendant was perpetrated by representatives of the United States Government'. International law which, it has often been said, is part of the law of the United States,[67] is, in this branch of the law, ignored by the Executive

[55] Ultimately the District Court to which the case was remanded held that the defendant had failed to prove that United States officials were involved in the abduction; 398 F. Supp. 916 (1974).

[56] Above note 15. [57] Ibid. 66. [58] Ibid. 65.

[59] *Davis* v. *Mueller*, 643 F.2d 521 (1981), a decision of the Court of Appeals, Eighth Circuit.

[60] Note 29. [61] Note 56. [62] Note 56. [63] Note 56.

[64] It is not admitted at all in the Fifth Circuit: *United States* v. *Lopez* 542, F.2d 283 (1976); see also, *United States* v. *Herrera*, 504 F.2d 859 (1974); *United States* v. *Winter* 509, F.2d 925 (1975).

[65] See, for instance, *Waits* v. *McGowan* 516 F.2d 203 (1975), Third Circuit; *United States* v. *Marzano* 537 F.2d 257 (1976), Seventh Circuit: *United States* v. *Reed*, 639 F.2d 896 (1981), Second Circuit.

[66] *United States* v. *Lira* 515 F.2d 68, 70 (1975).

[67] The case most frequently cited probably is *The Paquete Habana* 175 U.S., 677, 700 (1900), but the rule has been reaffirmed in numerous cases decided by the Supreme Court.

no less than by the Judiciary. Nor is any regard had to the human right to liberty and security of the person.

Admittedly, almost all the cases that came before the courts of the United States in recent years concerned drug dealers and smugglers who deserved no sympathy and whose conviction may well have served the public interest. Yet the lofty words of *Toscanino* express an eternal truth underlying the Due Process Clause of the Fourteenth Amendment:

> Society is the ulimate loser when, in order to convict the guilty, it uses methods that lead to decreased respect for the law.[68]

IV

At the end of this survey, it is apparent that the choice that has to be made is above all a moral or philosophical one. As a matter of legal reasoning—words, phrases, formulations—verbiage can be found for either or any solution of the problem discussed in these pages. Even if it is approached from the point of view of legal policies, the ambivalence of the possible attitudes is obvious: in these days of terrorism, violent crimes, traffic in drugs and consequent dangers to the public, one can understand and sympathize with the tendency of the authorities to pursue and combat the wrongdoers by any means, fair or foul, and to treat them as outcasts who have forfeited any right to consideration or indulgence. This line of argument is apt to overlook that among the persons so treated there may be an innocent one. This is a great danger, and it is believed that, for this reason alone, neither society nor the law must allow a departure from the great principle that no illegality must ever bear fruit. It does not matter whether the wrong done by or on behalf of the State prosecuting the defendant amounts to 'cruel, inhumane and outrageous treatment' or a 'mere illegality'. Nor does it matter whether the wrong committed is treated as a violation of international law (including human rights) or a deliberate breach of rules relating to the enforcement of municipal law. These are verbal distinctions unworthy of the great issue at stake. The skilful use of verbiage whereby the great case of *Toscanino* was reduced to the level of a technicality and 'erosion' of the rule in *Ker* v. *Illinois* was replaced by its 'recognition' is an impressive example of the adaptability of language. It is the underlying moral force, the respect for the law, that should prevail. Hardly any idea is greater than that of government by law rather than expediency. And law includes international law, even if there is no institution administering and enforcing it. Consequently, whether or no the injured State protests or otherwise objects, the abduction of the

[68] Above note 47, at 274.

accused from its territory, by force or by stealth, should be treated not as a bar to jurisdiction, but as a misuse of its exercise.

In these circumstances, it is deeply painful to read a German decision[69] which holds that the prosecution of an unlawfully abducted person is not contrary to the rule of law. The reason advanced by the Court is that that great constitutional principle requires only, on the one hand, that a criminal is being prosecuted and, if found guilty punished, and, on the other hand, that indispensable procedural requirements are observed. It is submitted that this is a remarkably superficial formulation which does not touch the specific question whether the exploitation of an admitted violation of public international law involving at the same time a clear infringement of human rights (which even a guilty person is entitled to enjoy) is not so fundamental an illegality as to render prosecution abusive, inconsistent with the rule of law or, as the Americans would say, contrary to due process of law.

A more practical argument of general significance should be added. It is strongly underscored by the remarkably large number of cases which since about 1975 have come before the American courts and in which unlawful abduction from a variety of countries in Central and South America and the Caribbean islands was alleged. They support the suspicion that there have been many more such cases which have not found their way into the law reports. The wrongful abduction from a foreign State's territory is bound to lead to international anarchy and friction, both in law and in fact. In particular, it will undermine the system of extradition treaties with its carefully elaborated provisions, including its exceptions such as that relating to political crimes. If the agent working in the foreign territory is discovered, he is liable to come into conflict with the local authorities. He may be criminally liable, his own State may be exposed to diplomatic protest and to claims for the international wrong done. If the government has had knowledge of the wrongful activity of its agents, its international responsibility may be heavy. If the agent operates on the instructions of inferior authorities such as police officers or public prosecutors, his government is likely to become greatly embarrassed. Serious consequences of this kind can only be avoided if the wrongful conduct is prevented or, alternatively, rendered futile. To reward it by allowing the prosecution of the abducted person is about the worst legal policy that can be imagined, for it amounts to an invitation to the injured State to commit similar illegalities in the wrongdoing State. Just as extradition treaties provide for reciprocity, their disregard or their replacement by unauthorized snatching of individuals from one Party's territory would tempt the other Party to reciprocate in kind. The international community should condemn such

[69] 3 June 1986, above note 34.

conduct. The policy of the United States, indeed the policy of all States in this field, needs careful re-examination in the light of Justice Brandeis' famous dictum:

> Decency, security and liberty alike demand that government officials shall be subjected to the same rules of conduct that are commands to the citizen. In a government of laws, existence of the government will be imperilled if it fails to observe the law scrupulously. But Government is the potent, the omnipresent teacher. For good or for ill, it teaches the whole people by its example. Crime is contagious. If the government becomes a lawbreaker it breeds contempt for law; it invites every man to become a law unto himself; it invites anarchy. To declare that in the administration of the criminal law the end justifies the means—to declare that the government may commit crimes in order to secure the conviction of a private criminal—would bring terrible retribution. Against that pernicious doctrine this court resolutely set its face.[70]

It is fitting to conclude with an observation by Justice Frankfurter, according to whom the Due Process clause of the American Constitution or, as we would say, the rule of law,

> inescapably imposes upon [the] court an exercise of judgment upon the whole course of the proceedings in order to ascertain whether they offend those canons of decency and fairness which express the notion of justice of English speaking peoples even toward those charged with the most heinous offences.[71]

NOTE

Since this paper went to press a further, highly illuminating decision of Germany's Federal Supreme Court was reported: 19 December 1986, NJW 1987, 3087. It involves a remarkable change of direction towards the view put forward in this paper. The accused was induced by a German agent provocateur acting in the Netherlands to enter German territory where he was taken into custody. He was sentenced to be imprisoned for a term of eleven years. On 23 October 1985 his appeal to the Federal Supreme Court failed as to the substance of the case, but succeeded in regard to the extent of punishment, so that the case was remitted to the lower court. On 6 January 1986 the Netherlands required the Federal Republic to arrange for 'the immediate restoration' of the defendant. Nethertheless on 3 June 1986 the Federal Constitutional Court refused leave to appeal: above n. 34. When the case came back to the lower court, it again sentenced the defendant to eleven years' imprisonment. A fresh appeal to the Federal Supreme Court led to an order that the proceedings be stayed so as to enable the Federal Republic to

[70] In *Olmstead* v. *United States*, 277 U.S. 436, 484, 485 (1928); Justice Holmes agreed with him. In the same sense, e.g. *Rochin* v. *California*, 342 U.S. 165 (1951).

[71] *Malinski* v. *New York*, 324 U.S. 401, 416, 417 (1944).

comply with the Dutch request. The Court asserted that public international law did not preclude the defendant's prosecution, but the Dutch right of restitution (which, of course, is founded on public international law) 'could preclude the exercise of German jurisdiction'. In order to permit restitution the Court, so it proclaimed, was doing all it could by staying the proceedings.

14

The International Enforcement of Public Rights

I

THE Restatement on the Conflict of Laws (First) which appeared in 1934 provided in s. 610 that 'no action can be maintained on a right created by the law of a foreign state as a method of furthering its own governmental interests'. This was supplemented by s. 611 which specifically excluded foreign penalties from enforcement. The Restatement (Second) of 1971 deleted the former, but in s. 89 retained the latter provision, the authors making it clear that they were not expressing an opinion on the recovery of foreign taxes.[1]

It is submitted that from the point of view of international relations with which these observations are exclusively concerned the old s. 610 could and ought to have been included in the Second Restatement, for it correctly states what was and is the law not only in the United States, but all over the world. To mention at this point only a few decisions which deny the *direct* enforcement[2] of a foreign State's public rights, it is free

[1] Comment b, p. 264.

[2] It should be made clear that the present observations are exclusively concerned with enforcement. The old adage according to which, for instance, no State 'takes notice' of the revenue laws of another State goes much too far in that we apply or have regard to foreign public laws in many connections. This is particularly so in cases involving the validity of the contract, impossibility of performance and so forth. The point was very well made by Sir Michael Mann, *I.C.L.Q.* 3 (1954), 465 who rightly also suggests (p. 469) that 'claims under foreign public law—manifestations of sovereign power—cannot be put in suit before an English court'. In view of the subject-matter and scope of the present article the contribution by Bermann, 'Public Law in the Conflict of Laws', *American Journal of Comparative Law*, 34 (1986) Suppl. p. 157, is hardly in point, because he does not primarily deal with international (as opposed to inter-state) aspects or with enforcement (as opposed to recognition and application).

For the author's earlier attempts at clarification of the subject, see 'Prerogative Rights of Foreign States and the Conflict of Laws', 40 *Transactions of the Grotius Society* (1955), 25, reprinted in *Studies in International Law* (1973) 492, and 'Conflict of Laws and Public Law', 132 (1971 i) *Recueil des Cours* 109. The present paper, much edited and 'Americanized' and in part even re-written, originally appeared in 19 (1987) *Journal of International Law and Politics*, 603; a German version appeared in *Festschrift for Gerhard Kegel* 365 and a French version appeared in *Revue Critique de Droit International Privé* 1988, 1. The present version is the original, unedited English text revised and supplemented in the light of events and research since 1987.

from doubt that fines cannot be recovered.[3] Although in remarkable circumstances to which it will be necessary to revert and in language which is perhaps neither judicial nor judicious the Court of Appeals of New York described the rule as 'an old chestnut',[4] in truth it is clear that not only in the United States,[5] but also in England[6] and in the British Commonwealth of Nations[7] as well as in all other countries which have ever been confronted with the problem,[8] claims by foreign States for taxes or customs duties[9] are not allowed or, as it is frequently put, foreign revenue laws are not enforced. Indeed, in England it was said by Lord Evershed[10] that 'it is not the practice of civilised countries, such as France and England, to enforce the revenue laws of the other of them'. Consequently compulsory contributions to national health insurance schemes are irrecoverable by a foreign State.[11] And the same applies to such public laws as export prohibitions,[12] exchange control restrictions[13] and securities control like the Securities Exchange Act 1934.[14] It should also be accepted that if a State confiscates a chattel situate within its territories, but does not obtain possession, it cannot recover it by action in a foreign country to

[3] This is generally accepted since Chief Justice Marshall said in 1825 'with no less brevity than force' (per Lord Watson in *Huntingdon* v. *Attrill*, [1893] A.C. 150, 156): 'The courts of no country execute the penal laws of another': *The Antelope*, 10 Wheat. (23 U.S.) 123. No attempt to recover a real fine has ever been made. But see below n. 89. The decisions which are available at least by implication accepted the principle, but related to 'penalties' which did not come within it: *Wisconsin* v. *Pelican Insurance Co.*, 127 US 265; *Huntingdon* v. *Attrill*, 146 U.S. 657; *Huntingdon* v. *Attrill*, [1893] A.C. 150.

[4] *Banco Frances e Brasileiro SA* v. *John Doe*, 36 NY 2d 592, 370 NYS 2d 536 (1975).

[5] See below n. 87.

[6] *Government of India* v. *Taylor*, [1955] A.C. 491, and since then, e.g., *Rossano* v. *Manufacturers Insurance Co.*, [1962] 3 W.L.R. 157.

[7] This follows from the numerous cases of attempted indirect enforcement to which reference will be made. Cases of direct enforcement are rare. See, however, South Africa: *Commissioners of Taxes* v. *McFarland*, 1965 (1) S.A. 470.

[8] *Austria*: Supreme Court, 29 October 1935, Sz. xvii No. 149; *Denmark*: 23 October 1924, Annual Digest 1923–4 No. 147; *Italy*: Court of Appeal Genoa, 14 January 1932, *Clunet* 1932, 1146; *Sweden*: 31 December 1924, *Annual Digest* 1923–4 No. 148.

[9] *Brocklaw* v. *Seatrain UK Ltd.*, [1971] 2 Q.B. 476.

[10] *In re Cohen*, [1950] 2 All E.R. 36, 39.

[11] *Scotland*: *Metal Industries (Salvage) Ltd.* v. *Harle*, 1962 S.L.T. 114; *Austria*: Supreme Court, 29 October 1935, Sz. xvii No. 149; *Italy*: Court of Appeal Palermo, 18 June 1966, *Rivista di diritto internazionale privato e processuale* 1968, 95, also Int. L.R. 71, 219, where it is correctly stated that the principle may be derogated from by treaty; *Germany*: see the decision below p. 47.

[12] *Ortiz* v. *Attorney-General of New Zealand*, [1984] A.C. 1 (CA)

[13] *Banco de Brasil, SA* v. *Israel Commodity Inc.* 12 N.Y. 2d 371, 107 N.E. 2d 448 (1952); *Menendez* v. *Saks & Co.*, 485 F.2d 1355, 1366 (1973). In the same sense *Sweden*: Supreme Court, 21 March 1961, Int.L.R. 47, 40.

[14] *Schemmer* v. *Property Resources Ltd.*, [1975] Ch. 273, 288. See *R.* v. *Pentonville Prison Governor, ex parte Budlong*, [1980] 1 W.L.R. 1110, at p. 1125 *per* Griffiths L.J. (as he then was): 'It is a well established rule that our courts will not enforce a foreign revenue, penal or public law. This means that our courts will not try and either punish or give a remedy for the breach of such law committed in a foreign country'.

which its original owner may have been able to take it.[15] Nor should a State be able any title based on its trading with the enemy legislation.[16] If and in so far as public rights are internationally unenforceable by action, they cannot, it is submitted, be enforced by counterclaim or set-off, a fact which in certain circumstances may appear harsh, but which for the sake of the principle and its legal basis must be accepted; and unenforceability extends to arbitration proceedings for this reason, among others, that arbitrators cannot be expected to render an award which cannot be enforced by judicial proceedings or execution.

The existence of the rule which in principle is supported by the Institute of International Law[17] derives some support from the fact that in general extradition treaties and treaties relating to legal assistance are not applicable if an offence against the type of legislation discussed in these pages is in issue. Thus Art. 5 of the European Extradition Treaty of 13 December 1957 provides that in criminal matters relating to contributions, taxes, customs duties or exchange control extradition will only be granted if the Contracting Parties have concluded special arrangements.[18] Or according to Art. 2 of the European Convention on Legal Assistance in Criminal Matters of 20 April 1959 assistance may be denied if the request relates to a criminal offence which in the State addressed is considered to be a fiscal offence.[19] A similar provision is included in the Convention between the United States of America and Switzerland of 25 May 1973.[20]

[15] There does not seem to be any judicial authority dealing with this point which was more fully developed in the 1955 paper (see *Studies in International Law*, pp. 503, 504). The suggestion then made is strongly supported by Lord Stowell in *The Fama* (1804) 5C. Rob. 106, at pp. 114, 115, who speaks of 'the necessary principle of jurisprudence that to complete the right of property, the right to the thing and the possession of the thing itself should be united . . . This is the general law of property'.

[16] Judicial practice seems to be opposed to this suggestion: *Lepage* v. *Sao Paolo Coffee Estates Company*, (1917) W.N. 216; *Jabbour* v. *Custodian of Absentee's Property of State of Israel*, (1954) 1 All. E.R. 145; *Brown, Gow, Wilson* v. *Beleggings-Societeit NV.*, (1961) Ontario R. 815, and the almost incomprehensible decision *United States* v. *Bank voor Handel en Scheepvaart, Int. LM.* 9 (1970) 759. In none of these cases the decisive point as developed in the text was put forward in argument. The correct result was reached by the Swedish Supreme Court *in re Hopf Products Ltd.*, A.D. 1943–45 No. 16. For a plainly wrong application of the principles see the decision of the Austrian Supreme Court, SZ xxxii, (1959), which was followed by the Supreme Court of the Principality of Liechtenstein, 9 September 1985, *I Prax* 1987, 379 (discussed by Mann ibid, p. 383): a German court order assessing the costs payable by an unsuccessful litigant was held to be unenforceable on the ground that the rights conferred by the order had their foundation in foreign public law.

[17] *Annuaire* 57 (1977) II 329 (Oslo): public law claims are in principle inadmissible in so far as, from the viewpoint of the State of the forum, the subject-matter of such claims is related to the exercise of governmental power.

[18] U.N.T.S. 359, 273. [19] U.N.T.S. 472, 185.

[20] Art. 2 (1) (c) (5), *Int. L.M.* 1973, 916. See now also the Treaty of 3 July 1986 between the United Kingdom of Great Britain and the United States of America relating to mutual legal assistance in criminal matters in the Cayman Islands (Cmnd. 9862) which (subject to certain exceptions) does not extend to 'any matter which relates directly or indirectly to the regulation, including the imposition, calculation and collection of taxes'.

Even more telling proof of the recognition of the rule comes from another type of treaty. Most treaties relating to jurisdiction as well as the recognition and enforcement of judgments include provisions which exclude from their scope claims based on public rights. Britain's treaties dealing with these subjects invariably contain such a clause, because s. 1 (2) (b) of the Foreign Judgments (Reciprocal Enforcement) Act 1933 so requires. Or Article 1 of the EEC Convention of 1968 states that it is limited to civil and commercial matters and, in particular, does not apply to revenue, customs or administrative matters.

II

In dealing with this branch of the law one should not be misled by terminological quibbles. The term 'public rights' seems to be entirely satisfactory. In England there exists authority for the use of the term 'prerogative rights'.[21] It has a longer history, but may today be a little unusual. What is considerably less satisfactory is the attempt to employ the words 'penal' and 'revenue' laws as the generic terms into which every public right has to be pressed. This happened with the Securities Exchange Act 1934. It has penal provisions, but it is not a penal statute, though an English judge so described it.[22] It created public rights. So did the New Zealand legislation relating to the export of works of art. Lord Denning in a seminal judgment described it as affording a public right to the Attorney-General of New Zealand;[23] the attempt of two other judges of the English Court of Appeal to categorize it as penal or revenue legislation is misleading.[24] In New York foreign currency exchange regulations have been described as revenue laws in order to bring them within the umbrella of the rule relating to them,[25] but, as Wachtler J. put it in a forceful dissenting judgment, the 'proper question is whether in the particular instance the claim sought to be enforced is a manifestation of such sovereign authority', for the 'bottom line is that the courts of one country will not enforce the laws adopted by another country in the exercise of its sovereign capacity for the purpose of fiscal regulation and management'.[26]

One point, however, should be clear beyond any peradventure. The rule applies to the extraterritorial enforcement of rights or claims asserted by a State. A mere interest of the State or government is not sufficient to bring it into operation. It is for this reason that one must deeply regret one of the most unfortunate decisions ever rendered by a supreme tribunal, i.e. the decision of the High Court of Australia in *Attorney-General (UK) v. Heinemann Publishers Australia Pty Ltd. and Peter*

[21] *Emperor of Austria v. Day* (1861), 3 De G.F. & J. 217, at p. 251 per Turner L.J.
[22] Above n. 14. [23] Above n. 12, at p. 24.
[24] Pp. 34, 35. [25] Above n. 4. [26] P. 510.

Wright, the *Spycatcher* case.[27] Wright was a former employee of the British secret service, who in his book *Spycatcher*, which Heinemann thought fit to publish in Australia, purported to disclose a large amount of secret and allegedly true information acquired by him in the course of his employment. Under English law he came 'under an obligation of confidence to the British Government'.[28] When the British Government attempted to enforce this obligation, the action which to many must have appeared irresistible failed on the ground[29] that allegedly the principle law 'renders unenforceable . . . actions to enforce the government interests of a foreign State'. Whatever the phrase 'government interests' may mean in other contexts (and the late Professor Currie, it will be remembered, has attributed to it a most unfortunate meaning and effect in the conflict of laws), it should be absolutely clear that there is no room for it in the formulation of the rule which is being discussed in this paper and which the High Court of Australia purported to follow. If this were not so, a State would be precluded from pursuing any claim of whatsoever nature in a foreign court, for any such claim necessarily touches governmental interests. The rule is limited to the pursuance of rights of a specific kind which do not comprise rights resulting from employment, even though they may have certain special features.

III

A much more important question than that of definition concerns the rationale of the rule relating to the unenforceability of foreign public laws. It is to be found in public international law, more specifically in the doctrine of international jurisdiction. As Lord Watson put it in 1893,[30] there exists a 'class of actions which, by the law of nations, are exclusively assigned to their domestic forum' and, therefore, cannot be brought in other States without infringing the latter's sovereign rights. The State which outside the confines of its own sovereignty pursues penal, tax or other public claims invokes its sovereign rights within the territory of the forum. Even the institution of legal proceedings implies the assertion that the plaintiff State is *entitled* to prosecute its public rights in the forum. It

[27] 78 (1988) *Australian L.R.* 449 discussed by Mann (1988) 104 *L.Q.R.* 497. The New Zealand Court of Appeal fortunately refused to follow the High Court of Australia on this point: *Attorney General for the United Kingdom* v. *Wellington Newspapers Ltd.*, [1988] 1 NZLR 166, 173. It was less fortunate that the court felt unable to adjudicate on the existence of British 'public interest' (p. 176). Why not?

[28] P. 455.

[29] p. 460. This is not the first time that the contrast between rights and interests has caused difficulties. See the International Court of Justice in the *Case Concerning Barcelona Traction*, *I.C.J. Reports*, 1970, 3, paras. 44, 46 and passim.

[30] *Huntingdon* v. *Attrill*, [1893] A.C. 150, at p. 156.

does not 'humbly and simply pray'[31] to make domestic courts available to it. It puts forward a *right* which is a sovereign or public right. It *demands* the recognition and enforcement of domestic jurisdiction or sovereignty and, accordingly, of public international law in so far as the consent of the State of the forum is lacking.[32] No judge can or may permit the prosecution of such a claim and the concomitant excess of foreign jurisdiction. Such consent can only be given by the sovereign and invariably presupposes a treaty and, probably, legislation. A judge who ventures to ignore the paramount rights of his sovereign would prejudice him, because he would deprive him of the possibility of insisting upon reciprocity. The explanation thus suggested is entirely in harmony with that given by Lord Keith of Avonholm:[33]

One explanation of the rule thus illustrated may be thought to be that enforcement of a claim for taxes is but an extension of the sovereign power which imposed the taxes, and that as assertion of sovereign authority by one State within the territory of another, as distinct from a patrimonial claim by a foreign sovereign, is (treaty or convention apart) contrary to all concepts of independent sovereignties.

It is quite true that other explanations have been put forward.[34] Of these the most significant is Judge Learned Hand's suggestion[35] that public laws affect a State in matters so vital to its existence that 'no court ought to undertake an inquiry which it cannot prosecute without determining whether those laws are consonant with its own notions of what is proper',

[31] This formulation was used by a German author (Frank, *RabelsZ* 30 (1970) 56, at p. 64).

[32] The author originally took the view that the attempt to enforce its public law extraterritorially involved a breach by the plaintiff State of public international law in that it committed an excess of its own jurisdiction: *Transactions of the Grotius Society* 40 (1955) 25, reprinted in *Studies in International Law* (1973) 492. This is not incorrect, but the essential point would seem to be the violation of the sovereign jurisdiction of the forum State.

[33] *Government of India* v. *Taylor*, [1955] A.C. 491, at p. 511. In support of the submissions in the text Van Hecke, *Travaux du Comité Français de droit international privé* 1983–4, p. 225 who speaks of 'la règle de non accueil des prétentions qui constituent une manifestation typique d' une souveraineté étrangère'. Lord Keith's explanation was probably approved by the House of Lords in *Re The State of Norway No. 1 and No. 2*, [1989] 2 W.L.R. 458, at p. 476 *per* Lord Goff of Chieveley.

[34] A variety of reasons was considered by *Oklahoma Tax Commission* v. *Rodgers*, (1946) 238 Mo. App. 1115, 193 S.W. 2d 919, at pp. 926, 927. It has been said, in particular, that the forum lacks local jurisdiction or competence. This is a wholly unconvincing explanation. Lipstein, *Festschrift für Zajtay* (1982) 357, 370 sqq. suggests difficulties of proof and procedure as a reason. But, to put it at its lowest, this is hardly exhaustive. Mr P. B. Carter, *British Year Book of International Law*, 1984, 111, at pp. 121, 122 opposes 'any general assertion that a court will not apply foreign public laws—an assertion of uncertain meaning and of possibly dangerous width'. The article which seems to doubt the rule relating to revenue laws (p. 117) and disregards Lord Denning's judgment in the case mentioned in n. 12 above suffers from the fact that it does not investigate the rationale of the rule and fails to distinguish bettween application and enforcement. Professor Castel, 42 (1964) *Canadian Bar Rev*. 277, 300, comes to the conclusion that 'no adequate justification has been offered for enforcing foreign tax laws directly or indirectly', but he ignores public international law.

[35] *Moore* v. *Mitchell*, 30 F. 2d 600, 604 (1929).

and which 'involves the relations between the States themselves'. In other words the eminent judge relied on an exaggerated, though not unfamiliar, effect of the act of state doctrine in that the mere possibility of judicial scrutiny ever becoming relevant should deny judicial enforcement to that large majority of cases in which the validity or morality of the foreign public law is not in issue at all. Such reasoning does not carry conviction. It certainly is not an acceptable substitute for the teachings of public international law or the foundation which they provide for the prevailing practice.

IV

If the prosecution of public rights involves the violation of the forum State's jurisdiction, it is open to it to give its consent in whatever manner its constitution permits, usually by treaty and legislation.[36]

Some such treaties have been concluded,[37] but they are rare.

In a recent decision of the House of Lords, which for many reasons is regrettable and indeed difficult to defend, there occurs the following *obiter dictum*:[38]

> There is another international rule whereby one state will not enforce the revenue and penal laws of another state. This rule with regard to revenue laws may in the future be modified by international convention or by the laws of the European Economic Community in order to prevent fraudulent practices which damage all states and benefit no state. But at the present time the international rule with regard to the non-enforcement of revenue and penal laws is absolute.

In so far as this dictum affirms the absolute character of the principle it can only be welcomed. On the other hand the prophecies about future developments seem to be without foundation. Nothing is known about a movement within the EEC to change the law; whether the problem falls within the scope of the EEC's purposes is perhaps not free from doubt. In 1981, it is true, the OECD submitted the draft of a model convention for mutual administrative assistance in the recovery of tax claims. But to date no State has adopted it. Nothing is known about the reasons. One can

[36] Van Hecke (above n. 33) p. 232 also emphasizes that derogation 'ne peut avoir lieu qu'en vertu d'un traité'.

[37] On 11 September 1970 the Federal Republic of Germany and Austria concluded a treaty about the recovery of customs duties. Germany's Federal Constitutional Court held that it had retrospective force so as to cover an Austrian customs assessment made in 1966: *BVerfGE* 63, 343. The decision is based on the view that before the treaty there existed only a procedural obstacle preventing enforcement in Germany. It is believed that this is wrong. There did not exist any debt. In 1966 the Austrian customs debt would not have been deducted for the purpose of calculating the 'debtor's' assets.

[38] *Williams and Humbert Ltd.* v. *W. & H. Trade Marks (Jersey) Ltd.*, [1986] A.C. 368, at p. 428.

only guess. One reason may be that according to Article 6 the convention applies only in the event of the tax claim having become unappealable in the country of origin. This compels the individual to resist such claims, possibly at great expense. Since the tax law of many States includes wholly unusual, sometimes even extreme and absurd tax burdens, this may be a serious prejudice for the taxpayer. It is conceivable that States regard it as intolerable. Another reason may be that according to the convention it is a matter for the requested State to enforce the claims of the requesting State in accordance with its own procedure. This may be considered a heavy burden on the administration of the requested State, particularly since the costs seem to be payable by the latter. The development expected by the House of Lords thus is likely to be remote, though a fresh draft was published in 1988.[39] In any case it only applies to tax claims *stricto sensu* with which the House was not concerned in the case before it. The dictum, therefore, had no legally relevant function. In 1984 Professor Van Hecke rightly included[39a] 'l'examen de cette bizarre invention–modèle en exprimant le souhait qu'elle ne connaisse aucun succès'.

Whatever the future may bring, for the moment it is clear that, as already mentioned, not only the judge, but also the defendant is disentitled to permit the exercise of sovereign acts in the forum to the foreign State, the plaintiff. For as an English judge has said in connection with claims arising from confiscation which, legally, are of the same character as any other public right, 'this is the application of a rule of public policy which involves a limitation of jurisdiction. No question of affirmation or ratification can therefore arise'.[40] In other words, the court must take the point *proprio motu*.

V

The question which legal system decides whether the plaintiff asserts a foreign public or private right, i.e., the question of classification,[41] was answered many years ago by Lord Watson:[42]

> Their Lordships cannot assent to the proposition that, in considering whether the present action was penal in such sense as to oust their jurisdiction, the courts of Ontario were bound to pay absolute deference to any interpretation which might have been put upon the Statute of 1875 in the State of New York. They had to construe and apply an international rule, which is a matter of law entirely within

[39] *International Legal Materials*, 1988, 1160.

[39a] Above n. 33, at p. 230.

[40] Wynn-Parry J. in *Novello* v. *Hinrichsen*, [1951] Ch. 595, 606.

[41] The terminology is uncertain: Scoles & Hay, *Conflict of Laws*, pp. 52 sqq. The learned authors prefer characterization.

[42] *Huntington* v. *Attrill*, [1893] A.C. 150, at p. 155.

> the cognizance of the foreign court whose jurisdiction is invoked . . . The court appealed to must determine for itself, in the first place the substance of the right sought to be enforced; and, in the second place, whether its enforcement would, either directly or indirectly, involve the execution of the penal laws of another state. Were any other principle to guide its decision, a court might find itself in the position of giving effect in one case and denying effect in another, to suits of the same character in consequence of the causes of action having arisen in different countries; or in the predicament of being constrained to give effect to laws which were, in its own judgment, strictly penal.

The reason why the law of the plaintiff State ought not to be decisive, cannot be stated more clearly. Nor ought the forum to apply its own conceptions or law.[43] Rather it must ascertain 'the substance of the right sought to be enforced', irrespective of labels and 'whatever device of nomenclature is used';[44] and it must apply 'an international rule', that is to say, not necessarily only its own law or its own municipal conceptions, but it must interpret the plaintiff State's asserted right in the light of the rule of public international law applicable to interference with the forum State's jurisdiction. Just as in connection with sovereign immunity acts done *jure imperii* are not subject to the jurisidiction of the forum, so claims, rights or causes of action accruing to the foreign State in the exercise of sovereign authority cannot be internationally enforced. Thus it is not simply for the law of the forum State to say whether the plaintiff State's claim is a revenue claim in the eyes of the forum.[45] The real question is whether that claim is regarded by international law as constituting an infringement of the sovereignty of the forum State. The difference may not always exist or be readily discernible. But there are likely to be cases in which its effect will make itself felt.[46]

An example is supplied by a decision of the Federal Republic of Germany's Federal Social Court, the highest tribunal dealing with appeals in matters of social security. A Dutchman had fraudulently obtained unemployment benefits from the Dutch State. He emigrated to Germany. Having ascertained that the payments ought not to have been made, the Dutch State sued in Germany for their return on the ground of unjustified

[43] But see above n. 15.

[44] Language of Viscount Simonds in *Adams* v. *National Bank of Greece*, [1961] A.C. 255, 274.

[45] This view, however, was taken by the New York Court of Appeals in *Banco Frances e Brasileiro* v. *John Doe*, 36 NY. 2d at pp. 597, 598, and Lord Cameron in *Metal Industries (Salvage) Ltd.* v. *S. T. 'Harle'*, (1962) S.L.T. 114, at p. 116. Carter (above n. 34) at p. 116 suggests that characterization 'of a law as revenue or otherwise is, of course, a matter for the forum'.

[46] The approach here outlined is, it is hoped, more precise than the few and superficial remarks in the 1955 paper mentioned above n. 32.

enrichment and tortious liability.[47] It will be necessary to revert to this case in another connection.[48] At this point it is material to say that the court expressly 'classified' or 'characterised' the claim according to German law the public law of which provides for the recovery of unjustifiably obtained unemployment benefits. Consequently the Dutch State's claim was to be defined as arising from public law and, therefore, inadmissible. The true question was whether as a matter of international law the Dutch claim involved the assertion of Dutch sovereign power within the Federal Republic. It did not. Even if the claim had been founded on a Dutch provision in a statute relating to social security rather than on unjustified enrichment and tort, in substance it would have been a right of the latter type that the plaintiff asserted. In the international sense it existed independently of the special provision relating to social security either in the Dutch or in the German legislation.

The point was most frequently considered in connection with the question whether a right asserted by a foreign State was penal in character. By exemplary reasoning both the Privy Council[49] and the Supreme Court of the United States[50] reached the conclusion that the test was whether the pecuniary penalties were recoverable in favour of the State on account of the violation of some statutory provision. In *British Airways v. Laker Airways*[51] Lord Diplock stated that it was common ground that if Laker proved its allegations, 'they disclose no cause of action . . . that is justiciable in an English Court. The Clayton Act which creates the civil remedy with threefold damages for criminal offences under the Sherman Act is, under English rules of conflict of laws, purely territorial in its application.' Indeed there is force in a dictum of the Court of Appeals, Fifth Circuit,[52] according to which 'a treble damages action . . . is designed at least in part to penalize wrongdoers and deter wrongdoing. Since it is a well-established principle of international law that the courts of no country execute the penal laws of another . . . we have little doubt that the Indonesian courts would quite properly refuse to entertain plaintiff's Sherman action'. Penalizing the defendant by the award of punitive damages to the plaintiff is, however, by no means unknown to the legal systems derived from English law, and if the plaintiff keeps the damage for himself, this, it is submitted, may be decisive. In any case, the Court of Appeal in England[53] was wholly justified in holding that a sum of 10,000 French francs awarded to the plaintiff for the defendant's 'résistance

[47] *BSGE*, 54, 250, also *IPRspr*. 1983 No. 130. [48] See below n. 93.

[49] *Huntington* v. *Attrill*, [1893] A.C. 150.

[50] *Wisconsin* v. *Pelican Insurance Company*, 127 U.S. 265 (1888). [51] [1985] A.C. 58.

[52] *Industrial Development* v. *Mitsui*, 704 F. 2d 785 (1983).

[53] *SA Consortium General Textiles* v. *Sun & Sand Agencies*, [1978] Q.B. 279, 299, 300 per Lord Denning M.R.

abusive' was not a penalty, but represented part of the costs or exemplary damages.

The problem of classification is particularly troublesome, when it arises in relation to those numerous treaties which employ the phrase 'civil and commercial matters', a phrase which in particular occurs in treaties relating to the recognition and enforcement of judgments and in the Hague Convention of 18 March 1970 about the taking of evidence abroad.[54] In a case relating to the former type the Belgian Cour de Cassation[55] had no difficulty in holding that a French judgment for taxes and fiscal penalties is not covered by the expression. The same term used in the EEC Convention of 1968 is subject to autonomous interpretation (whatever that may mean).[56] In relation to the Convention of 1970 and the United Kingdom legislation giving effect to it[57] the House of Lords was faced with an unusual problem. The estate of a Norwegian citizen instituted proceedings in a Norwegian civil court against the State of Norway to set aside an assessment of taxes. Both parties to the proceedings desired to take the evidence of two English bankers who objected on the ground, *inter alia*, that the proceedings were not 'in any civil or commercial matter'.[58] The Court, by a majority, dismissed the application on the indubitable ground that it involved 'fishing' and also the breach of the confidentiality of bankers. Kerr L.J. indicated that if the taxpayer had not consented to the application he would also have dismissed it on the ground of 'taxgathering'. But, and this is the point at present material, the Court also held, though 'reluctantly' and 'only with considerable doubt', that the application arose from 'proceedings in any civil or commercial matter'.[59]

A few months later, in response to a second application by Norway, another division of the Court of Appeal (May, Balcombe and Woolf L.JJ.) reached the opposite result and held that the words 'proceedings in any civil or commercial matter' were to be construed in accordance with a generally acceptable international interpretation which did not comprise matters of public, in particular, fiscal law.[60] Ultimately the House of Lords held, in effect, that the Act of 1975 applied, because in Norwegian law the claim was 'civil' and in English all claims except criminal ones were 'civil'.[61]

[54] Printed, e.g., by Ristau, *International Judicial Assistance*,Vol I, Appendix C or Cmnd. 3991.
[55] 18 February 1929, *Pasicrisie Belge* 1929. 1. 96.
[56] European Court of Justice, 14 October 1976, *ECR* 1976, 1541.
[57] Evidence (Proceedings in Other Jurisdictions) Act 1975.
[58] *In re Norway's Application*, [1987] Q.B. 433.
[59] [1986] 3 W.L.R. 452, discussed by Mann, [1986] 102 L.Q.R. 505.
[60] *In re State of Norway's Application (No. 2)* (1988) 3 W.L.R. 603.
[61] [1989] 2 W.L.R. 458. For further discussion, see Mann (1989) 105 *L.Q.R.*.

VI

The principle discussed in the preceding section is exemplified by the case in which the plaintiff is a foreign State or public authority and asserts a public right which in substance is so close to a private right that there should be no objection against its enforcement. This is so, for instance, where the State has conferred a benefit upon the defendant and is entitled to reimbursement. Even if the cause of action is supplied by a statutory provision of public law, it may be that the plaintiff could just as well, and perhaps does, rely upon unjustified enrichment or other quasi-contractual causes of action of a private law character.

Such a case was the decision of the Federal Social Court of Germany above referred to.[62] Another instructive example is supplied by a decision of the District Court of Hamburg.[63] The Municipality of Vienna carried out work on the defendant's house, while he was absent; this was done in order to prevent danger to adjoining properties. The Municipality sued in Hamburg to recover its outlays. Austrian provisions of public law entitled it to do so. But this is not relevant. As the Court put it, 'what is decisive is the nature of the substantive claim. It is similar to a claim for damages or the return of money paid for the defendant's benefit, i.e. a private law claim'.

A similar decision should be reached in those cases in which the State's payments are subject to the condition that in certain circumstances it is entitled to repayment. Thus a defendant who receives a social security on terms that the money is repayable in the event of his financial resources permitting it can be sued everywhere.[64] If, as happens in many countries, educational expenses are being advanced on condition that they are repayable by instalments when the pupil is in receipt of a salary, or if the defendant is liable for court fees[65] or telephone charges—in cases of this type a State's claim should succeed, because it concerns payment for, or repayment of, a benefit voluntarily accepted. The claim may have its basis in the State's sovereign rights, but in substance is of a commercial or private law character. The result should be the same where the State discharges the defendant's liabilities: thus it may pay maintenance to the

[62] N. 47. [63] 9 March 1977, *IPRspr.* 1977 No. 115.

[64] *Aliter* District Court Offenburg, 30 December 1960, *IPRspr.* 1960–1 No. 172, a decision rightly criticised by Frank (above n. 31).

[65] See the New Zealand case of *Connor* v. *Connor* (1974) 1 N.Z.L.R. 632. In a divorce case the plaintiff's costs were assessed by the Australian Court. Since the plaintiff had received Legal Aid, a payment recovered in New Zealand from the defendant would enure to the benefit of the Legal Aid Committee in Victoria, Australia. The court correctly held that recovery of the costs did not become a public right of the State of Victoria by reason of the mere fact that execution in New Zealand would result in the discharge of a foreign State's claim for costs.

defendant's wife or child and claim repayment. Or it pays damages to the victim of an accident and claims repayment from the wrongdoer; the statutory assignment may have its basis in public law, but can without difficulty be justified by rules of private law.[66]

Perhaps the decisive features of all these cases is that in the last resort the claim results from the voluntary act of the defendant or in other words it was open to him to avoid the assertion of claims against him. The distinction is illustrated by an English case:[67] the plaintiff Municipality of Sydney in Australia carried out improvement of a road in which the defendant's house was situate. By virtue of a local statute it claimed from the defendant payment of a proportionate contribution. The claim in England failed, because it concerned a payment in the nature of a tax. Although the defendant derived some advantage from the work carried out by the plaintiff, it was imposed upon him independently of his own attitude. There is, therefore, a marked difference between the Sydney and the Vienna case mentioned above. In Sydney the payment was imposed by statute upon a defined number of persons and was unavoidable. There was no question of the municipality acting for the benefit or at the (imputed) request of the defendant.

The suggested principle is also likely to provide the solution of the famous problem of what has been described as the escheat cases. A person dies intestate in, say, Sweden where he was domiciled. He leaves no next of kin. The Swedish State takes by virtue of what it regards as a right of escheat, i.e. a public right. Can it be asserted in the United States where the deceased also left property? American practice does not seem to be uniform.[68] The test, it is submitted, should be found in the fact that the effect of the law of the deceased's domicile is the same irrespective of the category which is said to include the State's right: whether it is a public right of escheat or a private right of succession, the State of the domicile takes as the universal successor of the deceased. This was Savigny's solution.[69] It was adopted by the Court of Appeal in England,[70] the Belgian Cour de Cassation[71] and the Court of Appeal in Vienna,[72] while the Court of Appeal in West Berlin[73] took the opposite view. The

[66] This is the law applicable within the EEC (see Soergel-Kegel, *Commentaries*, notes 448, sqq, before Art. 7) and see the Canadian case of *Weir* v. *Lohr*, 65 D.L.R. 2d 717 (1967): the plaintiff suffered an accident in Saskatchewan for which the defendant in Manitoba was responsible. The plaintiff's hospital expenses had been paid by the Saskatchewan Hospital Commission. By statute the plaintiff's claim was assigned to the Commission. The defendant's plea in Manitoba that the plaintiff was pursuing a public right failed.

[67] *Sydney Municipal Council* v. *Bull*, [1909] 1 K.B. 7.

[68] Scoles & Hay, *Conflict of Laws* (1982) p. 773 with references.

[69] *System* p. 315, 316. [70] *Re Maldonado* [1954] P. 233.

[71] *Clunet* 1954, 462 with a very detailed note by Hennebicq.

[72] *Österrreichische Zeitschrift für Rechtsvergleichung* 1981, 304.

[73] *I Prax* 1986, 41.

conceptualist approach should be abandoned. It should not matter how the right of the State of the deceased's domicile is described. That State takes the property in exactly the same way as if it were the next of kin. It is this effect which should be decisive.

The substance and real character and effect of the claim as the overriding test also assists where claims are made by a State against a present or former civil servant or vice versa.[74] According to the law of some countries a civil servant, perhaps even a soldier is or may be subject to an ordinary employment contract which may or may not have certain unusual features (such as the State's right of summary termination or the absence of the servant's right to remuneration enforceable by law), but does not in other respects fundamentally differ from the contract of any servant. There are other countries in which the relationship between the State and its servants belongs to public law, yet for many purposes has the characteristics of a contract of service or employment. For international purposes the classification adopted by the plaintiff State should not be decisive. The civil servant is in any real sense an employee. Whether he has a contract of employment or holds a public appointment may have no bearing upon the particular claims made: it may be material if the servant claims remuneration to which he has no enforceable right, it may be immaterial if the servant claims a testimonial or the State claims the return of documents or the observance of the confidentiality of information. The latter claim was made in the *Spycatcher* case.[75] It was in no sense typical of a civil servant's duties. Whether or no in English law the relationship between the Crown and its civil servants belongs to public law, in the international sense the United Kingdom did not assert a public right against the defendants in the Australian proceedings.

VII

A public right is being pursued only where the plaintiff is a State or a public authority or where the private plaintiff acts in the interest of or for the benefit of the State. For this reason claims by a private person for the repayment of expenditure are enforceable even if they originate from the payment of taxes, customs duties or penalties.

Thus the German Supreme Court was concerned with a case in which the plaintiff, an Austrian company, had acquired from the German

[74] Cf. s. 4 of the State Immunity Act 1978.

[75] Above n. 27. The fact that in English law a civil servant was held not to work under a contract of employment (*R. v. Civil Service Appeal Board, ex parte Bruce*, [1988] 3 All E.R. 686) should have no bearing upon the point discussed in the text. See also the interesting decision of the Court of Appeal at Aix-en-Provence, 25 April 1988, *Clunet* 1988, 779 (*Haiti v. Duvalier*).

defendant certain property situate in Czechoslovakia. Capital gains tax was payable there for which in the first place the vendor, alternatively the purchaser was liable. Since the German vendor had disregarded his obligations, the plaintiff paid the tax and claimed reimbursement from the German defendant. The Supreme Court upheld the claim.[76] In very similar circumstances a Palestinian Court arrived at the same result.[77] And an old decision of the French Cour de Cassation[78] decided correctly that an Italian forwarding agent could require his French customer to indemnify him in respect of Italian customs duties and customs penalties which he had been compelled to pay. But a later decision of the same court involving almost the same set of facts as the decision of the German Supreme Court above referred to reached the opposite result:[79] the court held that 's'agissant dans l'espèce du recouvrement d'une taxe instituée par le Gouvernement allemand', 'les lois fiscales sont strictement territoriales'. It is difficult to support such reasoning.

The point is particularly delicate, when it arises in the course of the winding-up of an estate with assets in more than one country. Thus the District Court at Dortmund allowed a Belgian residuary legatee who had paid Belgian estate duty to claim a proportionate contribution from residuary legatees in Germany.[80] The Court of Appeal in British Columbia[81] rendered a similar decision, when it held that the English executor of a testator who had died in England was entitled to such parts of the estate situate in British Colombia as were necessary to repay to him the English estate he had paid. The decisive point in these cases was that the plaintiff had paid, and was compelled to pay, the local estate duty. If no payment had been made, then the plaintiff would in substance have pursued the foreign State's claims for tax or fines. This would have been contrary to law. Accordingly it is impossible to support a decision of an English judge[82] which, incidentally, is inconsistent with decisions rendered in Australia[83] and South Africa.[84] The plaintiffs, resident in England, were entitled to substantial trust properties situate in England. The trustees,

[76] 28 March 1928, *IPRspr.* 1928 No. 37.

[77] *Ilgovski* v. *Shprinski*, Annual Digest 1941–2 No. 6.

[78] Cass.Civ. 22 November 1898, *Clunet* 1899, 136.

[79] Cass. Civ. 3 July 1928, *Clunet* 1929, 385. See now Cass. Civ. 21 January 1975, *Rev. Crit.* 1977, 120.

[80] 13 August 1976, *NJW* 1977, 2035.

[81] *Re Reid*, 17 D.L.R. 3d 199 (1971). Similarly the Scottish case of *Scottish & National Orchestra Society* v. *Thomson's Executors*, 1969 S.L.T. 199, where Lord Robertson held that in general the administrator of the Scottish estate of a testator who had died domiciled in Sweden, was not entitled to make payments to the Swedish executors in order to enable them to pay Swedish estate duty, but that a different decision was justified if such payments were required to permit the discharge of legacies in favour of Swedish legatees.

[82] *Re Lord Cable deceased*, [1976] 3 All E.R. 417.

[83] *Bath* v. *British & Malayan Trustees*, (1964) 2 N.S.W.R. 114.

[84] *Jones* v. *Borland*, (1969) 4 *South African LR.*, 29.

the defendants, were Indians who desired to transfer the property to India in order to pay Indian estate duty and to comply with Indian exchange control regulations. The judge refused to issue an injunction against the trustees. He accepted, it is true, the principle discussed in these pages, but refused to give effect to it, because the trustees were in India exposed to serious civil and criminal liability which they could not be expected to assume. Such reasoning, it is submitted, is not persuasive. Since the trustees had not made any payment in India, the decision is founded upon speculation about possible future developments. The decision meant that India secured the payment of her taxes and compliance with her exchange control regulations, while the plaintiffs were left in suspense as to whether or no any surplus would be made available to them in England. This was particularly so since it could not be assumed that in a civilized country the trustees were criminally liable if in the absence of any responsibility on their part an English court made compliance with Indian regulations impossible. It is reassuring to know that no less a judge than Lord Denning M.R. seems to share the view suggested here.[85]

As a State is not entitled to demand or enforce payment of a tax due to it from a foreign executor or trustee, the latter would commit a breach of his duties if he discharged it voluntarily. Rather he has to refrain from payment even if this means that he cannot travel or retain assets in the creditor State. A New York court had to decide a case[86] in which the settlement was governed by English law, but the trustee and all beneficiaries were in the United States. According to English law estate duty fell due in England. Yet the court held rightly that the trustee was not bound (and, one may assume, not entitled) to pay the tax, for 'our courts have consistently held that, in the absence of a treaty of reciprocal agreement, the courts of New York will not enforce the revenue laws of other jurisdictions'. It may be objected that it is too hard on a trustee to expect him to expose himself to inconvenience and possibly penalties in a foreign country. The answer is that in accordance with the traditional law of trusts the trustee must avoid a conflict of interests: if he wishes to let his own interests prevail over his duties as a trustee he should refuse to accept the trusteeship.

VIII

The next category comprises cases in which the indirect enforcement of public rights is being pursued. In principle such attempts should fail, but

[85] *Attorney-General of New Zealand* v. *Ortiz*, [1984] AC 1, 24.
[86] *In re Bliss' Trust*, 208 NYS 2d 725 (1960).

serious questions of delimitation arise. Here again the real character, the substance and effect of the claim should be decisive.

1. Where a judgment enforcing a public right such as a tax claim has been rendered in one country, it will not be recognized or enforced in another. The original claim has not lost its character by reason of the fact that it is incorporated into a judgment. This has been so held both in the United States[87] and in Canada[88] and is obviously correct.

The same rule applies, of course, to foreign judgments for a penal claim. Thus an American judgment for payment of an 'appearance bond' executed in the United States to obtain release from arrest clearly comes within the principle, as the English Court of Appeal held in *United States* v. *Inkley*.[89] It is remarkable that it was thought possible to bring such an action and that it succeeded before Gatehouse J. It is even more remarkable that the court was not referred to the relevant authorities, yet reached the correct conclusion that 'by whatever description it may be known, if the purpose of the action is the enforcement of a sanction, power or right at the instance of the State in its sovereign capacity it will not be entertained'.[90]

2. The guarantor who discharges the principal debtor's liabilities for the tax or customs duties cannot by virtue of subrogation obtain payment from the debtor. This was rightly so decided by the Court of Appeal in Hamburg,[91] when a Dutch bank which had guaranteed and discharged the tax liability of a German debtor *vis-à-vis* the Dutch authorities claimed reimbursement in Germany: the subrogation did not turn the claim into one of private law.[92] A different result may be reached if and in so far as the guarantor is in a position to found his claim upon a contractual duty to indemnify him. In such a case the guarantor does not try to enforce a tax claim in disguise, but invokes his contract with the principal debtor. On this ground the Hamburg Court of Appeal upheld the claim.

3. For similar reasons it must be emphasized again that the decision of the German Federal Social Court already referred to[93] cannot be supported. The claim was not only put upon unjustified enrichment and tort,

[87] *Her Majesty The Queen in Right of British Columbia* v. *Gilbertson*, 597 F. 2d 1161 (1979). § 483 of the Foreign Relations Law of the United States (Restatement Third, 1987): States are not required to recognize or to enforce judgments for the collection of tax, fines or penalties rendered by the courts of other States. If this suggested rule comprises truly international situations, then it would seem to be inconsistent with the decision referred to in this note (among others). It must be assumed that § 483 only applies to judgments of states of the Union.

[88] *United States* v. *Harden* (1963) S.C.R. 366.

[89] *United States of America* v. *Inkley* (1989) Q.B. 255.

[90] At p. 265 *per* Purchas L.J.

[91] *IPRspr*. 1958/59 No. 61.

[92] In a different connection the Federal Supreme Court of Germany decided that for the purpose of a privileged claim in a bankruptcy the subrogated claim of the guarantor was no longer a revenue claim: *NJW* 1973, 1077. This is a very doubtful point, but has no bearing upon the claims of foreign States.

[93] Above n. 47.

but in substance was derived from a right which did not by any means have the character of a public one.

A not wholly dissimilar case was decided by a New York court.[94] By virtue of the Compensation Law enacted by the Federal Republic of Germany the defendant had received payments to which he was not entitled. Section 7 of the Act entitled the State Nordrhein-Westfalen to repayment. The action succeeded. The Appellate Division accepted that section 7 created a public right. But it correctly held: 'The object of the action is not vindication of the public justice but reparation to one aggrieved'. This, indeed, is the decisive point: in substance it was damages for fraud that were in issue.

4. An indirect enforcement of a foreign public right occurs where the plaintiff pursues a claim for damages which in reality is designed to enforce a public right. Let it be assumed that in connection with his tax affairs the defendant has made fraudulent statements which under general common law rules would entitle the tax authorities to damages. If such a claim is pursued abroad, it is in truth the tax claim which the State attempts to enforce, and therefore the action should fail.

A very impressive example of this type of case is a decision of the Court of Appeals in New York.[95] Brazilian exchange control regulations included the familiar provision that the exporter of coffee had to surrender the dollars paid by the American importer to the plaintiff, the Brazilian Central Bank, an instrumentality of the Brazilian Government. The exporter would receive cruzeiros at the official rate of 90 to the dollar, while on the free market the rate was 200 to the dollar. The plaintiff alleged that the exporter and importer had fraudulently conspired in order to procure the free market rate to the former and deprive the plaintiff of the dollars, though it received cruzeiros. The plaintiff allegedly suffered damage and claimed payment in New York. The court was clearly right in dismissing the action for the compelling reason that the claim for damages merely disguised the plaintiff's public right flowing from the alleged violation of Brazilian exchange control regulations.

For the same reason it is impossible to support a later New York decision which in truth enabled the Brazilian State to enforce its exchange control regulations in the United States.[96] The facts are inadequately

[94] *Land Nordrhein-Westfalen* v. *Rosenthal*, 232 N.Y.S. 2d 963 (1963).

[95] *Banco do Brasil* v. *Israel Commodity Inc.*, 12 N.Y 2d 371, 190 N.E. 2d 235 (1963). On this case see Mann, *The Legal Aspect of Money* (4th edn. 1982) p. 429 with references. In this case as well as in the case to be mentioned next the plaintiffs also relied on Art. VIII (2) (b) of the IMF Articles of Agreement. This argument was untenable. The provision merely deals with the unenforceability of certain contracts, but has no bearing upon a right to damages or the entitlement of a State to pursue its public right abroad.

[96] *Banco Frances e Brasiliero* v. *John Doe*, 36 N.Y. 2d 592 (1975). On this case which, it is submitted, was wrongly decided, see Mann, loc. cit, pp. 429, 432. Williams, *American*

reported, but probably may be summarized as follows: The plaintiff was a Brazilian private bank. The defendants who were unidentified were somehow involved in submitting to the Brazilian authorities applications for exchange which included false statements. The plaintiff relied upon these applications and delivered to the defendants cheques in dollars against payment of Brazilian cruzeiros. The cheques were deposited with New York banks against which the plaintiff had obtained an injunction. In the Court of Appeals a majority of 6 to 1 upheld it. It is not easy to ascertain the majority's *ratio decidendi*. Certainly doubt was thrown upon the rule against the international enforcement of 'revenue laws'. Certainly it was held that nothing in the IMF Articles of Agreement 'prevents' a member State from assisting other member States in giving effect to their exchange regulations— a negative without affirmative value. Neither point can support the result, as the dissenting opinion conclusively establishes. Apart from a fine, the plaintiff apparently had suffered no damage, but seemingly the Brazilian authorities released dollars which, had the application been truthful, they would not have done, but for which they received the corresponding amount of cruzeiros. In reality, therefore, the court was concerned with nothing but the Brazilian authorities' claim to the return of dollars which had been obtained by means that according to Brazilian exchange control regulations were inadmissible. This, in short, was simply an attempt in a legally impermissible manner to enforce in New York Brazilian exchange control regulations. With the possible exception of the claim for damages in respect of the fine the action seems to have been without any foundation.

5. It should not be open to doubt that the foreign State cannot internationally enforce its revenue claim even if the action is based upon the debtor's written acknowledgment. As in the case of a judgment, this merely conceals the revenue claim which remains the real issue. As the Supreme Court of Canada put it[97]

> the argument that the claim asserted is simply for the performance of an agreement, made for good consideration, to pay a stated sum of money, must also fail. We are concerned not with form but with substance, and if it can properly be said that the respondent made an agreement it was simply an agreement to pay taxes which by the laws of the foreign State she was obliged to pay. Neither the foreign judgment nor the agreement does more than make certain the fact and the amount of the respondent's liability to the appellant. The nature of the liability is not altered. It is a liability to pay income tax.

Journal of International Law, 1976, 101, disregards what are believed to be the essential points.

[97] *United States of America* v. *Harden*, (1963) Can. Supreme Court 366, at p. 371. See also above n. 89.

The result should be the same if the debtor has contractually bound himself to make punctual payment of taxes which may become due in future. A contract whereby an American enterprise undertakes to construct and operate a factory in a foreign country may include a clause to the effect that the investor will punctually pay all duly assessed taxes. If the investor (allegedly) fails to make payment can the foreign State recover it by instituting proceedings in a foreign court or possibly before arbitrators sitting in a foreign country? Or is the case the same as that of an acknowledgment? It is submitted that the latter question should be answered in the affirmative. The assumed contractual provision is simply an anticipated acknowledgment of a debt. If the acknowledgment cannot be made the foundation of proceedings, the same should apply to the promise to pay in future. These submissions are supported by a decision of the Supreme Court of Sweden.[98] The question was whether a former resident of Bulgaria who had established himself in Sweden was bound to hand over to the Bulgarian State a sum of Swedish money collected by him and representing the price of tobacco exported from Bulgaria. When applying for an export licence in 1944 the plaintiff had undertaken in accordance with Bulgarian exchange control regulations to remit the proceeds of sale to the Bulgarian National Bank. The Bulgarian State's action based on this undertaking failed on the ground that the action 'must be regarded as predominantly of a public law character'.

And if a claim cannot be pursued before an ordinary court it is similarly excluded from prosecution before arbitrators whose awards may have to be enforced by a court. As mentioned above, it is unjustifiable in this respect to draw a distinction between a judgment and an award (which may become incorporated into a judgment). It is admitted that there have been cases in which States have raised tax claims before arbitrators, but there is no evidence that the points here discussed were taken either by the parties or by the arbitration tribunal.[99] The principle is that arbitrators cannot award what judges are precluded from adjudging. An award, frequently turned into a judgment, cannot have any other or greater force than a judgment.

The case is even more troublesome if the contract is so drafted as to impose upon the court or the arbitration tribunal the duty itself to assess the tax or the customs duty claimed by the State. This is an almost impossible task for a foreign lawyer and in such a case there in fact arise the specific arguments against the international enforcement of public rights which have sometimes been urged.[100]

[98] Int. L.R. 47, 40 (21 March 1961). This is the third decision of the Swedish Supreme Court in the famous litigation initiated by Takvarian against Bulgaria.

[99] This applies, in particular, to the *Aminoil* arbitration, Int. L.R. 66, 518.

[100] See above n. 34.

The situation is different where the plaintiff or the claimant in arbitration proceedings is asking for damages or compensation from the respondent State. In assessing the amount so claimed any sums due to the respondent, including taxes or fines, will have to be taken into account. There can be no objection, because the State does not claim payment to it, but merely argues about the assessment of the claimant's loss.[101] It is the net loss to which the victim of a breach of contract is entitled.

6. An obvious case of indirect enforcement arises where the liquidator of a company tries to recover from a director or shareholder sums exclusively required for the payment of taxes,[102] the emphasis being on 'exclusively',[103] for if part is required for the payment of trade creditors it is impossible to say that the action is brought for the enforcement of public rights. The same applies if all the shares in a company have been taken by tax or other authorities in payment of moneys due from shareholders and the proceedings are brought by new directors appointed by the foreign State of its own benefit.[104]. In such cases the wise principle applies which the Supreme Court of the United States formulated as follows:[105]

> Although a corporation and its shareholders are deemed separate entities for most purposes, the corporate form may be disregarded in the interests of justice where it is used to defeat an overriding public policy. . . Where equity would preclude the shareholders from maintaining the action in their own right, the corporation would also be precluded . . . The principal beneficiary of any recovery and itself estopped from complaining . . . cannot avoid the command of equity through the guise of proceeding in the name of . . . corporations which it owns and controls.

7. A question which has not been finally answered relates to extradition. Suppose that forgery or fraud are, but offences under revenue or exchange control laws are not included among those in respect of which extradition may be granted. Suppose also that forgery or fraud has been committed in

[101] In the arbitration between Kuwait and Aminoil, Int. L.R. 66, 518, the claimant State claimed 'royalties and taxes' (paragraph xix) and the tribunal in fact took a sum due under this heading into account (paragraph 176). The point made in the text does not seem to have been taken on behalf of Aminoil nor would it have been a good one, because the real issue in the case related to the compensation due to Aminoil and in assessing it the taxes (which like so many other items were not specified by the tribunal) were quite properly taken into account. On the Award see Mann, *British Year Book of International Law*, 1983, 213, or above pp. 252 sqq.

[102] *Peter Buchanan Ltd.* v. *McVey*, [1955] A.C. 516.

[103] *Ayres* v. *Evans*, 39 (1981–2) A.L.R. 129; Lord Mackay of Clashfern in *Williams and Humbert Ltd.* v. *W. & H. Trade Marks (Jersey) Ltd.* [1986] A.C. 368, at p. 440. This may be different in the United States: *Bandes* v. *Harlow & Jones*, 852, F.2d. 661 (1988).

[104] In England the decision of the House of Lords mentioned in the preceding note would at present be opposed to this suggestion.

[105] *Bangor Punta Operations Inc.* v. *Bangor & Arrostock Railroad Co.*, 417 U.S. 703, 713 (1974).

the course of and in connection with an offence under an enactment relating to revenue or exchange control. Can an order for extradition be made? Two Divisional Courts have given different answers.[106] It is submitted that the decisive question in such a case is whether, as it was put in the earlier of the two cases, 'in substance and in reality' it was the non-extraditable offence which was committed and to which the extraditable offence was merely incidental or whether the opposite is correct. If, for instance, the accused made an exchange control application which was fraudulent, it is likely that extradition for fraud should be refused. If, on the other hand, the accused committed a fraud and as a result, but quite separately, applied for exchange control permission, the offence is likely to be extraditable. No such question was asked in the second of the two cases.

IX

The conclusions to be drawn from the preceding discussions may be summarized shortly. The decisive question always is whether the plaintiff asserts a claim which in essence, in reality, by its nature, involves the assertion of a sovereign right. Where the State's claims arise from 'actus qui a rege sed ut a quovis alio' (Grotius), then they are capable of international enforcement. Careful assessment and delimitation is required. The decision will not always be an easy one. Nor will the results always be universally approved. They will in many cases depend upon legal judgment or instinct. What should not be open to dispute is the starting point and the purpose of the reasoning. In any case the Court of Appeals of New York was in error, when it felt able in somewhat non-judicial language to describe the non-enforceability of foreign 'revenue laws' as 'an old chestnut'.[107] Indeed, the English and American practice to ask whether a claim is founded upon 'a revenue law' is erroneous and misleading. The true question is whether in substance the claim asserts a public right. If it does then the rule stated by Dicey and Morris[108] in regard to English law is entitled to universal approval: 'English courts have no jurisdiction to entertain an action . . . for the enforcement either directly or indirectly of a penal, revenue or other public law of a foreign State.' Of that rule Lord Denning M.R. has said that 'no-one has ever doubted it'[109] and Kerr L.J. described it as being 'certainly a principle of general acceptation'.[110]

[106] *R.* v. *Governor of Pentonville Prison, ex parte Khubchandani* (1980) 71 Cr.App.R. 241; *R.* v. *Chief Metropolitan Stipendiary Magistrate, ex parte Secretary of State for the Home Department* (1989) 1 All E.R. 151.

[107] Above n. 96.

[108] *Conflict of Laws*, p. 89.

[109] Above n. 12, at pp. 19–24.

[110] *In re Norway's Application*, [1986] 3 W.L.R. 452, at p. 479.

15

Compound Interest as an Item of Damage in International Law

I

IN 1943 Miss Marjorie M. Whiteman wrote:

> There are few rules within the scope of the subject of damages in international law that are better settled than the one that compound interest is now allowable. Although in rare cases compound interest, or its equivalent, has been granted, tribunals have been almost unanimous in disapproval of its allowance.[1]

Forty years later, in 1983, Professor Charles Rousseau wrote:

> Arbitral tribunals generally reject this method [compound interest] of calculating damages, because they feel that the solution may only be adopted on the basis of the parties' express or implied intent.[2]

Numerous decisions, mainly arbitral awards, support both these statements. At the same time, however, it should be reçognized that, as an item of damage, the problem of compound interest apparently has never been fully analysed. Most learned writers ignore it[3] or fail to give any reason for their conclusions that compound interest is or is not payable.[4] Jean-Luc Subilia is the only author who has dealt with the problem of compound interest a little more carefully.[5] Subilia discusses all the relevant cases[6] and concludes:

[1] 3 *Damages in International Law* 1997 (1943).

[2] The original text stated: Les tribunaux arbitraux écartent généralement ce mode de calcul de l'indemnité, estimant qu'une telle solution ne peut résulter que de la volonté expresse ou tacite des parties. *Droit International Public* V § 242 (1983).

[3] See *I. Brownlie, State Responsibility* 227–29 (1983), which in n. 82 has an almost complete bibliography that confirms the statement in the text. See also L. Oppenheim, *International Law*, 353 (H. Lauterpacht, ed. 8th ed. 1963); D. O'Connell, 2 *International Law* 1122 (2nd ed. 1970); A. Verdross & B. Simma, *Universelles Völkerrecht* 876 (3d edn. 1984); L. Sohn & R. Baxter, *Convention on the International Responsibility of States for Injuries to Aliens*; Draft No. 12, with Explanation Notes, art. 38 (1959).

[4] See e.g. H. Lauterpacht, *Private Law Sources and Analogies of International Law* 146 n. 1 (1927); G. Dahm, *Völkerrecht* III 236 n. 9 (1961).

[5] *L'Allocation d'Intérêts dans la Jurisprudence International* (Lausanne 1972).

[6] Id. at 99, 163.

U. C. Davis Law Review, 21 (Festschrift in Honour of Edgar Bodenheimer), 1988, 577–86.

As far as compound interest is concerned, it seems that one cannot go further than to state that such recovery generally is not granted by international tribunals. Beyond that, the few precedents favourable to compound interest, which have been mentioned in Chapter VI, do not support the existence of a case law rule which would preclude them as a matter of international law.[7]

The position is similar when one looks at decisions. Some cases allow compound interest when awarding damages, although usually without any discussion. Thus, compound interest has been allowed in *Fabiani's* case,[8] in the *Affaire des Chemins de Fer Zeltweg-Wolfsburg,*[9] and more recently in the *Aminoi* case.[10] On the other hand, compound interest has been disallowed in a large number of cases, in particular in *France* v. *Peru*[11] and *Norway* v. *United States*.[12] In *Norway*, the tribunal stated:

The claimants have asked for compound interest with half-yearly adjustments, but compound interest has not been granted in previous arbitration cases, and the Tribunal is of the opinion that the claimants have not advanced sufficient reasons why an award of compound interest, in this case, should be made.[13]

Here, at least, there is an indication that if proper reasons had been advanced, the Tribunal might have awarded compound interest.

Perhaps the most significant decision on compound interest is the ruling given by Max Huber in *Great Britain* v. *Spain (Spanish Zone of Morocco)*.[14] The eminent jurist attempts an explanation and an analysis:

As regards the choice between simple and compound interest, the *Rapporteur* should first of all point out that the arbitral case law in matters involving compensation of one State by another for damages suffered by the nationals of one within the territory of the other—after all a particularly rich case law—is

[7] The original text stated:

Quant aux intérêts composés, il ne semble pas que l'on puisse aller au-delà de la constatation que la capitalisation n'est généralement pas admise par les tribunaux internationaux. Pour le surplus, les quelques précédents favorables à l'admission des intérêts composés que nous avons rapportés dans le chapitre VI nous interdisent de poser l'existence d'une règle jurisprudentielle qui les exclurait en droit international. Id. at 24.

[8] J. B. Moore, *Digest of International Law* 4878–4915 (1906).

[9] Affaire des Chemins de Fer Zeltweg-Wolfsburg et Unterdrauberg-Woellan (Austria and Yugoslavia), 3 R. Int'l Arb. Awards 1795, 1808 (1934).

[10] *Kuwait* v. *American Indep. Oil Co.*, 66 I.L.R. 518, 613 (Arb. Trib. 1982).

[11] Affaire des Réclamations Françaises Contre le Pérou (France v. Peru), 1 R. Int'l Arb. Awards 215, 220 (1920).

[12] Norwegian Shipowners' Claims (*Norway* v. *United States*), 1 R. Int'l Arb. Awards 307, 341 (1922).

[13] Id.

[14] Affaire des Biens Britanniques au Maroc Espagnol (*Great Britain* v. *Spain (Spanish Zone of Morocco)*), 2 R. Int'l Arb. Awards 615, 650 (1924).

> unanimous, as far as the *Rapporteur* knows, in disallowing compound interest. In these circumstances, very strong and quite specific arguments would be called for to grant such interest in this case. It seems, however, that such arguments do not exist, given the fact that the circumstances of the claims put before the *Rapporteur* do not differ in principle from those in the matters that have given rise to the pertinent case law.
>
> This is true in certain circumstances when compound interest would, because of the case presented, be more appropriate than simple interest, for instance in cases in which the goods that the damages awarded are supposed to replace increase by geometric rather than arithmetic progression, as with respect to herds of cattle.[15]

The reference to 'herds of cattle' is a little far-fetched, and, as we shall see, less telling than a claim to money, for such claims pre-eminently 's'augmentent par progression géométrique'.[16]

Recently, the problem acquired great practical importance in Arbitration Tribunal decisions dealing with the settlement of claims between the United States and Iran.[17] The issue arose for the first time in *R. J. Reynolds Tobacco Co.* v. *Iran*[18] which stated: 'The Tribunal, however, does not find that there are any special reasons for departing from international precedents which normally do not allow the awarding of compound interest'.[19] The word 'normally' is one of the unfortunate expressions which often occurs in the cases and gives rise to many unanswered questions.[20] In *Sylvana Technical Systems*[21] (Chamber I, Chairman: Professor Böckstiegel) it is stated that 'the Tribunal has never

[15] The original text stated:

> En ce qui concerne le choix entre les intérêts simples et les intérêts composés, le Rapporteur doit tout d'abord constater que la jurisprudence arbitrale en matière de compensations à accorder par un État à an autre pour dommages subis par les ressortissants de celui-ci sur le territoire de celui-là—jurisprudence pourtant particulièrement riche—est unanime, pour autant que le Rapporteur le sache, pour écarter les intérêts composés. Dans ces circonstances, il faudrait des arguments particulièrement forts et de nature toute spéciale pour admettre en l'espèce ce type d'intérêt. Pareils arguments ne sembleraient cependant pas exister, étant donné que les circonstances des réclamations dont le Rapporteur se trouve saisi ne diffèrent pas en principe de celles des cas qui ont donné lieu à la jurisprudence dont il s'agit.
>
> Cela est vrai entre autres de certaines èventualités où les intérêts composés sembleraient par ailleurs mieux correspondre à la nature des choses que les intérêts simples, savoir les cas où les biens que les indemnités accordées ont pour but de remplacer s'augmentent par progression géométrique plutôt qu'arithmétique, ce qui arrive par exemple pour les troupeaux de bétail. Id. at 650.

[16] '[I]ncrease by geometric progression.'

[17] This Article is based on an opinion that the author rendered to the claimants in *Starrett Housing Corp.* v. *Iran*.

[18] Iran-United States Claims Tribunal Reports 7, 181, 191 (Chamber III, Chairman: Mangard) [hereafter Iran–United States Tribunal].

[19] Id.

[20] What does it mean? Which are the abnormal cases? Why does this particular case come within the general rule rather than the exception?

[21] Iran–United States Claims Tribunal Reports 8, 298, 320.

awarded compound interest'.[22] This is a purely factual statement which is of little weight, because we do not know whether or on what legal grounds compound interest was claimed in previous cases and because the claimant in *Sylvana Technical Services* sought only simple interest.[23] Further, the Tribunal announced its intention to

> derive a rate of interest based approximately on the amount that the successful claimant would have been in a position to have earned if it had been paid in time and thus had the funds available to invest in a form of commercial investment in common use in its own country. Six-month certificates of deposit in the United States are such a form of investment for which average interest rates are available from an authoritative official source.[24]

It is not certain whether the Tribunal realized that investment in six-month certificates of deposit involves earning compound interest. *Anaconda-Iran* v. *Iran*[25] (Chamber III, Chairman: Virally) dealt with the point more fully:

> 139. The Tribunal notes that there are several reasons why judicial authorities, be it on a national or international level, generally do not award compound interest.
> 140. First of all, the inherent and essential effect of a contractual provision for compound interest is to dissuade the other party from defaulting in fulfilling its contractual obligations. Such an effect is particularly relevant in the context of a continuing relationship. If, however, a dispute emerges as to the scope and content of the contractual obligations and if, as in the present case, such a dispute leads to a termination of the contract in question, this purpose is mooted. Secondly, the mathematical result of a full application of contractual provisions such as Section 7.04, particularly in view of the delays that any adjudication of a dispute involves, is that the interest due could, by far, exceed the principal awards awarded. This is particularly relevant in the context of the proceedings before this Tribunal, as the great number of cases simultaneously under consideration causes the individual parties to incur additional delays. Consequently, to implement such a contractual clause would cause a benefit, and indeed a profit, to accrue to the successful party, which would be wholly out of proportion to the possible loss that the successful party might have incurred by not having the amounts due at its disposal.[26]

Contrary to the impression that these words conveyed, the contract did not include a provision relating to compound interest. It provided for simple interest at a defined rate plus two per cent, but the Tribunal did not attribute to it the full effect which it seems to contemplate.[27]

Finally, in an expropriation case, *Starrett Housing Corp.* v. *Iran* (Chairman: Lagergren),[28] the majority of the Tribunal, having received detailed

[22] Id. [23] Id. [24] Id. [25] Iran–United States Tribunal Reports 13, 199.
[26] At pp. 234, 235. [27] See the clause at p. 233.
[28] Iran–United States Tribunal Reports 16, 112.

arguments on the point, ignored all reasoning and simply stated that it was 'not persuaded to depart from' the practice referred to in *Sylvana Technical Systems*.[29] There was, however, a well-reasoned dissent by the American arbitrator, Mr Holtzmann.[30] Holtzmann pointed out that an award of compound interest was necessary 'to make Starrett whole for the actual damage it suffered', since

> the Respondents were fully aware that Starrett was borrowing money from its US banks on a compound basis in order to finance the Project . . . Starrett, like most contractors, operated on the basis of back-to-back loans and a substantial line of credit with their banks. It is normal commercial practice that banks customarily charge compound interest to finance credit facilities.[31]

Moreoever, an award of compound interest was 'in conformity with the Expert's valuation methods', and was also 'consistent with international law'.[32] If a rule against compound interest existed in 1943, 'it is no longer appropriate or justifiable . . . Modern economic reality, as well as equity, demands that injured parties who have themselves suffered actual compound interest charges be compensated on a compound basis in order to be made whole'.[33]

II

The solution of the compound interest problem in international law is made more difficult because the general principles of law recognized by civilized nations do not yield an unequivocal guidance. When a statute provides for the payment of interest, it is frequently expressly stated that such interest does not carry interest or, in other words, that the statute does not authorize (but does not prohibit) the payment of compound interest. This is the position in England,[34] France,[35] Germany,[36] Switzerland,[37] and the United States, where the point is usually dealt with by state legislation. However, the question is whether, independently of such provisions, compound interest may not become payable. First, authority exists for the proposition that compound interest is payable when the parties have by contract so stipulated.[38] Second, in the common law system the breach of a fiduciary duty may lead to the award of compound

[29] p. 235. [30] p. 249. [31] p. 252. [32] Id. [33] pp. 253, 254.
[34] Law Reform (Miscellaneous Provision) Act. 1934, s.3(1).
[35] Code Civil [C. Civ.] art. 1153.
[36] Section 289, first sentence of the Civil Code.
[37] Schweizerisches Obligationenrecht [OR] art. 105.
[38] See, e.g., Corbin *On Contracts* § 1047 (1964).

interest.[39] Third, compound interest may be an item of damage which, if not too remote, may be recoverable. This, in practice, is the most important case which in some countries, for instance in Germany, is dealt with by express provision for the payment of damages of any type flowing from the default.[40] In other countries, particularly the United States, it is frequently stated that compound interest is not allowed as damages for breach of contract or tort.[41]

However, the latter conclusion is not free from doubt. The specific compound interest problem occurs when the plaintiff could have earned such interest if the defendant had paid punctually or if the plaintiff has had to pay compound interest which, in the event of defendant's punctual payment, would have been avoided. The same result should follow in both alternatives from the general law of damages as it is understood in most countries: the failure to pay a debt when due is a breach of contract.[42] In practice, the two alternatives are likely to call for a distinction.

The former alternative must be treated with great care because it is usually highly speculative. Only when the plaintiff is a depositor of money which carried compound interest will a court find it possible to hold (and should hold) that the money due from the defendant also would have been deposited and would have earned interest and compound interest with clearly provable rests. By way of example, there is evidence in Canada that the principle according to which interest is payable when the payment of a just debt has been improperly withheld[43] was extended to cover the case of compound interest that could have been earned.[44]

[39] For an explanation of the United States system, see Williston *On Contracts* § 1417 (W. Jaeger ed., 3rd edn. 1968); for England's system, see *Wallersteiner* v. *Moir*, 1975 Q.B. 373 (CA).

[40] Section 289, second sentence of the Civil Code.

[41] *Cherokee Nation* v. *United States*, 270 U.S. 476, 490 (1926); see also Corbin, above note 38 and Williston, above note 40.

[42] In civil law systems this is likely to be undoubted, but the solution is probably the same in England, where Lord Brandon of the House of Lords recently stated that 'claims to recover . . . losses as damages for breach of contract, whether the breach relied on is late payment of a debt or any other breach, are subject to the same rules as apply to claims for damages for breach of contract generally'. See *President of India* v. *Lips Maritime Corp.*, [1987] 3 W.L.R. 572, 580. This is in line with *Lep Air Servs.* v. *Rolloswin Ltd.*, 1973 App. Cas. 331. See generally FA Mann, *The Legal Aspect of Money* 67, 68 (4th ed. 1982).

[43] This is the test for the award of interest, which was formulated by Lord Macnaghten in the Canadian appeal of *Toronto Ry. Co.* v. *City of Toronto*, 1906 App. Cas. 117 and which seems to have been accepted in Canada. See the Supreme Court of Canada in *Prince Albert Pulp Co.* v. *The Foundation Co. of Canada Ltd.*, 68 D.L.R. 3d 283 (1976).

[44] *Roman Catholic Diocese of Calgary* v. *Century Insurance Co. of Canada*, 8 D.L.R. 4th 435, 441 (1984), which extended the test mentioned in note 43 to compound interest. In British Columbia the Law Reform Commission has suggested that prejudgment interest should be compounded. *Report on the Court Order Interest Act 31* (1987). The English Law Commission rejected this suggestion as being 'either too crude to be fair in all cases or too intricate to be practicable'. See Cmnd. 7229 paragraph 85.

The later alternative is more easily proved and is exemplified by an important English Court of Appeal decision.[45] A building contract provided that if in the event of a variation of work the contractor has been involved 'in direct loss and/or expense' the amount of such loss or expense shall be recoverable from the building owner.[46] To finance this additional work, the contractors had borrowed money from their bank and paid interest and compound interest for the loan. Lord Goff, then Goff L. J. with whom O'Connor and Salde L.JJ. agreed, stated:

> There remains to be considered the question whether the respondents are entitled to recover their financing charges only on the basis of simple interest, or whether they are entitled to assess their claim on the basis of compound interest, calculated at quarterly rests, as they have done. Now here, it seems to me, we must adopt a realistic approach. We must bear in mind, moreover, that what we are here considering is a debt due under a contract . . . The respondents, like (I imagine) most building contractors, operated over the relevant period on the basis of a substantial overdraft at their bank, and their claim in respect of financing charges consists of a claim in respect of interest paid by them to the bank on the relevant amount during that period. It is notorious that banks do themselves, when calculating interest on overdrafts, operate on the basis of periodic rests; on the basis stated by the Court of Appeal in *F. L. Minter Ltd.* v. *Welsh Health Technical Services Organization*, 13 Building L.R. 1, which we here have to apply, I for my part can see no reason why that fact should not be taken into account when calculating the respondents' claim for loss or expense in the present case. It follows that, in order to calculate the respondents' contractual claim, it will be necessary to calculate it with reference to the total sum of £156,762.19 . . ., taking into account . . . the rates of interest charged by the bank to the respondents at various times over that period, and . . . the periodic rests on the basis of which the bank from time to time added outstanding interest to the capital sum outstanding for the purposes of calculating interest thereafter.[47]

It should be clear that 'direct loss and/or expense' is, independently of a contractual provision, also the prerequisite of a claim for damages flowing from a breach of contract or tort. It follows that even in the absence of a clause indemnifying a contracting party against 'direct loss and/or expense', compound interest reasonably incurred by the injured party should be recoverable as an item of damage. This, it is submitted, should not only be English law,[48] but should be accepted wherever damages are allowed and should, therefore, be treated as a general principle of law.

[45] *Rees and Kirby Ltd.* v. *Council of the City of Swansea*, 30 Building L.R. 8 (1985).

[46] Id. [47] Id. at 23.

[48] It is at present uncertain whether the submission made in the text will be accepted in England. On English law relating to interests, see Mann, 'On Interest, Compound Interest and Damages', 101 *Law Q. Rev.* 30 (1985).

III

The present uncertain state of international law described in part I, and the unsettled practice of municipal courts described in part II, render it necessary to base a decision applying international law on legal principle, that is, on reasoning derived from a rational appreciation of legal rules, and (in the words of the savant to whom these lines are dedicated in memory of more than sixty years of friendship) thus to inaugurate 'a new conception of justice in accord with the highest knowledge and truest insight perceptible to the human mind'.[49]

In this spirit it is necessary first to take account of modern economic conditions. It is a fact of universal experience that those who have a surplus of funds normally invest them to earn compound interest. This applies, in particular, to bank deposits or savings accounts. On the other hand, many are compelled to borrow from banks and therefore must pay compound interest. This applies, in particular, to business people whose own funds are frequently invested in brick and mortar, machinery and equipment, and whose working capital is obtained by way of loans or overdrafts from banks. The practice as to rests varies considerably. Monthly, quarterly, half-yearly, yearly rests occur, and in a specific case it may be necessary to investigate local practices. But it is likely that a judge who would award quarterly or half-yearly rests would not go far wrong.

If, in accordance with the usual formula, damages are intended to afford *restitutio in integrum* (complete compensation for the wrong suffered) such items of damage should not be excluded. One is not dealing with the payment or repayment of liquidated sums such as the price of goods or a loan or even arrears of agreed interest due in respect of a loan; in such circumstances the general practice of municipal laws or courts does not normally allow the payment of more than simple interest. But as soon as any liability for damages arises, different considerations apply and demand the elimination, by the payment of money, of all foreseeable injuries.

Nor can it be material that one function of a contractual provision for the payment of compound interest may be to deter the debtor from defaulting. This is certainly not necessarily or usually so. In fact it is an inappropriate idea in most cases because no contract exists in the case of damages, and when parties validly agree on compound interest, it is actually in the nature of liquidated damages.

Finally, it is completely wrong to attach any significance to the fact that the award of interest or compound interest may lead to the payment of a sum exceeding the capital due from the wrongdoer. This may happen in

[49] These are the concluding words of E. Bodenheimer, *Jurisprudence: The Philosophy and Method of the Law* 386 (1st edn. 1967).

many cases as a result of the wrongdoer's delaying tactics or the court's work load. But during that period the wrongdoer has enjoyed the fruits of the money withheld. Moreover, the classical Roman law doctrine forbidding the payment of interest *supra duplum* or, as it is put nowadays, *ultra alterum tantum*[50] has been long obsolete. On the international scene this idea made its sole appearance in the case of *Yuille Shortridge & Co.* in 1861,[51] when, under the influence of the then prevailing Roman law, the Senate of Hamburg as sole arbitrator stated: 'Since according to Roman law, the only one applicable here, cumulative back interest may not exceed the principal (Dig. de cond. indeb. 12.6), the interest in this case had to be limited to £2589'.[52] It is almost paradoxical that this was said in the very year in which the Universal German Commercial Code appeared. The Code applied in Hamburg and provided in Article 293: 'In the case of commercial transactions interest may exceed the total amount of the capital'.[53]

More modern systems of municipal law to which one must resort know nothing of restrictions that were revived, with inadequate reasoning, by Chamber III of the Iran-United States Arbitration Tribunal in 1985.[54] Of course, if the claimant is responsible for a delay, or if there is room in international practice for a doctrine corresponding to limitation of actions or prescription, any judge or arbitrator will disentitle the claimant from the interest or compound interest that is due. No such facts existed in *Anaconda-Iran*.[55] There was, therefore, no room for the revival of a principle peculiar to classical Roman law.[56] In conclusion, it is submitted that, on the basis of compelling evidence, compound interest may be and, in the absence of special circumstances, should be awarded to the claimant as damages by international tribunals.

[50] Digest XII.6.; C.4.32. See generally Windscheid-Kipp, *Pandektenrecht* II 82 (8th edn. 1906). For a general discussion of the problem, see L. Solidaro, 'Ultra Sortis Summam usurae non exiguntur', *Labeo* 28, 164 (1982).

[51] (Great Britain v. Portugal) Lapradelle-Politis, Recueil des arbitrages internationaux II 108 (1924).

[52] The original text stated: 'Comme d'après le droit commun, seul applicable ici, le cumul des intérêts arrièrés s'arrête lorqu'ils atteignent le principal (Dig. de cond. indeb. 12.6), on a dû restreindre les intérêts de ce chef à £2589. 1d.'

[53] Universal German Commercial Code art. 293.

[54] Iran-United States Tribunal, above note 18.

[55] See above note 25.

[56] Against the present recognition of the doctrine of *ultra alterum tantum* see J. Subilia, above note 5, at 101, 117.

16

The Judicial Recognition of an Unrecognized State

EVER since the House of Lords decided *Carl Zeiss Stiftung* v. *Rayner & Keeler Ltd.*[1] there was room to question whether the modern English judiciary had given thought to the rationale of the executive's refusal to recognize a foreign entity as a State. The meaning and purpose of non-recognition is simple and straightforward: the United Kingdom expresses its disapproval of the foreign entity, its origin and its policies. Therefore the UK regards it as non-existent, denies efficacy to its institutions, law and activities (though there may possibly be certain limited exceptions in matters of a purely private nature). In particular, the UK denies to an unrecognized State the right to become a party to a treaty, refuses to accept a diplomatic note or other official communication, or to recognize a passport issued by it.[2] In law, therefore, the non-recognized State does not exist. It is, if one prefers so to put it, a nullity. Of course, we all know that in fact or in the real world there is such an organizations as, say, the Turkish Republic of Cyprus, but in English eyes it does not exist. To a lawyer this is not an unfamiliar situation: in law a contract may be null and void and unenforceable, but in fact it may have been concluded and performed.

If this explanation is correct it must be obvious that if the courts are genuine in their determination to speak in foreign affairs with the same voice as the executive, as the Anglo-American tradition requires, they cannot allow the foreign organization to be admitted as a State through the back-door, by way of a fiction, by legal reasoning which makes nonsense of the executive's policy. This happened, however, in *Zeiss*. A statute passed by the unrecognized German Democratic Republic in its own name was given effect in England, because it was deemed to have been sanctioned by the alleged lawful sovereign, the Soviet Union. Such a result, condemned by the courts of the United States, and by many academic writers, was derived from a sentence in the Foreign Office certificate which was clearly misinterpreted and which, in the face of two

[1] [1967] A.C. 853.

[2] For references to such refusals see Mann, *Studies in International Law* pp. 673–4.

International and Comparative Law Quarterly, 36 (1987), 348–50.

applications, the House refused to have clarified by the Foreign Secretary: since the Foreign Office had certified that 'Her Majesty's government have recognized the State and government of the USSR as *de jure* entitled to exercise governing authority in respect' of the Soviet zone of occupation, everything done by the German Democratic Republic in its own name and under its own flag was deemed to be done by or with the authority of the Soviet Union, and thus carried the Soviet seal of validity and efficacy. The practical effect, therefore, was that the German Democratic Republic had in English courts exactly the same status as if it had been recognised *de jure*. A second decision similarly stultifying Britain's foreign policy has now been given in regard to the at present peculiarly delicate subject of South Africa. The Foreign and Commonwealth Office had obviously tried to find a form of words which would prevent such a result, but the Court of Appeal considered it had not succeeded.

In *GUR Corporation* v. *The Trust Bank of Africa Ltd.*[3] the plaintiffs had built a hospital and two schools for the Department of Public Works of the 'Republic of Ciskei'. The plaintiffs demanded from the defendant bank the return of a deposit of $300,000 in respect of a guarantee given by it to the building owners. The defendants appear to have joined the building owners as a third party and the question before the court was whether the latter could be sued in an English court. Steyn J. answered in the negative, the Court of Appeal (Sir John Donaldson M.R., Nourse and Glidewell L.JJ.) reversed. The Court of Appeal referred to the Status of Ciskei Act which was passed by the Republic of South Africa in 1981 to set up the Republic of Ciskei and to the Republic of Ciskei's Constitution Act 1981 whereby the 'Republic's Department of Public Works was created. Although the Foreign and Commonwealth Office had certified that Ciskei was not recognized as a State either *de jure* or *de facto*, the court looked at section 3 (1) of the South African Status of Ciskei Act 1981 according to which 'the legislative Assembly of Ciskei . . . may . . . make laws (including a constitiution) for the Ciskei' and regarded this as 'a straightforward delegation of legislative power' to Ciskei as a subordinate body of the Republic of South Africa, while in truth the Act intended to set up the independent and distinct Republic of Ciskei. Thus, the Court of Appeal (as, in *Zeiss* the House of Lords) fell into error: delegation means that the *delegatus* acts, not in his own name and for his own benefit, but on behalf, for the account and in the interest of the *delegans*. The 'Republic of Ciskei' certainly does not act and is not intended or authorized to act on behalf of South Africa. Section 3 purports to confer the power to act independently, as a sovereign, as a principal. The section cannot,

[3] [1986] 3 W.L.R. 583.

therefore, be relied upon in support of the Court of Appeal's theory. To read into it a delegation in the established sense of the law is pure fiction.

The result, of course, suited all three parties, in particular the defendant bank which, had Steyn J.'s judgment been upheld, would have had to sue the individual who signed the building contract as the agent of a non-existent person.

Yet in law the result is such as to be wholly inconsistent with UK policy. The effect of the decision is that the party before the court is not the Republic of South Africa, but the non-recognized Republic of Ciskei represented by its Department of Public Works.

Nourse L. J. sought to blame the Foreign and Commonwealth Office:

> The rule that the judiciary and the executive must speak with one voice presupposes that the judiciary can understand what the executive has said. In most cases there could hardly be any doubt in the matter. But in a case like the present, where there is a doubt, the judiciary must resolve it in the only way they know, which is to look at the question and then construe the answer given. It is not for the judiciary to criticise any obscurity in the expressions of the executive nor to inquire into their origin or policy. They must take them as they stand.[4]

This is not so. If there is any doubt the judiciary must ask the executive for clarification. In the present case the doubt was said to arise from the Foreign and Commonwealth Office's statement that 'Her Majesty's government has not taken and does not have a formal position as regards the exercise of governing authority over the territory of Ciskei'. The Foreign and Commonwealth Office will have to find a form of words which eliminates the judicial contrivances discovered in *Zeiss* and developed by the instant case. Perhaps the following formula would work:

> No State is recognized by Her Majesty's government as exercising any governing authority in the territory occupied by the organization describing itself as the Republic of Ciskei.

In truth, however, the sentence quoted above all did not need clarification. Since 1980 the Foreign and Commonwealth Office no longer recognizes, or has 'a formal position' in regard to, foreign governments. Neither did this matter in the present case. Where there is no State there cannot be a government. And it was the existence or non-existence of the State alone that was relevant in the instant case.

[4] Id., p. 604

17

The Effect in England of the Compulsory Acquisition by a Foreign State of the Shares in a Foreign Company

I

In *Williams and Humbert Ltd.* v. *W. & H. Trade Marks (Jersey) Ltd.*, *Rumasa SA* v. *Multinvest (UK) Ltd.*, [1986] A.C. 368, the House of Lords, in a speech delivered by Lord Templeman and concurred in by Lord Scarman, Lord Bridge of Harwich, Lord Brandon of Oakbrook and (probably) Lord Mackay of Clashfern, appear to decide that if Spain 'compulsorily acquires' all the shares in a Spanish company there is no legal principle that would prevent the company, represented by its new directors, from recovering its English assets.

If this is the principle established by the decision, it is impossible to dissent from it. Compulsory acquisition of property is an institution common to all civilized nations. It is, in the words of Lord Templeman, 'universally recognised and practised' (p. 30). It presupposes legislation and payment of full compensation equivalent to the loss suffered and assessed by an independent body. As Blackstone, adopting a lengthy analysis by Montesquieu, put it: 'The public is now considered as an individual, treating with an individual for an exchange.' (Or: 'Le public est à cet égard comme un particulier qui traite avec an particulier.') This is why one speaks of a compulsory sale creating at a certain point the relationship of vendor and purchaser. Such a principle to the evolution of which England made splendid contributions and which no English court could possibly condemn is contemplated by numerous constitutions and treaties since it was first formally proclaimed by the Constitution of Vermont in 1777 and taken up in 1789 by the French Déclaration des Droits de l'Homme et du Citoyen: 'La propriété étant un droit inviolable et sacré, nul ne peut en être privé, si ce n'est lorsque le nécessité publique, légalement constatée, l'exige évidemment, et sous la condition d'une juste et préalable indemnité'. Lord Templeman who at p. 30 refers to some of the provisions in constitutions and treaties cites the English translation of

---

The text reproduces three Notes which appeared in *Law Quarterly Review*, 102 (1986), 191–7, 103 (1987) 26–81, and 104 (1988) 346–7 respectively.

this text, but omits the important words 'et préalable' ('and antecedent'). The antithesis of compulsory acquisition has for centuries been confiscation or, as English law prefers to call it, forfeiture of property—an entirely different institution generally rejected by civilized nations. (For the foregoing see in much detail (1959) 75 LQR 188, particularly pp. 195 sqq.) Accordingly the decision which arose, in Lord Templeman's mysterious words, from the attempt 'to plead the compulsory acquisition as a defence' (p. 28) cannot be criticized on the ground that it enforces foreign public law, for 'a simple case of compulsory acquisition' (p. 36) in substance involves a sale and purchase.

Yet there is, unfortunately, room for the question whether in reality the decision does not have a different, an almost sinister effect. The doubt is due to three circumstances.

1. In order to appreciate the first of them it is necessary to know some of the few facts which are reported to have been pleaded by the defendants, but were struck out as failing to support a defence.

By a special law of 1983 all the shares in Rumasa SA, a Spanish company, 'were compulsorily acquired by the Spanish government' (p. 426). Control was 'vested in the general board of state ownership' (p. 426). The reason advanced by the Spanish legislator was that Rumasa 'threatened the stability of the Spanish economy' (p. 426). The law 'provided for the fair price of the shares thereby compulsorily acquired to be paid after a valuation' (p. 426). It does not seem that compensation was in fact paid or assessed; it certainly was not stated to have been 'préalable'. Apparently the defendants tried to plead that the proceedings brought in England by Rumasa SA to recover English property represented 'an attempt to enforce a foreign law which is penal or which otherwise ought not be enforced' (p. 426). It was this plea which, presumably, was supported by particulars that was not allowed to be made.

Lord Templeman's overriding and, indeed, sole ground was that what had occurred in Spain was a compulsory acquisition rather than a confiscation. When one remembers that the case concerned a point of pleading, the proposition is startling, for Lord Templeman seems to have interpreted the Spanish legislation as in fact amounting to compulsory acquisition, so that the defendants' proposed plea was demonstrably wrong in fact. Is this not an entirely novel approach? Is it not the law that for the purpose of striking out a pleading the facts alleged in it must be assumed to be true? By assuming 'a simple case of compulsory acquisition' such as is 'universally recognised and practised' Lord Templeman seems to answer this question in the negative. At the outset, therefore, his reasoning gives cause for concern, for the existence of a 'simple case of compulsory acquisition' is, of course, a question of fact on which, at the stage of pleading the court ought not to make a finding.

2. The reader's misgivings are in no way eliminated by the authorities on which Lord Templeman relied. They had nothing in common with a 'simple case of compulsory acquisition' and were far removed from what is 'universally recognised and practised'. This certainly applied, for instance, to *Princess Paley Olga* v. *Weisz*, [1929] 1 KB 718 and *Banco de Vizcaya* v. *Don Alfonso*, [1935] 1 KB 140, which were clear cases of confiscation and incidentally, were hardly in point, since they were in no way concerned with the recovery of their English property by Russian or Spanish companies respectively. Nor is it possible to support Lord Templeman's suggestion that American courts 'chose the same approach as that adopted by the English courts' in these two cases. The starting point of the development in the United States is *Zwack* v. *Kraus Bros. & Co. Ltd.*, 327 F.2d 255 (1956) which arose out of the events in Hungary in 1948. Oddly enough, Lord Templeman (p. 433) described it as a case of compulsory acquisition (which it was not) and as a partnership case (which it was only in a limited sense). In truth the case was on many subsequent occasions treated as the leading authority for the proposition that where a State *confiscates* all the shares or all the property of a foreign *corporation* the original shareholders can recover the corporation's property in the United States.

This was certainly so decided in numerous cases dealing with Cuban confiscations. Lord Templeman (p. 433) referred to only one of them at first instance, *Palicio y Compania SA* v. *Brush*, 256 F. Supp. 481 (1966); the decision was affirmed on appeal by the Second Circuit: 375 F.2d 1011 (1967), cert. denied 389 US 830, and closely related litigation ended in the United States Supreme Court: *Alfred Dunhill of London Inc.* v. *Republic of Cuba*, 425 US 682 (1976). These and other cases clearly establish that what happend in Cuba was confiscation, that the dispossessed shareholders of Cuban corporations were able to recover the corporations' trade marks in the United States as well as other pre-confiscation assets such as outstanding debts and that they were only precluded from recovering the price of post-confiscation sales of cigars. Lord Templeman attributes to the American judge of first instance the holding 'that the former owners were not entitled to the price of goods exported from Cuba', but were entitled to 'the United States trade marks which were situated in the United States and were therefore not affected by the Cuban decree of acquisition' (p. 434). The first part of this holding, as has been pointed out, is a misinterpretation, while the second part proved the appellants' case which Lord Templeman rejected: the point was that the former shareholders recovered the trade marks, among other assets, while in *Rumasa* the appellants were not even allowed to demand them by their pleading.

Lord Templeman also said that 'the United States recognised the Cuban law and its change of title to property situate in Cuba' (p. 434). Was he unaware of the case of *Banco Nacional de Cuba v. Sabbatino* which was concerned with sugar that had been confiscated in Cuba, but had belonged to a Cuban corporation 'whose capital stock was owned principally by United States residents', and the proceeds of sale of which were ultimately recovered by the latter? Was it not realized that the reason was that the Cuban confiscation violated international law: *Banco Nacional de Cuba* v. *Farr Whitlock & Co.*, 383 F.2d 172 (1967) or Int.L.R. 43, 14, cert. denied 390 US 956 (1968), and that it did so, although the sugar had been owned by a Cuban corporation 'over ninety per cent' of the shareholders of which were United States nationals: 307 F.2d 859 or Int.L.R. 35, 12? (In so far as international law is concerned, it may be that in *Rumasa* there was no room for its application, though the First Protocol to the European Convention on Human Rights may have been relevant.) If what occurred in Spain was confiscation rather than compulsory acquisition, the denial of the former shareholders' entitlement to the company's English property is clearly inconsistent with American cases of the highest persuasive authority, and would indeed be contrary to the law prevailing in Austria, France, the Federal Republic of Germany and Holland, among other countries. In France, in particular, the Cour de Cassation has stated on numerous occasions that 'aucun effet de droit ne peut être reconnu en France à une dépossession operée par un Etat étranger sans qu'aucune indemnité équitable soit préalablement fixée': above p. 176, n. 254 and p. 183, and see the recent and striking decision of March 14, 1984, *Semaine Juridique* 58 (1984) No. 20217.

Confiscation, as opposed to compulsory acquisition, is invariably characterized by the fact that the State acts suddenly, adopts special procedures and promises compensation, but never pays it. For many examples see Mann, *Studies in International Law* pp. 479–83. The full facts underlying the Spanish case are, perhaps fortunately, not known, but the indications referred to above raise a doubt about Lord Templeman's justification in speaking of compulsory acquisition.

3. The doubts are intensified by another puzzling aspect of the case. If this was, as Lord Templeman put it, 'a simple case of compulsory acquisition', i.e. of purchase and sale initiated by appropriate procedures, why was it relevant to refer at length to the rule against piercing the corporate veil? Why had *Peter Buchanan Ltd.* v. *McVeigh*, [1955] AC 516, approved in *Government of India* v. *Taylor*, [1955] AC 461 to be distinguished on the (illogical and unconvincing) ground that it concerned a revenue claim? Is it intended to imply that the Spanish case was one of confiscation, yet not covered by the great principle of English law that foreign public law will not be enforced either directly or indirectly? (See Dicey and Morris, Rule 3 and the illuminating judgment of Lord Denning

M.R. in *Attorney General of New Zealand* v. *Ortiz*, [1983] AC. 1, pp. 19–24, according to whom 'no one has ever doubted' that rule.)

The puzzlement is by no means reduced by the opinion delivered by Lord Mackay of Clashfern who was at pains to emphasize that *McVeigh's* case presupposed an unsatisfied revenue claim. If *Rumasa* was a case of compulsory acquisition *McVeigh*'s case was not in point at all. If it was a case of confiscation it is submitted that it cannot make any difference whether the claim is made for the benefit of the revenue department or some other governmental authority.

Nor is the reader's scepticism diminished by a number of dicta the justification of which cannot be assessed without a much more precise knowledge of the pleadings. The most remarkable passage is likely to be the following (p. 431):

> The English court will decline to consider the merits of compulsory acquisition. In their pleadings the appellants seek to attack the motives of the Spanish legislators, to allege oppression on the part of the Spanish government and to question the good faith of the Spanish administration in connection with the enactment, terms and implementation of the law of the 29 June 1983. No English judge could properly entertain such an attack launched on a friendly state which will shortly become a fellow member of the European Economic Community.

One can understand the reluctance of a court to find a foreign state, whether it be a fellow member of the EEC, NATO or the United Nations, guilty of oppressive conduct. But the refusal to allow such conduct to be pleaded and perhaps proved is an entirely different matter and, it is submitted, goes much too far; such reasoning would have compelled an English court to give effect, for instance, to many laws of Germany which up to September 3, 1939 was a friendly State. If a party is not allowed even to plead 'allegations and insinuations of oppression and bad faith' (p. 436) on the part of a foreign government, it is precluded *in limine* from setting up a violation of public policy as understood in England. Yet English public policy is autonomous and in no way subordinate to foreign notions. In *Luther* v. *Sagor & Co.*, [1921] 3 KB 532, 559, it is true, Scrutton L.J. suggested that the allegation that its legislation is contrary to essential principles of justice and morality 'might well with a susceptible foreign government become a *casus belli*'. Yet even so extreme a degree of juristic appeasement did not prevent the argument from being put. In modern conditions the dictum is in any event without any realistic basis.

In the result *Rumasa*'s case seems to have created grave uncertainty in a field which, in the interest of investors, requires that security of property in England should not be less than that which other great trading nations have achieved and granted. One only has to think of the numerous English companies which have large investments in foreign countries of every kind. Is it conceivable that if a foreign State confiscates the shares of the English parent's foreign subsidiary the latter, acting nominally in its own name, but obeying the dictates of the foreign State would be able to recover the subsidiary's assets in England? The attempt to show the courts the way to avoid so absurd a result by the appointment of a receiver was rejected by Lord Templeman. Although he speaks of a case of compulsory acqusition, the reader of his speech does not obtain the impression that he clearly distinguished it from the entirely different one of confiscatory foreign legislation or that he would necessarily deny direct or indirect effect to the latter.

In these circumstances it should be seriously considered whether the most desirable course would not be an immediate amendment of sections 666 (5), and 670 of the Companies Act 1985 which allow former shareholders of a foreign dissolved corporation to apply for a winding-up in England where this is 'just and equitable', for the appointment of a liquidator and ultimately for the distribution to them of the surplus of assets over liabilities. The same right should be assured to dispossessed shareholders of a foreign company which has property in this country. Such a step, previously thought to be unnecessary, would be in line with such cases as *Re Compania Merabello San Nicholas*, [1973] Ch. 75 and the earlier authorities there referred to; *Woronin Leutschig and Cheshire* v. *Frederick Huth & Co.*, (1946) 79 Ll.L.R. 262; and *A/S Tallina Laevauhisus* v. *Tallina Shipping Co.*, (1947) 80 Ll.L.R. 99. The fact that in this particular case the Spanish company sued the English defendants in tort and misfeasance and may perhaps be justified in doing so and that the dispossessed shareholders themselves would not have done so, cannot affect the principle that property in England should not be less protected against indirect confiscation than, for instance, in the United States, where the property of a closely controlled corporation could not in any case be obtained by the confiscator of its shares. If nothing is done English companies may have to be advised to transfer their shares in foreign subsidiaries to American, French, German or Dutch subsidiaries—at great expense and with serious tax consequences. If the House of Lords' decision should unfortunately and no doubt unwittingly give rise to the slightest danger of such steps becoming necessary, the public interest requires immediate intervention by Parliament.

II

In the course of the last few months two events occurred that render it unavoidable to revert to the *Rumasa* case, [1986] AC. 368.

The first concerns that part of the decision of the House of Lords which held the defence unarguable and therefore fit for striking out, although it was argued before Nourse J. for seven days, in the Court of Appeal for six days and in the House of Lords for three days. It is not easy to discover the precise principle of law on the basis of which the House rejected the appellants' argument that striking out was the improper procedure. Lord Templeman's remark that the investigation undertaken by the courts 'was no different from the investigation which would have been involved in the trial of an issue' (p. 436) is not free from difficulty, as the trial of an issue would have been a trial with all its incidents and safeguards involving discovery, cross-examination and so forth. But this is the very thing which according to Lord Templeman would have been 'harrassing to the plaintiffs and embarrassing to the court and designed to support the allegations and insinuations of oppression and bad faith on the part of the Spanish authorities' (ibid.). If and in so far as this ground was the *ratio decidendi* it was a departure from the narrow limits imposed by Order 18, r. 19. The point is mentioned here, because the remarks in the *Rumasa* case decided on December 12, 1985 and first reported on January 10, 1986 stand in stark contrast to the wholly traditional and convincing formulation in another case also involving Spain and decided on March 21, 1986 by Sir Nicolas Browne-Wilkinson V.-C.: *Kingdom of Spain* v. *Christie Manson & Woods Ltd.*, [1986] 1 WLR, 1120, at 1127, where Spain successfully resisted the striking-out of her statement of claim and where the principle was stated as follows:

> This is an application to strike out the proceedings before trial. That is an extreme step for a court to take and is only done when it is obvious and clear beyond doubt that the plaintiff has no claim fit to go to trial. To shut out somebody from the judgment seat has been said many times to be an extreme step. Only in exceptional circumstances, therefore, is it right on such an application finally to determine any difficult point of law. Normally, if a case involves sustained argument, it is not a case for striking out, but for a preliminary point of law to be set down.

The fact that it was Spain that succeeded on both occasions underlines the suspicion that on one occasion she was uncommonly lucky.

The second event is that the *Rumasa* case has now been reported in the Official Reports. The report includes more than ten pages reproducing the argument of counsel for the defendants-appellants. As a result some points, hitherto mysterious, have become even more perplexing.

Thus it now appears that counsel for the plaintiffs-respondents were not called upon. In an application for striking out this is as it should be: if a defence is unarguable this should be obvious at the conclusion of the argument for the defendants. But in the present case there arises a special and, indeed, fundamental problem: where is the origin of the view which can fairly be said to be the *ratio decidendi* and according to which the case was 'a simple case of compulsory acquisition' (p. 434) such as 'is universally recognised and practised' (p. 427)? There is no trace of such an argument in the judgments of Nourse J. (p. 375) or the Court of Appeal (p. 389) nor, as we now know, can it have been presented to the House of Lords. The inexorable conclusion must be that in a case in which the truth of the defence had to be assumed the House independently made findings which lacked any foundation in fact and the origin of which defies explanation.

Furthermore we are now told that the 'pleaded facts' included the allegation that the Spanish company, Rumasa, had become 'an organ of the State of Spain'; that the Spanish 'expropriation laws' were 'penal', and 'discriminatory' and 'confiscatory' in that, in particular, the purported right to compensation was 'illusory'; and that the action was brought 'by or at the instigation of the Spanish company which is now an organ of the State of Spain' (pp. 415, 416); in fact it is remarkable that at p. 427 the opinion twice speaks of allegations made by 'the representatives of the Spanish government now charged with the management of the Rumasa Group'. It is also clear that, among much further material, the appellants relied on *Carl Zeiss Stiftung* v. *Rayner & Keeler Ltd*. [1967] 1 AC 853, a decision not mentioned by Lord Templeman, although in that case Lords Reid, Upjohn and Wilberforce (pp. 924, 941, 962) described the question whether the Board of a confiscated foundation could recover its English property as an 'important' matter for defence. And the reporter tells us that the House was referred to an American decision which Lord Templeman also ignored, but which is of much greater significance than that mentioned by him, for it summarizes the whole of the American learning on the right of a dispossessed sharehold of a foreign corporation to recover American property: *Maltina Corporation* v. *Cawy Bottling Co. Inc*. 462 F. 2d 1021 (1972). The House could not require more than this case to obtain a picture of American practice and to ascertain that to say that the American courts 'chose the same approach as that adopted by the English courts' (p. 434) hardly does justice to the former.

The net result is that if Mr Frankfurther, the plaintiff in *Frankfurther* v. *W. L. Exner Ltd*., [1947] Ch. 629, had turned himself into a private limited company its new controller would have succeeded in claiming its English assets. At least Fox L.J. would have disliked such a result (p. 399). Most lawyers would indeed have been shocked. To distinguish this case by such play with words as recognition against enforcement would neither help nor be commensurate to the gravity of the problem. In *Rumasa* it had to be assumed for the purpose of the argument that the Spanish law was penal, disciminatory and confiscatory, i.e. of a type which English law, it was believed, would neither recognize nor enforce and which most certainly it would not judge in the light of terminological niceties. It follows that the appeal to the legislator with which the earlier observations concluded has become most urgent. There are in the world quite a few régimes which are capable of legislation such as Hitler initiated, though the number of the victims may be smaller and their nationality, race or religion may be different. Where the courts have tragically failed to provide such protection as a fair and rational legal system is expected to grant and as almost all civilized countries do grant, it is the duty of Parliament to intervene in good time.

III

For the reasons suggested above, the decision of the House of Lords in the *Rumasa* case, [1986] AC 368 is so singular that it will be of interest to British readers to learn how consequential litigation in the United States of America has fared.

Williams & Humbert Ltd., the 'great-grandchild' of Rumasa SA, a Spanish company the shares of which had been owned by the Ruiz-Mateos family, prior to 1976 owned the Dry Sack trademarks in Britain, the United States and elsewhere. In 1976, in order to protect them against Spanish confiscatory measures, these trade marks were transferred to W. & H. Trade Marks (Jersey) Ltd., all the shares of which were in turn held for the Ruiz-Mateos family. In 1983 Spain in fact transferred to itself all the shares in Rumasa SA without making any payment. Also in 1983, presumably at the direction of the new owners and certainly for the benefit of Rumasa SA, Williams & Humbert Ltd. brought the English action (which ended in the House of Lords) and an American action to recover the British and American trade marks respectively. In the latter action the Ruiz-Mateos family applied for leave to intervene. The Court of Appeals, District of Columbia Circuit, ordered the District Court to reconsider its original rejection of that application: 840 F.2d 72 (1988).

While, on the basis of pleadings only, Lord Templeman had arrived at the factual conclusion that Spain had embarked upon 'a simple case of compulsory acquisition' (p. 434) such as 'is universally recognised and practised' (p. 427), the Court of Appeals in Washington insisted that the family's application 'should be viewed on the tendered pleadings' which alleged (p. 75)

> that, through a four-link chain of corporate ownership, it is the sole owner of the United States Dry Sack trade marks and that the first link in that chain of ownership has been seized by the Spanish government without compensation in violation of fundamental principles of United States law.

namely, 'the bedrock principle prohibiting deprivation without compensation' (p. 75). The Court of Appeals then reviewed the two leading

American cases, one of which was ignored and the other one of which was misunderstood by Lord Templeman, and concluded (p. 76):

> These cases are persuasive, and the attempts of appellee to distinguish these cases and others cited by appellants as involving either citizens of this country or persons doing business here and as involving seizures by revolutionary, undemocratic régimes as ineffectual. Those incidents of the cited cases are merely coincidental and in no sense controlling of the decisions of the deciding courts. The general principle that a corporation and not its shareholders own its assets was considered and found not to be controlling in the context. *Maltina Corporation*, 462 F.2d 1021 at 1028. Cf. *Zwack*, 237 F.2d at 259. It is true that appellants have cited no case in which the owners of an expropriated entity were entitled to the United States assets of a subsidiary of the entity, but we find nothing in the cited cases or the circumstances revealed by the proposed pleadings in this case to indicate that the principles of the cited cases are exhausted by jumping the three entity hurdles here, rather than one.

There is, therefore, no doubt that the courts of the United States will not allow property in the United States to fall under the control of a confiscator even if what he has taken are the shares in a company created in his own country and hence situate there. One of the available methods, expressly sanctions in New York by s. 977b of the New York Civil Practice Act, is the appointment of a receiver.

On the earlier occasions it was suggested that the decision of the House of Lords in the *Rumasa* case had driven English law into unacceptable isolation. The Court of Appeals in Washington has confirmed that impression. The English legislature's intervention has become more urgent and will, it is hoped, not be delayed for long.

[1] See now the fascinating decision of *Bandes* v. *Harlow & Jones*, 852 F.2d 661 (1988), where the Court distributed an American fund by 'creating the fiction of a corporate dissolution' of the Nicaraguan corporation the majority of the share capital of which had been the plaintiffs' property, but was confiscated by the Sandanista Government.

Index